Foundations of Cryptography

Cryptography is concerned with the conceptualization, definition, and construction of computing systems that address security concerns. The design of cryptographic systems must be based on firm foundations. *Foundations of Cryptography* presents a rigorous and systematic treatment of foundational issues: defining cryptographic tasks and solving new cryptographic problems using existing tools. The emphasis is on the clarification of fundamental concepts and on demonstrating the feasibility of solving several central cryptographic problems, as opposed to describing ad hoc approaches.

This second volume contains a rigorous treatment of three basic applications: encryption, signatures, and general cryptographic protocols. It builds on the previous volume, which provides a treatment of one-way functions, pseudorandomness, and zero-knowledge proofs. It is suitable for use in a graduate course on cryptography and as a reference book for experts. The author assumes basic familiarity with the design and analysis of algorithms; some knowledge of complexity theory and probability is also useful.

Oded Goldreich is Professor of Computer Science at the Weizmann Institute of Science and incumbent of the Meyer W. Weisgal Professorial Chair. An active researcher, he has written numerous papers on cryptography and is widely considered to be one of the world experts in the area. He is an editor of *Journal of Cryptology* and *SIAM Journal on Computing* and the author of *Modern Cryptography, Probabilistic Proofs and Pseudorandomness.*

Foundations of Cryptography
II   Basic Applications

Oded Goldreich

Weizmann Institute of Science

CAMBRIDGE
UNIVERSITY PRESS

CAMBRIDGE UNIVERSITY PRESS
Cambridge, New York, Melbourne, Madrid, Cape Town, Singapore, São Paulo, Delhi

Cambridge University Press
The Edinburgh Building, Cambridge CB2 8RU, UK

Published in the United States of America by Cambridge University Press, New York

www.cambridge.org
Information on this title: www.cambridge.org/9780521119917

First published 2004
This digitally printed version 2009

A catalogue record for this publication is available from the British Library

ISBN 978-0-521-83084-3 hardback
ISBN 978-0-521-11991-7 paperback

To Dana

Contents
II   Basic Applications

Note: Asterisks indicate advanced material.

List of Figures

Preface

It is possible to build a cabin with no foundations,
but not a lasting building.
Eng. Isidor Goldreich (1906–1995)

Cryptography is concerned with the construction of schemes that withstand any abuse. Such schemes are constructed so as to maintain a desired functionality, even under malicious attempts aimed at making them deviate from their prescribed functionality.

The design of cryptographic schemes is a very difficult task. One cannot rely on intuitions regarding the typical state of the environment in which the system operates. For sure, the *adversary* attacking the system will try to manipulate the environment into untypical states. Nor can one be content with countermeasures designed to withstand specific attacks because the adversary (which acts after the design of the system is completed) will try to attack the schemes in ways that are typically different from the ones envisioned by the designer. The validity of the foregoing assertions seems self-evident; still, some people hope that in practice, ignoring these tautologies will not result in actual damage. Experience shows that these hopes rarely come true; cryptographic schemes based on make-believe are broken, typically sooner than later.

In view of these assertions, we believe that it makes little sense to make assumptions regarding the specific *strategy* that the adversary may use. The only assumptions that can be justified refer to the computational *abilities* of the adversary. Furthermore, it is our opinion that the design of cryptographic systems has to be based on *firm foundations,* whereas ad hoc approaches and heuristics are a very dangerous way to go. A heuristic may make sense when the designer has a very good idea about the environment in which a scheme is to operate, yet a cryptographic scheme has to operate in a maliciously selected environment that typically transcends the designer's view.

This work is aimed at presenting firm foundations for cryptography. The foundations of cryptography are the paradigms, approaches, and techniques used to conceptualize, define, and provide solutions to natural "security concerns." We will present some of these paradigms, approaches, and techniques, as well as some of the fundamental results obtained using them. Our emphasis is on the clarification of fundamental concepts and on demonstrating the feasibility of solving several central cryptographic problems.

Solving a cryptographic problem (or addressing a security concern) is a two-stage process consisting of a *definitional stage* and a *constructive stage*. First, in the definitional stage, the functionality underlying the natural concern is to be identified, and an adequate cryptographic problem has to be defined. Trying to list all undesired situations is infeasible and prone to error. Instead, one should define the functionality in terms of operation in an imaginary ideal model, and require a candidate solution to emulate this operation in the real, clearly defined model (which specifies the adversary's abilities). Once the definitional stage is completed, one proceeds to construct a system that satisfies the definition. Such a construction may use some simpler tools, and its security is proven relying on the features of these tools. In practice, of course, such a scheme may also need to satisfy some *specific* efficiency requirements.

This work focuses on several archetypical cryptographic problems (e.g., encryption and signature schemes) and on several central tools (e.g., computational difficulty, pseudorandomness, and zero-knowledge proofs). For each of these problems (resp., tools), we start by presenting the natural concern underlying it (resp., its intuitive objective), then define the problem (resp., tool), and finally demonstrate that the problem may be solved (resp., the tool can be constructed). In the last step, our focus is on demonstrating the feasibility of solving the problem, not on providing a practical solution. As a secondary concern, we typically discuss the level of practicality (or impracticality) of the given (or known) solution.

Computational Difficulty

The specific constructs mentioned earlier (as well as most constructs in this area) can exist only if some sort of computational hardness exists. Specifically, all these problems and tools require (either explicitly or implicitly) the ability to generate instances of hard problems. Such ability is captured in the definition of one-way functions (see further discussion in Section 2.1). Thus, one-way functions are the very minimum needed for doing most sorts of cryptography. As we shall see, one-way functions actually suffice for doing much of cryptography (and the rest can be done by augmentations and extensions of the assumption that one-way functions exist).

Our current state of understanding of efficient computation does not allow us to prove that one-way functions exist. In particular, the existence of one-way functions implies that $\mathcal{NP}$ is not contained in $\mathcal{BPP} \supseteq \mathcal{P}$ (not even "on the average"), which would resolve the most famous open problem of computer science. Thus, we have no choice (at this stage of history) but to assume that one-way functions exist. As justification for this assumption, we may only offer the combined beliefs of hundreds (or thousands) of researchers. Furthermore, these beliefs concern a simply stated assumption, and their validity follows from several widely believed conjectures that are central to various fields (e.g., the conjecture that factoring integers is hard is central to computational number theory).

Since we need assumptions anyhow, why not just assume what we want (i.e., the existence of a solution to some natural cryptographic problem)? Well, first we need to know what we want: As stated earlier, we must first clarify what exactly we want; that is, we must go through the typically complex definitional stage. But once this stage is completed, can we just assume that the definition derived can be met? Not really. Once a definition is derived, how can we know that it can be met at all? The way to demonstrate that a definition is viable (and so the intuitive security concern can be satisfied at all) is to construct a solution based on a *better-understood* assumption (i.e., one that is more common and widely believed). For example, looking at the definition of zero-knowledge proofs, it is not a priori clear that such proofs exist at all (in a non-trivial sense). The non-triviality of the notion was first demonstrated by presenting a zero-knowledge proof system for statements regarding Quadratic Residuosity that are believed to be hard to verify (without extra information). Furthermore, contrary to prior beliefs, it was later shown that the existence of one-way functions implies that any NP-statement can be proven in zero-knowledge. Thus, facts that were not at all known to hold (and were even believed to be false) were shown to hold by reduction to widely believed assumptions (without which most of modern cryptography collapses anyhow). To summarize, not all assumptions are equal, and so reducing a complex, new, and doubtful assumption to a widely believed simple (or even merely simpler) assumption is of great value. Furthermore, reducing the solution of a new task to the assumed security of a well-known primitive typically means providing a construction that, using the known primitive, solves the new task. This means that we not only know (or assume) that the new task is solvable but also have a solution based on a primitive that, being well known, typically has several candidate implementations.

Structure and Prerequisites

Our aim is to present the basic concepts, techniques, and results in cryptography. As stated earlier, our emphasis is on the clarification of fundamental concepts and the relationship among them. This is done in a way independent of the particularities of some popular number-theoretic examples. These particular examples played a central role in the development of the field and still offer the most practical implementations of all cryptographic primitives, but this does not mean that the presentation has to be linked to them. On the contrary, we believe that concepts are best clarified when presented at an abstract level, decoupled from specific implementations. Thus, the most relevant background for this work is provided by basic knowledge of algorithms (including randomized ones), computability, and elementary probability theory. Background on (computational) number theory, which is required for specific implementations of certain constructs, is not really required here (yet a short appendix presenting the most relevant facts is included in the first volume so as to support the few examples of implementations presented here).

Organization of the Work. This work is organized in two parts (see Figure 0.1): *Basic Tools* and *Basic Applications*. The first volume (i.e., [108]) contains an introductory chapter as well as the first part (Basic Tools), which consists of chapters on computational difficulty (one-way functions), pseudorandomness, and zero-knowledge proofs. These basic tools are used for the Basic Applications of the second part (i.e., the current

Volume 1: Introduction and Basic Tools
        Chapter 1: Introduction
        Chapter 2: Computational Difficulty (One-Way Functions)
        Chapter 3: Pseudorandom Generators
        Chapter 4: Zero-Knowledge Proof Systems
Volume 2: Basic Applications
        Chapter 5: Encryption Schemes
        Chapter 6: Digital Signatures and Message Authentication
        Chapter 7: General Cryptographic Protocols

Figure 0.1: Organization of this work.

volume), which consists of chapters on Encryption Schemes, Digital Signatures and Message Authentication, and General Cryptographic Protocols.

The partition of the work into two parts is a logical one. Furthermore, it has offered us the advantage of publishing the first part before the completion of the second part. Originally, a third part, entitled *Beyond the Basics,* was planned. That part was to have discussed the effect of Cryptography on the rest of Computer Science (and, in particular, complexity theory), as well as to have provided a treatment of a variety of more advanced security concerns. In retrospect, we feel that the first direction is addressed in [106], whereas the second direction is more adequate for a collection of surveys.

Organization of the Current Volume. The current (second) volume consists of three chapters that treat encryption schemes, digital signatures and message authentication, and general cryptographic protocols, respectively. Also included is an appendix that provides corrections and additions to Volume 1. Figure 0.2 depicts the high-level structure of the current volume. Inasmuch as this volume is a continuation of the first (i.e., [108]), one numbering system is used for both volumes (and so the first chapter of the current volume is referred to as Chapter 5). This allows a simple referencing of sections, definitions, and theorems that appear in the first volume (e.g., Section 1.3 presents the computational model used throughout the entire work). The only exception to this rule is the use of different bibliographies (and consequently a different numbering of bibliographic entries) in the two volumes.

Historical notes, suggestions for further reading, some open problems, and some exercises are provided at the end of each chapter. The exercises are *mostly* designed to help and test the basic understanding of the main text, not to test or inspire creativity. The open problems are fairly well known; still, we recommend a check on their current status (e.g., in our updated notices web site).

Web Site for Notices Regarding This Work. We intend to maintain a web site listing corrections of various types. The location of the site is

```
http://www.wisdom.weizmann.ac.il/~oded/foc-book.html
```

Chapter 5: Encryption Schemes
    The Basic Setting (Sec. 5.1)
    Definitions of Security (Sec. 5.2)
    Constructions of Secure Encryption Schemes (Sec. 5.3)
    Advanced Material (Secs. 5.4 and 5.5.1–5.5.3)
Chapter 6: Digital Signatures and Message Authentication
    The Setting and Definitional Issues (Sec. 6.1)
    Length-Restricted Signature Scheme (Sec. 6.2)
    Basic Constructions (Secs. 6.3 and 6.4)
    Advanced Material (Secs. 6.5 and 6.6.1–6.6.3)
Chapter 7: General Cryptographic Protocols
    Overview (Sec. 7.1)
    Advanced Material (all the rest):
        The Two-Party Case (Sec. 7.2–7.4)
        The Multi-Party Case (Sec. 7.5 and 7.6)
Appendix C: Corrections and Additions to Volume 1
Bibliography and Index

Figure 0.2: Rough organization of this volume.

Using This Work

This work is intended to serve as both a textbook and a reference text. That is, it is aimed at serving both the beginner and the expert. In order to achieve this aim, the presentation of the basic material is very detailed so as to allow a typical undergraduate in Computer Science to follow it. An advanced student (and certainly an expert) will find the pace (in these parts) far too slow. However, an attempt was made to allow the latter reader to easily skip details obvious to him/her. In particular, proofs are typically presented in a modular way. We start with a high-level sketch of the main ideas and only later pass to the technical details. Passage from high-level descriptions to lower-level details is typically marked by phrases such as "details follow."

> In a few places, we provide straightforward but tedious details in indented paragraphs such as this one. In some other (even fewer) places, such paragraphs provide technical proofs of claims that are of marginal relevance to the topic of the work.

More advanced material is typically presented at a faster pace and with fewer details. Thus, we hope that the attempt to satisfy a wide range of readers will not harm any of them.

Teaching. The material presented in this work, on the one hand, is way beyond what one may want to cover in a course and, on the other hand, falls very short of what one may want to know about Cryptography in general. To assist these conflicting needs, we make a distinction between *basic* and *advanced* material and provide suggestions for further reading (in the last section of each chapter). In particular, sections, subsections, and subsubsections marked by an asterisk (*) are intended for advanced reading.

Depending on the class, each lecture consists of 50–90 minutes. Lectures 1–15 are covered by the first volume. Lectures 16–28 are covered by the current (second) volume.

Lecture 1: Introduction, Background, etc. (depending on class)

Lectures 2–5: *Computational Difficulty* (*One-Way Functions*)
   Main: Definition (Sec. 2.2), Hard-Core Predicates (Sec. 2.5)
   Optional: Weak Implies Strong (Sec. 2.3), and Secs. 2.4.2–2.4.4

Lectures 6–10: *Pseudorandom Generators*
   Main: Definitional Issues and a Construction (Secs. 3.2–3.4)
   Optional: Pseudorandom Functions (Sec. 3.6)

Lectures 11–15: *Zero-Knowledge Proofs*
   Main: Some Definitions and a Construction (Secs. 4.2.1, 4.3.1, 4.4.1–4.4.3)
   Optional: Secs. 4.2.2, 4.3.2, 4.3.3–4.3.4, 4.4.4

Lectures 16–20: *Encryption Schemes*
   Main: Definitions and Constructions (Secs. 5.1, 5.2.1–5.2.4, 5.3.2–5.3.4)
   Optional: Beyond Passive Notions of Security (Overview, Sec. 5.4.1)

Lectures 21–24: *Signature Schemes*
   Definitions and Constructions (Secs. 6.1, 6.2.1–6.2.2, 6.3.1.1, 6.4.1–6.4.2)

Lectures 25–28: *General Cryptographic Protocols*
   The Definitional Approach and a General Construction (Overview, Sec. 7.1).

Figure 0.3: Plan for one-semester course on Foundations of Cryptography.

This work is intended to provide all material required for a course on Foundations of Cryptography. For a one-semester course, the teacher will definitely need to skip all advanced material (marked by an asterisk) and perhaps even some basic material; see the suggestions in Figure 0.3. Depending on the class, this should allow coverage of the basic material at a reasonable level (i.e., all material marked as "main" and some of the "optional"). This work can also serve as a textbook for a two-semester course. In such a course, one should be able to cover the entire basic material suggested in Figure 0.3, and even some of the advanced material.

Practice. The aim of this work is to provide sound theoretical foundations for cryptography. As argued earlier, such foundations are necessary for any *sound* practice of cryptography. Indeed, practice requires more than theoretical foundations, whereas the current work makes no attempt to provide anything beyond the latter. However, given a sound foundation, one can learn and evaluate various practical suggestions that appear elsewhere (e.g., in [149]). On the other hand, lack of sound foundations results in an inability to critically evaluate practical suggestions, which in turn leads to unsound decisions. Nothing could be more harmful to the design of schemes that need to with-stand adversarial attacks than misconceptions about such attacks.

Relationship to Another Book by the Author

A frequently asked question refers to the relationship of the current work to my text *Modern Cryptography, Probabilistic Proofs and Pseudorandomness* [106]. That text consists of three brief introductions to the related topics in its title. Specifically, Chapter 1 of [106] provides a brief (i.e., 30-page) summary of the current work. The other two chapters of [106] provide a wider perspective on two topics mentioned in the current work (i.e., Probabilistic Proofs and Pseudorandomness). Further comments on the latter aspect are provided in the relevant chapters of the first volume of the current work (i.e., [108]).

A Comment Regarding the Current Volume

There are no privileges without duties.
Adv. Klara Goldreich-Ingwer (1912–2004)

Writing the first volume was fun. In comparison to the current volume, the definitions, constructions, and proofs in the first volume were relatively simple and easy to write. Furthermore, in most cases, the presentation could safely follow existing texts. Consequently, the writing effort was confined to reorganizing the material, revising existing texts, and augmenting them with additional explanations and motivations.

Things were quite different with respect to the current volume. Even the simplest notions defined in the current volume are more complex than most notions treated in the first volume (e.g., contrast secure encryption with one-way functions or secure protocols with zero-knowledge proofs). Consequently, the definitions are more complex, and many of the constructions and proofs are more complex. Furthermore, in most cases, the presentation could not follow existing texts. Indeed, most effort had to be (and was) devoted to the actual design of constructions and proofs, which were only inspired by existing texts.

The mere fact that writing this volume required so much effort may imply that this volume will be very valuable: Even experts may be happy to be spared the hardship of trying to understand this material based on the original research manuscripts.

Acknowledgments

> ... very little do we have and inclose which we can call our own in the deep sense of the word. We all have to accept and learn, either from our predecessors or from our contemporaries. Even the greatest genius would not have achieved much if he had wished to extract everything from inside himself. But there are many good people, who do not understand this, and spend half their lives wondering in darkness with their dreams of originality. I have known artists who were proud of not having followed any teacher and of owing everything only to their own genius. Such fools!
>
> Goethe, *Conversations with Eckermann*, 17.2.1832

First of all, I would like to thank three remarkable people who had a tremendous influence on my professional development: Shimon Even introduced me to theoretical computer science and closely guided my first steps. Silvio Micali and Shafi Goldwasser led my way in the evolving foundations of cryptography and shared with me their constant efforts for further developing these foundations.

I have collaborated with many researchers, yet I feel that my collaboration with Benny Chor and Avi Wigderson had the most important impact on my professional development and career. I would like to thank them both for their indispensable contribution to our joint research and for the excitement and pleasure I had when collaborating with them.

Leonid Levin deserves special thanks as well. I had many interesting discussions with Leonid over the years, and sometimes it took me too long to realize how helpful these discussions were.

Special thanks also to four of my former students, from whom I have learned a lot (especially regarding the contents of this volume): to Boaz Barak for discovering the unexpected power of non-black-box simulations, to Ran Canetti for developing definitions and composition theorems for secure multi-party protocols, to Hugo Krawczyk for educating me about message authentication codes, and to Yehuda Lindell for significant simplification of the construction of a posteriori CCA (which enables a feasible presentation).

Next, I'd like to thank a few colleagues and friends with whom I had significant interaction regarding Cryptography and related topics. These include Noga Alon, Hagit Attiya, Mihir Bellare, Ivan Damgard, Uri Feige, Shai Halevi, Johan Hastad, Amir Herzberg, Russell Impagliazzo, Jonathan Katz, Joe Kilian, Eyal Kushilevitz, Yoad Lustig, Mike Luby, Daniele Micciancio, Moni Naor, Noam Nisan, Andrew Odlyzko, Yair Oren, Rafail Ostrovsky, Erez Petrank, Birgit Pfitzmann, Omer Reingold, Ron Rivest, Alon Rosen, Amit Sahai, Claus Schnorr, Adi Shamir, Victor Shoup, Madhu Sudan, Luca Trevisan, Salil Vadhan, Ronen Vainish, Yacob Yacobi, and David Zuckerman.

Even assuming I did not forget people with whom I had significant interaction on topics touching upon this book, the list of people I'm indebted to is far more extensive. It certainly includes the authors of many papers mentioned in the reference list. It also includes the authors of many Cryptography-related papers that I forgot to mention, and the authors of many papers regarding the Theory of Computation at large (a theory taken for granted in the current book).

Finally, I would like to thank Boaz Barak, Alex Healy, Vlad Kolesnikov, Yehuda Lindell, and Minh-Huyen Nguyen for reading parts of this manuscript and pointing out various difficulties and errors.

CHAPTER FIVE

Encryption Schemes

Up to the 1970s, Cryptography was understood as the art of building encryption schemes, that is, the art of constructing schemes allowing secret data exchange over insecure channels. Since the 1970s, other tasks (e.g., signature schemes) have been recognized as falling within the domain of Cryptography (and even being at least as central to Cryptography). Yet the construction of encryption schemes remains, and is likely to remain, a central enterprise of Cryptography.

In this chapter we review the well-known notions of private-key and public-key encryption schemes. More importantly, we define what is meant by saying that such schemes are secure. This definitional treatment is a cornerstone of the entire area, and much of this chapter is devoted to various aspects of it. We also present several constructions of secure (private-key and public-key) encryption schemes. It turns out that using randomness during the encryption process (i.e., not only at the key-generation phase) is essential to security.

Organization. Our main treatment (i.e., Sections 5.1–5.3) refers to security under "passive" (eavesdropping) attacks. In contrast, in Section 5.4, we discuss notions of security under active attacks, culminating in robustness against chosen ciphertext attacks. Additional issues are discussed in Section 5.5.

Teaching Tip. We suggest to focus on the basic definitional treatment (i.e., Sections 5.1 and 5.2.1–5.2.4) and on the the feasibility of satisfying these definitions (as demonstarted by the simplest constructions provided in Sections 5.3.3 and 5.3.4.1). The overview to security under active attacks (i.e., Section 5.4.1) is also recommended. We assume that the reader is familiar with the material in previous chapters (and specifically with Sections 2.2, 2.4, 2.5, 3.2–3.4, and 3.6). This familiarity is important not only because we use some of the notions and results presented in these sections but also because we use similar proof techniques (and do so while assuming that this is *not* the reader's first encounter with these techniques).

5.1. The Basic Setting

Loosely speaking, encryption schemes are supposed to enable private exchange of information between parties that communicate over an insecure channel. Thus, the basic setting consists of a *sender,* a *receiver,* and an *insecure channel* that may be tapped by an *adversary*. The goal is to allow the sender to transfer information to the receiver, over the insecure channel, without letting the adversary figure out this information. Thus, we distinguish between the actual (secret) information that the receiver wishes to transmit and the message(s) sent over the insecure communication channel. The former is called the *plaintext,* whereas the latter is called the *ciphertext*. Clearly, the ciphertext must differ from the plaintext or else the adversary can easily obtain the plaintext by tapping the channel. Thus, the sender must transform the plaintext into a corresponding ciphertext such that the receiver can retrieve the plaintext from the ciphertext, but the adversary cannot do so. Clearly, something must distinguish the receiver (who is able to retrieve the plaintext from the corresponding ciphertext) from the adversary (who cannot do so). Specifically, the receiver knows something that the adversary does not know. This thing is called a *key*.

An encryption scheme consists of a method of transforming plaintexts into ciphertexts and vice versa, using adequate keys. These keys are essential to the ability to effect these transformations. Formally, these transformations are performed by corresponding algorithms: an *encryption algorithm* that transforms a given plaintext and an adequate (encryption) key into a corresponding ciphertext, and a *decryption algorithm* that given the ciphertext and an adequate (decryption) key recovers the original plaintext. Actually, we need to consider a third algorithm, namely, a probabilistic algorithm used to generate keys (i.e., a *key-generation algorithm*). This algorithm must be probabilistic (or else, by invoking it, the adversary obtains the very same key used by the receiver). We stress that the encryption scheme itself (i.e., the aforementioned three algorithms) may be known to the adversary, and the scheme's security relies on the hypothesis that the adversary does not know the actual keys in use.[1]

In accordance with these principles, an encryption scheme consists of three algorithms. These algorithms are public (i.e., known to all parties). The two obvious algorithms are the *encryption algorithm,* which transforms plaintexts into ciphertexts, and the *decryption algorithm,* which transforms ciphertexts into plaintexts. By these principles, it is clear that the decryption algorithm must employ a *key* that is known to the receiver but is not known to the adversary. This key is generated using a third algorithm, called the *key-generator*. Furthermore, it is not hard to see that the encryption process must also depend on the key (or else messages sent to one party can be read by a different party who is also a potential receiver). Thus, the key-generation algorithm is used to produce a pair of (related) keys, one for encryption and one for decryption. The encryption algorithm, given an encryption-key and a plaintext, produces a ciphertext that when fed to the decryption algorithm, together with the corresponding

---

[1] In fact, in many cases, the legitimate interest may be served best by publicizing the scheme itself, because this allows an (independent) expert evaluation of the security of the scheme to be obtained.

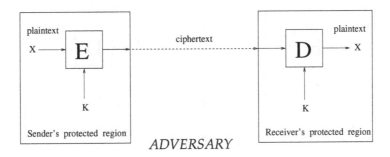

The key K is known to both receiver and sender, but is unknown to the adversary. For example, the receiver may generate K at random and pass it to the sender via a perfectly-private secondary channel (not shown here).

Figure 5.1: Private-key encryption schemes: an illustration.

decryption-key, yields the original plaintext. We stress that knowledge of the decryption-key is essential for the latter transformation.

5.1.1. Private-Key Versus Public-Key Schemes

A fundamental distinction between encryption schemes refers to the relation between the aforementioned pair of keys (i.e., the encryption-key and the decryption-key). The simpler (and older) notion assumes that the encryption-key equals the decryption-key. Such schemes are called private-key (or symmetric).

Private-Key Encryption Schemes. To use a private-key scheme, the legitimate parties must first agree on the secret key. This can be done by having one party generate the key at random and send it to the other party using a (secondary) channel that (unlike the main channel) is assumed to be secure (i.e., it cannot be tapped by the adversary). A crucial point is that the key is generated independently of the plaintext, and so it can be generated and exchanged prior to the plaintext even being determined. Assuming that the legitimate parties have agreed on a (secret) key, they can secretly communicate by using this key (see illustration in Figure 5.1): The sender encrypts the desired plaintext using this key, and the receiver recovers the plaintext from the corresponding ciphertext (by using the same key). Thus, private-key encryption is a way of extending a private channel over time: If the parties can use a private channel today (e.g., they are currently in the same physical location) but not tomorrow, then they can use the private channel today to exchange a secret key that they may use tomorrow for secret communication.

A simple example of a private-key encryption scheme is the *one-time pad*. The secret key is merely a uniformly chosen sequence of n bits, and an n-bit long ciphertext is produced by XORing the plaintext, bit-by-bit, with the key. The plaintext is recovered from the ciphertext in the same way. Clearly, the one-time pad provides

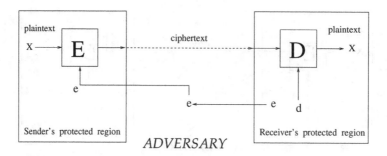

The key-pair (e, d) is generated by the receiver, who posts the encryption-key e on a public media, while keeping the decryption-key d secret.

Figure 5.2: Public-key encryption schemes: an illustration.

absolute security. However, its usage of the key is inefficient; or, put in other words, it requires keys of length comparable to the total length (or information contents) of the data being communicated. By contrast, the rest of this chapter will focus on encryption schemes in which n-bit long keys allow for the secure communication of data having an a priori unbounded (albeit polynomial in n) length. In particular, n-bit long keys allow for significantly more than n bits of information to be communicated securely.

Public-Key Encryption Schemes. A new type of encryption schemes emerged in the 1970s. In these so-called public-key (or asymmetric) encryption schemes, the decryption-key differs from the encryption-key. Furthermore, it is infeasible to find the decryption-key, given the encryption-key. These schemes enable secure communication without the use of a secure channel. Instead, each party applies the key-generation algorithm to produce a pair of keys. The party (denoted P) keeps the decryption-key, denoted d_P, secret and publishes the encryption-key, denoted e_P. Now, any party can send P private messages by encrypting them using the encryption-key e_P. Party P can decrypt these messages by using the decryption-key d_P, but nobody else can do so. (See illustration in Figure 5.2.)

5.1.2. The Syntax of Encryption Schemes

We start by defining the basic *mechanism of encryption schemes*. This definition says nothing about the security of the scheme (which is the subject of the next section).

Definition 5.1.1 (encryption scheme): *An* encryption scheme *is a triple, (G, E, D), of probabilistic polynomial-time algorithms satisfying the following two conditions:*

1. On input 1^n, algorithm G (called the key-generator*) outputs a pair of bit strings.*
2. For every pair (e, d) in the range of $G(1^n)$, and for every $\alpha \in \{0, 1\}^*$, algorithms E

(encryption) *and* D (decryption) *satisfy*

$$\Pr[D(d, E(e, \alpha)) = \alpha] = 1$$

where the probability is taken over the internal coin tosses of algorithms E and D.

The integer n serves as the security parameter *of the scheme. Each* (e, d) *in the range of* $G(1^n)$ *constitutes a pair of corresponding* encryption/decryption keys. *The string* $E(e, \alpha)$ *is the* encryption *of the plaintext* $\alpha \in \{0, 1\}^*$ *using the encryption-key e, whereas* $D(d, \beta)$ *is the* decryption *of the ciphertext* β *using the decryption-key d.*

We stress that Definition 5.1.1 says nothing about security, and so trivial (insecure) algorithms may satisfy it (e.g., $E(e, \alpha) \stackrel{\text{def}}{=} \alpha$ and $D(d, \beta) \stackrel{\text{def}}{=} \beta$). Furthermore, Definition 5.1.1 does not distinguish private-key encryption schemes from public-key ones. The difference between the two types is introduced in the security definitions: In a public-key scheme the "breaking algorithm" gets the encryption-key (i.e., e) as an additional input (and thus $e \neq d$ follows), while in private-key schemes e is not given to the "breaking algorithm" (and thus, one may assume, without loss of generality, that $e = d$).

We stress that this definition requires the scheme to operate for every plaintext, and specifically for plaintext of length exceeding the length of the encryption-key. (This rules out the information theoretic secure "one-time pad" scheme mentioned earlier.)

Notation. In the rest of this text, we write $E_e(\alpha)$ instead of $E(e, \alpha)$ and $D_d(\beta)$ instead of $D(d, \beta)$. Sometimes, when there is little risk of confusion, we drop these subscripts. Also, we let $G_1(1^n)$ (resp., $G_2(1^n)$) denote the first (resp., second) element in the pair $G(1^n)$. That is, $G(1^n) = (G_1(1^n), G_2(1^n))$. Without loss of generality, we may assume that $|G_1(1^n)|$ and $|G_2(1^n)|$ are polynomially related to n, and that each of these integers can be efficiently computed from the other. (In fact, we may even assume that $|G_1(1^n)| = |G_2(1^n)| = n$; see Exercise 6.)

Comments. Definition 5.1.1 may be relaxed in several ways without significantly harming its usefulness. For example, we may relax Condition (2) and allow a negligible decryption error (e.g., $\Pr[D_d(E_e(\alpha)) \neq \alpha] < 2^{-n}$). Alternatively, one may postulate that Condition (2) holds for all but a negligible measure of the key-pairs generated by $G(1^n)$. At least one of these relaxations is essential for some suggestions of (public-key) encryption schemes.

Another relaxation consists of restricting the domain of possible plaintexts (and ciphertexts). For example, one may restrict Condition (2) to α's of length $\ell(n)$, where $\ell : \mathbb{N} \to \mathbb{N}$ is some fixed function. Given a scheme of the latter type (with plaintext length ℓ), we may construct a scheme as in Definition 5.1.1 by breaking plaintexts into blocks of length $\ell(n)$ and applying the restricted scheme separately to each block. (Note that security of the resulting scheme requires that the security of the length-restricted scheme be preserved under multiple encryptions with the same key.) For more details see Sections 5.2.4 and 5.3.2.

5.2. Definitions of Security

In this section we present two fundamental definitions of security and prove their equivalence. The first definition, called *semantic security*, is the most natural one. Semantic security is a computational-complexity analogue of Shannon's definition of perfect privacy (which requires that the ciphertext yield no information regarding the plaintext). Loosely speaking, an encryption scheme is semantically secure if it is *infeasible* to learn anything about the plaintext from the ciphertext (i.e., impossibility is replaced by infeasibility). The second definition has a more technical flavor. It interprets security as the infeasibility of distinguishing between encryptions of a given pair of messages. This definition is useful in demonstrating the security of a proposed encryption scheme and for the analysis of cryptographic protocols that utilize an encryption scheme.

We stress that the definitions presented in Section 5.2.1 go far beyond saying that it is infeasible to recover the plaintext from the ciphertext. The latter statement is indeed a minimal requirement for a secure encryption scheme, but we claim that it is far too weak a requirement. For example, one should certainly not use an encryption scheme that leaks the first part of the plaintext (even if it is infeasible to recover the entire plaintext from the ciphertext). In general, an encryption scheme is typically used in applications where even obtaining partial information on the plaintext may endanger the security of the application. The question of which partial information endangers the security of a specific application is typically hard (if not impossible) to answer. Furthermore, we wish to design application-independent encryption schemes, and when doing so it is the case that each piece of partial information may endanger some application. Thus, we require that it be infeasible to obtain any information about the plaintext from the ciphertext. Moreover, in most applications the plaintext may not be uniformly distributed, and some a priori information regarding it may be available to the adversary. We thus require that the secrecy of all partial information be preserved also in such a case. That is, given any a priori information on the plaintext, it is infeasible to obtain any (new) information about the plaintext from the ciphertext (beyond what is feasible to obtain from the a priori information on the plaintext). The definition of semantic security postulates all of this.

Security of Multiple Plaintexts. Continuing the preceding discussion, the definitions are presented first in terms of the security of a single encrypted plaintext. However, in many cases, it is desirable to encrypt many plaintexts using the same encryption-key, and security needs to be preserved in these cases, too. Adequate definitions and discussions are deferred to Section 5.2.4.

A Technical Comment: Non-Uniform Complexity Formulation. To simplify the exposition, we define security in terms of non-uniform complexity (see Section 1.3.3 of Volume 1). Namely, in the security definitions we expand the domain of efficient adversaries (and algorithms) to include (explicitly or implicitly) non-uniform polynomial-size circuits, rather than only probabilistic polynomial-time machines. Likewise, we make no computational restriction regarding the probability distribution from which messages are taken, nor regarding the a priori information available on these messages. We note that employing such a non-uniform complexity formulation (rather than a uniform one) may only strengthen the definitions, yet it does weaken the implications proven between the definitions because these (simpler) proofs make free usage of non-uniformity. A uniform-complexity treatment is provided in Section 5.2.5.

5.2.1. Semantic Security

A good disguise should not reveal the person's height.
Shafi Goldwasser and Silvio Micali, 1982

Loosely speaking, semantic security means that nothing can be gained by looking at a ciphertext. Following the simulation paradigm, this means that whatever can be efficiently learned from the ciphertext can also be efficiently learned from scratch (or from nothing).

5.2.1.1. The Actual Definitions

To be somewhat more accurate, semantic security means that whatever can be efficiently computed from the ciphertext can be efficiently computed when *given only the length of the plaintext*. Note that this formulation does not rule out the possibility that the length of the plaintext can be inferred from the ciphertext. Indeed, some information about the length of the plaintext must be revealed by the ciphertext (see Exercise 4). We stress that other than information about the length of the plaintext, the ciphertext is required to yield nothing about the plaintext.

In the actual definitions, we consider only information regarding the plaintext (rather than information regarding the ciphertext and/or the encryption-key) that can be obtained from the ciphertext. Furthermore, we restrict our attention to functions (rather than randomized processes) applied to the plaintext. We do so because of the intuitive appeal of this special case, and are comfortable doing so because this special case implies the general one (see Exercise 13). We augment this formulation by requiring that the infeasibility of obtaining information about the plaintext remain valid even in the presence of other auxiliary partial information about the same plaintext. Namely, whatever can be efficiently computed from the ciphertext and additional partial information about the plaintext can be efficiently computed given only the length of the plaintext and the same partial information. In the definition that follows, the information regarding the plaintext that the adversary tries to obtain is represented by the function f, whereas the a priori partial information about the plaintext is represented by the function h. The infeasibility of obtaining information about the plaintext is required to hold for any distribution of plaintexts, represented by the probability ensemble $\{X_n\}_{n \in \mathbb{N}}$.

Security holds only for plaintexts of length polynomial in the security parameter. This is captured in the following definitions by the restriction $|X_n| \leq \text{poly}(n)$, where "poly" represents an arbitrary (unspecified) polynomial. Note that we cannot hope to provide computational security for plaintexts of unbounded length or for plaintexts of length that is exponential in the security parameter (see Exercise 3). Likewise, we restrict the functions f and h to be *polynomially-bounded*, that is, $|f(z)|, |h(z)| \leq \text{poly}(|z|)$.

The difference between private-key and public-key encryption schemes is manifested in the definition of security. In the latter case, the adversary (which is trying to obtain information on the plaintext) is given the encryption-key, whereas in the former case it is not. Thus, the difference between these schemes amounts to a difference in the adversary model (considered in the definition of security). We start by presenting the definition for private-key encryption schemes.

Definition 5.2.1 (semantic security – private-key): *An encryption scheme, (G, E, D), is* **semantically secure** (in the private-key model) *if for every probabilistic polynomial-time algorithm A there exists a probabilistic polynomial-time algorithm A' such that for every probability ensemble $\{X_n\}_{n \in \mathbb{N}}$, with $|X_n| \leq \text{poly}(n)$, every pair of polynomially bounded functions $f, h : \{0, 1\}^* \to \{0, 1\}^*$, every positive polynomial p and all sufficiently large n*

$$\Pr\left[A(1^n, E_{G_1(1^n)}(X_n), 1^{|X_n|}, h(1^n, X_n)) = f(1^n, X_n)\right]$$

$$< \Pr\left[A'(1^n, 1^{|X_n|}, h(1^n, X_n)) = f(1^n, X_n)\right] + \frac{1}{p(n)}$$

(The probability in these terms is taken over X_n as well as over the internal coin tosses of either algorithms G, E, and A or algorithm A'.)

We stress that all the occurrences of X_n in each of the probabilistic expressions refer to the same random variable (see the general convention stated in Section 1.2.1 in Volume 1). The security parameter 1^n is given to both algorithms (as well as to the functions h and f) for technical reasons.[2] The function h provides both algorithms with partial information regarding the plaintext X_n. Furthermore, h also makes the definition implicitly non-uniform; see further discussion in Section 5.2.1.2. In addition, both algorithms get the length of X_n. These algorithms then try to guess the value $f(1^n, X_n)$; namely, they try to infer information about the plaintext X_n. Loosely speaking, in a semantically secure encryption scheme the ciphertext does not help in this inference task. That is, the success probability of any efficient algorithm (i.e., algorithm A) that is given the ciphertext can be matched, up to a negligible fraction, by the success probability of an efficient algorithm (i.e., algorithm A') that is not given the ciphertext at all.

Definition 5.2.1 refers to private-key encryption schemes. To derive a definition of security for public-key encryption schemes, the encryption-key (i.e., $G_1(1^n)$) should be given to the adversary as an additional input.

---

[2] The auxiliary input 1^n is used for several purposes. First, it allows smooth transition to fully non-uniform formulations (e.g., Definition 5.2.3) in which the (polynomial-size) adversary depends on n. Thus, it is good to provide A (and thus also A') with 1^n. Once this is done, it is natural to allow also h and f to depend on n. In fact, allowing h and f to explicitly depend on n facilitates the proof of Proposition 5.2.7. In light of the fact that 1^n is given to both algorithms, we may replace the input part $1^{|X_n|}$ by $|X_n|$, because the former may be recovered from the latter in $\text{poly}(n)$-time.

Definition 5.2.2 (semantic security – public-key): *An encryption scheme, (G, E, D),* is semantically secure (in the public-key model) *if for every probabilistic polynomial-time algorithm A, there exists a probabilistic polynomial-time algorithm A' such that for every $\{X_n\}_{n \in \mathbb{N}}$, f, h, p, and n as in Definition 5.2.1*

$$\Pr\left[A(1^n, G_1(1^n), E_{G_1(1^n)}(X_n), 1^{|X_n|}, h(1^n, X_n)) = f(1^n, X_n)\right]$$

$$< \Pr\left[A'(1^n, 1^{|X_n|}, h(1^n, X_n)) = f(1^n, X_n)\right] + \frac{1}{p(n)}$$

Recall that (by our conventions) both occurrences of $G_1(1^n)$, in the first probabilistic expression, refer to the same random variable. We comment that it is pointless to give the random encryption-key (i.e., $G_1(1^n)$) to algorithm A' (because the task as well as the main inputs of A' are unrelated to the encryption-key, and anyhow A' could generate a random encryption-key by itself).

Terminology. For sake of simplicity, we refer to an encryption scheme that is semantically secure in the private-key (resp., public-key) model as a semantically secure private-key (resp., public-key) encryption scheme.

The reader may note that a semantically secure *public-key* encryption scheme cannot employ a deterministic encryption algorithm; that is, $E_e(x)$ must be a random variable rather than a fixed string. This is more evident with respect to the equivalent Definition 5.2.4. See further discussion following Definition 5.2.4.

5.2.1.2. Further Discussion of Some Definitional Choices

We discuss several secondary issues regarding Definitions 5.2.1 and 5.2.2. The interested reader is also referred to Exercises 16, 17, and 19, which present additional variants of the definition of semantic security.

Implicit Non-Uniformity of the Definitions. The fact that h is not required to be computable makes these definitions non-uniform. This is the case because both algorithms are given $h(1^n, X_n)$ as auxiliary input, and the latter may account for arbitrary (polynomially bounded) advice. For example, letting $h(1^n, \cdot) = a_n \in \{0, 1\}^{\text{poly}(n)}$ means that both algorithms are supplied with (non-uniform) advice (as in one of the common formulations of non-uniform polynomial-time; see Section 1.3.3). In general, the function h can code both information regarding its main input and non-uniform advice depending on the security parameter (i.e., $h(1^n, x) = (h'(x), a_n)$). We comment that these definitions are equivalent to allowing A and A' to be *related* families of non-uniform circuits, where by *related* we mean that the circuits in the family $A' = \{A'_n\}_{n \in \mathbb{N}}$ can be efficiently computed from the corresponding circuits in the family $A = \{A_n\}_{n \in \mathbb{N}}$. For further discussion, see Exercise 9.

Lack of Computational Restrictions Regarding the Function f. We do not even require that the function f be computable. This seems strange at first glance because (unlike the situation with respect to the function h, which codes a priori information given to the algorithms) the algorithms are asked to guess the value of f (at a plaintext implicit in the ciphertext given only to A). However, as we shall see in the sequel (see also Exercise 13), the actual technical content of semantic security is that the probability ensembles $\{(1^n, E(X_n), 1^{|X_n|}, h(1^n, X_n))\}_n$ and $\{(1^n, E(1^{|X_n|}), 1^{|X_n|}, h(1^n, X_n))\}_n$ are computationally indistinguishable (and so whatever A can compute can also be computed by A'). Note that the latter statement does not refer to the function f, which explains why we need not make any restriction regarding f.

Other Modifications of No Impact. Actually, inclusion of a priori information regarding the plaintext (represented by the function h) does not affect the definition of semantic security: Definition 5.2.1 remains intact if we restrict h to only depend on the security parameter (and so only provide plaintext-oblivious non-uniform advice). (This can be shown in various ways; e.g., see Exercise 14.1.) Also, the function f can be restricted to be a Boolean function having polynomial-size circuits, and the random variable X_n may be restricted to be very "dull" (e.g., have only two strings in its support): See proof of Theorem 5.2.5. On the other hand, Definition 5.2.1 implies stronger forms discussed in Exercises 13, 17 and 18.

5.2.2. Indistinguishability of Encryptions

A good disguise should not allow a mother to distinguish her own children.
Shafi Goldwasser and Silvio Micali, 1982

The following technical interpretation of security states that it is infeasible to distinguish the encryptions of two plaintexts (of the same length). That is, such ciphertexts are computationally indistinguishable as defined in Definition 3.2.7. Again, we start with the private-key variant.

Definition 5.2.3 (indistinguishability of encryptions – private-key): *An encryption scheme, (G, E, D), has* indistinguishable encryptions *(in the private-key model) if for every polynomial-size circuit family $\{C_n\}$, every positive polynomial p, all sufficiently large n, and every $x, y \in \{0, 1\}^{\text{poly}(n)}$ (i.e., $|x| = |y|$),*

$$|\Pr\left[C_n(E_{G_1(1^n)}(x)) = 1\right] - \Pr\left[C_n(E_{G_1(1^n)}(y)) = 1\right]| < \frac{1}{p(n)}$$

The probability in these terms is taken over the internal coin tosses of algorithms G and E.

Note that the potential plaintexts to be distinguished can be incorporated into the circuit C_n. Thus, the circuit models both the adversary's strategy and its a priori information: See Exercise 11.

Again, the security definition for public-key encryption schemes is derived by adding the encryption-key (i.e., $G_1(1^n)$) as an additional input to the potential distinguisher.

Definition 5.2.4 (indistinguishability of encryptions – public-key): *An encryption scheme, (G, E, D), has* indistinguishable encryptions (in the public-key model) *if for every polynomial-size circuit family* $\{C_n\}$*, and every p, n, x, and y as in Definition 5.2.3*

$$| \Pr\left[C_n(G_1(1^n), E_{G_1(1^n)}(x)) = 1\right] - \Pr\left[C_n(G_1(1^n), E_{G_1(1^n)}(y)) = 1\right] | < \frac{1}{p(n)}$$

Terminology. We refer to an encryption scheme that has indistinguishable encryptions in the private-key (resp., public-key) model as a ciphertext-indistinguishable private-key (resp., public-key) encryption scheme.

Failure of Deterministic Encryption Algorithms. A ciphertext-indistinguishable *public-key* encryption scheme cannot employ a deterministic encryption algorithm (i.e., $E_e(x)$ cannot be a fixed string). The reason is that for a public-key encryption scheme with a *deterministic* encryption algorithm E, given an encryption-key e and a pair of candidate plaintexts (x, y), one can easily distinguish $E_e(x)$ from $E_e(y)$ (by merely applying E_e to x and comparing the result to the given ciphertext). In contrast, in case the encryption algorithm itself is randomized, the same plaintext can be encrypted in many exponentially different ways, under the same encryption-key. Furthermore, the probability that applying E_e twice to the same message (while using independent randomization in E_e) results in the same ciphertext may be exponentially vanishing. (Indeed, as shown in Section 5.3.4, public-key encryption schemes having indistinguishable encryptions can be constructed based on any trapdoor permutation, and these schemes employ randomized encryption algorithms.)

5.2.3. Equivalence of the Security Definitions

The following theorem is stated and proven for private-key encryption schemes. A similar result holds for public-key encryption schemes (see Exercise 12).

Theorem 5.2.5 (equivalence of definitions – private-key): *A private-key encryption scheme is semantically secure if and only if it has indistinguishable encryptions.*

Let (G, E, D) be an encryption scheme. We formulate a proposition for each of the two directions of this theorem. Each proposition is in fact stronger than the corresponding direction stated in Theorem 5.2.5. The more useful direction is stated first: It asserts that the technical interpretation of security, in terms of ciphertext-indistinguishability, implies the natural notion of semantic security. Thus, the following proposition yields a methodology for designing semantically secure encryption schemes: Design and prove your scheme to be ciphertext-indistinguishable, and conclude (by applying the proposition) that it is semantically secure. The opposite direction (of Theorem 5.2.5) establishes the "completeness" of the latter methodology, and more generally asserts that requiring an encryption scheme to be ciphertext-indistinguishable does not rule out schemes that are semantically secure.

Proposition 5.2.6 (useful direction: "indistinguishability" implies "security"): *Suppose that (G, E, D) is a ciphertext-indistinguishable private-key encryption scheme. Then (G, E, D) is semantically secure. Furthermore, Definition 5.2.1 is satisfied by using $A' = M^A$, where M is a fixed oracle machine; that is, there exists a single M such that for every A letting $A' = M^A$ will do.*

Proposition 5.2.7 (opposite direction: "security" implies "indistinguishability"): *Suppose that (G, E, D) is a semantically secure private-key encryption scheme. Then (G, E, D) has indistinguishable encryptions. Furthermore, the conclusion holds even if the definition of semantic security is restricted to the special case satisfying the following four conditions:*

1. *The random variable X_n is uniformly distributed over a set containing two strings;*
2. *The value of h depends only on the length of its input or alternatively $h(1^n, x) = h'(n)$, for some h';*
3. *The function f is Boolean and is computable by a family of (possibly non-uniform) polynomial-size circuits;*
4. *The algorithm A is deterministic.*

In addition, no computational restrictions are placed on algorithm A' (i.e., A' can be any function), and moreover A' may depend on $\{X_n\}_{n\in\mathbb{N}}$, h, f, and A.

Observe that the four itemized conditions *limit the scope of the four universal quantifiers* in Definition 5.2.1, whereas the last sentence *removes a restriction on the existential quantifier* (i.e., removes the complexity bound on A') and reverses the order of quantifiers allowing the existential quantifier to depend on all universal quantifiers (rather than only on the last one). Thus, each of these modifications makes the resulting definition potentially weaker. Still, combining Propositions 5.2.7 and 5.2.6, it follows that a weak version of Definition 5.2.1 implies (an even stronger version than) the one stated in Definition 5.2.1.

5.2.3.1. Proof of Proposition 5.2.6

Suppose that (G, E, D) has indistinguishable encryptions. We will show that (G, E, D) is semantically secure by *constructing*, for every probabilistic polynomial-time algorithm A, a probabilistic polynomial-time algorithm A' such that the condition in Definition 5.2.1 holds. That is, *for every $\{X_n\}_{n\in\mathbb{N}}$, f and h, algorithm A' guesses $f(1^n, X_n)$ from $(1^n, 1^{|X_n|}, h(1^n, X_n))$ essentially as well as A guesses $f(1^n, X_n)$ from $E(X_n)$ and $(1^n, 1^{|X_n|}, h(1^n, X_n))$).* Our construction of A' consists of merely invoking A on input $(1^n, E(1^{|X_n|}), 1^{|X_n|}, h(1^n, X_n))$, and returning whatever A does. That is, A' invokes A with a dummy encryption rather than with an encryption of X_n (which A expects to get, but A' does not have). Intuitively, the indistinguishability of encryptions implies that A behaves nearly as well when invoked by A' (and given a dummy encryption) as when given the encryption of X_n, and this establishes that A' is adequate with respect to A. The main issue in materializing this plan is to show that the specific formulation of indistinguishability of encryptions indeed supports the implication (i.e., implies that

A guesses $f(1^n, X_n)$ essentially as well when given a dummy encryption as when given the encryption of X_n). Details follow.

The construction of A': Let A be an algorithm that tries to infer partial information (i.e., the value $f(1^n, X_n)$) from the encryption of the plaintext X_n (when also given 1^n, $1^{|X_n|}$ and a priori information $h(1^n, X_n)$). Intuitively, on input $E(\alpha)$ and $(1^n, 1^{|\alpha|}, h(1^n, \alpha))$, algorithm A tries to guess $f(1^n, \alpha)$. We construct a new algorithm, A', that performs essentially as well without getting the input $E(\alpha)$. The new algorithm consists of invoking A on input $E_{G_1(1^n)}(1^{|\alpha|})$ and $(1^n, 1^{|\alpha|}, h(1^n, \alpha))$, and outputting whatever A does. That is, on input $(1^n, 1^{|\alpha|}, h(1^n, \alpha))$, algorithm A' proceeds as follows:

1. A' invokes the key-generator G (on input 1^n), and obtains an encryption-key $e \leftarrow G_1(1^n)$.
2. A' invokes the encryption algorithm with key e and ("dummy") plaintext $1^{|\alpha|}$, obtaining a ciphertext $\beta \leftarrow E_e(1^{|\alpha|})$.
3. A' invokes A on input $(1^n, \beta, 1^{|\alpha|}, h(1^n, \alpha))$, and outputs whatever A does.

Observe that A' is described in terms of an oracle machine that makes a single oracle call to (any given) A, in addition to invoking the fixed algorithms G and E. Furthermore, the construction of A' depends neither on the functions h and f nor on the distribution of plaintexts to be encrypted (represented by the probability ensembles $\{X_n\}_{n\in\mathbb{N}}$). Thus, A' is probabilistic polynomial-time whenever A is probabilistic polynomial-time (and regardless of the complexity of h, f, and $\{X_n\}_{n\in\mathbb{N}}$).

Indistinguishability of encryptions will be used to prove that A' performs essentially as well as A. Specifically, the proof will use a reducibility argument.

Claim 5.2.6.1: Let A' be as in the preceding construction. Then, for every $\{X_n\}_{n\in\mathbb{N}}$, f, h, and p as in Definition 5.2.1, and all sufficiently large n's

$$\Pr\left[A(1^n, E_{G_1(1^n)}(X_n), 1^{|X_n|}, h(1^n, X_n)) = f(1^n, X_n)\right]$$
$$< \Pr\left[A'(1^n, 1^{|X_n|}, h(1^n, X_n)) = f(1^n, X_n)\right] + \frac{1}{p(n)}$$

Proof: To simplify the notations, let us incorporate $1^{|\alpha|}$ into $h_n(\alpha) \stackrel{\text{def}}{=} h(1^n, \alpha)$ and let $f_n(\alpha) \stackrel{\text{def}}{=} f(1^n, \alpha)$. Also, we omit 1^n from the inputs given to A, shorthanding $A(1^n, c, v)$ by $A(c, v)$. Using the definition of A', we rewrite the claim as asserting

$$\Pr\left[A(E_{G_1(1^n)}(X_n), h_n(X_n)) = f_n(X_n)\right] \tag{5.1}$$
$$< \Pr\left[A(E_{G_1(1^n)}(1^{|X_n|}), h_n(X_n)) = f_n(X_n)\right] + \frac{1}{p(n)}$$

Intuitively, Eq. (5.1) follows from the indistinguishability of encryptions. Otherwise, by fixing a violating value of X_n and hardwiring the corresponding values of $h_n(X_n)$ and $f_n(X_n)$, we get a small circuit that distinguishes an encryption of this value of X_n from an encryption of $1^{|X_n|}$. Details follow.

Assume toward the contradiction that for some polynomial p and infinitely many n's Eq. (5.1) is violated. Then, for each such n, we have $E[\Delta_n(X_n)] > 1/p(n)$, where

$$\Delta_n(x) \stackrel{\text{def}}{=} \left| \Pr\left[A(E_{G_1(1^n)}(x), h_n(x)) = f_n(x)\right] - \Pr\left[A(E_{G_1(1^n)}(1^{|x|}), h_n(x)) = f_n(x)\right]\right|$$

We use an averaging argument to single out a string x_n in the support of X_n such that $\Delta_n(x_n) \geq E[\Delta_n(X_n)]$: That is, let $x_n \in \{0, 1\}^{\text{poly}(n)}$ be a string for which the value of $\Delta_n(\cdot)$ is maximum, and so $\Delta_n(x_n) > 1/p(n)$. Using this x_n, we introduce a circuit C_n, which incorporates the fixed values $f_n(x_n)$ and $h_n(x_n)$, and distinguishes the encryption of x_n from the encryption of $1^{|x_n|}$. The circuit C_n operates as follows. On input $\beta = E(\alpha)$, the circuit C_n invokes $A(\beta, h_n(x_n))$ and outputs 1 if and only if A outputs the value $f_n(x_n)$. Otherwise, C_n outputs 0.

This circuit is indeed of polynomial size because it merely incorporates strings of polynomial length (i.e., $f_n(x_n)$ and $h_n(x_n)$) and emulates a polynomial-time computation (i.e., that of A). (Note that the circuit family $\{C_n\}$ is indeed non-uniform since its definition is based on a non-uniform selection of x_n's as well as on a hardwiring of (possibly uncomputable) corresponding strings $h_n(x_n)$ and $f_n(x_n)$.) Clearly,

$$\Pr\left[C_n(E_{G_1(1^n)}(\alpha)) = 1\right] = \Pr\left[A(E_{G_1(1^n)}(\alpha), h_n(x_n)) = f_n(x_n)\right] \tag{5.2}$$

Combining Eq. (5.2) with the definition of $\Delta_n(x_n)$, we get

$$\left| \Pr\left[C_n(E_{G_1(1^n)}(x_n)) = 1\right] - \Pr\left[C_n(E_{G_1(1^n)}(1^{|x_n|})) = 1\right]\right| = \Delta_n(x_n)$$
$$> \frac{1}{p(n)}$$

This contradicts our hypothesis that E has indistinguishable encryptions, and the claim follows. $\square$

We have just shown that A' performs essentially as well as A, and so Proposition 5.2.6 follows. ∎

Comments. The fact that we deal with a non-uniform model of computation allows the preceding proof to proceed regardless of the complexity of f and h. All that our definition of C_n requires is the hardwiring of the values of f and h on a single string, and this can be done regardless of the complexity of f and h (provided that $|f_n(x_n)|, |h_n(x_n)| \leq \text{poly}(n)$).

When proving the public-key analogue of Proposition 5.2.6, algorithm A' is defined exactly as in the present proof, but its analysis is slightly different: The distinguishing circuit, considered in the analysis of the performance of A', obtains the encryption-key as part of its input and passes it to algorithm A (upon invoking the latter).

5.2.3.2. Proof of Proposition 5.2.7

Intuitively, indistinguishability of encryption (i.e., of the encryptions of x_n and y_n) is a special case of semantic security in which f indicates one of the plaintexts and h does not distinguish them (i.e., $f(1^n, z) = 1$ iff $z = x_n$ and $h(1^n, x_n) = h(1^n, y_n)$). The only issue to be addressed by the actual proof is that semantic security refers to uniform (probabilistic polynomial-time) adversaries, whereas indistinguishability of encryption refers to non-uniform polynomial-size circuits. This gap is bridged by using the function h to provide the algorithms in the semantic-security formulation with adequate non-uniform advice (which may be used by the machine in the indistinguishability of encryption formulation).

The actual proof is by a reducibility argument. We show that if (G, E, D) has distinguishable encryptions, then it is not semantically secure (not even in the restricted sense mentioned in the furthermore-clause of the proposition). Toward this end, we assume that there exists a (positive) polynomial p and a polynomial-size circuit family $\{C_n\}$, such that for infinitely many n's there exists $x_n, y_n \in \{0, 1\}^{\text{poly}(n)}$ so that

$$\left| \Pr\left[C_n(E_{G_1(1^n)}(x_n)) = 1\right] - \Pr\left[C_n(E_{G_1(1^n)}(y_n)) = 1\right] \right| > \frac{1}{p(n)} \tag{5.3}$$

Using these sequences of C_n's, x_n's and y_n's, we define $\{X_n\}_{n \in \mathbb{N}}$, f and h (referred to in Definition 5.2.1) as follows:

- The probability ensemble $\{X_n\}_{n \in \mathbb{N}}$ is defined such that X_n is uniformly distributed over $\{x_n, y_n\}$.
- The (Boolean) function f is defined such that $f(1^n, x_n) = 1$ and $f(1^n, y_n) = 0$, for every n. Note that $f(1^n, X_n) = 1$ with probability $1/2$ and equals 0 otherwise.
- The function h is defined such that $h(1^n, X_n)$ equals the description of the circuit C_n. Note that $h(1^n, X_n) = C_n$ with probability 1, and thus $h(1^n, X_n)$ reveals no information on the value of X_n.

Note that X_n, f, and h satisfy the restrictions stated in the furthermore-clause of the proposition. Intuitively, Eq. (5.3) implies violation of semantic security with respect to the X_n, h, and f. Indeed, we will present a (deterministic) polynomial-time algorithm A that, given $C_n = h(1^n, X_n)$, guesses the value of $f(1^n, X_n)$ from the encryption of X_n, and does so with probability non-negligibly greater than $1/2$. This violates (even the restricted form of) semantic security, because no algorithm, regardless of its complexity, can guess $f(1^n, X_n)$ with probability greater than $1/2$ when only given $1^{|X_n|}$ (because given the constant values $1^{|X_n|}$ and $h(1^n, X_n)$, the value of $f(1^n, X_n)$ is uniformly distributed over $\{0, 1\}$). Details follow.

Let us assume, without loss of generality, that for infinitely many n's

$$\Pr\left[C_n(E_{G_1(1^n)}(x_n)) = 1\right] > \Pr\left[C_n(E_{G_1(1^n)}(y_n)) = 1\right] + \frac{1}{p(n)} \tag{5.4}$$

Claim 5.2.7.1: There exists a (deterministic) polynomial-time algorithm A such that for infinitely many n's

$$\Pr\left[A(1^n, E_{G_1(1^n)}(X_n), 1^{|X_n|}, h(1^n, X_n)) = f(1^n, X_n)\right] > \frac{1}{2} + \frac{1}{2p(n)}$$

Proof: The desired algorithm A merely uses $C_n = h(1^n, X_n)$ to distinguish $E(x_n)$ from $E(y_n)$, and thus given $E(X_n)$ it produces a guess for the value of $f(1^n, X_n)$. Specifically, on input $\beta = E(\alpha)$ (where α is in the support of X_n) and $(1^n, 1^{|\alpha|}, h(1^n, \alpha))$, algorithm A

recovers $C_n = h(1^n, \alpha)$, invokes C_n on input β, and outputs 1 if C_n outputs 1 (otherwise, A outputs 0).[3]

It is left to analyze the success probability of A. Letting $m = |x_n| = |y_n|$, $h_n(\alpha) \overset{\text{def}}{=} h(1^n, \alpha)$ and $f_n(\alpha) \overset{\text{def}}{=} f(1^n, \alpha)$, we have

$$\Pr\left[A(1^n, E_{G_1(1^n)}(X_n), 1^{|X_n|}, h_n(X_n)) = f_n(X_n)\right]$$

$$= \frac{1}{2} \cdot \Pr\left[A(1^n, E_{G_1(1^n)}(X_n), 1^{|X_n|}, h_n(X_n)) = f_n(X_n) \mid X_n = x_n\right]$$

$$+ \frac{1}{2} \cdot \Pr\left[A(1^n, E_{G_1(1^n)}(X_n), 1^{|X_n|}, h_n(X_n)) = f_n(X_n) \mid X_n = y_n\right]$$

$$= \frac{1}{2} \cdot \Pr\left[A(1^n, E_{G_1(1^n)}(x_n), 1^{|x_n|}, C_n) = 1\right]$$

$$+ \frac{1}{2} \cdot \Pr\left[A(1^n, E_{G_1(1^n)}(y_n), 1^{|y_n|}, C_n) = 0\right]$$

$$= \frac{1}{2} \cdot \left(\Pr\left[C_n(E_{G_1(1^n)}(x_n)) = 1\right] + 1 - \Pr\left[C_n(E_{G_1(1^n)}(y_n)) = 1\right]\right)$$

$$> \frac{1}{2} + \frac{1}{2p(n)}$$

where the inequality is due to Eq. (5.4). $\square$

In contrast, as aforementioned, no algorithm (regardless of its complexity) can guess $f(1^n, X_n)$ with success probability above $1/2$, when given only $1^{|X_n|}$ and $h(1^n, X_n)$. That is, we have the following:

Fact 5.2.7.2: For every n and every algorithm A'

$$\Pr\left[A'(1^n, 1^{|X_n|}, h(1^n, X_n)) = f(1^n, X_n)\right] \leq \frac{1}{2} \qquad (5.5)$$

Proof: Just observe that the output of A', on its constant input values 1^n, $1^{|X_n|}$ and $h(1^n, X_n)$, is stochastically independent of the random variable $f(1^n, X_n)$, which in turn is uniformly distributed in $\{0, 1\}$. Eq. (5.5) follows (and equality holds in case A' always outputs a value in $\{0, 1\}$). $\square$

Combining Claim 5.2.7.1 and Fact 5.2.7.2, we reach a contradiction to the hypothesis that the scheme is semantically secure (even in the restricted sense mentioned in the furthermore-clause of the proposition). Thus, the proposition follows. ∎

Comment. When proving the public-key analogue of Proposition 5.2.7, algorithm A is defined as in the current proof except that it passes the encryption-key, given to it as part of its input, to the circuit C_n. The rest of the proof remains intact.

---

[3] We comment that the value "1" output by C_n is an indication that α is more likely to be x_n, whereas the output of A is a guess of $f(\alpha)$. This point may be better stressed by redefining f such that $f(1^n, x_n) \overset{\text{def}}{=} x_n$ and $f(1^n, x) \overset{\text{def}}{=} y_n$ if $x \neq x_n$, and having A output x_n if C_n outputs 1 and output y_n otherwise.

5.2.4. Multiple Messages

Definitions 5.2.1–5.2.4 only refer to the security of an encryption scheme that is used to encrypt a single plaintext (per generated key). Since the plaintext may be longer than the key, these definitions are already non-trivial, and an encryption scheme satisfying them (even in the private-key model) implies the existence of one-way functions (see Exercise 2). Still, in many cases, it is desirable to encrypt many plaintexts using the same encryption-key. Loosely speaking, an encryption scheme is secure in the multiple-message setting if analogous definitions (to Definitions 5.2.1–5.2.4) also hold when polynomially many plaintexts are encrypted using the same encryption-key.

We show that *in the public-key model,* security in the single-message setting (discussed earlier) implies security in the multiple-message setting (defined in Section 5.2.4.1). We stress that this is not necessarily true *for the private-key model.*

5.2.4.1. Definitions

For a sequence of strings $\overline{x} = (x^{(1)}, ..., x^{(t)})$, we let $\overline{E}_e(\overline{x})$ denote the sequence of the t results that are obtained by applying the randomized process E_e to the t strings $x^{(1)}, ..., x^{(t)}$, respectively. That is, $\overline{E}_e(\overline{x}) = (E_e(x^{(1)}), ..., E_e(x^{(t)}))$. We stress that in each of these t invocations, the randomized process E_e utilizes independently chosen random coins. For the sake of simplicity, we consider the encryption of (polynomially) many plaintexts of the same (polynomial) length (rather than the encryption of plaintexts of various lengths as discussed in Exercise 20). The number of plaintexts as well as their total length (in unary) are given to all algorithms either implicitly or explicitly.[4]

Definition 5.2.8 (semantic security – multiple messages):

For private-key: *An encryption scheme, (G, E, D), is* semantically secure for multiple messages in the private-key model *if for every probabilistic polynomial-time algorithm A, there exists a probabilistic polynomial-time algorithm A' such that for every probability ensemble $\{\overline{X}_n = (X_n^{(1)}, ..., X_n^{(t(n))})\}_{n\in\mathbb{N}}$, with $|X_n^{(1)}| = \cdots = |X_n^{(t(n))}| \leq \mathrm{poly}(n)$ and $t(n) \leq \mathrm{poly}(n)$, every pair of polynomially bounded functions $f, h : \{0, 1\}^* \to \{0, 1\}^*$, every positive polynomial p and all sufficiently large n*

$$\Pr\left[A(1^n, \overline{E}_{G_1(1^n)}(\overline{X}_n), 1^{|\overline{X}_n|}, h(1^n, \overline{X}_n)) = f(1^n, \overline{X}_n)\right]$$

$$< \Pr\left[A'(1^n, t(n), 1^{|\overline{X}_n|}, h(1^n, \overline{X}_n)) = f(1^n, \overline{X}_n)\right] + \frac{1}{p(n)}$$

For public-key: *An encryption scheme, (G, E, D), is* semantically secure for multiple messages in the public-key model *if for A, A', t, $\{\overline{X}_n\}_{n\in\mathbb{N}}$, f, h, p, and n, as in the*

---

[4] For example, A can infer the number of plaintexts from the number of ciphertexts, whereas A' is given this number explicitly. Given the number of the plaintexts as well as their total length, both algorithms can infer the length of each plaintext.

private-key case, it holds that

$$\Pr\left[A(1^n, G_1(1^n), \overline{E}_{G_1(1^n)}(\overline{X}_n), 1^{|\overline{X}_n|}, h(1^n, \overline{X}_n)) = f(1^n, \overline{X}_n)\right]$$

$$< \Pr\left[A'(1^n, t(n), 1^{|\overline{X}_n|}, h(1^n, \overline{X}_n)) = f(1^n, \overline{X}_n)\right] + \frac{1}{p(n)}$$

(The probability in these terms is taken over $\overline{X}_n$ as well as over the internal coin tosses of the relevant algorithms.)

We stress that the elements of $\overline{X}_n$ are not necessarily independent; they may depend on one another. Note that this definition also covers the case where the adversary obtains some of the plaintexts themselves. In this case it is still infeasible for him/her to obtain information about the missing plaintexts (see Exercise 22).

Definition 5.2.9 (indistinguishability of encryptions – multiple messages):

For private-key: *An encryption scheme, (G, E, D), has* indistinguishable encryptions for multiple messages in the private-key model *if for every polynomial-size circuit family $\{C_n\}$, every positive polynomial p, all sufficiently large n, and every $x_1, ..., x_{t(n)}, y_1, ..., y_{t(n)} \in \{0, 1\}^{\text{poly}(n)}$, with $t(n) \leq \text{poly}(n)$, it holds that*

$$\left| \Pr\left[C_n(\overline{E}_{G_1(1^n)}(\bar{x})) = 1\right] - \Pr\left[C_n(\overline{E}_{G_1(1^n)}(\bar{y})) = 1\right] \right| < \frac{1}{p(n)}$$

where $\bar{x} = (x_1, ..., x_{t(n)})$ and $\bar{y} = (y_1, ..., y_{t(n)})$.

For public-key: *An encryption scheme, (G, E, D), has* indistinguishable encryptions for multiple messages in the public-key model *if for t, $\{C_n\}$, p, n, and $x_1, ..., x_{t(n)}, y_1, ..., y_{t(n)}$ as in the private-key case*

$$\left| \Pr\left[C_n(G_1(1^n), \overline{E}_{G_1(1^n)}(\bar{x})) = 1\right] - \Pr\left[C_n(G_1(1^n), \overline{E}_{G_1(1^n)}(\bar{y})) = 1\right] \right| < \frac{1}{p(n)}$$

The equivalence of Definitions 5.2.8 and 5.2.9 can be established analogously to the proof of Theorem 5.2.5.

Theorem 5.2.10 (equivalence of definitions – multiple messages): *A private-key (resp., public-key) encryption scheme is semantically secure for multiple messages if and only if it has indistinguishable encryptions for multiple messages.*

Thus, proving that single-message security implies multiple-message security for one definition of security yields the same for the other. We may thus concentrate on the ciphertext-indistinguishability definitions.

5.2.4.2. The Effect on the Public-Key Model

We first consider public-key encryption schemes.

Theorem 5.2.11 (single-message security implies multiple-message security): *A public-key* encryption scheme has indistinguishable encryptions *for multiple messages (i.e., satisfies Definition 5.2.9 in the public-key model) if and only if it has indistinguishable encryptions for a single message (i.e., satisfies Definition 5.2.4).*

Proof: Clearly, multiple-message security implies single-message security as a special case. The other direction follows by adapting the proof of Theorem 3.2.6 to the current setting.

Suppose, toward the contradiction, that there exist a polynomial t, a polynomial-size circuit family $\{C_n\}$, and a polynomial p, such that for infinitely many n's, there exists $x_1, ..., x_{t(n)}, y_1, ..., y_{t(n)} \in \{0, 1\}^{\mathrm{poly}(n)}$ so that

$$\left| \Pr\left[C_n(G_1(1^n), \overline{E}_{G_1(1^n)}(\bar{x})) = 1 \right] - \Pr\left[C_n(G_1(1^n), \overline{E}_{G_1(1^n)}(\bar{y})) = 1 \right] \right| > \frac{1}{p(n)}$$

where $\bar{x} = (x_1, ..., x_{t(n)})$ and $\bar{y} = (y_1, ..., y_{t(n)})$. Let us consider such a generic n and the corresponding sequences $x_1, ..., x_{t(n)}$ and $y_1, ..., y_{t(n)}$. We use a hybrid argument. Specifically, define

$$\bar{h}^{(i)} \stackrel{\text{def}}{=} (x_1, ..., x_i, y_{i+1}, ..., y_{t(n)})$$

$$\text{and} \quad H_n^{(i)} \stackrel{\text{def}}{=} (G_1(1^n), \overline{E}_{G_1(1^n)}(\bar{h}^{(i)}))$$

Since $H_n^{(0)} = (G_1(1^n), \overline{E}_{G_1(1^n)}(\bar{y}))$ and $H_n^{(t(n))} = (G_1(1^n), \overline{E}_{G_1(1^n)}(\bar{x}))$, it follows that there exists an $i \in \{0, ..., t(n) - 1\}$ so that

$$\left| \Pr\left[C_n(H_n^{(i)}) = 1 \right] - \Pr\left[C_n(H_n^{(i+1)}) = 1 \right] \right| > \frac{1}{t(n) \cdot p(n)} \tag{5.6}$$

We show that Eq. (5.6) yields a polynomial-size circuit that distinguishes the encryption of x_{i+1} from the encryption of y_{i+1}, and thus derive a contradiction to security in the single-message setting. Specifically, we construct a circuit D_n that incorporates the circuit C_n as well as the index i and the strings $x_1, ..., x_{i+1}, y_{i+1}, ..., y_{t(n)}$. On input an encryption-key e and (corresponding) ciphertext β, the circuit D_n operates as follows:

- For every $j \le i$, the circuit D_n generates an encryption of x_j using the encryption-key e. Similarly, for every $j \ge i + 2$, the circuit D_n generates an encryption of y_j using the encryption-key e.
  Let us denote the resulting ciphertexts by $\beta_1, ..., \beta_i, \beta_{i+2}, ..., \beta_{t(n)}$. That is, $\beta_j \leftarrow E_e(x_j)$ for $j \le i$ and $\beta_j \leftarrow E_e(y_j)$ for $j \ge i + 2$.
- Finally, D_n invokes C_n on input the encryption-key e and the sequence of ciphertexts $\beta_1, ..., \beta_i, \beta, \beta_{i+2}, ..., \beta_{t(n)}$, and outputs whatever C_n does.

We stress that the construction of D_n relies in an essential way on the fact that the encryption-key is given to D_n as input.

We now turn to the analysis of the circuit D_n. Suppose that β is a (random) encryption of x_{i+1} with (random) key e; that is, $\beta = E_e(x_{i+1})$. Then, $D_n(e, \beta) \equiv C_n(e, E_e(\bar{h}^{(i+1)})) = C_n(H_n^{(i+1)})$, where $X \equiv Y$ means that the random variables X and Y are identically distributed. Similarly, for $\beta = E_e(y_{i+1})$, we have $D_n(e, \beta) \equiv$

$C_n(e, E_e(\bar{h}^{(i)})) = C_n(H_n^{(i)})$. Thus, by Eq. (5.6), we have

$$\left| \Pr\left[D_n(G_1(1^n), E_{G_1(1^n)}(y_{i+1})) = 1\right]\right.$$
$$\left. -\Pr\left[D_n(G_1(1^n), E_{G_1(1^n)}(x_{i+1})) = 1\right]\right| > \frac{1}{t(n) \cdot p(n)}$$

in contradiction to our hypothesis that (G, E, D) is a ciphertext-indistinguishable public-key encryption scheme (in the single-message sense). The theorem follows. ∎

Discussion. The fact that we are in the public-key model is essential to this proof. It allows the circuit D_n to form encryptions relative to the same encryption-key used in the ciphertext given to it. In fact, as previously stated (and proven next), the analogous result does not hold in the private-key model.

5.2.4.3. The Effect on the Private-Key Model

In contrast to Theorem 5.2.11, *in the private-key model,* ciphertext-indistinguishability for a single message does *not* necessarily imply ciphertext-indistinguishability for multiple messages.

Proposition 5.2.12: *Suppose that there exist pseudorandom generators* (robust against polynomial-size circuits). *Then, there exists a private-key encryption scheme that satisfies Definition 5.2.3 but does not satisfy Definition 5.2.9.*

Proof: We start with the construction of the desired private-key encryption scheme. The encryption/decryption key for security parameter n is a uniformly distributed n-bit long string, denoted s. To encrypt a ciphertext, x, the encryption algorithm uses the key s as a seed for a (variable-output) pseudorandom generator, denoted g, that stretches seeds of length n into sequences of length $|x|$. The ciphertext is obtained by a bit-by-bit exclusive-or of x and $g(s)$. Decryption is done in an analogous manner.

We first show that this encryption scheme satisfies Definition 5.2.3. Intuitively, this follow from the hypothesis that g is a pseudorandom generator and the fact that $x \oplus U_{|x|}$ is uniformly distributed over $\{0, 1\}^{|x|}$. Specifically, suppose toward the contradiction that for some polynomial-size circuit family $\{C_n\}$, a polynomial p, and infinitely many n's

$$\left| \Pr[C_n(x \oplus g(U_n)) = 1] - \Pr[C_n(y \oplus g(U_n)) = 1]\right| > \frac{1}{p(n)}$$

where U_n is uniformly distributed over $\{0, 1\}^n$ and $|x| = |y| = m = \text{poly}(n)$. On the other hand,

$$\Pr[C_n(x \oplus U_m) = 1] = \Pr[C_n(y \oplus U_m) = 1]$$

Thus, without loss of generality

$$| \Pr[C_n(x \oplus g(U_n)) = 1] - \Pr[C_n(x \oplus U_m) = 1] | > \frac{1}{2 \cdot p(n)}$$

Incorporating x into the circuit C_n, we obtain a circuit that distinguishes U_m from $g(U_n)$, in contradiction to our hypothesis (regarding the pseudorandomness of g).

Next, we observe that this encryption scheme does not satisfy Definition 5.2.9. Specifically, given the ciphertexts of two plaintexts, one may easily retrieve the exclusive-or of the corresponding plaintexts. That is,

$$E_s(x_1) \oplus E_s(x_2) = (x_1 \oplus g(s)) \oplus (x_2 \oplus g(s)) = x_1 \oplus x_2$$

This clearly violates Definition 5.2.8 (e.g., consider $f(x_1, x_2) = x_1 \oplus x_2$) as well as Definition 5.2.9 (e.g., consider any $\bar{x} = (x_1, x_2)$ and $\bar{y} = (y_1, y_2)$ such that $x_1 \oplus x_2 \neq y_1 \oplus y_2$). Viewed in a different way, note that any plaintext-ciphertext pair yields a corresponding prefix of the pseudorandom sequence, and knowledge of this prefix violates the security of additional plaintexts. That is, given the encryption of a known plaintext x_1 along with the encryption of an unknown plaintext x_2, we can retrieve x_2.[5] ∎

Discussion. The single-message security of the scheme used in the proof of Proposition 5.2.12 was proven by considering an ideal version of the scheme in which the pseudorandom sequence is replaced by a truly random sequence. The latter scheme is secure in an information-theoretic sense, and the security of the actual scheme followed by the indistinguishability of the two sequences. As we show in Section 5.3.1, this construction can be modified to yield a private-key "stream-cipher" that is secure for multiple message encryptions. All that is needed in order to obtain multiple-message security is to make sure that (as opposed to this construction) the same portion of the pseudorandom sequence is never used twice.

An Alternative Proof of Proposition 5.2.12. Given an arbitrary private-key encryption scheme (G, E, D), consider the following private-key encryption scheme (G', E', D'):

- $G'(1^n) = ((k, r), (k, r))$, where $(k, k) \leftarrow G(1^n)$ and r is uniformly selected in $\{0, 1\}^{|k|}$;
- $E'_{(k,r)}(x) = (E_k(x), k \oplus r)$ with probability $1/2$ and $E'_{(k,r)}(x) = (E_k(x), r)$ otherwise;
- and $D'_{(k,r)}(y, z) = D_k(y)$.

If (G, E, D) is secure, then so is (G', E', D') (with respect to a single message); however, (G', E', D') is not secure with respect to two messages. For further discussion see Exercise 21.

---

[5] On input the ciphertexts β_1 and β_2, knowing that the first plaintext is x_1, we first retrieve the pseudorandom sequence (i.e., it is just $r \stackrel{\text{def}}{=} \beta_1 \oplus x_1$), and next retrieve the second plaintext (i.e., by computing $\beta_2 \oplus r$).

5.2.5.* A Uniform-Complexity Treatment

As stated at the beginning of this section, the non-uniform complexity formulation was adopted in this chapter for the sake of simplicity. In contrast, in this subsection, we outline an alternative definitional treatment of security based on a uniform (rather than a non-uniform) complexity formulation. We stress that by uniform or non-uniform complexity treatment of cryptographic primitives, we refer merely to the modeling of the adversary. The honest (legitimate) parties are always modeled by uniform complexity classes (most commonly probabilistic polynomial-time).

The notion of *efficiently constructible probability ensembles*, defined in Section 3.2.3 of Volume 1, is central to the uniform-complexity treatment. Recall that an ensemble, $X = \{X_n\}_{n \in \mathbb{N}}$, is said to be polynomial-time constructible if there exists a probabilistic polynomial-time algorithm S so that for every n, the random variables $S(1^n)$ and X_n are identically distributed.

5.2.5.1. The Definitions

We present only the definitions of security for multiple messages; the single-message variant can be easily obtained by setting the polynomial t (in Definitions 5.2.13 and 5.2.14) to be identically 1. Likewise, we present the public-key version, and the private-key analogue can be obtained by omitting $G_1(1^n)$ from the inputs to the various algorithms.

The uniformity of the following definitions is reflected in the complexity of the inputs given to the algorithms. Specifically, the plaintexts are taken from polynomial-time constructible ensembles and so are the auxiliary inputs given to the algorithms. For example, in the following definition we require the ensemble $\{\overline{X}_n\}$ to be polynomial-time constructible and the function h to be polynomial-time computable.

Definition 5.2.13 (semantic security – uniform-complexity version): *An encryption scheme, (G, E, D), is uniformly semantically secure in the public-key model if for every two polynomials t, ℓ, and every probabilistic polynomial-time algorithm A there exists a probabilistic polynomial-time algorithm A' such that for every polynomial-time constructible ensemble $\{\overline{X}_n = (X_n^{(1)}, ..., X_n^{(t(n))})\}_{n \in \mathbb{N}}$, with $|X_n^{(i)}| = \ell(n)$, every polynomial-time computable $h : \{0, 1\}^* \to \{0, 1\}^*$, every $f : \{0, 1\}^* \to \{0, 1\}^*$, every positive polynomial p, and all sufficiently large n's*

$$\Pr\left[A(1^n, G_1(1^n), \overline{E}_{G_1(1^n)}(\overline{X}_n), 1^{|\overline{X}_n|}, h(1^n, \overline{X}_n)) = f(1^n, \overline{X}_n)\right]$$

$$< \Pr\left[A'(1^n, t(n), 1^{|\overline{X}_n|}, h(1^n, \overline{X}_n)) = f(1^n, \overline{X}_n)\right] + \frac{1}{p(n)}$$

where $\overline{E}_e(\overline{x}) \stackrel{\text{def}}{=} (E_e(x^{(1)}), ..., E_e(x^{(t(n))}))$, for $\overline{x} = (x^{(1)}, ..., x^{(t(n))}) \in \{0, 1\}^{t(n) \cdot \ell(n)}$, is as in Definition 5.2.8.

Again, we stress that $\overline{X}_n$ is a sequence of random variables, which may depend on one another. Note that Definition 5.2.13 is seemingly weaker than the corresponding non-uniform definition (i.e., Definition 5.2.8). We stress that even here (i.e., in the uniform-complexity setting) no computational limitations are placed on the function f.

Definition 5.2.14 (indistinguishability of encryptions – uniform-complexity version): *An encryption scheme, (G, E, D), has* uniformly indistinguishable encryptions in the public-key model *if for every two polynomials t, ℓ, every probabilistic polynomial-time algorithm D', every polynomial-time constructible ensemble $\overline{T} \stackrel{\text{def}}{=} \{\overline{T}_n = \overline{X}_n \overline{Y}_n Z_n\}_{n\in\mathbb{N}}$, with $\overline{X}_n = (X_n^{(1)}, ..., X_n^{(t(n))})$, $\overline{Y}_n = (Y_n^{(1)}, ..., Y_n^{(t(n))})$, and $|X_n^{(i)}| = |Y_n^{(i)}| = \ell(n)$, it holds that*

$$| \Pr\left[D'(1^n, Z_n, G_1(1^n), \overline{E}_{G_1(1^n)}(\overline{X}_n)) = 1\right]$$

$$- \Pr\left[D'(1^n, Z_n, G_1(1^n), \overline{E}_{G_1(1^n)}(\overline{Y}_n)) = 1\right] | < \frac{1}{p(n)}$$

for every positive polynomial p and all sufficiently large n's. (The probability in these terms is taken over $\overline{T}_n = \overline{X}_n \overline{Y}_n Z_n$ as well as over the internal coin tosses of the relevant algorithms.)

The random variable Z_n represented a priori information about the plaintexts for which encryptions should be distinguished. A special case of interest is when $Z_n = \overline{X}_n \overline{Y}_n$. Uniformity is captured in the requirement that D' be a probabilistic polynomial-time algorithm (rather than a family of polynomial-size circuits) and that the ensemble $\{\overline{T}_n = \overline{X}_n \overline{Y}_n Z_n\}_{n\in\mathbb{N}}$ be polynomial-time constructible. Recall that in the non-uniform case (i.e., Definition 5.2.9), the random variable Z_n can be incorporated in the distinguishing circuit C_n (and thus be eliminated).[6] Thus, Definition 5.2.14 is seemingly weaker than the corresponding non-uniform definition (i.e., Definition 5.2.9).

5.2.5.2. Equivalence of the Multiple-Message Definitions

We prove the equivalence of the uniform-complexity definitions (presented earlier) for (multiple-message) security.

Theorem 5.2.15 (equivalence of definitions – uniform treatment): *A public-key encryption scheme satisfies Definition 5.2.13 if and only if it satisfies Definition 5.2.14. Furthermore, this holds even if Definition 5.2.14 is restricted to the special case where $Z_n = \overline{X}_n \overline{Y}_n$. Similarly, the equivalence holds even if Definition 5.2.13 is restricted to the special case where f is polynomial-time computable.*

An analogous result holds for the private-key model. The important direction of the theorem holds also for the single-message version (this is quite obvious from the

---

[6] Furthermore, in the case of non-uniform distinguishers, the auxiliary input 1^n is redundant.

following proof). In the other direction, we seem to use the multiple-message version (of semantic security) in an essential way. An alterative treatment is provided in Exercise 23.

Proof Sketch: Again, we start with the more important direction (i.e., "indistinguishability" implies semantic security). Specifically, assuming that (G, E, D) has indistinguishable encryptions in the uniform sense, even merely in the special case where $Z_n = \overline{X}_n \overline{Y}_n$, we show that it is semantically secure in the uniform sense. Our construction of algorithm A' is analogous to the construction used in the non-uniform treatment. Specifically, on input $(1^n, t(n), 1^{|\overline{\alpha}|}, h(1^n, \overline{\alpha}))$, algorithm A' generates a random encryption of a dummy sequence of plaintexts (i.e., $1^{|\overline{\alpha}|}$), feeds it to A, and outputs whatever A does.[7] That is,

$$A'(1^n, t(n), 1^{|\overline{\alpha}|}, u) = A(1^n, G_1(1^n), \overline{E}_{G_1(1^n)}(1^{|\overline{\alpha}|}), 1^{|\overline{\alpha}|}, u) \tag{5.7}$$

As in the non-uniform case, the analysis of algorithm A' reduces to the following claim.

Claim 5.2.15.1: For every two polynomials t and ℓ, every polynomial-time constructible ensemble $\{\overline{X}_n\}_{n \in \mathbb{N}}$, with $\overline{X}_n = (X_n^{(1)}, ..., X_n^{(t(n))})$ and $|X_n^{(i)}| = \ell(n)$, every polynomial-time computable h, every positive polynomial p, and all sufficiently large n's

$$\Pr\left[A(1^n, G_1(1^n), \overline{E}_{G_1(1^n)}(\overline{X}_n), 1^{|\overline{X}_n|}, h(1^n, \overline{X}_n)) = f(1^n, \overline{X}_n)\right]$$
$$< \Pr\left[A(1^n, G_1(1^n), \overline{E}_{G_1(1^n)}(1^{|\overline{X}_n|}), 1^{|\overline{X}_n|}, h(1^n, \overline{X}_n)) = f(1^n, \overline{X}_n)\right] + \frac{1}{p(n)}$$

Proof Sketch: Analogously to the non-uniform case, assuming toward the contradiction that the claim does not hold yields an algorithm that distinguishes encryptions of $\overline{X}_n$ from encryptions of $\overline{Y}_n = 1^{|\overline{X}_n|}$, when getting auxiliary information $Z_n = \overline{X}_n \overline{Y}_n = \overline{X}_n 1^{|\overline{X}_n|}$. Thus, we derive a contradiction to Definition 5.2.14 (even under the special case postulated in the theorem).

We note that the auxiliary information that is given to the distinguishing algorithm replaces the hardwiring of auxiliary information that was used in the non-uniform case (and is not possible in the uniform-complexity model). Specifically, rather than using a hardwired value of h (at some non-uniformly fixed sequence), the distinguishing algorithm will use the auxiliary information $Z_n = \overline{X}_n 1^{|\overline{X}_n|}$ in order to compute $h_n(\overline{X}_n) \overset{\text{def}}{=} (1^n, 1^{|\overline{X}_n|}, h(1^n, \overline{X}_n))$, which it will pass to A. Indeed, we rely on the hypothesis that h is efficiently computable.

The actual proof is quite simple in case the function f is also polynomial-time computable (which is not the case in general). In this special case, on input $(1^n, e, z, \overline{E}_e(\overline{\alpha}))$, where $z = (\overline{x}, 1^{|\overline{x}|})$ and $\overline{\alpha} \in \{\overline{x}, 1^{|\overline{x}|}\}$ for $\overline{x} \leftarrow \overline{X}_n$, the distinguishing algorithm computes $u = h(1^n, \overline{x})$ and $v = f(1^n, \overline{x})$, invokes A, and outputs 1 if and only if $A(1^n, e, \overline{E}_e(\overline{\alpha}), 1^{|\overline{x}|}, u) = v$.

---

[7] More accurately, algorithm A' proceeds as follows. Using $t(n)$, the algorithm breaks $1^{|\overline{\alpha}|}$ into a sequence of $t(n)$ equal-length (unary) strings, using 1^n it generates a random encryption-key, and using this key it generates the corresponding sequence of encryptions.

(Tedious comment: In case $\overline{\alpha} = 1^{|\overline{x}|}$, we actually mean that $\overline{\alpha}$ is a sequence of $t(n)$ strings of the form $1^{\ell(n)}$, where t and ℓ are as in $\overline{x} = (x^{(1)}, ..., x^{(t(n))}) \in (\{0, 1\}^{\ell(n)})^{t(n)}$.)

The proof becomes more involved in the case where f is not polynomial-time computable.[8] Again, the solution is in realizing that indistinguishability of encryption postulates a similar output profile (of A) in both cases, where the two cases correspond to whether A is given an encryption of $\overline{x}$ or an encryption of $1^{\overline{x}}$ (for $\overline{x} \leftarrow \overline{X}_n$). In particular, no value can occur as the output of A in one case with non-negligibly higher probability than in the other case. To clarify the point, for every fixed $\overline{x}$, we define $\Delta_{n,v}(\overline{x})$ to be the difference between $\Pr[A(G_1(1^n), \overline{E}_{G_1(1^n)}(\overline{x}), h_n(\overline{x})) = v]$ and $\Pr[A(G_1(1^n), \overline{E}_{G_1(1^n)}(1^{|\overline{x}|}), h_n(\overline{x})) = v]$, where $h_n(\overline{x}) \stackrel{\text{def}}{=} (1^n, 1^{|\overline{x}|}, h(1^n, \overline{x}))$ and the probability space is over the internal coin tosses of algorithms G, E, and A. Taking the expectation over $\overline{X}_n$, the contradiction hypothesis means that $\mathsf{E}[\Delta_{n,f(1^n,\overline{X}_n)}(\overline{X}_n)] > 1/p(n)$, and so with probability at least $1/2p(n)$ over the choice of $\overline{x} \leftarrow \overline{X}_n$ we have $\Delta_{n,f(1^n,\overline{x})}(\overline{x}) > 1/2p(n)$. The problem is that, given $\overline{x}$ (and 1^n), we cannot even approximate $\Delta_{n,f(1^n,\overline{x})}(\overline{x})$, because we do not have the value $f(1^n, \overline{x})$ (and we cannot compute it). Instead, we let $\Delta_n(\overline{x}) \stackrel{\text{def}}{=} \max_{v \in \{0,1\}^{\text{poly}(n)}}\{\Delta_{n,v}(\overline{x})\}$, and observe that $\mathsf{E}[\Delta_n(\overline{X}_n)] \geq \mathsf{E}[\Delta_{n,f(1^n,\overline{X}_n)}(\overline{X}_n)] > 1/p(n)$. Furthermore, given $(1^n, \overline{x})$, we can (efficiently) approximate $\Delta_n(\overline{x})$ as well as find a value v such that $\Delta_{n,v}(\overline{x}) > \Delta_n(\overline{x}) - (1/2p(n))$, with probability at least $1 - 2^{-n}$.

On approximating $\Delta_n(\overline{x})$ and finding an adequate v: Let $q(n)$ be a bound on the length of $f(1^n, \overline{x})$. Our goal is to approximate $\Delta_n(\overline{x})$, which is the maximum of $\Delta_{n,v}(\overline{x})$ taken over all $v \in \{0, 1\}^{q(n)}$, as well as find a value v for which $\Delta_{n,v}(\overline{x})$ is close to $\Delta_n(\overline{x})$. For each fixed v, it is easy to approximate $\Delta_{n,v}(\overline{x})$, but we cannot afford to seperately compute each of these approximations. Yet we can efficiently compute an implicit representation of all the $2^{q(n)}$ approximations, where all but polynomially many of the $\Delta_{n,v}(\overline{x})$'s will be approximated by zero. This is possible because the $\Delta_{n,v}(\overline{x})$'s are the differences between corresponding two sequences of positive numbers (where each sequence has a sum equal to one). Specifically, we obtain $m \stackrel{\text{def}}{=} O((n + q(n)) \cdot p(n)^2)$ outputs of $A(G_1(1^n), \overline{E}_{G_1(1^n)}(\overline{x}), h_n(\overline{x}))$ and m outputs of $A(G_1(1^n), \overline{E}_{G_1(1^n)}(1^{|\overline{x}|}), h_n(\overline{x}))$, where in each of the invocations we use new coin tosses for algorithms A, G, and E. For each v, the quantity $\Delta_{n,v}(\overline{x})$ is approximated by the difference between the fraction of times that v occurs as output in the first case and the fraction of times it occurs as output in the second case. Indeed, at most, $2m$ values may occur as outputs, and for all other v's the quantity $\Delta_{n,v}(\overline{x})$ is implicitly approximated by zero. Let us denote by $\widetilde{\Delta}_{n,v}(\overline{x})$ the approximation computed (explicitly or implicitly) for $\Delta_{n,v}(\overline{x})$. Note that for every fixed v, the probability that $|\Delta_{n,v}(\overline{x}) - \widetilde{\Delta}_{n,v}(\overline{x})| > 1/4p(n)$ is at most $2^{-(n+q(n))}$; hence, with probability at least $1 - 2^{-n}$, $|\Delta_{n,v}(\overline{x}) - \widetilde{\Delta}_{n,v}(\overline{x})| \leq 1/4p(n)$ holds for all v's. Having computed all these approximations, we just select a string $\tilde{v}$ for which the approximated quantity $\widetilde{\Delta}_{n,\tilde{v}}(\overline{x})$ is the largest. To analyze the quality of

---

[8] Unlike in the non-uniform treatment, here we cannot hardwire values (such as the values of h and f on good sequences) into the algorithm D', because D' is required to be uniform.

our selection, let us denote by v_n a string s that maximizes $\Delta_{n,s}(\overline{x})$ (i.e., $\Delta_{n,v_n}(\overline{x}) = \Delta_n(\overline{x})$). Then, with probability at least $1 - 2^{-n}$, the string $\tilde{v}$ satisfies

$$\Delta_{n,\tilde{v}}(\overline{x}) \geq \widetilde{\Delta}_{n,\tilde{v}}(\overline{x}) - (1/4p(n))$$

$$\geq \widetilde{\Delta}_{n,v_n}(\overline{x}) - (1/4p(n))$$

$$\geq \Delta_{n,v_n}(\overline{x}) - (1/4p(n)) - (1/4p(n))$$

where the first and last inequalities are due to the quality of our approximations, and the second inequality is due to the fact that $\tilde{v}$ maximizes $\widetilde{\Delta}_{n,\cdot}(\overline{x})$. Thus, $\Delta_{n,\tilde{v}}(\overline{x}) \geq \Delta_n(\overline{x}) - (1/2p(n))$.

Thus, on input $(1^n, e, z, \overline{E}_e(\overline{\alpha}))$, where $z = (\overline{x}, 1^{|\overline{x}|})$, the distinguisher, denoted D', operates in two stages.

1. In the first stage, D' ignores the ciphertext $\overline{E}_e(\overline{\alpha})$. Using z, algorithm D' recovers $\overline{x}$, and computes $u = h_n(\overline{x}) \overset{\text{def}}{=} (1^n, 1^{|\overline{x}|}, h(1^n, \overline{x}))$. Using $\overline{x}$ and u, algorithm D' estimates $\Delta_n(\overline{x})$, and finds a value v as noted. That is, with probability at least $1 - 2^{-n}$, it holds that $\Delta_{n,v}(\overline{x}) > \Delta_n(\overline{x}) - (1/2p(n))$.
2. In the second stage (using u and v, as determined in the first stage), algorithm D' invokes A, and outputs 1 if and only if $A(e, \overline{E}_e(\overline{\alpha}), u) = v$.

Let $V_n(\overline{x})$ be the value found in the first stage of algorithm A (i.e., obliviously of the ciphertext $\overline{E}_e(\overline{\alpha})$). The reader can easily verify that

$$\Big| \Pr\Big[D'(1^n, G_1(1^n), Z_n, \overline{E}_{G_1(1^n)}(\overline{X}_n)) = 1\Big]$$

$$- \Pr\Big[D'(1^n, G_1(1^n), Z_n, \overline{E}_{G_1(1^n)}(1^{\overline{X}_n})) = 1\Big] \Big|$$

$$= \mathsf{E}\Big[\Delta_{n, V_n(\overline{X}_n)}(\overline{X}_n)\Big]$$

$$\geq (1 - 2^{-n}) \cdot \mathsf{E}\Big[\Delta_n(\overline{X}_n) - \frac{1}{2p(n)}\Big] - 2^{-n}$$

$$> \mathsf{E}\Big[\Delta_n(\overline{X}_n)\Big] - \frac{2}{3p(n)} > \frac{1}{3p(n)}$$

where the first inequality is due to the quality of the first stage (and the 2^{-n} factors account for the probability that the value found in that stage is bad). Thus, we have derived a probabilistic polynomial-time algorithm (i.e., D') that distinguishes encryptions of $\overline{X}_n$ from encryptions of $\overline{Y}_n = 1^{|\overline{X}_n|}$, when getting auxiliary information $Z_n = \overline{X}_n 1^{|\overline{X}_n|}$. By hypothesis, $\{\overline{X}_n\}$ is polynomial-time constructible, and it follows that so is $\{\overline{X}_n \overline{Y}_n Z_n\}$ Thus, we derive contradiction to Definition 5.2.14 (even under the special case postulated in the theorem), and the claim follows. $\square$

Having established the important direction, we now turn to the opposite one. That is, we assume that (G, E, D) is (uniformly) semantically secure and prove that it has (uniformly) indistinguishable encryptions. Again, the proof is by contradiction. However, the proof is more complex than in the non-uniform case, because here "distinguishable encryptions" means distinguishing between two plaintext-distributions (rather than between two fixed sequences of plaintexts), when also given a possibly related auxiliary input Z_n. Thus, it seems that we need to incorporate Z_n into the input given to the (semantic-security) adversary, and the only way to do so seems to be by letting Z_n be part of the a priori information given to that adversary (i.e., letting $h(\text{plaintext}) = Z_n$). Indeed, this will be part of the construction presented next.

Suppose, without loss of generality, that there exists a probabilistic polynomial-time algorithm D', a polynomial-time constructible ensemble $\overline{T} \stackrel{\text{def}}{=} \{T_n = \overline{X}_n \overline{Y}_n Z_n\}_{n \in \mathbb{N}}$ (as in Definition 5.2.14), a positive polynomial p, and infinitely many n's such that

$$\Pr\left[D'(Z_n, G_1(1^n), \overline{E}_{G_1(1^n)}(\overline{X}_n)) = 1\right]$$
$$> \Pr\left[D'(Z_n, G_1(1^n), \overline{E}_{G_1(1^n)}(\overline{Y}_n)) = 1\right]| + \frac{1}{p(n)}$$

Let $t(n)$ and $\ell(n)$ be such that $\overline{X}_n$ (resp., $\overline{Y}_n$) consists of $t(n)$ strings, each of length $\ell(n)$. Suppose, without loss of generality, that $|Z_n| = m(n) \cdot \ell(n)$, and parse Z_n into $\overline{Z}_n = (Z_n^{(1)}, ..., Z_n^{(m(n))}) \in (\{0, 1\}^{\ell(n)})^{m(n)}$ such that $Z_n = Z_n^{(1)} \cdots Z_n^{(m(n))}$. We define an auxiliary polynomial-time constructible ensemble $\overline{Q} \stackrel{\text{def}}{=} \{\overline{Q}_n\}_{n \in \mathbb{N}}$ such that

$$\overline{Q}_n = \begin{cases} 0^{\ell(n)} \overline{Z}_n \overline{X}_n \overline{Y}_n & \text{with probability } \frac{1}{2} \\ 1^{\ell(n)} \overline{Z}_n \overline{Y}_n \overline{X}_n & \text{with probability } \frac{1}{2} \end{cases} \tag{5.8}$$

That is, $\overline{Q}_n$ is a sequence of $1 + m(n) + 2t(n)$ strings, each of length $\ell(n)$, that contains $\overline{Z}_n \overline{X}_n \overline{Y}_n$ in addition to a bit (encoded in the $\ell(n)$-bit long prefix) indicating whether or not the order of $\overline{X}_n$ and $\overline{Y}_n$ is switched. We define the function f to be equal to this "switch"-indicator bit, and the function h to provide all information in $\overline{Q}_n$ except this switch bit. That is, we define f and h as follows:

- We define $f(1^n, \overline{q}) \stackrel{\text{def}}{=} f_n(\overline{q})$, where f_n returns the first bit of its input; that is, $f_n(\sigma^{\ell(n)} z \alpha \beta) = \sigma$, for $(z, \alpha, \beta) \in (\{0, 1\})^{l(n)})^{m(n)+2t(n)}$.
- We define $h(1^n, \overline{q}) \stackrel{\text{def}}{=} h_n(\overline{q})$, where h_n reorders the suffix of its input according to the first bit; that is, $h_n(0^{\ell(n)} z \alpha \beta) = z \alpha \beta$ and $h_n(1^{\ell(n)} z \alpha \beta) = z \beta \alpha$. Thus, $h(1^n, \overline{Q}_n) = \overline{Z}_n \overline{X}_n \overline{Y}_n$, where $\overline{Z}_n \overline{X}_n \overline{Y}_n$ is determined by $\overline{T}_n = \overline{X}_n \overline{Y}_n Z_n$ (and is independent of the switch-case chosen in Eq. (5.8)).

We stress that both h and f are polynomial-time computable.

We will show that the distinguishing algorithm D' (which distinguishes $\overline{E}(\overline{X}_n)$ from $\overline{E}(\overline{Y}_n)$, when also given $Z_n \equiv \overline{Z}_n$) can be transformed into a polynomial-time algorithm A that guesses the value of $f(1^n, \overline{Q}_n)$, from the encryption of $\overline{Q}_n$ (and the value of $h(1^n, \overline{Q}_n)$), and does so with probability non-negligibly greater than $1/2$. This violates semantic security, since no algorithm (regardless of its running time) can guess $f(1^n, \overline{Q}_n)$ with probability greater than $1/2$ when only given $h(1^n, \overline{Q}_n)$ and $1^{|\overline{Q}_n|}$ (because, conditioned on the value of $h(1^n, \overline{Q}_n)$ (and $1^{|\overline{Q}_n|}$), the value of $f(1^n, \overline{Q}_n)$ is uniformly distributed over $\{0, 1\}$).

On input $(e, \overline{E}_e(\overline{\alpha}), 1^{|\overline{\alpha}|}, h(1^n, \overline{\alpha}))$, where $\overline{\alpha} = \sigma^{\ell(n)} \overline{z} \overline{u} \overline{v} \in (\{0, 1\}^{l(n)})^{1+m(n)+2t(n)}$ equals either $(0^{\ell(n)}, \overline{z}, \overline{x}, \overline{y})$ or $(1^{\ell(n)}, \overline{z}, \overline{y}, \overline{x})$, algorithm A proceeds in two stages:

1. In the first stage, algorithm A ignores the ciphertext $\overline{E}_e(\overline{\alpha})$. It first extracts $\overline{x}, \overline{y}$ and $z \equiv \overline{z}$ out of $h(1^n, \overline{\alpha}) = \overline{z} \overline{x} \overline{y}$, and approximates $\Delta_n(z, \overline{x}, \overline{y})$, which is

defined to equal

$$\Pr\left[D'(z, G_1(1^n), \overline{E}_{G_1(1^n)}(\overline{x})) = 1\right] - \Pr\left[D'(z, G_1(1^n), \overline{E}_{G_1(1^n)}(\overline{y})) = 1\right]$$

Specifically, using $O(n \cdot p(n)^2)$ samples, algorithm A obtains an approximation, denoted $\widetilde{\Delta}_n(z, \overline{x}, \overline{y})$, such that $|\widetilde{\Delta}_n(z, \overline{x}, \overline{y}) - \Delta_n(z, \overline{x}, \overline{y})| < 1/3p(n)$ with probability at least $1 - 2^{-n}$.

Algorithm A sets $\xi = 1$ if $\widetilde{\Delta}_n(z, \overline{x}, \overline{y}) > 1/3p(n)$, sets $\xi = -1$ if $\widetilde{\Delta}_n(z, \overline{x}, \overline{y}) < -1/3p(n)$, and sets $\xi = 0$ otherwise (i.e., $|\widetilde{\Delta}_n(z, \overline{x}, \overline{y})| \leq 1/3p(n)$). Intuitively, ξ indicates the sign of $\widetilde{\Delta}_n(z, \overline{x}, \overline{y})$, provided that the absolute value of the latter is large enough, and is set to zero otherwise. In other words, with overwhelmingly high probability, ξ indicates whether the value of $\Pr[D'(z, \cdot, \overline{E}.(\overline{x})) = 1]$ is significantly greater, smaller, or about the same as $\Pr[D'(z, \cdot, \overline{E}.(\overline{y})) = 1]$.

In case $\xi = 0$, algorithm A halts with an arbitrary reasonable guess (say a randomly selected bit). (We stress that all this is done obliviously of the ciphertext $\overline{E}_e(\overline{\alpha})$, which is only used next.)

2. In the second stage, algorithm A extracts the last block of ciphertexts (i.e., $\overline{E}_e(\overline{v})$) out of $\overline{E}_e(\overline{\alpha}) = \overline{E}_e(\sigma^{\ell(n)}\overline{z}\,\overline{u}\,\overline{v})$, and invokes D' on input $(z, e, \overline{E}_e(\overline{v}))$, where z is as extracted in the first stage. Using the value of ξ as determined in the first stage, algorithm A decides (i.e., determines its output bit) as follows:

   - In case $\xi = 1$, algorithm A outputs 1 if and only if the output of D' is 1.
   - In case $\xi = -1$, algorithm A outputs 0 if and only if the output of D' is 1.

   That is, $\xi = 1$ (resp., $\xi = -1$) indicates that D' is more (resp., less) likely to output 1 when given the encryption of $\overline{x}$ than when given the encryption of $\overline{y}$.

Claim 5.2.15.2: Let $p, \overline{Q}_n, h, f$, and A be as in Eq. (5.8) and the text that follows it.

$$\Pr\left[A(G_1(1^n), \overline{E}_{G_1(1^n)}(\overline{Q}_n), h(1^n, \overline{Q}_n)) = f(1^n, \overline{Q}_n)\right] > \frac{1}{2} + \frac{1}{7 \cdot p(n)}$$

Proof Sketch: We focus on the case in which the approximation of $\Delta_n(z, \overline{x}, \overline{y})$ computed by (the first stage of) A is within $1/3p(n)$ of the correct value. Thus, in case $\xi \neq 0$, the sign of ξ agrees with the sign of $\Delta_n(z, \overline{x}, \overline{y})$. It follows that for every possible $(z, \overline{x}, \overline{y})$ such that $\xi = 1$ (it holds that $\Delta_n(z, \overline{x}, \overline{y}) > 0$ and) the following holds:

$$\Pr\left[A(G_1(1^n), \overline{E}_{G_1(1^n)}(\overline{Q}_n), h(1^n, \overline{Q}_n)) = f(1^n, \overline{Q}_n) \mid (Z_n, \overline{X}_n, \overline{X}_n) = (z, \overline{x}, \overline{y})\right]$$

$$= \frac{1}{2} \cdot \Pr\left[A(G_1(1^n), \overline{E}_{G_1(1^n)}(0^{\ell(n)}, z, \overline{x}, \overline{y}), h_n(0^{\ell(n)}, z, \overline{x}, \overline{y})) = 0\right]$$

$$+ \frac{1}{2} \cdot \Pr\left[A(G_1(1^n), \overline{E}_{G_1(1^n)}(1^{\ell(n)}, z, \overline{y}, \overline{x}), h_n(1^{\ell(n)}, z, \overline{y}, \overline{x})) = 1\right]$$

$$= \frac{1}{2} \cdot \Pr\left[D'(z, G_1(1^n), \overline{E}_{G_1(1^n)}(\overline{y})) = 0\right]$$

$$+ \frac{1}{2} \cdot \Pr\left[D'(z, G_1(1^n), \overline{E}_{G_1(1^n)}(\overline{x})) = 1\right]$$

$$= \frac{1}{2} \cdot (1 + \Delta_n(z, \overline{x}, \overline{y}))$$

Similarly, for every possible $(z, \overline{x}, \overline{y})$ such that $\xi = -1$ (it holds that $\Delta_n(z, \overline{x}, \overline{y}) < 0$ and) the following holds:

$$\Pr\left[A(G_1(1^n), \overline{E}_{G_1(1^n)}(\overline{Q}_n), h(1^n, \overline{Q}_n)) = f(1^n, \overline{Q}_n) \mid (Z_n, \overline{X}_n, \overline{X}_n) = (z, \overline{x}, \overline{y})\right]$$

$$= \frac{1}{2} \cdot (1 - \Delta_n(z, \overline{x}, \overline{y}))$$

Thus, in both cases where $\xi \neq 0$, algorithm A succeeds with probability

$$\frac{1 + \xi \cdot \Delta_n(z, \overline{x}, \overline{y})}{2} = \frac{1 + |\Delta_n(z, \overline{x}, \overline{y})|}{2}$$

and in case $\xi = 0$ it succeeds with probability $1/2$, which is (artificially) lower-bounded by $(1 + |\Delta_n(z, \overline{x}, \overline{y})| - (2/3p(n)))/2$ (because $|\Delta_n(z, \overline{x}, \overline{y})| \leq 2/3p(n)$ for $\xi = 0$).[9] Thus, *ignoring the negligible probability that the approximation deviated from the correct value by more than* $1/3p(n)$, the overall success probability of algorithm A is

$$\mathsf{E}\left[\frac{1 + |\Delta_n(Z_n, \overline{X}_n, \overline{Y}_n)| - (2/3p(n))}{2}\right] \geq \frac{1 + \mathsf{E}[\Delta_n(Z_n, \overline{X}_n, \overline{Y}_n)] - (2/3p(n))}{2}$$

$$> \frac{1 + (1/p(n)) - (2/3p(n))}{2} = \frac{1}{2} + \frac{1}{6p(n)}$$

where the last inequality follows by the contradiction hypothesis (i.e., that $\mathsf{E}[\Delta_n(Z_n, \overline{X}_n, \overline{Y}_n)] > \frac{1}{p(n)}$). The claim follows (because the negligible probability ignored in the last [displayed] inequality is certainly upper-bounded by $(1/6p(n)) - (1/7p(n))$). $\square$

This completes the proof of the opposite direction. ∎

Discussion. The proof of the first (i.e., important) direction holds also in the single-message setting. In general, for any function t, in order to prove that semantic security holds with respect to t-long sequences of ciphertexts, we just use the hypothesis that t-long message-sequences have indistinguishable encryptions. In contrast, the proof of the second (i.e., opposite) direction makes an essential use of the multiple-message setting. In particular, in order to prove that t-long message-sequences have indistinguishable encryptions, we use the hypothesis that semantic security holds with respect to $(1 + m + 2t)$-long sequences of ciphertexts, where m depends on the length of the auxiliary input in the claim of ciphertext-indistinguishability. Thus, even if we only want to establish ciphertext-indistinguishability in the single-message setting, we do so by using semantic security in the multiple-message setting. Furthermore, we use the fact that given a sequence of ciphertexts, we can extract a certain subsequence of ciphertexts.

---

[9] This analysis looks somewhat odd but is nevertheless valid. Our aim is to get a "uniform" expression for the success probability of A in all cases (i.e., for all values of ξ). In case $|\xi| = 1$, we have the lower-bound $(1 + |\Delta_n(z, \overline{x}, \overline{y})|)/2$, which is certainly lower-bounded by $(1 + |\Delta_n(z, \overline{x}, \overline{y})| - (2/3p(n)))/2$, whereas in case $\xi = 0$ we artificially lower-bound $1/2$ by the same expression. Once we have such a "uniform" expression, we may take expectation over it (without breaking it to cases).

5.2.5.3. Single-Message Versus Multiple-Message Definitions

As in the non-uniform case, for the public-key model, single-message security implies multiple-message security. Again, this implication does *not* hold in the private-key model. The proofs of both statements are analogous to the proofs provided in the non-uniform case. Specifically:

1. For the public-key model, single-message uniform-indistinguishability of encryptions implies multiple-message uniform-indistinguishability of encryptions, which in turn implies multiple-message uniform-semantic security.

   In the proof of this result, we use the fact that all hybrids are polynomial-time constructible, and that we may select a random pair of neighboring hybrids (as in the proof of Theorem 3.2.6). We also use the fact that an ensemble of triplets, $\{\overline{T}_n = \overline{X}_n \overline{Y}_n Z'_n\}_{n \in \mathbb{N}}$, with $\overline{X}_n = (X_n^{(1)}, ..., X_n^{(t(n))})$, $\overline{Y}_n = (Y_n^{(1)}, ..., Y_n^{(t(n))})$, as in Definition 5.2.14, induces an ensemble of triplets, $\{T_n = X_n Y_n Z_n\}_{n \in \mathbb{N}}$, for the case $t \equiv 1$. Specifically, we shall use $X_n = X_n^{(i)}$, $Y_n = Y_n^{(i)}$, and $Z_n = (\overline{X}_n, \overline{Y}_n, Z'_n, i)$, where i is uniformly distributed in $\{1, ..., t(n)\}$.

2. For the private-key model, single-message uniform-indistinguishability of encryptions does *not* imply multiple-message uniform-indistinguishability of encryptions. The proof is exactly as in the non-uniform case.

5.2.5.4. The Gain of a Uniform Treatment

Suppose that one is content with the uniform-complexity level of security, which is what we advocate in the following paragraph. Then the gain in using the uniform-complexity treatment is that a uniform-complexity level of security can be obtained using only uniform-complexity assumptions (rather than non-uniform-complexity assumptions). Specifically, the results presented in Section 5.3 are based on non-uniform assumptions such as the existence of functions that cannot be inverted by polynomial-size circuits (rather than by probabilistic polynomial-time algorithms). These non-uniform assumptions are used in order to satisfy the non-uniform definitions presented in Sections 5.2.1 and 5.2.2. Using any of these constructions, while making the analogous uniform assumptions, yields encryption schemes with the analogous uniform-complexity security. (We stress that this is no coincidence, but is rather an artifact of these construction being proven secure via a *uniform* reducibility argument.)

However, something is lost when relying on these (seemingly weaker) uniform-complexity assumptions. Namely, the security we obtain is only against the (seemingly weaker) uniform adversaries. We believe that this loss in security is immaterial. In particular, schemes secure against probabilistic polynomial-time adversaries can be used in any setting consisting of probabilistic polynomial-time machines with inputs generated by probabilistic polynomial-time procedures. We believe that the cryptographic setting is such a case. That is, we believe that the world should be modeled as a probabilistic polynomial-time procedure; namely, each object in the world was generated at some point by a uniform and efficient procedure (possibly depending on previously existing objects), rather than handed down from heaven (where it might have been selected non-uniformly or using non-recursive procedures).

5.2.5.5. An Alternative Treatment

An alternative uniform-complexity treatment of security (in the current passive setting) can be derived from the treatment of security under chosen plaintext attacks (presented in Section 5.4.3). Specifically, the definitions presented in Section 5.4.3.1 should be modified as follows:

- Replace the input pair (e, z), which is given to the attacker's first part (i.e., A_1), by 1^n. That is, eliminate the (non-uniform) auxiliary input z, and omit the encryption-key e (also in the public-key version).
- Remove the encryption oracle (i.e., E_e) from the definitions; that is, model the attacker by an ordinary (probabilistic polynomial-time) algorithm, rather than by an oracle machine.

Consequently, the definition of semantic security (Definition 5.4.8) can be simplified by using $A_1' = A_1$ and omitting Condition 2 (which refers to the distributions produced by A_1 and A_1'). Doing so requires a minor change in the first part of the proof of Theorem 5.4.11 (i.e., letting A_2' rather than A_1' generate a random encryption-key).

In the resulting definitions, the first part of the attacker is confined to an oblivious selection of a challenge template (i.e., the challenge template is selected independently of the encryption-key), whereas the second part of the attacker is given an adequate challenge (and nothing else). In the case of semantic security, this means that the adversary first selects the "application" that consists of the plaintext distribution, the partial information function h, and the desired information function f. These three objects are represented by circuits. Next, a plaintext x is selected according to the specified distribution, and the adversary is given a corresponding ciphertext (i.e., $E_e(x)$), as well as the corresponding partial information $h(x)$.

5.3. Constructions of Secure Encryption Schemes

In this section we present constructions of secure private-key and public-key encryption schemes. Here and throughout this section security means *semantic security in the multiple-message setting*. Recall that this is equivalent to ciphertext-indistinguishability (in the multiple-message setting). Also recall that for public-key schemes it suffices to prove ciphertext-indistinguishability in the single-message setting. Following are the main results of this section:

- Using any (non-uniformly robust) pseudorandom function, one can construct secure private-key encryption schemes. Recall that the former can be constructed using any (non-uniformly strong) one-way function.
- Using any (non-uniform strong) trapdoor one-way permutation, one can construct secure public-key encryption schemes.

In addition, we review some popular suggestions for private-key and public-key encryption schemes.

Probabilistic Encryption. Before starting, we recall that a secure *public-key* encryption scheme must employ a probabilistic (i.e., randomized) encryption algorithm. Otherwise, given the encryption-key as (additional) input, it is easy to distinguish the encryption of the all-zero message from the encryption of the all-ones message. The same holds for *private-key* encryption schemes when considering the multi-message setting.[10] For example, using a deterministic (private-key) encryption algorithm allows the adversary to distinguish two encryptions of the same message from the encryptions of a pair of different messages. Thus, the common practice of using pseudorandom permutations as "block-ciphers" (see definition in Section 5.3.2) is *not* secure (again, one can distinguish two encryptions of the same message from encryptions of two different messages). This explains the linkage between our security definitions and *randomized* (aka *probabilistic*) encryption schemes. Indeed, all our encryption schemes will employ randomized encryption algorithms.[11]

5.3.1.* Stream-Ciphers

It is common practice to use "pseudorandom generators" as a basis for private-key stream-ciphers (see definition in Section 5.3.1.1). Specifically, the pseudorandom generator is used to produce a stream of bits that are XORed with the corresponding plaintext bits to yield corresponding ciphertext bits. That is, the generated pseudorandom sequence (which is determined by the a priori shared key) is used as a "one-time pad" instead of a truly random sequence, with the advantage that the generated sequence may be much longer than the key (whereas this is not possible for a truly random sequence). This common practice is indeed sound, provided one actually uses pseudorandom generators (as defined in Section 3.3 of Volume 1), rather than programs that are called "pseudorandom generators" but actually produce sequences that are easy to predict (such as the linear congruential generator or some modifications of it that output a constant fraction of the bits of each resulting number).

As we shall see, by using any pseudorandom generator one may obtain a secure *private-key stream-cipher* that allows for the encryption of a stream of plaintext bits. We note that such a stream-cipher does not conform to our formulation of an encryption scheme (i.e., as in Definition 5.1.1), because in order to encrypt several messages one is required to maintain a counter (to prevent reusing parts of the pseudorandom "one-time pad"). In other words, we obtain a secure encryption scheme with a *variable state* that is modified after the encryption of each message. We stress that constructions of secure

---

[10] We note that this does not hold with respect to private-key schemes in the single-message setting (or for the augmented model of state-based ciphers discussed in Section 5.3.1). In such a case, the private-key can be augmented to include a seed for a pseudorandom generator, the output of which can be used to eliminate randomness from the encryption algorithm. (Question: Why does the argument fail in the public-key setting and in the multi-message private-key setting?)

[11] The (private-key) stream-ciphers discussed in Section 5.3.1 are an exception, but (as further explained in Section 5.3.1) these schemes do not adhere to our (basic) formulation of encryption schemes (as in Definition 5.1.1).

and *stateless* encryption schemes (i.e., conforming with Definition 5.1.1) are known and are presented in Sections 5.3.3 and 5.3.4. The traditional interest in stream-ciphers is due to efficiency considerations. We discuss this issue at the end of Section 5.3.3. But before doing so, let us formalize the discussion.

5.3.1.1. Definitions

We start by extending the simple mechanism of encryption schemes (as presented in Definition 5.1.1). The key-generation algorithm remains unchanged, but both the encryption and decryption algorithm take an additional input and emit an additional output, corresponding to their state before and after the operation. The length of the state is not allowed to grow by too much during each application of the encryption algorithm (see Item 3 in Definition 5.3.1), or else the efficiency of the entire "repeated encryption" process cannot be guaranteed. For the sake of simplicity, we incorporate the key in the state of the corresponding algorithm. Thus, the initial state of each of the algorithms is set to equal its corresponding key. Furthermore, one may think of the intermediate states as updated values of the corresponding key. For clarity, the reader may consider the special case in which the state contains the initial key, the number of times the scheme was invoked (or the total number of bits in such invocations), and auxiliary information that allows a speedup of the computation of the next ciphertext (or plaintext).

For simplicity, we assume that the decryption algorithm (i.e., D) is deterministic (otherwise formulating the reconstruction condition would be more complex). Intuitively, the main part of the reconstruction condition (i.e., Item 2 in Definition 5.3.1) is that the (proper) iterative encryption–decryption process recovers the original plaintexts. The additional requirement in Item 2 is that the state of the decryption algorithm is updated correctly so long as it is fed with strings of length equal to the length of the valid ciphertexts. The reason for this additional requirement is discussed following Definition 5.3.1. We comment that in traditional stream-ciphers, the plaintexts (and ciphertexts) are individual bits or blocks of a fixed number of bits (i.e., $|\alpha^{(i)}| = |\beta^{(i)}| = \ell$ for all i's).

Definition 5.3.1 (state-based cipher – the mechanism): A state-based encryption scheme *is a triple,* (G, E, D), *of probabilistic polynomial-time algorithms satisfying the following three conditions:*

1. *On input 1^n, algorithm G outputs a pair of bit strings.*
2. *For every pair $(e^{(0)}, d^{(0)})$ in the range of $G(1^n)$, and every sequence of plaintexts $\alpha^{(i)}$'s, the following holds: If $(e^{(i)}, \beta^{(i)}) \leftarrow E(e^{(i-1)}, \alpha^{(i)})$ and $(d^{(i)}, \gamma^{(i)}) \leftarrow D(d^{(i-1)}, \beta^{(i)})$, for $i = 1, 2, \ldots$, then $\gamma^{(i)} = \alpha^{(i)}$ for every i. Furthermore, for every i and every $\beta \in \{0, 1\}^{|\beta^{(i)}|}$, it holds that $D(d^{(i-1)}, \beta) = (d^{(i)}, \cdot)$. That is, $d^{(i)}$ is actually determined by $d^{(i-1)}$ and $|\beta^{(i)}|$.*[12]

---

[12] Alternatively, we may decompose the decryption (resp., encryption) algorithm into two algorithms, where the first takes care of the actual decryption (resp., encryption) and the second takes care of updating the state. For details see Exercise 24.

3. *There exists a polynomial p such that for every pair $(e^{(0)}, d^{(0)})$ in the range of $G(1^n)$, and every sequence of $\alpha^{(i)}$'s and $e^{(i)}$'s as in Item 2, it holds that $|e^{(i)}| \leq |e^{(i-1)}| + |\alpha^{(i)}| \cdot p(n)$. Similarly for the $d^{(i)}$'s.*

That is, as in Definition 5.1.1, the encryption–decryption process operates properly (i.e., the decrypted message equals the plaintext), provided that the corresponding algorithms get the corresponding keys (or states). Note that in Definition 5.3.1, the keys are modified by the encryption–decryption process, and so correct decryption requires holding the correctly updated decryption-key. We stress that the furthermore-clause in Item 2 guarantees that the decryption-key is correctly updated so long as the decryption process is fed with strings of the correct lengths (but not necessarily with the correct ciphertexts). This extra requirement implies that given the initial decryption-key and the current ciphertext, as well as the lengths of all previous ciphertexts (which may be actually incorporated in the current ciphertext), one may recover the current plaintext. This fact is interesting for two reasons:

A theoretical reason: It implies that without loss of generality (albeit with possible loss in efficiency), the decryption algorithm may be stateless. Furthermore, without loss of generality (again, with possible loss in efficiency), the state of the encryption algorithm may consist of the initial encryption-key and the lengths of the plaintexts encrypted so far.

A practical reason: It allows for recovery from the loss of some of the ciphertexts. That is, assuming that all ciphertexts have the same (known) length (which is typically the case in the relevant applications), if the receiver knows (or is given) the total number of ciphertexts sent so far, then it can recover the current plaintext from the current ciphertext, even if some of the previous ciphertexts were lost. See the special provision in Construction 5.3.3.

We comment that in Construction 5.3.3, it holds that $|e^{(i)}| \leq |e^{(0)}| + \log_2 \sum_{j=1}^{i} |\alpha^{(j)}|$, which is much stronger than the requirement in Item 3 (of Definition 5.3.1).

We stress that Definition 5.3.1 refers to the encryption of multiple messages (and meaningfully extends Definition 5.1.1 only when considering the encryption of multiple messages). However, Definition 5.3.1 by itself does not explain why one should encrypt the ith message using the updated encryption-key $e^{(i-1)}$, rather than reusing the initial encryption-key $e^{(0)}$ in all encryptions (where decryption is done by reusing the initial decryption-key $d^{(0)}$). Indeed, the reason for updating these keys is provided by the following security definition that refers to the encryption of multiple messages, and holds only in case the encryption-keys in use are properly updated (in the multiple-message encryption process). Here we present only the semantic security definition for private-key schemes.

Definition 5.3.2 (semantic security – state-based cipher): *For a state-based encryption scheme, (G, E, D), and any $\overline{x} = (x^{(1)}, ..., x^{(t)})$, we let $\overline{E}_e(\overline{x}) = (y^{(1)}, ..., y^{(t)})$ be the result of the following t-step (possibly random) process, where $e^{(0)} \stackrel{\text{def}}{=} e$. For $i = 1, ..., t$, we let $(e^{(i)}, y^{(i)}) \leftarrow E(e^{(i-1)}, x^{(i)})$, where each of the t invocations E utilizes* *independently chosen random coins. The scheme (G, E, D) is* semantically secure in the state-based private-key model *if for every polynomial t and every probabilistic polynomial-time algorithm A there exists a probabilistic polynomial-time algorithm A' such that for every $\{\overline{X}_n = (X_n^{(1)}, ..., X_n^{(t(n))})\}_{n \in \mathbb{N}}$, f, h, p, and n as in Definition 5.2.8, it holds that*

$$\Pr\left[A(1^n, \overline{E}_{G_1(1^n)}(\overline{X}_n), 1^{|\overline{X}_n|}, h(1^n, \overline{X}_n)) = f(1^n, \overline{X}_n)\right]$$

$$< \Pr\left[A'(1^n, t(n), 1^{|\overline{X}_n|}, h(1^n, \overline{X}_n)) = f(1^n, \overline{X}_n)\right] + \frac{1}{p(n)}$$

Note that Definition 5.3.2 (only) differs from Definition 5.2.8 in the preamble defining the random variable $\overline{E}_e(\overline{x})$, which mandates that the encryption-key $e^{(i-1)}$ is used in the ith encryption. Furthermore, Definition 5.3.2 guarantees nothing regarding an encryption process in which the plaintext sequence $x^{(1)}, ..., x^{(t)}$ is encrypted by $E(e, x^{(1)}), E(e, x^{(2)}), ..., E(e, x^{(t)})$ (i.e., the initial encryption-key e itself is used in all encryptions, as in Definition 5.2.8).

5.3.1.2. A Sound Version of a Common Practice

Using any (on-line) pseudorandom generator, one can easily construct a secure state-based private-key encryption scheme. Recall that on-line pseudorandom generators are a special case of variable-output pseudorandom generators (see Section 3.3.3), in which a hidden state is maintained and updated so as to allow generation of the next output bit in time polynomial in the length of the initial seed, regardless of the number of bits generated so far. Specifically, the next (hidden) state and output bit are produced by applying a (polynomial-time computable) function $g : \{0, 1\}^n \to \{0, 1\}^{n+1}$ to the current state (i.e., $s'\sigma \leftarrow g(s)$, where s is the current state, s' is the next state and σ is the next output bit). The suggested state-based private-key encryption scheme will be initialized with a key equal to the seed of such a generator, and will maintain and update a state allowing it to quickly produce the next output bit of the generator. The stream of plaintext bits will be encrypted by XORing these bits with the corresponding output bits of the generator.

Construction 5.3.3 (how to construct stream-ciphers [i.e., state-based private-key encryption schemes]): *Let g be a polynomial-time computable function such that $|g(s)| = |s| + 1$ for all $s \in \{0, 1\}^*$.*

Key-generation and initial state: *On input 1^n, uniformly select $s \in \{0, 1\}^n$, and output the key-pair (s, s). The initial state of each algorithm is set to $(s, 0, s)$.*

(We maintain the initial key s and a step-counter in order to allow recovery from loss of ciphertexts.)

Encrypting the next plaintext bit x with state (s, t, s'): *Let $s''\sigma = g(s')$, where $|s''| = |s'|$ and $\sigma \in \{0, 1\}$. Output the ciphertext bit $x \oplus \sigma$, and set the new state to $(s, t + 1, s'')$.*

407

Decrypting the ciphertext bit y with state (s, t, s'): *Let $s''\sigma = g(s')$, where $|s''| = |s'|$ and $\sigma \in \{0, 1\}$. Output the plaintext bit $y \oplus \sigma$, and set the new state to $(s, t + 1, s'')$.*

Special recovery procedure: *When notified that some ciphertext bits may have been lost and that the current ciphertext bit has index t', the decryption procedure first recovers the correct current state, denoted $s_{t'}$, to be used in decryption instead of s'. This can be done by computing $s_i\sigma_i = g(s_{i-1})$, for $i = 1, ..., t'$, where $s_0 \overset{\text{def}}{=} s$.[13]*

Note that both the encryption and decryption algorithms are deterministic, and that the state after encryption of t bits has length $2n + \log_2 t < 3n$ (for $t < 2^n$).

Recall that g (as in Construction 5.3.3) is called a next-step function of an on-line pseudorandom generator if for every polynomial p the ensemble $\{G_n^p\}_{n\in\mathbb{N}}$ is pseudorandom (with respect to polynomial-size circuits), where G_n^p is defined by the following random process:

> *Uniformly select $s_0 \in \{0, 1\}^n$;*
> *For $i = 1$ to $p(n)$, let $s_i\sigma_i \leftarrow g(s_{i-1})$, where $\sigma_i \in \{0, 1\}$ (and $s_i \in \{0, 1\}^n$);*
> *Output $\sigma_1\sigma_2 \cdots \sigma_{p(n)}$.*

Also recall that if g is itself a pseudorandom generator, then it constitutes a next-step function of an on-line pseudorandom generator (see Exercise 21 of Chapter 3). We have:

Proposition 5.3.4: *Suppose that g is a next-step function of an on-line pseudorandom generator. Then Construction 5.3.3 constitutes a secure state-based private-key encryption scheme.*

Proof Idea: Consider an ideal version of Construction 5.3.3 in which a truly random sequence is used instead of the output produced by the on-line pseudorandom generator defined by g. The ideal version coincides with the traditional one-time pad, and thus is perfectly secure. The security of the actual Construction 5.3.3 follows by the pseudorandomness of the on-line generator. ∎

5.3.2. Preliminaries: Block-Ciphers

Many encryption schemes are conveniently presented by first constructing a restricted type of encryption scheme that we call a *block-cipher*.[14] In contrast to encryption schemes (as defined in Definition 5.1.1), block-ciphers (as defined in Definition 5.3.5) are only required to operate on plaintexts of a specific length (which is a function of the security parameter). As we shall see, given a secure block-cipher, we can easily construct a (general) secure encryption scheme.

---

[13] More generally, if the decryption procedure holds the state at time $t < t'$ then it needs only compute $s_{t+1}, ..., s_{t'}$.

[14] In using the term *block-cipher,* we abuse standard terminology by which a block-cipher must, in addition to operating on plaintext of specific length, produce ciphertexts of a length that equals the length of the corresponding plaintexts. We comment that the latter cannot be semantically secure; see Exercise 25.

5.3.2.1. Definitions

We start by considering the syntax (cf. Definition 5.1.1).

Definition 5.3.5 (block-cipher): *A* block-cipher *is a triple, (G, E, D), of probabilistic polynomial-time algorithms satisfying the following two conditions:*

1. *On input 1^n, algorithm G outputs a pair of bit strings.*
2. *There exists a polynomially bounded function $\ell : \mathbb{N} \to \mathbb{N}$, called the* block length, *so that for every pair (e, d) in the range of $G(1^n)$, and for each $\alpha \in \{0, 1\}^{\ell(n)}$, algorithms E and D satisfy*

$$\Pr[D_d(E_e(\alpha)) = \alpha] = 1$$

Typically, we use either $\ell(n) = \Theta(n)$ or $\ell(n) = 1$. Analogously to Definition 5.1.1, this definition does not distinguish private-key encryption schemes from public-key ones. The difference between the two types is captured in the security definitions, which are essentially as before, with the modification that we only consider plaintexts of length $\ell(n)$. For example, the analogue of Definition 5.2.8 (for private-key schemes) reads:

Definition 5.3.6 (semantic security – private-key block-ciphers): *A block-cipher, (G, E, D), with block length ℓ is* semantically secure *(in the private-key model) if for every probabilistic polynomial-time algorithm A there exists a probabilistic polynomial-time algorithm A' such that for every ensemble $\{\overline{X}_n = (X_n^{(1)}, ..., X_n^{(t(n))})\}_{n \in \mathbb{N}}$, with $|X_n^{(1)}| = \cdots = |X_n^{(t(n))}| = \ell(n)$ and $t(n) \leq \mathrm{poly}(n)$, every pair of polynomially bounded functions f, h, every positive polynomial p, and all sufficiently large n, it holds that*

$$\Pr\left[A(1^n, \overline{E}_{G_1(1^n)}(\overline{X}_n), 1^{|\overline{X}_n|}, h(1^n, \overline{X}_n)) = f(1^n, \overline{X}_n)\right]$$

$$< \Pr\left[A'(1^n, t(n), 1^{|\overline{X}_n|}, h(1^n, \overline{X}_n)) = f(1^n, \overline{X}_n)\right] + \frac{1}{p(n)}$$

where $\overline{E}_e(x^{(1)}, ..., x^{(t)}) = (E_e(x^{(1)}), ..., E_e(x^{(t)}))$, as in Definition 5.2.8.

Note that, in case ℓ is polynomial-time computable, we can omit the auxiliary input $1^{|X_n|} = 1^{t(n) \cdot \ell(n)}$, because it can be reconstructed from the security parameter n and the value $t(n)$.

5.3.2.2. Transforming Block-Ciphers into General Encryption Schemes

There are obvious ways of transforming a block-cipher into a general encryption scheme. The basic idea is to break the plaintexts (for the resulting scheme) into blocks and encode each block separately by using the block-cipher. Thus, the security of the block-cipher (in the multiple-message settings) implies the security of the resulting encryption scheme. The only technicality we need to deal with is how to encrypt plaintexts of length that is not an integer multiple of the block-length (i.e., of $\ell(n)$). This is easily resolved by padding the last block (while indicating the end of the actual plaintext).[15]

Construction 5.3.7 (from block-ciphers to general encryption schemes): *Let (G, E, D) be a block-cipher with block length function ℓ. We construct an encryption scheme, (G', E', D'), as follows. The key-generation algorithm, G', is identical to G. To encrypt a message α* (with encryption-key e generated under security parameter n), *we break it into consecutive blocks of length $\ell(n)$, while possibly augmenting the last block. Let $\alpha_1, ..., \alpha_t$ be the resulting blocks. Then*

$$E'_e(\alpha) \stackrel{\text{def}}{=} (|\alpha|, E_e(\alpha_1), ..., E_e(\alpha_t))$$

To decrypt the ciphertext $(m, \beta_1, ..., \beta_t)$ (with decryption-key d), *we let $\alpha_i = D_d(\beta_i)$ for $i = 1, ..., t$, and let the plaintext be the m-bit long prefix of the concatenated string $\alpha_1 \cdots \alpha_t$.*

This construction yields ciphertexts that reveal the exact length of the plaintext. Recall that this is not prohibited by the definitions of security, and that we cannot hope to totally hide the plaintext length. However, we can easily construct encryption schemes that hide some information about the length of the plaintext; see examples in Exercise 5. Also, note that the above construction applies even to the special case where ℓ is identically 1.

Proposition 5.3.8: *Let (G, E, D) and (G', E', D') be as in Construction 5.3.7. Suppose that the former is a secure private-key[16]* (resp., public-key) *block-cipher. Then the latter is a secure private-key* (resp., public-key) *encryption scheme.*

Proof Sketch: The proof is by a reducibility argument. Assuming toward the contradiction that the encryption scheme (G', E', D') is not secure, we conclude that neither is (G, E, D), contradicting our hypothesis. Specifically, we rely on the fact that in both schemes, security means security in the multiple-message setting. Note that in case the security of (G', E', D') is violated via $t(n)$ messages of length $L(n)$, the security of (G, E, D) is violated via $t(n) \cdot \lceil L(n)/\ell(n) \rceil$ messages of length $\ell(n)$. Also, the argument may utilize any of the two notions of security (i.e., semantic security or ciphertext-indistinguishability). ■

5.3.3. Private-Key Encryption Schemes

Secure private-key encryption schemes can be easily constructed using any efficiently computable pseudorandom function ensemble (see Section 3.6). Specifically, we present a block-cipher with block length $\ell(n) = n$. The key-generation algorithm consists of

---

[15] We choose to use a very simple indication of the end of the actual plaintext (i.e., to include its length in the ciphertext). In fact, it suffices to include the length of the plaintext modulo $\ell(n)$. Another natural alternative is to use a padding of the form $10^{(\ell(n)-|\alpha|-1) \bmod \ell(n)}$, while observing that no padding is ever required in case $\ell(n) = 1$.

[16] Recall that throughout this section *security* means security in the multiple-message setting.

selecting a seed, denoted s, for such a function, denoted f_s. To encrypt a message $x \in \{0, 1\}^n$ (using key s), the encryption algorithm uniformly selects a string $r \in \{0, 1\}^n$ and produces the ciphertext $(r, x \oplus f_s(r))$. To decrypt the ciphertext (r, y) (using key s), the decryption algorithm just computes $y \oplus f_s(r)$. Formally, we have:

Construction 5.3.9 (a private-key block-cipher based on pseudorandom functions): *Let $F = \{F_n\}$ be an efficiently computable function ensemble and let I and V be the algorithms associated with it. That is, $I(1^n)$ selects a function with distribution F_n and $V(s, x)$ returns $f_s(x)$, where f_s is the function associated with the string s. We define a private-key block-cipher, (G, E, D), with block length $\ell(n) = n$ as follows:*

Key-generation: $G(1^n) = (k, k)$, where $k \leftarrow I(1^n)$.

Encrypting plaintext $x \in \{0, 1\}^n$ (using the key k): $E_k(x) = (r, V(k, r) \oplus x)$, where r is uniformly chosen in $\{0, 1\}^n$.

Decrypting ciphertext (r, y) (using the key k): $D_k(r, y) = V(k, r) \oplus y$.

Clearly, for every k (in the range of $I(1^n)$) and $x \in \{0, 1\}^n$,

$$D_k(E_k(x)) \;=\; D_k(U_n, f_k(U_n) \oplus x) \;=\; f_k(U_n) \oplus (f_k(U_n) \oplus x) \;=\; x$$

We assume that F is *pseudorandom with respect to polynomial-size circuits*, meaning that no polynomial-size circuit having "oracle gates" can distinguish the case in which the answers are provided by a random function from the case in which the answers are provided by a function in F. Alternatively, one may consider probabilistic polynomial-time oracle machines that obtain a non-uniform polynomially long auxiliary input. That is, *for every probabilistic polynomial-time oracle machine M, for every pair of positive polynomials p and q, and for all sufficiently large n's and all $z \in \{0, 1\}^{p(n)}$,*

$$\left| \Pr\left[M^\phi(z) = 1\right] - \Pr\left[M^{f_{I(1^n)}}(z) = 1\right] \right| \;<\; \frac{1}{q(n)}$$

where ϕ is a uniformly selected function mapping $\{0, 1\}^n$ to $\{0, 1\}^n$.

Analogously to Corollary 3.6.7, such (non-uniformly strong) pseudorandom functions can be constructed using any non-uniformly strong one-way function.

Proposition 5.3.10: *Let F and (G, E, D) be as in Construction 5.3.9, and suppose that F is pseudorandom with respect to polynomial-size circuits. Then (G, E, D) is secure.*

The proof of Proposition 5.3.10 follows. Combining Propositions 5.3.8 and 5.3.10 (with a non-uniform version of Corollary 3.6.7), we obtain:

Theorem 5.3.11: *If there exist (non-uniformly strong) one-way functions, then there exist secure private-key encryption schemes.*

The converse holds too; see Exercise 2.

Proof of Proposition 5.3.10: The proof consists of two steps (suggested as a general methodology in Section 3.6):

1. Prove that an idealized version of the scheme, in which one uses a uniformly selected function $\phi : \{0, 1\}^n \to \{0, 1\}^n$, rather than the pseudorandom function f_s, is secure (in the sense of ciphertext-indistinguishability).
2. Conclude that the real scheme (as presented in Construction 5.3.9) is secure (because otherwise one could distinguish a pseudorandom function from a truly random one).

Specifically, in the ideal version, the messages $x^{(1)}, \ldots, x^{(t)}$ are encrypted by $(r^{(1)}, \phi(r^{(1)}) \oplus x^{(1)}), \ldots, (r^{(t)}, \phi(r^{(t)}) \oplus x^{(t)})$, where the $r^{(j)}$'s are independently and uniformly selected, and ϕ is a random function. Thus, with probability greater than $1 - t^2 \cdot 2^{-n}$, the $r^{(j)}$'s are all distinct, and so the values $\phi(r^{(j)}) \oplus x^{(j)}$ are independently and uniformly distributed, regardless of the $x^{(j)}$'s. It follows that the ideal version is ciphertext-indistinguishable; that is, for any $x^{(1)}, \ldots, x^{(t)}$ and $y^{(1)}, \ldots, y^{(t)}$, the statistical difference between the distributions $(U_n^{(1)}, \phi(U_n^{(1)}) \oplus x^{(1)}), \ldots, (U_n^{(t)}, \phi(U_n^{(t)}) \oplus x^{(t)})$ and $(U_n^{(1)}, \phi(U_n^{(1)}) \oplus y^{(1)}), \ldots, (U_n^{(t)}, \phi(U_n^{(t)}) \oplus y^{(t)})$ is at most $t^2 \cdot 2^{-n}$.

Now, if the actual scheme is not ciphertext-indistinguishable, then for some sequence of $r^{(j)}$'s and $v^{(j)}$'s, a polynomial-size circuit can distinguish the $\phi(r^{(j)}) \oplus v^{(j)}$'s from the $f_s(r^{(j)}) \oplus v^{(j)}$'s, where ϕ is random and f_s is pseudorandom.[17] But this contradicts the hypothesis that polynomial-size circuits cannot distinguish between the two cases. ∎

Discussion. Note that we could have gotten rid of the randomization if we had allowed the encryption algorithm to be history dependent (as discussed in Section 5.3.1). Specifically, in such a case, we could have used a counter in the role of r. Furthermore, if the encryption scheme is used for FIFO communication between the parties and both can maintain the counter-value, then there is no need for the sender to send the counter-value. However, in the latter case, Construction 5.3.3 is preferable (because the adequate pseudorandom *generator* may be more efficient than a pseudorandom *function* as used in Construction 5.3.9). We note that in case the encryption scheme is not used for FIFO communication and one may need to decrypt messages with arbitrary varying counter-values, it is typically better to use Construction 5.3.9. Furthermore, in many cases it may be preferable to select a value (i.e., r) at random, rather, than rely on a counter that must be stored in a reliable manner between applications (of the encryption algorithm).

The ciphertexts produced by Construction 5.3.9 are longer than the corresponding plaintexts. This is unavoidable in the case of secure (history-independent) encryption schemes (see Exercise 25). In particular, the common practice of using pseudorandom

---

[17] The $v^{(j)}$'s either equal the $x^{(j)}$'s or the $y^{(j)}$'s, whereas the $r^{(j)}$'s are random (or are fixed by an averaging argument). The conclusion follows by considering the actual encryptions of the $x^{(j)}$'s and the $y^{(j)}$'s versus their ideal encryptions. Since the actual encryptions are distinguishable whereas the ideals are not, the actual encryption of either the $x^{(j)}$'s or the $y^{(j)}$'s must be distinguishable from the corresponding ideal version.

permutations as block-ciphers[18] is *not* secure (e.g., one can distinguish two encryptions of the same message from encryptions of two different messages).

Recall that by combining Constructions 5.3.7 and 5.3.9 (and referring to Propositions 5.3.8 and 5.3.10), we obtain a (full-fledged) private-key encryption scheme. A more efficient scheme is obtained by a direct combination of the ideas underlying both constructions:

Construction 5.3.12 (a private-key encryption scheme based on pseudorandom functions): *Let $F = \{F_n\}$ be as in Construction 5.3.9 (that is, $F = \{F_n\}$ is an efficiently computable function ensemble) and I and V be the selection and evaluation algorithms associated with it (e.g., $V(s, x) = f_s(x)$). We define a private-key encryption scheme, (G, E, D), as follows:*

Key-generation: $G(1^n) = (k, k)$, *where $k \leftarrow I(1^n)$.*

Encrypting plaintext $\alpha \in \{0, 1\}^*$ (using the key k): *Break α into consecutive blocks of length n, while possibly augmenting the last block. Let $\alpha_1, ..., \alpha_t$ be the resulting blocks. Associate $\{0, 1\}^n$ with the set of integer residues modulo 2^n, select uniformly $r \in \{0, 1\}^n$, and compute $r_i = r + i \bmod 2^n$, for $i = 1, ..., t$. Finally, form the ciphertext $(r, |\alpha|, V(k, r_1) \oplus \alpha_1, ..., V(k, r_t) \oplus \alpha_t)$. That is,*

$$E_k(x) = (r, |\alpha|, f_k(r + 1 \bmod 2^n) \oplus \alpha_1, ..., f_k(r + t \bmod 2^n) \oplus \alpha_t)$$

Decrypting ciphertext $(r, m, y_1, ..., y_t)$ (using the key k): *For $i = 1, ..., t$, compute $\alpha_i = V(k, (r + i \bmod 2^n)) \oplus y_i$, and output the m-bit long prefix of $\alpha_1 \cdots \alpha_t$. That is, $D_k(r, m, y_1, ..., y_t)$ is the m-bit long prefix of*

$$(V(k, (r + 1 \bmod 2^n)) \oplus y_1) \cdots (V(k, (r + t \bmod 2^n)) \oplus y_t)$$
$$= (f_k(r + 1 \bmod 2^n) \oplus y_1) \cdots (f_k(r + t \bmod 2^n) \oplus y_t)$$

Clearly, Construction 5.3.12 constitutes a secure private-key encryption scheme (provided that F is pseudorandom with respect to polynomial-size circuits). See Exercise 26.

5.3.4. Public-Key Encryption Schemes

As mentioned earlier, randomization during the encryption process can be avoided in private-key encryption schemes that employ a varying state (not allowed in our basic Definition 5.1.1). In the case of public-key encryption schemes, randomization during the encryption process is essential (even if the encryption scheme employs a varying state). Thus, the *randomized encryption paradigm* plays an even more pivotal role in the construction of public-key encryption schemes. To demonstrate this paradigm, we start with a very simple (and quite wasteful) construction. But before doing so, we recall the notion of trapdoor permutations.

---

[18] That is, letting $E_k(x) = p_k(x)$, where p_k is the permutation associated with the string k.

Trapdoor permutations. All our constructions employ a collection of trapdoor permutations, as in Definition 2.4.5. Recall that such a collection, $\{p_\alpha\}_\alpha$, comes with four probabilistic polynomial-time algorithms, denoted here by I, S, F, and B (for *index*, *sample*, *forward*, and *backward*), such that the following (syntactic) conditions hold:

1. On input 1^n, algorithm I selects a random n-bit long *index* α of a permutation p_α, along with a corresponding trapdoor τ;
2. On input α, algorithm S *samples* the domain of p_α, returning a random element in it;
3. For x in the domain of p_α, given α and x, algorithm F returns $p_\alpha(x)$ (i.e., $F(\alpha, x) = p_\alpha(x)$);
4. For y in the range of p_α, if (α, τ) is a possible output of $I(1^n)$, then given τ and y, algorithm B returns $p_\alpha^{-1}(y)$ (i.e., $B(\tau, y) = p_\alpha^{-1}(y)$).

The hardness condition refers to the difficulty of inverting p_α on a random element of its range, when given only the range-element and α. That is, let $I_1(1^n)$ denote the first element in the output of $I(1^n)$ (i.e., the index); then for every polynomial-size circuit family $\{C_n\}$, every polynomial p and all sufficiently large n's

$$\Pr[C_n(I_1(1^n), p_{I_1(1^n)}(S(I_1(1^n)))) = S(I_1(1^n))] \; < \; \frac{1}{p(n)}$$

Namely, C_n fails to invert p_α on $p_\alpha(x)$, where α and x are selected by I and S as in the previous paragraph. Recall that the collection can be easily modified to have a hard-core predicate (see Theorem 2.5.2). For simplicity, we continue to refer to the collection as $\{p_\alpha\}$, and *let b denote the corresponding hard-core predicate.*

5.3.4.1. Simple Schemes

We are now ready to present a very simple (alas quite wasteful) construction of a secure public-key encryption scheme. Actually, we present a block-cipher with block-length $\ell \equiv 1$.

Construction 5.3.13 (a simple public-key block-cipher scheme): *Let $\{p_\alpha\}$, I, S, F, B, and b be as in the paragraph entitled "trapdoor permutations."*

Key-generation: *The key-generation algorithm consists of selecting at random a permutation p_α together with a trapdoor τ for it: The permutation (or rather its description) serves as the public-key, whereas the trapdoor serves as the private-key. That is, $G(1^n) = I(1^n)$, which means that the index-trapdoor pair generated by I is associated with the key-pair of G.*

Encryption: *To encrypt a bit σ, using the encryption-key α, the encryption algorithm randomly selects an element, r, in the domain of p_α, and produces the ciphertext $(p_\alpha(r), \sigma \oplus b(r))$. That is, $E_\alpha(\sigma) = (F(\alpha, r), \sigma \oplus b(r))$, where $r \leftarrow S(\alpha)$.*

Decryption: *To decrypt the ciphertext (y, ς), using the decryption-key τ, the decryption algorithm just computes $\varsigma \oplus b(p_\alpha^{-1}(y))$, where the inverse is computed using the trapdoor τ of p_α. That is, $D_\tau(y, \varsigma) = \varsigma \oplus b(B(\tau, y))$.*

Clearly, for every possible (α, τ) output of G and for every $\sigma \in \{0, 1\}$, it holds that

$$
\begin{aligned}
D_\tau(E_\alpha(\sigma)) &= D_\tau(F(\alpha, S(\alpha)), \sigma \oplus b(S(\alpha))) \\
&= (\sigma \oplus b(S(\alpha))) \oplus b(B(\tau, F(\alpha, S(\alpha)))) \\
&= \sigma \oplus b(S(\alpha)) \oplus b(p_\alpha^{-1}(p_\alpha(S(\alpha)))) \\
&= \sigma \oplus b(S(\alpha)) \oplus b(S(\alpha)) = \sigma
\end{aligned}
$$

The security of this public-key encryption scheme follows from the (non-uniform) one-way feature of the collection $\{p_\alpha\}$ (or rather from the hypothesis that b is a corresponding hard-core predicate).

Proposition 5.3.14: *Suppose that b is a (non-uniformly strong) hard-core of the collection $\{p_\alpha\}$. Then Construction 5.3.13 constitutes a secure public-key block-cipher (with block-length $\ell \equiv 1$).*

Proof: Recall that by the equivalence theorems (i.e., Theorems 5.2.5 and 5.2.11), it suffices to show single-message ciphertext-indistinguishability. Furthermore, by the fact that here there are only two plaintexts (i.e., 0 and 1), it suffices to show that one cannot distinguish the encryptions of these two plaintexts. That is, all we need to prove is that, given the encryption-key α, it is infeasible to distinguish $E_\alpha(0) = (p_\alpha(r), b(r))$ from $E_\alpha(1) = (p_\alpha(r), 1 \oplus b(r))$, where $r \leftarrow S(\alpha)$. But this is easily implied by the hypothesis that b is a hard-core of the collection $\{p_\alpha\}$. Details follow.

Recall that by saying that b is a hard-core of $\{p_\alpha\}$, we mean that for every polynomial-size circuit family $\{C_n\}$, every polynomial p and all sufficiently large n's

$$
\Pr[C_n(I_1(1^n), p_{I_1(1^n)}(S(I_1(1^n)))) = b(S(I_1(1^n)))] < \frac{1}{2} + \frac{1}{p(n)} \tag{5.9}
$$

However, analogously to the second proof of Theorem 3.4.1, it can be shown that this implies that for every polynomial-size circuit family $\{C_n'\}$, every polynomial p', and all sufficiently large n's

$$
|\Pr[C_n'(\alpha, p_\alpha(r), b(r)) = 1] - \Pr[C_n'(\alpha, p_\alpha(r), 1 \oplus b(r)) = 1]| < \frac{1}{p'(n)}
$$

where $\alpha \leftarrow I_1(1^n)$ and $r \leftarrow S(\alpha)$. Thus, $(\alpha, E_\alpha(0))$ is computationally indistinguishable from $(\alpha, E_\alpha(1))$, and the proposition follows. ∎

Using Propositions 5.3.8 and 5.3.14, and recalling that Theorem 2.5.2 applies also to collections of one-way permutations and to the non-uniform setting, we obtain:

Theorem 5.3.15: *If there exist collections of (non-uniformly hard) trapdoor permutations, then there exist secure public-key encryption schemes.*

A generalization. As admitted earlier, Construction 5.3.13 is quite wasteful. Specifically, it is wasteful in *bandwidth,* which is defined to be the relationship between the length of the plaintext and the length of the ciphertext. In Construction 5.3.13, the relationship between these lengths equals the security parameter (i.e., the length of description of individual elements in the domain of the permutation). However, the idea underlying Construction 5.3.13 can yield efficient public-key schemes, provided we use trapdoor permutations having hard-core functions with large range (see Section 2.5.3). To demonstrate the point, we use the following assumption relating to the RSA collection of trapdoor permutations (cf. Subsections 2.4.3 and 2.4.4).

Large Hard-Core Conjecture for RSA: *The first $n/2$ least-significant bits of the argument constitute a* (non-uniformly strong) *hard-core function of the RSA function when applied with n-bit long moduli.*

We stress that the conjecture is *not* known to follow from the assumption that the RSA collection is (non-uniformly) hard to invert. What is known to hold under the latter assumption is only that the first $O(\log n)$ least-significant bits of the argument constitute a (non-uniformly strong) hard-core function of RSA (with n-bit long moduli). Still, if the large hard-core conjecture holds, then one obtains a secure public-key encryption scheme with efficiency comparable to that of "plain RSA" (see the following discussion). Furthermore, this scheme is related (but not identical) to the common practice of randomly padding messages (using padding equal in length to the message) before encrypting them (by applying the RSA function).[19] That is, we consider the following scheme:

Construction 5.3.16 (Randomized RSA – a public-key block-cipher scheme): *This scheme employs the RSA collection of trapdoor permutations (cf. Subsections 2.4.3 and 2.4.4). The following description is, however, self-contained.*

Key-generation: *The key-generation algorithm consists of selecting at random two n-bit primes, P and Q, setting $N = P \cdot Q$, selecting at random a pair (e, d) such that $e \cdot d \equiv 1 \pmod{(P-1) \cdot (Q-1)}$, and outputting the pair $((N, e), (N, d))$, where (N, e) is the encryption-key and (N, d) is the decryption-key. That is, $((N, e), (N, d)) \leftarrow G(1^n)$, where N, e, and d are as specified here.*

(Note that N is $2n$-bits long.)

Encryption: *To encrypt an n-bit string σ (using the encryption-key (N, e)), the encryption algorithm randomly selects an element $r \in \{0, ..., N-1\}$, and produces the ciphertext $(r^e \bmod N, \sigma \oplus \mathrm{LSB}(r))$, where $\mathrm{LSB}(r)$ denotes the n least-significant bits of r. That is, $E_{(N,e)}(\sigma) = (r^e \bmod N, \sigma \oplus \mathrm{LSB}(r))$.*

Decryption: *To decrypt the ciphertext $(y, \varsigma) \in \{0, ..., N-1\} \times \{0, 1\}^n$ (using the decryption-key (N, d)), the decryption algorithm just computes $\varsigma \oplus \mathrm{LSB}(y^d \bmod N)$, where $\mathrm{LSB}(\cdot)$ is as in the Encryption procedure. That is, $D_{(N,d)}(y, \varsigma) = \varsigma \oplus \mathrm{LSB}(y^d \bmod N)$.*

The bandwidth of this scheme is much better than in Construction 5.3.13: A plaintext of length n is encrypted via a ciphertext of length $2n + n = 3n$. Furthermore, Randomized RSA is almost as efficient as "plain RSA" (or the RSA function itself).

---

[19] The conjectured security of the common practice relies on a seemingly stronger assumption; that is, the assumption is that for every $x \in \{0, ..., 2^n - 1\}$, given (N, e) as generated in Construction 5.3.16, it is infeasible to distinguish $r^e \bmod N$ from $(x + s2^n)^e \bmod N$, where r (resp., s) is uniformly distributed in $\{0, ..., N-1\}$ (resp., in $\{0, ..., \lfloor N/2^n \rfloor - 1\}$).

To see that Randomized RSA satisfies the syntactic requirements of an encryption scheme, consider any possible output of $G(1^n)$, denoted $((N, e), (N, d))$, and any $\sigma \in \{0, 1\}^n$. Then, for any $r \in \{0, ..., N - 1\}$, it holds that

$$D_{(N,d)}(E_{(N,e)}(\sigma)) = D_{(N,d)}((r^e \bmod N), \sigma \oplus \mathrm{LSB}(r))$$
$$= (\sigma \oplus \mathrm{LSB}(r)) \oplus \mathrm{LSB}((r^e \bmod N)^d \bmod N)$$
$$= \sigma \oplus \mathrm{LSB}(r) \oplus \mathrm{LSB}(r^{ed} \bmod N) = \sigma$$

where the last equality is due to $r^{ed} \equiv r \pmod{N}$. The security of Randomized RSA (as a public-key encryption scheme) follows from the large hard-core conjecture for RSA, analogously to the proof of Proposition 5.3.14.

Proposition 5.3.17: *Suppose that the large hard-core conjecture for RSA does hold. Then Construction 5.3.16 constitutes a secure public-key block-cipher (with block-length $\ell(n) = n$).*

Proof Sketch: Recall that by the equivalence theorems (i.e., Theorems 5.2.5 and 5.2.11), it suffices to show single-message ciphertext-indistinguishability. Considering any two strings x and y, we need to show that $((N, e), r^e \bmod N, x \oplus \mathrm{LSB}(r))$ and $((N, e), r^e \bmod N, y \oplus \mathrm{LSB}(r))$ are indistinguishable, where N, e and r are selected at random as in the construction. It suffices to show that for every fixed x, the distributions $((N, e), r^e \bmod N, x \oplus \mathrm{LSB}(r))$ and $((N, e), r^e \bmod N, x \oplus s)$ are indistinguishable, where $s \in \{0, 1\}^n$ is uniformly distributed, independently of anything else. The latter claim follows from the hypothesis that the n least-significant bits are a hard-core function for RSA with moduli of length $2n$. ∎

Discussion. We wish to stress that *encrypting messages by merely applying the RSA function to them (without randomization) yields an insecure encryption scheme.* Unfortunately, this procedure (previously referred to as "plain RSA") is quite common in practice. The fact that plain RSA is definitely insecure is a special case of the fact that any public-key encryption scheme that employs a deterministic encryption algorithm is insecure. We warn that the fact that in such deterministic encryption schemes one can distinguish encryptions of two specific messages (e.g., the all-zero message and the all-one message) is not "merely of theoretical concern"; it may seriously endanger some applications! In contrast, Randomized RSA (as defined in Construction 5.3.16) *may be* secure, provided a quite reasonable conjecture (i.e., the large hard-core conjecture for RSA) holds. We comment that the more common practice of applying the RSA function to a randomly padded version of the plaintext is secure if and only if a seemingly stronger (and yet reasonable) assumption holds; see footnote 19. Thus, the latter practice is far superior to using the RSA function directly (i.e., without randomization): *The randomized version is likely to be secure, whereas the non-randomized (or plain) version is definitely insecure.*

We note that Construction 5.3.16 (or, alternatively, Construction 5.3.13) generalizes to any collection of trapdoor permutations having a corresponding large hard-core function. Suppose that $\{p_\alpha\}$ is such a collection, and h (or rather $\{h_\alpha\}$) is a corresponding hard-core function (resp., a corresponding collection of hard-core functions), such that any element in the domain of p_α is mapped by h (or h_α) to an $\ell(|\alpha|)$-bit long string. Then we can encrypt an $\ell(|\alpha|)$-bit long plaintext, x, by $(p_\alpha(r), h(r) \oplus x)$ (resp., $(p_\alpha(r), h_\alpha(r) \oplus x)$), where $r \leftarrow S(\alpha)$ (as in Construction 5.3.13). This yields a secure public-key encryption scheme with bandwidth related to the ratio of $\ell(|\alpha|)$ over the length of the description of an individual element in the domain of p_α.

5.3.4.2. An Alternative Scheme

An alternative construction of a public-key encryption scheme is presented in Construction 5.3.18. Rather than encrypting each plaintext bit (or block of bits) by an independently selected element in the domain of the trapdoor permutation (as done in Construction 5.3.13), we select only one such element (for the entire plaintext) and generate from it additional bits, one per each bit of the plaintext. These additional bits are determined by successive applications of the trapdoor permutation, and only the last result is included in the ciphertext. In a sense, the construction of this encryption scheme augments the construction of a pseudorandom generator based on one-way permutations (i.e., Construction 3.4.4).

Construction 5.3.18 (a public-key encryption scheme): *Let $\{p_\alpha\}$, I, S, F, B, and b be as in Construction 5.3.13. We use the notation $p_\alpha^{i+1}(x) = p_\alpha(p_\alpha^i(x))$ and $p_\alpha^{-(i+1)}(x) = p_\alpha^{-1}(p_\alpha^{-i}(x))$.*

Key-generation: *The key-generation algorithm consists of selecting at random a permutation p_α together with a trapdoor, exactly as in Construction 5.3.13. That is, $G(1^n) = I(1^n)$, which means that the index-trapdoor pair generated by I is associated with the key-pair of G.*

Encryption: *To encrypt a string σ, using the encryption-key α, the encryption algorithm randomly selects an element, r, in the domain of p_α and produces the ciphertext $(p_\alpha^{|\sigma|}(r), \sigma \oplus G_\alpha^{(|\sigma|)}(r))$, where*

$$G_\alpha^{(\ell)}(r) \stackrel{\text{def}}{=} b(r) \cdot b(p_\alpha(r)) \cdots b(p_\alpha^{\ell-1}(r)) \tag{5.10}$$

That is, $E_\alpha(\sigma) = (p_\alpha^{|\sigma|}(S(\alpha)), \sigma \oplus G_\alpha^{(|\sigma|)}(S(\alpha)))$.

Decryption: *To decrypt the ciphertext (y, ς), using the decryption-key τ, the decryption algorithm just computes $\varsigma \oplus G_\alpha^{(|\varsigma|)}(p_\alpha^{-|\varsigma|}(y))$, where the inverse is computed using the trapdoor τ of p_α. That is, $D_\tau(y, \varsigma) = \varsigma \oplus G_\alpha^{(|\varsigma|)}(p_\alpha^{-|\varsigma|}(y))$.*

We stress that this encryption scheme is a full-fledged one (rather than a block-cipher). Its bandwidth tends to 1 with the length of the plaintext; that is, a plaintext of length $\ell = \text{poly}(n)$ is encrypted via a ciphertext of length $m + \ell$, where m denotes the length of the description of individual elements in the domain of p_α. Clearly, for every possible (α, τ) output of G (and $r \leftarrow S(\alpha)$), it holds that

$$D_\tau(E_\alpha(\sigma)) = D_\tau(p_\alpha^{|\sigma|}(r), \sigma \oplus G_\alpha^{(|\sigma|)}(r))$$

$$= (\sigma \oplus G_\alpha^{(|\sigma|)}(r)) \oplus G_\alpha^{(|\sigma|)}(p_\alpha^{-|\sigma \oplus G_\alpha^{(|\sigma|)}(r)|}(p_\alpha^{|\sigma|}(r)))$$

$$= \sigma \oplus G_\alpha^{(|\sigma|)}(r) \oplus G_\alpha^{(|\sigma|)}(r) = \sigma$$

The security of this public-key encryption scheme follows from the (non-uniform) one-way feature of the collection $\{p_\alpha\}$, but here we restrict the sampling algorithm S to produce almost uniform distribution over the domain (so that this distribution is preserved under successive applications of p_α).

Proposition 5.3.19: *Suppose that b is a (non-uniformly strong) hard-core of the trapdoor collection $\{p_\alpha\}$. Furthermore, suppose that this trapdoor collection utilizes a domain sampling algorithm S so that the statistical difference between $S(\alpha)$ and the uniform distribution over the domain of p_α is negligible in terms of $|\alpha|$. Then Construction 5.3.18 constitutes a secure public-key encryption scheme.*

Proof: Again, we prove single-message ciphertext-indistinguishability. It suffices to show that for every σ, the distributions $(\alpha, p_\alpha^{|\sigma|}(S(\alpha)), \sigma \oplus G_\alpha^{(|\sigma|)}(S(\alpha)))$ and $(\alpha, p_\alpha^{|\sigma|}(S(\alpha)), \sigma \oplus s)$ are indistinguishable, where $s \in \{0, 1\}^{|\sigma|}$ is uniformly distributed, independently of anything else. The latter claim holds by a minor extension to Proposition 3.4.6: This proposition refers to the case where $S(\alpha)$ is uniform over the domain of p_α, but can be extended to the case in which there is a negligible statistical difference between the distributions.

Details: We need to prove that for every polynomial ℓ and every sequence of pairs $(\sigma'_n, \sigma''_n) \in \{0, 1\}^{\ell(n)} \times \{0, 1\}^{\ell(n)}$, the distributions $D'_n \stackrel{\text{def}}{=} (\alpha, p_\alpha^{\ell(n)}(S(\alpha)), \sigma'_n \oplus G_\alpha^{(\ell(n))}(S(\alpha)))$ and $D''_n \stackrel{\text{def}}{=} (\alpha, p_\alpha^{\ell(n)}(S(\alpha)), \sigma''_n \oplus G_\alpha^{(\ell(n))}(S(\alpha)))$ are indistinguishable, where $\alpha \leftarrow I_1(1^n)$. We prove this in two steps:

1. We first prove that for every sequence of σ_n's, the distributions $D_n \stackrel{\text{def}}{=} (\alpha, p_\alpha^{\ell(n)}(S(\alpha)), \sigma_n \oplus G_\alpha^{(\ell(n))}(S(\alpha)))$ and $R_n \stackrel{\text{def}}{=} (\alpha, p_\alpha^{\ell(n)}(S(\alpha)), \sigma_n \oplus U_{\ell(n)})$ are indistinguishable, where $U_{\ell(n)}$ denotes a random variable uniformly distributed over $\{0, 1\}^{\ell(n)}$ and $\alpha \leftarrow I_1(1^n)$.

   Suppose first that $S(\alpha)$ is uniform over the domain of p_α. Then the indistinguishability of $\{D_n\}_{n \in \mathbb{N}}$ and $\{R_n\}_{n \in \mathbb{N}}$ follows directly from Proposition 3.4.6 (as adapted to circuits): The adapted form refers to the indistinguishability of $(\alpha, p_\alpha^{\ell(n)}(S(\alpha)), G_\alpha^{(\ell(n))}(S(\alpha)))$ and $(\alpha, p_\alpha^{\ell(n)}(S(\alpha)), U_{\ell(n)})$, and yields the desired claim by noting that σ_n can be incorporated in the prospective distinguisher. The extension (to the case that $S(\alpha)$ has negligible statistical difference to the uniform distribution over the domain of p_α) is straightforward.

2. Applying the previous item to D'_n and $R'_n \stackrel{\text{def}}{=} (\alpha, p_\alpha^{\ell(n)}(S(\alpha)), \sigma'_n \oplus U_{\ell(n)})$, we conclude that $\{D'_n\}_{n \in \mathbb{N}}$ and $\{R'_n\}_{n \in \mathbb{N}}$ are indistinguishable. Similarly, $\{D''_n\}_{n \in \mathbb{N}}$ and $\{R''_n\}_{n \in \mathbb{N}}$, where $R''_n \stackrel{\text{def}}{=} (\alpha, p_\alpha^{\ell(n)}(S(\alpha)), \sigma''_n \oplus U_{\ell(n)})$, are indistinguishable. Furthermore, $\{R'_n\}_{n \in \mathbb{N}}$ and $\{R''_n\}_{n \in \mathbb{N}}$ are identically distributed. Thus, $\{D'_n\}_{n \in \mathbb{N}}$ and $\{D''_n\}_{n \in \mathbb{N}}$ are indistinguishable.

The proposition follows. ∎

An instantiation. Assuming that factoring Blum Integers (i.e., products of two primes each congruent to 3 (mod 4)) is hard, one may use the modular squaring function (which induces a permutation over the quadratic residues modulo the product of these integers) in the role of the trapdoor permutation used in Construction 5.3.18. This yields a secure public-key encryption scheme with efficiency comparable to that of plain RSA (see further discussion later in this section).

Construction 5.3.20 (the Blum-Goldwasser Public-Key Encryption Scheme): *Consult Appendix A in Volume 1 for the relevant number-theoretic background, and note that for $P \equiv 3$ (mod 4) the number $(P + 1)/4$ is an integer. For simplicity, we present a block-cipher with arbitrary block-length $\ell(n) \leq \text{poly}(n)$; a full-fledged encryption scheme can be derived by an easy modification (see Exercise 27).*

Key-generation: *The key-generation algorithm consists of selecting at random two n-bit primes, P and Q, each congruent to 3 mod 4, and outputting the pair $(N, (P, Q))$, where $N = P \cdot Q$.*

> *Actually, for sake of efficiency, the key-generator also computes*
>
> $$d_P = ((P + 1)/4)^{\ell(n)} \bmod P - 1 \quad (in \{0, ..., P - 2\})$$
>
> $$d_Q = ((Q + 1)/4)^{\ell(n)} \bmod Q - 1 \quad (in \{0, ..., Q - 2\})$$
>
> $$c_P = Q \cdot (Q^{-1} \bmod P) \qquad\qquad (in \{0, ..., N - Q\})$$
>
> $$c_Q = P \cdot (P^{-1} \bmod Q) \qquad\qquad (in \{0, ..., N - P\})$$

> *It outputs the pair (N, T), where N serves as the encryption-key and $T = (P, Q, N, c_P, d_P, c_Q, d_Q)$ serves as decryption-key.*

Encryption: *To encrypt the message $\sigma \in \{0, 1\}^{\ell(n)}$, using the encryption-key N:*

1. *Uniformly select $s_0 \in \{1, ..., N\}$.*
   (Note that if $\text{GCD}(s_0, N) = 1$, then $s_0^2 \bmod N$ is a uniformly distributed quadratic residue modulo N.)
2. *For $i = 1, .., \ell(n) + 1$, compute $s_i \leftarrow s_{i-1}^2 \bmod N$ and $b_i = \text{lsb}(s_i)$, where $\text{lsb}(s)$ is the least-significant bit of s.*

The ciphertext is $(s_{\ell(n)+1}, \varsigma)$, where $\varsigma = \sigma \oplus b_1 b_2 \cdots b_{\ell(n)}$.

Decryption: *To decrypt the ciphertext (r, ς) using the decryption-key $T = (P, Q, N, c_P, d_P, c_Q, d_Q)$, one first retrieves s_1 and then computes the b_i's as in the Encryption procedure. Instead of successively extracting modular square roots $\ell(n)$ times, we extract the $2^{\ell(n)}$-th root, which can be done as efficiently as extracting a single square root. Extracting the $2^{\ell(n)}$-th root modulo N is done by extracting the corresponding root modulo P and modulo Q (by raising to power d_P modulo P and d_Q modulo Q, respectively) and combining the results via the Chinese Reminder Theorem:*

1. *Let $s' \leftarrow r^{d_P} \bmod P$, and $s'' \leftarrow r^{d_Q} \bmod Q$.*
2. *Let $s_1 \leftarrow c_P \cdot s' + c_Q \cdot s'' \bmod N$.*
3. *For $i = 1, ..., \ell(n)$, compute $b_i = \text{lsb}(s_i)$ and $s_{i+1} \leftarrow s_i^2 \bmod N$.*

The plaintext is $\varsigma \oplus b_1 b_2 \cdots b_{\ell(n)}$.

Again, one can easily verify that this construction constitutes an encryption scheme: The main fact to verify is that the value of s_1 as reconstructed in the decryption stage equals the value used in the encryption stage. This follows by combining the Chinese Reminder Theorem with the fact that for every quadratic residue s mod N, it holds that $s \equiv (s^{2^{\ell(n)}} \bmod N)^{d_P} \pmod{P}$ and $s \equiv (s^{2^{\ell(n)}} \bmod N)^{d_Q} \pmod{Q}$.

Details: Recall that for a prime $P \equiv 3 \pmod{4}$, and every quadratic residue r, we have $r^{(P+1)/2} \equiv r \pmod{P}$. Thus, for every quadratic residue s (modulo N) and every ℓ, we have

$$(s^{2^\ell} \bmod N)^{d_P} \equiv \left(s^{2^\ell} \bmod N \right)^{((P+1)/4)^\ell} \pmod{P}$$

$$\equiv s^{((P+1)/2)^\ell} \pmod{P}$$

$$\equiv s \pmod{P}$$

Similarly, $(s^{2^\ell} \bmod N)^{d_Q} \equiv s \pmod{Q}$. Finally, observing that c_P and c_Q are as in the Chinese Reminder Theorem,[20] we conclude that s_1 as recovered in Step 2 of the decryption process equals s_1 as first computed in Step 2 of the encryption process.

Encryption amounts to $\ell(n) + 1$ modular multiplications, whereas decryption amounts to $\ell(n) + 2$ such multiplications and 2 modular exponentiations (relative to half-sized moduli). Counting modular exponentiations with respect to n-bit moduli as $O(n)$ (i.e., at least n, typically $1.5n$, and at most $2n$) modular multiplications (with respect to n-bit moduli), we conclude that the entire encryption–decryption process requires work comparable to $2\ell(n) + 3n$ modular multiplications. For comparison to (Randomized) RSA, note that encrypting/decrypting $\ell(n)$-bit messages (in Randomized RSA) amounts to $\lceil \ell(n)/n \rceil$ modular exponentiations, and so the total work is comparable to $2 \cdot (\ell(n)/n) \cdot 1.5n = 3\ell(n)$ modular multiplications (for general exponent e, or $(\ell(n)/n) \cdot (2 + 1.5n) \approx 1.5\ell(n)$ modular multiplications in case $e = 3$).

The security of the Blum-Goldwasser scheme (i.e., Construction 5.3.20) follows immediately from Proposition 5.3.19 and the fact that the least-significant bit (i.e., lsb) is a hard-core for the modular squaring function. Recalling that inverting the latter is computationally equivalent to factoring, we get:

Corollary 5.3.21: *Suppose that factoring is infeasible in the sense that for every polynomial-size circuit $\{C_n\}$, every positive polynomial p, and all sufficiently large n's*

$$\Pr[C_n(P_n \cdot Q_n) = P_n] < \frac{1}{p(n)}$$

where P_n and Q_n are uniformly distributed n-bit long primes. Then Construction 5.3.20 constitutes a secure public-key encryption scheme.

Thus, the conjectured infeasibility of factoring (which is a necessary condition for security of RSA) yields a secure public-key encryption scheme with efficiency comparable

---

[20] That is, $i \equiv c_P \cdot (i \bmod P) + c_Q \cdot (i \bmod Q) \pmod{N}$, for every integer i.

to that of (plain or Randomized) RSA. In contrast, recall that plain RSA itself is not secure (as it employs a deterministic encryption algorithm), whereas Randomized RSA (i.e., Construction 5.3.16) is not known to be secure under a standard assumption such as intractability of factoring (or even of inverting the RSA function).[21]

5.4.* Beyond Eavesdropping Security

Our treatment so far has referred only to a "passive" attack in which the adversary merely eavesdrops on the line over which ciphertexts are being sent. Stronger types of attacks, culminating in the so-called Chosen Ciphertext Attack, may be possible in various applications. Specifically, in some settings it is feasible for the adversary to make the sender encrypt a message of the adversary's choice, and in some settings the adversary may even make the receiver decrypt a ciphertext of the adversary's choice. This gives rise to *chosen plaintext attacks* and to *chosen ciphertext attacks,* respectively, which are not covered by the security definitions considered in previous sections. Thus, our main goal in this section is to provide a treatment of such types of "active" attacks. In addition, we also discuss the related notion of non-malleable encryption schemes (see Section 5.4.5).

5.4.1. Overview

We start with an overview of the type of attacks and results considered in the current (rather long) section.

5.4.1.1. Types of Attacks

The following mini-taxonomy of attacks is certainly not exhaustive.

Passive attacks. We first reconsider passive attacks as referred to in the definitions given in previous sections. In the case of public-key schemes we distinguish two sub-cases:

1. A *key-oblivious,* passive attack, as captured in the aforementioned definitions. By "key-obliviousness" we refer to the postulation that the choice of plaintext does not depend on the public-key.
2. A *key-dependent,* passive attack, in which the choice of plaintext may depend on the public-key.

(In Definition 5.2.2, the choice of plaintext means the random variable X_n, whereas in Definition 5.2.4, it means the pair (x_n, y_n). In both these definitions, the choice of the plaintext is key-oblivious.)

---

[21] Recall that Randomized RSA is secure provided that the $n/2$ least-significant bits constitute a hard-core function for n-bit RSA moduli. This is a reasonable conjecture, but it seems stronger than the conjecture that RSA is hard to invert: Assuming that RSA is hard to invert, we only know that the $O(\log n)$ least-significant bits constitute a hard-core function for n-bit moduli.

Chosen Plaintext Attacks. Here the attacker may obtain encryptions of plaintexts of its choice (under the key being attacked). Indeed, such an attack does not add power in the case of public-key schemes.

Chosen Ciphertext Attacks. Here the attacker may obtain decryptions of ciphertexts of its choice (under the key being attacked). That is, the attacker is given oracle access to the decryption function corresponding to the decryption-key in use. We distinguish two types of such attacks.

1. In an *a priori chosen* ciphertext attack, the attacker is given access to the decryption oracle only prior to being presented with the ciphertext that it should attack (i.e., the ciphertext for which it has to learn partial information). That is, the attack consists of two stages: In the first stage, the attacker is given the above oracle access, and in the second stage, the oracle is removed and the attacker is given a "test ciphertext" (i.e., a test of successful learning).

2. In an *a posteriori chosen* ciphertext attack, after being given the test ciphertext, the decryption oracle is not removed, but rather the adversary's access to this oracle is restricted in the natural way (i.e., the adversary is allowed to query the oracle on any ciphertext except for the test ciphertext).

In both cases, the adversary may make queries that do not correspond to a legitimate ciphertext, and the answer will be accordingly (i.e., a special "failure" symbol). Furthermore, in both cases the adversary may effect the selection of the test ciphertext (by specifying a distribution from which the corresponding plaintext is to be drawn).

Formal definitions of all these types of attacks are given in the following subsections (i.e., in Sections 5.4.2, 5.4.3, and 5.4.4, respectively). In addition, in Section 5.4.5, we consider the related notion of *malleability,* that is, attacks aimed at generating encryptions of plaintexts related to the secret plaintext, rather than gaining information about the latter.

5.4.1.2. Constructions

As in the basic case (i.e., Section 5.3), actively secure private-key encryption schemes can be constructed based on the existence of one-way functions, whereas actively secure public-key encryption schemes are based on the existence of (enhanced) trapdoor permutations. In both cases, withstanding a posteriori chosen ciphertext attacks is harder than withstanding a priori chosen ciphertext attacks. We will present the following results.

For Private-Key Schemes. In Section 5.4.4.3, we show that the private-key encryption scheme based on pseudorandom functions (i.e., Construction 5.3.9) is secure also under *a priori chosen ciphertext attacks,* but is not secure under an *a posteriori chosen ciphertext attack.* We also show how to transform any passively secure private-key encryption scheme into a scheme *secure under (a posteriori) chosen ciphertext attacks* by using a message-authentication scheme on top of the basic encryption. Thus, the latter construction relies on message-authentication schemes as defined in Section 6.1. We mention that message-authentication schemes can be constructed using pseudorandom functions; see Section 6.3.

For Public-Key Schemes. Assuming the existence of enhanced trapdoor permutations (see Section C.1 in Appendix C), we will present constructions of public-key encryption schemes that are secure against (a priori and a posteriori) chosen ciphertext attacks. The constructions utilize various forms of non-interactive zero-knowledge proofs (see Section 4.10 in Volume 1), which can be constructed under the former assumption. We warn that these constructions, which are presented in Section 5.4.4.4, are rather complex.

As a corollary to the relation between these strong notions of security and non-malleable encryption schemes, we will conclude that the schemes withstanding a posteriori chosen ciphertext attacks are non-malleable. For details, see Section 5.4.5.

5.4.1.3. Methodological Comments

As hinted, we do not cover all possible intermediate types of attacks but, rather, focus on some natural ones. For example, we only consider key-dependent attacks on public-key encryption schemes (but not on private-key schemes).

The attacks are presented in increasing order of strength; hence, resilience against such attacks yields increasingly stronger notions of security.[22] This fact may be best verified when considering the indistinguishability variants of these security definitions.

A uniform-complexity treatment seems more appealing in the current section (i.e., more than in the previous sections). However, for the sake of consistency with the basic definitions (i.e., the previous sections of this chapter), we use non-uniform formulations of the various definitions. In fact, our treatment of the active attacks (i.e., in Sections 5.4.3 and 5.4.4) only uses non-uniformity in referring to (non-uniform) auxiliary inputs, and so non-uniformity can be easily eliminated in that case (i.e., by just eliminating these auxiliary inputs from all the definitions). (In Section 5.4.2 we refer to non-uniform families of [polynomial-size] circuits, but also in this case, all results extend to the uniform-complexity setting [because all the reductions are actually uniform].)

As mentioned, non-interactive zero-knowledge proofs play a central role in the construction of public-key encryption schemes that are secure under chosen ciphertext attacks. Thus, we will assume that the reader is fairly comfortable with the notion of zero-knowledge proofs. Furthermore, although we recall the relevant definition of non-interactive zero-knowledge, which will serve as our starting point toward stronger notions, we recommend that the more basic definitions (and results) regarding non-interactive zero-knowledge proofs (as presented in Section 4.10) be studied first. In our constructions of encryption schemes that are secure under a posteriori chosen

---

[22] Indeed, an alternative presentation may start with the strongest notion of security (i.e., corresponding to a-posteriori chosen ciphertext attacks), and obtain the weaker notions by imposing various restrictions (on the attacks).

ciphertext attacks, we will use some results from Chapter 6. In the case of private-key encryption schemes (treated in Section 5.4.4.3), we will use a message-authentication scheme, but do so in a self-contained way. In the case of public-key encryption schemes (treated in Section 5.4.4.4), we will use signature schemes (having an extra property) in order to construct a certain non-interactive zero-knowledge proof, which we use for the construction of the encryption scheme. At that point we will refer to a specific result proved in Chapter 6.

5.4.2. Key-Dependent Passive Attacks

The following discussion, as well as the entire subsection, *refers only to public-key encryption schemes*. For sake of simplicity, we present the single-message definitions of security. We note that, as in the basic case (for public-key encryption schemes), the single-message definitions of security are equivalent to the multiple-message ones.

In Definitions 5.2.2 and 5.2.4, the plaintext distribution (or pair) is fixed obliviously of the encryption-key. This suffices for the natural case in which the (high-level) application (using the encryption scheme) is oblivious of the encryption-key.[23] However, in some settings, the adversary may have partial control on the application. Furthermore, in the public-key case, the adversary knows the encryption-key in use, and so (if it may partially control the application then) it may be able to cause the application to invoke the encryption scheme on plaintexts that are related to the encryption-key in use. Thus, for such settings, we need stronger definitions of security that postulate that partial information about the plaintext remains secret even if the plaintext does depend on the encryption-key in use. Note that here we merely consider the dependence of the "test" plaintext (i.e., the one for which the adversary wishes to obtain partial information) on the encryption-key, and ignore the fact that the foregoing motivation also suggests that the adversary can obtain the encryptions of additional plaintexts chosen by it (as discussed in Section 5.4.3). However, it is easy to see that (in the public-key setting discussed here) these additional encryptions are of no use because the adversary can generate them by itself (see Section 5.4.3).

5.4.2.1. Definitions

Recall that we seek a definition that guarantees that partial information about the plaintext remains secret even if the plaintext does depend on the encryption-key in use. That is, we seek a strengthening of semantic security (as defined in Definition 5.2.2) in which one allows the plaintext distribution ensemble (denoted $\{X_n\}_{n\in\mathbb{N}}$ in Definition 5.2.2) to depend on the encryption-key in use (i.e., for encryption-key e, we consider the distribution X_e over $\{0, 1\}^{\text{poly}(|e|)}$). Furthermore, we also allow the partial information functions (denoted f and h in Definition 5.2.2) to depend on the encryption-key in use (i.e., for encryption-key e, we consider the functions f_e and h_e). In the actual definition

---

[23] Indeed, it is natural (and even methodologically imperative) that a high-level application that uses encryption as a tool be oblivious of the keys used by that tool. However, this refers only to a proper operation of the application, and deviation may be caused (in some settings) by an improper behavior (i.e., an adversary).

it is important to restrict the scope of the functions $\{h_e\}_e$ and the distributions $\{X_e\}_e$ so that their dependency on e is polynomial-time computable (see Exercise 28). This yields the definition presented in Exercise 29, which is equivalent to the following formulation.[24]

Definition 5.4.1 (semantic security under key-dependent passive attacks): *The sequence* $\{(f_e, h_e, X_e)\}_{e \in \{0,1\}^*}$ is admissible *for the current definition if*

1. *The functions* $f_e : \{0,1\}^* \to \{0,1\}^*$ *are polynomially bounded; that is, there exists a polynomial ℓ such that $|f_e(x)| \le \ell(|x| + |e|)$.*
2. *There exists a non-uniform family of polynomial-size (h-evaluation) circuits $\{H_n\}_{n \in \mathbb{N}}$ such that for every e in the range of $G_1(1^n)$ and every x in the support of X_e, it holds that $H_n(e, x) = h_e(x)$.*
3. *There exists a non-uniform family of* (probabilistic) *polynomial-size* (sampling) *circuits $\{S_n\}_{n \in \mathbb{N}}$ such that for every e in the range of $G_1(1^n)$ and for some $m = \mathrm{poly}(|e|)$, the random variables $S_n(e, U_m)$ and X_e are identically distributed.*[25]

An encryption scheme, (G, E, D), is semantically secure under key-dependent passive attacks *if for every probabilistic polynomial-time algorithm A, there exists a probabilistic polynomial-time algorithm A' such that for every admissible sequence $\{(f_e, h_e, X_e)\}_{e \in \{0,1\}^*}$, every positive polynomial p, and all sufficiently large n it holds that*

$$\Pr\left[A(e, E_e(X_e), 1^{|X_e|}, h_e(X_e)) = f_e(X_e) \right]$$
$$< \Pr\left[A'(e, 1^{|X_e|}, h_e(X_e)) = f_e(X_e) \right] + \frac{1}{p(n)}$$

where $(e, d) \leftarrow G(1^n)$, and the probability is taken over the internal coin tosses of algorithms G, E, A, and A', as well as over X_e.

We stress that the performance of A' is measured against the same distribution of triplets (f_e, h_e, X_e) (i.e., $e \leftarrow G_1(1^n)$) as the one considered for algorithm A. Unlike in other versions of the definition of semantic security, here it is important to let A' have the encryption-key e because the task (i.e., the evaluation of $f_e(X_e)$) as well as its main input (i.e., the value $h_e(X_e)$) are related to e. (Indeed, if e were not given to A', then no encryption scheme (G, E, D) could have satisfied the revised Definition 5.4.1: Considering $h_e(x) = x \oplus e$ (for $|x| = |e|$) and $f_e(x) = x$, note that it is easy for A to compute x from e and $h_e(x)$, which are explicit in $(e, E_e(x), 1^{|x|}, h_e(x))$, whereas no A' can compute x from $(1^n, 1^{|x|}, h_e(x))$.)

Using Exercise 14.2, one may verify that Definition 5.2.2 is a special case of Definition 5.4.1. An analogous modification (or generalization) of Definition 5.2.4 yields the following:

---

[24] Recall that without loss of generality, we may assume that the keys generated by $G(1^n)$ have length n. Thus, there is no point in providing the algorithms with 1^n as an auxiliary input (as done in Definition 5.2.2).

[25] As usual, $S_n(e, r)$ denotes the output of the circuit S_n on input e and coins r. We stress that for every e, the length of X_e is fixed.

Definition 5.4.2 (indistinguishability of encryptions under key-dependent passive attacks): *The sequence* $\{(x_e, y_e)\}_{e \in \{0,1\}^*}$ *is* admissible *for the current definition if there exists a non-uniform family of polynomial-size circuits* $\{P_n\}_{n \in \mathbb{N}}$ *that maps each encryption-key* $e \in \{0, 1\}^*$ *to the corresponding pair of* (equal-length) *strings* (x_e, y_e). *That is, for every* e *in the range of* $G_1(1^n)$, *it holds that* $P_n(e) = (x_e, y_e)$. *An encryption scheme,* (G, E, D), *has* indistinguishable encryptions under key-dependent passive attacks *if for every non-uniform family of polynomial-size circuits* $\{C_n\}$, *every admissible sequence* $\{(x_e, y_e)\}_{e \in \{0,1\}^*}$, *every positive polynomial* p, *and all sufficiently large* n *it holds that*

$$| \Pr[C_n(e, E_e(x_e)) = 1] - \Pr[C_n(e, E_e(y_e)) = 1] | < \frac{1}{p(n)}$$

where $(e, d) \leftarrow G(1^n)$, *and the probability is taken over the internal coin tosses of algorithms* G *and* E.

As in the basic case (i.e., Section 5.2), the two definitions are equivalent.

Theorem 5.4.3 (equivalence of definitions for key-dependent passive attacks): *A public-key encryption scheme* (G, E, D) *is semantically secure under key-dependent passive attacks if and only if it has indistinguishable encryptions under key-dependent passive attacks.*

Proof Sketch: In order to show that indistinguishability of encryptions implies semantic security, we follow the proof of Proposition 5.2.6. Specifically, A' is constructed and analyzed almost as before, with the exception that A' gets and uses the encryption-key e (rather than letting it generate a random encryption-key by itself).[26] That is, we let $A'(e, 1^{|x|}, h_e(x)) = A(e, E_e(1^{|x|}), 1^{|x|}, h_e(x))$, and show that for all (deterministic) polynomial-size circuit families $\{S'_n\}_{n \in \mathbb{N}}$ and $\{H_n\}_{n \in \mathbb{N}}$ it holds that

$$\Pr\left[A(e, E_e(S'_n(e)), 1^{|S'_n(e)|}, H_n(e, S'_n(e))) = f_e(S'_n(e)) \right] \qquad (5.11)$$

$$< \Pr\left[A(e, E_e(1^{|S'_n(e)|}), 1^{|S'_n(e)|}, H_n(e, S'_n(e))) = f_e(S'_n(e)) \right] + \frac{1}{\text{poly}(n)}$$

where $e \leftarrow G_1(1^n)$ and $\mu : \mathbb{N} \rightarrow [0,1]$ is a negligible function. Once established, Eq. (5.11) implies that (G, E, D) satisfies Definition 5.4.1.

On how Eq. (5.11) implies Definition 5.4.1: The issue is that Eq. (5.11) refers to deterministic plaintext-selecting circuits (i.e., the S'_n's), whereas Definition 5.4.1 refers to probabilistic plaintext-sampling circuits (i.e., the S_n's). This small gap can be bridged by fixing a sequence of coins for the latter probabilistic (sampling) circuits. Specifically, starting with any admissible (for Definition 5.4.1) sequence $\{(f_e, h_e, X_e)\}_{e \in \{0,1\}^*}$, where $H_n(e, x) = h_e(x)$ and $X_e \equiv S_n(e, U_{\text{poly}(n)})$, we consider some sequence of coins r_n (for S_n) that maximizes the gap between $\Pr[A(e, E_e(x_e), 1^{|x_e|}, H_n(e, x_e)) = f_e(x_e)]$ and $\Pr[A'(e, 1^{|x_e|}, H_n(e, x_e)) = f_e(x_e)]$,

---

[26] Here we use the convention by which A' gets e along with $h_e(x)$ (and $1^{|x|}$). This is important because A' must feed a matching pair $(e, h_e(x))$ to A.

where e is random and $x_e = S_n(e, r_n)$. Recalling that $A'(e, 1^\ell, \gamma) = A(e, E_e(1^\ell), 1^\ell, \gamma)$ and incorporating the sequence of r_n's in A, we obtain a contradiction to Eq. (5.11) (i.e., by letting $S'_n(e) = S_n(e, r_n) = x_e$).

Assuming (to the contrary of the above claim) that Eq. (5.11) does not hold, we obtain a sequence of admissible pairs $\{(x_e, y_e)\}_{e \in \{0,1\}^*}$ for Definition 5.4.2 such that their encryptions can be distinguished (in contradiction to our hypothesis). Specifically, we set $x_e \overset{\text{def}}{=} S'_n(e)$ and $y_e \overset{\text{def}}{=} 1^{|x_e|}$, and let $C'_n(e, \alpha) \overset{\text{def}}{=} A(e, \alpha, 1^{|x_e|}, H_n(e, x_e))$. Thus, we obtain a (poly(n)-size) circuit C'_n such that for some positive polynomial p and infinitely many n's

$$\left| \Pr[C'_n(e, E_e(x_e)) = f_e(x_e)] - \Pr[C'_n(e, E_e(y_e)) = f_e(x_e)] \right| > \frac{1}{p(n)}$$

where e is distributed according to $G_1(1^n)$. Using an idea as in the proof of Theorem 5.2.15, we derive a (poly(n)-size) circuit C_n that distinguishes $(e, E_e(x_e))$ from $(e, E_e(y_e))$, where $e \leftarrow G_1(1^n)$, in contradiction to our hypothesis.

> Details: We refer to the proof of Claim 5.2.15.1 (contained in the proof of Theorem 5.2.15). Recall that the idea was to proceed in two stages. First, using only e (which also yields x_e and y_e), we find an arbitrary value v such that $\left| \Pr[C'_n(e, E_e(x_e)) = v] - \Pr[C'_n(e, E_e(y_e)) = v] \right|$ is large. In the second stage, we use this value v in order to distinguish the case in which we are given an encryption of x_e from the case in which we are given an encryption of y_e. (We comment if $(e, x) \mapsto f_e(x)$ were computable by a poly(n)-size circuit, then converting C'_n into a distinguisher C_n would have been much easier; we further comment that as a corollary to the current proof, one can conclude that the restricted form is equivalent to the general one.)

This concludes the proof that indistinguishability of encryptions (as per Definition 5.4.2) implies semantic security (as per Definition 5.4.1), and we now turn to the opposite direction.

Suppose that (G, E, D) does not have indistinguishable encryptions, and consider an admissible sequence $\{(x_e, y_e)\}_{e \in \{0,1\}^*}$ that witnesses this failure. Following the proof of Proposition 5.2.7, we define a probability ensemble $\{X_e\}_{e \in \{0,1\}^*}$ and function ensembles $\{h_e\}_{e \in \{0,1\}^*}$ and $\{f_e\}_{e \in \{0,1\}^*}$ in an analogous manner:

- The distribution X_e is uniformly distributed over $\{x_e, y_e\}$.
- The function f_e satisfies $f_e(x_e) = 1$ and $f_e(y_e) = 0$.
- The function h_e is defined such that $h_e(X_e)$ equals the description of the circuit C_n that distinguishes $(e, E_e(x_e))$ from $(e, E_e(y_e))$, where $e \leftarrow G_1(1^n)$ (and $(x_e, y_e) = P_n(e)$).

Using the admissibility of the sequence $\{(x_e, y_e)\}_e$ (for Definition 5.4.2), it follows that $\{(f_e, h_e, X_e)\}_e$ is admissible for Definition 5.4.1. Using the same algorithm A as in the proof of Proposition 5.2.7 (i.e., $A(e, \beta, C_n) = C_n(e, \beta)$, where β is a ciphertext and $C_n = h_e(X_e)$), and using the same analysis, we derive a contradiction to the hypothesis that (G, E, D) satisfies Definition 5.4.1.

Details: Without loss of generality, suppose that

$$\Pr[C_n(e, E_e(x_e))=1] > \Pr[C_n(e, E_e(y_e))=1] + \frac{1}{p(n)}$$

for $e \leftarrow G_1(1^n)$. Then, as shown in Claim 5.2.7.1,

$$\Pr[A(e, E_e(X_e), h_e(X_e))=f_e(X_e)] > \frac{1}{2} + \frac{1}{2p(n)}$$

On the other hand, as shown in Fact 5.2.7.2, for every algorithm A'

$$\Pr[A'(e, 1^{|X_e|}, h_e(X_e))=f_e(X_e)] \le \frac{1}{2}$$

because $(e, 1^{|X_e|}, h_e(X_e))$ contains no information about the value of $f_e(X_e)$ (which is uniformly distributed in $\{0, 1\}$). This violates Definition 5.4.1, and so our initial contradiction hypothesis (i.e., that one can distinguish encryptions under (G, E, D)) must be false.

The theorem follows. ∎

Multiple-Message Security. Definitions 5.4.1 and 5.4.2 can be easily generalized to handle the encryption of many messages (as in Section 5.2.4), yielding again two equivalent definitions. Since we are in the public-key setting, one can show (analogously to Theorem 5.2.11) that the single-message definitions of security are equivalent to the multiple-message ones (i.e., by showing that Definition 5.4.2 implies its multiple-message generalization). One important observation is that admissibility for the multiple-message definition enables one to carry out a hybrid argument (as in the proof of Theorem 5.2.11). For details, see Exercise 31. The bottom-line is that *we can freely use any of the four security definitions for key-dependent passive attacks, and security under that definition implies security under any of the other definitions.*

5.4.2.2. Constructions

All the results presented in Section 5.3.4 extend to security under key-dependent passive attacks. That is, for each of the constructions presented in Section 5.3.4, the same assumption used to prove security under key-oblivious passive attacks actually suffices for proving security under key-dependent passive attacks. Before demonstrating this fact, we comment that (in general) security under key-oblivious passive attacks *does not* necessarily imply security under key-dependent passive attacks; see Exercise 32.

Initial observations. We start by observing that Construction 5.3.7 (i.e., the transformation of block-ciphers to general encryption schemes) maintains its security in our context. That is:

Proposition 5.4.4: (extension of Proposition 5.3.8): *Let (G, E, D) and (G', E', D') be as in Construction 5.3.7; that is, let (G', E', D') be the full-fledged encryption constructed based on the block-cipher (G, E, D). Then if (G, E, D) is secure under key-dependent passive attacks, then so is (G', E', D').*

Proof Idea: As in the proof of Proposition 5.3.8, we merely observe that multiple-message security of (G', E', D') is equivalent to multiple-message security of (G, E, D). ∎

We next observe that Construction 5.3.13 (a block-cipher with block-length $\ell \equiv 1$) maintains its security also under a key-dependent passive attack. This is a special case of the following observation:

Proposition 5.4.5: *Let (G, E, D) be a block-cipher with logarithmically bounded block-length (i.e., $\ell(n) = O(\log n)$). If (G, E, D) is secure under key-oblivious passive attacks, then it is also secure under key-dependent passive attacks.*

Proof Sketch: Here we use the definition of ciphertext-indistinguishability in the single-message setting. The key observation is that the set of possible messages is relatively small, and so selecting a message in a key-dependent manner does not give much advantage over selecting a message at random (i.e., obliviously of the key).

Consider an arbitrary admissible (for Definition 5.4.2) set of pairs, $\{(x_e, y_e)\}_{e \in \{0,1\}^*}$, where $|x_e| = |y_e| = O(\log |e|)$, and a circuit family $\{C_n\}$ that tries to distinguish $(e, E_e(x_e))$ from $(e, E_e(y_e))$. We shall show that $\{C_n\}$ necessarily fails by relating its distinguishing gap to the distinguishing gap of a key-oblivious attack (represented in the next paragraph by the $C_n^{x,y}$'s).

Let $\{P_n\}_{n \in \mathbb{N}}$ be the circuit family producing the aforementioned admissible set (i.e., $P_n(e) = (x_e, y_e)$). Fixing some $n \in \mathbb{N}$ and an arbitrary $(x, y) \in \{0, 1\}^* \times \{0, 1\}^*$, we consider a circuit $C_n^{x,y}$ (depending on the circuits C_n and P_n and the pair (x, y)) that, on input (e, α), operates as follows:

1. Using the hard-wired circuit P_n and the input (key) e, the circuit $C_n^{x,y}$ checks whether (x_e, y_e) equals the hard-wired pair (x, y) (i.e., $C_n^{x,y}$ checks whether $P_n(e) = (x, y)$). In case the check fails, $C_n^{x,y}$ outputs an arbitrary value (e.g., 1) obliviously of the ciphertext α.
2. Otherwise (i.e., $P_n(e) = (x, y)$), the circuit $C_n^{x,y}$ invokes C_n on its own input and answers accordingly (i.e., outputs $C_n(e, \alpha)$).

Since (G, E, D) is secure under key-oblivious passive attacks, it follows that (for every $(x, y) \in \{0, 1\}^m \times \{0, 1\}^m$, where $m \leq \text{poly}(n)$) the circuit $C_n^{x,y}$ cannot distinguish the case $\alpha = E_e(x)$ from the case $\alpha = E_e(y)$. Thus, for some negligible function $\mu : \mathbb{N} \to [0,1]$ and every pair $(x, y) \in \{0, 1\}^m \times \{0, 1\}^m$, the following holds:

$$\mu(n) > \left| \text{Pr}_e[C_n^{x,y}(e, E_e(x)) = 1] - \text{Pr}_e[C_n^{x,y}(e, E_e(y)) = 1] \right|$$

$$= \left| \text{Pr}_e \left[\begin{array}{c} C_n(e, E_e(x_e)) = 1 \\ \wedge \ (x_e, y_e) = (x, y) \end{array} \right] - \text{Pr}_e \left[\begin{array}{c} C_n(e, E_e(y_e)) = 1 \\ \wedge \ (x_e, y_e) = (x, y) \end{array} \right] \right|$$

where $e \leftarrow G_1(1^n)$, and equality holds because in case $(x_e, y_e) \neq (x, y)$, the output of $C_n^{x,y}(e, \alpha)$ is independent of α (and so in this case $C_n^{x,y}(e, E_e(x)) = C_n^{x,y}(e, E_e(y))$). Since this holds for any pair $(x, y) \in \{0, 1\}^m \times \{0, 1\}^m$, and since $|x_e| = |y_e| = \ell(n)$, it follows that

$$|\Pr_e[C_n(e, E_e(x_e)) = 1] - \Pr_e[C_n(e, E_e(y_e)) = 1]|$$

$$\leq \sum_{|x|=|y|=\ell(n)} \left| \Pr_e \left[\begin{array}{c} C_n(e, E_e(x_e)) = 1 \\ \wedge\ (x_e, y_e) = (x, y) \end{array} \right] - \Pr_e \left[\begin{array}{c} C_n(e, E_e(y_e)) = 1 \\ \wedge\ (x_e, y_e) = (x, y) \end{array} \right] \right|$$

$$< 2^{2\ell(n)} \cdot \mu(n)$$

and the proposition follows (because $\ell(n) = O(\log n)$). ∎

A Feasibility Result. Combining Theorem 5.3.15 with Propositions 5.4.4 and 5.4.5, we obtain a feasibility result:

Theorem 5.4.6: *If there exist collections of (non-uniformly hard) trapdoor permutations, then there exist public-key encryption schemes that are secure under key-dependent passive attacks.*

More Efficient Schemes. In order to obtain more efficient schemes, we directly analyze the efficient constructions presented in Section 5.3.4. For example, extending the proof of Proposition 5.3.19, we obtain:

Proposition 5.4.7: *Suppose that b is a (non-uniformly strong) hard-core of the trapdoor collection $\{p_\alpha\}$. Furthermore, suppose that this trapdoor collection utilizes a domain sampling algorithm S so that the statistical difference between $S(\alpha)$ and the uniform distribution over the domain of p_α is negligible in terms of $|\alpha|$. Then Construction 5.3.18 constitutes a public-key encryption scheme that is secure under key-dependent passive attacks.*

Proof Sketch: Again, we prove single-message ciphertext-indistinguishability. We rely heavily on the admissibility condition. In analogy to the proof of Proposition 5.3.19, it suffices to show that for every polynomial-size circuit family $\{C_n\}$, the distributions $(\alpha, p_\alpha^\ell(S(\alpha)), C_n(\alpha) \oplus G_\alpha^{(\ell)}(S(\alpha)))$ and $(\alpha, p_\alpha^\ell(S(\alpha)), C_n(\alpha) \oplus U_\ell)$ are indistinguishable, for a randomly generated (encryption-key) α, where $\ell = |C_n(\alpha)|$ and U_ℓ is uniformly distributed (independently of anything else).[27] Incorporating $\{C_n\}$ in the potential distinguisher, it suffices to show that the distributions $(\alpha, p_\alpha^\ell(S(\alpha)), G_\alpha^{(\ell)}(S(\alpha)))$ and $(\alpha, p_\alpha^\ell(S(\alpha)), U_\ell)$ are indistinguishable. The latter claim follows as in the proof of Proposition 5.3.19 (i.e., by a minor extension to Proposition 3.4.6). The proposition follows. ∎

5.4.3. Chosen Plaintext Attack

So far, we have discussed only passive attacks (in two variants: key-oblivious versus key-dependent, discussed in Section 5.2 and 5.4.2, respectively). Turning to active

---

[27] Recall that here α serves as an encryption-key and $C_n(\alpha)$ is a key-dependent plaintext. Typically, $C_n(\alpha)$ would be the first or second element in the plaintext pair $(x_\alpha, y_\alpha) = P_n(\alpha)$.

attacks, we start with mild active attacks in which the adversary may obtain (from some legitimate user) ciphertexts corresponding to plaintexts of the adversary's choice. Such attacks will be called *chosen plaintext attacks*, and they characterize the adversary's abilities in some applications. For example, in some settings, the adversary may (directly or indirectly) control the encrypting module (but not the decrypting module).

Intuitively, a chosen plaintext attack poses additional threat in the case of private-key encryption schemes (see Exercise 33), but not in the case of public-key encryption schemes. In fact, we will show that in the case of public-key encryption schemes, a chosen plaintext attack can be emulated by a passive key-dependent attack.

5.4.3.1. Definitions

We start by rigorously formulating the framework of chosen plaintext attacks. Intuitively, such attacks proceed in four stages corresponding to the generation of a key (by a legitimate party), the adversary's requests (answered by the legitimate party) to encrypt plaintexts under this key, the generation of a challenge ciphertext (under this key and according to a template specified by the adversary), and additional requests to encrypt plaintexts (under the same key). That is, a chosen plaintext attack proceeds as follows:

1. *Key generation:* A key-pair $(e, d) \leftarrow G(1^n)$ is generated (by a legitimate party). In the *public-key setting* the adversary is given $(1^n, e)$, whereas in the *private-key setting* the adversary is only given 1^n. Actually, assuming (without loss of generality) that $|e| = n$, we may replace $(1^n, e)$ by e in the former case.
2. *Encryption requests:* Based on the information obtained so far, the adversary may request (the legitimate party) to encrypt plaintexts of its (i.e., the adversary's) choice. A request to encrypt the plaintext x is answered with a value taken from the distribution $E_e(x)$, where e is as determined in Step 1. After making several such requests, the adversary moves to the next stage.
3. *Challenge generation:* Based on the information obtained so far, the adversary specifies a challenge template and is given an actual challenge.
   When defining semantic security, the challenge template is a triplet of circuits (S_m, h_m, f_m), where S_m specifies a distribution of m-bit long plaintexts (and $h_m, f_m : \{0, 1\}^m \to \{0, 1\}^*$), and the actual challenge is a pair $(E_e(x), h_m(x))$ where x is distributed according to $S_m(U_{\text{poly}(n)})$. When defining indistinguishability of encryptions, the challenge template is merely a pair of equal-length strings, and the actual challenge is an encryption of one of these two strings.
4. *Additional encryption requests:* Based on the information obtained so far, the adversary may request the encryptions of additional plaintexts of its choice. These requests are handled as in Step 2. After making several such requests, the adversary produces an output and halts.

In the actual definition, the adversary's strategy will be decoupled into two parts corresponding to its actions before and after the generation of the actual challenge. Each part will be represented by a (probabilistic polynomial-time) oracle machine, where the oracle is an "encryption oracle" (with respect to the key generated in Step 1). The first part, denoted A_1, represents the adversary's behavior during Step 2. It is given a security parameter (and possibly an encryption-key), and its output is a pair (τ, σ), where τ is the template generated in the beginning of Step 3 and σ is state information passed to the second part of the adversary. The second part of the adversary, denoted A_2, represents the adversary's behavior during Step 4. It is given the state σ (of the first part), as well as the actual challenge (generated Step 3), and produces the actual output of the adversary.

In accordance with the use of non-uniform formulations, we let each of the two oracle machines have a (non-uniform) auxiliary input. In fact, it suffices to provide only the first machine with such a (non-uniform) auxiliary input, because it can pass auxiliary input to the second machine in the state information σ. (Similarly, in the case of public-key schemes, it suffices to provide only the first machine with the encryption-key.) We comment that we provide these machines with probabilistic oracles; that is, in response to a plaintext query x, the oracle E_e returns a random ciphertext $E_e(x)$ (i.e., the result of a probabilistic process applied to e and x). Thus, in the case of public-key schemes, the four-step attack process can be written as follows:

$$(e, d) \leftarrow G(1^n)$$
$$(\tau, \sigma) \leftarrow A_1^{E_e}(e, z)$$
$$c \stackrel{\text{def}}{=} \text{an actual challenge generated according to the template } \tau$$
$$\text{output} \leftarrow A_2^{E_e}(\sigma, c)$$

where z denotes (non-uniform) auxiliary input given to the adversary. In the case of private-key schemes, the adversary (i.e., A_1) is given 1^n instead of e.

Semantic Security. Instantiating this framework to derive a definition of semantic security amounts to specifying the challenge generation and to postulating that the success probability in such an attack should be met by a corresponding benign process. As hinted in the preceding discussion, the challenge generation consists of the adversary specifying a triplet of circuits, denoted (S_m, h_m, f_m), and being presented with an encryption of $x \leftarrow S_m(U_{\text{poly}(n)}) \in \{0, 1\}^m$ along with the partial information $h_m(x)$. The adversary's goal is to guess $f_m(x)$, and semantic security amounts to saying that the adversary's success probability can be matched by a *corresponding algorithm* that is only given $h_m(x)$ and $1^{|x|} = 1^m$. Like the adversary, the corresponding algorithm is decoupled into two parts; the first is in charge of outputting a challenge template, and the second is in charge of solving the challenge (without being given a ciphertext), where state information is passed from the first part to the second part. It is important to require that *the challenge template produced by the corresponding algorithm be distributed exactly as the challenge template produced by the adversary.* (See further discussion following Definition 5.4.8.)

Definition 5.4.8 (semantic security under chosen plaintext attacks):

For public-key schemes: *A public-key encryption scheme, (G, E, D), is said to be se-mantically secure under chosen plaintext attacks if for every pair of probabilistic* *polynomial-time* oracle machines, A_1 and A_2, *there exists a pair of probabilistic polynomial-time algorithms,* A_1' *and* A_2', *such that the following two conditions hold:*

1. *For every positive polynomial p, and all sufficiently large n and* $z \in \{0, 1\}^{\mathrm{poly}(n)}$ *it holds that*

$$
\Pr \left[\begin{array}{ll} v = f_m(x) & \text{where} \\ & (e, d) \leftarrow G(1^n) \\ & ((S_m, h_m, f_m), \sigma) \leftarrow A_1^{E_e}(e, z) \\ & c \leftarrow (E_e(x), h_m(x)), \text{ where } x \leftarrow S_m(U_{\mathrm{poly}(n)}) \\ & v \leftarrow A_2^{E_e}(\sigma, c) \end{array} \right]
$$

$$
< \Pr \left[\begin{array}{ll} v = f_m(x) & \text{where} \\ & ((S_m, h_m, f_m), \sigma) \leftarrow A_1'(1^n, z) \\ & x \leftarrow S_m(U_{\mathrm{poly}(n)}) \\ & v \leftarrow A_2'(\sigma, 1^{|x|}, h_m(x)) \end{array} \right] + \frac{1}{p(n)}
$$

Recall that (S_m, h_m, f_m) *is a triplet of circuits produced as in Step 3 of the foregoing description, and that x is a sample from the distribution induced by* S_m.

2. *For every n and z, the first elements* (i.e., *the* (S_m, h_m, f_m) *part*) *in the random variables* $A_1'(1^n, z)$ *and* $A_1^{E_{G_1(1^n)}}(G_1(1^n), z)$ *are identically distributed.*

For private-key schemes: *The definition is identical except that algorithm* A_1 *gets the security parameter* 1^n *instead of the encryption-key e.*

Note that as in almost all other definitions of semantic security (with the exception of Definition 5.4.1), algorithm A_1' does not get a (random) encryption-key as input (but may rather generate one by itself).[28] Since the challenge template is not fixed (or determined by e) but, rather, is chosen by A and A' themselves, it is very important to require that in both cases, the challenge template be distributed identically (or approximately so): There is no point in relating the success probability of A and A', unless these probabilities refer to same distribution of problems (i.e., challenge templates).[29] (The issue arises also in Definition 5.4.1 where it was resolved by forcing A' to refer to the challenge template determined by the public-key e.)[30]

Definition 5.4.8 implies Definition 5.4.1, but this may not be evident from the definitions themselves (most importantly, because here f_m is computationally bounded whereas in Definition 5.4.1 the function is computationally unbounded). Still, the validity of the claim follows easily from the equivalence of the two definitions to the

---

[28] In fact, A_1' is likely to start by generating $e \leftarrow G_1(1^n)$, because it has to generate a challenge template that is distributed as the one produced by A_1 on input $e \leftarrow G_1(1^n)$.

[29] Failure to make this requirement would have resulted in a fundamentally bad definition (by which every encryption scheme is secure). For example, algorithm A_1' could have set h_m to equal the function f_m selected by A_1 (in a corresponding attack). Doing so, the success of A to guess the value of $f_m(x)$ from the (insecure) encryption of x and a (possibly) useless value $h_m(x)$ (e.g., for a constant function h_m) would have been met by the success of A' to "guess" the value of $f_m(x)$ from $f_m(x)$ itself (without being given the encryption of x). An alternative approach, which follows the formulation of Definition 5.4.1, is presented in Exercise 34.

[30] Indeed, an alternative solution could have been the one adopted here and in the sequel; that is, in an alternative to Definition 5.4.1, one may allow A' to select the challenge template by itself, provided that the selection yields a distribution similar to the one faced by A (as induced by the public-key e). For details, see Exercise 30.

corresponding notions of indistinguishability of encryptions (and the fact that the implication is evident for the latter formulations).

Indistinguishability of Encryptions. Deriving the corresponding definition of indistinguishability of encryptions (from the previous framework) is considerably simpler. Here, the challenge generation consists of the adversary specifying two equal-length strings and the adversary being presented with the encryption of one of them. The adversary's goal is to distinguish the two possible cases.

Definition 5.4.9 (indistinguishability of encryptions under chosen plaintext attacks):

For public-key schemes: *A public-key encryption scheme, (G, E, D), is said to have* indistinguishable encryptions under chosen plaintext attacks *if for every pair of probabilistic polynomial-time oracle machines, A_1 and A_2, for every positive polynomial p, and for all sufficiently large n and $z \in \{0, 1\}^{\mathrm{poly}(n)}$ it holds that*

$$|p_{n,z}^{(1)} - p_{n,z}^{(2)}| < \frac{1}{p(n)}$$

where

$$p_{n,z}^{(i)} \stackrel{\text{def}}{=} \Pr \begin{bmatrix} v = 1 \text{ where} \\ \quad (e, d) \leftarrow G(1^n) \\ \quad ((x^{(1)}, x^{(2)}), \sigma) \leftarrow A_1^{E_e}(e, z) \\ \quad c \leftarrow E_e(x^{(i)}) \\ \quad v \leftarrow A_2^{E_e}(\sigma, c) \end{bmatrix}$$

where $|x^{(1)}| = |x^{(2)}|$.

For private-key schemes: *The definition is identical except that A_1 gets the security parameter 1^n instead of the encryption-key e.*

Clearly, Definition 5.4.9 implies Definition 5.4.2 as a special case. Furthermore, for public-key schemes, the two definitions are equivalent (see Proposition 5.4.10), whereas for private-key schemes, Definition 5.4.9 is strictly stronger (see Exercise 33).

Proposition 5.4.10: *Let (G, E, D) be a* public-key *encryption scheme that has indistinguishable encryptions under key-dependent passive attacks. Then (G, E, D) has indistinguishable encryptions under chosen plaintext attack.*

Proof Sketch: The key observation is that in the public-key model, a chosen plaintext attack can be emulated by a passive key-dependent attack. Specifically, the (passive) attacker can emulate access to an encryption oracle by itself (by using the encryption-key given to it). Thus, we obtain an attacker as in Definition 5.4.9, with the important exception that it never makes oracle calls (but rather emulates E_e by itself). In other words, we have an attacker as in Definition 5.4.2, with the minor exception that it is a probabilistic polynomial-time machine with auxiliary input z (rather than being a polynomial-size circuit) and that it distinguishes a pair of plaintext distributions rather than a pair of (fixed) plaintexts (which depend on the encryption-key). However, fixing the best-possible coins for this attacker (and incorporating them as well as z in an adequate circuit), we obtain an attacker exactly as in Definition 5.4.2 such that its distinguishing gap is at least as large as the one of the (initial) chosen plaintext attacker. (For details, see Exercise 30.) ∎

Equivalence of Semantic Security and Ciphertext-Indistinguishability. As in previous cases, we show that the two formulations of (chosen plaintext attack) security (i.e., semantic security and indistinguishability of encryptions) are in fact equivalent.

Theorem 5.4.11 (equivalence of definitions for chosen plaintext attacks): *A public-key (resp., private-key) encryption scheme (G, E, D) is semantically secure under chosen plaintext attacks if and only if it has indistinguishable encryptions under chosen plaintext attacks.*

Proof Sketch: In order to show that indistinguishabity of encryptions implies semantic security, we follow again the ideas underlying the proof of Proposition 5.2.6. Specifically, for both the private-key and public-key cases, A_1' and A_2' are constructed as follows:

1. $A_1'(1^n, z) \stackrel{\text{def}}{=} (\tau, \sigma')$, where (τ, σ') is generated as follows:

   First, A_1' generates an instance of the encryption scheme; that is, A_1' lets $(e, d) \leftarrow G(1^n)$. Next, A_1' invokes A_1, while emulating the oracle E_e, and sets $(\tau, \sigma) \leftarrow A_1^{E_e}(1^n, z)$. Finally, A_1' sets $\sigma' \stackrel{\text{def}}{=} (e, \sigma)$.

   We warn that the generation of the key-pair by A_1' should not be confused with the generation of the key-pair in the probabilistic experiment referring to the combined algorithm $A = (A_1, A_2)$. In particular, the generated encryption-key e allows A_1' to emulate the encryption oracle E_e (also in the private-key case). Furthermore, A_1' outputs the encryption-key e as part of the state passed by it to A_2', whereas A_1 does not necessarily do so (and, in fact, cannot do so in the case of the private-key model). This will allow A_2', too, to emulate the encryption oracle E_e.

2. $A_2'((e, \sigma), 1^m, \gamma) \stackrel{\text{def}}{=} A_2^{E_e}(\sigma, (E_e(1^m), \gamma))$, where typically $\gamma = h_m(x)$ and $m = |x|$.

Since A_1' merely emulates the generation of a key-pair and the actions of A_1 with respect to such a pair, the equal distribution condition (i.e., Item 2 in Definition 5.4.8) holds. Using the (corresponding) indistinguishability of encryption hypothesis, we show that (even in the presence of an encryption oracle E_e) the distributions $(\sigma, (E_e(x), h(x)))$ and $(\sigma, (E_e(1^{|x|}), h(x)))$ are indistinguishable, where $(e, d) \leftarrow G(1^n)$, $((S, h, f), \sigma) \leftarrow A_1^{E_e}(y, z)$ (with $y = e$ or $y = 1^n$ depending on the model), and $x \leftarrow S(U_{\text{poly}(n)})$.

> Details: Suppose that given $((S, h, f), \sigma)$ generated by $A_1^{E_e}(y, z)$ and oracle access to E_e, where $e \leftarrow G_1(1^n)$, one can distinguish $(\sigma, (E_e(x), h(x)))$ and $(\sigma, (E_e(1^{|x|}), h(x)))$, where $x \leftarrow S(U_{\text{poly}(n)})$. Then we obtain a distinguisher as in Definition 5.4.9 as follows. The first part of the distinguisher invokes A_1 (while answering its oracle queries by forwarding these queries to its own E_e oracle), and obtains $((S, h, f), \sigma) \leftarrow A_1^{E_e}(y, z)$. It sets $x^{(1)} \leftarrow S(U_{\text{poly}(n)})$ and $x^{(2)} = 1^{|x^{(1)}|}$,

and outputs $((x^{(1)}, x^{(2)}), (\sigma, h(x^{(1)})))$. That is, $(x^{(1)}, x^{(2)})$ is the challenge template, and it is answered with $E_e(x^{(i)})$, where i is either 1 or 2. The second part of the new distinguisher gets as input a challenge ciphertext $\alpha \leftarrow E_e(x^{(i)})$ and the state generated by the first part $(\sigma, h(x^{(1)}))$, and invokes the distinguisher of the contradiction hypothesis with input $(\sigma, (\alpha, h(x^{(1)})))$, while answering its oracle queries by forwarding these queries to its own E_e oracle. Thus, the new distinguisher violates the condition in Definition 5.4.9, in contradiction to the hypothesis that (G, E, D) has indistinguishable encryptions.

It follows that indistinguishability of encryptions (as per Definition 5.4.9) implies semantic security (as per Definition 5.4.8). (Here, this implication is easier to prove than in previous cases because the function f is computable via a circuit that is generated as part of the challenge template [and, without loss of generality, is part of σ].)

We now turn to the opposite direction. Suppose that (G, E, D) does not have indistinguishable encryptions, and consider the pairs $(x^{(1)}, x^{(2)})$ produced as a challenge template by the distinguishing adversary. Following the ideas of the proof of Proposition 5.2.7, we let the semantic-security adversary generate a corresponding challenge template (S, h, f) such that

- The circuit S samples uniformly in $\{x^{(1)}, x^{(2)}\}$.
- The function f satisfies $f(x^{(1)}) = 1$ and $f(x^{(2)}) = 0$.
- The function h is defined arbitrarily subject to $h(x^{(1)}) = h(x^{(2)})$.

Note that here we do not need to use h for passing non-uniform information (e.g., a description of the distinguisher). Instead, non-uniform information (i.e., the auxiliary input z to the distinguisher) is passed explicitly by other means (i.e., as the auxiliary input to the semantic-security adversary).

We stress that when the semantic-security adversary invokes the distinguishing adversary, the former uses its own oracle to answer the queries made by the latter. (Likewise, the former passes its auxiliary input z to the latter.) The reader may easily verify that the semantic-security adversary has a noticeable advantage in guessing $f(S(U_{\text{poly}(n)}))$ (by using the distinguishing gap between $E_e(x^{(1)})$ and $E_e(x^{(2)})$), whereas no algorithm that only gets $h(S(U_{\text{poly}(n)}))$ can have any advantage in such a guess. We derive a contradiction to the hypothesis that (G, E, D) satisfies Definition 5.4.8, and the theorem follows. ∎

Multiple-Message Security. Definitions 5.4.8 and 5.4.9 can be easily generalized to handle challenges in which multiple plaintexts are encrypted. As in previous cases, the corresponding (multiple-plaintext) definitions are equivalent. Furthermore, *the multiple-plaintext definitions are equivalent to the single-plaintext definition, both for public-key and private-key schemes*. We stress the equivalence for private-key schemes (which does not hold for the basic definitions presented in Section 5.1; see Proposition 5.2.12). To see the equivalence, it is best to consider the notion of indistinguishability of encryptions. In this case, the argument used in the proof of Theorem 5.2.11 (i.e., the public-key case) can be applied here by using the encryption oracle in order to produce the ciphertexts needed for the hybrid argument (rather than by generating these ciphertexts using knowledge of the encryption-key, which is only possible in the public-key setting).

5.4.3.2. Constructions

In view of Proposition 5.4.10 (and Theorem 5.4.11), we focus on private-key encryption schemes (because a public-key encryption scheme is secure under chosen plaintext attacks if and only if it is secure under passive key-dependent attacks). All the results presented in Section 5.3.3 extend to security under chosen plaintext attacks. Specifically, we prove that Constructions 5.3.9 and 5.3.12 remain secure also under a chosen plaintext attack.

Proposition 5.4.12: *Let F and (G, E, D) be as in Construction 5.3.9, and suppose that F is pseudorandom with respect to polynomial-size circuits. Then the private-key encryption scheme (G, E, D) is secure under chosen plaintext attacks. The same holds with respect to Construction 5.3.12.*

Proof Sketch: We focus on Construction 5.3.9 and follow the technique underlying the proof of Proposition 5.3.10. That is, we consider an idealized version of the scheme, in which one uses a uniformly selected function $\phi : \{0, 1\}^n \to \{0, 1\}^n$, rather than the pseudorandom function f_s. Essentially, all that the adversary obtains by encryption queries in the ideal version is pairs $(r, \phi(r))$, where the r's are uniformly and independently distributed in $\{0, 1\}^n$. As to the challenge itself, the plaintext is "masked" by the value of ϕ at another uniformly and independently distributed element in $\{0, 1\}^n$. Thus, unless the latter element happens to equal one of the r's used by the encryption oracle (which happens with negligible probability), the challenge plaintext is perfectly masked. Thus, the ideal version is secure under a chosen plaintext attack, and the same holds for the real scheme (since otherwise one derives a contradiction to the hypothesis that F is pseudorandom). ∎

Summary. Private-key and public-key encryption schemes that are secure under chosen plaintext attacks exist if and only if corresponding schemes that are secure under passive (key-dependent) attacks exist.[31]

5.4.4. Chosen Ciphertext Attack

We now turn to stronger forms of active attacks in which the adversary may obtain (from some legitimate user) plaintexts corresponding to ciphertexts of its choice. We consider two types of such attacks, called *chosen ciphertext attacks:* In the milder type, called *a priori chosen ciphertext attacks*, such decryption requests can be made only before the challenge ciphertext (for which the adversary should gain knowledge) is presented. In the stronger type, called *a posteriori chosen ciphertext attacks*, such decryption requests can also be made after the challenge ciphertext is presented, so long as one does not request a decryption of this very (challenge) ciphertext.

---

[31] Hint: When establishing the claim for the private-key case, use Exercise 2.

Both types of attacks address security threats in realistic applications: In some settings, the adversary may experiment with the decryption module, before the actual ciphertext in which it is interested is sent. Such a setting corresponds to an a priori chosen ciphertext attack. In other settings, one may invoke the decryption module on inputs of one's choice at any time, but all these invocations are recorded, and real damage is caused only by knowledge gained with respect to a ciphertext for which a decryption request was not recorded. In such a setting, protection against a posteriori chosen ciphertext attacks is adequate. Furthermore, in both cases, decryption requests can also be made with respect to strings that are not valid ciphertexts, in which case the decryption module returns a special error symbol.

Typically, in settings in which a mild or strong form of a chosen *ciphertext* attack is possible, a chosen *plaintext* attack is possible, too. Thus, we actually consider combined attacks in which the adversary may ask for encryption and decryption of strings of its choice. Indeed (analogously to Proposition 5.4.10), in the case of public-key schemes (but not in the case of private-key schemes), the combined attack is equivalent to a "pure" chosen *ciphertext* attack.

Organization. We start by providing security definitions for the two types of attacks discussed here. In Section 5.4.4.2, we further extend the definitional treatment of security (and derive a seemingly stronger notion that is in fact equivalent to the notions in Section 5.4.4.1). In Section 5.4.4.3 (resp., Section 5.4.4.4) we discuss the construction of private-key (resp., public-key) encryption schemes that are secure under chosen ciphertext attacks.

5.4.4.1. Definitions for Two Types of Attacks

Following Section 5.4.3.1 and bearing in mind that we wish to define two types of chosen ciphertext attacks (i.e., a priori and a posteriori ones), we first formulate the framework of chosen ciphertext attacks. As in the case of chosen plaintext attacks, we consider attacks that proceed in four stages corresponding to the generation of a pair of keys (by a legitimate party), the adversary's requests (answered by the legitimate party) to encrypt and/or decrypt strings under the corresponding key, the generation of a challenge ciphertext (under this key and according to a template specified by the adversary), and additional requests to encrypt and/or decrypt strings. That is, a chosen ciphertext attack proceeds as follows:

1. *Key generation:* A key-pair $(e, d) \leftarrow G(1^n)$ is generated (by a legitimate party). In the *public-key setting* the adversary is given e, whereas in the *private-key setting* the adversary is only given 1^n.

2. *Encryption and decryption requests:* Based on the information obtained so far, the adversary may request (the legitimate party) to encrypt and/or decrypt strings of its (i.e., the adversary's) choice. A request to encrypt the plaintext x is answered with a value taken from the distribution $E_e(x)$, where e is as determined in Step 1. A request to decrypt a valid (with respect to E_e) ciphertext y is answered with the value $D_d(y)$, where d is as determined in Step 1. A request to decrypt a string y that

is not a valid ciphertext (with respect to E_e) is answered with a special error symbol. After making several such requests, the adversary moves to the next stage.

3. *Challenge generation:* Based on the information obtained so far, the adversary specifies a challenge template and is given an actual challenge. This is done as in the corresponding step in the framework of chosen plaintext attacks.

4. *Additional encryption and decryption requests:* Based on the information obtained so far, the adversary may request the encryptions of additional plaintexts of its choice. In addition, in the case of an a posteriori chosen ciphertext attack (but not in the case of an a priori chosen ciphertext attack), the adversary may make additional decryption requests with the only (natural) restriction that it not be allowed to ask for a decryption of the challenge ciphertext. All requests are handled as in Step 2. After making several such requests, the adversary produces an output and halts.

In the actual definition, as in the case of chosen plaintext attacks, the adversary's strategy will be decoupled into two parts corresponding to its actions before and after the generation of the actual challenge. Each part will be represented by a (probabilistic polynomial-time) two-oracle machine, where the first oracle is an "encryption oracle" and the second is a "decryption oracle" (both with respect to the corresponding key generated in Step 1). As in the case of chosen plaintext attacks, the two parts are denoted A_1 and A_2, and A_1 passes state information (denoted σ) to A_2. Again, in accordance with the use of non-uniform formulations, we provide A_1 with a (non-uniform) auxiliary input. Thus, in the case of (a posteriori chosen ciphertext attacks on) public-key schemes, the four-step attack process can be written as follows:

$$(e, d) \leftarrow G(1^n)$$

$$(\tau, \sigma) \leftarrow A_1^{E_e, D_d}(e, z)$$

$$c \stackrel{\text{def}}{=} \text{an actual challenge generated according to the template } \tau$$

$$\text{output} \leftarrow A_2^{E_e, D_d}(\sigma, c)$$

where A_2 is not allowed to make a query regarding the ciphertext in c, and z denotes the (non-uniform) auxiliary input given to the adversary. In the case of private-key schemes, the adversary (i.e., A_1) is given 1^n instead of e. In the case of a priori chosen ciphertext attacks, A_2 is not allowed to query D_d (or, equivalently, A_2 is only given oracle access to the oracle E_e).

Semantic Security. As in the case of chosen plaintext attacks, a definition of semantic security is derived by an adequate specification of the challenge generation and the meaning of success. As before, the challenge generation consists of the adversary specifying a triplet of circuits, denoted (S, h, f), and being presented with an encryption of $x \leftarrow S(U_{\text{poly}(n)})$ along with the partial information $h(x)$. The adversary's goal is to guess $f(x)$, and semantic security amounts to saying that the adversary's success probability can be matched by a *corresponding algorithm* that is only given $h(x)$ and $1^{|x|}$. Again, the corresponding algorithm is decoupled into two parts; the first is in charge of outputting a challenge template, and the second is in charge of solving the challenge, where state information is passed from the first part to the second part. Furthermore, it is again important to require that the challenge template produced by the corresponding algorithm be distributed exactly as the challenge template produced by the adversary.

Definition 5.4.13 (Semantic Security under Chosen Ciphertext Attacks):

For public-key schemes: *A public-key encryption scheme, (G, E, D), is said to be* se-mantically secure under a priori chosen ciphertext attacks *if for every pair of probabilistic polynomial-time oracle machines, A_1 and A_2, there exists a pair of probabilistic polynomial-time algorithms, A_1' and A_2', such that the following two conditions hold:*

1. *For every positive polynomial p, and all sufficiently large n and $z \in \{0, 1\}^{\text{poly}(n)}$ it holds that*

$$\Pr \left[\begin{array}{l} v = f(x) \text{ where} \\ \quad (e, d) \leftarrow G(1^n) \\ \quad ((S, h, f), \sigma) \leftarrow A_1^{E_e, D_d}(e, z) \\ \quad c \leftarrow (E_e(x), h(x)), \text{ where } x \leftarrow S(U_{\text{poly}(n)}) \\ \quad v \leftarrow A_2^{E_e}(\sigma, c) \end{array} \right]$$

$$< \Pr \left[\begin{array}{l} v = f(x) \text{ where} \\ \quad ((S, h, f), \sigma) \leftarrow A_1'(1^n, z) \\ \quad x \leftarrow S(U_{\text{poly}(n)}) \\ \quad v \leftarrow A_2'(\sigma, 1^{|x|}, h(x)) \end{array} \right] + \frac{1}{p(n)}$$

2. *For every n and z, the first elements (i.e., the (S, h, f) part) in the random variables $A_1'(1^n, z)$ and $A_1^{E_{G_1(1^n)}, D_{G_2(1^n)}}(G_1(1^n), z)$ are identically distributed.*

Semantic security under a posteriori chosen ciphertext attacks *is defined analogously, except that A_2 is given oracle access to both E_e and D_d with the restriction that when given the challenge $c = (c', c'')$, machine A_2 is not allowed to make the query c' to the oracle D_d.*

For private-key schemes: *The definition is identical except that algorithm A_1 gets the security parameter 1^n instead of the encryption-key e.*

Clearly, the a posteriori version of Definition 5.4.13 implies its a priori version, which in turn implies Definition 5.4.8. Furthermore, these implications are strict (see Exercises 36 and 35, respectively).

Indistinguishability of Encryptions. As in the case of chosen plaintext attacks, deriving the corresponding definition of indistinguishability of encryptions (from the previous framework) is considerably simpler: The challenge generation consists of the adversary specifying two equal-length strings, and the adversary is presented with the encryption of one of them.

Definition 5.4.14 (indistinguishability of encryptions under chosen ciphertext attacks):

For public-key schemes: *A public-key encryption scheme, (G, E, D), is said to have* indistinguishable encryptions under a priori chosen ciphertext attacks *if for every pair of probabilistic polynomial-time oracle machines, A_1 and A_2, for every positive polynomial p, and for all sufficiently large n and $z \in \{0, 1\}^{\mathrm{poly}(n)}$ it holds that*

$$|p_{n,z}^{(1)} - p_{n,z}^{(2)}| < \frac{1}{p(n)}$$

where

$$p_{n,z}^{(i)} \stackrel{\text{def}}{=} \Pr \begin{bmatrix} v = 1 \text{ where} \\ \quad (e, d) \leftarrow G(1^n) \\ \quad ((x^{(1)}, x^{(2)}), \sigma) \leftarrow A_1^{E_e, D_d}(e, z) \\ \quad c \leftarrow E_e(x^{(i)}) \\ \quad v \leftarrow A_2^{E_e}(\sigma, c) \end{bmatrix}$$

where $|x^{(1)}| = |x^{(2)}|$.

Indistinguishability of encryptions under a posteriori chosen ciphertext attacks *is defined analogously, except that A_2 is given oracle access to both E_e and D_d with the restriction that when given the challenge c, machine A_2 is not allowed to make the query c to the oracle D_d.*

For private-key schemes: *The definition is identical, except that A_1 gets the security parameter 1^n instead of the encryption-key e.*

Clearly, the a posteriori version of Definition 5.4.14 implies its a priori version, which in turn implies Definition 5.4.9 as a special case. Again, these implications are strict (see again Exercises 36 and 35, respectively).

Terminology. We use CCA as a shorthand for chosen ciphertext attack.

Equivalence of Semantic Security and Ciphertext-Indistinguishability. Again, we show that the two formulations of security (i.e., semantic security and indistinguishability of encryptions) are in fact equivalent.

Theorem 5.4.15 (equivalence of definitions for CCA): *A public-key (resp., private-key) encryption scheme (G, E, D) is semantically secure under a priori CCA if and only if it has indistinguishable encryptions under a priori CCA. An analogous claim holds for a posteriori CCA.*

Proof Sketch: We adapt the proof of Theorem 5.4.11 to the current setting. The adaptation is straightforward, and we focus on the case of a posteriori CCA security (while commenting on the case of a priori CCA security).

In order to show that indistinguishability of encryptions implies semantic security, given an adversary (A_1, A_2) we construct the following matching algorithm A_1', A_2':

1. $A_1'(1^n, z) \stackrel{\text{def}}{=} (\tau, \sigma')$, where (τ, σ') is generated as follows:
   First, A_1' generates an instance of the encryption scheme; that is, A_1' lets $(e, d) \leftarrow G(1^n)$. Next, A_1' invokes A_1, while emulating the oracles E_e and D_d, and sets $(\tau, \sigma) \leftarrow A_1^{E_e, D_d}(1^n, z)$. Finally, A_1' sets $\sigma' \stackrel{\text{def}}{=} ((e, d), \sigma)$. (In the case of a-priori CCA security, we may set $\sigma' \stackrel{\text{def}}{=} (e, \sigma)$, as in the proof of Theorem 5.4.11.)

   We comment that the generated key-pair (e, d), allows A_1' to emulate the encryption and decryption oracles E_e and D_d.

2. $A_2'(((e, d), \sigma), 1^m, \gamma) \stackrel{\text{def}}{=} A_2^{E_e, D_d}(\sigma, (E_e(1^m), \gamma))$, where typically $\gamma = h(x)$ and $m = |x|$. (In the case of a priori CCA security, we may set $A_2'((e, \sigma), 1^m, \gamma) \stackrel{\text{def}}{=} A_2^{E_e}(\sigma, (E_e(1^m), \gamma))$, as in the proof of Theorem 5.4.11.)

Again, since A_1' merely emulates the generation of a key-pair and the actions of A_1 with respect to such a pair, the equal distribution condition (i.e., Item 2 in Definition 5.4.13) holds. Using the (corresponding) indistinguishability of encryption hypothesis, we show that (even in the presence of the encryption oracle E_e and a restricted decryption oracle D_d) the distributions $(\sigma, (E_e(x), h(x)))$ and $(\sigma, (E_e(1^{|x|}), h(x)))$ are indistinguishable, where $(e, d) \leftarrow G(1^n)$, $((S, h, f), \sigma) \leftarrow A_1^{E_e}(y, z)$ (with $y = e$ or $y = 1^n$ depending on the model), and $x \leftarrow S(U_{\text{poly}(n)})$. The main thing to notice is that the oracle queries made by a possible distinguisher of these distributions can be handled by a distinguisher of encryptions (as in Definition 5.4.14), by passing these queries to its own oracles. It follows that indistinguishability of encryptions (as per Definition 5.4.14) implies semantic security (as per Definition 5.4.13).

We now turn to the opposite direction. Here, the construction of a challenge template (as per Definition 5.4.13) is exactly as the corresponding construction in the proof of Theorem 5.4.11. Again, the thing to notice is that the oracle queries made by a possible distinguisher of encryptions (as in Definition 5.4.14) can be handled by the semantic-security adversary, by passing these queries to its own oracles. We derive a contradiction to the hypothesis that (G, E, D) satisfies Definition 5.4.13, and the theorem follows. ∎

Multiple-Message Security. Definitions 5.4.13 and 5.4.14 can be easily generalized to handle challenges in which multiple plaintexts are encrypted. We stress that in the case of a posteriori CCA, the adversary is not allowed to make a decryption query that equals *any* of the challenge ciphertexts. As in previous cases, the corresponding (multiple-plaintext) definitions are equivalent. Furthermore, as in the case of chosen plaintext attacks, the multiple-plaintext definitions are equivalent to the single-plaintext definitions (both for public-key and private-key schemes). We stress that this notion of multiple-message CCA security refers to a *single* challenge-generation step in which a sequence of messages (rather than a single message) can be specified. A more general notion of multiple-message CCA security allows multiple challenge-generation steps that may be interleaved with the query steps. This notion generalizes the notion of chosen ciphertext attacks and is discussed next (i.e., in Subsection 5.4.4.2). Actually, we will focus on this generalization when applied to a posteriori chosen ciphertext attacks, although a similar generalization can be applied to a priori chosen ciphertext attacks (and in fact also to chosen plaintext attacks).

5.4.4.2. A Third Equivalent Definition of a posteriori CCA Security

In continuation of the last paragraph, we consider general attacks during which several challenge templates may be produced (at arbitrary times and possibly interleaved with encryption and decryption queries).[32] Each of these challenge templates will be answered similarly to the way such templates were answered previously (i.e., by selecting a plaintext from the specified distribution and providing its encryption together with the specified partial information). Unlike in Section 5.4.4.1, we will even allow attacks that make decryption queries regarding ciphertexts obtained as (part of) the answer to previous challenge templates. After such an attack, the adversary will try to obtain information about the unrevealed plaintexts, and security holds if its success probability can be met by a corresponding benign adversary that does not see the ciphertexts. Indeed, the discussion requires clarification and careful formulation, provided next.

We start with a description of *the actual attacks*. It will be convenient to change the formalism and consider the generation of challenge templates as challenge queries that are answered by a special oracle called the tester, and denoted $T_{e,r}$, where e is an encryption-key and r is a random string of adequate length. On query a *challenge template* of the form (S, h), where S is a sampling circuit and h is (an evaluation circuit for) a function, the (randomized) oracle $T_{e,r}$ returns the pair $(E_e(x), h(x))$, where $x = S(r)$. (Indeed, we may assume without loss of generality that for all queries (S, h), it holds that S is a sampling circuit that generates strings of length that fits h's input.) We stress that r is not known to the adversary, and that this formalism supports the generation of dependent challenges as well as of independent ones.[33] A multiple-challenge CCA is allowed queries to $T_{e,r}$, as well as *unrestricted* queries to both E_e and the corresponding D_d, including decryption queries referring to previously obtained challenge ciphertexts. It terminates by outputting a function f and a value v, hoping that $f(x^1, ..., x^t) = v$, where $x^i = S^i(r)$ and (S^i, h^i) is the i-th challenge query made by the adversary. Note that the description of f (in terms of an evaluation circuit) may encode various information gathered by the adversary during its attack (e.g., it may even encode its entire computation transcript).[34]

---

[32] Note that in this section we generalize the notion of an a posteriori chosen ciphertext attack. When generalizing the notion of an a priori chosen ciphertext attack, we disallow decryption queries after the first challenge template is produced.

[33] Independently distributed plaintexts can be obtained by sampling circuits that refer to disjoint parts of the random string r. On the other hand, we can obtain a pair of plaintexts such that the second plaintext is a function of the first one by letting the second sampling circuit equal the composition of the first sampling circuit with the said function. That is, making queries of the form $(S, \cdot)$ and $(C \circ S, \cdot)$, where C is a deterministic circuit, we obtain answers that refer to the plaintexts $x \stackrel{\text{def}}{=} S(r)$ and $C(x)$.

[34] In general, the description of functions in terms of circuits that are not of minimal size is redundant, and opens the door for encoding of additional information.

We now turn to describe *the benign adversary* (which does not see the ciphertexts). Such an adversary is given oracle access to a corresponding oracle, T_r, that behaves as follows. On query a challenge template of the form (S, h), the oracle returns $h(x)$, where $x = S(r)$. (Again, r is not known to the adversary.) Like the real adversary, the benign adversary also terminates by outputting a function f and a value v, hoping that $f(x^1, ..., x^t) = v$, where $x^i = S^i(r)$ and (S^i, h^i) is the i-th challenge query made by the adversary.

Security amounts to asserting that the effect of any efficient multiple-challenge CCA can be simulated by an efficient benign adversary that does not see the ciphertexts. As in Definition 5.4.13, the simulation has to satisfy two conditions: First, the probability that $f(x^1, ..., x^t) = v$ in the CCA must be met by the probability that a corresponding event holds in the benign model (where the adversary does not see ciphertexts). Second, the challenge queries, as well as the function f, should be distributed similarly in the two models. Actually, the second condition should be modified in order to account for the case that the real CCA adversary makes a *decryption query* that refers to a ciphertext that is contained in the answer given to a *previous challenge query*, denoted (S, h). Note that such a decryption query (i.e., $E_e(S(r))$) reveals $S(r)$ to the attacker, and that this has nothing to do with the security of the encryption scheme. Thus, it is only fair to also allow the benign adversary (which sees no ciphertexts) to make the corresponding query, which is equivalent to the challenge query (S, id), where id is the identity function. (Indeed, the answer will be $\mathrm{id}(S(r)) = S(r)$.)

In order to obtain the actual definition, we need to define the trace of the execution of these two types of adversaries. *For a multiple-challenge CCA adversary,* denoted A, the trace is defined as the sequence of challenge queries made during the attack, augmented by fictitious challenge queries such that the (fictitious challenge) query (S, id) is included if and only if the adversary made a decryption query c such that $(c, \cdot)$ is the answer given to a previous challenge query of the form $(S, \cdot)$. (This convention is justified by the fact that the answer $(E_e(S(r)), \mathrm{id}(S(r)))$ to the fictitious challenge query (S, id) is efficiently computable from the answer $S(r)$ to the decryption query $c = E_e(S(r))$.)[35] In fact, for simplicity, we will assume in the following definition that A (or rather a minor modification of A) actually makes these fictitious challenge queries. *For the benign adversary,* denoted B, the trace is defined as the sequence of challenge queries made during the attack.

Definition 5.4.16 (multiple-challenge CCA security):

For public-key schemes: *A public-key encryption scheme, (G, E, D), is said to be* se-cure under multiple-challenge-chosen ciphertext attacks *if for every probabilistic polynomial-time oracle machine A there exists a probabilistic polynomial-time oracle machine B such that the following two conditions hold:*

1. *For every positive polynomial p, and all sufficiently large n and $z \in \{0, 1\}^{\mathrm{poly}(n)}$*

---

[35] Indeed, the value $(E_e(S(r)), \mathrm{id}(S(r)))$ is obtained from $S(r)$ by making an encryption query $S(r)$.

it holds that

$$\Pr \begin{bmatrix} v = f(x^1, ..., x^t) \text{ where} \\ \qquad (e, d) \leftarrow G(1^n) \text{ and } r \leftarrow U_{\text{poly}(n)} \\ \qquad (f, v) \leftarrow A^{E_e, D_d, T_{e,r}}(e, z) \\ \qquad x^i \leftarrow S^i(r), \text{ for } i = 1, ..., t. \end{bmatrix}$$

$$< \Pr \begin{bmatrix} v = f(x^1, ..., x^t) \text{ where} \\ \qquad r \leftarrow U_{\text{poly}(n)} \\ \qquad (f, v) \leftarrow B^{T_r}(1^n, z) \\ \qquad x^i \leftarrow S^i(r), \text{ for } i = 1, ..., t. \end{bmatrix} + \frac{1}{p(n)}$$

where t is the number of challenge queries made by A (resp., B), and S^i is the first part of the i-th challenge query made by A (resp., B) to $T_{e,r}$ (resp., to T_r).

2. *The following two probability ensembles, indexed by $n \in \mathbb{N}$ and $z \in \{0, 1\}^{\text{poly}(n)}$, are computationally indistinguishable:*

   (a) *The trace of $A^{E_{G_1(1^n)}, D_{G_2(1^n)}, T_{G_1(1^n)}, U_{\text{poly}(n)}}(G_1(1^n), z)$ augmented by the first element of its output pair (i.e., the function f).*

   (b) *The trace of $B^{T_{U_{\text{poly}(n)}}}(1^n, z)$ augmented by the first element of its output pair.*

That is, in both cases, we refer to the corresponding sequence

$$((S^1, h^1), ..., (S^t, h^t), f)$$

where (S^i, h^i) denotes the i-th challenge query.

For private-key schemes: *The definition is identical, except that machine A gets the security parameter 1^n instead of the encryption-key e.*

To get more comfortable with Definition 5.4.16, consider the special case in which the real CCA adversary does not make decryption queries to ciphertexts obtained as part of answers to challenge queries. (In the proof of Theorem 5.4.17, such adversaries will be called canonical and will be showed to be as powerful as the general ones.) The trace of such adversaries equals the sequence of actual challenge queries made during the attack (without any fictitious challenge queries), which simplifies the meaning of Condition 2. Furthermore, the special case in which such an adversary makes a single challenge query is very similar to Definition 5.4.13, with the exception that here Condition 2 allows computational indistinguishability (rather than requiring identical distributions). Still, this very restricted case (of Definition 5.4.16) does imply security under a posteriori CCA (see Exercise 37). More importantly, the following holds:

Theorem 5.4.17 (a posteriori CCA implies Definition 5.4.16): *Let (G, E, D) be a public-key (resp., private-key) encryption scheme that is secure under a posteriori CCA. Then (G, E, D) is secure under multiple-challenge CCA.*

Proof Sketch: As a bridge between the multiple-challenge CCA and the corresponding benign adversary that does not see the ciphertext, we consider canonical adversaries that can *perfectly simulate* any multiple-challenge CCA *without making decryption queries to ciphertexts obtained as part of answers to challenge queries*. Instead, these canonical adversaries make corresponding queries of the form (S, id), where id is the identity function and $(S, \cdot)$ is the challenge-query that was answered with the said ciphertext. Specifically, suppose that a multiple-challenge CCA has made the challenge query (S, h), which was answered by (c, v) where $c = E_e(x)$, $v = h(x)$ and $x = S(r)$, and at a later stage makes the decryption query c, which is to be answered by $D_d(c) = x$. Then, the corresponding canonical adversary makes the challenge query (S, h) as the original adversary, receiving the same pair (c, v), but later (instead of making the decryption query c) the canonical adversary makes the challenge query (S, id), which is answered by $\text{id}(S(r)) = x = D_d(c)$. Note that the trace of the corresponding canonical adversary is identical to the trace of the original CCA adversary (and the same holds with respect to their outputs).

Thus, given an a posteriori CCA–secure encryption scheme, it suffices to establish Definition 5.4.16 when the quantification is restricted to *canonical* adversaries A. Indeed, as in previous cases, we construct a benign adversary B in the natural manner: On input $(1^n, z)$, machine B generates $(e, d) \leftarrow G(1^n)$, and invokes A on input (y, z), where $y = e$ if we are in the public-key case and $y = 1^n$ otherwise. Next, B emulates all oracles expected by A, while using its own oracle T_r. Specifically, the oracles E_e and D_d are perfectly emulated by using the corresponding keys (known to B), and the oracle $T_{e,r}$ is (imperfectly) emulated using the oracle T_r; that is, the query (S, h) is forwarded to T_r, and the answer $h(S(r))$ is augmented with $E_e(1^m)$, where m is the number of output bits in S. Note that the latter emulation (i.e., the answer $(E_e(1^{|S(r)|}), h(S(r)))$) is imperfect since the answer of $T_{e,r}$ would have been $(E_e(S(r)), h(S(r)))$, yet (as we shall show) A cannot tell the difference.

In order to show that B satisfies both conditions of Definition 5.4.16 (with respect to this A), we will show that the following two ensembles are computationally indistinguishable:

1. The global view in a real attack of A on (G, E, D). That is, we consider the output of the following experiment:

   (a) $(e, d) \leftarrow G(1^n)$ and $r \leftarrow U_{\text{poly}(n)}$.
   (b) $(f, v) \leftarrow A^{E_e, D_d, T_{e,r}}(y, z)$, where $y = e$ if we are in the public-key case and $y = 1^n$ otherwise. Furthermore, we let $((S^1, h^1), ..., (S^t, h^t))$ denote the trace of the execution $A^{E_e, D_d, T_{e,r}}(y, z)$.
   (c) The output is $((S^1, h^1), ..., (S^t, h^t)), (f, v), r$.

2. The global view in an attack emulated by B. That is, we consider the output of an experiment as in Item 1, except that $A^{E_e, D_d, T_{e,r}}(y, z)$ is replaced by $A^{E_e, D_d, T'_{e,r}}(y, z)$, where on query (S, h) the oracle $T'_{e,r}$ replies with $(E_e(1^{|S(r)|}), h(S(r)))$ rather than with $(E_e(S(r)), h(S(r)))$.

Note that computational indistinguishability of these ensembles immediately implies Condition 2 of Definition 5.4.16, whereas Condition 1 also follows because using r, we can determine whether or not $f(S^1(r), ..., S^t(r)) = v$ holds (for (f, v) and $S^1, ..., S^t$ that appear in the ensemble's output). Also note that these ensembles may be computationally indistinguishable only in the case where A is *canonical* (which we have assumed to be the case).[36]

The computational indistinguishability of these two ensembles is proven using a hybrid argument, which in turn relies on the hypothesis that (G, E, D) has indistinguishable encryptions under a posteriori CCAs. Specifically, we introduce $t + 1$ *mental experiments* that are hybrids of the two ensembles (which we wish to relate). Each of these mental experiments is given oracle access to E_e and D_d, where $(e, d) \leftarrow G(1^n)$ is selected from the outside. The i-th hybrid experiment uses these two oracles (in addition to y, which equals e in the public-key case and 1^n otherwise) in order to emulate an execution of $A^{E_e, D_d, \Pi^i_{e,r}}(y, z)$, where r is selected by the experiment itself and $\Pi^i_{e,r}$ is a hybrid of $T_{e,r}$ and $T'_{e,r}$. Specifically, $\Pi^i_{e,r}$ is a history-dependent process that answers like $T_{e,r}$ on the first i queries and like $T'_{e,r}$ on the rest. Thus, for $i = 0, ..., t$, we define the i-th hybrid experiment as a process that, given y (which equals e or 1^n) and oracle access to E_e and D_d, where $(e, d) \leftarrow G(1^n)$, behaves as follows:

1. The process selects $r \leftarrow U_{\text{poly}(n)}$.
2. The process emulates an execution of $A^{E_e, D_d, \Pi^i_{e,r}}(y, z)$, where $y = e$ if we are in the public-key case and $y = 1^n$ otherwise, by using the oracles E_e and D_d. Specifically, the answers of $\Pi^i_{e,r}$ are emulated using the knowledge of r and oracle access to E_e: the j-th query to $\Pi^i_{e,r}$, denoted (S^j, h^j), is answered by $(E_e(S^j(r)), h^j(S^j(r)))$ if $j \leq i$ and is answered by $(E_e(1^{|S^j(r)|}), h^j(S^j(r)))$ otherwise. (The process answers A's queries to E_e and D_d by forwarding them to its own corresponding oracles.)
3. As before, (f, v) denotes the output of $A^{E_e, D_d, \Pi^i_{e,r}}(y, z)$, and $((S^1, h^1), ..., (S^t, h^t))$ denotes its trace. The process outputs $((S^1, h^1), ..., (S^t, h^t)), (f, v), r$.

We stress that since A is *canonical*, none of the D_d-queries equals a ciphertext obtained as part of the answer of a $\Pi^i_{e,r}$-query.

Clearly, the distribution of the 0-hybrid is identical to the distribution of the global view in an attack emulated by B, whereas the distribution of the t-hybrid is identical to the distribution of the global view in a real attack by A. On the other hand, distinguishing the i-hybrid from the $(i + 1)$-hybrid yields a successful *a posteriori CCA* (in the sense of distinguishing encryptions). That is, assuming that one can distinguish the i-hybrid from the $(i + 1)$-hybrid, we construct an a posteriori CCA adversary (as per Definition 5.4.14)

---

[36] Non-canonical adversaries can easily distinguish the two types of views by distinguishing the oracle $T_{e,r}$ from oracle $T'_{e,r}$. For example, suppose we make a challenge query with a sampling-circuit S that generates some distribution over $\{0, 1\}^m \setminus \{1^m\}$, next make a decryption query on the ciphertext obtained in the challenge query, and output the answer. Then, in case we query the oracle $T_{e,r}$, we output $D_d(E_e(S(r))) \neq 1^m$; whereas in case we query the oracle $T'_{e,r}$, we output $D_d(E_e(1^m)) = 1^m$. Recall, however, that at this point of the proof, we are guaranteed that A is canonical (and indeed A might have been derived by perfectly emulating some non-canonical A'). An alternative way of handling non-canonical adversaries is to let B handle the disallowed (decryption) queries by making the corresponding challenge query, and returning its answer rather than the decryption value. (Note that B, which emulates $T'_{r,e}$, can detect which queries are disallowed.)

as follows. For $(e, d) \leftarrow G(1^n)$, given $y = e$ if we are in the public-key case and $y = 1^n$ otherwise, the attacker (having oracle access to E_e and D_d) behaves as follows:

1. The attacker selects $r \leftarrow U_{\text{poly}(n)}$.

2. The attacker emulates an execution of $A^{E_e, D_d, \Pi_{e,r}^j}(y, z)$, where $j \in \{i, i + 1\}$ (is unknown to the attacker), as follows. The queries to E_e and D_d are answered by using the corresponding oracles available to the attacker, and the issue is answering the queries to $\Pi_{e,r}^j$. The first i queries to $\Pi_{e,r}^j$ are answered as in both $\Pi_{e,r}^i$ and $\Pi_{e,r}^{i+1}$ (i.e., query (S, h) is answered by $(E_e(S(r)), h(S(r)))$), and the last $t - (i + 1)$ queries are also answered as in both $\Pi_{e,r}^i$ and $\Pi_{e,r}^{i+1}$ (i.e., by $(E_e(1^{|S(r)|}), h(S(r)))$, this time). The $i + 1^{\text{st}}$ query, denoted (S^{i+1}, h^{i+1}), is answered by producing the *challenge template* $(S^{i+1}(r), 1^{|S^{i+1}(r)|})$, which is answered by the challenge ciphertext c (where $c \in \{E_e(S^{i+1}(r)), E_e(1^{|S^{i+1}(r)|})\}$), and replying with $(c, h^{i+1}(S^{i+1}(r)))$.

   Note that if $c = E_e(S^{i+1}(r))$, then we emulate $\Pi_{e,r}^{i+1}$, whereas if $c = E_e(1^{|S^{i+1}(r)|})$ then we emulate $\Pi_{e,r}^i$.

3. Again, (f, v) denotes the output of $A^{E_e, D_d, \Pi_{e,r}^j}(y, z)$, and $((S^1, h^1), ..., (S^t, h^t))$ denotes its trace. The attacker feeds $((S^1, h^1), ..., (S^t, h^t)), (f, v), r$ to the hybrid distinguisher (which we have assumed to exist toward the contradiction), and outputs whatever the latter does.

This is an a posteriori CCA as in Definition 5.4.14: It produces a *single* challenge (i.e., the pair of plaintexts $(S^{i+1}(r), 1^{|S^{i+1}(r)|})$), and distinguishes the case that it is given the ciphertext $c = E_e(S^{i+1}(r))$ from the case that it is given the ciphertext $c = E_e(1^{|S^{i+1}(r)|})$, without querying D_d on the challenge ciphertext c. The last assertion follows by the hypothesis that A is *canonical*, and so none of the D_d-queries that A makes equals the ciphertext c obtained as (part of) the answer to the $i + 1^{\text{st}}$ $\Pi_{e,r}^j$-query. Thus, distinguishing the $i + 1^{\text{st}}$ and i-th hybrids implies distinguishing encryptions under an a posteriori CCA, which contradicts our hypothesis regarding (G, E, D). The theorem follows. ∎

Further Generalization. Recall that we have allowed arbitrary challenge queries of the form (S, h) that were answered by $(E_e(S(r)), h(S(r)))$. Instead, we may allow queries of the form (S, h) that are answered by $(E_e(S(r)), h(r))$; that is, h is applied to r itself rather than to $S(r)$. Actually, given the "independence" of h from S, one could have replaced the challenge queries by two types of queries: partial-information (on r) queries that correspond to the h's (and are answered by $h(r)$), and encrypted partial-information queries that correspond to the S's (and are answered by $E_e(S(r))$). As shown in Exercise 38, all these forms are in fact equivalent.

5.4.4.3. Constructing CCA-Secure Private-Key Schemes

In this section we present simple constructions of CCA-secure *private-key* encryption schemes. We start with a priori CCA, and next turn to a posteriori CCA.

Security under a-priori CCA. All the results presented in Section 5.3.3 extend to security under a priori chosen ciphertext attacks. Specifically, we prove that Constructions 5.3.9 and 5.3.12 remain secure also under an a priori CCA.

Proposition 5.4.18: *Let F and (G, E, D) be as in Construction 5.3.9, and suppose that F is pseudorandom with respect to polynomial-size circuits. Then the private-key encryption scheme (G, E, D) is secure under a priori chosen ciphertext attacks. The same holds with respect to Construction 5.3.12.*

Proof Sketch: As in the proof of 5.4.12, we focus on Construction 5.3.9, and consider an idealized version of the scheme in which one uses a uniformly selected function $\phi : \{0, 1\}^n \to \{0, 1\}^n$ (rather than the pseudorandom function f_s). Again, all that the adversary obtains by *encryption queries* in the ideal version is pairs $(r, \phi(r))$, where the r's are uniformly and independently distributed in $\{0, 1\}^n$. Similarly, *decryption queries* provide the adversary with pairs $(r, \phi(r))$, but here the r's are selected by the adversary. Still in an a priori CCA, all decryption queries are made before the challenge is presented, and so these r's are selected (by the adversary) independent of the challenge. Turning to the challenge itself, we observe that the plaintext is "masked" by the value of ϕ at another uniformly and independently distributed element in $\{0, 1\}^n$, denoted r_C. We stress that r_C is independent of all r's selected in decryption queries (because these occur before r_C is selected), as well as being independent of all r's selected by the encryption oracle (regardless of whether these queries are made prior or subsequently to the challenge). Now, unless r_C happens to equal one of the r's that appear in the pairs $(r, \phi(r))$ obtained by the adversary (which happens with negligible probability), the challenge plaintext is perfectly masked. Thus, the ideal version is secure under an a priori CCA. The same holds for the real scheme, because pseudorandom functions are indistinguishable from truly random ones (even by machines that adaptively query the function at arguments of their choice). ∎

Security under a-posteriori CCA. Unfortunately, Constructions 5.3.9 and 5.3.12 are not secure under a posteriori chosen ciphertext attacks: Given a challenge ciphertext $(r, x \oplus f_s(r))$, the adversary may obtain $f_s(r)$ by making the query (r, y'), for any $y' \neq x \oplus f_s(r)$. This query is allowed and is answered with x' such that $y' = x' \oplus f_s(r)$. Thus, the adversary may recover the challenge plaintext x from the challenge ciphertext (r, y), where $y \overset{\text{def}}{=} x \oplus f_s(r)$, by computing $y \oplus (y' \oplus x')$. Thus, we should look for new private-key encryption schemes if we want to obtain one that is secure under a posteriori CCA. Actually, we show how to transform any private-key encryption scheme that is secure under chosen *plaintext* attack (CPA) into one that is secure under a posteriori CCA.

The idea underlying our transformation (of CPA-secure schemes into CCA-secure ones) is to eliminate the adversary's gain from chosen ciphertext attacks by making it infeasible to produce a legitimate ciphertext (other than the ones given explicitly to the adversary). Thus, an a posteriori CCA adversary can be emulated by a chosen *plaintext* attack (CPA) adversary, while almost preserving the success probability.

The question is indeed how to make it infeasible for the (a posteriori CCA) adversary to produce a legitimate ciphertext (other than the ones explicitly given to it). One answer is to use "Message Authentication Codes" (MACs) as defined in Section 6.1.[37] That is, we augment each ciphertext with a corresponding authentication tag (which is "hard to forge"), and consider an augmented ciphertext to be valid only if it consists of a valid (string,tag)-pair. For the sake of self-containment (and concreteness), we will use a specific implementation of such MACs via pseudorandom functions. Incorporating this MAC in Construction 5.3.9, we obtain the following:

Construction 5.4.19 (a private-key block-cipher secure against a-posteriori CCA): *As in Construction 5.3.9, let $F = \{F_n\}$ be an efficiently computable function ensemble and let I be the function-selection algorithm associated with it; i.e., $I(1^n)$ selects a function f_s with distribution F_n. We define a private-key block-cipher, (G, E, D), with block-length $\ell(n) = n$ as follows:*

Key-generation: $G(1^n) = ((k, k'), (k, k'))$, *where k and k' are generated by two independent invocations of $I(1^n)$.*

Encrypting plaintext $x \in \{0, 1\}^n$ (using the key (k, k')):

$$E_{k,k'}(x) = ((r, f_k(r) \oplus x), f_{k'}(r, f_k(r) \oplus x)),$$

where r is uniformly chosen in $\{0, 1\}^n$.

Decrypting ciphertext (r, y) (using the key (k, k')): $D_{k, k'}((r, y), t) = f_k(r) \oplus y$ *if $f_{k'}(r, y) = t$ and $D_{k,k'}((r, y), t) = \bot$ otherwise.*

Proposition 5.4.20: *Let F and (G, E, D) be as in Construction 5.4.19, and suppose that F is pseudorandom with respect to polynomial-size circuits. Then the private-key encryption scheme (G, E, D) is secure under a posteriori chosen ciphertext attacks.*

Proof Sketch: Following the motivation preceding the construction, we emulate any a posteriori CCA adversary by a CPA adversary. Specifically, we need to show how to answer *decryption queries* made by the CCA adversary. Let us denote such a generic query by $((r, y), t)$, and consider the following three cases:

1. If $((r, y), t)$ equals the answer given to some (previous) *encryption query* x, then we answer the current query with x.
   Clearly, the answer we give is always correct.
2. If $((r, y), t)$ equals the challenge ciphertext, then this query is not allowed.
3. Otherwise, we answer that $((r, y), t)$ is not a valid ciphertext.
   We need to show that our answer is indeed correct. Recall that in this case, $((r, y), t)$ neither appeared before as an answer to an encryption query nor equals the challenge ciphertext. Since for every (r, y) there is a *unique* t' such that $((r, y), t')$ is a valid ciphertext, the case hypothesis implies that one of the following sub-cases

---

[37] In fact, we need to use secure Message Authentication Codes that have unique valid tags (or at least are super-secure), as discussed in Section 6.5.1 (resp., Section 6.5.2).

must occur:

Case 1: Some $((r, y), t')$, with $t' \neq t$, has appeared before either as an answer to an encryption query or as the challenge ciphertext. In this case, $((r, y), t)$ is definitely not a valid ciphertext, because $((r, y), t')$ is the unique valid ciphertext of the form $((r, y), \cdot)$.

Case 2: No triple of the form $((r, y), \cdot)$ has appear before (as such an answer to an encryption query or as the challenge ciphertext). In this sub-case, the ciphertext is valid if and only if $t = f_{k'}(r, y)$. That is, in order to produce such a valid ciphertext, the adversary must guess the value of $f_{k'}$ at (r, y), when only seeing the value of $f_{k'}$ at other arguments. By the pseudorandomness of the function $f_{k'}$, the adversary may succeed in such a guess only with negligible probability, and hence our answer is wrong only with negligible probability.

Finally, note that the CPA-security of Construction 5.3.9 (see Proposition 5.4.12) implies the CPA-security of Construction 5.4.19. The proposition follows. ■

An Alternative Proof of Proposition 5.4.20. Augmenting the proof of Proposition 5.4.18, we (need to) consider here also *decryption queries* made after the challenge ciphertext, denoted $((r_C, y_C), t_C)$, is presented. Let us denote such a generic decryption query by $((r, y), t)$. We consider four cases, ignoring the unlikely case that some encryption query is answered by a pair of the form $((r_C, \cdot), \cdot)$:

1. If $r \neq r_C$ then the query $((r, y), t)$ can be treated as in the proof of Proposition 5.4.18, because it reveals nothing on $f_k(r_C)$. Indeed, such a query is not more dangerous than a query made during an a priori CCA attack.
2. If $r = r_C$ and $y \neq y_C$ then, except with negligible probability, the query $((r, y), t)$ is not a valid ciphertext, because it is infeasible to guess the value of $f_{k'}(r, y)$ (which is the only value of t' such that $((r, y), t')$ is valid). Thus, such queries (which are almost always answered by $\bot$) can be ignored.
3. If $(r, y) = (r_C, y_C)$ and $t \neq t_C$ then (surely) the query $((r, y), t)$ is not a valid ciphertext, and can be ignored (as in the previous case).
4. If $(r, y, t) = (r_C, y_C, t_C)$ then the query $((r, y), t)$ is not allowed.

The proposition follows. ■

The same construction and analysis can be applied to Construction 5.3.12. Combining Proposition 5.4.20 with Corollary 3.6.7, we get:

Theorem 5.4.21: *If there exist (non-uniformly hard) one-way functions, then there exist private-key encryption schemes that are secure under a posteriori chosen ciphertext attacks.*

5.4.4.4. Constructing CCA-Secure Public-Key Schemes

In this section we present fairly complicated constructions of CCA-secure *public-key* encryption schemes. Again, we start by considering a priori CCA, and then augment the constructions in order to handle a posteriori CCA. Specifically, we will show how to transform any public-key encryption scheme that is secure in the passive (key-dependent) sense into one that is secure under a posteriori CCA. As in the case of private-key schemes, the idea underlying the transformation is to eliminate the adversary's gain from chosen ciphertext attacks.

Recall that in the case of private-key schemes, the adversary's gain from a CCA was eliminated by making it infeasible (for the adversary) to produce legitimate ciphertexts (other than those explicitly given to it). However, in the context of public-key schemes, the adversary can easily generate legitimate ciphertexts (by applying the keyed encryption algorithm to any plaintext of its choice). Thus, in the current context, the adversary's gain from a CCA is eliminated by making it infeasible (for the adversary) to produce legitimate ciphertexts without "knowing" the corresponding plaintext. This, in turn, will be achieved by augmenting the plaintext with a non-interactive zero-knowledge "proof of knowledge" of the corresponding plaintext.

NIZK: Preliminaries. Strong forms of Non-Interactive Zero-Knowledge (NIZK) proofs will play a key role in our transformation, and we will assume that the reader is familiar with the main notions and results that are presented in Section 4.10. Since the notion of a *proof-of-knowledge* is quite complex in general (cf. Section 4.7), and more so in the *non-interactive* (zero-knowledge) context (let alone that we will need strengthenings of it), we will not make explicit use of this notion (i.e., of proof-of-knowledge). Instead, we will use non-interactive (zero-knowledge) *proofs of membership* (NIZK) as defined in Section 4.10. In fact, our starting point is the definition of *adaptive* NIZK systems (i.e., Definition 4.10.15), when extended to handle assertions of a priori unbounded length (as discussed at the beginning of Section 4.10.3.1). We focus on proof systems in which the prover is implemented by a probabilistic polynomial-time algorithm that is given a suitable auxiliary-input (e.g., an NP-witness). For the sake of clarity, let us reproduce the resulting definition.

Definition 5.4.22 (adaptive NIZK): *An* adaptive non-interactive zero-knowledge proof system (adaptive NIZK) *for a language* $L \in \mathcal{NP}$, *with an NP-relation* R_L, *consists of a pair of probabilistic polynomial-time algorithms, denoted* (P, V), *that satisfy the following:*

- Syntax: *Both machines are given the same uniformly selected* reference string $r \in \{0, 1\}^m$ *along with an actual input* $x \in \{0, 1\}^*$ *such that* $|x| = \text{poly}(m)$ *and an auxiliary input. Specifically, on input* r, x *and* w *(supposedly,* $(x, w) \in R_L$), *the prover* P *outputs an alleged proof* $\pi \leftarrow P(x, w, r)$; *whereas on input* r, x *and* π, *the verifier* V *decides according to* $V(x, r, \pi) \in \{0, 1\}$.
- Completeness: *For every* $(x, w) \in R_L$ *with* $|x| = \text{poly}(m)$, *the probability that* V *does not accept the input* x *(based on the proof* $P(x, w, U_m)$ *and the reference string* U_m) *is negligible; that is,* $\Pr[V(x, U_m, P(x, w, U_m)) \neq 1]$ *is negligible. (Typically, the error probability here is zero, in which case we say that the proof has* perfect completeness.)

- **Adaptive Soundness:** *For every* $\Xi : \{0, 1\}^m \to (\{0, 1\}^{\mathrm{poly}(m)} \setminus L)$ *and every* $\Pi :$ $\{0, 1\}^m \to \{0, 1\}^{\mathrm{poly}(m)}$, *the probability that* V *accepts the input* $\Xi(U_m)$ (*based on the proof* $\Pi(U_m)$ *and the reference string* U_m) *is negligible; that is,* $\Pr[V(\Xi(U_m), U_m, \Pi(U_m)) = 1]$ *is negligible.*

- **Adaptive Zero-Knowledge:** *There exist two probabilistic polynomial-time algorithms,* S_1 *and* S_2, *such that for every pair of functions* $\Xi : \{0, 1\}^m \to (\{0, 1\}^{\mathrm{poly}(m)} \cap L)$ *and* $W : \{0, 1\}^m \to \{0, 1\}^{\mathrm{poly}(m)}$ *such that* Ξ *and* W *are both implementable by polynomial-size circuits and* $(\Xi(r), W(r)) \in R_L$ ($\forall r \in \{0, 1\}^m$), *the ensembles* $\{(U_m, \Xi(U_m), P(\Xi(U_m), W(U_m), U_m))\}_{m \in \mathbb{N}}$ *and* $\{S^{\Xi}(1^m)\}_{m \in \mathbb{N}}$ *are computationally indistinguishable* (*by non-uniform families of polynomial-size circuits*), *where* $S^{\Xi}(1^m)$ *denotes the output of the following randomized process:*

  1. $(r, s) \leftarrow S_1(1^m)$;
  2. $x \leftarrow \Xi(r)$;
  3. $\pi \leftarrow S_2(x, s)$;
  4. Output (r, x, π).

  Indeed, S is a two-stage simulator that first produces (*obliviously of the actual input*) *an alleged reference string r* (*along with the auxiliary information s*),[38] *and then, given an actual input* (*which may depend on r*), *simulates the actual proof.*

Note that it is important that in the zero-knowledge condition, the function Ξ is required to be implementable by polynomial-size circuits (because otherwise only languages in $\mathcal{BPP}$ can have such proof systems; see Exercise 39). In the rest of this subsection, whenever we refer to an adaptive NIZK, we mean this definition. Actually, we may relax the adaptive soundness condition so that it only applies to functions Ξ and Π that are implementable by polynomial-size circuits. That is, computational soundness will actually suffice for the rest of this subsection.

Additional Conventions. Note that (analogously to Proposition 5.4.10) in the case of public-key schemes, the combined chosen plaintext and ciphertext attack (as in Definitions 5.4.13 and 5.4.14) is equivalent to a "pure" chosen *ciphertext* attack. Thus, in this subsection we consider only attacks of the latter type. Another technical point is that in our construction we can use any public-key encryption scheme that is secure in the passive (key-dependent) sense, *provided that for all but a negligible measure of the key-pairs that it generates, there is no decryption error.* For simplicity of presentation, we will assume that the basic encryption scheme has no decryption error at all (i.e., on all key-pairs).

The General Framework. The following schema (for constructing CCA-secure public-key encryption schemes) uses a passively secure public-key encryption

---

[38] The auxiliary information s may explicitly contain r. Alternatively, s may just equal the coins used by S_1. In the constructions that follow, we do not follow either of these conventions, but rather let s equal the very information about r that S_2 needs.

scheme, denoted (G, E, D), and an adaptive NIZK, denoted (P, V), for a related NP-set.

Construction 5.4.23 (CCA-security construction framework): *Let $E_e(x, s)$ denote the ciphertext produced by E when given the encryption-key e, the plaintext x, and the coins s; that is, $E_e(x) \leftarrow E_e(x, s)$, where s is selected uniformly among the set of poly($|e|$, $|x|$)-long bit strings. We use an adaptive NIZK (P, V) for the language L_R defined by the following NP-relation:*

$$R \stackrel{\text{def}}{=} \{((e_1, e_2, y_1, y_2), (x, s_1, s_2)) : y_1 = E_{e_1}(x, s_1) \ \& \ y_2 = E_{e_2}(x, s_2)\} \quad (5.12)$$

That is, $(e_1, e_2, y_1, y_2) \in L_R$ if y_1 and y_2 are encryptions of the same plaintext, produced using the encryption-keys e_1 and e_2, respectively.

Key-generation: $G'(1^n) \stackrel{\text{def}}{=} ((e_1, e_2, r), (d_1, d_2, r))$, *where (e_1, d_1) and (e_2, d_2) are selected at random by invoking $G(1^n)$ twice, and r is uniformly distributed in $\{0, 1\}^n$.*

Encrypting plaintext $x \in \{0, 1\}^*$ (using the key $\overline{e} = (e_1, e_2, r)$):

$E'_{\overline{e}}(x) \stackrel{\text{def}}{=} (y_1, y_2, \pi)$, *where s_1, s_2 are uniformly selected poly(n)-long bit strings, $y_1 = E_{e_1}(x, s_1)$, $y_2 = E_{e_2}(x, s_2)$, and $\pi \leftarrow P((e_1, e_2, y_1, y_2), (x, s_1, s_2), r)$.*

Decrypting ciphertext (y_1, y_2, π) (using the key $\overline{d} = (d_1, d_2, r)$):

If $V((e_1, e_2, y_1, y_2), r, \pi) = 1$, then return $D_{d_1}(y_1)$ or else return an error symbol indicating that the ciphertext is not valid.

Indeed, our choice to decrypt according to y_1 (in case π is a valid proof) is immaterial, and we could as well decrypt according to y_2. Another alternative could be to decrypt according to both y_1 and y_2 and return a result only if both outcomes are identical (and π is a valid proof). We stress that, here as well as in the following analysis, we rely on the hypothesis that decryption is error-free, which implies that $D_d(E_e(x)) = x$ for every (e, d) in the range of G. Thus, $D_{d_1}(y_1) = D_{d_2}(y_2)$, for any $(e_1, e_2, y_1, y_2) \in L_R$, where the (e_i, d_i)'s are in the range of G.

Clearly, Construction 5.4.23 constitutes a public-key encryption scheme; that is, $D'_{\overline{d}}(E'_{\overline{e}}(x)) = x$, provided that the NIZK proof generated during the encryption stage was accepted during the decryption stage. Indeed, if the NIZK system enjoys perfect completeness (which is typically the case), then the decryption error is zero. By the zero-knowledge property, the passive security of the original encryption scheme (G, E, D) is preserved by Construction 5.4.23. Intuitively, creating a valid ciphertext seems to imply "knowledge" of the corresponding plaintext, but this appealing claim should be examined with more care (and in fact is not always valid). Furthermore, as stated previously, our actual proof will not refer to the notion of "knowledge." Instead, the actual proof will proceed by showing how a chosen ciphertext attack on Construction 5.4.23 can be transformed into a (key-dependent) passive attack on (G, E, D). In fact, we will need to *augment* the notion of (adaptive) NIZK in order to present such a transformation. We will do so in two steps. The first augmentation will be used to deal with a priori CCA, and further augmentation will be used to deal with a posteriori CCA.

Step I: a-priori CCA

Let us start by considering an a priori CCA. Given such an adversary A, we construct a passive adversary B that attacks (G, E, D) by emulating the attack of A on Construction 5.4.23. One important observation is that the latter encryption scheme uses two keys of the original scheme. Thus, given an encryption-key of the original scheme, B generates another encryption-key (while storing the corresponding decryption-key) and invokes A, giving it the pair of encryption-keys (along with a reference string to be generated as discussed in the next paragraph). When A makes a decryption query, B may answer the query by using the stored decryption-key (generated by B before). This works provided that the query ciphertext contains a pair of ciphertexts of the same plaintext according to the two keys, which is the reason we augmented the ciphertext pairs by a *proof of consistency*. Thus, actually, B should examine the latter proof and act analogously to the decryption process of Construction 5.4.23.

The next problem arises when A asks to be given a challenge. Algorithm B forwards the request as its own challenge template, but the challenge given to B is a single ciphertext of the original scheme, and so B needs to augment it into something that looks like a ciphertext of Construction 5.4.23. Here is where we rely on the zero-knowledge property of the proof of consistency (for producing the required proof that relates to a plaintext we do not know), but in order to do so, the reference string needs to be generated by the simulator (rather than be uniformly distributed). But this leads to the following problem: When referring (in the previous paragraph) to the soundness of the proofs of consistency, we assumed that the reference string is uniformly distributed (since soundness was stated for that case), and it is not clear whether soundness holds when the reference string is generated by the simulator (who must use a different[39] distribution). This issue is addressed by the notion of (weak) *simulationsoundness*.

Defining and Constructing Adaptive NIZKs with a Weak Simulation-Soundness Property. This discussion leads to the following definition:

Definition 5.4.24 (weak simulation-soundness): *Let (P, V) be an adaptive NIZK for a language L, and (S_1, S_2) be a corresponding two-stage simulator. We say that* **weak simulation-soundness** *holds if for all polynomial-size implementable functions Ξ and Π, it holds that*

$$\Pr[\Xi(r) \notin L \text{ and } V(\Xi(r), r, \Pi(r)) = 1, \text{ where } (r, s) \leftarrow S_1(1^n)] < \mu(n)$$

where $\mu : \mathbb{N} \rightarrow [0,1]$ is a negligible function.

Note that the computational limitation on Π is essential to the viability of the definition (see Exercise 40). It is tempting to conjecture that every adaptive NIZK (or rather its simulator) satisfies weak simulation-soundness; however, this is not true (for further discussion see Exercise 41). Nevertheless, adaptive NIZK (for $\mathcal{NP}$) with a simulator

---

[39] Indeed, prove that the distribution produced by the simulator must be far away from uniform. See related Exercises 39 and 40.

satisfying weak simulation-soundness can be constructed given any adaptive NIZK (for $\mathcal{NP}$).

Construction 5.4.25 (from adaptive NIZK to weak simulation-soundness): *Let (P, V) be an adaptive NIZK for some language L, and let (S_1, S_2) be the corresponding two-stage simulator. We construct the following adaptive NIZK that works with reference string $((r_1^0, r_1^1), ..., (r_n^0, r_n^1))$, where $r_i^\sigma \in \{0, 1\}^n$.*

Prover P': On common input x and auxiliary-input w (s.t., $(x, w) \in R_L$), (and reference string $((r_1^0, r_1^1), ..., (r_n^0, r_n^1)))$, uniformly select $b_1, ..., b_n \in \{0, 1\}$, compute $\pi_i \leftarrow P(x, w, r_i^{b_i})$ for $i = 1, ..., n$, and output $\overline{\pi} \stackrel{\text{def}}{=} (b_1, ..., b_n, \pi_1, ..., \pi_n)$.

Verifier V': On common input x (and reference string $((r_1^0, r_1^1), ..., (r_n^0, r_n^1)))$, given an alleged proof $\overline{\pi} = (b_1, ..., b_n, \pi_1, ..., \pi_n)$, accept if and only if $V(x, r_i^{b_i}, \pi_i) = 1$ for each $i \in \{1, ..., n\}$.

Simulator's first stage S_1': On input 1^n, select uniformly $c_1, ..., c_n \in \{0, 1\}$, generate $(r_i^{c_i}, s_i) \leftarrow S_1(1^n)$ for $i = 1, ..., n$, select uniformly $r_1^{1-c_1}, ..., r_n^{1-c_n} \in \{0, 1\}^n$, and output $(\overline{r}, \overline{s})$, where $\overline{r} \stackrel{\text{def}}{=} ((r_1^0, r_1^1), ..., (r_n^0, r_n^1))$ and $\overline{s} \stackrel{\text{def}}{=} (c_1, ..., c_n, s_1, ..., s_n)$.

Simulator's second stage S_2': On input $(\overline{s}, x)$, where $\overline{s} = (c_1, ..., c_n, s_1, ..., s_n)$, compute $\pi_i \leftarrow S_2(x, s_i)$ for $i = 1, ..., n$, and output $(c_1, ..., c_n, \pi_1, ..., \pi_n)$.

It is easy to see that Construction 5.4.25 preserves the adaptive NIZK features of (P, V, S_1, S_2). Furthermore, as will be shown, Construction 5.4.25 is weak simulation-sound.

Proposition 5.4.26: *Construction 5.4.25 is an adaptive NIZK for L, and weak simulation-soundness holds with respect to the prescribed simulator.*

Proof Sketch: Completeness and soundness follow by the corresponding properties of (P, V). To see that the simulation is indistinguishable from the real execution of (P', V'), note that the two probability ensembles differ in two aspects: First, the simulation uses $r_i^{c_i}$'s generated by $S_1(1^n)$, whereas in the real execution, the $r_i^{c_i}$'s are uniformly distributed; and second, the simulation uses simulated proofs produced by $S_2(x, s_i)$, rather than real proofs produced by $P(x, w, r_i^{b_i})$. Still, the indistinguishability of the output of the original simulator from the real execution of (P, V) can be used to prove that the current ensembles are indistinguishable, too. Specifically, we consider a *hybrid distribution* in which all r_i^b's are generated by $S_1(1^n)$ but the individual proofs (i.e., π_i's) are produced by $P(x, w, r_i^{b_i})$. Using the fact that indistinguishability (by small circuits) is preserved under repeated sampling, we show that this hybrid ensemble is indistinguishable from each of the two original ensembles (i.e., the real execution of (P', V') and the simulation by (S_1', S_2')).

To establish the weak simulation-soundness property, we consider an arbitrary cheating prover $C = (\Xi, \Pi)$ that is implementable by a family of small circuits. We say that $C(\overline{r}) = (\Xi(\overline{r}), \Pi(\overline{r}))$ succeeds if it holds that $\Xi(\overline{r}) \notin L$ and $V'(\Xi(\overline{r}), \overline{r}, \Pi(\overline{r})) = 1$. We are interested in the probability that $C(\overline{r})$ succeeds when $(\overline{r}, \overline{s}) \leftarrow S_1'(1^n)$. Recall that $\bar{s} = (c_1, ..., c_n, s_1, ..., s_n)$, where the c_i's are selected uniformly in $\{0, 1\}$, whereas $\Pi(\bar{r})$ has the form $(b_1, ..., b_n, \pi_1, ..., \pi_n)$. Let us denote the latter sequence of b_i's by $B(\bar{r})$; that is, $\Pi(\bar{r}) = (B(\bar{r}), \Pi'(\bar{r}))$. We distinguish two cases according to whether or not $B(\bar{r}) = \bar{c} \overset{\text{def}}{=} (c_1, ..., c_n)$:

$$\Pr[C(\bar{r}) = (\Xi(\bar{r}), (B(\bar{r}), \Pi'(\bar{r}))) \text{ succeeds, when } (\bar{r}, \bar{s}) \leftarrow S'_1(1^n)]$$

$$= \Pr[C(\bar{r}) \text{ succeeds and } B(\bar{r}) = \bar{c}, \text{ when } (\bar{r}, (\bar{c}, \bar{s}')) \leftarrow S'_1(1^n)] \qquad (5.13)$$

$$+ \Pr[C(\bar{r}) \text{ succeeds and } B(\bar{r}) \neq \bar{c}, \text{ when } (\bar{r}, (\bar{c}, \bar{s}')) \leftarrow S'_1(1^n)] \qquad (5.14)$$

Eq. (5.13), which corresponds to the first case, must be negligible because the corresponding probability that refers to a uniformly selected reference string (as appearing in the real proof) is negligible, and the indistinguishability of a simulated reference string from a uniformly distributed one was established previously.

> Details: For a uniformly distributed reference string $\bar{r}$, we have $\Pr[B(\bar{r}) = \bar{c}] = 2^{-n}$ by information-theoretic considerations (i.e., $\bar{r}$ is statistically independent of $\bar{c}$). On the other hand, for a simulated reference string $\bar{r}$ and a corresponding $\bar{c}$, the quantity $q \overset{\text{def}}{=} \Pr[B(\bar{r}) = \bar{c}]$ is lower-bounded by Eq. (5.13). The quality of the simulator's output (established in the first paragraph of the proof) implies that the simulated reference string is computationally indistinguishable from a uniformly distributed reference string, which in turn implies that $q - 2^{-n}$ is negligible. It follows that Eq. (5.13) is negligible.

Eq. (5.14) must be negligible because in this case, at least one of the alleged proofs (to a false assertion) is with respect to a uniformly distributed reference string.

> Details: By the case hypothesis (i.e., $B(\bar{r}) \neq \bar{c}$), there exists an i such that the i-th bit of $B(\bar{r})$ is different from c_i (i.e., $b_i \neq c_i$). Thus, the i-th alleged proof (i.e., π_i) is with respect to a uniformly distributed reference string, that is, with respect to $r_i^{b_i} = r_i^{1-c_i}$, where $r_i^{1-c_i}$ is selected uniformly in $\{0, 1\}^n$. By the (adaptive) soundness of (P, V), this proof for a false assertion can be valid only with negligible probability, which in turn implies that Eq. (5.14) is negligible.

Having established that both Eq. (5.13) and Eq. (5.14) are negligible, the proposition follows. ∎

Using Adaptive NIZKs with Weak Simulation-Soundness. Following the foregoing motivating discussion, we show that if the adaptive NIZK used in Construction 5.4.23 has the weak simulation-soundness property, then the resulting encryption scheme (G', E', D') is secure under a priori CCA.

Theorem 5.4.27: *Suppose that the adaptive NIZK (P, V) used in Construction 5.4.23 has the weak simulation-soundness property and that the public-key encryption scheme (G, E, D) is passively secure in the key-dependent sense. Further suppose that the probability that $G(1^n)$ produces a pair (e, d) such that $\Pr[D_d(E_e(x)) = x] < 1$, for some $x \in \{0, 1\}^{\text{poly}(n)}$, is negligible. Then Construction 5.4.23 constitutes a public-key encryption scheme that is secure under a priori CCA.*

Combining the above with Theorem 4.10.16 and Proposition 5.4.26, it follows that public-key encryption schemes that are secure under a priori CCA exist, provided that enhanced[40] trapdoor permutations exists.

Proof Sketch: Assuming toward the contradiction that the scheme (G', E', D') is not secure under a priori CCA, we show that the scheme (G, E, D) is not secure under a (key-dependent) passive attack. Specifically, we refer to the definitions of security in the sense of indistinguishability of encryptions (as in Definitions 5.4.14 and 5.4.2, respectively). To streamline the proof, we reformulate Definition 5.4.2, incorporating both circuits (i.e., the one selecting message pairs and the one trying to distinguish their encryptions) into one circuit and allow this circuit to be probabilistic. (Certainly, this model of a key-dependent passive attack is equivalent to the one in Definition 5.4.2.)

Let (A_1', A_2') be an a priori CCA adversary attacking the scheme (G', E', D') (as per Definition 5.4.14), and (S_1, S_2) be the two-stage simulator for (P, V). We construct a (key-dependent) passive adversary A (attacking (G, E, D)) that, given an encryption-key e (in the range of $G_1(1^n)$), behaves as follows:

1. *Initialization*: A generates $(e_1, d_1) \leftarrow G(1^n)$, $(r, s) \leftarrow S_1(n)$, and sets $\overline{e} = (e_1, e, r)$. (We assume that $(e, d) \leftarrow G(1^n)$, and let $(e_2, d_2) \stackrel{\text{def}}{=} (e, d)$, so $\overline{e} = (e_1, e_2, r)$.)

2. *Emulation of $A_1'^{D_{\overline{d}}}(\overline{e})$*: A invokes A_1' on input $\overline{e}$, and answers its (decryption) queries as follows. When asked to decrypt the alleged ciphertext (q_1, q_2, q_3), adversary A checks if q_3 is a valid proof of consistency of q_1 and q_2 (with respect to the reference string r). If the proof is valid, then A answers with $D_{d_1}(q_1)$ or else A returns the error symbol.

   (Note that the emulation of the oracle $D_{\overline{d}}$ by A is perfect, although A only knows part of the corresponding decryption-key $\overline{d}$. Also note that A emulates A_1' on an input and oracle access that are computationally indistringuishable from the input and oracle access given to A_1' in a real attack.)

3. *Using A_2' for the final decision*: Let $((x^{(1)}, x^{(2)}), \sigma)$ denote the challenge template output by A_1'. Then, A outputs $(x^{(1)}, x^{(2)})$ as its own challenge pair. Next, given a ciphertext $y = E_e(x)$, where $x \in \{x^{(1)}, x^{(2)}\}$, adversary A forms a corresponding (almost certainly illegal) ciphertext under E', denoted (y_1, y, π), by letting $y_1 \leftarrow E_{e_1}(0^{|x^{(1)}|})$ and $\pi \leftarrow S_2(s, (e_1, e, y_1, y))$. Finally, A invokes A_2' on input $(\sigma, (y_1, y, \pi))$, and outputs whatever the latter does. Recall that here (in the case of a priori CCA), A_2' is an ordinary machine (rather than an oracle machine).

   (Note that A emulates A_2' on an input that is computationally indistringuishable from the input given to A_2' in a real attack. In particular, A typically invokes A_2' with an illegal ciphertext, whereas in a real attack, A_2' is always given a legal ciphertext.)

In order to analyze the performance of A, we introduce the following hybrid process, denoted H, as a *mental experiment*. The hybrid process behaves as A, with the only exception that (in Step 3) $y_1 \leftarrow E_{e_1}(x)$ (rather than $y_1 \leftarrow E_{e_1}(0^{|x|})$). Thus, unlike A,

---

[40] See Section C.1 in Appendix C

the hybrid process invokes A_2' with a legal ciphertext. (The question of how the hybrid process "knows" or gets this y_1 is out of place; we merely define a mental experiment.) Let $p_A^{(j)} = p_A^{(j)}(n)$ (resp., $p_H^{(j)} = p_H^{(j)}(n)$) denote the probability that A (resp., the hybrid process H) outputs 1 when $x = x^{(j)}$, where the probability is taken over the choices of $(e, d) \leftarrow G(1^n)$ and the internal coin tosses of A (resp., H).

Claim 5.4.27.1: For both j's, the absolute difference between $p_A^{(j)}(n)$ and $p_H^{(j)}(n)$ is a negligible function in n.

Proof: Define an auxiliary hybrid process that behaves as the hybrid process, except that when emulating $D_{\overline{q}}$, the auxiliary process answers according to D_{d_2} (rather than according to D_{d_1}). (Again, this is a mental experiment.) Let $p_{HH}^{(j)}$ denote the probability that this auxiliary process outputs 1 when $x = x^{(j)}$. Similarly, define another *mental experiment* that behaves as A, except that when emulating $D_{\overline{q}}$, this process answers according to D_{d_2} (rather than according to D_{d_1}), and let $p_{AA}^{(j)}$ denote the probability that the latter process outputs 1 when $x = x^{(j)}$. We stress that in Step 3, the latter mental experiment behaves exactly like A; the only aspect in which this mental experiment differs from A is in its decryption operations at Step 2. The various processes are tabulated next.

	answers dec-queries	the challenge ciphertext for A'	nature of process
A	by using D_{d_1}	$(E_{e_1}(0^{|x|}), E_e(x), \cdot)$	a real (passive) attack on (G, E, D) (w.r.t. key e)
H	by using D_{d_1}	$(E_{e_1}(x), E_e(x), \cdot)$	a mental experiment
HH	by using D_{d_2}	$(E_{e_1}(x), E_e(x), \cdot)$	a mental experiment
AA	by using D_{d_2}	$(E_{e_1}(0^{|x|}), E_e(x), \cdot)$	a mental experiment

We establish the following facts regarding these processes:

Fact 1. For both j's, the absolute difference between $p_H^{(j)}$ and $p_{HH}^{(j)}$ is negligible.

The reason is that the two processes differ only in the way they answer the decryption queries: In the first process the decryption is according to D_{d_1}, and in the second it is according to D_{d_2}. However, by weak simulation-soundness, it is infeasible to produce triples (q_1, q_2, q_3) such that $(e_1, e, q_1, q_2) \notin L_R$ and yet q_3 is a valid proof (with respect to r, for the false assertion that (e_1, e, q_1, q_2) is in L_R). Thus, except with negligible probability, either $D_{d_1}(q_1) = D_{d_2}(q_2)$ or q_3 is not valid, and so it does not matter whether one decrypts according to D_{d_1} or to D_{d_2}.[41]

Fact 2. Similarly, for both j's, the absolute difference between $p_A^{(j)}$ and $p_{AA}^{(j)}$ is negligible.

Fact 3. Finally, for both j's, the absolute difference between $p_{HH}^{(j)}$ and $p_{AA}^{(j)}$ is negligible.

---

[41] Here, we rely on the hypothesis that except with negligible probability over the key-generation process, the decryption is error-less (i.e., always yields the original plaintext).

The reason is that the experiments AA and HH differ only in the input $(\sigma, (y_1, y, \pi))$ that they feed to A_2'; whereas AA forms $y_1 \leftarrow E_{e_1}(0^{|x|})$ (and $\pi \leftarrow S_2(s, (e_1, e, y_1, y)))$, the process HH forms $y_1 \leftarrow E_{e_1}(x)$ (and $\pi \leftarrow S_2(s, (e_1, e, y_1, y)))$. However, A_2' cannot distinguish the two cases because this would have violated the security of E_{e_1}.

That is, to establish Fact 3, we construct a passive attack, denoted B, that behaves similarly to A except that it *switches its reference to the two basic keys* (i.e., the first two components of the encryption-key $\bar{e}$) and *acts very differently in Step 3* (e.g., B produces a different challenge template). Specifically, given an attacked encryption-key e, adversary B generates $(e_2, d_2) \leftarrow G(1^n)$, sets $\bar{e} = (e, e_2, \cdot)$, and emulates $A_1'^{D_{\bar{d}}}(\bar{e})$ using the decryption-key d_2 to answer queries. For a fixed j, when obtaining (from A_1') the challenge template $((x^{(1)}, x^{(2)}), \sigma)$, adversary B produces the challenge template $((0^{|x^{(j)}|}, x^{(j)}), \sigma)$, and invokes A_2' on input $(\sigma, (y, y_2, \pi))$, where $y = E_e(x)$ $(x \in \{0^{|x^{(j)}|}, x^{(j)}\})$ is the challenge ciphertext given to B, and B computes $y_2 \leftarrow E_{e_2}(x^{(j)})$ and $\pi \leftarrow S_2(s, (e, e_2, y, y_2))$. (Finally, B outputs the output obtained from A_2'.) Note that when given the challenge ciphertext $E_e(x^{(j)})$, the adversary B effectively behaves as experiment HH (for the same j), whereas when given $E_e(0^{|x^{(j)}|})$, it effectively behaves as experiment AA (for the same j). Thus, if $p_{HH}^{(j)}$ and $p_{AA}^{(j)}$ differ in a non-negligible manner, then B violates the passive security of the encryption scheme (G, E, D).

Combining these three facts, the current claim follows. □

Let us denote by $p_{\text{cca}}^{(j)}(n)$ the probability that the CCA adversary (A_1', A_2') outputs 1 when given a ciphertext corresponding to the jth plaintext in its challenge template (see Definitions 5.4.14). Recall that *by the contradiction hypothesis, $|p_{\text{cca}}^{(1)}(n) - p_{\text{cca}}^{(2)}(n)|$ is not negligible.*

Claim 5.4.27.2: For both j's, the absolute difference between $p_{\text{cca}}^{(j)}(n)$ and $p_H^{(j)}(n)$ is a negligible function in n.

Proof: The only difference between the output in a real attack of (A_1', A_2') and the output of the hybrid process is that in the hybrid process, a "simulated reference string" and a "simulated proof" are used instead of a uniformly distributed reference string and a real NIZK proof. However, this difference is indistinguishable.[42] □

Combining Claims 5.4.27.1 and 5.4.27.2, we obtain that for some negligible function μ it holds that

$$|p_A^{(1)}(n) - p_A^{(2)}(n)| > |p_H^{(1)}(n) - p_H^{(2)}(n)| - \mu(n)$$
$$> |p_{\text{cca}}^{(1)}(n) - p_{\text{cca}}^{(2)}(n)| - 2\mu(n)$$

We conclude that (the passive attack) A violates the passive security of (G, E, D). This contradicts the hypothesis (regarding (G, E, D)), and so the theorem follows. ■

---

[42] We stress that the current claim relies only on the fact that the simulated reference-string and proof are indistinguishable from the corresponding real objects.

Step II: a-posteriori CCA

In order to use Construction 5.4.23 in the context of a posteriori CCA security, we need to further strengthen the NIZK proof in use. The reason is that in an a posteriori CCA, the adversary may try to generate proofs of false claims (as part of the ciphertext queries in the second stage) after being given a (single) simulated proof (as part of the challenge ciphertext). Specifically, when trying to extend the proof of Theorem 5.4.27, we need to argue that, given a simulated proof (to either a false or a true statement), it is infeasible to generate a proof to a false statement (so long as one does not just copy the given simulated proof [in case it is to a false statement]). The notion of weak simulation-soundness does not suffice to bound the probability of success in such attempts, because the former notion refers to what one can do when only given the simulated reference string (without a corresponding simulated proof). The following definition addresses the situation in which one is given a *single* simulated proof (along with the simulated reference string). (We comment that a more general notion that refers to a situation in which one is given *many* simulated proofs is not necessary for the current application.)

Definition 5.4.28 (1-proof simulation-soundness): *Let (P, V) be an adaptive NIZK for a language L, and (S_1, S_2) be a corresponding two-stage simulator. We say that* 1-proof simulation-soundness *holds if for every triplet of polynomial-size circuit families (Ξ^1, Ξ^2, Π^2), the probability of the following event is negligible:*

The event: *For r and (x^1, π^1, x^2, π^2) generated as described next, the following three conditions hold: $x^2 \notin L$, $(x^2, \pi^2) \neq (x^1, \pi^1)$, and $V(x^2, r, \pi^2) = 1$.*

The generation process: *First $(r, s) \leftarrow S_1(1^n)$, then $x^1 \leftarrow \Xi^1(r)$, next $\pi^1 \leftarrow S_2(s, x^1)$, and finally $(x^2, \pi^2) \leftarrow (\Xi^2(r, \pi^1), \Pi^2(r, \pi^1))$.*

That is, the adversary is represented by three circuits, and the process considered is as follows. Given a simulated reference string r, the adversary selects an input x^1, gets a corresponding simulated proof π^1, and tries to form a (valid with respect to r) proof π^2 for some NO-instance x^2. Note that x^1 is not required to be a YES-instance. In case $x^2 = x^1$, we consider only $\pi^2 \neq \pi^1$ (and in case $x^2 \neq x^1$, we also consider $\pi^2 = \pi^1$). Definition 5.4.28 requires that the success probability of any such feasible adversary be negligible. Note that weak simulation-soundness is obtained as a special case of Definition 5.4.28 (by setting $\Xi(r) = \Xi^2(r, \lambda)$ and $\Pi(r) = \Pi^2(r, \lambda)$, where λ denotes the empty string).

Theorem 5.4.29: *Suppose that the adaptive NIZK (P, V) used in Construction 5.4.23 has the 1-proof simulation-soundness property and that the encryption scheme (G, E, D) is as in Theorem 5.4.27. Then Construction 5.4.23 constitutes a public-key encryption scheme that is secure under a posteriori CCA.*

Proof Sketch: The proof follows the structure of the proof of Theorem 5.4.27. Specifically, given an a posteriori CCA adversary (A'_1, A'_2) (attacking (G', E', D')), we first construct a passive adversary A (attacking (G, E, D)). The construction is as in the proof of Theorem 5.4.27, with the exception that in Step 3 we need to emulate the decryption oracle (for A'_2). This emulation is performed exactly as the one performed in Step 2 (for A_1'). Next, we analyze this passive adversary as in the proof of Theorem 5.4.27, while referring to an A_2' that may make decryption queries.[43] The analysis of the handling of these (additional) queries relies on the 1-proof simulation-soundness property.

In particular, when proving a claim analogous to Claim 5.4.27.1, we have to establish two facts (corresponding to Facts 1 and 2) that refer to the difference in the process's output when decrypting according to D_{d_1} and D_{d_2}, respectively. Both facts follow from the fact (established next) that, except with negligible probability, neither A_1' nor A_2' can produce a query (q_1, q_2, q_3) such that q_3 is a *valid proof that q_1 and q_2 are consistent* and yet $D_{d_1}(q_1) \neq D_{d_2}(q_2)$. (We stress that in the current context we refer also to A_2', which may try to produce such a query based on the challenge ciphertext given to it.)

Fact 5.4.29.1: The probability that A_1' produces a query (q_1, q_2, q_3) such that q_3 is a valid proof (with respect to reference string r) that (supposedly) there exists x, s_1, s_2 such that $q_i = E_{e_i}(x, s_i)$ (for $i = 1, 2$), and yet $D_{d_1}(q_1) \neq D_{d_2}(q_2)$ is negligible. The same holds for A_2' so long as the query is different from the challenge ciphertext given to it. This holds regardless of whether the challenge ciphertext (given to A_2') is produced as in A (i.e., $y_1 = E_{e_1}(0^m)$) or as in the hybrid process H (i.e., $y_1 = E_{e_1}(x)$).

Proof: Recall that one of our hypotheses is that the encryption (G, E, D) is error-free (except for a negligible measure of the key-pairs). Thus, the current fact refers to a situation that either A_1' or A_2' produces a valid proof for a false statement. The first part (i.e., referring to A_1') follows from the weak simulation-soundness of the NIZK, which in turn follows from its 1-proof simulation-soundness property. We focus on the second part, which refers to A_2'.

Let (y_1, y_2, π) denote the challenge ciphertext given to A_2'; that is, $y_2 = y$ is the challenge ciphertext given to $A(e)$ (or to $H(e)$), which augments it with y_1 and $\pi \leftarrow S_2(s, (e_1, e_2, y_1, y_2))$. Recall that $(r, s) \leftarrow S_1(1^n)$ and that $e_2 = e$. Suppose that A_2' produces a query (q_1, q_2, q_3) as in the claim; that is, $(q_1, q_2, q_3) \neq (y_1, y_2, \pi)$, the encryptions q_1 and q_2 are not consistent (with respect to e_1 and e_2, respectively), and yet $V((e_1, e_2, q_1, q_2), r, q_3) = 1$. Specifically, it holds that $x^2 \stackrel{\text{def}}{=} (e_1, e_2, q_1, q_2) \notin L_R$, where L_R is as in Construction 5.4.23 (see Eq. (5.12)), and yet $V(x^2, r, q_3) = 1$ (i.e., $\pi^2 \stackrel{\text{def}}{=} q_3$ is a valid proof of the false statement regarding x^2). Since (y_1, y_2, π) is produced by letting $\pi \leftarrow S_2(s, (e_1, e_2, y_1, y_2))$, it follows that $\pi^1 \stackrel{\text{def}}{=} \pi$ is a simulated proof (with respect to the reference string r) for the alleged membership of $x^1 \stackrel{\text{def}}{=} (e_1, e_2, y_1, y_2)$ in L_R, where $(r, s) \leftarrow S_1(1^n)$. Furthermore, given such a proof (along with the reference string r), A_2' produces a query (q_1, q_2, q_3) that yields a pair (x^2, π^2), where $\pi^2 = q_3$, such that $x^2 = (e_1, e_2, q_1, q_2) \notin L_R$ and yet $V(x^2, r, \pi^2) = 1$ and $(x^2, \pi^2) \neq (x^1, \pi^1)$. Thus, using A_1' and A_2' (along with (G, E, D)), we obtain circuits Ξ^1, Ξ^2, Π^2 that violate the hypothesis that (S_1, S_2) is 1-proof simulation-sound.

Details: On input a (simulated) reference string r, the circuit Ξ^1 selects (e_1, d_1) and (e_2, d_2) in the range of $G(1^n)$, and emulates the execution of $A_1'^{D_{\overline{d}}}(\overline{e})$, where $\overline{e} = (e_1, e_2, r)$ and $\overline{d} = (d_1, d_2, r)$. (Indeed, we fix the best possible choice of

---

[43] Indeed, in the proof of Theorem 5.4.27, where (A_1', A_2') is an a priori CCA, A_2' makes no such queries.

(e_1, d_1) and (e_2, d_2), rather than selecting both at random, and emulate the oracle $D_{\bar{d}}$ using $\bar{d}$ that is known to the circuit.) When A_1' outputs a challenge template, Ξ^1 emulates the selection of the challenge x, sets $y_1 \leftarrow E_{e_1}(0^{|x|})$ (or $y_1 \leftarrow E_{e_1}(x)$ when we argue about the hybrid process H), $y_2 \leftarrow E_{e_2}(x)$, and outputs $x^1 \stackrel{\text{def}}{=} (e_1, e_2, y_1, y_2)$. (Again, we may fix the best choice of x_1, y_1, and y_2, rather than generating them at random.) The challenge ciphertext is formed by augmenting y_1, y_2 with $\pi^1 \leftarrow S_2(s, x^1)$, where s is the auxiliary information generated by $S(1^n)$ (i.e., $(r, s) \leftarrow S(1^n)$). Next, we describe the circuits Ξ^2 and Π^2, which obtain $x^1 = (e_1, e_2, y_1, y_2)$ (as produced by Ξ^1) along with a simulated proof $\pi^1 = S_2(s, x^1)$. On input a reference string r and x^1, π^1 (as just discussed), these circuits emulate $A_2'^{D_{\bar{d}}}(\sigma, (y_1, y_2, \pi^1))$, where σ is the state information generated by A_1'. For some i (fixed as the best choice), we consider the i-th decryption query made during the emulation (i.e., we emulate the answers to previous queries by emulating $D_{\bar{d}}$). Denoting this (i.e., i-th) query by (q_1, q_2, q_3), the circuit Ξ^2 outputs $x^2 \stackrel{\text{def}}{=} (e_1, e_2, q_1, q_2)$ and Π^2 outputs $\pi^2 \stackrel{\text{def}}{=} q_3$. Since $(q_1, q_2, q_3) \neq (y_1, y_2, \pi^1)$, it follows that $(x^2, \pi^2) = ((e_1, e_2, q_1, q_2), \pi^2) \neq ((e_1, e_2, y_1, y_2), \pi^1) = (x^1, \pi^1)$. The event stated in the claim refers to the case that $x^2 \notin L_R$ and yet π^2 is accepted as a proof (with respect to the reference string r). But this event and the current process are exactly as in the definition of 1-proof simulation soundness. We stress that the argument applies to the process defined by the actual attack, as well as to the process defined by the hybrid H. In the first case $x^1 \notin L_R$, whereas in the second case $x^1 \in L_R$, but 1-proof simulation soundness applies to both cases.

It follows that a query (q_1, q_2, q_3) as in the claim can be produced only with negligible probability. $\square$

Fact 5.4.29.1 implies (an adequate extension of) the first two facts in the proof of a claim analogous to Claim 5.4.27.1. The third fact in that proof, as well as the proof of the analogue of Claim 5.4.27.2, do not refer to the soundness of the NIZK-proofs, and are established here exactly as in the proof of Theorem 5.4.27. The current theorem follows. ∎

Constructing Adaptive NIZK with 1-Proof Simulation-Soundness Property. We construct the desired NIZK by using a standard (adaptive) NIZK proof, a weak form of a signature scheme, and a specific commitment scheme. Since all ingredients can be implemented using enhanced trapdoor permutations (see Definition C.1.1 in Appendix C), we obtain:

Theorem 5.4.30: *If there exist collections of (non-uniformly hard) enhanced trapdoor permutations, then every language in $\mathcal{NP}$ has an adaptive NIZK with 1-proof simulation-soundness property.*

Proof Sketch: Let $L \in \mathcal{NP}$. We construct a suitable NIZK for L using the following three ingredients:

1. An *adaptive Non-Interactive Witness-Indistinguishable* (*NIWI*) *proof,* denoted $(P^{\text{WI}}, V^{\text{WI}})$, for a suitable language in $\mathcal{NP}$. We stress that we mean a proof system

that operates with a reference string of length n and can be applied to prove (adaptively chosen) statements of length poly(n), where the adaptivity refers both to the soundness and witness-indistinguishability requirements.

As shown in Section 4.10.3.2,[44] the existence of enhanced trapdoor permutations implies that every language in $\mathcal{NP}$ has an adaptive NIZK that operates with a reference string of length n and can be applied to prove statements of length poly(n). Indeed, in analogy to discussions in Section 4.6, any NIZK is a NIWI.

2. A *super-secure one-time signature scheme*, denoted $(G^{\mathrm{OT}}, S^{\mathrm{OT}}, V^{\mathrm{OT}})$. Specifically, one-time security (see Section 6.4.1) means that we consider only attacks in which the adversary may obtain a signature to a *single* document of its choice (rather than signatures to polynomially many documents of its choice). On the other hand, super-security (see Section 6.5.2) means that the adversary should fail to produce a valid document-signature that is different from the query-answer pair that appeared in the attack. (We stress that unlike in ordinary security, the adversary is deemed successful even if it produces a *different signature to the same document* for which it has obtained a signature during the attack.)

By Theorem 6.5.2, super-secure one-time signature schemes can be constructed on the basis of any one-way function. (If we were willing to assume the existence of collision-free hashing functions, then we could have used instead the easier-to-establish Theorem 6.5.1.)

3. A *perfectly-binding commitment scheme*, denoted C, as defined in Section 4.4.1, with the following two additional properties: The first additional property is that the commitment strings are pseudorandom; that is, the ensembles $\{C(x)\}_{x \in \{0,1\}^*}$ and $\{U_{|C(x)|}\}_{x \in \{0,1\}^*}$ are computationally indistinguishable. The second property is that the support of $C(U_n)$ is a negligible portion of $\{0, 1\}^{|C(U_n)|}$.

Using any collection of one-way permutations (e.g., the one in the hypothesis), we may obtain the desired commitment scheme. Specifically, Construction 4.4.2 constitutes a commitment scheme that satisfies the pseudorandomness property (but not the "negligible portion" property). To obtain the additional "negligible portion" property, we merely let $C(x)$ equal a pair of two independent commitments to x (and it follows that the support of $C(U_n)$ is at most a $2^n \cdot (2^{-n})^2 = 2^{-n}$ fraction of $\{0, 1\}^{|C(U_n)|}$).[45] We denote by $C(x, r)$ the commitment to value x produced using coins r; that is, $C(x) = C(x, r)$, where r is uniformly chosen in $\{0, 1\}^{\ell(|x|)}$, for some polynomial ℓ.

Given these ingredients, we construct an adaptive (1-proof simulation-sound) NIZK for L (with witness relation R) as follows. The NIZK proof uses a *reference string* of the form $\bar{r} = (r_1, r_2)$, where $n \stackrel{\text{def}}{=} |r_2|$ and $m \stackrel{\text{def}}{=} |r_1| = \text{poly}(n)$. (The length of r_1 is set to equal the length of $C(v)$, where $(s, v) \leftarrow G^{\mathrm{OT}}(1^n)$.)

---

[44] See Theorem 4.10.16 and comment following it, as well as Sections C.1 and C.4 in Appendix C.

[45] This presupposes that in the original commitment scheme, the support of $C(x)$ is at most a $2^{-|x|}$ fraction of $\{0, 1\}^{|C(x)|}$, which does hold for Construction 4.4.2. An alternative construction of a commitment scheme satisfying both additional properties can be obtained using any one-way function. Specifically, Construction 4.4.4 will do, except that it uses two messages. However, since the first message (i.e., sent by the receiver) is a random string, we may incorporate it in the reference string (of the NIZK scheme presented next).

Prover P: On common input $x \in \{0, 1\}^{\text{poly}(n)}$ and auxiliary-input w (and reference string $\bar{r} = (r_1, r_2)$), where supposedly $(x, w) \in R$, the prover behaves as follows:

1. Generates a key-pair for the one-time signature scheme; that is, $(s, v) \leftarrow G^{\text{OT}}(1^n)$.
2. Computes a pre-proof $p \leftarrow P^{\text{WI}}((x, r_1, v), w, r_2)$, where $(P^{\text{WI}}, V^{\text{WI}})$ is a proof system (using r_2 as reference string) for the following NP-language L':

$$L' \stackrel{\text{def}}{=} \{(x, y, v) : (x \in L) \vee (\exists w' \; y = C(v, w'))\} \tag{5.15}$$

The corresponding NP-relation is

$$R' \stackrel{\text{def}}{=} \{((x, y, v), w') : ((x, w') \in R) \vee (y = C(v, w'))\} \tag{5.16}$$

Note that P indeed feeds P^{WI} with an adequate NP-witness (i.e., $((x, r_1, v), w) \in R'$ since $(x, w) \in R$). The first part of the reference string of P is part of the statement fed to P^{WI}, whereas the second part of P's reference string serves as a reference string for P^{WI}. The behavior of V (with respect to V^{WI}) will be analogous.

3. The prover computes a signature σ to (x, p) relative to the signing-key s (generated in Step 1). That is, P computes $\sigma \leftarrow S_s^{\text{OT}}(x, p)$.

The prover outputs the triplet (v, p, σ).

Verifier V: On common input x and an alleged proof (v, p, σ) (and reference string $\bar{r} = (r_1, r_2)$), the verifier accepts if and only if the following two conditions hold:

1. σ is a valid signature, with respect to the verification-key v, of the pair (x, p). That is, $V_v^{\text{OT}}((x, p), \sigma) = 1$.
2. p is a valid proof, with respect to the reference string r_2, of the statement $(x, r_1, v) \in L'$. That is, $V^{\text{WI}}((x, r_1, v), r_2, p) = 1$.

Simulator's first stage S_1: On input 1^{m+n} (from which S_1 determines n and m), the first stage produces a reference string and auxiliary information as follows:

1. Like the real prover, $S_1(1^{m+n})$ starts by generating a key-pair for the one-time signature scheme; that is, $(s, v) \leftarrow G^{\text{OT}}(1^n)$.
2. Unlike in the real setting, $S_1(1^{m+n})$ selects s_1 uniformly in $\{0, 1\}^{\ell(|v|)}$, and sets $r_1 = C(v, s_1)$. (Note that in the real setting, r_1 is uniformly distributed independently of v, and thus in the real setting, r_1 is unlikely to be in the support of C, let alone in that of $C(v)$.)
3. Like in the real setting, $S_1(1^{m+n})$ selects r_2 uniformly in $\{0, 1\}^n$.

$S_1(1^{m+n})$ outputs the pair $(\bar{r}, \bar{s})$, where $\bar{r} = (r_1, r_2)$ is a simulated reference string and $\bar{s} = (v, s, s_1, r_2)$ is auxiliary information to be passed to S_2.

Simulator's second stage S_2: On input a statement x and auxiliary input $\bar{s} = (v, s, s_1, r_2)$ (as generated by S_1), S_2 proceeds as follows:

1. Using (the NP-witness) s_1, the simulator computes a pre-proof $p \leftarrow P^{\text{WI}}((x, C(v, s_1), v), s_1, r_2)$. Note that indeed, $((x, C(v, s_1), v), s_1) \in R'$.

2. Using (the signing-key) s, the simulator computes a signature σ to (x, p) relative to s, where p is as computed in the first step. That is, $\sigma \leftarrow S_s^{\text{OT}}(x, p)$.

$S_2(\bar{s}, x)$ outputs (v, p, σ) as a simulated proof (with respect to $\bar{r}$) for membership of x in L.

As we will show in Claim 5.4.30.2, the above (two-stage) simulator produces output that is indistinguishable from the output of the real execution. Intuitively, the first stage of the simulator enables cheating by entities (such as the second stage of the simulator) that can produce signatures with respect to the verification-key committed to in the string r_1 (which is part of the reference string generated by S_1). This allows the simulation (which gets the signing-key) to cheat, but does not allow cheating by an adversary that sees only the verification-key as well as a single valid signature (which are both part of the single proof given to the adversary in the definition of 1-proof simulation-soundness). We now turn to the actual proof of these properties.

Claim 5.4.30.1: (P, V) satisfies completeness and adaptive soundness.

Proof: Completeness follows by combining the syntactic properties of the one-time signature scheme, the completeness property of the proof system $(P^{\text{WI}}, V^{\text{WI}})$, and the definition of R'. Adaptive soundness follows by combining the (adaptive) soundness of $(P^{\text{WI}}, V^{\text{WI}})$ with the fact that r_1 is unlikely to be a commitment to any string. Specifically, using the additional property by which $C(G_2^{\text{OT}}(1^n))$ covers a negligible portion of $\{0, 1\}^m$, it follows that for a uniformly selected $r_1 \in \{0, 1\}^m$, there exist no v such that r_1 is in the support of $C(v)$. Thus, except with negligible probability (over the random choice of r_1), if $(x, r_1, v) \in L'$ holds for some v, then $x \in L$. On the other hand, using the (adaptive) soundness of $(P^{\text{WI}}, V^{\text{WI}})$, except with negligible probability (over the random choice of r_2), the existence of a valid proof (v, p, σ) for some $x \in \{0, 1\}^{\text{poly}(n)}$ implies that $(x, r_1, v) \in L'$. Thus, for a *uniformly distributed* reference string $\bar{r} = (r_1, r_2) \in \{0, 1\}^{m+n}$, except with negligible probability, there exists no $x \in \{0, 1\}^{\text{poly}(n)} \setminus L$ and π such that $V(x, \bar{r}, \pi) = 1$. The claim follows. $\square$

Claim 5.4.30.2 (adaptive zero-knowledge): For every efficient way of selecting inputs Ξ, the output produced by the two-stage simulator (S_1, S_2) is indistinguishable from the one produced by P. That is, the ensembles $\{S^{\Xi}(1^{m+n})\}$ and $R^{\Xi, W} \stackrel{\text{def}}{=} \{(U_{m+n}, \Xi(U_{m+n}), P(\Xi(U_{m+n}), W(U_{m+n}), U_{m+n}))\}$ are computationally indistinguishable, where S^{Ξ} is defined as in Definition 5.4.22.

Proof: Consider a hybrid distribution $H^{\Xi}(1^{m+n})$, in which everything except the pre-proof is produced as by $S^{\Xi}(1^{m+n})$, and the pre-proof is computed as by the real prover. That is, $(\bar{r}, \bar{s}) \leftarrow S_1(1^{m+n})$ (where $\bar{r} = (r_1, r_2)$ and $\bar{s} = (v, s, s_1, r_2)$) is produced as by S^{Ξ}, but then for $(x, w) = (\Xi(\bar{r}), W(\bar{r}))$, the pre-proof is computed using the witness w; that is, $p \leftarrow P^{\text{WI}}((x, r_1, v), w, r_2)$, rather than $p \leftarrow P^{\text{WI}}((x, r_1, v), s_1, r_2)$. The final proof $\pi = (v, p, \sigma)$ is obtained (as in both cases) by letting $\sigma \leftarrow S_s^{\text{OT}}(x, p)$. We now relate the hybrid ensemble to each of the two ensembles referred to in the claim.

1. By the (adaptive) witness-indistinguishability of P^{WI}, the ensembles H^Ξ and S^Ξ are computationally indistinguishable. (Recall that these ensembles differ only in the way the pre-proof is produced; specifically, they differ only in the NP-witness used by P^{WI} to prove the very same claim.)
2. By the pseudorandomness of the commitments produced for any fixed value, H^Ξ and $R^{\Xi, W}$ are computationally indistinguishable. (Recall that these ensembles differ only in the way the first part of the reference string (i.e., r_1) is produced.)

The claim follows. $\square$

Claim 5.4.30.3 (1-proof simulation-soundness): For every triplet of polynomial-size circuit families (Ξ^1, Ξ^2, Π^2), consider the following process: First $(\bar{r}, \bar{s}) \leftarrow S_1(1^{m+n})$, then $x^1 \leftarrow \Xi^1(\bar{r})$, next $\pi^1 \leftarrow S_2(\bar{s}, x^1)$, and finally $(x^2, \pi^2) \leftarrow (\Xi^2(\bar{r}, \pi^1), \Pi^2(\bar{r}, \pi^1))$. Then, the probability that the following three conditions hold simultaneously is negligible: (1) $x^2 \notin L$, (2) $(x^2, \pi^2) \neq (x^1, \pi^1)$, and (3) $V(x^2, \bar{r}, \pi^2) = 1$.

Proof: Recall that $\bar{r} = (r_1, r_2)$ and $\bar{s} = (v, s, s_1, r_2)$, where $(s, v) \leftarrow G^{OT}(1^n)$ and $r_1 = C(v, s_1)$ for a uniformly chosen $s_1 \in \{0, 1\}^{\ell(|v|)}$ (and r_2 is selected uniformly in $\{0, 1\}^n$). Also recall that $\pi^1 = (v^1, p^1, \sigma^1)$, where $v^1 = v$, $p^1 \leftarrow P^{WI}((x, C(v, s_1), v), s_1, r_2)$ and $\sigma^1 \leftarrow S_s^{OT}(x^1, p^1)$. Let us denote $(v^2, p^2, \sigma^2) \stackrel{\text{def}}{=} \pi^2$. We need to upper-bound the following:

$$\Pr\left[(x^2 \notin L) \wedge ((x^2, \pi^2) \neq (x^1, \pi^1)) \wedge (V(x^2, \bar{r}, \pi^2) = 1)\right]$$

$$= \Pr\left[\begin{array}{l} (x^2 \notin L) \wedge ((x^2, \pi^2) \neq (x^1, \pi^1)) \\ \wedge (V_{v^2}^{OT}((x^2, p^2), \sigma^2) = 1) \\ \wedge (V^{WI}((x^2, r_1, v^2), r_2, p^2) = 1) \end{array}\right] \tag{5.17}$$

where the equality is due to the definition of V. We consider two cases (in which the event in Eq. (5.17) may hold):

$v^2 = v^1$: In this case, either $(x^2, p^2) \neq (x^1, p^1)$ or $\sigma^2 \neq \sigma^1$ must hold (because otherwise $(x^2, \pi^2) = (x^2, (v^2, p^2, \sigma^2)) = (x^1, (v^1, p^1, \sigma^1)) = (x^1, \pi^1)$ follows). But this means that (Ξ^2, Π^2), given a single valid signature σ^1 (to the document (x^1, p^1)) with respect to a randomly generated verification-key $v = v^1 = v^2$, is able to produce a valid document-signature pair $((x^2, p^2), \sigma^2)$ (with respect to the same verification-key) such that $((x^2, p^2), \sigma^2) \neq ((x^1, p^1), \sigma^1)$, in contradiction to the super-security of the one-time signature scheme.

Details: It suffices to upper-bound

$$\Pr\left[\begin{array}{l} (v^2 = v^1) \wedge ((x^2, \pi^2) \neq (x^1, \pi^1)) \\ \wedge (V_{v^2}^{OT}((x^2, p^2), \sigma^2) = 1) \end{array}\right] \tag{5.18}$$

As explained in the previous paragraph, the first two conditions in Eq. (5.18) imply that $((x^2, p^2), \sigma^2) \neq ((x^1, p^1), \sigma^1)$. Using (S_1, S_2) and (Ξ^1, Ξ^2, Π^2), we derive an attacker, A, that violates the super-security of the (one-time) signature scheme. The attacker just emulates the process described in the claim's hypothesis, except that it obtains v as input (rather than generating the pair (s, v)

by invoking G^{OT}) and uses oracle access to S_s^{OT} (rather than s itself) in order to produce the signature σ^1. Specifically, on input v, the attacker A first selects $s_1 \in \{0, 1\}^\ell$ and $r_2 \in \{0, 1\}^n$ uniformly, sets $r_1 = C(v, s_1)$ and $\bar{r} = (r_1, r_2)$, and obtains $x^1 \leftarrow \Xi^1(\bar{r})$. Next, A computes $p^1 \leftarrow P^{WI}((x^1, r_1, v), s_1, r_2)$ and queries S_s^{OT} on (x^1, p^1), obtaining the answer $\sigma^1 \leftarrow S_s^{OT}(x^1, p^1)$ and setting $\pi^1 = (v, p^1, \sigma^1)$. (Indeed, π^1 so produced is distributed exactly as $S_2(\bar{s}, x^1)$, where $\bar{s} = (v, s, s_1, r_2)$, although A does not know s; the argument relies on the fact that $S_2(\bar{s}, x^1)$ can be implemented without knowledge of s and while making a single query to the signing oracle S_s^{OT}.) Finally, A sets $(x^2, \pi^2) \leftarrow (\Xi^2(\bar{r}, \pi^1), \Pi^2(\bar{r}, \pi^1))$, and outputs $((x^2, p^2), \sigma^2)$, where $\pi^2 = (v^2, p^2, \sigma^2)$. Note that A queries its signing oracle only once. (Recall that A queries S_s^{OT} on (x^1, p^1), obtains the answer σ^1, and produces the output pair $((x^2, p^2), \sigma^2)$.) On the other hand, the probability that A produces a *valid* document-signature pair (with respect to the verification-key v) that is different from the (single) query-answer pair it makes equals Eq. (5.18). Thus, the super-security of the one-time signature scheme implies that Eq. (5.18) is negligible.

$v^2 \neq v^1$: Since $r_1 = C(v^1, s_1)$, it follows (by the perfect binding property of C) that r_1 is not in the support of $C(v^2)$ (i.e., for every w', $r_1 \neq C(v^2, w')$). Thus, if $x^2 \notin L$, then $(x^2, r_1, v^2) \notin L'$. Now, by the adaptive soundness of (P^{WI}, V^{WI}) and the fact that r_2 was selected uniformly in $\{0, 1\}^n$, it follows that, except with negligible probability, p^2 is not a valid proof (with respect to the reference string r_2) of the false statement "$(x^2, r_1, v^2) \in L'$."

Details: It suffices to upper-bound

$$
\Pr\left[
\begin{array}{c}
(v^2 \neq v^1) \wedge (x^2 \notin L) \\
\wedge (V^{WI}((x^2, r_1, v^2), r_2, p^2) = 1)
\end{array}
\right]
\tag{5.19}
$$

As explained in the previous paragraph, the first two conditions in Eq. (5.19) imply $(x^2, r_1, v^2) \notin L'$. The key observation is that r_2 (generated by S_1) is uniformly distributed in $\{0, 1\}^n$, and thus the adaptive soundness of the NIWI system applies. We conclude that Eq. (5.19) is upper-bounded by the (negligible) soundness error of the NIWI system, and the claim follows also in this case.

Combining both cases, the claim follows. □

Combining Claims 5.4.30.1–5.4.30.3, the current theorem follows. ∎

Conclusion. Combining Theorems 5.4.6, 5.4.30 and 5.4.29, we get:

Theorem 5.4.31: *If there exist collections of (non-uniformly hard) enhanced trapdoor permutations, then there exist public-key encryption schemes that are secure under a posteriori chosen ciphertext attacks.*

(See Section C.1 in Appendix C for a discussion of the notion of enhanced trapdoor permutations.)

5.4.5. Non-Malleable Encryption Schemes

So far, our treatment has referred to an adversary that, when given a ciphertext, tries to gain explicit information about the plaintext. A less explicit gain, captured by the so-called notion of *malleability,* is the ability to generate an encryption of a related plaintext (possibly without learning anything about the original plaintext). Loosely speaking, an encryption scheme is called *non-malleable* if, given a ciphertext, it is infeasible (for an adversary) to produce a (different) valid ciphertext for a related plaintext. For example, given a ciphertext of a plaintext of the form $1x$, for an unknown x, it should be infeasible to produce a ciphertext to the plaintext $0x$.

Non-malleability may relate to any of the types of attacks considered earlier (e.g., passive attacks, chosen ciphertext attacks, etc). Thus, we have a "matrix" of adversaries, with one dimension (parameter) being the *type of attack* and the second being its *purpose*. So far, we have discussed the first dimension (i.e., the type of the attack) when focusing on a particular purpose (i.e., of violating the secrecy of the plaintext). We now turn to the second dimension (i.e., the purpose of the attack) and consider also the purpose of malleability. That is, we make a distinction between the following two notions (or purposes of attack):

1. Standard *security:* the infeasibility of *obtaining information regarding the plaintext.* As defined in Section 5.2, such information is captured by a function of the bare plaintext,[46] and it may not depend on the encryption-key (or decryption-key).
2. In contrast, the notion of *non-malleability* refers to the generating of a string depending on both the plaintext and the current encryption-key. Specifically, one requires that it be infeasible for an adversary, given a ciphertext, to produce a valid ciphertext (under the same encryption-key) for a related plaintext.

We shall show that with the exception of passive attacks on private-key schemes, non-malleability always implies security against attempts to obtain information on the plaintext. We shall also show that security and non-malleability are equivalent under a posteriori chosen ciphertext attack. Thus, the results of the previous sections imply that non-malleable (under a posteriori chosen ciphertext attack) encryption schemes can be constructed based on the same assumptions used to construct passively secure encryption schemes.

5.4.5.1. Definitions

For the sake of brevity, we present only a couple of definitions. Specifically, focusing on the public-key model, we consider only the simplest and strongest types of attacks; that is, we first consider (key-oblivious) passive attacks, and then we turn to chosen ciphertext attacks. The definitions refer to an adversary that is given a ciphertext and tries to generate a (different) ciphertext to a plaintext related to the original one. That is, given $E_e(x)$, the adversary tries to output $E_e(y)$ such that $(x, y) \in R$ with respect to

---

[46] Note that considering a randomized process applied to the plaintext does not make the definition stronger.

some (efficiently recognizable)[47] relation R. Loosely speaking, the adversary's success probability in such an attempt is compared to the success probability of generating such $E_e(y)$ when given e but not $E_e(x)$. In fact, we prefer an equivalent formulation in which the latter algorithm is required to output the plaintext y itself.[48] As in the case of semantic security, we strengthen the definition by considering all possible partial information functions h.

Definition 5.4.32 (passive non-malleability): *A public-key encryption scheme* (G, E, D) *is said to be* non-malleable under passive attacks *if for every probabilistic polynomial-time algorithm A there exists a probabilistic polynomial-time algorithm A' such that for every ensemble $\{X_n\}_{n\in\mathbb{N}}$, with $|X_n| = \mathrm{poly}(n)$, every polynomially bounded $h : \{0, 1\}^* \to \{0, 1\}^*$, every polynomially bounded relation R that is recognizable by a (non-uniform) family of polynomial-size circuits, every positive polynomial p, and all sufficiently large n, it holds that*

$$\Pr\left[\begin{array}{l} (x, y) \in R \text{ where} \\ \quad (e, d) \leftarrow G(1^n) \text{ and } x \leftarrow X_n \\ \quad c \leftarrow E_e(x) \text{ and } c' \leftarrow A(e, c, 1^{|x|}, h(x)) \\ \quad y \leftarrow D_d(c') \text{ if } c' \neq c \text{ and } y \leftarrow 0^{|x|} \text{ otherwise} \end{array}\right]$$

$$< \Pr\left[\begin{array}{l} (x, y) \in R \text{ where} \\ \quad x \leftarrow X_n \\ \quad y \leftarrow A'(1^n, 1^{|x|}, h(x)) \end{array}\right] + \frac{1}{p(n)}$$

We stress that the definition effectively prevents the adversary A from just outputting the ciphertext given to it (because in this case, its output is treated as if it were $E_e(0^{|x|})$). This provision is important because otherwise no encryption scheme could have satisfied the definition (see Exercise 42). A more subtle issue, which was hand-waved in the definition, is how to handle the case in which A produces an illegal ciphertext (i.e., is y defined in such a case to be a standard string [e.g., $1^{|d|}$] or a special error symbol).[49] The rest of our text holds under both conventions. Note that A' can certainly produce plaintexts, but its information regarding X_n is restricted to $h(X_n)$ (and $1^{|X_n|}$). Thus, if when given $h(X_n)$ and $1^{|X_n|}$ it is infeasible to generate y such that $(X_n, y) \in R$, then A' as in Definition 5.4.32 may produce such a y only with negligible probability. Consequently, Definition 5.4.32 implies that in this case, given $E_e(X_n)$ (and e, $h(X_n)$, $1^{|X_n|}$), it is infeasible to produce $E_e(y)$ such that $(X_n, y) \in R$.

---

[47] The computational restriction on R is essential here; see Exercise 16, which refers to a related definition of semantic security.

[48] Potentially, this can only make the definition stronger, because the ability to produce plaintexts implies the ability to produce corresponding ciphertexts (with respect to a given or a randomly chosen encryption-key).

[49] It is interesting to note that in the case of passive attacks, the two possible conventions seem to yield non-equivalent definitions. The issue is whether the adversary can correlate the generation of an illegal ciphertext to the encrypted plaintext handed to it. The question of whether this issue is important or not seems to depend on the type of application. (In contrast, in the case of a posteriori CCA, the two conventions yield equivalent definitions, because without loss of generality, the attacker may check whether the ciphertext produced by it is legal.)

Definition 5.4.32 cannot be satisfied by encryption schemes in which one can modify bits in the ciphertext without changing the corresponding plaintext (i.e., consider the identity relation). We stress that such encryption schemes may be semantically secure under passive attacks (e.g., given a semantically secure encryption scheme (G, E, D), consider $E'_e(x) = E_e(x)\sigma$, for randomly chosen $\sigma \in \{0, 1\}$). However, such encryption schemes may not be (semantically) secure under a posteriori CCA.

Turning to the definition of non-malleability under chosen ciphertext attacks, we adopt the definitional framework of Section 5.4.4.1. Specifically, analogous to Definition 5.4.13, the challenge template produced by A_1 (and A'_1) is a triplet of circuits representing a distribution S (represented by a sampling circuit), a function h (represented by an evaluation circuit), and a relation R (represented by a membership recognition circuit). The goal of A_2 (and A'_2) will be to produce a ciphertext of a plaintext that is R-related to the challenge plaintext $S(U_{\text{poly}(n)})$.

Definition 5.4.33 (non-malleability under chosen ciphertext attacks): *A public-key encryption scheme is said to be* non-malleable under a priori chosen ciphertext attacks *if for every pair of probabilistic polynomial-time oracle machines, A_1 and A_2, there exists a pair of probabilistic polynomial-time algorithms, A'_1 and A'_2, such that the following two conditions hold:*

1. *For every positive polynomial p and all sufficiently large n and $z \in \{0, 1\}^{\text{poly}(n)}$:*

$$\Pr \left[\begin{array}{l} (x, y) \in R \text{ where} \\ \quad (e, d) \leftarrow G(1^n) \\ \quad ((S, h, R), \sigma) \leftarrow A_1^{E_e, D_d}(e, z) \\ \quad (c, v) \leftarrow (E_e(x), h(x)), \text{ where } x \leftarrow S(U_{\text{poly}(n)}) \\ \quad c' \leftarrow A_2^{E_e}(\sigma, c, v) \\ \quad y \leftarrow D_d(c') \text{ if } c' \neq c \text{ and } y \leftarrow 0^{|x|} \text{ otherwise.} \end{array} \right]$$

$$< \Pr \left[\begin{array}{l} (x, y) \in R \text{ where} \\ \quad ((S, h, R), \sigma) \leftarrow A'_1(1^n, z) \\ \quad x \leftarrow S(U_{\text{poly}(n)}) \\ \quad y \leftarrow A'_2(\sigma, 1^{|x|}, h(x)) \end{array} \right] + \frac{1}{p(n)}$$

2. *For every n and z, the first element* (i.e., the (S, h, R) part) *in the random variables $A'_1(1^n, z)$ and $A_1^{E_{G_1(1^n)}}(G_1(1^n), z)$ are identically distributed.*

Non-malleability under a posteriori chosen ciphertext attacks *is defined analogously, except that A_2 is given oracle access to both E_e and D_d, with the restriction that when given the challenge (c, v), machine A_2 is not allowed to make the query c to the oracle D_d.*

We comment that the definitional treatment can be extended to multiple-message non-malleability, but we refrain from doing so here.[50]

---

[50] We warn that even in the case of public-key schemes, (single-message) non-malleability (under some type of attacks) does not necessarily imply the corresponding notion of multiple-message non-malleability.

5.4.5.2. Relation to Semantic Security

With the exception of passive attacks on private-key schemes, for each type of attack considered in this chapter (and for both private-key and public-key schemes), non-malleability under this type of attack implies semantic security under the same type. For example, we show the following:

Proposition 5.4.34: *Let (G, E, D) be a public-key encryption scheme that is non-malleable under passive attacks* (resp., *under a posteriori chosen ciphertext attacks*). *Then, (G, E, D) is semantically secure under passive attacks* (resp., *under a posteriori chosen ciphertext attacks*).

Proof Sketch: For clarity, the reader may consider the case of passive attacks, but the same argument holds also for a posteriori chosen ciphertext attacks. Furthermore, the argument only relies on the hypothesis that (G, E, D) is "non-malleable with respect to a single (simple) relation."[51]

Suppose (toward the contradiction) that (G, E, D) is not semantically secure (under the relevant type of attack). Using the equivalence to indistinguishability of encryptions, it follows that under such attacks, one can distinguish encryption to x_n from encryption to y_n. Consider the relation $R = \{(x, \bar{x}) : x \in \{0, 1\}^*\}$, where $\bar{x}$ is the complement of x, and the uniform distribution Z_n on $\{x_n, y_n\}$. We construct an algorithm that, given a ciphertext (as well as an encryption-key e), runs the said distinguisher and produces $E_e(\bar{x}_n)$ in case the distinguisher "votes" for x_n (and produces $E_e(\bar{y}_n)$ otherwise). Indeed, given $E_e(Z_n)$, our algorithm outputs $E_e(\bar{Z}_n)$ (and thus "hits" R) with probability that is non-negligibly higher than $1/2$. This performance cannot be met by any algorithm that is not given $E_e(Z_n)$. Thus, we derive a contradiction to the hypothesis that (G, E, D) is non-malleable. ■

We stress that this argument relies only on the fact that in the public-key model, we can produce the encryption of any string, since we are explicitly given the encryption-key. In fact, it suffices to have access to an encryption oracle, and thus the argument extends also to active attacks in the private-key model (in which the attacker is allowed encryption queries). On the other hand, under most types of attacks considered here, non-malleability is strictly stronger than semantic security. Still, in the special case of a posteriori chosen ciphertext attacks, the two notions are equivalent. Specifically, we prove that in the case of a posteriori CCA, semantic security implies non-malleability.

Proposition 5.4.35: *Let (G, E, D) be a public-key encryption scheme that is semantically secure under a posteriori chosen ciphertext attacks. Then, (G, E, D) is non-malleable under a posteriori chosen ciphertext attacks. The same holds for private-key encryption schemes.*

Proof Sketch: Suppose toward the contradiction that (G, E, D) is not non-malleable under a posteriori chosen ciphertext attacks, and let $A = (A_1, A_2)$ be an adversary demonstrating this. We construct a semantic-security (a posteriori CCA) adversary

---

[51] In order to avoid certain objections, we refrain from using the simpler relation $R = \{(x, x) : x \in \{0, 1\}^*\}$.

$B = (B_1, B_2)$ that emulates A (while using its own oracles) and produces its own output by querying its own decryption oracle on the ciphertext output by A, which is assumed (without loss of generality) to be different from the challenge ciphertext given to A. The key point is that B can make this extra query because it is an a posteriori CCA adversary, and thus the difference between outputting a ciphertext and outputting the corresponding plaintext disappears. Intuitively, B violates semantic security (with respect to relations and a posteriori CCA, as can be defined analogously to Exercise 16). Details follow.

Given an encryption-key e, algorithm B_1 invokes $A_1(e)$, while answering A_1's queries by querying its own oracles, and obtains the challenge template (S, h, R) (and state σ), which it outputs as its own challenge template. Algorithm B_2 is given a ciphertext c (along with the adequate auxiliary information) and invokes A_2 on the very same input, while answering A_2's queries by querying its own oracles. When A_2 halts with output $c' \neq c$, algorithm B_2 forwards c' to its decryption oracle and outputs the answer. Thus, for every relation R, the plaintext output by B "hits" the relation R with the same probability that the decryption of A's output "hits" R. We have to show that this hitting probability cannot be met by a corresponding benign algorithm that does not get the ciphertext; but this follows from the hypothesis regarding A (and the fact that in both cases, the corresponding benign algorithm [i.e., A' or B'] outputs a plaintext [rather than a ciphertext]). Finally, we have to establish, analogously to Exercise 16, that semantic security with respect to relations holds (in our current context of chosen ciphertext attacks) if and only if semantic security (with respect to functions) holds. The latter claim follows as in Exercise 16 by relying on the fact that in the current context, the relevant relations have polynomial-size circuits. (A similar argument holds for private-key schemes.) ∎

Conclusion. Combining Theorem 5.4.31 and Proposition 5.4.35 we get:

Theorem 5.4.36: *If there exist collections of (non-uniformly hard) enhanced trapdoor permutations, then there exist* public-key *encryption schemes that are non-malleable under a posteriori chosen ciphertext attacks.*

Analogously, using Theorem 5.4.21, we get:

Theorem 5.4.37: *If there exist (non-uniformly hard) one-way functions, then there exist* private-key *encryption schemes that are non-malleable under a posteriori chosen ciphertext attacks.*

5.5. Miscellaneous

5.5.1. On Using Encryption Schemes

Once defined and constructed, encryption schemes may be (and actually are) used as building blocks toward various goals that are different from the original motivation.

Still, the original motivation (i.e., secret communication of information) is of great importance, and in this section we discuss several issues regarding the use of encryption schemes toward achieving this goal.

Using Private-Key Schemes: The Key-Exchange Problem. As discussed in Section 5.1.1, using a private-key encryption scheme requires the communicating parties to share a secret key. This key can be generated by one party and secretly communicated to the other party by an alternative (expensive) secure channel. Often, a preferable solution consists of employing a key-exchange (or rather key-generation) protocol, which is executed over the standard (insecure) communication channel. An important distinction refers to the question of whether the insecure communication channel, connecting the legitimate parties, is tapped by a *passive* adversary or may even be subject to *active* attacks in which an adversary may modify the messages sent over the channel (and even delete and insert such messages). Protocols that are secure against passive (resp., active) adversaries are often referred to by the term authenticated key-exchange (resp., unauthenticated key-exchange), because in the passive case, one refers to the messages received over the channel as being authentic (rather than possibly modified by the adversary).

A simple (generic) *authenticated* key-exchange protocol consists of using a public-key encryption scheme in order to secretly communicate a key (for the private-key encryption scheme, which is used in the actual communication).[52] Specifically, one party generates a random instance of a public-key encryption scheme, sends the encryption-key to the other party, which generates a random key (for the private-key encryption scheme), and sends an encryption (using the received encryption-key) of the newly generated key to the first party. A famous alternative is the so-called Diffie-Hellman Key-Exchange [75]: For a (large) prime P and primitive element g, which are universal or generated on the fly (by one party that openly communicates them to the other), the first (resp., second) party uniformly selects $x \in \mathbb{Z}_P$ (resp., $y \in \mathbb{Z}_P$) and sends $g^x \bmod P$ (resp., $g^y \bmod P$) to the other party, and both parties use $g^{xy} \bmod P$ as their common key, relying on the fact that $g^{xy} \equiv (g^x \bmod P)^y \equiv (g^y \bmod P)^x \pmod{P}$. (The security of this protocol relies on the assumption that given a prime P, a primitive element g, and the triplet $(P, g, (g^x \bmod P), (g^y \bmod P), (g^z \bmod P))$, it is infeasible to decide whether or not $z \equiv xy \pmod{P-1}$, for $x, y, z \in \mathbb{Z}_P$.) The construction of *unauthenticated* key-exchange protocols is far more complex, and the interested reader is referred to [29, 30, 15].

Using State-Dependent Private-Key Schemes. In many communication settings, it is reasonable to assume that the encryption device may maintain (and modify) a state (e.g., a counter). In such a case, the stream-ciphers discussed in Section 5.3.1 become relevant. Furthermore, using a stream-cipher is particularly appealing in applications where decryption is performed in the same order as encryption (e.g., in FIFO communication). In such applications, the stream-cipher of Construction 5.3.3 is preferable to

---

[52] One reason not to use the public-key encryption scheme itself for the actual (encrypted) communication is that private-key encryption schemes tend to be much faster.

the (pseudorandom function-based) encryption scheme of Construction 5.3.9 for a couple of reasons. First, applying an on-line pseudorandom generator is likely to be more efficient than applying a pseudorandom function. Second, for an ℓ-bit long counter (or random value), Construction 5.3.3 allows for securely encrypting 2^ℓ messages (or bits), whereas Construction 5.3.9 definitely becomes insecure when $\sqrt{2^\ell}$ messages (or bits) are encrypted. For small values of ℓ (e.g., $\ell = 64$), this difference is crucial.

Using Public-Key Schemes: Public-Key Infrastructure. As in the case of private-key schemes, an important distinction refers to the question of whether the insecure communication channel between the legitimate parties is tapped by a *passive* adversary or may even be subject to *active* attacks. In typical applications of public-key encryption schemes, the parties communicate through a communication network (and not via a point-to-point channel), in which case active attacks are very realistic (e.g., it is easy to send mail over the Internet pretending to be somebody else). Thus, the standard use of public-key encryption schemes in real-life communication requires a mechanism for providing the sender with the *receiver's authentic encryption-key* (rather than trusting an "unauthenticated" incoming message to specify an encryption-key). In small systems, one may assume that each user holds a local record of the encryption-keys of all other users. However, this is not realistic in large-scale systems, and so the sender must obtain the relevant encryption-key on the fly in a "reliable" way (i.e., typically, certified by some trusted authority). In most theoretical work, one assumes that the encryption-keys are posted and can be retrieved from a public-file that is maintained by a trusted party (which makes sure that each user can post only encryption-keys bearing its own identity). Alternatively, such a trusted party may provide each user with a (signed) certificate stating the authenticity of the user's encryption-key. In practice, maintaining such a public-file (and/or handling such certificates) is a major problem, and mechanisms that implement this abstraction are typically referred to by the generic term "public-key infrastructure" (PKI). For a discussion of the practical problems regarding PKI deployment see, e.g., [149, Chap. 13].

5.5.2. On Information-Theoretic Security

In contrast to the bulk of our treatment, which focuses on computationally bounded adversaries, in this section we consider computationally unbounded adversaries. We stress that also in this case, the length (and number) of the plaintexts is bounded. The resulting notion of security is the one suggested by Shannon: A (private-key or public-key) encryption scheme is called perfectly secure (or information-theoretically secure) if the ciphertext yields no information regarding the plaintext. That is, perfect-security is derived from Definitions 5.2.1 and 5.2.2 by allowing computationally unbounded algorithms (in the roles of A and A').

It is easy to see that no public-key encryption scheme may be perfectly secure: A computationally unbounded adversary that is given a encryption-key can find a corresponding decryption-key, which allows it to decrypt any ciphertext.

In contrast, restricted types of private-key encryption schemes may be perfectly secure. Specifically, the traditional "one-time pad" yields such a (private-key) scheme, which can be used to securely communicate an a priori bounded number of bits. Furthermore, multiple messages may be handled provided that their total length is a priori bounded and that we use a state (as in Construction 5.3.3). We stress that this state-based private-key perfectly secure encryption scheme uses a key of length equal to the total length of plaintexts to be encrypted. Indeed, the key must be at least that long (to allow perfect-security), and a state is essential for allowing several plaintexts to be securely encrypted.

Partial Information Models. Note that in the case of private-key encryption schemes, the limitations of perfect-security hold only if the adversary has full information of the communication over the channel. On the other hand, perfectly secure private channels can be implemented on top of channels to which the adversary has limited access. We mention three types of channels of the latter type, which have received a lot of attention.

- The *bounded-storage model,* where the adversary can freely tap the communication channel(s) but is restricted in the amount of data it can store (cf., [148, 48, 187]).[53]
- The *noisy channel model* (which generalizes the *wiretap channel* of [189]), where both the communication between the legitimate parties and the tapping channel of the adversary are subjected to noise (cf., [148, 69] and the references therein).
- *Quantum channels,* where an adversary is (supposedly) prevented from obtaining full information by the (currently believed) laws of quantum mechanics (cf., [45] and the references therein).

Following are the author's subjective opinions regarding these models (as a possible basis for actual secure communication). The bounded-storage model is very appealing, because it clearly states its *reasonable assumptions* regarding the *abilities of the adversary.* In contrast, making absolute assumptions about the noise level at any point in time seems (overly) optimistic, and thus not adequate in the context of cryptography. Basing cryptography on quantum mechanics sounds like a very appealing idea, but attempts to implement this idea have often stumbled over unjustified hidden assumptions (which are to be expected, given the confusing nature of quantum mechanics and the discrepancy between its scientific culture and cryptography).

5.5.3. On Some Popular Schemes

The reader may note that we have avoided the presentation of several popular encryption schemes. We regret to say that most of these schemes are proposed without any reference to a satisfactory notion of security.[54] Thus, it is not surprising that we have nothing to say about the contents of such proposals. In contrast, we highlight a few things that we

---

[53] Typically, this model postulates the existence of an auxiliary (uni-directional) public channel on which a trusted party (called a beacon) transmits a huge amount of random bits.

[54] Typically, these schemes are not (semantically) secure. Furthermore, these proposals fail to suggest a weaker definition of security that is supposedly satisfied by the proposed schemes.

have said about other popular schemes and common practices:

- The common practice of using "pseudorandom generators" as a basis for private-key stream-ciphers (i.e., Construction 5.3.3) is sound, provided that one actually uses pseudorandom generators (rather than programs that are called "pseudorandom generators" but actually produce sequences that are easy to predict).[55]
- Whereas the *plain* RSA public-key encryption scheme (which employs a deterministic encryption algorithm) is not secure, the *randomized* RSA encryption scheme (i.e., Construction 5.3.16) is secure, provided that the *large hard-core conjecture* holds (see Section 5.3.4.1). Some support for the latter (clearly stated) conjecture may be derived from the fact that a related function (i.e., much fewer least-significant bits) constitutes a hard-core of the RSA.

  We comment that the common practice of randomly padding messages before encrypting them (by applying the RSA function) is secure under a seemingly stronger conjecture; see footnote 19 (in Section 5.3.4.1).

- Assuming the intractability of factoring, there exists a *secure* public-key encryption scheme with efficiency comparable to that of plain RSA: We refer to the Blum-Goldwasser public-key encryption scheme (i.e., Construction 5.3.20).

Finally, we warn that encryption schemes *proved to be secure in the random oracle model* are not necessarily secure (in the standard sense). For further discussion of the Random Oracle Methodology, we refer the reader to Section 6.6.3.

5.5.4. Historical Notes

The notion of private-key encryption scheme seems almost as ancient as the alphabet itself. Furthermore, it seems that the development of encryption methods went along with the development of communication media. As the amounts of communication grew, more efficient and sophisticated encryption methods were required. Computational complexity considerations were explicitly introduced into the arena by Shannon [185]: In his seminal work, Shannon considered the classical setting where no computational considerations are present. He showed that in this information-theoretic setting, secure communication of information is possible only so long as its entropy is lower than the entropy of the key. He thus concluded that if one wishes to have an encryption scheme that is capable of handling messages with total entropy exceeding the length of the key, then one must settle for a computational relaxation of the secrecy condition. That is, rather than requiring that the ciphertext yield no information on the plaintext, one has to settle for the requirement that such information cannot be efficiently computed from the ciphertext. The latter requirement indeed coincides with the definition of semantic security.

The notion of a public-key encryption scheme was introduced by Diffie and Hellman [75]. The first concrete candidates were suggested by Rivest, Shamir, and

---

[55] The linear congruential generator is easy to predict [43]. The same holds for some modifications of it that output a constant fraction of the bits of each resulting number [94]. We warn that sequences having large linear-complexity (LFSR-complexity) are *not* necessarily hard to predict.

Adleman [176] and by Merkle and Hellman [154]. The abstract notion, as well as the concrete candidate implementations (especially the RSA scheme of [176]), have been the driving force behind the theoretical study of encryption schemes. However, the aforementioned pioneering works did not provide a definition of security. Such satisfactory definitions were provided (only a few years later) by Goldwasser and Micali [123]. The two definitions presented in Section 5.2 originate in [123], where it was shown that ciphertext-indistinguishability implies semantic security. The converse direction is due to [156].

Regarding the seminal paper of Goldwasser and Micali [123], a few additional comments are in place. Arguably, this paper is the basis of the entire rigorous approach to cryptography (presented in the current work): It introduced general notions such as computational indistinguishability, definitional approaches such as the simulation paradigm, and techniques such as the hybrid argument. Its title ("Probabilistic Encryption") is due to the authors' realization that public-key encryption schemes in which the encryption algorithm is deterministic cannot be secure in the sense defined in their paper. Indeed, this led the authors to (explicitly) introduce and justify the paradigm of "randomizing the plaintext" as part of the encryption process. Technically speaking, the paper only presents security definitions for public-key encryption schemes, and furthermore, some of these definitions are syntactically different from the ones we have presented here (yet all these definitions are equivalent). Finally, the term "ciphertext-indistinguishability" used here replaces the (generic) term "polynomial-security" used in [123]. Many of our modifications (to the definitions in [123]) are due to Goldreich [104], which is also the main source of our uniform-complexity treatment.[56]

The first construction of a secure public-key encryption scheme based on a simple complexity assumption was given by Goldwasser and Micali [123].[57] Specifically, they constructed a public-key encryption scheme assuming that deciding Quadratic Residiousity modulo composite numbers is intractable. The condition was weakened by Yao [190], who showed that any trapdoor permutation will do. The efficient public-key encryption scheme of Construction 5.3.20 is due to Blum and Goldwasser [41]. The security is based on the fact that the least-significant bit of the modular squaring function is a hard-core predicate, provided that factoring is intractable, a result mostly due to [1].

For decades, it has been common practice to use "pseudorandom generators" in the design of stream-ciphers. As pointed out by Blum and Micali [42], this practice is sound *provided* that one uses pseudorandom generators (as defined in Chapter 3 of this work). The construction of private-key encryption schemes based on pseudorandom functions is due to [111].

We comment that it is indeed peculiar that the rigorous study of (the security of) private-key encryption schemes has lagged behind the corresponding study of public-key encryption schemes. This historical fact may be explained by the very thing that

---

[56] Section 5.2.5.5 was added during the copyediting stage, following discussions with Johan Håstad.

[57] Recall that plain RSA is not secure, whereas Randomized RSA is based on the Large Hard-Core Conjecture for RSA (which is less appealing that the standard conjecture referring to the intractability of inverting RSA).

makes it peculiar; that is, private-key encryption schemes are less complex than public-key ones, and hence, the problematics of their security (when applied to popular candidates) is less obvious. In particular, the need for a rigorous study of (the security of) public-key encryption schemes arose from observations regarding some of their concrete applications (e.g., doubts raised by Lipton concerning the security of the "mental poker" protocol of [184], which used "plain RSA" as an encryption scheme). In contrast, the need for a rigorous study of (the security of) private-key encryption schemes arose later and by analogy to the public-key case.

Credits for the Advanced Section (i.e., Section 5.4)

Definitional Issues. The original definitional treatment of Goldwasser and Micali [123] actually refers to key-dependent passive attacks (rather than to key-oblivious passive attacks). Chosen ciphertext attacks (of the a priori and a posteriori type) were first considered in [164] (and [174], respectively). However, these papers focused on the formulation in terms of indistinguishability of encryptions, and formulations in terms of semantic security have not appeared before. Section 5.4.4.2 is based on [116]. The study of the *non-malleability* of the encryption schemes was initiated by Dolev, Dwork, and Naor [77].

Constructions. The framework for constructing public-key encryption schemes that withstand Chosen Ciphertext Attacks (i.e., Construction 5.4.23) is due to Naor and Yung [164], who used it to construct public-key schemes that withstand a priori CCA (under suitable assumptions). This framework was applied to the setting of a posteriori CCA by Sahai [179, 180], who followed and improved the ideas of Dolev, Dwork, and Noar [77] (which were the first to construct public-key schemes that withstand a posteriori CCA and prove Theorem 5.4.31). Our presentation of the proof of Theorem 5.4.31 follows subsequent simplification due to [142]. The key role of non-interactive zero-knowledge proofs in this context was suggested by Blum, Feldman, and Micali [40]. The fact that security and non-malleability are equivalent under a posteriori chosen ciphertext attack was proven in [77, 16].

5.5.5. Suggestions for Further Reading

For discussion of Non-Malleable Cryptography, which actually transcends the domain of encryption, see [77]. Specifically, we wish to highlight the notion of non-malleable commitment schemes, which is arguably the most appealing instantiation of the "non-malleability paradigm": It is infeasible for a party that is given a non-malleable commitment to produce a commitment to a related string. Note that ability to produce related commitments may endanger some applications (see, e.g., [115]), even if this ability is not decoupled from the ability to properly decommit (to the produced commitment) once a decommitment to the original commitment is obtained.

Recall that there is a gap between the assumptions currently required for the construction of private-key and public-key encryption schemes: Whereas the former can be constructed based on any one-way functions, the latter seem to require a trapdoor permutation (or, actually, a "trapdoor predicate" [123]). A partial explanation to this gap was provided by Impagliazzo and Rudich, who showed that generic (black-box) constructions of public-key encryption schemes cannot rely on one-way functions [133] (or even on one-way permutations [135]). This may explain the gap in our current state of knowledge, but it does not indicate that this gap is inherent; that is, it is possible that non-black-box constructions of public-key encryption schemes based on one-way functions do exist. Indeed, Barak's recent demonstrations of the power of non-block-box proofs of security [5, 6] are a good lesson.

For a detailed discussion of the relationship among the various notions of secure private-key and public-key encryption schemes, the reader is referred to [136] and [16], respectively.

5.5.6. Open Problems

Secure public-key encryption schemes exist if there exist collections of (non-uniformly hard) trapdoor permutations (cf. Theorem 5.3.15). It is not known whether the converse holds (although secure public-key encryption schemes easily imply one-way functions). Note that trapdoor permutations differ from general one-way functions in both the 1-to-1 and trapdoor properties, and the former property should not be discarded (see [23]).

Randomized RSA (i.e., Construction 5.3.16) is commonly believed to be a secure public-key encryption scheme. It would be of great practical importance to gain additional support for this belief. As shown in Proposition 5.3.17, the security of Randomized RSA follows from the *Large Hard-Core Conjecture for RSA,* but the latter is not known to follow from a more standard assumption, such as that RSA is hard to invert. This is indeed the third place in the current work where we suggest the establishment of the latter implication as an important open problem.

The constructions of *public-key* encryption schemes (*secure against chosen ciphertext attacks*) that are presented in Section 5.4 should be considered plausibility results (which also offer some useful construction paradigms). Presenting "reasonably-efficient" public-key encryption schemes that are secure against (a posteriori) chosen ciphertext attacks, under general widely believed assumptions, is an important open problem.[58]

5.5.7. Exercises

Exercise 1: *Secure encryption schemes imply secure communication protocols:* A secure communication protocol is a two-party protocol that allows the parties to communicate in secrecy (i.e., as in Definition 5.2.1). We stress that the sender

---

[58] We comment that the "reasonably-efficient" scheme of [68] is based on a strong assumption regarding a specific computational problem related to the *Diffie-Hellman Key Exchange.* Specifically, it is assumed that for a prime P and primitive element g, given $(P, g, (g^x \bmod P), (g^y \bmod P), (g^z \bmod P))$, it is infeasible to decide whether $z \equiv xy \pmod{P-1}$.

enters such a protocol with input that equals the message to be delivered, and the receiver enters with no input (or with input that equals the security parameter).

1. Show that any secure public-key encryption scheme yields a (two-message) secure communication protocol.
2. Define secure communication protocol with initial set-up, and show that any secure private-key encryption scheme yields such a (one-message) protocol. (Here, the communicating parties obtain an [equal] auxiliary input that is generated at random according to some pre-determined process.)

Advanced: Show that a secure communication protocol (even with initial set-up but with a priori unbounded messages) implies the existence of one-way functions.

Guideline (advanced part): See guideline for Exercise 2.

Exercise 2: *Secure encryption schemes imply one-way function* [132]: Show that the existence of a secure private-key encryption scheme (i.e., as in Definition 5.2.1) implies the existence of one-way functions.

> **Guideline:** Recall that, by Exercise 11 of Chapter 3 in Volume 1, it suffices to prove that the former implies the existence of a pair of polynomial-time constructible probability ensembles that are statistically far apart and still are computationally indistinguishable. To prove the existence of such ensembles, consider the encryption of $(n + 1)$-bit plaintexts relative to a random n-bit long key, denoted K_n. Specifically, let the first ensemble be $\{(U_{n+1}, E(U_{n+1}))\}_{n\in\mathbb{N}}$, where $E(x) = E_{K_n}(x)$, and the second ensemble be $\{(U_{n+1}^{(1)}, E(U_{n+1}^{(2)}))\}_{n\in\mathbb{N}}$, where $U_{n+1}^{(1)}$ and $U_{n+1}^{(2)}$ are independently distributed. It is easy to show that these ensembles are computationally indistinguishable and are both polynomial-time constructible. The more interesting part is to show that these ensembles are statistically far apart. Note that the correct decryption condition implies that $(K_n, E_{K_n}(U_{n+1}))$ contains $n + 1 - o(1)$ bits of information about U_{n+1}. On the other hand, if these ensembles are statistically close, then $E_{K_n}(U_{n+1})$ contains $o(1)$ bits of information about U_{n+1}. Contradiction follows, because K_n may contain at most n bits of information.

Exercise 3: *Encryption schemes with unbounded-length plaintexts:* Suppose that the definition of semantic security is modified so that no bound is placed on the length of plaintexts. Prove that in such a case there exists no semantically secure encryption scheme.

> **Guideline:** A plaintext of length exponential in the security parameter allows the adversary, which runs in time polynomial in its input, to find the decryption-key by exhaustive search. In the case of public-key schemes, we merely search for a choice of coins that make the key-generator algorithm output a key-pair with an encryption-key that fits the one given to us. In the case of private-key schemes, we assume that we are given all but the first bit of the plaintext (i.e., we refer to $h(1^n, \sigma x) = x$ where $\sigma \in \{0, 1\}$), and search for an adequate key as well as the value of σ.

Exercise 4: *Encryption schemes must leak information about the length of the plaintext:* Suppose that the definition of semantic security is modified so that the algorithms are not given the length of the plaintext. Prove that in such a case there exists no semantically secure encryption scheme.

> **Guideline:** First show that for some polynomial p, $|E(1^n)| < p(n)$ (always holds), whereas for some $x \in \{0, 1\}^{p(n)}$ it must hold that $\Pr[|E(x)| < p(n)] < 1/2$.

Exercise 5: *Hiding partial information about the length of the plaintext:* Using an arbitrary secure encryption scheme, construct a correspondingly secure encryption scheme that hides the exact length of the plaintext. In particular, construct an encryption scheme that reveals only the following function h' of the length of the plaintext:

1. $h'(m) = \lceil m/n \rceil \cdot n$, where n is the security parameter.
2. $h'(m) = 2^{\lceil \log_2 m \rceil}$.

(Hint: Just use an adequate padding convention, making sure that it always allows correct decryption.)

Exercise 6: *Length parameters:* Assuming the existence of a secure public-key (resp., private-key) encryption scheme, prove the existence of such a scheme in which the length of the keys equal the security parameter. Furthermore, show that (without loss of generality) the length of ciphertexts may be a fixed polynomial in the length of the plaintext and the security parameter.

Exercise 7: *On the distribution of public-keys:* Let (G, E, D) be a secure public-key encryption scheme. Prove that for every positive polynomial p, and all sufficiently large n, it holds that $\max_e\{\Pr[G_1(1^n) = e]\} < 1/p(n)$.

> **Guideline:** Show that for any encryption-key e in the range of $G_1(1^n)$, one can find a corresponding decryption-key in expected time $1/\Pr[G_1(1^n) = e]$.

Exercise 8: *Deterministic encryption schemes:* Prove that a semantically secure public-key encryption scheme must employ a probabilistic encryption algorithm.

> **Guideline:** For any public-key encryption scheme having a deterministic encryption algorithm, given the encryption-key, one can distinguish the encryptions of two candidate plaintexts by computing the unique ciphertext corresponding to each of them.

Exercise 9: *An alternative formulation of Definition 5.2.1:* Prove that the following definition, in which we use non-uniform families of polynomial-size circuits (rather than probabilistic polynomial-time algorithms) is equivalent to Definition 5.2.1.

> There exists a probabilistic polynomial-time transformation T such that for every polynomial-size circuit family $\{C_n\}_{n\in\mathbb{N}}$, and for every $\{X_n\}_{n\in\mathbb{N}}$, $f, h : \{0, 1\}^* \to \{0, 1\}^*$, p and n as in Definition 5.2.1
>
> $$\Pr\left[C_n(E_{G_1(1^n)}(X_n), 1^{|X_n|}, h(1^n, X_n)) = f(1^n, X_n)\right]$$
>
> $$< \Pr\left[C'_n(1^{|X_n|}, h(1^n, X_n)) = f(1^n, X_n)\right] + \frac{1}{p(n)}$$

where $C'_n \leftarrow T(C_n)$ and the probability is also taken over the internal coin tosses of T.

Formulate and show an analogous result for public-key encryption.

Guideline: The alternative view of non-uniformity, discussed in Section 1.3 of Volume 1, is useful here. That is, we can view a circuit family as a sequence of advices given to a universal machine. Thus, the alternative formulation of the definition states that advices for a machine that gets the ciphertext can be efficiently transformed into advices for a machine that does not get the ciphertext. However, we can incorporate the (probabilistic) transformation program into the second universal algorithm (which then become probabilistic). Consequently, the advices are identical for both machines (and can be incorporated in the auxiliary input $h(1^n, X_n)$ used in Definition 5.2.1). Viewed this way, the alternative formulation is equivalent to asserting that for some (universal) deterministic polynomial-time algorithm U, there exists a probabilistic polynomial-time algorithm U' such that for every $\{X_n\}_{n \in \mathbb{N}}$, $f, h : \{0, 1\}^* \rightarrow \{0, 1\}^*$, p, and n as in Definition 5.2.1

$$\Pr\left[U(1^n, E_{G_1(1^n)}(X_n), 1^{|X_n|}, h(1^n, X_n)) = f(1^n, X_n)\right]$$
$$< \Pr\left[U'(1^n, 1^{|X_n|}, h(1^n, X_n)) = f(1^n, X_n)\right] + \frac{1}{p(n)}$$

Still, a gap remains between Definition 5.2.1 and this definition: The last refers only to one possible deterministic algorithm U, whereas Definition 5.2.1 refers to all probabilistic polynomial-time algorithms. To close the gap, we first observe that (by Propositions 5.2.7 and 5.2.6), Definition 5.2.1 is equivalent to a form in which one only quantifies over deterministic polynomial-time algorithms A. We conclude by observing that one can code any algorithm A (and polynomial time-bound) referred to by Definition 5.2.1 in the auxiliary input (i.e., $h(1^n, X_n)$) given to U.

Exercise 10: *In continuation of Exercise 9,* consider a definition in which the transformation T (of the circuit family $\{C_n\}_{n \in \mathbb{N}}$ to the circuit family $\{C'_n\}_{n \in \mathbb{N}}$) is not even required to be computable.[59] Clearly, the new definition is not stronger than the one in Exercise 9. Show that the two definitions are in fact equivalent.

Guideline: Use the furthermore-clause of Proposition 5.2.7 to show that the new definition implies indistinguishability of encryptions, and conclude by applying Proposition 5.2.6 and invoking Exercise 9.

Exercise 11: *An alternative formulation of Definition 5.2.3:* Prove that Definition 5.2.3 remains unchanged when supplying the circuit with auxiliary input. That is, an encryption scheme satisfies the modified Definition 5.2.3 if and only if

---

[59] Equivalently, one may require that for any polynomial-size circuit family $\{C_n\}_{n \in \mathbb{N}}$ there exists a polynomial-size circuit family $\{C'_n\}_{n \in \mathbb{N}}$ satisfying the relevant inequality.

for every polynomial-size circuit family $\{C_n\}$, every positive polynomial p, all sufficiently large n, and every $x, y \in \{0, 1\}^{\mathrm{poly}(n)}$ (i.e., $|x| = |y|$) and $z \in \{0, 1\}^{\mathrm{poly}(n)}$,

$$\left| \Pr\left[C_n(z, E_{G_1(1^n)}(x)) = 1 \right] - \Pr\left[C_n(z, E_{G_1(1^n)}(y)) = 1 \right] \right| < \frac{1}{p(n)}$$

(Hint: Incorporate z in the circuit C_n.)

Exercise 12: *Equivalence of the security definitions in the public-key model:* Prove that a public-key encryption scheme is semantically secure if and only if it has indistinguishable encryptions.

Exercise 13: *The technical contents of semantic security:* The following explains the lack of computational requirements regarding the function f, in Definition 5.2.1. Prove that an encryption scheme, (G, E, D), is (semantically) secure (in the private-key model) if and only if the following holds:

There exists a probabilistic polynomial-time algorithm A'' such that for every $\{X_n\}_{n \in \mathbb{N}}$ and h as in Definition 5.2.1, the following two ensembles are computationally indistinguishable:

1. $\{E_{G_1(1^n)}(X_n), 1^{|X_n|}, h(1^n, X_n)\}_{n \in \mathbb{N}}$.
2. $\{A''(1^n, 1^{|X_n|}, h(1^n, X_n))\}_{n \in \mathbb{N}}$.

Formulate and prove an analogous claim for the public-key model.

Guideline: We care mainly about the fact that the latter formulation implies semantic security. The other direction can be proven analogously to the proof of Proposition 5.2.7.

Exercise 14: *Equivalent formulations of semantic security:*

1. Prove that Definition 5.2.1 remains unchanged if we restrict the function h to depend only on the length of its input or, alternatively, $h(1^n, x) = h'(n)$ for some $h' : \mathbb{N} \to \{0,1\}^*$.
2. Prove that Definition 5.2.1 remains unchanged if we may restrict the function h and the probability ensemble $\{X_n\}_{n \in \mathbb{N}}$ such that they are computable (resp., sampleable) by polynomial-size circuits.

Guideline (Part 1): Prove that this special case (i.e., obtained by the restriction on h) is equivalent to the general one. This follows by combining Propositions 5.2.7 and 5.2.6. Alternatively, this follows by considering all possible probability ensembles $\{X_n'\}_{n \in \mathbb{N}}$ obtained from $\{X_n\}_{n \in \mathbb{N}}$ by conditioning that $h(1^n, X_n) = a_n$ (for every possible sequence of a_n's).

Guideline (Part 2): The claim regarding h follows from Part 1. To establish the claim regarding X_n, observe that (by Propositions 5.2.7 and 5.2.6) we may consider the case in which X_n ranges over two strings.

Exercise 15: *A variant on Exercises 13 and 14.1:* Prove that an encryption scheme, (G, E, D), is (semantically) secure (in the private-key model) if and only if the following holds:

> For every probabilistic polynomial-time algorithm A there exists a probabilistic polynomial-time algorithm A' such that for every ensemble $\{X_n\}_{n \in \mathbb{N}}$, with $|X_n| = \text{poly}(n)$, and polynomially-bounded h', the following two ensembles are computationally indistinguishable.
>
> 1. $\{A(1^n, E_{G_1(1^n)}(X_n), 1^{|X_n|}, h'(1^n))\}_{n \in \mathbb{N}}$.
> 2. $\{A'(1^n, 1^{|X_n|}, h'(1^n))\}_{n \in \mathbb{N}}$.

An equivalent form is obtained by replacing $h'(1^n)$ with a poly(n)-bit long string v_n. Formulate and prove an analogous claim for the public-key model.

> **Guideline:** Again, we care mainly about the fact that this variant implies semantic security. The easiest proof of this direction is by applying Propositions 5.2.7 and 5.2.6. A more interesting proof is obtained by using Exercise 13: Indeed, the current formulation is a special case of the formulation in Exercise 13, and so we need to prove that it implies the general case. The latter is proven by observing that otherwise – using an averaging argument – we derive a contradiction in one of the residual probability spaces defined by conditioning on $h(1^n, X_n)$ (i.e., $(X_n | h(1^n, X_n) = v)$ for some v).

Exercise 16: *Semantic security with respect to relations:* The formulation of semantic security in Definition 5.2.1 refers to computing a function (i.e., f) of the plaintext. Here we present a (related) definition that refers to finding strings that are in a certain relation to the plaintext. Note that, unlike in Definition 5.2.1, here we consider only efficiently recognizable relations. Specifically, we require the following:

> For every probabilistic polynomial-time algorithm A there exists a probabilistic polynomial-time algorithm A' such that for every ensemble $\{X_n\}_{n \in \mathbb{N}}$, with $|X_n| = \text{poly}(n)$, every polynomially bounded function h, every polynomially bounded relation R that is recognizable by a (non-uniform) family of polynomial-size circuits, every positive polynomial p, and all sufficiently large n
>
> $$\Pr\left[(X_n, A(1^n, E_{G_1(1^n)}(X_n), 1^{|X_n|}, h(1^n, X_n))) \in R\right]$$
> $$< \Pr\left[(X_n, A'(1^n, 1^{|X_n|}, h(1^n, X_n))) \in R\right] + \frac{1}{p(n)}$$

1. Prove that this definition is in fact equivalent to the standard definition of semantic security.
2. Show that if the computational restriction on the relation R is removed, then no encryption scheme can satisfy the resulting definition.

Formulate and prove analogous claims for the public-key model.

> **Guideline (for Part 1):** Show that the new definition is equivalent to indistinguishability of encryptions. Specifically, follow the proofs of Propositions 5.2.6 and 5.2.7, using the circuits guaranteed for R in the first proof, and noting that the second proof holds intact.

> **Guideline (for Part 2):** Consider the relation $R = \{(x, E_e(x)) : |x| = 2|e|\}$, and the distribution $X_n = U_{2n}$. (Note that if the encryption scheme is semantically secure, then this R is not recognizable by small circuits.)

Exercise 17: *Semantic security with a randomized h:* The following syntactic strengthening of semantic security is important in some applications. Its essence is in considering information *related* to the plaintext, in the form of a related random variable, rather than partial information about the plaintext (in the form of a function of it). Prove that an encryption scheme, (G, E, D), is (semantically) secure (in the private-key model) if and only if the following holds:

> For every probabilistic polynomial-time algorithm A there exists a probabilistic polynomial-time algorithm A' such that for every $\{(X_n, Z_n)\}_{n \in \mathbb{N}}$, with $|(X_n, Z_n)| = \text{poly}(n)$, where Z_n may depend arbitrarily on X_n, and f, p, and n as in Definition 5.2.1
>
> $$\Pr\left[A(1^n, E_{G_1(1^n)}(X_n), 1^{|X_n|}, Z_n) = f(1^n, X_n)\right]$$
> $$< \Pr\left[A'(1^n, 1^{|X_n|}, Z_n) = f(1^n, X_n)\right] + \frac{1}{p(n)}$$

That is, the auxiliary input $h(1^n, X_n)$ of Definition 5.2.1 is replaced by the random variable Z_n. Formulate and prove an analogous claim for the public-key model.

> **Guideline:** Definition 5.2.1 is clearly a special case of the latter formulation. On the other hand, the proof of Proposition 5.2.6 extends easily to this (seemingly stronger) formulation of semantic security.

Exercise 18: *Semantic Security with respect to Oracles* (suggested by Boaz Barak): Consider an extended definition of semantic security in which, in addition to the regular inputs, the algorithms have oracle access to a function $H_{1^n,x} : \{0, 1\}^* \to \{0, 1\}^*$ (instead of being given the value $h(1^n, x)$). The $H_{1^n,x}$'s have to be restricted to have polynomial (in $n + |x|$) size circuits. That is, *an encryption scheme, (G, E, D), is* extended-semantically secure (in the private-key model) *if the following holds*:

> *For every probabilistic polynomial-time algorithm A there exists a probabilistic polynomial-time algorithm B such that for every ensemble $\{X_n\}_{n \in \mathbb{N}}$, with $|X_n| = \text{poly}(n)$, every polynomially bounded function f, every family of polynomial-sized circuits $\{H_{1^n,x}\}_{n \in \mathbb{N}, x \in \{0,1\}^*}$, every positive polynomial p, and all sufficiently large n*
>
> $$\Pr\left[A^{H_{1^n,X_n}}(1^n, E_{G_1(1^n)}(X_n), 1^{|X_n|}) = f(1^n, X_n)\right]$$
> $$< \Pr\left[B^{H_{1^n,X_n}}(1^n, 1^{|X_n|}) = f(1^n, X_n)\right] + \frac{1}{p(n)}$$

The definition of public-key security is analogous.

1. Show that if (G, E, D) has indistinguishable encryptions, then it is extended-semantically secure.

2. Show that if no restrictions are placed on the $H_{1^n,x}$'s, then no scheme can be extended-semantically secure (in this unrestricted sense).

Guideline (for Part 1): The proof is almost identical to the proof of Proposition 5.2.6: The algorithm B forms an encryption of $1^{|X_n|}$, and invokes A on it. Indistinguishability of encryptions is used in order to establish that $B^{H_{1^n,x_n}}(1^n, 1^{|X_n|})$ performs essentially as well as $A^{H_{1^n,x_n}}(1^n, 1^{|X_n|}, E(X_n))$. Otherwise, we obtain a distinguisher of $E(x_n)$ from $E(1^{|x_n|})$, for some infinite sequence of x_n's. In particular, the oracle H_{1^n,x_n} (being implementable by a small circuit) can be incorporated into a distinguisher.

Guideline (for Part 2): In such a case, $H_{1^n,x}$ may be defined such that, when queried about a ciphertext, it reveals the decryption-key in use.[60] Such an oracle allows A (which is given a ciphertext) to recover the corresponding plaintext, but does not help A' (which is only given 1^n, $1^{|X_n|}$) to find any information about the value of X_n.

Exercise 19: *Another equivalent definition of security:* The following exercise is interesting mainly for historical reasons. In the definition of semantic security appearing in [123], the term $\max_{u,v}\{\Pr[f(1^n, X_n)=v|h(1^n, X_n)=u]\}$ appears instead of the term $\Pr[A'(1^n, 1^{|X_n|}, h(1^n, X_n)) = f(1^n, X_n)]$. That is, it is required that the following holds:

For every probabilistic polynomial-time algorithm A, every ensemble $\{X_n\}_{n\in\mathbb{N}}$, with $|X_n| = \text{poly}(n)$, every pair of polynomially bounded functions $f, h : \{0, 1\}^* \to \{0, 1\}^*$, every positive polynomial p, and all sufficiently large n

$$\Pr\left[A(1^n, E_{G_1(1^n)}(X_n), 1^{|X_n|}, h(1^n, X_n))= f(1^n, X_n)\right]$$
$$< \max_{u,v} \left\{\Pr[f(1^n, X_n)=v|h(1^n, X_n)=u]\right\} + \frac{1}{p(n)}$$

Prove that this formulation is in fact equivalent to Definition 5.2.1.

Guideline: First, note that this definition is implied by Definition 5.2.1 (because $\max_{u,v}\{\Pr[f(1^n, X_n) = v|h(1^n, X_n) = u]\} \geq \Pr[A'(1^n, 1^{|X_n|}, h(1^n, X_n)) = f(1^n, X_n)]$, for every algorithm A'). Next note that in the *special case,* in which X_n satisfies $\Pr[f(1^n, X_n)=0|h(1^n, X_n)=u] = \Pr[f(1^n, X_n)=1|h(1^n, X_n)=u] = \frac{1}{2}$, for all u's, the previous terms are equal (because A' can easily achieve success probability $1/2$ by simply always outputting 1). Finally, combining Propositions 5.2.7 and 5.2.6, infer that it suffices to consider only the latter special case.

---

[60] This refers to the private-key case, whereas in the public-key case, $H_{1^n,x}$ may be defined such that, when queried about an encryption-key, it reveals the decryption-key in use.

Exercise 20: *Multiple messages of varying lengths:* In continuation of Section 5.2.4, generalize the treatment to the encryption of multiple messages of varying lengths. That is, provide adequate definitions and analogous results.

> **Guideline:** For example, a generalization of the first item of Definition 5.2.8 postulates that for every probabilistic polynomial-time algorithm A, there exists a probabilistic polynomial-time algorithm A' such that for every ensemble $\{\overline{X}_n = (X_n^{(1)}, ..., X_n^{(t(n))})\}_{n \in \mathbb{N}}$, with $t(n) \leq \text{poly}(n)$ and $|X_n^{(i)}| \leq \text{poly}(n)$, every pair of polynomially bounded functions $f, h : \{0, 1\}^* \to \{0, 1\}^*$, every positive polynomial p, and all sufficiently large n
>
> $$\Pr\left[A(1^n, \overline{E}_{G_1(1^n)}(\overline{X}_n), (1^{|X_n^{(1)}|}, ..., 1^{|X_n^{(t(n))}|}), h(1^n, \overline{X}_n)) = f(1^n, \overline{X}_n)\right]$$
>
> $$< \Pr\left[A'(1^n, (1^{|X_n^{(1)}|}, ..., 1^{|X_n^{(t(n))}|}), h(1^n, \overline{X}_n)) = f(1^n, \overline{X}_n)\right] + \frac{1}{p(n)}$$

Exercise 21: *Private-key encryption secure with respect to exactly t messages.* In continuation of Proposition 5.2.12, show that if secure private-key encryption schemes exist, then for every t there are such schemes that are secure with respect to the encryption of t messages but not with respect to the encryption of $t + 1$ messages.

> **Guideline:** Given an arbitrary private-key encryption scheme (G, E, D), consider the following private-key encryption scheme (G', E', D'):
>
> - $G'(1^n) = (\overline{k}, \overline{k})$, where $\overline{k} = (k_0, k_1, ..., k_t)$ such that $(k_0, k_0) \leftarrow G(1^n)$ and $k_1, ..., k_t$ are uniformly and independently selected in $\{0, 1\}^n$ (without loss of generality, $n = |k_0|$);
> - $E'_{(k_0, k_1, ..., k_t)}(x) = (E_{k_0}(x), r, \sum_{i=0}^t k_i r^i)$, where r is uniformly selected in $\{0, 1\}^n$, and the arithmetics is of the field $GF(2^n)$;
> - and $D'_{(k_0, k_1, ..., k_t)}(y, r, v) = D_{k_0}(y)$.
>
> Essentially, the original scheme is augmented with a $(t + 1)$-out-of-2^n secret sharing scheme (see Definition 7.5.34), such that a share of the original key is revealed by each encryption.

Exercise 22: *Known plaintext attacks:* Loosely speaking, in a known plaintext attack on a private-key (resp., public-key) encryption scheme, the adversary is given some plaintext/ciphertext pairs in addition to some extra ciphertexts (without corresponding plaintexts). Semantic security in this setting means that whatever can be efficiently computed about the missing plaintexts can also be efficiently computed given only the length of these plaintexts.

1. Provide formal definitions of *security under known plaintext attacks,* treating both the private-key and public-key models and referring to both the single-message and multiple-message settings.
2. Prove that any secure *public-key* encryption scheme is also secure in the presence of known plaintext attacks.
3. Prove that any private-key encryption scheme that is *secure in the multiple-message setting* is also secure in the presence of known plaintext attacks.

Guideline (for Part 3): Consider a function h in the multiple-message setting that reveals some of the plaintexts.

Exercise 23: *A variant on the uniform-complexity treatment* (suggested by Johan Håstad): The original motivation for the following variant of semantic security was to allow equivalence to indistinguishability of encryptions also in the single-message case. Intuitively, the definition asserts that whatever can be efficiently inferred from the encryption of one piece of partial information and a second piece of partial information can be efficiently inferred only from the latter. (This should be contrasted with Definition 5.2.13, in which the encryption is applied to the entire information.) That is, as a variant of Definition 5.2.13, we say that an encryption scheme, (G, E, D), is uniformly semantically secure *in the public-key model* if

for every probabilistic polynomial-time algorithm A there exists a probabilistic polynomial-time algorithm A' such that for every polynomial ℓ, every polynomial-time computable functions $h_1, h_2 : \{0, 1\}^* \to \{0, 1\}^*$, every $f : \{0, 1\}^* \to \{0, 1\}^*$, every positive polynomial p, and all sufficiently large n's

$$\Pr\left[A(1^n, G_1(1^n), E_{G_1(1^n)}(h_1(U_{\ell(n)})), 1^{|h_1(U_{\ell(n)})|}, h_2(U_{\ell(n)})) = f(U_{\ell(n)})\right]$$
$$< \Pr\left[A'(1^n, 1^{|h_1(U_{\ell(n)})|}, h_2(U_{\ell(n)})) = f(U_{\ell(n)})\right] + \frac{1}{p(n)}$$

where, for simplicity of notation, we have omitted the argument 1^n from all functions.

Show that this definition is equivalent to the single-message version of Definition 5.2.14 (i.e., its restriction to the case of $t \equiv 1$). Show that the non-uniform variant of this definition (i.e., allowing h_1 and h_2 to be any polynomially bounded functions) is equivalent to Definition 5.2.1. (Provide two alternative proofs to the latter statement, with and without invoking Theorem 5.2.5.)

Exercise 24: *Alterntaive formulation of state-based ciphers:* For $E = (E', E'')$ and $D = (D', D'')$, consider the following reformulation of Item 2 of Definition 5.3.1: For every pair $(e^{(0)}, d^{(0)})$ in the range of $G(1^n)$, every sequence of plaintexts $\alpha^{(i)}$'s, and every i, it holds that $D'(d^{(i-1)}, E'(e^{(i-1)}, \alpha^{(i)})) = \alpha^{(i)}$, where $e^{(j)} = E''(e^{(j-1)}, 1^{|\alpha^{(j)}|})$ and $d^{(j)} = D''(d^{(j-1)}, 1^{|E'(e^{(j-1)}, 1^{|\alpha^{(j)}|})|})$ for $j = 1, ..., i-1$. Prove the equivalence of the two formulations.

Exercise 25: *On the standard notion of block-cipher:* A standard block-cipher is a triple, (G, E, D), of probabilistic polynomial-time algorithms that satisfies Definition 5.3.5 as well as $|E_e(\alpha)| = \ell(n)$ for every pair (e, d) in the range of $G(1^n)$ and every $\alpha \in \{0, 1\}^{\ell(n)}$.

1. Prove that a standard block-cipher cannot be semantically secure (in the multiple-message private-key model). Furthermore, show that any semantically secure encryption scheme must employ ciphertexts that are longer than the corresponding plaintexts.

2. Present a state-based version of the definition of a (secure) standard (private-key) block-cipher, and note that Construction 5.3.3 satisfies it.

   Guideline (for Part 1): Consider the encryption of a pair of two identical messages versus the encryption of a pair of two different messages, and use the fact that E_e must be a permutation of $\{0, 1\}^{\ell(n)}$. Extend the argument to any encryption scheme in which plaintexts of length $\ell(n)$ are encrypted by ciphertexts of length $\ell(n) + O(\log n)$, observing that in this case most plaintexts have only poly(n)-many ciphertexts under E_e.

Exercise 26: *A secure private-key encryption scheme:* Assuming that F is pseudo-random with respect to polynomial-size circuits, prove that Construction 5.3.12 constitutes a secure private-key encryption scheme.

   Guideline: Adapt the proof of Proposition 5.3.10. When referring to the security of $t = \text{poly}(n)$ messages, each of length $\ell = \text{poly}(n)$, the adaptation requires bounding the probability that for t uniformly selected $r^{(j)}$'s there exists $j_1, j_2 \in \{1, ..., t\}$ and $i_1, i_2 \in \{1, ..., \ell/n\}$ such that $r^{(j_1)} + i_1 \equiv r^{(j_2)} + i_2 \pmod{2^n}$.

Exercise 27: *The Blum-Goldwasser public-key encryption scheme* was presented in Construction 5.3.20 as a block-cipher (with arbitrary block-length). Provide an alternative presentation of this scheme as a full-fledged encryption scheme (rather than a block-cipher), and prove its security (under the factoring assumption).

   Guideline: In the alternative presentation, the values of d_P and d_Q cannot be determined at key-generation time, but are rather computed by the decryption process. (This means that decryption requires two additional modular exponentiations.)

Exercise 28: *On the importance of restricting the ensembles $\{h_e\}_{e \in \{0,1\}^*}$ and $\{X_e\}_{e \in \{0,1\}^*}$ in Definition 5.4.1:*

1. Show that if one allows arbitrary function ensembles $\{h_e\}_{e \in \{0,1\}^*}$ in Definition 5.4.1, then no encryption scheme can satisfy it.
2. Show that if one allows arbitrary probability ensembles $\{X_e\}_{e \in \{0,1\}^*}$ in Definition 5.4.1, then no encryption scheme can satisfy it, even if one uses only a single function h that is polynomial-time computable.

   Guideline: For Part 1, consider the functions $h_e(x) = d$, where d is a decryption-key corresponding to the encryption-key e. For Part 2, consider the random variable $X_e = (d, U_{|e|})$, where d is as before, and the function $h(x', x'') = x'$.

Exercise 29: *An alternative formulation of Definition 5.4.1:* Show that the following formulation of the definition of admissible ensembles $\{h_e\}_e$ and $\{X_e\}_e$ is equivalent to the one in Definition 5.4.1:

- There is a non-uniform family of polynomial-size circuits $\{T_n\}$ that transform encryption-keys (i.e., e in $G_1(1^n)$) into circuits that compute the corresponding functions (i.e., h_e). That is, on input $e \leftarrow G_1(1^n)$, the circuit T_n outputs a circuit C_e such that $C_e(x) = h_e(x)$ holds for all strings of adequate length (i.e., $\leq \text{poly}(|e|)$).

- There is a non-uniform family of polynomial-size circuits $\{T_n\}$ that transform encryption-keys (i.e., e in $G_1(1^n)$) into circuits that sample the corresponding distributions (i.e., X_e). That is, on input $e \leftarrow G_1(1^n)$, the circuit T_n outputs a circuit S_e such that $S_e(U_m)$ is distributed identically to X_e, where U_m denotes the uniform distribution over the set of strings of length $m = m(e)$.

Note that this formulation is in greater agreement with the motivating discussion preceding Definition 5.4.1. The formulation in Definition 5.4.1 was preferred because of its relative simplicity.

> **Guideline:** Consider, for example, the condition regarding $\{h_e\}$. The formulation in Definition 5.4.1 is shown to imply the one in this exercise by considering the circuit family $\{T_n\}$ such that on input e (in the range of $G_1(1^n)$), the circuit T_n outputs the circuit $C_e(\cdot) \stackrel{\text{def}}{=} H_n(e, \cdot)$, where H_n is the circuit guaranteed by Definition 5.4.1. That is, T_n has the description of H_n hard-wired, and outputs the description of the circuit obtained from H_n by fixing its first input to be e. On the other hand, given a circuit family $\{T_n\}$ that transforms $e \mapsto C_e$ as here, we obtain a circuit H_n as required in the formulation of Definition 5.4.1 as follows. The circuit H_n has T_n hard wired, and so, on input (e, x), the circuit H_n first reconstructs the circuit $C_e \leftarrow T_n(e)$, and then emulates the computation of the value $C_e(x)$.

Exercise 30: *Alternative formulations of Definitions 5.4.1 and 5.4.2:* Following the framework of Section 5.4.3, present alternative definitions of security for key-dependent passive attacks (by replacing the oracle machines A_1 and A_2 in Definitions 5.4.8 and 5.4.9 with ordinary machines). Show that these definitions are equivalent to Definitions 5.4.1 and 5.4.2.

> **Guideline:** For example, show how to derive circuits P_n and C_n (as in Definition 5.4.2) from the machines A_1, A_2 and the auxiliary input z (of Definition 5.4.9).

Exercise 31: *Multiple-message security in the context of key-dependent passive attacks on public-key schemes:* Formulate multiple-message generalizations of Definitions 5.4.1 and 5.4.2, and prove that both are equivalent (in the public-key model) to the single-message definitions.

> **Guideline:** Note that admissibility for the multiple-message generalization of Definition 5.4.2 means that, given an encryption-key e, one can compute (via a polynomial-size circuit that depends only on $|e|$) a corresponding pair of sequences $((x_e^{(1)}, ..., x_e^{(t(|e|))}), (y_e^{(1)}, ..., y_e^{(t(|e|))}))$. Thus, ability to distinguish corresponding sequences of encryptions yields ability to distinguish, for some i, the encryption of $x_e^{(i)}$ from the encryption of $y_e^{(i)}$, where the latter distinguisher generates the corresponding x-y hybrid (by using the circuit guaranteed by the admissibility condition and the input encryption-key e), and invokes the former distinguisher on the resulting sequence of encryptions.

Exercise 32: *Key-oblivious versus key-dependent passive attacks:* Assuming the existence of secure public-key encryption schemes, show that there exists one that satisfies the basic definition (i.e., as in Definition 5.2.2) but is insecure under key-dependent passive attacks (i.e., as in Definition 5.4.1).

Guideline: Given a scheme (G, E, D), define (G, E', D') such that $E'_e(x) = (1, E_e(x))$ if $x \neq e$ and $E'_e(x) = (0, x)$ otherwise (i.e., for $x = e$). Using Exercise 7 (which establishes that each encryption-key is generated with negligible probability), show that (G, E', D') satisfies Definition 5.2.2. Alternatively, use $G'(1^n) = ((r, G_1(1^n)), G_2(1^n))$, where r is uniformly distributed in $\{0, 1\}^n$, which immediately implies that each encryption-key is generated with negligible probability.

Exercise 33: *Passive attacks versus Chosen Plaintext Attacks:* Assuming the existence of secure private-key encryption schemes, show that there exists one that is secure in the standard (multi-message) sense (i.e., as in Definition 5.2.8) but is insecure under a chosen plaintext attack (i.e., as in Definition 5.4.8).

Guideline: Given a scheme (G, E, D), define (G', E', D') such that

1. $G'(1^n) = ((k, r), (k, r))$, where $(k, k) \leftarrow G(1^n)$ and r is selected uniformly in $\{0, 1\}^n$.
2. $E'_{(k,r)}(x) = (1, r, E_k(x))$ if $x \neq r$ and $E'_{(k,r)}(x) = (0, k, x)$ otherwise (i.e., for $x = r$).

Show that (G', E', D') is secure in the standard sense, and present a (simple but very "harmful") chosen plaintext attack on it.

Exercise 34: *Alternative formulations of semantic security for CPA and CCA:* Consider an alternative form of Definition 5.4.8 (resp., Definition 5.4.13) in which $A'_1(1, z)$ is replaced by $A_1^{E_e}(e, z)$ (resp., $A_1^{E_e, D_d}(e, z)$), where $(e, d) \leftarrow G(1^n)$ and Condition 2 is omitted. Show that the current form is equivalent to the one presented in the main text.

Guideline: The alternative forms presented here restrict the choice of A'_1 (to a canonical one), and thus the corresponding definitions are at least as strong as the ones in the main text. However, since Theorem 5.4.11 (resp., Theorem 5.4.15) is established using the canonical A'_1, it follows that the current definitions are actually equivalent to the ones in the main text. We comment that we consider the formulation in the main text to be more natural, alas more cumbersome.

Exercise 35: *Chosen Plaintext Attacks versus Chosen Ciphertext Attacks:* Assuming the existence of private-key (resp., public-key) encryption schemes that are secure under a chosen plaintext attack, show that there exists one that is secure in the former sense but is not secure under a chosen ciphertext attack (not even in the a priori sense).

Guideline: Given a scheme (G, E, D), define (G', E', D') such that $G' = G$ and

1. $E'_e(x) = (1, E_e(x))$ with probability $1 - 2^{-|e|}$ and $E'_e(x) = (0, x)$ otherwise.
2. $D'_d(1, y) = D_d(y)$ and $D'_d(0, y) = (d, y)$.

Recall that decryption is allowed to fail with negligible probability, and note that the construction is adequate for both public-key and private-key schemes. Alternatively, to obtain error-free decryption, define $E'_e(x) = (1, E_e(x))$, $D'_d(1, y) = D_d(y)$ and

$D'_d(0, y) = (d, y)$. In the case of private-key schemes, we may define $E'_k(k) = (0, 1^{|k|})$ and $E'_k(x) = (1, E_k(x))$ for $x \neq k$.

Exercise 36: *Chosen Ciphertext Attacks: a priori versus a posteriori:* Assuming the existence of private-key (resp., public-key) encryption schemes that are secure under an a priori chosen plaintext attack, show that there exists one that is secure in the former sense but is not secure under an a posteriori chosen ciphertext attack.

Guideline: Given a scheme (G, E, D), define (G', E', D') such that $G' = G$ and

1. $E'_e(x) \stackrel{\text{def}}{=} (b, E_e(x))$, where b is uniformly selected in $\{0, 1\}$.
2. $D'_d(b, y) \stackrel{\text{def}}{=} D_d(y)$.

Exercise 37: *Multiple-challenge CCA security implies a posteriori CCA security.* Show that Definition 5.4.16 implies security under a posteriori CCA.

Guideline: It is tempting to claim that Definition 5.4.13 is a special case of Definition 5.4.16 (obtained when allowing only one challenge query). However, things are not so simple: In Definition 5.4.13 the challenges are required to be identically distributed (in the two cases), whereas in Definition 5.4.16 only computational indistinguishability is required. Instead, we suggest showing that Definition 5.4.14 (which is equivalent to Definition 5.4.13) is implied by the (very) restricted case of Definition 5.4.16 discussed following the definition (i.e., a canonical adversary that makes a single challenge query).[61]

Exercise 38: *Equivalent forms of multiple-challenge CCA security:*

1. Consider a modification of Definition 5.4.16 in which challenge queries of the form (S, h) are answered by $(E_e(S(r)), h(r))$, rather than by $(E_e(S(r)), h(S(r)))$. Prove that the original definition is equivalent to the modified one.
2. Consider a modification of Definition 5.4.16 in which the challenge queries of the form (S, h) are replaced by two types of queries: partial-information queries of the form (leak, h) that are answered by $h(r)$, and partial-encryption queries of the form (enc, S) that are answered by $E_e(S(r))$. Prove that the original definition is equivalent to the modified one.

Guideline: Show how the modified model of Part 1 can emulate the original model (that's easy), and how the original model can emulate the modified model of Part 1 (e.g., replace the query (S, h) by the pair of queries $(S, 0)$ and (id, h)). Next relate the models in Parts 1 and 2.

Exercise 39: *On the computational restriction on the choice of input in the definition of adaptive NIZK:* Show that if Definition 5.4.22 is strengthened by waiving the computational bounds on Ξ, then only trivial NIZKs (i.e., languages in $\mathcal{BPP}$) can satisfy it.

---

[61] Furthermore, we may even restrict this challenge query to be of the form $(S, 0)$, where 0 is the all-zero function (which yields no information).

Guideline: Show that allowing a computationally unbounded Ξ forces the simulator to generate a reference string that is statistically close to the uniform distribution. Thus, soundness implies weak simulation-soundness in the strong sense of Exercise 40 (i.e., with respect to a computationally unbounded Π as in Definition 5.4.22), and by applying Exercise 40 we are done.

Exercise 40: *Weak simulation-soundness can hold only with respect to computationally bounded cheating provers.* Show that if Definition 5.4.24 is strengthened by waiving the computational bounds on Π, then only trivial NIZKs (i.e., for languages in $\mathcal{BPP}$) can satisfy it.

Guideline: Show that otherwise the two-stage simulation procedure, $S = (S_1, S_2)$, can be used to distinguish inputs in the language L from inputs outside the language, because in the first case it produces a valid proof whereas in the second case it cannot do so. The latter fact is proved by showing that if S_2 (which also gets an auxiliary input s produced by S_1 along with the reference string) produces a valid proof for some $x \notin L$, then a computationally unbounded prover may do the same by first generating s according to the conditional distribution induced by the reference string (and then invoking S_2).

Exercise 41: *Does weak simulation-soundness hold for all adaptive NIZKs?*

1. Detect the flaw in the following argument toward an affirmative answer: If weak simulation-soundness does not hold, then we can distinguish a uniformly selected reference string (for which soundness holds) from a reference string generated by S_1 (for which soundness does not hold).
2. Assuming the existence of one-way permutations (and adaptive NIZKs), show an adaptive NIZK with a suitable simulator such that weak simulation-soundness does not hold.
3. (Suggested by Boaz Barak and Yehuda Lindell): Consider languages containing pairs (α, x) such that one can generate α's along with suitable trapdoors $t(\alpha)$'s that allow for determining whether or not inputs of the form $(\alpha, \cdot)$ are in the language. For such languages, define a weaker notion of simulation-soundness that refers to the setting in which a random α is generated and then one attempts to produce valid proofs for a no-instance of the form $(\alpha, \cdot)$ with respect to a reference-string generated by S_1. (The weaker notion asserts that in this setting it is infeasible to produce a valid proof for such a no-instance.) Provide a clear definition, prove that it is satisfied by *any* adaptive NIZK for the corresponding language, and show that this definition suffices for proving Theorem 5.4.27.

Guideline (Part 1): The existence of an efficient $C = (\Xi, \Pi)$ that violates weak simulation-soundness only means that for a reference string generated by S_1, the cheating Π generates a *valid proof for a no-instance* selected by Ξ. When C is given a uniformly selected reference string, it either may fail to produce a valid proof or *may produce a valid proof for a yes-instance*. However, we cannot necessarily distinguish no-instances from yes-instances (see, for example, Part 2). This gap is eliminated in Part 3.

Guideline (Part 2): Given a one-way permutation f with a corresponding hard-core predicate b, consider the pseudorandom generator $G(s) \stackrel{\text{def}}{=} (G'(s), f^{2|s|}(s))$, where $G'(s) \stackrel{\text{def}}{=} b(s)b(f(s)) \cdots b(f^{2|s|-1}(s))$ (see proof of Proposition 5.3.19). Let L denote the set of strings that are *not* images of G, and note that L is in $\mathcal{NP}$ (because $L = \{(\alpha, \beta) : \exists s \text{ s.t. } \beta = f^{2|s|}(s) \wedge \alpha \neq G'(s)\}$). Given any adaptive NIZK for L, denoted (P, V), consider the modification (P', V') such that $P'(x, w, (r_1, r_2)) = P(x, w, r_1)$ and $V'(x, (r_1, r_2), \pi) = 1$ if either $V(x, \pi, r_1) = 1$ or $x = r_2$. The modified simulator is derived by $S'_1(1^n) \stackrel{\text{def}}{=} ((r_1, r_2), s)$, where $(r_1, s) \leftarrow S_1(1^n)$ and $r_2 \leftarrow G(U_n)$ (and $S'_2(x, s) \stackrel{\text{def}}{=} S_2(x, s)$). Verify that the modified algorithms satisfy the definition of an adaptive NIZK, and note that weak simulation-soundness is easily violated by $\Xi(r_1, r_2) = r_2 \notin L$ (and any Π).

Exercise 42: *On defining non-malleability:* Show that when defining non-malleability (i.e., in Definitions 5.4.32 and 5.4.33), it is essential to prevent A from outputting the ciphertext that is given to it.

Guideline: Consider the identity relation, a constant function h, and let X_n be uniform over $\{0, 1\}^n$. Note that A gets $(e, E_e(X_n), 1^n)$, whereas A' only gets 1^n.

CHAPTER SIX

Digital Signatures and Message Authentication

Message authentication and (digital) signatures were the first tasks that joined encryption to form modern cryptography. Both message authentication and digital signatures are concerned with the "authenticity" of data, and the difference between them is analogous to the difference between private-key and public-key encryption schemes.

In this chapter, we define message authentication and digital signatures, and the security notions associated with them. We show how to construct message-authentication schemes using pseudorandom functions, and how to construct signature schemes using one-way permutations. We stress that the latter construction employs arbitrary one-way permutations, which do not necessarily have a trapdoor.

Organization. The basic definitions are presented in Section 6.1. Constructions of message-authentication schemes and signature schemes are presented in Sections 6.3 and 6.4, respectively. Toward presenting these constructions, we discuss restricted types of message authentication and signature schemes, which are of independent interest, such as length-restricted schemes (see Section 6.2) and one-time signature schemes (see Section 6.4.1). Additional issues are discussed in Sections 6.5 and 6.6.

Teaching Tip. In contrast to the case of encryption schemes (cf. Chapter 5), the definitional treatment of signatures (and message authentication) is quite simple. The treatment of length-restricted schemes (see Section 6.2) plays an important role in the construction of standard schemes, and thus we strongly recommend highlighting this treatment. We suggest focusing on the presentation of the simplest construction of message-authentication schemes (provided in Section 6.3.1) and on the (not-so-simple) construction of signature schemes that is provided in Sections 6.4.1 and 6.4.2. As in Chapter 5, we assume that the reader is familiar with the material in Chapters 2 and 3 of Volume 1 (and specifically with Sections 2.2, 2.4, and 3.6). This familiarity is important not only because we use some of the notions and results presented in these sections but also because we use similar proof techniques (and do so while assuming that this is *not* the reader's first encounter with these techniques).

6.1. The Setting and Definitional Issues

Both signature schemes and message-authentication schemes are methods for "validating" data, that is, verifying that the data was approved by a certain party (or set of parties). The difference between signature schemes and message-authentication schemes is that "signatures" should be "universally verifiable," whereas "authentication tags" are only required to be verifiable by parties that are also able to generate them. It is customary to discuss each of these two types of schemes separately, and we start by providing a brief overview of such a nature. We then turn to our actual treatment, which applies to both types of schemes in a unified manner.

6.1.1. The Two Types of Schemes: A Brief Overview

The need to discuss "digital signatures" has arisen with the introduction of computer communication to the business environment (in which parties need to commit themselves to proposals and/or declarations that they make). Discussions of "unforgeable signatures" also took place in previous centuries, but the objects of discussion were handwritten signatures (and not digital ones), and the discussion was not perceived as related to "cryptography." Loosely speaking, a *scheme for unforgeable signatures* should satisfy the following:

- Each user can *efficiently produce his/her own signature* on documents of his/her choice;
- every user can *efficiently verify* whether a given string is a signature of another (specific) user on a specific document; but
- *it is infeasible to produce signatures of other users* to documents that they did not sign.

We note that the formulation of unforgeable digital signatures also provides a clear statement of the essential ingredients of handwritten signatures. The ingredients are each person's ability to sign for him/herself, a universally agreed-upon verification procedure, and the belief (or assertion) that it is infeasible (or at least hard) to forge signatures in a manner that passes the verification procedure. It is not clear to what extent handwritten signatures do meet these requirements. In contrast, our treatment of digital-signature schemes provides precise statements concerning the extend to which digital signatures meet these requirements. Furthermore, unforgeable digital signature schemes can be constructed based on the existence of one-way functions.

Message authentication is a task related to the setting considered for encryption schemes; that is, communication over an insecure channel. This time, we consider an active adversary that is monitoring the channel and may alter the messages sent on it. The parties communicating through this insecure channel wish to authenticate the messages they send so that their counterpart can tell an original message (sent by the sender) from a modified one (i.e., modified by the adversary). Loosely speaking, a *scheme for message authentication* should satisfy the following:

- Each of the communicating parties can *efficiently produce an authentication tag* to any message of his/her choice;
- each of the communicating parties can *efficiently verify* whether a given string is an authentication tag of a given message; but
- *it is infeasible for an external adversary* (i.e., a party other than the communicating parties) *to produce authentication tags* to messages not sent by the communicating parties.

Note that in contrast to the specification of signature schemes, we do not require universal verification: Only the designated receiver is required to be able to verify the authentication tags. Furthermore, we do not require that the receiver be unable to produce authentication tags by itself (i.e., we only require that *external parties* not be able to do so). Thus, message-authentication schemes cannot convince *a third party* that the sender has indeed sent the information (rather than the receiver having generated it by itself). In contrast, signatures can be used to convince third parties. In fact, a signature to a document is typically sent to a second party so that in the future, this party may (by merely presenting the signed document) convince third parties that the document was indeed generated (or sent or approved) by the signer.

6.1.2. Introduction to the Unified Treatment

Loosely speaking, message-authentication and signature schemes are supposed to enable reliable transmission of data between parties. That is, the basic setting consists of a *sender* and a *receiver*, where the receiver may be either predetermined or determined only after the data was sent. Loosely speaking, the receiver wishes to be guaranteed that the data received was actually sent by the sender, rather than modified (or even concocted) by somebody else (i.e., an adversary). The receiver may be a party that shares an explicit (unreliable) point-to-point communication line with the sender; this is indeed the typical setting in which message authentication is employed. However, in other cases (typically when signature schemes are employed), the receiver may be any party that obtains the data in the future and wishes to verify that it was indeed sent by the declared sender. In both cases, the reliability (or authenticity) of the data is established by an authentication process that consists of two main procedures:

1. A signing procedure that is employed by the alleged sender in order to produce signatures to data of its choice.
2. A verification procedure that is employed by the receiver in order to determine the authenticity of the data using the provided signature.

As in case of encryption schemes, the authentication process presupposes also a third procedure called key-generation that allows the sender to generate a signing-key (to be used in the signing procedure), along with a verification-key (to be used in the verification procedure). The key-generation procedure is typically invoked by the sender, and the possession of the signing-key constitutes the sender's advantage over the adversary (see analogous discussion in Chapter 5). That is, without the signing-key, it is infeasible to generate valid signatures (with respect to the corresponding verification-key). Furthermore, even after receiving signatures to messages of its choice, an adversary (lacking the signing-key) cannot generate a valid signature to any other message.

As previously stated, the ability to produce valid signatures is linked to the knowledge of the signing-key. Loosely speaking, "security" (or "unforgeability") means the infeasibility of producing valid signatures without knowledge of the signing-key, where validity means passing verification with respect to the corresponding verification-key. The difference between message-authentication and signature schemes amounts to the question of whether "security" also holds when the verification-key is publicly known: In the case of message-authentication schemes, the verification-key is assumed to be kept secret (and so these schemes are of the "private-key" type), whereas in the case of signature schemes, the verification-key may be made public (and so these schemes are of the "public-key" type). Thus, the difference between message-authentication and signature schemes is captured by the security definition, and effects the possible applications of these schemes.

From the point of view of their functionality, the difference between message-authentication and signature schemes arises from the difference in the settings for which they are intended, which amounts to a difference in the identity of the receiver and in the level of trust that the sender has in the receiver. Typically, message-authentication schemes are employed in cases where the receiver is predetermined (at the time of message transmission) and is fully trusted by the sender, whereas signature schemes allow verification of the authenticity of the data by anybody (which is certainly not trusted by the sender). In other words, signature schemes allow for *universal verification,* whereas message-authentication schemes may *only allow predetermined parties to verify* the authenticity of the data. Thus, in signature schemes the verification-key must be known to anybody, and in particular is known to the adversary. In contrast, in message-authentication schemes, the verification-key is only given to a set of predetermined receivers that are all trusted not to abuse this knowledge; that is, in such schemes it is postulated that the verification-key is not (a priori) known to the adversary. (See Figure 6.1.)

Summary and Terminology. Message-authentication and signature schemes differ in the question of whether the verification-key is "private" (i.e., a secret unknown to the adversary) or "public" (i.e., known to everybody and in particular known to the adversary). Thus, in a sense, these are private-key and public-key versions of a task that

Type	Verification-key known	Verification possible
Message auth. schemes	to the designated (trusted) receiver(s) only	for the designated (trusted) receiver(s) only
Signature schemes	to everybody (including the adversary)	for anybody (including the adversary)

Figure 6.1: Message-authentication versus signature schemes.

lacks a good name (since both authentication and signatures are already taken by one of the two versions). Still, seeking a uniform terminology, we shall sometimes refer to message-authentication schemes (also known as *Message Authentication Codes* [MAC]) as to private-key signature schemes. Analogously, we shall sometimes refer to signature schemes as to public-key signature schemes.

6.1.3. Basic Mechanism

We start by defining the basic *mechanism of message-authentication and signature schemes*. Recall that this basic mechanism will support both the private-key and public-key versions, and the difference between the two versions will only be reflected in the definition of security. Indeed, the definition of the basic mechanism says nothing about the security of the scheme (which is the subject of the next section), and thus is the same for both the private-key and public-key versions. In both cases, the scheme consists of three efficient algorithms: *key generation, signing* (or *authenticating*), and *verification*. The basic requirement is that signatures that are produced by the signing algorithm be accepted as valid by the verification algorithm, when fed a verification-key corresponding to the signing-key used by the signing algorithm.

Definition 6.1.1 (signature scheme): *A* signature scheme *is a triple, (G, S, V), of probabilistic polynomial-time algorithms satisfying the following two conditions:*

1. *On input 1^n, algorithm G (called the* key-generator*) outputs a pair of bit strings.*
2. *For every pair (s, v) in the range of $G(1^n)$, and for every $\alpha \in \{0, 1\}^*$, algorithms S (*signing*) and V (*verification*) satisfy*

$$\Pr[V(v, \alpha, S(s, \alpha)) = 1] = 1$$

where the probability is taken over the internal coin tosses of algorithms S and V.

The integer n serves as the security parameter *of the scheme. Each (s, v) in the range of $G(1^n)$ constitutes a pair of corresponding* signing/verification keys.

We sometimes call $S(s, \alpha)$ a signature to the document α produced using the signing-key s. Likewise, when $V(v, \alpha, \beta) = 1$, we say that β is a valid signature to α with respect to the verification-key v. (Indeed, at this point, we may assume that algorithm V is deterministic, but see subsequent comments.) This definition asserts that any signature to α produced using the signing-key s is a valid signature to α with respect to the corresponding verification-key v. Note that there may be valid signatures (with respect to v) that are not produced by the signing process (using the corresponding s).

We stress that Definition 6.1.1 says nothing about security, and so trivial (i.e., insecure) triples of algorithms may satisfy it (e.g., $S(s, \alpha) \stackrel{\text{def}}{=} 0$ and $V(v, \alpha, \beta) \stackrel{\text{def}}{=} 1$, for all s, v, α and β). Furthermore, Definition 6.1.1 does not distinguish private-key signature schemes from public-key ones. The difference between the two types is introduced in the security definitions: In a public-key scheme, the "adversary" gets the verification-key (i.e., v) as an additional input (and thus $v \neq s$ follows), whereas in private-key schemes, v is not given to the "adversary" (and thus one may assume, without loss of generality, that $v = s$).

Notation. In the rest of this work, we shall write $S_s(\alpha)$ instead of $S(s, \alpha)$ and $V_v(\alpha, \beta)$ instead of $V(v, \alpha, \beta)$. Also, we let $G_1(1^n)$ (resp., $G_2(1^n)$) denote the first (resp., second) element in the pair $G(1^n)$. That is, $G(1^n) = (G_1(1^n), G_2(1^n))$. Without loss of generality, we may assume that $|G_1(1^n)|$ and $|G_2(1^n)|$ are polynomially related to n, and that each of these integers can be efficiently computed from the other.

Comments: A Few Relaxations

Definition 6.1.1 may be relaxed in several ways without significantly harming its usefulness. For example, we may relax Condition (2) and allow a negligible verification error (e.g., $\Pr[V_v(\alpha, S_s(\alpha)) \neq 1] < 2^{-n}$). Alternatively, one may postulate that Condition (2) holds for all but a negligible measure of the key-pairs generated by $G(1^n)$. At least one of these relaxations is essential for many suggestions of (public-key) signature schemes.

Especially in the case where we adopt the first relaxation of Condition (2), it makes sense to consider also randomized verification algorithms. However, all natural signature schemes happen to employ a deterministic verification algorithm (see Exercise 1). Still, in the case of probabilistic verification algorithms, we may define β as a valid signature of α (with respect to v) if $\Pr[V_v(\alpha, \beta) = 1] \geq 1/2$. The threshold $1/2$ used here is quite arbitrary, and the definition is essentially robust under the replacement of $1/2$ by either $1/\mathrm{poly}(n)$ or $1 - 2^{-\mathrm{poly}(n)}$.[1] Alternatively, we may view β as a "fractionally valid" signature of α with respect to v (i.e., valid with probability $\Pr[V_v(\alpha, \beta) = 1]$).

Another relaxation of Definition 6.1.1 consists of restricting the domain of possible documents. However, unlike the situation with respect to encryption schemes, such a restriction is non-trivial in the current context, and is discussed at length in Section 6.2.

6.1.4. Attacks and Security

Loosely speaking, secure signature schemes should prevent an adversary from generating valid signatures to "unauthentic" documents (i.e., documents that were not approved by the legitimate signer). Thus, the potential adversary is "active" at least in the mild sense that it attempts to "generate" something new and different from all that it holds (rather than to "extract" information that is implicit in something that is given to it).[2]

---

[1] Indeed, robustness follows by "amplification" (i.e., error- reduction) of the verification algorithm. For example, given V as here, one may consider V' that applies V to the tested pair for a linear number of times and accepting if and only if V has accepted in all tries.

[2] Indeed, in general, the distinction between "generating something new" and "extracting something implicit" cannot be placed on firm grounds. However, our reference to this distinction is merely at the motivational level. Furthermore, this distinction can be formalized in the context that we care about, which is the context of comparing encryption and signature schemes (or, rather, the adversaries attacking these schemes). In the case of encryption schemes, we consider adversaries that try to extract information about the plaintext from the ciphertext. That is, the desired object is a function of the given input. In contrast, in the case of signature schemes, we consider adversaries that try to generate a valid signature with respect to a certain verification-key. That is, the desired object is not a function of the given input.

Furthermore, the typical applications of signature schemes are to setting in which the adversary may obtain from the legitimate signer valid signatures to some documents of the adversary's choice. For this reason, the basic definition of security of signature schemes refers to such "chosen message attacks" (to be discussed and defined next). (Indeed, the situation here is different from the case of encryption schemes, where the basic definition refers to a "passive" adversary that only wire-taps a communication line, in encrypted form, over this line.)

We shall consider a very strong definition of security (against "chosen message attacks"). That is, we consider very powerful attacks on the signature scheme, as well as a very liberal notion of breaking it. Specifically, during the course of the attack, the attacker is allowed to obtain signatures to *any* document of its choice. One may argue that in many applications, such a general attack is not possible (because, in these applications, documents to be signed must have a specific format). Yet our view is that it is impossible to define a general (i.e., application-independent) notion of admissible documents, and thus a general/robust definition of an attack seems to have to be formulated as suggested here. (Note that at worst, our approach is overly cautious.) Likewise, the attacker is said to be successful if it can produce a valid signature to *any* document for which it has not asked for a signature during its attack. Again, this defines the ability to form signatures to possibly "nonsensical" documents as a breaking of the scheme. Yet, again, we see no way to have a general (i.e., application-independent) notion of "meaningful" documents (so that only forging signatures to them will be considered a breaking of the scheme). This discussion leads to the following (slightly informal) formulation:

- A chosen message attack is a process that can obtain signatures to strings of its choice, relative to some fixed signing-key that is generated by G. We distinguish two cases:

  The private-key case: Here the attacker is given 1^n as input, and the signatures are produced relative to s, where $(s, v) \leftarrow G(1^n)$.

  The public-key case: Here the attacker is given v as input, and the signatures are produced relative to s, where $(s, v) \leftarrow G(1^n)$.

- Such an attack is said to succeed (in existential forgery) if it outputs a valid signature to a string for which it has *not* requested a signature during the attack. That is, the attack is successful if it outputs a pair (α, β) such that $V_v(\alpha, \beta) = 1$ (where v is as in the previous item) and α is different from all strings for which a signature has been required during the attack.

- A signature scheme is secure (or unforgeable) if every feasible chosen message attack succeeds with at most negligible probability.

Formally, a chosen message attack is modeled by a probabilistic polynomial-time oracle machine that is given oracle access to a "keyed signing process" (i.e., the signing algorithm combined with a signing-key). Depending on the version (i.e., public-key or not), the attacker may get the corresponding verification-key as input. We stress that this is the *only* difference between the two cases (i.e., private-key and public-key), which are spelled out in Definition 6.1.2. We refer the reader to the clarifying discussion that follows Definition 6.1.2; in fact, some readers may prefer to read that discussion first.

Definition 6.1.2 (unforgeable signatures): *For a probabilistic oracle machine, M, we denote by $Q_M^O(x)$ the set of queries made by M on input x and access to oracle O. As usual, $M^O(x)$ denotes the output of the corresponding computation. We stress that $Q_M^O(x)$ and $M^O(x)$ are dependent random variables that represents two aspects of the same probabilistic computation.*

The private-key case: *A private-key signature scheme is* secure *if for every probabilistic polynomial-time oracle machine M, every positive polynomial p, and all sufficiently large n, it holds that*

$$\Pr\left[\begin{array}{l} V_v(\alpha, \beta) = 1 \ \& \ \alpha \notin Q_M^{S_s}(1^n) \\ \text{where } (s, v) \leftarrow G(1^n) \ \text{and } (\alpha, \beta) \leftarrow M^{S_s}(1^n) \end{array}\right] < \frac{1}{p(n)}$$

where the probability is taken over the coin tosses of algorithms G, S, and V, as well as over the coin tosses of machine M.

The public-key case: *A public-key signature scheme is* secure *if for every probabilistic polynomial-time oracle machine M, every positive polynomial p, and all sufficiently large n, it holds that*

$$\Pr\left[\begin{array}{l} V_v(\alpha, \beta) = 1 \ \& \ \alpha \notin Q_M^{S_s}(v) \\ \text{where } (s, v) \leftarrow G(1^n) \ \text{and } (\alpha, \beta) \leftarrow M^{S_s}(v) \end{array}\right] < \frac{1}{p(n)}$$

where the probability is taken over the coin tosses of algorithms G, S, and V, as well as over the coin tosses of machine M.

The definition refers to the following experiment. First a pair of keys, (s, v), is generated by invoking $G(1^n)$, and is fixed for the rest of the discussion. Next, an attacker is invoked on input 1^n or v, depending on whether we are in the private-key or public-key case. In both cases, the attacker is given oracle access to S_s, where the latter may be a probabilistic oracle rather than a standard deterministic one (e.g., if queried twice for the same value, then the probabilistic signing-oracle may answer in different ways). Finally, the attacker outputs a pair of strings (α, β). The attacker is deemed successful if and only if the following two conditions hold:

1. The string α is different from all queries (i.e., requests for signatures) made by the attacker; that is, the first string in the output pair $(\alpha, \beta) = M^{S_s}(x)$ is different from any string in $Q_M^{S_s}(x)$, where $x = 1^n$ or $x = v$, depending on whether we are in the private-key or public-key case.
   We stress that both $M^{S_s}(x)$ and $Q_M^{S_s}(x)$ are random variables that are defined based on the *same* random execution of M (on input x and oracle access to S_s).
2. The pair (α, β) corresponds to a valid document-signature pair relative to the verification key v. In case V is deterministic (which is typically the case) this means that

$V_v(\alpha, \beta) = 1$. The same applies also in case V is probabilistic, and when viewing $V_v(\alpha, \beta) = 1$ as a random variable. (Alternatively, in the latter case, a condition such as $\Pr[V_v(\alpha, \beta) = 1] \geq 1/2$ may replace the condition $V_v(\alpha, \beta) = 1$.)

6.1.5.* Variants

Clearly, any signature scheme that is secure in the public-key model is also secure in the private-key model. The converse is not true: Consider, for example, the private-key scheme presented in Construction 6.3.1 (as well as any other "natural" message-authentication scheme). Following are a few other comments regarding the definitions.

6.1.5.1. Augmenting the Attack with a Verification Oracle

It is natural to augment Definition 6.1.2 by providing the adversary with unlimited access to the corresponding verification-oracle V_v. We stress that (in this augmented definition) the documents that (only) appear in the verification queries are not added to the set $Q_M^{S_s}$; that is, the output (α, β) is considered a successful forgery even if the adversary made a *verification-query* of the form $(\alpha, \cdot)$, but provided (as in Definition 6.1.2) that the adversary did not make the *signing-query* α (and that $V_v(\alpha, \beta) = 1$).

Indeed, in the public-key case, the verification-oracle adds no power to the adversary, because the adversary (which is given the verification-key) can emulate the verification-oracle by itself. Furthermore, *typically*, also in the private-key model, the verification-oracle does not add much power. Specifically, we have:

Proposition 6.1.3 (cases in which security extends to the augmented model):

1. *Any secure* public-key *signature scheme is secure also under attacks that utilize a verification-oracle (in addition to the signing-oracle).*
2. *Any secure* private-key *signature scheme that has unique valid signatures* (as defined next) *is secure also under attacks that utilize a verification-oracle (in addition to the signing-oracle).*

A signature scheme (G, S, V) is said to have unique valid signatures if for every verification-key v and document α, there exists a unique β such that $V_v(\alpha, \beta) = 1$ (or, such that $\Pr[V_v(\alpha, \beta) = 1] > 1/poly(|v|)$). As discussed in Section 6.5.1 (see also Exercises 1 and 2), any secure private-key signature scheme can be transformed into one having a deterministic verification algorithm and unique valid signatures. In fact, all private-key signature schemes presented in Section 6.3 have unique valid signatures. We comment that the unique signature property is essential for the validity of Part 2; see Exercise 3.

Proof Sketch: As stated previously, Part 1 is obvious (because a standard adversary can emulate the verification-oracle by using the verification-key given to it). We prove Part 2 by showing that also in that case, a standard adversary can emulate the verification-oracle. However, in this case, the emulation is less obvious, because the standard adversary cannot test the validity of signatures by itself. Still, considering an arbitrary combined attack on such a private-key signature scheme, we emulate the verification-queries (in the standard model) as follows:

- For a verification-query (α, β), if α equals a previous signing-query, then we can emulate the answer by ourselves. Specifically, if the signing-query α was answered with β, then we answer the verification-query positively; otherwise we answer it negatively. The correctness of the emulation follows from the hypothesis that this signature scheme has unique valid signatures.
- Otherwise (i.e., for a verification-query (α, β) such that α does not equal any previous signing-query), we may choose to either halt and output (α, β) as a candidate forgery (gambling on $V_v(\alpha, \beta) = 1$) or continue and emulate a negative answer by ourselves (gambling on $V_v(\alpha, \beta) = 0$). Specifically, for every such verification-query, we may choose the first possibility with probability $1/t(n)$ and the second possibility otherwise, where $t(n)$ is a bound on the number of verification-queries performed by the original augmented attack (which we emulate). It can be shown that the success probability of the resulting standard adversary is at least a $1/t(n)$ fraction of the success probability of the given adversary. For details see Exercise 3.

Thus, insecurity in the augmented model implies insecurity in the original model, and the proposition follows. ∎

6.1.5.2. Inessential Generalities

The definitions presented here (specifically, Definition 6.1.1) were aimed at generality and flexibility. We comment that several levels of freedom can be eliminated without loss of generality (but with some loss of convenience). Firstly, as in the case of encryption schemes, one may modify the key-generation algorithm so that on input 1^n it outputs a pair of n-bit long keys. Two more fundamental restrictions, which actually do not affect the existence of secure schemes, follow.

Randomization in the Signing Process. In contrast to the situation with respect to encryption schemes (see Sections 5.2 and 5.3), randomization is not essential to the actual signing and verifying processes (but is, as usual, essential to key-generation). That is, without loss of generality (but with possible loss in efficiency), the signing algorithm may be *deterministic,* and in all of the schemes we present (in the current chapter), the verification algorithm is deterministic. For further discussion, see Exercise 1.

Canonical Verification in the Private-Key Version. As hinted earlier, in the private-key case, we may just identify the signing and verification keys (i.e., $k \stackrel{\text{def}}{=} s = v$). Furthermore (following the comment about deterministic signing), without loss of generality, verification may amount to comparing the alleged signature to one produced by the verification algorithm itself (which may just produce signatures exactly as the signing algorithm). That is, for a deterministic signing process S_k, we may let $V_k(\alpha, \beta) \stackrel{\text{def}}{=} 1$ if and only if $\beta = S_k(\alpha)$. For details, see Exercise 2.

6.1.5.3. Weaker Notions of Security and Some Popular Schemes

Weaker notions of security have been considered in the literature. The various notions refer to two parameters: (1) the type of attack, and (2) when the adversary is considered to be successful. Indeed, Definition 6.1.2 refers to the most severe type of attacks (i.e., unrestricted chosen message attacks) and to the most liberal notion of success (i.e., the ability to produce a valid signature to any new message). For further discussion, the interested reader is referred to Section 6.6.3. In particular, we note that *plain RSA*, as well as plain versions of Rabin's scheme and the DSS, are *not* secure under Definition 6.1.2. However, these schemes satisfy weaker notions of security, provided that some (standard) intractability assumptions hold. Furthermore, variants of these signature schemes (in which the function is not applied directly to the document itself) may be secure (under Definition 6.1.2).

6.2. Length-Restricted Signature Scheme

Restricted types of (public-key and private-key) signature schemes play an important role in our exposition. The first restriction we consider is the restriction of signature schemes to (apply only to) documents of a certain predetermined length. We call the resulting schemes length-restricted. The effect of the length-restriction is more dramatic here (in the context of signature schemes) than it is in the context of encryption schemes; this can be appreciated by comparing (the length of) Section 6.2.2 to (the length of) Section 5.3.2.2. Nevertheless, as we shall show (see Theorem 6.2.2), if the length restriction is not too low, then the full power of signature schemes can be regained; that is, length-restricted signature schemes yield full-fledged ones.

6.2.1. Definition

The essence of the length-restriction is that security is guaranteed only with respect to documents of the predetermined length. Note that the question of what is the result of invoking the signature algorithm on a document of improper length is immaterial. What is important is that an attacker (of a length-restricted scheme) is deemed successful only if it produces a signature *to a* (different) *document of proper length*. Still, for the sake of concreteness (and simplicity of subsequent treatment), we define the basic mechanism only for documents of proper length.

Definition 6.2.1 (signature scheme for fixed-length documents): *Let $\ell : \mathbb{N} \to \mathbb{N}$. An ℓ-restricted signature scheme is a triple, (G, S, V), of probabilistic polynomial-time algorithms satisfying the following two conditions:*

1. *As in Definition 6.1.1, on input 1^n, algorithm G outputs a pair of bit strings.*
2. *Analogously to Definition 6.1.1, for every n and every pair (s, v) in the range of $G(1^n)$, and for every $\alpha \in \{0, 1\}^{\ell(n)}$, algorithms S and V satisfy $\Pr[V_v(\alpha, S_s(\alpha)) = 1] = 1$.*

Such a scheme is called secure (*in the private-key or public-key model*) *if the* (corresponding) *requirements of Definition 6.1.2 hold when restricted to attackers that only make queries of length* $\ell(n)$ *and output a pair* (α, β) *with* $|\alpha| = \ell(n)$.

We stress that the essential modification is presented in the security condition. The latter considers an adversary to be successful only in case it forges a signature to a (different) document α *of the proper length* (i.e., $|\alpha| = \ell(n)$).

6.2.2. The Power of Length-Restricted Signature Schemes

We comment that ℓ-restricted private-key signature schemes for $\ell(n) = O(\log n)$ are trivial (since the signing and verification keys may contain a table look-up associating a secret with each of the $2^{\ell(n)} = \text{poly}(n)$ possible documents).[3] In contrast, this triviality does not hold for public-key signature schemes. (For details on both claims, see Exercise 5.) On the other hand, in both (private-key and public-key) cases, ℓ-restricted signature schemes for any super-logarithmic ℓ (e.g., $\ell(n) = n$ or even $\ell(n) = \log_2^2 n$) are as powerful as ordinary signature schemes:

Theorem 6.2.2: *Suppose that ℓ is a super-logarithmically growing function. Then, given an ℓ-restricted signature scheme that is secure in the private-key* (resp., public-key) *model, one can construct a full-fledged signature scheme that is secure in the same model.*

Results of this flavor can be established in two different ways, corresponding to two methods of converting an ℓ-restricted signature scheme into a full-fledged one. Both methods are applicable both to private-key and public-key signature schemes. The first method (presented in Section 6.2.2.1) consists of parsing the original document into blocks (with *adequate* "linkage" between blocks), and applying the ℓ-restricted scheme to each block. The second method (presented in Section 6.2.2.2) consists of hashing the document into an $\ell(n)$-bit long value (via an *adequate* hashing scheme), and applying the restricted scheme to the resulting value. Thus, the second method requires an additional assumption (i.e., the existence of "collision-free" hashing), and so Theorem 6.2.2 (as stated) is actually proved using the first method. The second method is presented because it offers other benefits; in particular, *it yields signatures of fixed length* (i.e., the signature-length only depends on the key-length) and *uses a single invocation of the restricted scheme*. The latter feature will play an important role in subsequent sections (e.g., in Sections 6.3.1.2 and 6.4.1.3).

6.2.2.1. Signing (Augmented) Blocks

In this subsection we present a simple method for constructing general signature schemes out of length-restricted ones, and in doing so we establish Theorem 6.2.2.

---

[3] Recall that such triviality does not hold in the context of encryption schemes, not even in the private-key case. See Section 5.3.2.

Loosely speaking, the method consists of parsing the original document into blocks (with *adequate* "linkage" between blocks), and applying the length-restricted scheme to each (augmented) block.

Let ℓ and (G, S, V) be as in Theorem 6.2.2. We construct a general signature scheme, (G', S', V'), with $G' = G$, by viewing documents as sequences of strings, each of length $\ell'(n) = \ell(n)/O(1)$. That is, we associate $\alpha = \alpha_1 \cdots \alpha_t$ with the sequence $(\alpha_1, ..., \alpha_t)$, where each α_i has length $\ell'(n)$. (At this point, the reader may think of $\ell'(n) = \ell(n)$, but actually we will use $\ell'(n) = \ell(n)/4$ in order to make room for some auxiliary information.)

To motivate the actual construction, we consider first the following simpler schemes all aimed at producing secure signatures for arbitrary (documents viewed as) sequences of $\ell'(n)$-bit long strings. The simplest scheme consists of *just signing each of the strings in the sequence*. That is, the signature to the sequence $(\alpha_1, ..., \alpha_t)$, is a sequence of β_i's, each being a signature (with respect to the length-restricted scheme) to the corresponding α_i. This will not do, because an adversary, given the (single) signature (β_1, β_2) to the sequence (α_1, α_2) with $\alpha_1 \neq \alpha_2$, can present (β_2, β_1) as a valid signature to $(\alpha_2, \alpha_1) \neq (\alpha_1, \alpha_2)$. So how about foiling this forgery by preventing a reordering of the "atomic" signatures (i.e., the β_i's); that is, how about signing the sequence $(\alpha_1, ..., \alpha_t)$ by applying the restricted scheme to each pair (i, α_i), rather than to α_i itself? This will not do either, because an adversary, given a signature to the sequence $(\alpha_1, \alpha_2, \alpha_3)$, can easily present a signature to the sequence (α_1, α_2). So we also need to include in each $\ell(n)$-bit string the total number of α_i's in the sequence. But even this is not enough, because given signatures to the sequences (α_1, α_2) and (α_1', α_2'), with $\alpha_1 \neq \alpha_1'$ and $\alpha_2 \neq \alpha_2'$, an adversary can easily generate a signature to (α_1, α_2'). Thus, we have to prevent the forming of new sequences of "basic signatures" by combining elements from different signature sequences. This can be done by associating (say, at random) an identifier with each sequence and incorporating this identifier in each $\ell(n)$-bit string to which the basic (restricted) signature scheme is applied. This discussion yields the signature scheme presented next, where a signature to a message $(\alpha_1, ..., \alpha_t)$ consists of a sequence of (basic) signatures to statements of the (effective) form *"the string α_i is the i-th block, out of t blocks, in a message associate with identifier r."*

Construction 6.2.3 (signing augmented blocks): *Let ℓ and (G, S, V) be as in Theorem 6.2.2. We construct a general signature scheme, (G', S', V'), with $G' = G$, by considering documents as sequences of strings. We construct S' and V' as follows, using $G' = G$ and $\ell'(n) = \ell(n)/4$:*

Signing with S': *On input a signing-key s (in the range of $G_1(1^n)$) and a document $\alpha \in \{0, 1\}^*$, algorithm S' first parses α into a sequence of blocks $(\alpha_1, ..., \alpha_t)$, such that α is uniquely reconstructed from the α_i's and each α_i is an $\ell'(n)$-bit long string.*[4]

---

[4] The *parsing rule* should apply to strings of arbitrary length, regardless of whether or not this length is a multiple of $\ell'(n)$. For example, we may parse α as $(\alpha_1, ..., \alpha_t)$ such that $\alpha_1 \cdots \alpha_t = \alpha \cdot 10^j$ and $j \in \{0, 1, ..., \ell'(n) - 1\}$. (Note that under this parsing rule, if $|\alpha|$ is a multiple of $\ell'(n)$, then $|\alpha_1 \cdots \alpha_t| = |\alpha| + \ell'(n)$.)

Next, S' uniformly selects $r \in \{0, 1\}^{\ell'(n)}$. For $i = 1, ..., t$, algorithm S' computes

$$\beta_i \leftarrow S_s(r, t, i, \alpha_i)$$

where i and t are represented as $\ell'(n)$-bit long strings. That is, β_i is essentially a signature to the statement "α_i is the i-th block, out of t blocks, in a sequence associate with identifier r." Finally, S' outputs as signature the sequence

$$(r, t, \beta_1, ..., \beta_t)$$

Verification with V': On input a verifying-key v (in the range of $G_2(1^n)$), a document $\alpha \in \{0, 1\}^*$, and a sequence $(r, t, \beta_1, ..., \beta_t)$, algorithm V' first parses α into $\alpha_1, ..., \alpha_{t'}$, using the same parsing rule as used by S'. Algorithm V' accepts if and only if the following two conditions hold:

1. *$t' = t$, where t' is obtained in the parsing of α and t is part of the alleged signature.*
2. *For $i = 1, ..., t$, it holds that $V_v((r, t, i, \alpha_i), \beta_i) = 1$, where α_i is obtained in the parsing of α and the rest are as in the corresponding parts of the alleged signature.*

Clearly, the triplet (G', S', V') satisfies Definition 6.1.1. We need to show that is also inherits the security of (G, S, V). That is:

Proposition 6.2.4: *Suppose that (G, S, V) is an ℓ-restricted signature scheme that is secure in the private-key (resp., public-key) model. Then (G', S', V'), as defined in Construction 6.2.3, is a full-fledged signature scheme that is secure in the private-key (resp., public-key) model.*

Theorem 6.2.2 follows immediately from Proposition 6.2.4.

Proof: Intuitively, ignoring the unlikely case that two messages signed by S'_s were assigned the same random identifier, a forged signature with respect to (G', S', V') must contain some S_s-signature that was not contained in any of the S'_s-signatures (provided in the attack). Thus, forgery with respect to (G', S', V') yields forgery with respect to (G, S, V). Indeed, the proof is by a reducibility argument, and it holds for both the private-key and the public-key models.

Given an adversary A' attacking the complex scheme (G', S', V'), we construct an adversary A that attacks the ℓ-restricted scheme, (G, S, V). In particular, A invokes A' with input identical to its own input (which is the security parameter or the verification-key, depending on the model), and uses its own oracle in order to emulate the oracle S'_s for A'. This can be done in a straightforward manner; that is, algorithm A will act as S'_s does by using the oracle S_s. Specifically, A parses each query α' of A' into a corresponding sequence $(\alpha'_1, ..., \alpha'_{t'})$, uniformly selects an identifier r', and obtains S_s-signatures to (r', t', j, α'_j), for $j = 1, ..., t'$. When A' outputs a document-signature pair relative to the complex scheme (G', S', V'), algorithm A tries to use this pair in order to form a document-signature pair relative to the ℓ-restricted scheme, (G, S, V).

We stress that from the point of view of adversary A', the distribution of keys and oracle answers that A provides it with is exactly as in a real attack on (G', S', V').

This is a crucial point, because we use the fact that events that occur in a real attack of A' on (G', S', V') occur with the same probability in the emulation of (G', S', V') by A.

Assume that with (non-negligible) probability $\varepsilon'(n)$, the (probabilistic polynomial-time) algorithm A' succeeds in existentially forging relative to the complex scheme (G', S', V'). We consider the following cases regarding the forging event:

1. The identifier supplied in the forged signature is different from all the random identifiers supplied (by A) as part of the signatures given to A'. In this case, each ℓ-restricted valid signature supplied as part of the forged (complex) signature yields existential forgery relative to the ℓ-restricted scheme.

   Formally, let $\alpha^{(1)}, ..., \alpha^{(m)}$ be the sequence of queries made by A', and let $(r^{(1)}, t^{(1)}, \overline{\beta}^{(1)}), ..., (r^{(m)}, t^{(m)}, \overline{\beta}^{(m)})$ be the corresponding (complex) signatures supplied to A' by A (using S_s to form the $\overline{\beta}^{(i)}$'s). It follows that each $\overline{\beta}^{(i)}$ consists of a sequence of S_s-signatures to $\ell(n)$-bit strings starting with $r^{(i)} \in \{0, 1\}^{\ell(n)/4}$, and that the oracle S_s was invoked (by A) only on strings of this form. Let $(\alpha, (r, t, \beta_1, ..., \beta_t))$ be the output of A', where α is parsed as $(\alpha_1, ..., \alpha_t)$, and suppose that applying V'_v to the output of A' yields 1 (i.e., the output is a valid document-signature pair for the complex scheme). The case hypothesis states that $r \neq r^{(i)}$, for all i's. It follows that each of the β_j's is an S_s-signature to a string starting with $r \in \{0, 1\}^{\ell(n)/4}$, and thus different from all queries made to the oracle S_s. Thus, each pair $((r, t, i, \alpha_i), \beta_i)$ is a valid document-signature pair (because $V'_v(\alpha, (r, t, \beta_1, ..., \beta_t)) = 1$ implies $V_v((r, t, i, \alpha_i), \beta_i) = 1$), with a document different from all queries made to S_s. This yields a successful forgery with respect to the ℓ-restricted scheme.

2. The identifier supplied in the forged signature equals the random identifier supplied (by A) as part of *exactly one* of the signatures given to A'. In this case, existential forgery relative to the ℓ-restricted scheme is obtained by considering the relation between the output of A' and the single supplied signature having the same identifier.

   As in the previous case, let $\alpha^{(1)}, ..., \alpha^{(m)}$ be the sequence of queries made by A', and let $(r^{(1)}, t^{(1)}, \overline{\beta}^{(1)}), ..., (r^{(m)}, t^{(m)}, \overline{\beta}^{(m)})$ be the corresponding (complex) signatures supplied to A' by A. Let $(\alpha, (r, t, \beta_1, ..., \beta_t))$ be the output of A', where α is parsed as $(\alpha_1, ..., \alpha_t)$, and suppose that $\alpha \neq \alpha^{(i)}$ for all i's and that $V'_v(\alpha, (r, t, \beta_1, ..., \beta_t)) = 1$. The hypothesis of the current case is that there exists a unique i so that $r = r^{(i)}$. We consider two subcases regarding the relation between t and $t^{(i)}$:

   - $t \neq t^{(i)}$. In this subcase, each ℓ-restricted signature supplied as part of the forged (complex) signature yields existential forgery relative to the ℓ-restricted scheme. The argument is analogous to the one employed in the previous case. Specifically, here each of the β_j's is an S_s-signature to a string starting with (r, t), and thus different from all queries made to the oracle S_s (because these queries either start with $r^{(i')} \neq r$ or start with $(r^{(i)}, t^{(i)}) \neq (r, t)$). Thus, each pair $((r, t, j, \alpha_j), \beta_j)$ is a valid document-signature pair with a document different from all queries made to S_s.
   - $t = t^{(i)}$. In this subcase, we use the hypothesis $\alpha \neq \alpha^{(i)}$, which (combined with $t = t^{(i)}$) implies that there exists a j such that $\alpha_j \neq \alpha_j^{(i)}$, where $\alpha_j^{(i)}$ is the jth

block in the parsing of $\alpha^{(i)}$. For this j, the string β_j (supplied as part of the forged complex-signature) yields existential forgery relative to the ℓ-restricted scheme. Specifically, we have $V_v((r, t, j, \alpha_j), \beta_j) = 1$, whereas (r, t, j, α_j) is different from each query $(r^{(i')}, t^{(i')}, j', \alpha_{j'}^{(i')})$ made by A to S_s.

> Justification for $(r, t, j, \alpha_j) \neq (r^{(i')}, t^{(i')}, j', \alpha_{j'}^{(i')})$: In case $i' \neq i$, it must hold that $r^{(i')} \neq r$ (by the [Case 2] hypothesis regarding the uniqueness of i s.t. $r^{(i)} = r$). Otherwise (i.e., in case $i' = i$), either $j' \neq j$ or $\alpha_{j'}^{(i')} = \alpha_j^{(i)} \neq \alpha_j$, where the inequality is due to the hypothesis regarding j.

Thus, $((r, t, j, \alpha_j), \beta_j)$ is a valid document-signature pair with a document different from all queries made to S_s.

3. The identifier supplied in the forged signature equals the random identifiers supplied (by A) as part of *at least two* signatures given to A'. In particular, it follows that two signatures given to A use the same random identifier. The probability that this event occurs is at most

$$\binom{m}{2} \cdot 2^{-\ell'(n)} < m^2 \cdot 2^{-\ell(n)/4}$$

However, $m = \text{poly}(n)$ (since A' runs in polynomial-time), and $2^{-\ell(n)/4}$ is negligible (since ℓ is super-logarithmic). So this case occurs with negligible probability and may be ignored.

Note that A can easily determine which of the cases occurs and act accordingly.[5] Thus, assuming that A' forges relative to the complex scheme with non-negligible probability $\varepsilon'(n)$, it follows that A forges relative to the length-restricted scheme with non-negligible probability $\varepsilon(n) \geq \varepsilon'(n) - \text{poly}(n) \cdot 2^{-\ell(n)/4}$, in contradiction to the proposition's hypothesis. ∎

Comment. We call the reader's attention to the essential role of the hypothesis that ℓ is super-logarithmic in the proof of Proposition 6.2.4. Indeed, Construction 6.2.3 is insecure in case $\ell(n) = O(\log n)$. The reason is that by asking for polynomially many signatures, the adversary may obtain two S_s'-signatures that use the same (random) identifier. Furthermore, with some care, these signatures yield existential forgery (see Exercise 6).

6.2.2.2. Signing a Hash Value

In this subsection, we present an alternative method for constructing general signature schemes out of length-restricted ones. Loosely speaking, the method consists of hashing the document into a short (fixed-length) string (via an adequate hashing scheme), and applying the length-restricted signature scheme to the resulting hash-value. This two-stage process is referred to as the hash and sign paradigm.

---

[5] This observation only saves us a polynomial factor in the forging probability. That is, if A did not know which part of the forged complex-signature to use for its own forgery, it could have just selected one at random (and be correct with probability $1/\text{poly}(n)$ because there are only $\text{poly}(n)$-many possibilities).

Let ℓ and (G, S, V) be as in Theorem 6.2.2. The second method of constructing a general signature scheme out of (G, S, V) consists of first hashing the document into an $\ell(n)$-bit long value and then applying the ℓ-restricted scheme to the hashed value. Thus, in addition to an ℓ-restricted scheme, this method employs an adequate hashing scheme. In particular, one way of implementing this method is based on "collision-free hashing" (defined next). An alternative implementation, based on "universal one-way hashing," is deferred to Section 6.4.3.

Collision-Free Hashing Functions. Loosely speaking, a *collision-free hashing scheme* (aka *a collision-resistent hashing scheme*) consists of a collection of functions $\{h_s : \{0, 1\}^* \to \{0, 1\}^{|s|}\}_{s \in \{0,1\}^*}$ such that given s and x it is easy to compute $h_s(x)$, but given a random s it is hard to find $x \neq x'$ such that $h_s(x) = h_s(x')$.

Definition 6.2.5 (collision-free hashing functions): *Let $\ell : \mathbb{N} \to \mathbb{N}$. A collection of functions $\{h_s : \{0, 1\}^* \to \{0, 1\}^{\ell(|s|)}\}_{s \in \{0,1\}^*}$ is called* collision-free hashing *if there exists a probabilistic polynomial-time algorithm I such that the following holds:*

1. *(admissible indexing – technical):*[6] *For some polynomial p, all sufficiently large n's, and every s in the range of $I(1^n)$, it holds that $n \leq p(|s|)$. Furthermore, n can be computed in polynomial-time from s.*
2. *(efficient evaluation): There exists a polynomial-time algorithm that, given s and x, returns $h_s(x)$.*
3. *(hard-to-form collisions): We say that the pair (x, x') forms a* collision under the function h *if $h(x) = h(x')$ but $x \neq x'$. We require that every probabilistic polynomial-time algorithm, given $I(1^n)$ as input, outputs a collision under $h_{I(1^n)}$ with negligible probability. That is, for every probabilistic polynomial-time algorithm A, every positive polynomial p, and all sufficiently large n's,*

$$\Pr\left[A(I(1^n)) \text{ is a collision under } h_{I(1^n)}\right] < \frac{1}{p(n)}$$

where the probability is taken over the internal coin tosses of algorithms I and A.

The function ℓ is called the range specifier *of the collection.*

Note that the range specifier must be super-logarithmic (or else one may easily find a collision by selecting $2^{\ell(n)} + 1$ different pre-images and computing their image under the function). In Section 6.2.3, we show how to construct collision-free hashing functions using claw-free collections. But first, we show how to use the former in order to convert a length-restricted signature scheme into a full-fledged one.

---

[6] This condition is made merely in order to avoid annoying technicalities. In particular, this condition allows the collision-forming adversary to run for poly(n)-time (because by this condition $n = $ poly($|s|$)), as well as allows for determining n from s. Note that $|s| = $ poly(n) holds by definition of I.

Construction 6.2.6 (hash and sign): *Let ℓ and (G, S, V) be as in Theorem 6.2.2, and let $\{h_r : \{0, 1\}^* \to \{0, 1\}^{\ell(|r|)}\}_{r \in \{0,1\}^*}$ be as in Definition 6.2.5. We construct a general signature scheme, (G', S', V'), as follows:*

Key-generation with G': *On input 1^n, algorithm G' first invokes G to obtain $(s, v) \leftarrow G(1^n)$. Next, it invokes I, the indexing algorithm of the collision-free hashing collection, to obtain $r \leftarrow I(1^n)$. Finally, G' outputs the pair $((r, s), (r, v))$, where (r, s) serves as a signing-key and (r, v) serves as a verification-key.*

Signing with S': *On input a signing-key (r, s) (in the range of $G_1'(1^n)$) and a document $\alpha \in \{0, 1\}^*$, algorithm S' invokes S once to produce and output $S_s(h_r(\alpha))$.*

Verification with V': *On input a verifying-key (r, v) (in the range of $G_2'(1^n)$), a document $\alpha \in \{0, 1\}^*$, and an alleged signature β, algorithm V' invokes V and outputs $V_v(h_r(\alpha), \beta)$.*

Note that the resulting signature scheme applies the original one once (per each invocation of the resulting scheme). We stress that the length of resulting signatures only depend on the length of the signing-key and is independent of the document being signed; that is, $|S'_{r,s}(\alpha)| = |S_s(h_r(\alpha))|$, which in turn is bounded by $\text{poly}(|s|, \ell(|r|))$.

Proposition 6.2.7: *Suppose that (G, S, V) is an ℓ-restricted signature scheme that is secure in the private-key (resp., public-key) model. Suppose that $\{h_r : \{0, 1\}^* \to \{0, 1\}^{\ell(|r|)}\}_{r \in \{0,1\}^*}$ is indeed a collision-free hashing collection. Then (G', S', V'), as defined in Construction 6.2.6, is a full-fledged signature scheme that is secure in the private-key (resp., public-key) model.*

Proof: Intuitively, the security of (G', S', V') follows from the security of (G, S, V) and the collision-freeness property of the collection $\{h_r\}$. Specifically, forgery relative to (G', S', V') can be obtained either by a forged S-signature to a hash-value different from all hash-values that appeared in the attack or by forming a collision under the hash function. The actual proof is by a reducibility argument. Given an adversary A' attacking the complex scheme (G', S', V'), we construct an adversary A that attacks the ℓ-restricted scheme, (G, S, V), as well as an algorithm B forming collisions under the hashing collection $\{h_r\}$. Both A and B will have running time related to that of A'. We show if A' is successful with non-negligible probability, than the same holds for either A or B. Thus, in either case, we reach a contradiction. We start with the description of algorithm A, which is designed to attack the ℓ-restricted scheme (G, S, V). We stress that almost the same description applies in both the private-key and public-key case.

On input x, which equals the security parameter 1^n in the private-key case and a verification-key v otherwise (i.e., in the public-key case), the adversary A operates as follows. First, A uses I (the indexing algorithm of the collision-free hashing collection) to obtain $r \leftarrow I(1^n)$, exactly as done in the second step of G'. Next, A invokes A' (on input 1^n or (r, v), depending on the case) and uses r as well as its own oracle S_s in order to emulate the oracle $S'_{r,s}$ for A'. The emulation is done in a straightforward manner; that is, algorithm A will act as $S'_{r,s}$ does by using the oracle S_s (i.e., to answer query q, algorithm A makes the query $h_r(q)$). When A' outputs a document-signature pair relative to the complex scheme (G', S', V'), algorithm A tries to use this pair in order to form a document-signature pair relative to the ℓ-restricted scheme, (G, S, V). That is, if A' outputs the document-signature pair (α, β), then A will output the document-signature pair $(h_r(\alpha), \beta)$.

As in the proof of Proposition 6.2.4, we stress that the distribution of keys and oracle answers that A provides A' is exactly as in a real attack of A' on (G', S', V'). This is a crucial point, because we use the fact that events that occur in a real attack of A' on (G', S', V') occur with the same probability in the emulation of (G', S', V') by A.

Assume that with (non-negligible) probability $\varepsilon'(n)$, the (probabilistic polynomial-time) algorithm A' succeeds in existentially forging relative to the complex scheme (G', S', V'). We consider the following two cases regarding the forging event, letting $(\alpha^{(i)}, \beta^{(i)})$ denote the i-th query and answer pair made by A', and (α, β) denote the forged document-signature pair that A' outputs (in case of success):

Case 1: $h_r(\alpha) \neq h_r(\alpha^{(i)})$ for all i's. (That is, the hash-value used in the forged signature is different from all hash-values used in the queries to S_s.) In this case, the pair $(h_r(\alpha), \beta)$ constitutes a success in existential forgery relative to the ℓ-restricted scheme.

Case 2: $h_r(\alpha) = h_r(\alpha^{(i)})$ for some i. (That is, the hash-value used in the forged signature equals the hash-value used in the i-th query to S_s, although $\alpha \neq \alpha^{(i)}$.) In this case, the pair $(\alpha, \alpha^{(i)})$ forms a collision under h_r (and we do *not* obtain success in existential forgery relative to the ℓ-restricted scheme).

Thus, if Case 1 occurs with probability at least $\varepsilon'(n)/2$, then A succeeds in its attack on (G, S, V) with probability at least $\varepsilon'(n)/2$, which contradicts the security of the ℓ-restricted scheme (G, S, V). On the other hand, if Case 2 occurs with probability at least $\varepsilon'(n)/2$, then we derive a contradiction to the collision-freeness of the hashing collection $\{h_r : \{0, 1\}^* \to \{0, 1\}^{\ell(|r|)}\}_{r \in \{0,1\}^*}$. Details (regarding the second case) follow.

We construct an algorithm, denoted B, that given $r \leftarrow I(1^n)$, attempts to form collisions under h_r as follows. On input r, algorithm B generates $(s, v) \leftarrow G(1^n)$ and emulates the attack of A on this instance of the ℓ-restricted scheme, with the exception that B does not invoke algorithm I to obtain an index of a hash function but rather uses the index r (given to it as input). Recall that A, in turn, emulates an attack of A' on the signing-oracle $S'_{r,s}$, and that A answers the query q' made by A' by forwarding the query $q = h_r(q')$ to S_s. Thus, B actually emulates the attack of A' (on the signing-oracle $S'_{r,s}$) and does so in a straightforward manner; that is, to answer query q' made by A', algorithm B first obtains $q = h_r(q')$ (using its knowledge of r) and then answers with $S_s(q)$ (using its knowledge of s). Finally, when A' outputs a forged document-signature pair, algorithm B checks whether Case 2 occurs (i.e., whether $h_r(\alpha) = h_r(\alpha^{(i)})$ holds for some i), in which case it obtains (and outputs) a collision under h_r. (Note that in the public-key case, B invokes A' on input (r, v), whereas in the private-key case, B invokes A' on input 1^n. Thus, in the private-key case, B actually does not use r but rather only uses an oracle access to h_r.)

We stress that from the point of view of the emulated adversary A, the execution is distributed exactly as in its attack on (G, S, V). Thus, since we assumed that the second case occurs with probability at least $\varepsilon'(n)/2$ in a real attack, it follows that B succeeds in forming a collision under $h_{I(1^n)}$ with probability at least $\varepsilon'(n)/2$. This contradicts the collision-freeness of the hashing functions, and the proposition follows. ∎

Comment. For the private-key case, the proof of Proposition 6.2.7 actually established a stronger claim than stated. Specifically, the proof holds even for a weaker definition of collision-free hashing in which the adversary is *not* given a description of the hashing function, but can rather obtain its value at any pre-image of its choice. This observation is further pursued in Section 6.3.1.3.

On Using the Hash-and-Sign Paradigm in Practice. The *hash-and-sign paradigm*, underlying Construction 6.2.6, is often used in practice. Specifically, a document is signed using a two-stage process: First, the document is hashed into a (relatively) short bit string, and next, a basic signature scheme is applied to the resulting string. One appealing feature of this process is that the length of resulting signatures only depends on the length of the signing-key (and is independent of the document being signed). We stress that this process yields a secure signature scheme only if the hashing scheme is *collision-free* (as defined previously). In Section 6.2.3, we present several constructions of collision-free hashing functions (based on general assumptions). Alternatively, one may indeed postulate that certain off-the-shelf products (such as MD5 or SHA) are collision-free, but such assumptions need to be seriously examined (and indeed may turn out false).[7] We stress that using a hashing scheme, in the two-stage (hash-and-sign) process, without seriously evaluating whether or not it is collision-free is a very dangerous practice.

We comment that a variant on the hash-and-sign paradigm will be presented in Construction 6.4.30. The two variants are compared in Section 6.4.3.4.

6.2.3.* Constructing Collision-Free Hashing Functions

In view of the relevance of collision-free hashing to signature schemes, we now take a small detour from the main topic and consider the construction of collision-free hashing. Most importantly, we show how to construct collision-free hashing functions using a claw-free collection of permutations. In addition, we show two different constructions that use a restricted type of collision-free hashing in order to obtain full-fledged collision-free hashing.

6.2.3.1. A Construction Based on Claw-Free Permutations

In this subsection, we show how to construct collision-free hashing functions using a claw-free collection of permutations as defined in Section 2.4.5 of Volume 1. Recall that such a collection consists of pairs of permutations, (f_s^0, f_s^1), such that both f_s^σ's

---

[7] See, for example, [76].

are permutations over a set D_s, augmented with a probabilistic polynomial-time index selection algorithm I such that the following conditions hold:

1. *The domain is easy to sample:* There exists a probabilistic polynomial-time algorithm that, given s, outputs a string uniformly distributed over D_s.
2. *The permutations are easy to evaluate:* There exists a polynomial-time algorithm that, given s, σ and $x \in D_s$, outputs $f_s^\sigma(x)$.
3. *It is hard to form claws:* Every probabilistic polynomial-time algorithm, given $s \leftarrow I(1^n)$, outputs a pair (x, y) such that $f_s^0(x) = f_s^1(y)$ with at most negligible probability. That is, a pair (x, y) satisfying $f_s^0(x) = f_s^1(y)$ is called a claw for index s. (We stress that $x = y$ may hold.) Then, it is required that for every probabilistic polynomial-time algorithm, A', every positive polynomial $p(\cdot)$, and all sufficiently large n's

$$\Pr\left[A'(I(1^n)) \in C_{I(1^n)}\right] < \frac{1}{p(n)}$$

where C_s denote the set of claws for index s.

Note that since f_s^0 and f_s^1 are permutations over the same set, many claws do exists (i.e., $|C_s| = |D_s|$). However, the third condition postulates that for s generated by $I(1^n)$, such claws are hard to find. We may assume, without loss of generality, that for some $\ell : \mathbb{N} \rightarrow \mathbb{N}$ and all s's, it holds that $D_s \subseteq \{0, 1\}^{\ell(|s|)}$. Indeed, ℓ must be polynomially bounded. For simplicity, we assume that $I(1^n) \in \{0, 1\}^n$. Recall that such collections of permutation pairs can be constructed based on the standard DLP or factoring intractability assumptions (see Section 2.4.5).

Construction 6.2.8 (collision-free hashing based on claw-free permutations pairs): *Given an index selecting algorithm I for a collection of permutation pairs $\{(f_s^0, f_s^1)\}_s$ as in the foregoing discussion, we construct a collection of hashing functions $\{h_{(s,r)} : \{0, 1\}^* \rightarrow \{0, 1\}^{|r|}\}_{(s,r) \in \{0,1\}^* \times \{0,1\}^*}$ as follows:*

Index selection algorithm: *On input 1^n, we first invoke I to obtain $s \leftarrow I(1^n)$, and next use the domain sampler to obtain a string r that is uniformly distributed in D_s. We output the index $(s, r) \in \{0, 1\}^n \times \{0, 1\}^{\ell(n)}$, which corresponds to the hashing function*

$$h_{(s,r)}(x) \stackrel{\text{def}}{=} f_s^{y_1} f_s^{y_2} \cdots f_s^{y_t}(r)$$

where $y_1 \cdots y_t$ is a prefix-free encoding of x; that is, for any $x \neq x'$ the coding of x is not a prefix of the coding of x'. For example, we may code $x_1 x_2 \cdots x_m$ by $x_1 x_1 x_2 x_2 \cdots x_m x_m 01$.

Evaluation algorithm: *Given an index (s, r) and a string x, we compute $h_{(s,r)}(x)$ in a straightforward manner. That is, first we compute the prefix-free encoding of x, denoted $y_1 \cdots y_t$. Next, we use the evaluation algorithm of the claw-free collection to compute $f_s^{y_1} f_s^{y_2} \cdots f_s^{y_t}(r)$, which is the desired output.*

Actually, as will become evident from the proof of Proposition 6.2.9, as far as Construction 6.2.8 is concerned, the definition of claw-free permutations can be relaxed: We do not need an algorithm that, given an index s, generates a uniformly distributed element in D_s; any efficient algorithm that generates elements in D_s will do (regardless of the distribution induced on D_s, and in particular, even if the algorithm always outputs the same element in D_s).

Proposition 6.2.9: *Suppose that the collection of permutation pairs $\{(f_s^0, f_s^1)\}_s$, together with the index-selecting algorithm I, constitutes a claw-free collection. Then, the function ensemble $\{h_{(s,r)} : \{0, 1\}^* \to \{0, 1\}^{|r|}\}_{(s,r)\in\{0,1\}^*\times\{0,1\}^*}$ as defined in Construction 6.2.8 constitutes a collision-free hashing with a range specifying function ℓ' satisfying $\ell'(n + \ell(n)) = \ell(n)$.*

Proof: Intuitively, forming collisions under $h_{(s,r)}$ means finding two different sequences of functions from $\{f_s^0, f_s^1\}$ that (when applied to r) yield the same image (e.g., $f_s^1 \circ f_s^0 \circ f_s^0(r) = f_s^1 \circ f_s^1(r) \circ f_s^1(r)$). Since these two sequences cannot be a prefix of one another, it must be that somewhere along the process (of applying these f_s^σ's), the application of two different functions yields the same image (i.e., a claw).

The proof is by a reducibility argument. Given an algorithm A' that on input (s, r) forms a collision under $h_{(s,r)}$, we construct an algorithm A that on input s forms a claw for index s. On input s (supposedly generated by $I(1^n)$), algorithm A selects r (uniformly) in D_s, and invokes algorithm A' on input (s, r). Suppose that A' outputs a pair (x, x') so that $h_{(s,r)}(x) = h_{(s,r)}(x')$ but $x \neq x'$. Without loss of generality,[8] assume that the coding of x equals $y_1 \cdots y_{i-1} 0 z_{i+1} \cdots z_t$, and that the coding of x' equals $y_1 \cdots y_{i-1} 1 z'_{i+1} \cdots z'_{t'}$. By the definition of $h_{(s,r)}$, it follows that

$$f_s^{y_1} \cdots f_s^{y_{i-1}} f_s^0 f_s^{z_{i+1}} \cdots f_s^{z_t}(r) = f_s^{y_1} \cdots f_s^{y_{i-1}} f_s^1 f_s^{z'_{i+1}} \cdots f_s^{z'_{t'}}(r) \qquad (6.1)$$

Since each of the f_s^σ's is 1-1, Eq. (6.1) implies that

$$f_s^0 f_s^{z_{i+1}} \cdots f_s^{z_t}(r) = f_s^1 f_s^{z'_{i+1}} \cdots f_s^{z'_{t'}}(r) \qquad (6.2)$$

Computing $w \stackrel{\text{def}}{=} f_s^{z_{i+1}} \cdots f_s^{z_t}(r)$ and $w' \stackrel{\text{def}}{=} f_s^{z'_{i+1}} \cdots f_s^{z'_{t'}}(r)$, algorithm A obtains a pair (w, w') such that $f_s^0(w) = f_s^1(w')$. Thus, algorithm A forms claws for index $I(1^n)$ with probability that is lower-bounded by the probability that A' forms a collision under $h_{I'(1^n)}$, where I' is the index-selection algorithm as defined in Construction 6.2.8. Using the hypothesis that the collection of pairs (together with I) is claw-free, the proposition follows. ∎

---

[8] Let $C(x)$ (resp., $C(x')$) denote the prefix-free coding of x (resp., x'). Then $C(x)$ is not a prefix of $C(x')$, and $C(x')$ is not a prefix of $C(x)$. It follows that $C(x) = uv$ and $C(x') = uv'$, where v and v' differ in their leftmost bit. Without loss of generality, we may assume that the leftmost bit of v is 0, and the leftmost bit of v' is 1.

6.2.3.2. Collision-Free Hashing via Block-Chaining

In this subsection, we show how a restricted type of Collision-Free Hashing (CFH) can be used to obtain full-fledge collision-free hashing (CFH). Specifically, we refer to the following restriction of Definition 6.2.5:

Definition 6.2.10 (length-restricted collision-free hashing functions): *Let $\ell', \ell : \mathbb{N} \to$* $\mathbb{N}$. *A collection of functions* $\{h_s : \{0, 1\}^{\ell'(|s|)} \to \{0, 1\}^{\ell(|s|)}\}_{s \in \{0,1\}^*}$ *is called* ℓ'-restricted collision-free hashing *if there exists a probabilistic polynomial-time algorithm I such that the following holds:*

1. (admissible indexing – technical): *As in Definition 6.2.5.*
2. (efficient evaluation): *There exists a polynomial-time algorithm that, given s and $x \in \{0, 1\}^{\ell'(|s|)}$, returns $h_s(x)$.*
3. (hard-to-form collisions): *As in Definition 6.2.5, we say that the pair (x, x') forms a collision under the function h if $h(x) = h(x')$ but $x \neq x'$. We require that every probabilistic polynomial-time algorithm, given $I(1^n)$ as input, outputs a pair in $\{0, 1\}^{\ell'(|s|)} \times \{0, 1\}^{\ell'(|s|)}$ that forms a collision under $h_{I(1^n)}$ with negligible probability. That is, for every probabilistic polynomial-time algorithm A, every positive polynomial p, and all sufficiently large n's,*

$$\Pr\left[A(I(1^n)) \in \{0, 1\}^{2 \cdot \ell'(|I(1^n)|)} \text{ is a collision under } h_{I(1^n)}\right] < \frac{1}{p(n)}$$

where the probability is taken over the internal coin tosses of algorithms I and A.

Indeed, we focus on the case $\ell'(n) = \text{poly}(n)$, or else the hardness condition holds vacuously (since no polynomial-time algorithm can print a pair of strings of super-polynomial length). On the other hand, we only care about the case $\ell'(n) > \ell(n)$ (otherwise the functions may be 1-1). Finally, recall that ℓ must be super-logarithmic. Following is a simple construction of full-fledge collision-free hashing based on any 2ℓ-restricted collision-free hashing (see also Figure 6.2).

Construction 6.2.11 (from 2ℓ-restricted CFH to full-fledged CFH): *Let $\{h'_s : \{0, 1\}^{2\ell(|s|)} \to \{0, 1\}^{\ell(|s|)}\}_{s \in \{0,1\}^*}$ be a collection of functions. Consider the collection $\{h_s : \{0, 1\}^* \to \{0, 1\}^{2\ell(|s|)}\}_{s \in \{0,1\}^*}$, where $h_s(x)$ is defined by the following process, which we call block-chaining:*

1. *Break x into $t \stackrel{\text{def}}{=} \lceil |x|/\ell(|s|) \rceil$ consecutive blocks, while possibly padding the last block with 0's, such that each block has length $\ell(|s|)$. Denote these $\ell(|s|)$-bit long blocks by $x_1, ..., x_t$. That is, $x_1 \cdots x_t = x0^{t \cdot \ell(|s|) - |x|}$.*

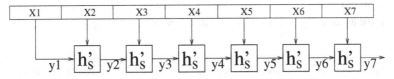

Figure 6.2: Collision-free hashing via block-chaining (for $t = 7$).

For the sake of uniformity, in case $|x| \leq \ell(|s|)$, we let $t = 2$ and $x_1 x_2 = x 0^{2\ell(|s|)-|x|}$.
On the other hand, we may assume that $|x| < 2^{\ell(|s|)}$, and so $|x|$ can be represented
by an $\ell(|s|)$-bit long string.[9]

2. *Let $y_1 \overset{\text{def}}{=} x_1$. For $i = 2, ..., t$, compute $y_i = h'_s(y_{i-1}x_i)$.*
3. *Set $h_s(x)$ to equal $(y_t, |x|)$.*

An interesting property of Construction 6.2.11 is that it allows for computing the hash-value of an input string while *processing the input in an on-line fashion*; that is, the implementation of the hashing process may process the input x in a block-by-block manner, while storing only the current block and a small amount of state information (i.e., the current y_i and the number of blocks encountered so far). *This property is important in applications in which one wishes to hash a long stream of input bits.*

Proposition 6.2.12: *Let* $\{h'_s : \{0, 1\}^{2\ell(|s|)} \rightarrow \{0, 1\}^{\ell(|s|)}\}_{s \in \{0,1\}^*}$ *and* $\{h_s : \{0, 1\}^* \rightarrow \{0, 1\}^{2\ell(|s|)}\}_{s \in \{0,1\}^*}$ *be as in Construction 6.2.11, and suppose that the former is a collection of 2ℓ-restricted collision-free hashing functions. Then the latter constitutes a (full-fledged) collection of collision-free hashing functions.*

Proof: Recall that forming a collision under h_s means finding $x \neq x'$ such that $h_s(x) = h_s(x')$. By the definition of h_s, this means that $(y_t, |x|) = h_s(x) = h_s(x') = (y'_{t'}, |x'|)$, where t, t' and $y_t, y'_{t'}$ are determined by $h_s(x)$ and $h_s(x')$. In particular, it follows that $|x| = |x'|$ and so $t = t'$ (where, except when $|x| \leq \ell(|s|)$, it holds that $t = \lceil |x|/\ell(|s|) \rceil = \lceil |x'|/\ell(|s|) \rceil = t'$). Recall that $y_t = y'_t$ and consider two cases:

Case 1: If $(y_{t-1}, x_t) \neq (y'_{t-1}, x'_t)$, then we obtain a collision under h'_s (since $h'_s(y_{t-1}x_t) = y_t = y'_t = h'_s(y'_{t-1}x'_t)$), and derive a contradiction to its collision-free hypothesis.

Case 2: Otherwise $(y_{t-1}, x_t) = (y'_{t-1}, x'_t)$, and we consider the two *corresponding* cases with respect to the relation of (y_{t-2}, x_{t-1}) to (y'_{t-2}, x'_{t-1}); that is, we further consider whether or not (y_{t-2}, x_{t-1}) equals (y'_{t-2}, x'_{t-1}).

Eventually, since $x \neq x'$, we get to a situation in which $y_i = y'_i$ and $(y_{i-1}, x_i) \neq (y'_{i-1}, x'_i)$, which is handled as in the first case.

We now provide a formal implementation of this intuitive argument. Suppose toward the contradiction that there exists a probabilistic polynomial-time algorithm A that on input s forms a collision under h_s (with certain probability). Then, we construct an algorithm that will, with similar probability, succeed to form a suitable (i.e., length-restricted) collision under h'_s. Algorithm $A'(s)$ operates as follows:

1. $A'(s)$ invokes $A(s)$ and obtains $(x, x') \leftarrow A(s)$.

If either $h_s(x) \neq h_s(x')$ or $x = x'$, then A failed, and A' halts without output. In the sequel, we assume that $h_s(x) = h_s(x')$ and $x \neq x'$.

---

[9] The adversary trying to form collisions with respect to h_s runs in poly($|s|$)-time. Using $\ell(|s|) = \omega(\log |s|)$, it follows that such an adversary cannot output a string of length $2^{\ell(|s|)}$. (The same also holds, of course, for legitimate usage of the hashing function.)

2. $A'(s)$ computes $t, x_1, ..., x_t$ and $y_1, ..., y_t$ (resp., $t', x'_1, ..., x'_t$ and $y'_1, ..., y'_t$) as in Construction 6.2.11. Next, $A'(s)$ finds an $i \in \{2, ..., t\}$ such that $y_i = y'_i$ and $(y_{i-1}, x_i) \neq (y'_{i-1}, x'_i)$, and outputs the pair $(y_{i-1}x_i, y'_{i-1}x'_i)$. (We will show next that such an i indeed exists.)

Note that (since $h_s(x) = h_s(x')$) it holds that $t = t'$ and $y_t = y'_t$. On the other hand, $(x_1, ..., x_t) \neq (x'_1, ..., x'_t)$. As argued in the motivating discussion, it follows that there exists an $i \in \{2, ..., t\}$ such that $y_i = y'_i$ and $(y_{i-1}, x_i) \neq (y'_{i-1}, x'_i)$.

> On the existence of a suitable i (more details): Suppose, toward the contradiction that, for every $i \in \{2, ..., t\}$, it holds that either $y_i \neq y'_i$ or $(y_{i-1}, x_i) = (y'_{i-1}, x'_i)$. Using the hypothesis $y_t = y'_t$, it follows (by descending induction on j) that $(y_{j-1}, x_j) = (y'_{j-1}, x'_j)$, for $j = t, ..., 2$. Using $y_1 = x_1$ and $y'_1 = x'_1$, it follows that $x_j = x'_j$ for every $j = 1, ..., t$, which contradicts the hypothesis $(x_1, ..., x_t) \neq (x'_1, ..., x'_t)$.

Clearly, the output pair $(y_{i-1}x_i, y'_{i-1}x'_i)$ constitutes a collision under h'_s (because $h'_s(y_{i-1}x_i) = y_i = y'_i = h'_s(y'_{i-1}x'_i)$, whereas $y_{i-1}x_i \neq y'_{i-1}x'_i$).

Thus, whenever $A(s)$ forms a collision under h_s, it holds that $A'(s)$ outputs a pair of $2\ell(s)$-bit long strings that form a collision under h'_s. The proposition follows. ∎

Variants on Construction 6.2.11. The said construction can be generalized to use any (non-trivial) length-restricted collision-free hashing. That is, for any $\ell' > \ell$, let $\{h'_s : \{0, 1\}^{\ell'(|s|)} \to \{0, 1\}^{\ell(|s|)}\}_{s \in \{0,1\}^*}$ be a collection of ℓ'-restricted collision-free hashing functions, and consider a parsing of the input string x into a sequence $x_1, ..., x_t$ of $(\ell'(|s|) - \ell(|s|))$-bit long blocks. Then we get a full-fledged collision-free hashing family $\{h_s : \{0, 1\}^* \to \{0, 1\}^{2\ell(|s|)}\}$ by letting $h_s(x) = (y_t, |x|)$, where $y_i = h'_s(y_{i-1}x_i)$ for $i = 2, ..., t$. (Construction 6.2.11 is obtained as a special case, for $\ell'(n) = 2\ell(n)$.) In case $\ell'(n) - \ell(n) = \omega(\log n)$, we obtain another variant by letting $h_s(x) = h'_s(y_t, |x|)$ (rather than $h_s(x) = (y_t, |x|)$), where y_t is as in Construction 6.2.11. The latter variant is quite popular. In establishing its security, when considering a collision $h_s(x) = h_s(x')$, we distinguish the case $(y_t, |x|) = (y'_{t'}, |x'|)$ (which is handled as in the proof of Proposition 6.2.12) from the case $(y_t, |x|) \neq (y'_{t'}, |x'|)$ (which yields an immediate collision under h'_s).

6.2.3.3. Collision-Free Hashing via Tree-Hashing

Using 2ℓ-restricted collision-free hashing functions, we now present an alternative construction of (full-fledged) collision-free hashing functions. The alternative construction will have the extra property of supporting verification of a bit in the input (with respect to the hash-value) within complexity that is independent of the length of the input.

Construction 6.2.13 (from 2ℓ-restricted CFH to full-fledged CFH – an alternative construction (see also Figure 6.3.)): *Let* $\{h'_s : \{0, 1\}^{2\ell(|s|)} \to \{0, 1\}^{\ell(|s|)}\}_{s \in \{0,1\}^*}$ *be a*

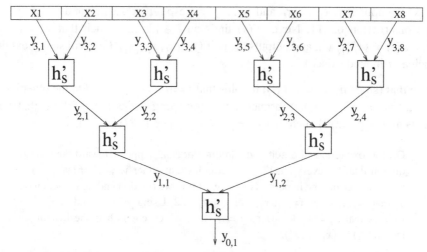

Figure 6.3: Collision-free hashing via tree-chaining (for $t = 8$).

collection of functions. Consider the collection $\{h_s : \{0, 1\}^* \to \{0, 1\}^{2\ell(|s|)}\}_{s \in \{0,1\}^*}$, *where* $h_s(x)$ *is defined by the following process, called* tree-hashing:

1. *Break x into $t \stackrel{\text{def}}{=} 2^{\lceil \log_2(|x|/\ell(|s|)) \rceil}$ consecutive blocks, while possibly adding dummy 0-blocks and padding the last block with 0's, such that each block has length $\ell(|s|)$. Denote these $\ell(|s|)$-bit long blocks by $x_1, ..., x_t$. That is, $x_1 \cdots x_t = x 0^{t \cdot \ell(|s|) - |x|}$.*

   Let $d = \log_2 t$, and note that d is a positive integer.

   Again, for the sake of uniformity, in case $|x| \leq \ell(|s|)$, we let $t = 2$ and $x_1 x_2 = x 0^{2\ell(|s|) - |x|}$. On the other hand, again, we assume that $|x| < 2^{\ell(|s|)}$, and so $|x|$ can be represented by an $\ell(|s|)$-bit long string.

2. *For $i = 1, ..., t$, let $y_{d,i} \stackrel{\text{def}}{=} x_i$.*
3. *For $j = d-1, ..., 1, 0$ and $i = 1, ..., 2^j$, compute $y_{j,i} = h'_s(y_{j+1,2i-1} y_{j+1,2i})$.*
4. *Set $h_s(x)$ to equal $(y_{0,1}, |x|)$.*

That is, hashing is performed by placing the $\ell(|s|)$-bit long blocks of x at the leaves of a binary tree of depth d, and computing the values of internal nodes by applying h'_s to the values associated with the two children (of the node). The final hash-value consists of the value associated with the root (i.e., the only level-0 node) and the length of x.

Proposition 6.2.14: *Let* $\{h'_s : \{0, 1\}^{2\ell(|s|)} \to \{0, 1\}^{\ell(|s|)}\}_{s \in \{0,1\}^*}$ *and* $\{h_s : \{0, 1\}^* \to \{0, 1\}^{2\ell(|s|)}\}_{s \in \{0,1\}^*}$ *be as in Construction 6.2.13, and suppose that the former is a collection of 2ℓ-restricted collision-free hashing functions. Then the latter constitutes a (full-fledged) collection of collision-free hashing functions.*

Proof Sketch: Recall that forming a collision under h_s means finding $x \neq x'$ such that $h_s(x) = h_s(x')$. By the definition of h_s, this means that $(y_{0,1}, |x|) = h_s(x) = h_s(x') = (y'_{0,1}, |x'|)$, where (t, d) and $y_{0,1}$ (resp., (t', d') and $y'_{0,1}$) are determined by $h_s(x)$ (resp., $h_s(x')$). In particular, it follows that $|x| = |x'|$ and so $d = d'$ (because $2^d = t = t' =$

$2^{d'}$). Recall that $y_{0,1} = y'_{0,1}$, and let us state this fact by saying that for $j = 0$ and for every $i \in \{1, ..., 2^j\}$, it holds that $y_{j,i} = y'_{j,i}$. Starting with $j = 0$, we consider two cases (for level $j + 1$ in the tree):

Case 1: If for some $i \in \{1, ..., 2^{j+1}\}$ it holds that $y_{j+1,i} \neq y'_{j+1,i}$, then we obtain a collision under h'_s, and derive a contradiction to its collision-free hypothesis. Specifically, the collision is obtained because $z \stackrel{\text{def}}{=} y_{j+1,2\lceil i/2 \rceil - 1} y_{j+1,2\lceil i/2 \rceil}$ is different from $z' \stackrel{\text{def}}{=} y'_{j+1,2\lceil i/2 \rceil - 1} y'_{j+1,2\lceil i/2 \rceil}$, whereas $h'_s(z) = y_{j,\lceil i/2 \rceil} = y'_{j,\lceil i/2 \rceil} = h'_s(z')$.

Case 2: Otherwise for every $i \in \{1, ..., 2^{j+1}\}$, it holds that $y_{j+1,i} = y'_{j+1,i}$. In this case, we consider the next level.

Eventually, since $x \neq x'$, we get to a situation in which for some $j \in \{1, ..., d - 1\}$ and some $i \in \{1, ..., 2^{j+1}\}$, it holds that $z \stackrel{\text{def}}{=} y_{j+1,2\lceil i/2 \rceil - 1} y_{j+1,2\lceil i/2 \rceil}$ is different from $z' \stackrel{\text{def}}{=} y'_{j+1,2\lceil i/2 \rceil - 1} y'_{j+1,2\lceil i/2 \rceil}$, whereas $h'_s(z) = y_{j,\lceil i/2 \rceil} = y'_{j,\lceil i/2 \rceil} = h'_s(z')$. This situation is handled as in the first case.

The actual argument proceeds as in the proof of Proposition 6.2.12. ∎

A Local Verification Property. Construction 6.2.13 has the extra property of supporting efficient verification of bits in x with respect to the hash-value. That is, suppose that for a randomly selected h_s, one party holds x and the other party holds $h_s(x)$. Then, for every i, the first party may provide a short (efficiently verifiable) certificate that x_i is indeed the i-th block of x. The certificate consists of the sequence of pairs $(y_{d,2\lceil i/2 \rceil - 1}, y_{d,2\lceil i/2 \rceil}), ..., (y_{1,2\lceil i/2^d \rceil - 1}, y_{1,2\lceil i/2^d \rceil})$, where d and the $y_{j,k}$'s are computed as in Construction 6.2.13 (and $(y_{0,1}, |x|) = h_s(x)$). The certificate is verified by checking whether or not $y_{j-1,\lceil i/2^{d-j+1} \rceil} = h'_s(y_{j,2\lceil i/2^{d-j+1} \rceil - 1} y_{j,2\lceil i/2^{d-j+1} \rceil})$, for every $j \in \{1, ..., d\}$. Note that if the first party can present two different values for the i-th block of x along with corresponding certificates, then it can also form collisions under h'_s. Construction 6.2.13 and its local-verification property were already used in this work (i.e., in the construction of highly- efficient argument systems, presented in Section 4.8.4 of Volume 1). Jumping ahead, we note the similarity between the local-verification property of Construction 6.2.13 and the authentication-tree of Section 6.4.2.2.

6.3. Constructions of Message-Authentication Schemes

In this section, we present several constructions of secure message-authentication schemes (referred to earlier as secure private-key signature schemes). Here, we sometimes refer to such a scheme by the popular abbreviation MAC (which actually abbreviates the more traditional term of a Message Authentication Code).

6.3.1. Applying a Pseudorandom Function to the Document

A scheme for message authentication can be obtained by applying a pseudorandom function (specified by the key) to the message (which one wishes to authenticate). The simplest implementation of this idea is presented in Section 6.3.1.1, whereas more sophisticated implementations are presented in Sections 6.3.1.2 and 6.3.1.3.

6.3.1.1. A Simple Construction and a Plausibility Result

Message-authentication schemes can be easily constructed using pseudorandom functions (as defined in Section 3.6 of Volume 1). Specifically, by Theorem 6.2.2, it suffices to construct an ℓ-restricted message-authentication scheme for any super-logarithmically growing ℓ. Indeed, this is our starting point.

Construction 6.3.1 (an ℓ-restricted MAC based on pseudorandom functions): *Let ℓ be a super-logarithmically growing function, and $\{f_s : \{0, 1\}^{\ell(|s|)} \to \{0, 1\}^{\ell(|s|)}\}_{s \in \{0,1\}^*}$ be as in Definition 3.6.4. We construct an ℓ-restricted message-authentication scheme, (G, S, V), as follows:*

Key-generation with G: *On input 1^n, we uniformly select $s \in \{0, 1\}^n$, and output the key-pair (s, s). (Indeed, the verification-key equals the signing-key.)*

Signing with S: *On input a signing-key $s \in \{0, 1\}^n$ and an $\ell(n)$-bit string α, we compute and output $f_s(\alpha)$ as a signature of α.*

Verification with V: *On input a verification-key $s \in \{0, 1\}^n$, an $\ell(n)$-bit string α, and an alleged signature β, we accept if and only if $\beta = f_s(\alpha)$.*

Indeed, signing amounts to applying f_s to the given document string, and verification amounts to comparing a given value to the result of applying f_s to the document. Analogous constructions can be presented by using the generalized notions of pseudorandom functions defined in Definitions 3.6.9 and 3.6.12 (see further comments in the following subsections). In particular, using a pseudorandom function ensemble of the form $\{f_s : \{0, 1\}^* \to \{0, 1\}^{|s|}\}_{s \in \{0,1\}^*}$, we obtain a general message-authentication scheme (rather than a length-restricted one). In the following proof, we only demonstrate the security of the ℓ-restricted message-authentication scheme of Construction 6.3.1. (The security of the general message-authentication scheme can be established analogously; see Exercise 8.)

Proposition 6.3.2: *Suppose that $\{f_s : \{0, 1\}^{\ell(|s|)} \to \{0, 1\}^{\ell(|s|)}\}_{s \in \{0,1\}^*}$ is a pseudorandom function, and that ℓ is a super-logarithmically growing function. Then Construction 6.3.1 constitutes a secure ℓ-restricted message-authentication scheme.*

Proof: The proof follows the general methodology suggested in Section 3.6.3. Specifically, we consider the security of an ideal scheme in which the pseudorandom function is replaced by a truly random function (mapping $\ell(n)$-bit long strings to $\ell(n)$-bit long strings). Clearly, an adversary that obtains the values of this *random* function at arguments of its choice cannot predict its value at a new point with probability greater than $2^{-\ell(n)}$. Thus, an adversary attacking the *ideal scheme* may succeed in existential forgery with at most negligible probability. The same must hold for any efficient adversary that attacks the *actual scheme,* because otherwise such an adversary yields a violation of the pseudorandomness of $\{f_s : \{0, 1\}^{\ell(|s|)} \to \{0, 1\}^{\ell(|s|)}\}_{s\in\{0,1\}^*}$. Details follow.

The actual proof is by a reducibility argument. Given a probabilistic polynomial-time A attacking the scheme (G, S, V), we consider what happens when A attacks an ideal scheme in which a random function is used instead of a pseudorandom one. That is, we refer to two experiments:

1. *Machine A attacks the actual scheme:* On input 1^n, machine A is given oracle access to (the signing process) $f_s : \{0, 1\}^{\ell(n)} \to \{0, 1\}^{\ell(n)}$, where s is uniformly selected in $\{0, 1\}^n$. After making some queries of its choice, A outputs a pair (α, β), where α is different from all its queries. Machine A is deemed successful if and only if $\beta = f_s(\alpha)$.

2. *Machine A attacks the ideal scheme:* On input 1^n, machine A is given oracle access to a function $\phi : \{0, 1\}^{\ell(n)} \to \{0, 1\}^{\ell(n)}$, uniformly selected among all such possible functions. After making some queries of its choice, A outputs a pair (α, β), where α is different from all its queries. Again, A is deemed successful if and only if $\beta = \phi(\alpha)$.

   Clearly, A's success probability in this experiment is at most $2^{-\ell(n)}$, which is a negligible function (since ℓ is super-logarithmic).

Assuming that A's success probability in the actual attack is non-negligible, we derive a contradiction to the pseudorandomness of the function ensemble $\{f_s\}$. Specifically, we consider a distinguisher D that, on input 1^n and oracle access to a function $f : \{0, 1\}^{\ell(n)} \to \{0, 1\}^{\ell(n)}$, behaves as follows: First D emulates the actions of A, while answering A's queries using its oracle f. When A outputs a pair (α, β), the distinguisher makes one additional oracle query to f and outputs 1 if and only if $f(\alpha) = \beta$.

Note that when f is selected uniformly among all possible $\{0, 1\}^{\ell(n)} \to \{0, 1\}^{\ell(n)}$ functions, D emulates an attack of A on the ideal scheme, and thus outputs 1 with negligible probability (as explained in the beginning of the proof). On the other hand, if f is uniformly selected in $\{f_s\}_{s\in\{0,1\}^n}$, then D emulates an attack of A on the actual scheme, and thus (due to the contradiction hypothesis) outputs 1 with non-negligible probability. We reach a contradiction to the pseudorandomness of $\{f_s\}_{s\in\{0,1\}^n}$. The proposition follows. ∎

A Plausibility Result. Combining Theorem 6.2.2, Proposition 6.3.2, and Corollary 3.6.7, it follows that the existence of one-way functions implies the existence of message-authentication schemes. The converse also holds; see Exercise 7. Thus, we have:

Theorem 6.3.3: *Secure message-authentication schemes exist if and only if one-way functions exist.*

In contrast to the feasibility result stated in Theorem 6.3.3, we now present alternative ways of using pseudorandom functions to obtain secure message-authentication schemes (MACs). These alternatives yield more efficient schemes, where efficiency is measured in terms of the *length of the signatures* and the *time* it takes to produce and verify them.

6.3.1.2.* Using the Hash-and-Sign Paradigm

Theorem 6.3.3 was proved by combining the length-restricted MAC of Construction 6.3.1 with the simple but wasteful idea of providing signatures (authentication tags) for each block of the document (i.e., Construction 6.2.3). In particular, the signature produced this way is longer than the document. Instead, here we suggest using the second method of converting length-restricted MACs into full-fledged ones; that is, the hash-and-sign method of Construction 6.2.6. This will yield *signatures of a fixed length* (i.e., independent of the length of the document). Combining the hash-and-sign method with a length-restricted MAC of Construction 6.3.1 (which is based on pseudorandom functions), we obtain the following construction:

Construction 6.3.4 (hash and sign using pseudorandom functions): *Let* $\{f_s : \{0, 1\}^{|s|} \to \{0, 1\}^{|s|}\}_{s \in \{0,1\}^*}$ *be a pseudorandom function ensemble and* $\{h_r : \{0, 1\}^* \to \{0, 1\}^{|r|}\}_{r \in \{0,1\}^*}$ *be a collection of collision-free hashing functions. Furthermore, for simplicity we assume that, when invoked on input* 1^n, *the indexing algorithm* I *of the collision-free hashing collection outputs an n-bit long index. The general message-authentication scheme,* (G, S, V), *is as follows*:

Key-generation with G: *On input* 1^n, *algorithm* G *selects uniformly* $s \in \{0, 1\}^n$, *and invokes the indexing algorithm* I *to obtain* $r \leftarrow I(1^n)$. *The key-pair output by* G *is* $((r, s), (r, s))$.

Signing with S: *On input a signing-key* (r, s) *in the range of* $G_1(1^n)$ *and a document* $\alpha \in \{0, 1\}^*$, *algorithm* S *outputs the signature/tag* $f_s(h_r(\alpha))$.

Verification with V: *On input a verification-key* (r, s) *in the range of* $G_2(1^n)$, *a document* $\alpha \in \{0, 1\}^*$, *and an alleged signature* β, *algorithm outputs 1 if and only if* $f_s(h_r(\alpha)) = \beta$.

Combining Propositions 6.2.7 and 6.3.2, it follows that *Construction 6.3.4 constitutes a secure message-authentication scheme* (MAC), provided that the ingredients are as postulated. In particular, this means that Construction 6.3.4 yields a secure MAC, provided that collision-free hashing functions exist (and are used in Construction 6.3.4). While this result uses a seemingly stronger assumption than the existence of one-way functions (used to establish the Theorem 6.3.3), it yields more efficient MACs, both in terms of signature length (as discussed previously) and authentication time (to be discussed next).

Construction 6.3.4 yields faster signing and verification algorithms than the construction resulting from combining Constructions 6.2.3 and 6.3.1, provided that hashing a long string is less time-consuming than applying a pseudorandom function to it (or to all its blocks). The latter assumption is consistent with the current state of the art regarding the implementation of both primitives. Further speed improvements are discussed in Section 6.3.1.3.

An Alternative Presentation. Construction 6.3.4 was analyzed by invoking the hash-and-sign paradigm (i.e., Proposition 6.2.7), while referring to the fixed-length MAC arising from the pseudorandom function ensemble $\{f_s : \{0, 1\}^{|s|} \to \{0, 1\}^{|s|}\}_{s \in \{0,1\}^*}$. An alternative analysis may proceed by first establishing that $\{g_{s,r} = f_s \circ h_r\}_{s \in \{0,1\}^*, r \leftarrow I(1^{|s|})}$ is a generalized pseudorandom function (as per Definition 3.6.12), and next observing that any such ensemble yields a full-fledged MAC (see Exercise 8).

6.3.1.3.* A Variation on the Hash-and-Sign Paradigm (or Using Non-Cryptographic Hashing Plus Hiding)

Construction 6.3.4 combines the use of a collision-free hashing function with the application of a pseudorandom function. Here we take another step toward speeding-up message authentication by showing that the collision-free hashing can be replaced with *ordinary* (i.e., non-cryptographic) *hashing,* provided that a pseudorandom function (rather than a generic MAC) is applied to the result. Consequently, we also reduce the intractability assumptions used in the analysis of the construction. Before getting into details, let us explain why we can use non-cryptographic hashing and why this may lead to reduced intractability assumptions and to efficiency improvements.

- Since we are in the private-key setting, the adversary does not get the description of the hash function used in the hash-and-sign process. Furthermore, applying the pseudorandom function to the hash-value hides it from the adversary. Thus, when trying to form collisions under the hash function, the adversary is in "total darkness" and may only rely on the collision probability of the hashing function (as defined next). (Recall that in case the adversary fails to form a collision, it must succeed in forging with respect to the length-restricted scheme if it wishes to forge with respect to the full-fledged scheme.)
- Using an ordinary hashing instead of a collision-free hash function means that the only intractability assumption used is the existence of pseudorandom functions (or, equivalently, of one-way functions).

  The reason that applying an ordinary hashing, rather than a collision-free hash function, may yield an efficiency improvement is that the former is likely to be more efficient than the latter. This is to be expected, given that ordinary hashing need only satisfy a weak (probabilistic) condition, whereas collision-free hashing refers to a more complicated (intractability) condition.[10]

By ordinary hashing we mean function ensembles as defined in Section 3.5.1.1 of Volume 1. For starters, recall that these are collections of functions mapping $\ell(n)$-bit strings to $m(n)$-bit strings. These collections are associated with a set of strings, denoted $S_{\ell(n)}^{m(n)}$, and we may assume that $S_{\ell(n)}^{m(n)} \equiv \{0, 1\}^n$. Specifically, we call $\{S_{\ell(n)}^{m(n)}\}_{n \in \mathbb{N}}$

---

[10] This intuition may not hold when comparing a construction of ordinary hashing that is rigorously analyzed with an ad hoc suggestion of a collision-free hashing. But it certainly holds when comparing the former to the constructions of collision-free hashing that are based on a well-established intractability assumption.

a hashing ensemble if it satisfies the following three conditions:

1. *Succinctness:* $n = \text{poly}(\ell(n), m(n))$.
2. *Efficient evaluation:* There exists a polynomial-time algorithm that, on input a representation of a function, h (in $S_{\ell(n)}^{m(n)}$), and a string $x \in \{0, 1\}^{\ell(n)}$, returns $h(x)$.
3. *Pairwise independence:* For every $x \neq y \in \{0, 1\}^{\ell(n)}$, if h is uniformly selected in $S_{\ell(n)}^{m(n)}$, then $h(x)$ and $h(y)$ are independent and uniformly distributed in $\{0, 1\}^{m(n)}$. That is, for every $\alpha, \beta \in \{0, 1\}^{m(n)}$,

$$\Pr_h[h(x) = \alpha \ \wedge \ h(y) = \beta] \ = \ 2^{-2m(n)}$$

In fact, for the current application, we can replace the third condition by the following weaker condition, parameterized by a function $\text{cp} : \mathbb{N} \to [0, 1]$ (s.t. $\text{cp}(n) \geq 2^{-m(n)}$): For every $x \neq y \in \{0, 1\}^{\ell(n)}$,

$$\Pr_h[h(x) = h(y)] \ \leq \ \text{cp}(n) \tag{6.3}$$

Indeed, the pairwise independence condition implies that Eq. (6.3) is satisfied with $\text{cp}(n) = 2^{-m(n)}$. Note that Eq. (6.3) asserts that the collision probability of $S_{\ell(n)}^{m(n)}$ is at most $\text{cp}(n)$, where the collision probability refers to the probability that $h(x) = h(y)$ when h is uniformly selected in $S_{\ell(n)}^{m(n)}$ and $x \neq y \in \{0, 1\}^{\ell(n)}$ are arbitrary fixed strings.

Hashing ensembles with $n \leq \ell(n) + m(n)$ and $\text{cp}(n) = 2^{-m(n)}$ can be constructed (for a variety of functions $\ell, m : \mathbb{N} \to \mathbb{N}$, e.g., $\ell(n) = 2n/3$ and $m(n) = n/3$; see Exercise 22. Using such ensembles, we first present a construction of length-restricted message-authentication schemes (and later show how to generalize the construction to obtain full-fledged message-authentication schemes).

Construction 6.3.5 (Construction 6.3.4, revisited – length-restricted version): *Let* $\{h_r : \{0, 1\}^{\ell(|r|)} \to \{0, 1\}^{m(|r|)}\}_{r \in \{0,1\}^*}$ *and* $\{f_s : \{0, 1\}^{m(|s|)} \to \{0, 1\}^{m(|s|)}\}_{s \in \{0,1\}^*}$ *be efficiently computable function ensembles. We construct the following ℓ-restricted scheme,* (G, S, V):

Key-generation with G: *On input 1^n, algorithm G selects independently and uniformly $r, s \in \{0, 1\}^n$. The key-pair output by G is $((r, s), (r, s))$.*

Signing with S: *On input a signing-key (r, s) in the range of $G_1(1^n)$ and a document $\alpha \in \{0, 1\}^{\ell(n)}$, algorithm S outputs the signature/tag $f_s(h_r(\alpha))$.*

Verification with V: *On input a verifying-key (r, s) in the range of $G_2(1^n)$, a document $\alpha \in \{0, 1\}^{\ell(n)}$, and an alleged signature β, algorithm outputs 1 if and only if $f_s(h_r(\alpha)) = \beta$.*

Note that a generalization of Construction 6.3.5 in which the pseudorandom function is replaced by an arbitrary (length-restricted) secure message-authentication scheme may be insecure; see Exercise 9.

Proposition 6.3.6: *Suppose that $\{f_s : \{0, 1\}^{m(|s|)} \to \{0, 1\}^{m(|s|)}\}_{s \in \{0,1\}^*}$ is a pseudorandom function, and that the collision probability of the collection $\{h_r : \{0, 1\}^{\ell(|r|)} \to$*

$\{0, 1\}^{m(|r|)}\}_{r\in\{0,1\}^*}$ *is a negligible function of* $|r|$. *Then Construction 6.3.5 constitutes a secure ℓ-restricted message-authentication scheme.*

In particular, the second hypothesis requires that $2^{-m(n)}$ be a negligible function in n. By the previous discussion, adequate collections of hashing functions (i.e., with collision probability $2^{-m(n)}$) exists for $\ell(n) = 2n/3$ (and $m(n) = n/3$). We comment that, under the hypothesis of Proposition 6.3.6, the collection $\{g_{s,r} : f_s \circ h_r\}_{|s|=|r|}$ constitutes a pseudorandom function ensemble. This is implicitly shown in the following proof, and is related to Exercise 31 in Chapter 3.

Proof Sketch: As in the proof of Proposition 6.3.2, we first consider the security of an ideal scheme in which the pseudorandom function is replaced by a truly random function (mapping $m(n)$-bit long strings to $m(n)$-bit long strings). Consider any (probabilistic polynomial-time) adversary attacking the *ideal scheme*. Such an adversary may obtain the signatures to polynomially -many $\ell(n)$-bit long strings of its choice. However, except with negligible probability, these strings are hashed to *different* $m(n)$-bit long strings, which in turn are mapped by the random function to totally independent and uniformly distributed $m(n)$-bit long strings. Furthermore, except with negligible probability, the $\ell(n)$-bit long string α contained in the adversary's (alleged message-signature) output pair is hashed to an $m(n)$-bit long string that is different from all the previous hash-values, and so the single valid signature corresponding to α is a uniformly distributed $m(n)$-bit long string that is independent of all previously seen signatures.

On the distribution of signatures in the ideal scheme: Suppose that the hashing collection $\{h_r : \{0, 1\}^{\ell(|r|)} \to \{0, 1\}^{m(|r|)}\}_{r\in\{0,1\}^n}$ has collision probability $\mathrm{cp}(n)$, and $\phi : \{0, 1\}^{m(n)} \to \{0, 1\}^{m(n)}$ is a random function. Then, we claim that an adversary that obtains signatures to $t(n) - 1$ strings of its choice succeeds in forging a signature to a new string with probability at most $t(n)^2 \cdot \mathrm{cp}(n) + 2^{-m(n)}$, regardless of its computational powers. The claim is proved by showing that, except with probability at most $t(n)^2 \cdot \mathrm{cp}(n)$, the $t(n)$ strings selected by the adversary are mapped by h_r to distinct values. The latter claim is proved by induction on the number of selected strings, denoted i, where the base case (i.e., $i = 1$) holds vacuously. Let $s_1, ..., s_i$ denote the strings selected so far, and suppose that with probability at least $1 - i^2 \cdot \mathrm{cp}(n)$, the i hash-values $h_r(s_j)$'s are distinct. The adversary only sees the corresponding $\phi(h_r(s_j))$'s, which are uniformly and independently distributed (in a way independent of the values of the $h_r(s_j)$'s). Thus, loosely speaking, the adversary's selection of the next string, denoted s_{i+1}, is independent of the values of the $h_r(s_j)$'s, and so a collision of $h_r(s_{i+1})$ with one of the previous $h_r(s_j)$'s occurs with probability at most $i \cdot \mathrm{cp}(n)$. The induction step follows (since $1 - i^2 \cdot \mathrm{cp}(n) - i \cdot \mathrm{cp}(n) > 1 - (i + 1)^2 \cdot \mathrm{cp}(n)$).

It follows that any adversary attacking the *ideal scheme* may succeed in existential forgery with at most negligible probability (provided it makes at most polynomially many queries). The same must hold for any efficient adversary that attacks the *actual scheme,* since otherwise such an adversary yields a violation of the pseudorandomness of $\{f_s : \{0, 1\}^{m(|s|)} \to \{0, 1\}^{m(|s|)}\}_{s\in\{0,1\}^*}$. The exact implementation of this argument follows the details given in the proof of Proposition 6.3.2. ∎

Obtaining Full-Fledged MACs. Construction 6.3.5 can be generalized to obtain full-fledged MACs by using generalized hashing families that map arbitrary strings (rather than fixed-length ones) to fixed-length strings. Specifically, for $\ell : \mathbb{N} \to \mathbb{N}$ and $\mathsf{cp} : \mathbb{N} \to [0,1]$, we call $\{h_r : \{0, 1\}^* \to \{0, 1\}^{m(|r|)}\}_{n \in \mathbb{N}}$ a generalized hashing ensemble with a (ℓ, cp)-collision property if it satisfies the following two conditions:

1. *Efficient evaluation:* There exists a polynomial-time algorithm that, on input r (representing the function h_r) and a string $x \in \{0, 1\}^*$, returns $h_r(x)$.
2. *Collision probability:*[11] For every $n \in \mathbb{N}$ and $x \neq y$ such that $|x|, |y| \leq \ell(n)$, the probability that $h_r(x) = h_r(y)$ when r is uniformly selected in $\{0, 1\}^n$ is at most $\mathsf{cp}(n)$.

For our construction of a full-fledged MAC, we need a generalized hashing ensemble with an (ℓ, cp)-collision property for some super-polynomial $\ell(n)$ and negligible $\mathsf{cp}(n)$ (e.g., $\ell(n) = 1/\mathsf{cp}(n) = 2^{n^\varepsilon}$ for some constant $\varepsilon > 0$). The existence of such ensembles will be discussed after the proof of Proposition 6.3.7.

Proposition 6.3.7 (Construction 6.3.4, revisited – full-fledged version): *Suppose that $\{f_s : \{0, 1\}^{m(|s|)} \to \{0, 1\}^{m(|s|)}\}_{s \in \{0,1\}^*}$ is a pseudorandom function ensemble. For some super-polynomial $\ell : \mathbb{N} \to \mathbb{N}$ and negligible $\mathsf{cp} : \mathbb{N} \to [0, 1]$, suppose that $\{h_r : \{0, 1\}^* \to \{0, 1\}^{m(|r|)}\}_{r \in \{0,1\}^*}$ is a generalized hashing ensemble with an (ℓ, cp)-collision property. Then (G, S, V) as in Construction 6.3.4 constitutes a secure MAC. That is, we refer to the following scheme:*

Key-generation with G: *On input 1^n, algorithm G selects independently and uniformly $r, s \in \{0, 1\}^n$, and outputs $((r, s), (r, s))$.*

Signing with S: *On input a signing-key (r, s) and a document $\alpha \in \{0, 1\}^*$, algorithm S outputs the signature/tag $f_s(h_r(\alpha))$.*

Verification with V: *On input a verifying-key (r, s), a document $\alpha \in \{0, 1\}^*$, and an alleged signature β, algorithm outputs 1 if and only if $f_s(h_r(\alpha)) = \beta$.*

Proof Sketch: The proof is identical to the proof of Proposition 6.3.6, except that here the (polynomial-time) adversary attacking the scheme may query for the signatures of strings of various lengths. Still, all these queries (as well as the final output) are of polynomial length and thus shorter than $\ell(n)$. Thus, the (ℓ, cp)-collision property implies that, except with negligible probability, all these queries (as well as the relevant part of the output) are hashed to different values. ∎

On Constructing Adequate Hashing Ensembles. For some $\varepsilon > 0$ and $f(n) = 2^{n^\varepsilon}$, generalized hashing ensembles with a $(f, 1/f)$-collision property can be constructed is several ways. One such way is by applying a tree-hashing scheme as in Construction 6.2.13; see Exercise 23. For further details about constructions of generalized

---

[11] Note that it is essential to restrict the collision condition to strings of bounded length. In contrast, for every finite family of functions H, there exist two different strings that are mapped to the same image by each function in H. For details, see Exercise 21.

hashing ensembles, see Section 6.6.5. Combining any of these constructions with Proposition 6.3.7, we get:

Theorem 6.3.8: *Assuming the existence of one-way functions, there exist message-authentication schemes with fixed-length signatures; that is, signatures of length that depend on the length of the signing-key but not on the length of the document.*

An Alternative Presentation. The proofs of Propositions 6.3.6 and 6.3.7 actually establish that $\{g_{s,r} = f_s \circ h_r\}_{s \in \{0,1\}^*, r \in \{0,1\}^{|s|}}$ is a generalized pseudorandom function (as per Definition 3.6.12). For further discussion of this aspect, see Section C.2 in Appendix C. Hence, the actual claim of these propositions (i.e., the security of the constructed MAC) can be derived from the fact that any generalized pseudorandom function yields a full-fledged MAC (see Exercise 8).

6.3.2.* More on Hash-and-Hide and State-Based MACs

The basic idea underlying Construction 6.3.5 (as well as Proposition 6.3.7) is to combine a "weak tagging scheme" with an adequate "hiding scheme." Specifically, the weak tagging scheme should be secure against forgery *provided that the adversary does not have access to the scheme's outcome*, and the hiding scheme implements the latter provision in a setting in which the actual adversary does obtain the value of the MAC. In Construction 6.3.5 (and in Proposition 6.3.7), the tagging scheme was implemented by ordinary hashing and hiding was obtained by applying a pseudorandom function to the string that one wishes to hide.[12]

One more natural "hiding scheme" (which can also be implemented using pseudorandom functions) is obtained by using certain private-key encryption schemes. For example, we may use Construction 5.3.9 (in which the plaintext x is encrypted/hidden by the pair $(u, x \oplus f_s(u))$, where u is uniformly selected), instead of hiding x by the value $f_s(x)$ (as in Construction 6.3.5 and Proposition 6.3.7). The resulting MAC is as follows:

Key-generation: On input 1^n, we select independently and uniformly $r, s \in \{0, 1\}^n$, where r specifies a hashing[13] function $h_r : \{0, 1\}^* \to \{0, 1\}^{m(|r|)}$ and s specifies a pseudorandom function $f_s : \{0, 1\}^{m(|s|)} \to \{0, 1\}^{m(|s|)}$. We output the key-pair $((r, s), (r, s))$.

Signing: On input a signing-key (r, s) and a document $\alpha \in \{0, 1\}^*$, we uniformly select $u \in \{0, 1\}^{m(|s|)}$, and output the signature/tag $(u, h_r(\alpha) \oplus f_s(u))$.

Verification: On input a verifying-key (r, s), a document $\alpha \in \{0, 1\}^*$, and an alleged signature (u, v), we output 1 if and only if $v = h_r(\alpha) \oplus f_s(u)$.

Alternative implementations of the same underlying idea are more popular, especially in the context of state-based MACs. We start by defining state-based MACs, and

---

[12] We comment that this specific hiding method is not 1-1, and furthermore, it is not clear whether it can also be efficiently inverted when given the "secret key" (i.e., the seed of the pseudorandom function). In contrast, the alternative hiding method described next is 1-1 and can be efficiently inverted when given the secret key.

[13] The hashing function should belong to an AXU family, as defined in Section 6.3.2.2.

then show how to construct them based on the hash-and-hide (or rather tag-and-hide) paradigm.

6.3.2.1. The Definition of State-Based MACs

As in the case of steam-ciphers discussed in Section 5.3.1, we extend the mechanism of message-authentication schemes (MACs) by allowing the signing and verification processes to maintain and update a state. Formally, both the signing and the verification algorithms take an additional input and emit an additional output, corresponding to their state before and after the operation. The length of the state is not allowed to grow by too much during each application of the algorithm (see Condition 3 in Definition 6.3.9), or else efficiency of the entire "repeated signing" process cannot be guaranteed. For the sake of simplicity, we incorporate the key in the state of the corresponding algorithm. Thus, the initial state of each of the algorithms is set to equal its corresponding key. Furthermore, one may think of the intermediate states as of updated values of the corresponding key.

In the following definition, we follow conventions similar to those used in defining state-based ciphers (i.e., Definition 5.3.1). Specifically, for simplicity, we assume that the verification algorithm (i.e., V) is deterministic (otherwise the formulation would be more complex). Intuitively, the main part of the verification condition (i.e., Condition 2) is that the (proper) iterative signing-verifying process always accepts. The additional requirement in Condition 2 is that the state of the verification algorithm be updated correctly as long as it is fed with strings of length equal to the length of the valid document-signature pairs. The importance of this condition was discussed in Section 5.3.1 and is further discussed following Definition 6.3.9.

Definition 6.3.9 (state-based MAC – the mechanism): *A* state-based message-authentication scheme *is a triple,* (G, S, V), *of probabilistic polynomial-time algorithms satisfying the following three conditions:*

1. *On input* 1^n, *algorithm G outputs a pair of bit strings.*
2. *For every pair* $(s^{(0)}, v^{(0)})$ *in the range of* $G(1^n)$, *and every sequence of* $\alpha^{(i)}$'s, the *following holds: If* $(s^{(i)}, \beta^{(i)}) \leftarrow S(s^{(i-1)}, \alpha^{(i)})$ *and* $(v^{(i)}, \gamma^{(i)}) \leftarrow V(v^{(i-1)}, \alpha^{(i)}, \beta^{(i)})$ *for* $i = 1, 2, ...,$ *then* $\gamma^{(i)} = 1$ *for every i.*
   Furthermore, for every i and every $(\alpha, \beta) \in \{0, 1\}^{|\alpha^{(i)}|} \times \{0, 1\}^{|\beta^{(i)}|}$, *it holds that* $V(v^{(i-1)}, \alpha, \beta) = (v^{(i)}, \cdot)$. *That is,* $v^{(i)}$ *is actually determined by* $v^{(i-1)}$ *and* $(|\alpha^{(i)}|, |\beta^{(i)}|)$.[14]
3. *There exists a polynomial p such that for every pair* $(s^{(0)}, v^{(0)})$ *in the range of* $G(1^n)$, *and every sequence of* $\alpha^{(i)}$'s *and* $s^{(i)}$'s *as in Condition 2, it holds that* $|s^{(i)}| \leq |s^{(i-1)}| + |\alpha^{(i)}| \cdot p(n)$. *Similarly for the* $v^{(i)}$'s.

---

[14] Alternatively, we may decompose the verification (resp., signing) algorithm into two algorithms, where the first takes care of the actual verification (resp., signing) and the second takes care of updating the state. For details, see Exercise 18.

That is, as in Definition 6.1.1, the signing-verification process operates properly provided that the corresponding algorithms get the corresponding keys (states). Note that in Definition 6.3.9, the keys are modified by the signing-verification process, and so correct verification requires holding the correctly updated verification-key. We stress that the furthermore-clause in Condition 2 guarantees that the verification-key is correctly updated as long as the verification process is fed with strings of the correct lengths (but not necessarily with the correct document-signature pairs). This extra requirement implies that, given the initial verification-key and the current document-signature pair, as well as the lengths of all previous pairs (which may be actually incorporated in the current signature), one may correctly decide whether or not the current document-signature pair is valid. As in the case of state-based ciphers (cf. Section 5.3.1), this fact is interesting for two reasons:

A theoretical reason: It implies that without loss of generality (alas, with possible loss in efficiency), the verification algorithm may be stateless. Furthermore, without loss of generality (alas, with possible loss in efficiency), the state of the signing algorithm may consist of the initial signing-key and the lengths of the messages signed so far. (We assume here that the length of the signature is determined by the length of the message and the length of the signing-key.)

A practical reason: It allows for recovery from the loss of some of the message-signature pairs. That is, assuming that all messages have the same length (which is typically the case in MAC applications), if the receiver knows (or is given) the total number of messages sent so far, then it can verify the authenticity of the current message-signature pair, even if some of the previous message-signature pairs were lost.

We stress that Definition 6.3.9 refers to the signing of multiple messages (and is meaningless when considering the signing of a single message). However, Definition 6.3.9 (by itself) does not explain why one should sign the i-th message using the updated signing-key $s^{(i-1)}$, rather than by reusing the initial signing-key $s^{(0)}$ (where all corresponding verifications are done by reusing the initial verification-key $v^{(0)}$). Indeed, the reason for updating these keys is provided by the following security definition that refers to the signing of multiple messages, and holds only in case the signing-keys in use are properly updated (in the multiple-message authentication process).

Definition 6.3.10 (security of state-based MACs):

- *A* chosen message attack on a state-based MAC, *(G, S, V), is an interactive process that is initiated with $(s^{(0)}, v^{(0)}) \leftarrow G(1^n)$, and proceeds as follows: In the i-th iteration, based on the information gathered so far, the attacker selects a string $\alpha^{(i)}$, and obtains $\beta^{(i)}$, where $(s^{(i)}, \beta^{(i)}) \leftarrow S(s^{(i-1)}, \alpha^{(i)})$.*
- *Such an attack is said to* succeed *if it outputs a valid signature to a string for which it has* not *requested a signature during the attack. That is, the attack is successful if it outputs a pair (α, β) such that α is different from all signature-queries made*

during the attack, and $V(v^{(i-1)}, \alpha, \beta) = (\cdot, 1)$ *holds for some intermediate state* (*verification-key*) $v^{(i-1)}$ (*as in Definition 6.3.9*).[15]

- *A state-based MAC is* secure *if every probabilistic polynomial-time chosen message attack as in the first item succeeds with at most negligible probability.*

Note that Definition 6.3.10 (only) differs from Definition 6.1.2 in the way that the signatures $\beta^{(i)}$'s are produced (i.e., using the updated signing-key $s^{(i-1)}$, rather than the initial signing-key $s^{(0)}$). Furthermore, Definition 6.3.10 guarantees nothing regarding a signing process in which the signature to the i-th message is obtained by invoking $S(s^{(0)}, \cdot)$ (as in Definition 6.1.2).

6.3.2.2. State-Based Hash-and-Hide MACs

We are now ready to present alternative implementations of the hash-and-hide paradigm. Recall that in Section 6.3.1.3, the document was hashed (by using an adequate hashing function), and the resulting hash-value was (authenticated and) hidden by applying a pseudorandom function to it. In the current subsection, hiding will be obtained in a more natural (and typically more efficient) way, that is, by XORing the hash-value with a new portion of a (pseudorandom) one-time pad. Indeed, the state is used in order to keep track of what part of the (one-time) pad was already used (and should not be used again). Furthermore, to obtain improved efficiency, we let the state encode information that allows fast generation of the next portion of the (pseudorandom) one-time pad. This is obtained using an (on-line) pseudorandom generator (see Sections 3.3.3 and 5.3.1).

Recall that *on-line pseudorandom generators* are a special case of variable-output pseudorandom generators (see Section 3.3.3), in which a hidden state is maintained and updated so as to allow generation of the next output bit in time polynomial in the length of the initial seed, regardless of the number of bits generated so far. Specifically, the next (hidden) state and output bit are produced by applying a (polynomial-time computable) function $g : \{0, 1\}^n \to \{0, 1\}^{n+1}$ to the current state (i.e., $(s', \sigma) \leftarrow g(s)$, where s is the current state, s' is the next state and σ is the next output bit). Analogously to Construction 5.3.3, the suggested state-based MAC will use an on-line pseudorandom generator in order to generate the required pseudorandom one-time pad, and the latter will be used to hide (and authenticate) the hash-value (obtained by hashing the original document).

Construction 6.3.11 (a state-based MAC): *Let* $g : \{0, 1\}^* \to \{0, 1\}^*$ *such that* $|g(s)| = |s| + 1$, *for every* $s \in \{0, 1\}^*$. *Let* $\{h_r : \{0, 1\}^* \to \{0, 1\}^{m(|r|)}\}_{r \in \{0,1\}^*}$ *be a family of functions having an efficient evaluation algorithm.*

---

[15] In fact, one may strengthen the definition by using a weaker notion of success in which it is only required that $\alpha \neq \alpha^{(i)}$ (rather than requiring that $\alpha \notin \{\alpha^{(j)}\}_j$). That is, the attack is successful if, for some i, it outputs a pair (α, β) such that $\alpha \neq \alpha^{(i)}$ and $V(v^{(i-1)}, \alpha, \beta) = (\cdot, 1)$, where the $\alpha^{(j)}$'s and $v^{(j)}$'s are as in Definition 6.3.9. The stronger definition provides "replay protection" (i.e., even if the adversary obtains a valid signature that authenticates α as the j-th message, it cannot produce a valid signature that authenticates α as the i-th message, unless α was actually authenticated as the i-th message).

Key-generation and initial state: *Uniformly select $s, r \in \{0, 1\}^n$, and output the key-pair $((s, r), (s, r))$. The initial state of each algorithm is set to $(s, r, 0, s)$.*

(We maintain the initial key (s, r) and a step-counter in order to allow recovery from loss of message-signature pairs.)

Signing message α with state (s, r, t, s'): *Let $s_0 \overset{\text{def}}{=} s'$. For $i = 1, ..., m(n)$, compute $s_i \sigma_i = g(s_{i-1})$, where $|s_i| = n$ and $\sigma_i \in \{0, 1\}$. Output the signature $h_r(\alpha) \oplus \sigma_1 \cdots \sigma_{m(n)}$, and set the new state to $(s, r, t + m(n), s_{m(n)})$.*

Verification of the pair (α, β) with respect to the state (s, r, t, s'): *Compute $\sigma_1 \cdots \sigma_{m(n)}$ and $s_{m(n)}$ as in the signing process; that is, for $i = 1, ..., m(n)$, compute $s_i \sigma_i = g(s_{i-1})$, where $s_0 \overset{\text{def}}{=} s'$. Set the new state to $(s, r, t + m(n), s_{m(n)})$, and accept if and only if $\beta = h_r(\alpha) \oplus \sigma_1 \cdots \sigma_{m(n)}$.*

Special recovery procedure: *When notified that some message-signature pairs may have been lost and that the current message-signature pair has index t', one first recovers the correct current state, which as in the ordinary verification (of the previous paragraph) will be denoted s_0. This is done by setting $s_{-t'} \overset{\text{def}}{=} s$ and computing $s_{i-t'} \sigma_{i-t'} = g(s_{i-t'-1})$, for $i = 1, ..., t'$. Indeed, recovery of s_0 is required only if $t' \neq t$.*[16]

Note that both the signing and verification algorithms are deterministic, and that the state after authentication of t messages has length $3n + \log_2(t \cdot m(n)) < 4n$, provided that $t < 2^n/m(n)$.

We now turn to the analysis of the security of Construction 6.3.11. The hashing property of the collection of h_r's should be slightly stronger than the one used in Section 6.3.1.3. Specifically, rather than a bound on the collision probability (i.e., the probability that $h_r(x) = h_r(y)$ for any relevant fixed x, y and a random r), we need a bound on the probability that $h_r(x) \oplus h_r(y)$ equals any fixed string (again, for any relevant fixed x, y and a random r). This property is commonly referred to by the name Almost-Xor-Universal (AXU). That is, $\{h_r : \{0, 1\}^* \to \{0, 1\}^{m(|r|)}\}_{r \in \{0,1\}^*}$ is called an (ℓ, ε)-AXU family if for every $n \in \mathbb{N}$, every $x \neq y$ such that $|x|, |y| \leq \ell(n)$, and every z, it holds that

$$\Pr[h_{U_n}(x) \oplus h_{U_n}(y) = z] \leq \varepsilon(n) \tag{6.4}$$

References to constructions of such families are provided in Section 6.6.5.

Proposition 6.3.12: *Suppose that g is a pseudorandom generator,[17] and that $\{h_r\}$ is a (ℓ, ε)-AXU family, for some super-polynomial ℓ and negligible ε. Then Construction 6.3.11 constitutes a secure state-based MAC. Furthermore, security holds even with respect to the stronger notion discussed in footnote 15.*

---

[16] More generally, if the verification procedure holds the state at time $t < t'$, then it need only compute $s_{t+1-t'}, ..., s_0$.

[17] In fact, as shown in the proof, it suffices to assume that g is a next-step function of an on-line pseudorandom generator.

Proof Sketch: By Exercise 21 of Chapter 3, if g is a pseudorandom generator, then for every polynomial p the ensemble $\{G_n^p\}_{n \in \mathbb{N}}$ is pseudorandom, where G_n^p is defined by the following random process:

Uniformly select $s_0 \in \{0, 1\}^n$;
For $i = 1$ to $p(n)$, let $s_i \sigma_i \leftarrow g(s_{i-1})$, where $\sigma_i \in \{0, 1\}$ (and $s_i \in \{0, 1\}^n$);
Output $\sigma_1 \sigma_2 \cdots \sigma_{p(n)}$.

Recall that, in such a case, we said that g is a next-step function of an on-line pseudorandom generator.

As in previous cases, it suffices to establish the security of an ideal scheme in which the sequence (of $m(n)$-bit long blocks) produced by iterating the next-step function g is replaced by a truly random sequence (of $m(n)$-bit long blocks). In the ideal scheme, all that the adversary may obtain via a chosen message attack is a sequence of $m(n)$-bit long blocks, which is uniformly distributed among all such possible sequences. Note that each of the signatures obtained during the attack, as well as the forged signature, refers to a single block in this sequence (e.g., the i-th obtained signature refers to the i-th block). We consider two types of forgery attempts:

1. In case the adversary tries to forge a signature referring to an *unused* (during the attack) block, it may succeed with probability at most $2^{-m(n)}$, because we may think of this block as being chosen after the adversary makes its forgery attempt. Note that $2^{-m(n)}$ is negligible, because $\varepsilon(n) \geq 2^{-m(n)}$ must hold (i.e., $2^{-m(n)}$ lower-bounds the collision probability).

2. The more interesting case is when the adversary tries to forge a signature referring to a block, say the i-th one, that was used (to answer the i-th query) during the attack. Denote the j-th query by $\alpha^{(j)}$, the (random) j-th block by $b^{(j)}$, and the forged document by α. Then, at the time of outputting the forgery attempt (α, β), the adversary only knows the sequence of $b^{(j)} \oplus h_r(\alpha^{(j)})$'s (as well as the $\alpha^{(j)}$'s that were chosen by it), but this yields no information on r (because the $b^{(j)}$'s are random and unknown to the adversary). Note that the adversary succeeds if and only if $b^{(i)} \oplus h_r(\alpha) = \beta$, where $\beta^{(i)} \stackrel{\text{def}}{=} b^{(i)} \oplus h_r(\alpha^{(i)})$ is known to it. Thus, the adversary succeeds if and only if $h_r(\alpha^{(i)}) \oplus h_r(\alpha) = \beta^{(i)} \oplus \beta$, where $\alpha^{(i)}, \beta^{(i)}, \alpha, \beta$ are known to the adversary and r is uniformly distributed.

> **Further clarification:** Considering the distribution of r conditioned on partial transcripts of the attack (i.e., the sequence of queries and answers), we claim that at any time, r is uniformly distributed in $\{0, 1\}^n$. The claim holds because, for each possible value of r, the answers to the different queries are all uniformly distributed (because they are XORed with random $b^{(j)}$'s). Thus, r is uniformly distributed also conditioned on the transcript at the time that the adversary outputs its forgery attack, which in turn is successful if and only if $b^{(i)} \oplus h_r(\alpha) = \beta$ holds, where $b^{(i)} = h_r(\alpha^{(i)}) \oplus \beta^{(i)}$ and $\alpha^{(i)}, \beta^{(i)}, \alpha, \beta$ are fixed by this transcript. Thus, a successful forgery implies $h_r(\alpha^{(i)}) \oplus h_r(\alpha) = \beta^{(i)} \oplus \beta$, for fixed $\alpha^{(i)}, \beta^{(i)}, \alpha, \beta$ and uniformly distributed r.

Hence, by the AXU property, the probability that the adversary succeeds is at most $\varepsilon(n)$.

The security of the real scheme follows (or else one could have distinguished the sequence produced by iterating the next-step function g from a truly random sequence). ∎

Construction 6.3.11 Versus the Constructions of Section 6.3.1.3: Recall that all these schemes are based on the hash-and-hide paradigm. The difference between the schemes is that in Section 6.3.1.3, a pseudorandom function is applied to the hash-value (i.e., the signature to α is $f_s(h_r(\alpha))$), whereas in Construction 6.3.11, the hash-value is XORed with a pseudorandom value (i.e., we may view the signature as consisting of $(c, h_r(\alpha) \oplus f_s(c))$, where c is a counter value and $f_s(c)$ is the c-th block produced by iterating the next-step function g starting with the initial seed s). We note two advantages of the state-based MAC over the MACs presented in Section 6.3.1.3: First, applying an on-line pseudorandom generator is likely to be more efficient than applying a pseudorandom function. Second, a counter allows for securely authenticating more messages than can be securely authenticated by applying a pseudorandom function to the hashed value. Specifically, the use of an an m-bit long counter allows for securely authenticating 2^m messages, whereas using an m-bit long hash-value suffers from the "birthday effect" (i.e., collisions are likely to occur when $\sqrt{2^m}$ messages are authenticated). Indeed, these advantages are relevant only in applications in which using state-based MACs is possible, and are most advantageous in applications where verification is performed in the same order as signing (e.g., in FIFO communication). In the latter case, Construction 6.3.11 offers another advantage: "replay protection" (as discussed in footnote 15).

6.4. Constructions of Signature Schemes

In this section, we present several constructions of secure *public-key* signature schemes. In the sequel, we refer to such schemes as *signature schemes,* which is indeed the traditional term.

Two central paradigms in the construction of signature schemes are the "refreshing" of the "effective" signing-key (see Section 6.4.2.1), and the usage of an "authentication-tree" (see Section 6.4.2.2). In addition, the "hash-and-sign paradigm" (employed also in the construction of message-authentication schemes) plays an even more crucial role in the following presentation. In addition, we use the notion of a *one-time signature scheme* (see Section 6.4.1).

The current section is organized as follows. In Section 6.4.1 we define and construct various types of one-time signature schemes. The hash-and-sign paradigm plays a crucial role in one of these constructions, which in turn is essential for Section 6.4.2. In Section 6.4.2 we show how to use one-time signature schemes to construct general signature schemes. This construction utilizes the "refreshing paradigm" (as applied to one-time signature schemes) and an authentication-tree. Thus, *assuming the existence of collision-free hashing, we obtain* (general) *signature schemes.*

In Section 6.4.3, wishing to relax the conditions under which signature schemes can be constructed, we define *universal one-way hashing functions,* and show how to use them instead of collision-free hashing (in the aforementioned constructions and, in particular, within a modified hash-and-sign paradigm). Indeed, the gain in using universal one-way hashing (rather than collision-free hashing) is that the former can be constructed based on any one-way function (whereas this is not known for collision-free hashing). Thus, we obtain:

Theorem 6.4.1: *Secure signature schemes exist if and only if one-way functions exist.*

The difficult direction is to show that the existence of one-way functions implies the existence of signature schemes. For the opposite direction, see Exercise 7.

6.4.1. One-Time Signature Schemes

In this section we define and construct various types of one-time signature schemes. Specifically, we first define one-time signature schemes, next define a length-restricted version of this notion (analogous to Definition 6.2.1), then present a simple construction of the latter, and finally show how such a construction, combined with collision-free hashing, yields a general one-time signature scheme.

6.4.1.1. Definitions

Loosely speaking, one-time signature schemes are signature schemes for which the security requirement is restricted to attacks in which the adversary asks for at most one string to be signed. That is, the mechanics of one-time signature schemes is as of ordinary signature schemes (see Definition 6.1.1), but the security requirement is relaxed as follows:

- A chosen one-message attack is a process that can obtain a signature to *at most one* string of its choice. That is, the attacker is given v as input, and obtains a signature relative to s, where $(s, v) \leftarrow G(1^n)$ for an adequate n.
  (Note that in this section, we focus on public-key signature schemes and thus present only the definition for this case.)
- Such an attack is said to succeed (*in existential forgery*) if it outputs a valid signature to a string for which it has *not* requested a signature during the attack.
  (Indeed, the notion of success is exactly as in Definition 6.1.2.)
- A one-time signature scheme is secure (or unforgeable) if every feasible chosen *one*-message attack succeeds with at most negligible probability.

Moving to the formal definition, we again model a chosen message attack as a probabilistic oracle machine; however, since here we care only about *one*-message attacks, we consider only oracle machines that make at most one query. Let M be such a machine. As before, we denote by $Q_M^O(x)$ the set of queries made by M on input x and access to oracle O, and let $M^O(x)$ denote the output of the corresponding computation. Note that here $|Q_M^O(x)| \leq 1$ (i.e., M may make either no queries or a single query).

Definition 6.4.2 (security for one-time signature schemes): *A one-time signature scheme is* secure *if for every probabilistic polynomial-time oracle machine M that makes at most one query, every positive polynomial p, and all sufficiently large n, it holds that*

$$\Pr\left[\begin{array}{c} V_v(\alpha, \beta) = 1 \ \& \ \alpha \notin Q_M^{S_s}(1^n) \\ \text{where } (s, v) \leftarrow G(1^n) \text{ and } (\alpha, \beta) \leftarrow M^{S_s}(v) \end{array} \right] < \frac{1}{p(n)}$$

where the probability is taken over the coin tosses of algorithms G, S, and V, as well as over the coin tosses of machine M.

We now define a length-restricted version of one-time signature schemes. The definition is indeed analogous to Definition 6.2.1:

Definition 6.4.3 (length-restricted one-time signature schemes): *Let $\ell : \mathbb{N} \to \mathbb{N}$. An ℓ-restricted one-time signature scheme is a triple, (G, S, V), of probabilistic polynomial-time algorithms satisfying the the mechanics of Definition 6.2.1. That is, it satisfies the following two conditions:*

1. *As in Definition 6.1.1, on input 1^n, algorithm G outputs a pair of bit strings.*
2. *Analogously to Definition 6.1.1, for every n and every pair (s, v) in the range of $G(1^n)$, and for every $\alpha \in \{0, 1\}^{\ell(n)}$, algorithms S and D satisfy $\Pr[V_v(\alpha, S_s(\alpha)) = 1] = 1$.*

Such a scheme is called secure *(in the one-time model) if the requirement of Definition 6.4.2 holds when restricted to attackers that only make queries of length $\ell(n)$ and output a pair (α, β) with $|\alpha| = \ell(n)$. That is, we consider only attackers that make at most one query, with the requirements that this query be of length $\ell(n)$ and that the output (α, β) satisfies $|\alpha| = \ell(n)$.*

Note that even the existence of secure 1-restricted one-time signature schemes implies the existence of one-way functions, see Exercise 13.

6.4.1.2. Constructing Length-Restricted One-Time Signature Schemes

We now present a simple construction of length-restricted one-time signature schemes. The construction works for any length-restriction function ℓ, but the keys will have length greater than ℓ. The latter fact limits the applicability of such schemes and will be removed in the next subsection. But first, we construct ℓ-restricted one-time signature schemes that are based on any one-way function f. Loosely speaking, the verification-key will consist of ℓ *pairs* of images (of f), and a signature will consist of ℓ pre-images (under f) corresponding to ℓ out of these 2ℓ images, where the selection of images is determined by the corresponding bits of the message. We may assume for simplicity that f is length-preserving.

Construction 6.4.4 (an ℓ-restricted one-time signature scheme): *Let $\ell : \mathbb{N} \to \mathbb{N}$ be polynomially bounded and polynomial-time computable, and $f : \{0, 1\}^* \to \{0, 1\}^*$ be* *polynomial-time computable and length-preserving. We construct an ℓ-restricted one-time signature scheme, (G, S, V), as follows:*

Key-generation with G: *On input 1^n, we uniformly select $s_1^0, s_1^1, ..., s_{\ell(n)}^0, s_{\ell(n)}^1 \in \{0, 1\}^n$, and compute $v_i^j = f(s_i^j)$, for $i = 1, ..., \ell(n)$ and $j = 0, 1$. We let $s = ((s_1^0, s_1^1), ..., (s_{\ell(n)}^0, s_{\ell(n)}^1))$, and $v = ((v_1^0, v_1^1), ..., (v_{\ell(n)}^0, v_{\ell(n)}^1))$, and output the key-pair (s, v).*
(Note that $|s| = |v| = 2 \cdot \ell(n) \cdot n$.)

Signing with S: *On input a signing-key $s = ((s_1^0, s_1^1), ..., (s_{\ell(n)}^0, s_{\ell(n)}^1))$ and an $\ell(n)$-bit string $\alpha = \sigma_1 \cdots \sigma_{\ell(n)}$, we output $(s_1^{\sigma_1}, ..., s_{\ell(n)}^{\sigma_{\ell(n)}})$ as a signature of α.*

Verification with V: *On input a verification-key $v = ((v_1^0, v_1^1), ..., (v_{\ell(n)}^0, v_{\ell(n)}^1))$, an $\ell(n)$-bit string $\alpha = \sigma_1 \cdots \sigma_{\ell(n)}$, and an alleged signature $\beta = (\beta_1, ..., \beta_{\ell(n)})$, we accept if and only if $v_i^{\sigma_i} = f(\beta_i)$, for $i = 1, ..., \ell(n)$.*

Proposition 6.4.5: *If f is a one-way function, then Construction 6.4.4 constitutes a secure ℓ-restricted one-time signature scheme.*

Note that Construction 6.4.4 does *not* constitute a (general) ℓ-restricted signature scheme: An attacker that obtains signatures to *two* strings (e.g., to the strings $0^{\ell(n)}$ and $1^{\ell(n)}$), can present a valid signature to any $\ell(n)$-bit long string (and thus totally break the system). However, here we consider only attackers that may ask for at most one string (of their choice) to be signed. As a corollary to Proposition 6.4.5, we obtain:

Corollary 6.4.6: *If there exist one-way functions, then for every polynomially bounded and polynomial-time computable $\ell : \mathbb{N} \to \mathbb{N}$, there exist secure ℓ-restricted one-time signature schemes.*

Proof of Proposition 6.4.5: Intuitively, forging a signature (after seeing at most one signature to a different message) requires inverting f on some random image (corresponding to a bit location on which the two $\ell(n)$-bit long messages differ). The actual proof is by a reducibility argument. Given an adversary A attacking the scheme (G, S, V), while making at most one query, we construct an algorithm A' for inverting f.

As a warm-up, let us first deal with the case in which A makes no queries at all. In this case, on input y (supposedly in the range of f), algorithm A' proceeds as follows. First A' selects uniformly and independently a position p in $\{1, ..., \ell(n)\}$, a bit b, and a sequence of ($2\ell(n)$ many) n-bit long strings $s_1^0, s_1^1, ..., s_{\ell(n)}^0, s_{\ell(n)}^1$. (Actually, s_p^b is not used and needs not be selected.) For every $i \in \{1, ..., \ell(n)\} \setminus \{p\}$, and every $j \in \{0, 1\}$, algorithm A' computes $v_i^j = f(s_i^j)$. Algorithm A' also computes $v_p^{1-b} = f(s_p^{1-b})$, and sets $v_p^b = y$ and $v = ((v_1^0, v_1^1), ..., (v_{\ell(n)}^0, v_{\ell(n)}^1))$. Note that if $y = f(x)$, for a uniformly distributed $x \in \{0, 1\}^n$, then for each possible choice of p and b, the sequence v is distributed identically to the public-key generated by $G(1^n)$. Next, A' invokes A on input v, hoping that A will forge a signature, denoted $\beta = \tau_1 \cdots \tau_{\ell(n)}$, to a message $\alpha = \sigma_1 \cdots \sigma_{\ell(n)}$ so that $\sigma_p = b$. If this event occurs, A' obtains a pre-image of y under

f, because the validity of the signature implies that $f(\tau_p) = v_p^{\sigma_p} = v_p^b = y$. Observe that conditioned on the value of v and the internal coin tosses of A, the value b is uniformly distributed in $\{0, 1\}$. Thus, A' inverts f with probability $\varepsilon(n)/2$, where $\varepsilon(n)$ denotes the probability that A succeeds in forgery.

We turn back to the actual case in which A may make a single query. Without loss of generality, we assume that A always makes a single query; see Exercise 11. In this case, on input y (supposedly in the range of f), algorithm A' selects p, b and the s_i^j's, and forms the v_i^j's and v exactly as in the previous warm-up discussion. Recall that if $y = f(x)$, for a uniformly distributed $x \in \{0, 1\}^n$, then for each possible choice of p and b, the sequence v is distributed identically to the public-key generated by $G(1^n)$. Also note that for each v_i^j other than $v_p^b = y$, algorithm A' holds a random pre-image (of v_i^j) under f. Next, A' invokes A on input v, and tries to answer its query, denoted $\alpha = \sigma_1 \cdots \sigma_{\ell(n)}$. We consider two cases regarding this query:

1. If $\sigma_p = b$, then A' cannot supply the desired signature because it lacks a pre-image of $s_p^b = y$ under f. Thus, in this case A' aborts. However, this case occurs with probability $\frac{1}{2}$, independently of the actions of A (because v yields no information on either p or b).

   (That is, conditioned on the value of v and the internal coin tosses of A, this case occurs with probability $\frac{1}{2}$.)[18]

2. If $\sigma_p = 1 - b$, then A' can supply the desired signature because it holds all the relevant s_i^j's (i.e., random pre-images of the relevant v_i^j's under f). In particular, A' holds both s_i^j's, for $i \neq p$, as well as s_p^{1-b}. Thus, A' answers with $(s_1^{\sigma_1}, ..., s_{\ell(n)}^{\sigma_{\ell(n)}})$.

Note that conditioned on the value of v, on the internal coin tosses of A, and on the second case occuring, p is uniformly distributed in $\{1, ..., \ell(n)\}$. When the second case occurs, A obtains a signature to α, and this signature is distributed exactly as in a real attack. We stress that since A asks at most one query, no additional query will be asked by A. Also note that, in this case (i.e., $\sigma_p = 1 - b$), algorithm A outputs a forged message-signature pair, denoted (α', β'), with probability exactly as in a real attack.

We now turn to the analysis of A', and consider first the emulated attack of A. Recall that $\alpha = \sigma_1 \cdots \sigma_{\ell(n)}$ denotes the (single) query[19] made by A, and let $\alpha' = \sigma_1' \cdots \sigma_{\ell(n)}'$ and $\beta' = s_1' \cdots s_{\ell(n)}'$, where (α', β') is the forged message-signature pair output by A. By our hypothesis (that this is a forgery-success event), it follows that $\alpha' \neq \alpha$ and that $f(s_i') = v_i^{\sigma_i'}$ for all i's. Now, considering the emulation of A by A', recall that (under all these conditions) p is uniformly distributed in $\{1, ..., \ell(n)\}$. Hence, with probability $\frac{|\{i : \sigma_i' \neq \sigma_i\}|}{\ell(n)} \geq \frac{1}{\ell(n)}$, it holds that $\sigma_p' \neq \sigma_p$, and in that case, A' obtains a pre-image of y under f (since s_p' satisfies $f(s_p') = v_p^{\sigma_p'}$, which in turn equals $v_p^{1-\sigma_p} = v_p^b = y$).

---

[18] This follows from an even stronger statement by which conditioned on the value of v, on the internal coin tosses of A, and on the value of p, the current case happens with probability $\frac{1}{2}$. The stronger statement holds because under all these conditions, b is uniformly distributed in $\{0, 1\}$ (and so $\sigma_p = b$ happens with probability exactly $\frac{1}{2}$).

[19] Recall that, without loss of generality, we may assume that A always makes a single query; see Exercise 11.

To summarize, assuming that A succeeds in a single-message attack on (G, S, V) with probability $\varepsilon(n)$, algorithm A' inverts f on a random image (i.e., on $f(U_n)$) with probability

$$\varepsilon(n) \cdot \frac{1}{2} \cdot \frac{|\{i : \sigma_i' \neq \sigma_i\}|}{\ell(n)} \geq \frac{\varepsilon(n)}{2\ell(n)}$$

Thus, if A is a probabilistic polynomial-time *chosen one-message* attack that forges signatures with non-negligible probability, then A' is a probabilistic polynomial-time algorithm that inverts f with non-negligible probability (in violation of the hypothesis that f is a one-way function). The proposition follows. ■

6.4.1.3. From Length-Restricted Schemes to General Ones

Using the hash-and-sign paradigm (i.e., Construction 6.2.6), we transform *length-restricted* one-time signature schemes into one-time signature schemes. That is, we use collision-free hashing and apply Construction 6.2.6, except that here (G, S, V) is an ℓ-restricted *one-time* signature scheme, rather than an ℓ-restricted (general) signature scheme. Analogously to Proposition 6.2.7, we obtain:

Proposition 6.4.7: *Suppose that (G, S, V) is a secure ℓ-restricted one-time signature scheme, and that $\{h_r : \{0, 1\}^* \to \{0, 1\}^{\ell(|r|)}\}_{r \in \{0,1\}^*}$ is a collision-free hashing collection. Then (G', S', V'), as defined in Construction 6.2.6, is a secure one-time signature scheme.*

Proof: The proof is identical to the proof of Proposition 6.2.7; we merely notice that if the adversary A', attacking (G', S', V'), makes at most one query, then the same holds for the adversary A that we construct (in that proof) to attack (G, S, V). In general, the adversary A constructed in the proof of Proposition 6.2.7 makes a single query per each query of the adversary A'. ■

Combining Proposition 6.4.7, Corollary 6.4.6, and the fact that collision-free hashing collections, imply one-way functions (see Exercise 14), we obtain:

Corollary 6.4.8: *If there exist collision-free hashing collections, then there exist secure one-time signature schemes. Furthermore, the length of the resulting signatures depends only on the length of the signing-key.*

Comments. We stress that when using Construction 6.2.6, signing each document under the (general) scheme (G', S', V') only requires signing a single string under the ℓ-restricted scheme (G, S, V). This is in contrast to Construction 6.2.3, in which signing a document under the (general) scheme (G', S', V') requires signing many strings under the ℓ-restricted scheme (G, S, V), where the number of such strings depends (linearly) on the length of the original document.

Construction 6.2.6 calls for the use of collision-free hashing. The latter can be constructed using any claw-free permutation collection (see Proposition 6.2.9); however, it is not know whether collision-free hashing can be constructed based on any one-way function. Wishing to construct signature schemes based on any one-way function, we later avoid (in Section 6.4.3) the use of collision-free hashing. Instead, we use "universal one-way hashing functions" (to be defined), and present a variant of Construction 6.2.6 that uses these functions, rather than collision-free ones.

6.4.2. From One-Time Signature Schemes to General Ones

In this section we show how to construct general signature schemes using one-time signature schemes. That is, we shall prove:

Theorem 6.4.9: *If there exist secure* one-time *signature schemes, then secure* (general) *signature schemes exist as well.*

Actually, we can use length-restricted one-time signature schemes, *provided that the length of the strings being signed is at least twice the length of the verification-key.* Unfortunately, Construction 6.4.4 does not satisfy this condition. Nevertheless, Corollary 6.4.8 does provide one-time signature schemes. Thus, combining Theorem 6.4.9 and Corollary 6.4.8, we obtain:

Corollary 6.4.10: *If there exist collision-free hashing collections, then there exist secure signature schemes.*

Note that Corollary 6.4.10 asserts the existence of secure (public-key) signature schemes, based on an assumption that does *not* mention trapdoors. We stress this point because of the contrast to the situation with respect to public-key encryption schemes, where a trapdoor property seems necessary for the construction of secure schemes.

6.4.2.1. The Refreshing Paradigm

The so-called "refreshing paradigm" plays a central role in the proof of Theorem 6.4.9. Loosely speaking, the refreshing paradigm suggests reducing the dangers of a chosen message attack on the signature scheme by using "fresh" instances of the scheme for signing each new document. Of course, these fresh instances should be authenticated by the original instance (corresponding to the verification-key that is publicly known), but such an authentication refers to a string selected by the legitimate signer, rather than by the adversary.

Example. To demonstrate the refreshing paradigm, consider a basic signature scheme (G, S, V) used as follows. Suppose that the user U has generated a key-pair, $(s, v) \leftarrow G(1^n)$, and has placed the verification-key v on a public-file. When a party asks U to sign some document α, the user U generates a new (fresh) key-pair, $(s', v') \leftarrow G(1^n)$, signs v' using the original signing-key s, signs α using the new (fresh) signing-key s', and presents $(S_s(v'), v', S_{s'}(\alpha))$ as a signature to α. An alleged signature, (β_1, v', β_2), is verified by checking whether both $V_v(v', \beta_1) = 1$ and $V_{v'}(\alpha, \beta_2) = 1$ hold. Intuitively, the gain in terms of security is that a full-fledged chosen message attack cannot be launched on (G, S, V). All that an attacker may obtain (via a chosen message attack on the new scheme) is signatures, relative to the original signing-key s, to randomly chosen strings (taken from the distribution $G_2(1^n)$), as well as additional signatures each relative to a random and independently chosen signing-key.

We refrain from analyzing the features of the signature scheme presented in this example. Instead, as a warm-up to the actual construction used in the next section (in order to establish Theorem 6.4.9), we present and analyze a similar construction (which is, in some sense, a hybrid of the two constructions). The reader may skip this warm-up, and proceed directly to Section 6.4.2.2.

Construction 6.4.11 (a warm-up): *Let (G, S, V) be a signature scheme and (G', S', V') be a one-time signature scheme. Consider a signature scheme, (G'', S'', V''), with $G'' = G$, as follows:*

Signing with S'': *On input a signing-key s (in the range of $G_1''(1^n)$) and a document $\alpha \in \{0, 1\}^*$, first invoke G' to obtain $(s', v') \leftarrow G'(1^n)$. Next, invoke S to obtain $\beta_1 \leftarrow S_s(v')$, and S' to obtain $\beta_2 \leftarrow S'_{s'}(\alpha)$. The final output is (β_1, v', β_2).*

Verification with V'': *On input a verifying-key v, a document $\alpha \in \{0, 1\}^*$, and an alleged signature $\beta = (\beta_1, v', \beta_2)$, we output 1 if and only if both $V_v(v', \beta_1) = 1$ and $V'_{v'}(\alpha, \beta_2) = 1$.*

Construction 6.4.11 differs from the previous example only in that a one-time signature scheme is used to generate the "second signature" (rather than using the same ordinary signature scheme). The use of a one-time signature scheme is natural here, because it is unlikely that the same signing-key s' will be selected in two invocations of S''.

Proposition 6.4.12: *Suppose that (G, S, V) is a secure signature scheme, and that (G', S', V') is a secure one-time signature scheme. Then (G'', S'', V''), as defined in Construction 6.4.11, is a secure signature scheme.*

We comment that the proposition holds even if (G, S, V) is secure only against attackers that select queries according to the distribution $G_2'(1^n)$. Furthermore, (G, S, V) need only be ℓ-restricted, for some suitable function $\ell : \mathbb{N} \to \mathbb{N}$.

Proof Sketch: Consider an adversary A'' attacking the scheme (G'', S'', V''). We may ignore the case in which two queries of A'' are answered by triplets containing the same one-time verification-key v' (because if this event occurs with non-negligible probability, then the one-time scheme (G', S', V') cannot be secure). We consider two cases regarding the relation of the one-time verification-keys included in the signatures provided by S''_s and the one-time verification-key included in the signature forged by A''.

1. In case, *for some i,* the one-time verification-key v' contained in the forged message equals the one-time verification-key $v^{(i)}$ contained in the answer to the i-th query, we derive violation to the security of the one-time scheme (G', S', V').

Specifically, consider an adversary A' that on input a verification-key v' for the one-time scheme (G', S', V'), generates $(s, v) \leftarrow G(1^n)$ at random, selects i at random (among polynomially many possibilities), invokes A'' on input v, and answers its queries as follows. The i-th query of A'', denoted $\alpha^{(i)}$, is answered by making the only query to $S'_{s'}$, obtaining $\beta' = S'_{s'}(\alpha^{(i)})$, and returning $(S_s(v'), v', \beta')$ to A''. (Note that A' holds s.) Each other query of A'', denoted $\alpha^{(j)}$, is answered by invoking G' to obtain $(s^{(j)}, v^{(j)}) \leftarrow G'(1^n)$, and returning $(S_s(v^{(j)}), v^{(j)}, S'_{s^{(j)}}(\alpha^{(j)}))$ to A''. If A'' answers with a forged signature and v' is the verification-key contained in it, then A' obtains a forged signature relative to the one-time scheme (G', S', V') (i.e., a signature to a message different from $\alpha^{(i)}$, which is valid with respect to the verification-key v'). Furthermore, conditioned on the case hypothesis and a forgery event, the second event (i.e., v' is the verification-key contained in the forged signature) occurs with probability $1/\text{poly}(n)$. Note that, indeed, A' makes at most one query to $S'_{s'}$, and that the distribution seen by A'' is exactly as in an actual attack on (G'', S'', V'').

2. In case, *for all i*, the one-time verification-key v' contained in the forged message is different from the one-time verification-key $v^{(i)}$ contained in the answer to the i-th query, we derive violation to the security of the scheme (G, S, V).

   Specifically, consider an adversary A that on input a verification-key v for the scheme (G, S, V), invokes A'' on input v, and answers its queries as follows. To answer the j-th query of A'', denoted $\alpha^{(j)}$, algorithm A invokes G' to obtain $(s^{(j)}, v^{(j)}) \leftarrow G'(1^n)$, queries S_s for a signature to $v^{(j)}$, and returns $(S_s(v^{(j)}), v^{(j)}, S'_{s^{(j)}}(\alpha^{(j)}))$ to A''. When A'' answers with a forged signature and $v' \notin \{v^{(j)} : j = 1, ..., \text{poly}(n)\}$ is the one-time verification-key contained in it, A obtains a forged signature relative to the scheme (G, S, V) (i.e., a signature to a string v' different from all $v^{(j)}$'s, which is valid with respect to the verification-key v). (Note again that the distribution seen by A'' is exactly as in an actual attack on (G'', S'', V'').)[20]

Thus, in both cases we derive a contradiction to some hypothesis, and the proposition follows. ■

6.4.2.2. Authentication-Trees

The refreshing paradigm by itself (i.e., as employed in Construction 6.4.11) does not seem to suffice for establishing Theorem 6.4.9. Recall that our aim is to construct a general signature scheme based on a one-time signature scheme. The refreshing paradigm suggests using a fresh instance of a one-time signature scheme in order to sign the actual document; however, whenever we do so (as in Construction 6.4.11), we must authenticate this fresh instance relative to the single verification-key that is public. A straightforward implementation of this scheme (as presented in Construction 6.4.11) calls for many signatures to be signed relative to the single verification-key that is public, and so a one-time signature scheme cannot be used (for this purpose). Instead, a more sophisticated method of authentication is called for.

---

[20] Furthermore, all queries to S_s are distributed according to $G_2(1^n)$, justifying the comment made just before the proof sketch.

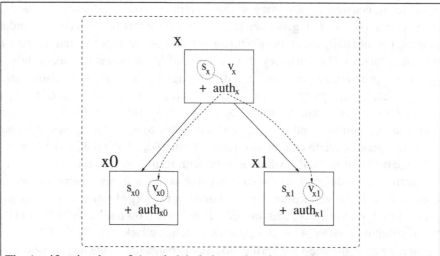

The (verification-key of a) node labeled x authenticates (the verification-keys of) its children, labeled $x0$ and $x1$, respectively. The authentication is via a one-time signature of the text $v_{x0}v_{x1}$ using the signing-key s_x, and it is verifiable with respect to the verification-key v_x.

Figure 6.4: Authentication-trees: the basic authentication step.

Let us try to sketch the basic idea underlying the new authentication method. The idea is to use the public verification-key (of a one-time signature scheme) in order to authenticate several (e.g., two) fresh instances (of the one-time signature scheme), use each of these instances to authenticate several fresh instances, and so on. We obtain a tree of fresh instances of the one-time signature, where each internal node authenticates its children. We can now use the leaves of this tree in order to sign actual documents, where each leaf is used at most once. Thus, a signature to an actual document consists of (1) a one-time signature to this document authenticated with respect to the verification-key associated with some leaf, and (2) a sequence of one-time verification-keys associated with the nodes along the path from the root to this leaf, where each such verification-key is authenticated with respect to the verification-key of its parent (see Figures 6.4 and 6.5). We stress that each instance of the one-time signature scheme is used to sign at most one string (i.e., several verification-keys if the instance resides in an internal node, and an actual document if the instance resides in a leaf).

This description may leave the reader wondering how one actually signs (and verifies signatures) using the process outlined here. We start with a description that does not fit our definition of a signature scheme, because it requires the signer to keep a record of its actions during all previous invocations of the signing process.[21] We refer to such a scheme as *memory dependent,* and define this notion first.

---

[21] This (memory) requirement will be removed in the next section.

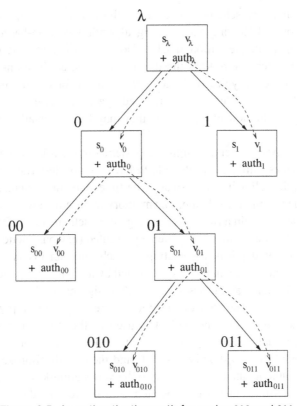

Figure 6.5: An authentication path for nodes 010 and 011.

Definition 6.4.13 (memory-dependent signature schemes):

Mechanics: *Item 1 of Definition 6.1.1 stays as it is, and the* initial state (of the signing algorithm) *is defined to equal the output of the key-generator. Item 2 is modified such that the signing algorithm is given a state, denoted γ, as auxiliary input and returns a modified state, denoted δ, as auxiliary output. It is required that for every pair (s, v) in the range of $G(1^n)$, and for every $\alpha, \gamma \in \{0, 1\}^*$, if $(\beta, \delta) \leftarrow S_s(\alpha, \gamma)$, then $V_v(\alpha, \beta) = 1$ and $|\delta| \leq |\gamma| + |\alpha| \cdot \text{poly}(n)$.*

(That is, the verification algorithm accepts the signature β and the state does not grow by too much.)

Security: *The notion of a chosen message attack is modified so that the oracle S_s now maintains a state that it updates in the natural manner; that is, when in state γ and faced with query α, the oracle sets $(\beta, \delta) \leftarrow S_s(\alpha, \gamma)$, returns β, and updates its state to δ. The notions of success and security are defined as in Definition 6.1.2, except that they now refer to the modified notion of an attack.*

The definition of memory-dependent signature schemes (i.e., Definition 6.4.13) is related to the definition of state-based MACs (i.e., Definition 6.3.10). However, there are two differences between these two definitions: First, Definition 6.4.13 refers to (public-key) signature schemes, whereas Definition 6.3.10 refers to MACs. Second, in Definition 6.4.13, only the signing algorithm is state-based (or memory-dependent), whereas in Definition 6.3.10 also the verification algorithm is state-based. The latter difference reflects the difference in the applications envisioned for both types of schemes. (Typically, MACs are intended for communication between a predetermined set of "mutually synchronized" parties, whereas signature schemes are intended for production of signatures that may be universally verifiable at any time.)

We note that memory-dependent signature schemes may suffice in many applications of signature schemes. Still, it is preferable to have memoryless (i.e., ordinary) signature schemes. In the following, we use any one-time signature schemes to construct a memory-dependent signature scheme. The memory requirement will be removed in the next section, so as to obtain a (memoryless) signature scheme (as in Definition 6.1.1).

The memory-dependent signature scheme presented (in Construction 6.4.14) maintains a binary tree of depth n, associating to each node an instance of a one-time signature scheme. Each node in the tree is labeled by a binary string, denoted $\sigma_1 \cdots \sigma_i$ for some $i \in \{0, 1, ..., n\}$, and is associated with a (signing and verification) key-pair, denoted $(s_{\sigma_1 \cdots \sigma_i}, v_{\sigma_1 \cdots \sigma_i})$. The root of the tree is labeled by the empty string, λ, and the verification-key v_λ associated with it is used as the verification-key of the entire (memory-dependent) signature scheme. The children of an internal node labeled $\sigma_1 \cdots \sigma_i$ are labeled $\sigma_1 \cdots \sigma_i 0$ and $\sigma_1 \cdots \sigma_i 1$, and their verification-keys (i.e., $v_{\sigma_1 \cdots \sigma_i 0}$ and $v_{\sigma_1 \cdots \sigma_i 1}$) are authenticated with respect to the verification-key $v_{\sigma_1 \cdots \sigma_i}$. With the exception of the (one-time) instance associated with the root of the tree, all the other instances are generated (when needed) on the fly, and are stored in memory (along with their authentication with respect to their parents). A new document is signed by allocating a new leaf, authenticating the actual document with respect to the verification-key associated with this leaf, and authenticating each *relevant* verification-key with respect to the verification-key associated with its parent. The relevant key-pairs (as well as their authentication with respect to their parents) are generated on the fly, unless they are already stored in memory (which means that they were generated in the course of signing a previous document). Thus, the verification-key associated with the relevant leaf is authenticated with respect to the verification-key associated with its parent, which in turn is authenticated with respect to the verification-key associated with its own parent, and so on up to the authentication (of the verification-keys of the root's children) with respect to the verification-key associated with the root. The latter sequence of authentications (of each node's verification-key with respect to the verification-key of its parent) is called an authentication path (see Figure 6.5). We stress that the (one-time) instance associated with each node is used to authenticate at most one string. A formal description of this memory-dependent signature scheme follows:

Construction 6.4.14 (a memory-dependent signature scheme): *Let (G, S, V) be a one-time signature scheme. Consider the following memory-dependent signature scheme, (G', S', V'), with $G' = G$. On security parameter n, the scheme uses a full binary tree of depth n. Each of the nodes in this tree is* labeled *by a binary string so that the root is labeled by the empty string, denoted λ, and the left (resp., right) child of a node labeled* *by x is labeled by $x0$ (resp., $x1$). Here we refer to the current state of the signing process as to a* record.

Initiating the scheme: *To initiate the scheme, on security parameter n, we invoke $G(1^n)$ and let $(s, v) \leftarrow G(1^n)$. We record (s, v) as the key-pair associated with the root, and output v as the (public) verification-key.*

In the rest of the description, we denote by (s_x, v_x) the key-pair associated with the node labeled x; thus, $(s_\lambda, v_\lambda) = (s, v)$.

Signing with S' using the current record: *Recall that the current record contains the signing-key $s = s_\lambda$, which is used to produce auth_λ (defined in the sequel).*

To sign a new document, denoted α, we first allocate an unused leaf. Let $\sigma_1 \cdots \sigma_n$ be the label of this leaf. For example, we may keep a counter of the number of documents signed, and determine $\sigma_1 \cdots \sigma_n$ according to the counter value (e.g., if the counter value is c, then we use the c-th string in lexicographic order).[22]

Next, for every $i = 1, \ldots, n$ and every $\tau \in \{0, 1\}$, we try to retrieve from our record the key-pair associated with the node labeled $\sigma_1 \cdots \sigma_{i-1}\tau$. In case such a pair is not found, we generate it by invoking $G(1^n)$ and store it (i.e., add it to our record) for future use; that is, we let $(s_{\sigma_1 \cdots \sigma_{i-1}\tau}, v_{\sigma_1 \cdots \sigma_{i-1}\tau}) \leftarrow G(1^n)$.

Next, for every $i = 1, \ldots, n$, we try to retrieve from our record a signature to the string $v_{\sigma_1 \cdots \sigma_{i-1}0} v_{\sigma_1 \cdots \sigma_{i-1}1}$ relative to the signing-key $s_{\sigma_1 \cdots \sigma_{i-1}}$. In case such a signature is not found, we generate it by invoking $S_{s_{\sigma_1 \cdots \sigma_{i-1}}}$, and store it for future use; that is, we obtain $S_{s_{\sigma_1 \cdots \sigma_{i-1}}}(v_{\sigma_1 \cdots \sigma_{i-1}0} v_{\sigma_1 \cdots \sigma_{i-1}1})$. (The ability to retrieve this signature from memory, for repeated use, is the most important place in which we rely on the memory dependence of our signature scheme.)[23] *We let*

$$\text{auth}_{\sigma_1 \cdots \sigma_{i-1}} \stackrel{\text{def}}{=} \left(v_{\sigma_1 \cdots \sigma_{i-1}0}, \; v_{\sigma_1 \cdots \sigma_{i-1}1}, \; S_{s_{\sigma_1 \cdots \sigma_{i-1}}}(v_{\sigma_1 \cdots \sigma_{i-1}0} v_{\sigma_1 \cdots \sigma_{i-1}1}) \right)$$

(Intuitively, via $\text{auth}_{\sigma_1 \cdots \sigma_{i-1}}$, the node labeled $\sigma_1 \cdots \sigma_{i-1}$ authenticates the verification-keys associated with its children.)

Finally, we sign α by invoking $S_{s_{\sigma_1 \cdots \sigma_n}}$, and output

$$(\sigma_1 \cdots \sigma_n, \text{auth}_\lambda, \text{auth}_{\sigma_1}, \ldots, \text{auth}_{\sigma_1 \cdots \sigma_{n-1}}, S_{s_{\sigma_1 \cdots \sigma_n}}(\alpha))$$

Verification with V': *On input a verification-key v, a document α, and an alleged signature β, we accept if and only if the following conditions hold:*

1. *β has the form*

$$(\sigma_1 \cdots \sigma_n, (v_{0,0}, v_{0,1}, \beta_0), (v_{1,0}, v_{1,1}, \beta_1), \ldots, (v_{n-1,0}, v_{n-1,1}, \beta_{n-1}), \beta_n)$$

---

[22] Alternatively, as done in Construction 6.4.16, we may select the leaf at random (while ignoring the negligible probability that the selected leaf is not unused).

[23] This allows the signing process S_s' to use each (one-time) signing-key s_x for producing a single S_{s_x}-signature. In contrast, the use of a counter for determining a new leaf can be easily avoided, by selecting a leaf at random.

where the σ_i's are bits and all other symbols represent strings.

(Jumping ahead, we mention that $v_{i,\tau}$ is supposed to equal $v_{\sigma_1\cdots\sigma_i\tau}$; that is, the verification-key associated by the signing process with the node labeled $\sigma_1\cdots\sigma_i\tau$. In particular, v_{i-1,σ_i} is supposed to equal $v_{\sigma_1\cdots\sigma_i}$.)

2. $V_v(v_{0,0}v_{0,1}, \beta_0) = 1$.

(That is, the public-key (i.e., v) authenticates the two strings $v_{0,0}$ and $v_{0,1}$ claimed to correspond to the instances of the one-time signature scheme associated with the nodes labeled 0 and 1, respectively.)

3. *For $i = 1, ..., n - 1$, it holds that $V_{v_{i-1,\sigma_i}}(v_{i,0}v_{i,1}, \beta_i) = 1$.*

(That is, the verification-key v_{i-1,σ_i}, which is already believed to be authentic and supposedly corresponds to the instance of the one-time signature scheme associated with the node labeled $\sigma_1\cdots\sigma_i$, authenticates the two strings $v_{i,0}$ and $v_{i,1}$ that are supposed to correspond to the instances of the one-time signature scheme associated with the nodes labeled $\sigma_1\cdots\sigma_i 0$ and $\sigma_1\cdots\sigma_i 1$, respectively.)

4. $V_{v_{n-1,\sigma_n}}(\alpha, \beta_n) = 1$.

(That is, the verification-key v_{n-1,σ_n}, which is already believed to be authentic, authenticates the actual document α.)

Regarding the verification algorithm, note that Conditions 2 and 3 establish that $v_{i,\sigma_{i+1}}$ is authentic (i.e., equals $v_{\sigma_1\cdots\sigma_i\sigma_{i+1}}$). That is, $v = v_\lambda$ authenticates v_{σ_1}, which authenticates $v_{\sigma_1\sigma_2}$, and so on up-to $v_{\sigma_1\cdots\sigma_n}$. The fact that the $v_{i,\bar{\sigma}_{i+1}}$'s are also proven to be authentic (i.e., equal to the $v_{\sigma_1\cdots\sigma_i\bar{\sigma}_{i+1}}$'s, where $\bar{\sigma} = 1 - \sigma$) is not really useful (when signing a message using the leaf associated with $\sigma_1\cdots\sigma_n$). This excess is merely an artifact of the need to use $s_{\sigma_1\cdots\sigma_i}$ only once during the entire operation of the memory-dependent signature scheme: In the currently (constructed) S'_s-signature, we may not care about the authenticity of some $v_{\sigma_1\cdots\sigma_i\bar{\sigma}_{i+1}}$, but we may care about it in some other S'_s-signatures. For example, if we use the leaf labeled 0^n to sign the first document and the leaf labeled $0^{n-1}1$ to sign the second, then in the first S'_s-signature we care only about the authenticity of v_{0^n}, whereas in the second S'_s-signature we care about the authenticity of $v_{0^{n-1}1}$.

Proposition 6.4.15: *If (G, S, V) is a secure one-time signature scheme, then Construction 6.4.14 constitutes a secure memory-dependent signature scheme.*

Proof: Recall that a S'_{s_λ}-signature to a document α has the form

$$(\sigma_1\cdots\sigma_n, \text{auth}_\lambda, \text{auth}_{\sigma_1}, ..., \text{auth}_{\sigma_1\cdots\sigma_{n-1}}, S_{s_{\sigma_1\cdots\sigma_n}}(\alpha)) \qquad (6.5)$$

where the auth_x's, v_x's, and s_x's satisfy

$$\text{auth}_x = \left(v_{x0}, v_{x1}, S_{s_x}(v_{x0}\,v_{x1})\right) \qquad (6.6)$$

(See Figure 6.4.) In this case, we say that this S'_s-signature uses the leaf labeled $\sigma_1\cdots\sigma_n$. For every $i = 1, ..., n$, we call the sequence $(\text{auth}_\lambda, \text{auth}_{\sigma_1}, ..., \text{auth}_{\sigma_1\cdots\sigma_{i-1}})$

an authentication path for $v_{\sigma_1 \cdots \sigma_i}$; see Figure 6.5. (Note that this sequence is also an authentication path for $v_{\sigma_1 \cdots \sigma_{i-1} \bar{\sigma}_i}$, where $\bar{\sigma} = 1 - \sigma$.) Thus, a valid S_s'-signature to a document α consists of an n-bit string $\sigma_1 \cdots \sigma_n$, authentication paths for each $v_{\sigma_1 \cdots \sigma_i}$ ($i = 1, ..., n$), and a signature to α with respect to the one-time scheme (G, S, V) using the signing-key $s_{\sigma_1 \cdots \sigma_n}$.

Intuitively, forging an S_s'-signature requires either using only verification-keys supplied by the signer (i.e., supplied by S_s' as part of an answer to a query) or producing an authentication path for a verification-key that is different from all verification-keys supplied by the signer. In both cases, we reach a contradiction to the security of the one-time signature scheme (G, S, V). Specifically, in the *first case,* the forged S_s'-signature contains a one-time signature that is valid with respect to the one-time verification-key associated by the signing process with a leaf labeled $\sigma_1 \cdots \sigma_n$, because by the case's hypothesis, the forged signature utilizes only verification-keys supplied by the signer. This yields forgery with respect to the instance of the one-time signature scheme associated with the leaf labeled $\sigma_1 \cdots \sigma_n$ (because the document that is S_s'-signed by the forger must be different from all S_s'-signed documents, and thus the forged document is different from all strings to which a one-time signature associated with a leaf was applied).[24] We now turn to the *second case* (i.e., forgery with respect to (G', S', V') is obtained by producing an authentication path for a verification-key that is different from all verification-keys supplied by the signer). As in the first case, we denote by $\sigma_1 \cdots \sigma_n$ the label of the leaf used for the (forged) signature. Let $i \in \{0, ..., n - 1\}$ be the largest integer such that the signature produced by the forger refers to the verification-key $v_{\sigma_1 \cdots \sigma_i}$ (as supplied by the signer), rather than to a different value (claimed by the forger to be the verification-key associated with the node labeled $\sigma_1 \cdots \sigma_i$). (Note that $i = 0$ corresponds to the forger not even using v_{σ_1}, whereas $i < n$ by the case hypothesis.) For this i, the triple $\mathrm{auth}_{\sigma_1 \cdots \sigma_i} = (v_{i,0}', v_{i,1}', \beta_i')$ that is contained in the S_s'-signature produced by the forger contains a one-time signature (i.e., β_i') that is valid with respect to the one-time verification-key associated by the signing process with the node labeled $\sigma_1 \cdots \sigma_i$ (where v_λ is always used by the signing process). Furthermore, by maximality of i, the latter signature is to a string (i.e., $v_{i,0}' v_{i,1}'$) that is different from the string to which the S_s'-signer has applied $S_{s_{\sigma_1 \cdots \sigma_i}}$ (i.e., $v_{i,\sigma_{i+1}}' \neq v_{\sigma_1 \cdots \sigma_{i+1}}$). This yields forgery with respect to the instance of the one-time signature scheme associated with the node labeled $\sigma_1 \cdots \sigma_i$.

The actual proof is by a reducibility argument. Given an adversary A' attacking the complex scheme (G', S', V'), we construct an adversary A that attacks the one-time signature scheme, (G, S, V). In particular, the adversary A will use its (one-time) oracle access to S_s in order to emulate the memory-dependent signing oracle for A'. We stress that the adversary A may make at most one query to its S_s-oracle. Following is a detailed description of the adversary A. Since we care only about probabilistic polynomial-time adversaries, we may assume that A' makes at most $t = \mathrm{poly}(n)$ many queries, where n is the security parameter.

---

[24] Note that what matters is merely that the document S_s'-signed by the forger is different from the (single) document to which $S_{s_{\sigma_1 \cdots \sigma_n}}$ was applied by the S_s'-signer, in case $S_{s_{\sigma_1 \cdots \sigma_n}}$ was ever applied by the S_s'-signer.

The Construction of Adversary A: Suppose that (s, v) is in the range of $G(1^n)$. On input v and one-query oracle access to S_s, adversary A proceeds as follows:

1. *Initial choice:* A uniformly selects $j \in \{1, \ldots, (2n + 1) \cdot t\}$.

   (The integer j specifies an instance of (G, S, V) generated during the emulated attack of A' on (G', S', V'). This instance will be attacked by A. Note that since $2n + 1$ instances of (G, S, V) are referred to in each signature relative to (G', S', V'), the quantity $(2n + 1) \cdot t$ upper-bounds the total number of instances of (G, S, V) that appear during the entire attack of A'. This upper bound is not tight.)

2. *Invoking A':* If $j = 1$, then A sets $v_\lambda = v$ and invokes A' on input v. In this case A does not know s_λ, which is defined to equal s, yet A can obtain a *single* signature relative to the signing-key s by making a (single) query to its own oracle (i.e., the oracle S_s).

   Otherwise (i.e., $j > 1$), machine A invokes G, obtains $(s', v') \leftarrow G(1^n)$, sets $(s_\lambda, v_\lambda) = (s', v')$, and invokes A' on input v'. We stress that in this case A knows s_λ.

   Indeed, in both cases, A' is invoked on input v_λ. Also, in both cases, the one-time instance associated with the root (i.e., the node labeled λ) is called the first instance.

3. *Emulating the memory-dependent signing oracle for A':* The emulation is analogous to the operation of the signing procedure as specified in Construction 6.4.14. The only exception refers to the j-th instance of (G, S, V) that occurs in the memory-dependent signing process. Here, A uses the verification key v, and if an S_s-signature needs to be produced, then A queries S_s for it. We stress that at most one signature need ever be produced with respect to each instance of (G, S, V) that occurs in the memory-dependent signing process, and therefore S_s is queried at most once. Details follow.

   Machine A maintains a record of all key-pairs and one-time signatures it has generated and/or obtained from S_s. When A is asked to supply a signature to a new document, denoted α, it proceeds as follows:

   (a) A allocates a new leaf-label, denoted $\sigma_1 \cdots \sigma_n$, exactly as done by the signing process.

   (b) For every $i = 1, \ldots, n$ and every $\tau \in \{0, 1\}$, machine A tries to retrieve from its record the one-time instance associated with the node labeled $\sigma_1 \cdots \sigma_{i-1}\tau$. If such an instance does not exist in the record (i.e., the one-time instance associated with the node labeled $\sigma_1 \cdots \sigma_{i-1}\tau$ did not appear so far), then A distinguishes two cases:

       i. If the record so far contains exactly $j - 1$ one-time instances (i.e., the current instance is the j-th one to be encountered), then A sets $v_{\sigma_1 \cdots \sigma_{i-1}\tau} \leftarrow v$, and adds it to its record. In this case, A does not know $s_{\sigma_1\cdots\sigma_{i-1}\tau}$, which is defined to equal s, yet A can obtain a *single* signature relative to s by making a (single) query to its own oracle (i.e., the oracle S_s).

From this point on, the one-time instance associated with the node labeled $\sigma_1\cdots\sigma_{i-1}\tau$ will be called the j-th instance.

ii. Otherwise (i.e., the current instance is *not* the j-th one to be encountered), A acts as the signing process: It invokes $G(1^n)$, obtains $(s_{\sigma_1\cdots\sigma_{i-1}\tau}, v_{\sigma_1\cdots\sigma_{i-1}\tau}) \leftarrow G(1^n)$, and adds it to the record. (Note that in this case, A knows $s_{\sigma_1\cdots\sigma_{i-1}\tau}$ and can generate by itself signatures relative to it.)

The one-time instance just generated is given the next serial number. That is, the one-time instance associated with the node labeled $\sigma_1\cdots\sigma_{i-1}\tau$ will be called the k-th instance if the current record (i.e., after the generation of the one-time key-pair associated with the node labeled $\sigma_1\cdots\sigma_{i-1}\tau$) contains exactly k instances.

(c) For every $i = 1, ..., n$, machine A tries to retrieve from its record a (one-time) signature to the string $v_{\sigma_1\cdots\sigma_{i-1}0}\, v_{\sigma_1\cdots\sigma_{i-1}1}$, relative to the signing-key $s_{\sigma_1\cdots\sigma_{i-1}}$. If such a signature does not exist in the record then A distinguishes two cases:

i. If the one-time signature instance associated with the node labeled $\sigma_1\cdots\sigma_{i-1}$ is the j-th such instance, then A obtains the one-time signature $S_{s_{\sigma_1\cdots\sigma_{i-1}}}(v_{\sigma_1\cdots\sigma_{i-1}0}\, v_{\sigma_1\cdots\sigma_{i-1}1})$ by querying S_s, and adds this signature to the record.

Note that by the previous steps (i.e., Step 3(b)i as well as Step 2), s is identified with $s_{\sigma_1\cdots\sigma_{i-1}}$, and that the instance associated with a node labeled $\sigma_1\cdots\sigma_{i-1}$ is only used to produce a single signature; that is, to the string $v_{\sigma_1\cdots\sigma_{i-1}0}\, v_{\sigma_1\cdots\sigma_{i-1}1}$. Thus, in this case, A queries S_s at most once.

We stress that this makes crucial use of the fact that, for every τ, the verification-key associated with the node labeled $\sigma_1\cdots\sigma_{i-1}\tau$ is identical in all executions of the current step. This fact guarantees that A only needs a single signature relative to the instance associated with a node labeled $\sigma_1\cdots\sigma_{i-1}$, and thus queries S_s at most once (and retrieves this signature from memory if it ever needs this signature again).

ii. Otherwise (i.e., the one-time signature instance associated with the node labeled $\sigma_1\cdots\sigma_{i-1}$ is *not* the j-th such instance), A acts as the signing process: It invokes $S_{s_{\sigma_1\cdots\sigma_{i-1}}}$, obtains the one-time signature $S_{s_{\sigma_1\cdots\sigma_{i-1}}}(v_{\sigma_1\cdots\sigma_{i-1}0}\, v_{\sigma_1\cdots\sigma_{i-1}1})$, and adds it to the record. (Note that in this case, A knows $s_{\sigma_1\cdots\sigma_{i-1}}$ and can generate by itself signatures relative to it.)

Thus, in both cases, A obtains $\text{auth}_{\sigma_1\cdots\sigma_{i-1}} = (v_{\sigma_1\cdots\sigma_{i-1}0}, v_{\sigma_1\cdots\sigma_{i-1}1}, \beta_{i-1})$, where $\beta_{i-1} = S_{s_{\sigma_1\cdots\sigma_{i-1}}}(v_{\sigma_1\cdots\sigma_{i-1}0}\, v_{\sigma_1\cdots\sigma_{i-1}1})$.

(d) Machine A now obtains a one-time signature of α relative to $S_{s_{\sigma_1\cdots\sigma_n}}$. (Since a new leaf is allocated for each query made by A', we need to generate at most one signature relative to the one-time instance $S_{s_{\sigma_1\cdots\sigma_n}}$ associated with the leaf $\sigma_1 \cdots \sigma_n$.) This is done analogously to the previous step (i.e., Step 3c). Specifically:

    i. If the one-time signature instance associated with the (leaf) node labeled $\sigma_1 \cdots \sigma_n$ is the j-th instance, then A obtains the one-time signature $S_{s_{\sigma_1 \cdots \sigma_n}}(\alpha)$ by querying S_s.

    Note that in this case, s is identified with $s_{\sigma_1 \cdots \sigma_n}$, and that an instance associated with a leaf is only used to produce a single signature. Thus, also in this case (which is disjoint of Case 3(c)i), A queries S_s at most once.

    ii. Otherwise (i.e., the one-time signature instance associated with the node labeled $\sigma_1 \cdots \sigma_n$ is *not* the j-th instance), A acts as the signing process: It invokes $S_{s_{\sigma_1 \cdots \sigma_n}}$ and obtains the one-time signature $S_{s_{\sigma_1 \cdots \sigma_n}}(\alpha)$. (Again, in this case A knows $s_{\sigma_1 \cdots \sigma_n}$ and can generate by itself signatures relative to it.)

    Thus, in both cases, A obtains $\beta_n = S_{s_{\sigma_1 \cdots \sigma_n}}(\alpha)$.

(e) Finally, A answers the query α with

$$(\sigma_1 \cdots \sigma_n, \text{auth}_\lambda, \text{auth}_{\sigma_1}, \ldots, \text{auth}_{\sigma_1 \cdots \sigma_{n-1}}, \beta_n)$$

4. *Using the output of A':* When A' halts with output (α', β'), machine A checks whether this is a valid document-signature pair with respect to V'_{v_λ} and whether the document α' did not appear as a query of A'. If both conditions hold, then A tries to obtain forgery with respect to S_s. To explain how this is done, we need to take a closer look at the valid document-signature pair, (α', β'), output by A'. Specifically, suppose that β' has the form

$$(\sigma'_1 \cdots \sigma'_n, (v'_{0,0}, v'_{0,1}, \beta'_0), (v'_{1,0}, v'_{1,1}, \beta'_1), \ldots, (v'_{n-1,0}, v'_{n-1,1}, \beta'_{n-1}), \beta'_n)$$

and that the various components satisfy all conditions stated in the verification procedure. (In particular, the sequence $(v'_{0,0}, v'_{0,1}, \beta'_0), \ldots, (v'_{n-1,0}, v'_{n-1,1}, \beta'_{n-1})$ is the authentication path (for v'_{n-1,σ'_n}) output by A'.) Recall that strings of the form $v'_{k,\tau}$ denote the verification-keys included in the output of A', whereas strings of the form v_x denote the verification-keys (as used in the answers given to A' by A and) as recorded by A.

Let i be *maximal* such that the sequence of key-pairs $(v'_{0,0}, v'_{0,1}), \ldots, (v'_{i-1,0}, v'_{i-1,1})$ appears in *some* authentication path supplied to A' (by A).[25] Note that $i \in \{0, \ldots, n\}$, where $i = 0$ means that $(v'_{0,0}, v'_{0,1})$ differs from (v_0, v_1), and $i = n$ means that the sequence $((v'_{0,0}, v'_{0,1}), \ldots, (v'_{n-1,0}, v'_{n-1,1}))$ equals the sequence $((v_0, v_1), \ldots, (v_{\sigma'_1 \cdots \sigma'_{n-1} 0}, v_{\sigma'_1 \cdots \sigma'_{n-1} 1}))$. In general, the sequence $((v'_{0,0}, v'_{0,1}), \ldots, (v'_{i-1,0}, v'_{i-1,1}))$ equals the sequence $((v_0, v_1), \ldots, (v_{\sigma'_1 \cdots \sigma'_{i-1} 0}, v_{\sigma'_1 \cdots \sigma'_{i-1} 1}))$. In particular, for $i \geq 1$, it holds that $v'_{i-1,\sigma'_i} = v_{\sigma'_1 \cdots \sigma'_i}$, whereas for $i = 0$ we shall only

---

[25] That is, i is such that for *some* $\beta_0, \ldots, \beta_{i-1}$ (which may but need not equal $\beta'_0, \ldots, \beta'_{i-1}$), the sequence $(v'_{0,0}, v'_{0,1}, \beta_0), \ldots, (v'_{i-1,0}, v'_{i-1,1}, \beta_{i-1})$ is a prefix of *some* authentication path (for some $v_{\sigma'_1 \cdots \sigma'_i \sigma_{i+1} \cdots \sigma_n}$) supplied to A' by A. We stress that here we only care about whether or not some $v'_{k,\tau}$'s equal the corresponding verification-keys supplied by A, and ignore the question of whether (in case of equality) the verification-keys were authenticated using the very same (one-time) signature. We mention that things will be different in the analogous part of the proof of Theorem 6.5.2 (which refers to super-security).

refer to v_λ (which is the verification-key attacked by A'). In both cases, the output of A' contains a one-time signature relative to $v_{\sigma'_1 \cdots \sigma'_i}$, and this signature is to a string different from the (possibly) only one to which a signature was supplied to A' by A. Specifically, as in the motivating discussion (in the beginning of the proof), we distinguish the cases $i = n$ and $i < n$:

(a) In case $i = n$, the output of A' contains the (one-time) signature β'_n that satisfies $V_{v_{\sigma'_1 \cdots \sigma'_n}}(\alpha', \beta'_n) = 1$. Furthermore, α' is different from the (possibly) only document to which $S_{s_{\sigma'_1 \cdots \sigma'_n}}$ was applied during the emulation of the S'-signer by A, since by our hypothesis the document α' did not appear as a query of A'. (Recall that by the construction of A, instances of the one-time signature scheme associated with leaves are only applied to the queries of A'.)

(b) In case $i < n$, the output of A' contains the (one-time) signature β'_i that satisfies $V_{v_{\sigma'_1 \cdots \sigma'_i}}(v'_{i,0} v'_{i,1}, \beta'_i) = 1$. Furthermore, $v'_{i,0} v'_{i,1}$ is different from $v_{\sigma'_1 \cdots \sigma'_i 0} v_{\sigma'_1 \cdots \sigma'_i 0}$, which is the (possibly) only string to which $S_{s_{\sigma'_1 \cdots \sigma'_i}}$ was applied during the emulation of the S'-signer by A, where the last assertion is due to the maximality of i (and the construction of A).

Thus, in both cases, A obtains from A' a valid (one-time) signature relative to the (one-time) instance associated with the node labeled $\sigma'_1 \cdots \sigma'_i$. Furthermore, in both cases, this (one-time) signature is to a string that did not appear in the record of A. The question is whether the instance associated with the node labeled $\sigma'_1 \cdots \sigma'_i$ is the j-th instance, for which A set $v = v_{\sigma'_1 \cdots \sigma'_i}$. In case the answer is yes, A obtains forgery with respect to the (one-time) verification-key v (which it attacks).

In view of this discussion, A acts as follows. It determines i as in the beginning of the current step (i.e., Step 4), and checks whether $v = v_{\sigma'_1 \cdots \sigma'_i}$ (or, almost equivalently, whether the j-th instance is the one associated with the node labeled $\sigma'_1 \cdots \sigma'_i$). In case $i = n$, machine A outputs the string-signature pair (α', β'_n); otherwise (i.e., $i < n$) it outputs the string-signature pair $(v'_{i,0} v'_{i,1}, \beta'_i)$.

This completes the (admittingly long) description of adversary A. We repeat again some obvious observations regarding this construction. Firstly, A makes at most one query to its (one-time) signing oracle S_s. Secondly, assuming that A' is probabilistic polynomial-time, so is A. Thus, all that remains is to relate the success probability of A (when attacking a random instance of (G, S, V)) to the success probability of A' (when attacking a random instance of (G', S', V')). As usual, the main observation is that the view of A', during the emulation of the memory-dependent signing process (by A), is identically distributed to its view in an actual attack on (G', S', V'). Furthermore, this holds conditioned on any possible fixed value of j (selected in the first step of A). It follows that if A' succeeds in forging signatures in an actual attack on (G', S', V') with probability $\varepsilon'(n)$, then A succeeds in forging signatures with respect to (G, S, V) with probability at least $\frac{\varepsilon'(n)}{(2n+1) \cdot t}$, where the $(2n + 1) \cdot t$ factor is due to the probability that the choice of j is a good one (i.e., so that the j-th instance is the one associated with the node labeled $\sigma'_1 \cdots \sigma'_i$, where $\sigma'_1 \cdots \sigma'_n$ and i are as defined in Step 4 of A's construction).

We conclude that if (G', S', V') can be broken by a probabilistic polynomial-time chosen message attack with non-negligible probability, then (G, S, V) can be broken by a probabilistic polynomial-time single-message attack with non-negligible probability, in contradiction to the proposition's hypothesis. The proposition follows. ∎

6.4.2.3. The Actual Construction

In this section, we remove the memory dependency of Construction 6.4.14 and obtain an ordinary (rather than memory-dependent) signature scheme. Toward this end, we use pseudorandom functions (as defined in Definition 3.6.4). The basic idea is that the record maintained in Construction 6.4.14 can be determined (on the fly) by an application of a pseudorandom function to certain strings. For example, instead of generating and storing an instance of a (one-time) signature scheme for each node that we encounter, we can determine the randomness for the (corresponding invocation of the) key-generation algorithm as a function of the label of that node. Thus, there is no need to store the key-pair generated, because if we ever need it again, then regenerating it (in the very same way) will yield exactly the same result. The same idea applies also to the generation of (one-time) signatures. In fact, the construction is simplified, because we need not check whether or not we are generating an object for the first time.

For simplicity, let us assume that on security parameter n, both the key-generation and signing algorithms (of the one-time signature scheme (G, S, V)) use exactly n internal coin tosses. (This assumption can be justified by using pseudorandom generators, which exist anyhow under the assumptions used here.) For $r \in \{0, 1\}^n$, we denote by $G(1^n, r)$ the output of G on input 1^n and internal coin-tosses r. Likewise, for $r \in \{0, 1\}^n$, we denote by $S_s(\alpha, r)$ the output of S, on input a signing-key s and a document α, when using internal coin-tosses r. For simplicity, we shall actually be using generalized pseudorandom functions as in Definition 3.6.12 (rather than pseudorandom functions as defined in Definition 3.6.4).[26] Furthermore, for simplicity, we shall consider applications of such pseudorandom functions to sequences of characters containing $\{0, 1\}$, as well as a few additional special characters.

Construction 6.4.16 (Removing the memory requirement from Construction 6.4.14): *Let (G, S, V) be a one-time signature scheme, and $\{f_r : \{0, 1\}^* \to \{0, 1\}^{|r|}\}_{r \in \{0,1\}^*}$ be a generalized pseudorandom function ensemble as in Definition 3.6.12. Consider the following signature scheme, (G', S', V'), which refers to a full binary tree of depth n as in Construction 6.4.14:*

Key-generation algorithm G': *On input 1^n, algorithm G' obtains $(s, v) \leftarrow G(1^n)$ and selects uniformly $r \in \{0, 1\}^n$. Algorithm G' outputs the pair $((r, s), v)$, where (r, s) is the signing-key and v is the verification-key.[27]*

---

[26] We shall make comments regarding the minor changes required in order to use ordinary pseudorandom functions. The first comment is that we shall consider an encoding of strings of length up to $n + 2$ by strings of length $n + 3$ (e.g., for $i \leq n + 2$, the string $x \in \{0, 1\}^i$ is encoded by $x10^{n+2-i}$).

[27] In case we use ordinary pseudorandom functions, rather than generalized ones, we select r uniformly in $\{0, 1\}^{n+3}$ such that $f_r : \{0, 1\}^{n+3} \to \{0, 1\}^{n+3}$. Actually, we shall be using the function $f_r : \{0, 1\}^{n+3} \to \{0, 1\}^n$ derived from the original f_r by dropping the last 3 bits of the function value.

Signing algorithm S': *On input a signing-key (r, s) (in the range of $G'_1(1^n)$) and a document α, the algorithm proceeds as follows:*

1. *It selects uniformly $\sigma_1 \cdots \sigma_n \in \{0, 1\}^n$.*

   (Algorithm S' will use the leaf labeled $\sigma_1 \cdots \sigma_n \in \{0, 1\}^n$ to sign the current document. Indeed, with exponentially vanishing probability, the same leaf may be used to sign two different documents, and this will lead to forgery [but only with negligible probability].)

   (Alternatively, to obtain a deterministic signing algorithm, one may set $\sigma_1 \cdots$ $\sigma_n \leftarrow f_r(\texttt{select-leaf}, \alpha)$, where $\texttt{select-leaf}$ is a special character.)[28]

2. *Next, for every $i = 1, ..., n$ and every $\tau \in \{0, 1\}$, the algorithm invokes G and sets*

$$(s_{\sigma_1 \cdots \sigma_{i-1}\tau}, v_{\sigma_1 \cdots \sigma_{i-1}\tau}) \leftarrow G(1^n, f_r(\texttt{key-gen}, \sigma_1 \cdots \sigma_{i-1}\tau))$$

   where $\texttt{key-gen}$ is a special character.[29]

3. *For every $i = 1, ..., n$, the algorithm invokes $S_{s_{\sigma_1 \cdots \sigma_{i-1}}}$ and sets*

$$\text{auth}_{\sigma_1 \cdots \sigma_{i-1}} \overset{\text{def}}{=} \big(v_{\sigma_1 \cdots \sigma_{i-1}0}, v_{\sigma_1 \cdots \sigma_{i-1}1},$$
$$S_{s_{\sigma_1 \cdots \sigma_{i-1}}}(v_{\sigma_1 \cdots \sigma_{i-1}0} \, v_{\sigma_1 \cdots \sigma_{i-1}1}, f_r(\texttt{sign}, \sigma_1 \cdots \sigma_{i-1}))\big)$$

   where $\texttt{sign}$ is a special character.[30]

4. *Finally, the algorithm invokes $S_{s_{\sigma_1 \cdots \sigma_n}}$ and outputs*[31]

$$(\sigma_1 \cdots \sigma_n, \text{auth}_\lambda, \text{auth}_{\sigma_1}, ..., \text{auth}_{\sigma_1 \cdots \sigma_{n-1}}, S_{s_{\sigma_1 \cdots \sigma_n}}(\alpha, f_r(\texttt{sign}, \sigma_1 \cdots \sigma_n)))$$

Verification algorithm V': *On input a verification-key v, a document α, and an alleged signature β, algorithm V' behaves exactly as in Construction 6.4.14. Specifically, assuming that β has the form*

$$(\sigma_1 \cdots \sigma_n, (v_{0,0}, v_{0,1}, \beta_0), (v_{1,0}, v_{1,1}, \beta_1), ..., (v_{n-1,0}, v_{n-1,1}, \beta_{n-1}), \beta_n)$$

algorithm V' accepts if and only if the following three conditions hold:

- $V_v(v_{0,0}v_{0,1}, \beta_0) = 1$.
- *For $i = 1, ..., n - 1$, it holds that $V_{v_{i-1,\sigma_i}}(v_{i,0}v_{i,1}, \beta_i) = 1$.*
- $V_{v_{n-1,\sigma_n}}(\alpha, \beta_n) = 1$.

Proposition 6.4.17: *If (G, S, V) is a secure one-time signature scheme and $\{f_r : \{0, 1\}^* \to \{0, 1\}^{|r|}\}_{r \in \{0,1\}^*}$ is a generalized pseudorandom function ensemble, then Construction 6.4.16 constitutes a secure (general) signature scheme.*

---

[28] In case we use ordinary pseudorandom functions, rather than generalized ones, this alternative can be (directly) implemented only if it is guaranteed that $|\alpha| \leq n$. In such a case, we apply the f_r to the $(n + 3)$-bit encoding of 00α.

[29] In case we use ordinary pseudorandom functions, rather than generalized ones, the argument to f_r is the $(n + 3)$-bit encoding of $10\sigma_1 \cdots \sigma_{i-1}\tau$.

[30] In case we use ordinary pseudorandom functions, rather than generalized ones, the argument to f_r is the $(n + 3)$-bit encoding of $11\sigma_1 \cdots \sigma_{i-1}$.

[31] In case we use ordinary pseudorandom functions, rather than generalized ones, the argument to f_r is the $(n + 3)$-bit encoding of $11\sigma_1 \cdots \sigma_n$.

Proof: Following the general methodology suggested in Section 3.6.3, we consider an *ideal version* of Construction 6.4.16 in which a truly random function is used (rather than a pseudorandom one). The ideal version is almost identical to Construction 6.4.14, with the only difference being the way in which $\sigma_1 \cdots \sigma_n$ is selected. Specifically, applying a truly random function to determine (one-time) key-pairs and (one-time) signatures is equivalent to generating these keys and signatures at random (on the fly) and reusing the stored values whenever necessary. Regarding the way in which $\sigma_1 \cdots \sigma_n$ is selected, observe that the proof of Proposition 6.4.15 is oblivious of this way, except for the assumption that the same leaf is never used to sign two different documents. However, the probability that the same leaf is used twice by the (memoryless) signing algorithm, when serving polynomially many signing requests, is exponentially vanishing and thus can be ignored in our analysis. We conclude that *the ideal scheme* (in which a truly random function is used instead of f_r) *is secure*. It follows that also the actual signature scheme (as in Construction 6.4.16) is secure, or else one can efficiently distinguish a pseudorandom function from a truly random one (which is impossible). Details follow.

Assume toward the contradiction that there exists a probabilistic polynomial-time adversary A' that succeeds in forging signatures with respect to (G', S', V') with non-negligible probability, but succeeds only with negligible probability when attacking the ideal scheme. We construct a distinguisher D that on input 1^n and oracle access to $f : \{0, 1\}^* \to \{0, 1\}^n$ behaves as follows. Machine D generates $((r', s), v) \leftarrow G'(1^n)$ and invokes A' on input v. Machine D answers the queries of A' by running the signing process, using the signing-key (r', s), with the exception that it replaces the values $f_{r'}(x)$ by $f(x)$. That is, whenever the signing process calls for the computation of the value of the function $f_{r'}$ on some string x, machine D queries its oracle (i.e., f) on the string x, and uses the response $f(x)$ instead of $f_{r'}(x)$. When A' outputs an alleged signature to a new document, machine M evaluates whether or not the signature is valid (with respect to V_v) and outputs 1 if and only if A' has indeed succeeded (i.e., the signature is valid). Observe that if D is given oracle access to a truly random function, then the emulated A' attacks the ideal scheme, whereas if D is given oracle access to a pseudorandom function f_r, then the emulated A' attacks the real scheme. It follows that D distinguishes the two cases, in contradiction to the pseudorandomness of the ensemble $\{f_r\}$. ∎

6.4.2.4. Conclusions and Comments

Theorem 6.4.9 follows by combining Proposition 6.4.17 with the fact that the existence of secure one-time signature schemes implies the existence of one-way functions (see Exercise 13), which in turn implies the existence of (generalized) pseudorandom functions. Recall that by combining Theorem 6.4.9 and Corollary 6.4.8, we obtain Corollary 6.4.10, which states that *the existence of collision-free hashing collections implies the existence of secure signature schemes*. Furthermore, the length of the resulting signatures depends only on the length of the signing-key.

We comment that Constructions 6.4.14 and 6.4.16 can be generalized as follows. Rather than using a (depth n) full binary tree, one can use any tree that has a super-polynomial (in n) number of leaves, provided that one can enumerate the leaves (resp., uniformly select a leaf) and generate the path from the root to a given leaf. We consider a few possibilities:

- For any $d : \mathbb{N} \to \mathbb{N}$ bounded by a polynomial in n (e.g., $d \equiv 2$ or $d(n) = n$ are indeed "extreme" cases), we may consider a full $d(n)$-ary tree of depth $e(n)$ so that $d(n)^{e(n)}$ is greater than any polynomial in n. The choice of parameters in Constructions 6.4.14 and 6.4.16 (i.e., $d \equiv 2$ and $e(n) = n$) is probably the simplest one.

  Natural complexity measures for a signature scheme include the length of signatures and the signing and verification times. In a generalized construction, the length of the signatures is linear in $d(n) \cdot e(n)$, and the number of applications of the underlying one-time signature scheme (per each general signature) is linear in $e(n)$, where in internal nodes the one-time signature scheme is applied to a string of length linear in $d(n)$. Assuming that the complexity of one-time signatures is linear in the document length, all complexity measures are linear in $d(n) \cdot e(n)$, and so $d \equiv 2$ is the best generic choice. However, this assumption may not hold when some specific one-time signatures are used. For example, the complexity of producing a signature to an ℓ-bit long string in a one-time signature scheme may be of the form $p(n) + p'(n) \cdot \ell$, where $p'(n) \ll p(n)$. In such (special) cases, one may prefer to use a larger $d : \mathbb{N} \to \mathbb{N}$ (see Section 6.6.5).

- For the memory-dependent construction, it may be preferable to use unbalanced trees (i.e., having leaves at various levels). The advantage is that if one utilizes first the leaves closer to the root, then one can obtain a saving on the cost of signing the first documents.

  For example, consider using a ternary tree of super-logarithmic depth (i.e., $d \equiv 3$ and $e(n) = \omega(\log n)$), in which each internal node of level $i \in \{0, 1, ..., e(n) - 2\}$ has two children that are internal nodes and a single child that is a leaf (and the internal nodes of level $e(n) - 1$ have only leaves as children). Thus, for $i \geq 1$, there are 3^{i-1} leaves at level i. If we use all leaves of level i before using any leaf of level $i + 1$, then the length of the j-th signature in this scheme is linear in $\log_3 j$ (and so is the number of applications of the underlying one-time signature scheme).

When actually applying these constructions, one should observe that in variants of Construction 6.4.14, the size of the tree determines the number of documents that can be signed, whereas in variants of Construction 6.4.16, the tree size has an even more drastic effect on the number of documents that can be signed.[32] In some cases, a hybrid of Constructions 6.4.14 and 6.4.16 may be preferable: We refer to a memory-dependent scheme in which leaves are assigned as in Construction 6.4.14 (i.e., according to a counter), but the rest of the operation is done as in Construction 6.4.16 (i.e., the one-time instances are regenerated on the fly, rather than being recorded and retrieved

---

[32] In particular, the number of documents that can be signed should definitely be smaller than the square root of the size of the tree (or else two documents are likely to be assigned the same leaf). Furthermore, we cannot use a small tree (e.g., of size 1,000) even if we know that the total number of documents that will ever be signed is small (e.g., 10), because in this case, the probability that two documents are assigned the same leaf is too big (e.g., 1/20).

from memory). In some applications, the introduction of a document-counter may be tolerated, and the gain is the ability to use a smaller tree (i.e., of size merely greater than the number of documents that should be ever signed).

More generally, we wish to stress that each of the following ingredients of the previous constructions is useful in a variety of related and unrelated settings. We refer specifically to the *refreshing paradigm,* the *authentication-tree construction,* and the notion (and constructions) of *one-time signatures.* For example:

- It is common practice to authenticate messages sent during a "communication session" via a (*fresh*) session-key that is typically authenticated by a master-key. One of the reasons for this practice is the prevention of a chosen message attack on the (more valuable) master-key. (Other reasons include allowing the use of a faster (alas, less secure) authentication scheme for the actual communication and introducing independence between sessions.)
- Observe the analogy between the tree-hashing (of Construction 6.2.13) and the *authentication-tree* (of Construction 6.4.14). Despite the many differences, in both cases the value of each internal node authenticates the values of its children. Thus, the value of the root may be used to authenticate a very large number of values (associated with the leaves). Furthermore, the value associated with each leaf can be verified within complexity that is linear in the depth of the tree.
- Recall the application of *one-time signatures* to the construction of CCA-secure public-key encryption schemes (see the proof of Theorem 5.4.30).

6.4.3.* Universal One-Way Hash Functions and Using Them

So far, we have established that *the existence of collision-free hashing collections implies the existence of secure signature schemes* (cf. Corollary 6.4.10). We seek to weaken the assumption under which secure signature schemes can be constructed, and bear in mind that the existence of one-way functions is certainly a necessary condition (cf., for example, Exercise 13). In view of Theorem 6.4.9, we may focus on constructing secure *one-time* signature schemes. Furthermore, recall that secure length-restricted one-time signature schemes can be constructed based on any one-way function (cf. Corollary 6.4.6). Thus, the only bottleneck we face (with respect to the assumption used) is the transformation of length-restricted one-time signature schemes into (general) one-time signature schemes. For the latter transformation, we have used a specific incarnation of the "hash-and-sign paradigm" (i.e., Proposition 6.4.7, which refers to Construction 6.2.6). This incarnation utilizes collision-free hashing, and our goal is to replace it by a variant (of Construction 6.2.6) that uses a seemingly weaker notion called *Universal One-Way Hash Functions.*

6.4.3.1. Definition

A collection of universal one-way hash functions is defined analogously to a collection of collision-free hash functions. The only difference is that the hardness (to form collisions) requirement is relaxed. Recall that in the case of (a collection of) collision-free hash functions, it was required that, given the function's description, it is hard to form an *arbitrary* collision under the function. In the case of (a collection of) universal one-way hash functions, we only require that, given the function's description h and a pre-image x_0, it is hard to find an $x \neq x_0$ so that $h(x) = h(x_0)$. We refer to this requirement as to *hardness to form designated collisions.*

Our formulation of the hardness to form designated collisions is actually seemingly stronger. Rather than being supplied with a (random) pre-image x_0, the collision-forming algorithm is allowed to select x_0 by itself, but must do so *before being presented with the function's description.* That is, the attack of the collision-forming algorithm proceeds in three stages: First the algorithm selects a pre-image x_0, next it is given a description of a randomly selected function h, and finally it is required to output $x \neq x_0$ such that $h(x) = h(x_0)$. We stress that the third stage in the attack is also given the random coins used for producing the initial pre-image (at the first stage). This yields the following definition, where the first stage is captured by a deterministic polynomial-time algorithm A_0 (which maps a sequence of coin tosses, denoted $U_{q(n)}$, to a pre-image of the function), and the third stage is captured by algorithm A (which is given the very same coins $U_{q(n)}$ as well as the function's description).

Definition 6.4.18 (universal one-way hash functions – UOWHF): *Let* $\ell : \mathbb{N} \to \mathbb{N}$. *A collection of functions* $\{h_s : \{0, 1\}^* \to \{0, 1\}^{\ell(|s|)}\}_{s \in \{0,1\}^*}$ *is called* universal one-way hashing (UOWHF) *if there exists a probabilistic polynomial-time algorithm I so that the following holds:*

1. (admissible indexing – technical):[33] *For some polynomial p, all sufficiently large n's, and every s in the range of $I(1^n)$, it holds that $n \leq p(|s|)$. Furthermore, n can be computed in polynomial-time from s.*
2. (efficient evaluation): *There exists a polynomial-time algorithm that, given s and x, returns $h_s(x)$.*
3. (hard-to-form designated collisions): *For every polynomial q, every deterministic polynomial-time algorithm A_0, every probabilistic polynomial-time algorithm A, every positive polynomial p, and all sufficiently large n's*

$$\Pr\left[\begin{array}{c} h_{I(1^n)}(A(I(1^n), U_{q(n)})) = h_{I(1^n)}(A_0(U_{q(n)})) \\ \text{and} \quad A(I(1^n), U_{q(n)}) \neq A_0(U_{q(n)}) \end{array}\right] < \frac{1}{p(n)} \qquad (6.7)$$

where the probability is taken over $U_{q(n)}$ and the internal coin tosses of algorithms I and A.

The function ℓ is called the range specifier *of the collection.*

We stress that the *hardness to form designated collisions* condition refers to the following three-stage process: First, using a uniformly distributed $r \in \{0, 1\}^{q(n)}$, the (initial) adversary generates a pre-image $x_0 = A_0(r)$; next, a function h is selected (by invoking $I(1^n)$); and, finally, the (residual) adversary A is given h (as well as r used

---

[33] This condition is made merely to avoid annoying technicalities. Note that $|s| = \text{poly}(n)$ holds by definition of I.

at the first stage) and tries to find a pre-image $x \neq x_0$ such that $h(x) = h(x_0)$. Indeed, Eq. (6.7) refers to the probability that $x \stackrel{\text{def}}{=} A(h, r) \neq x_0$ and yet $h(x) = h(x_0)$.

Note that the range specifier (i.e., ℓ) must be super-logarithmic (or else, given s and $x_0 \leftarrow U_n$, one is too likely to find an $x \neq x_0$ such that $h_s(x) = h_s(x_0)$, by uniformly selecting x in $\{0, 1\}^n$). Also note that any UOWHF collection yields a collection of one-way functions (see Exercise 19). Finally, note that any collision-free hashing is universally one-way hashing, but the converse is false (see Exercise 20). Furthermore, it is not known whether collision-free hashing can be constructed based on any one-way functions (in contrast to Theorem 6.4.29, to follow).

6.4.3.2. Constructions

We construct UOWHF collections in several steps, starting with a related but restricted notion, and relaxing the restriction gradually (until we reach the unrestricted notion of UOWHF collections). The aforementioned restriction refers to the length of the arguments to the function. Most importantly, the hardness (to form designated collisions) requirement will refer only to an argument of this length. That is, we refer to the following technical definition:

Definition 6.4.19 $((d, r)$-UOWHFs): *Let $d, r : \mathbb{N} \to \mathbb{N}$. A collection of functions $\{h_s : \{0, 1\}^{d(|s|)} \to \{0, 1\}^{r(|s|)}\}_{s \in \{0,1\}^*}$ is called (d, r)-UOWHF if there exists a probabilistic polynomial-time algorithm I so that the following holds:*

1. *For all sufficiently large n's and every s in the range of $I(1^n)$, it holds that $|s| = n$.[34]*
2. *There exists a polynomial-time algorithm that, given s and $x \in \{0, 1\}^{d(|s|)}$, returns $h_s(x)$.*
3. *For every polynomial q, every deterministic polynomial-time algorithm A_0 mapping $q(n)$-bit long strings to $d(|s|)$-bit long strings, every probabilistic polynomial-time algorithm A, every positive polynomial p, and all sufficiently large n's, Eq. (6.7) holds.*

Of course, we care only about (d, r)-UOWHF for functions $d, r : \mathbb{N} \to \mathbb{N}$ satisfying $d(n) > r(n)$. (The case $d(n) \leq r(n)$ is trivial since collisions can be avoided altogether, say, by the identity map.) The "minimal" non-trivial case is when $d(n) = r(n) + 1$. Indeed, this is our starting point. Furthermore, the construction of such a minimal $(d, d - 1)$-UOWHF (undertaken in the following first step) is the most interesting step to be taken on our entire way toward the construction of full-fledged UOWHF. We start with an overview of the steps taken along the way.

Step I: Constructing $(d, d - 1)$-UOWHFs: This construction utilizes a one-way permutation f and a family of hashing functions mapping n-bit long strings to $(n - 1)$-bit long strings. A generic function in the constructed collection is obtained by

---

[34] Here we chose to make a more stringent condition, requiring that $|s| = n$, rather than $n \leq \text{poly}(|s|)$. In fact, one can easily enforce this more stringent condition by modifying I into I' so that $I'(1^{l(n)}) = I(1^n)$ for a suitable function $l : \mathbb{N} \to \mathbb{N}$ satisfying $l(n) \leq \text{poly}(n)$ and $n \leq \text{poly}(l(n))$.

composing a hashing function with f; that is, the resulting function is $h \circ f$: $\{0, 1\}^n \rightarrow \{0, 1\}^{n-1}$, where $h : \{0, 1\}^n \rightarrow \{0, 1\}^{n-1}$ is a hashing function. Hence, the constructed functions shrink their input by a single bit.

Intuitively, a random hashing function h maps the f-images in a random manner, whereas the pre-images under $h \circ f$ are the f-inverses of the pre-images under h. Thus, seeking to invert f on y, we may select $x_0 \in \{0, 1\}^n$ and h at random such that $h(f(x_0)) = h(y)$, and seek a collision with the designated pre-image x_0 under $h \circ f$. It follows that the ability to form designated collisions can be translated to inverting f on a random image. Transforming this intuition into an actual proof is the most technically challenging part of the current section.

Step II: Constructing $(d', d'/2)$-UOWHFs: Here we merely compose random functions taken from collections as constructed in Step I. Successively applying $d'/2$ such functions, we map the d'-bit long pre-image to a $d'/2$-bit long image.

Intuitively, the ability to form designated collisions with respect to the constructed collection yields such an ability with respect to (one of) the original collections. (In the actual argument, we rely on the fact that the definition of $(d, d - 1)$-UOWHF refers also to adversaries that get the random coins used for producing the designated pre-image, and not merely the designated preimage itself.)

Step III: In this step, we construct (length-unrestricted) quasi-UOWHFs that shrink their input by a factor of two. These functions are constructed by applying a (single) random function taken from a collection as constructed in Step II to each block of d' consecutive bits of the pre-image. (Clearly, a collision of the entire sequence of blocks yields collisions at some block.)

Step IV: Obtaining full-fledged UOWHFs: This construction is analogous to the one used in Step II. We merely compose random functions taken from a collection as constructed in Step III. Successively applying t such functions, we essentially map $2^t n$-bit long pre-images to n-bit long images.

Detailed descriptions of these four steps follow:

Step I: Constructing $(d, d - 1)$-UOWHFs. We show how to construct length-restricted UOWHFs that shrink their input by a single bit. Our construction can be carried out using any one-way permutation. In addition, we use a family of hashing functions, S_n^{n-1}, as defined in Section 3.5.1.1. Recall that a function selected uniformly in S_n^{n-1} maps $\{0, 1\}^n$ to $\{0, 1\}^{n-1}$ in a pairwise independent manner, that the functions in S_n^{n-1} are easy to evaluate, and that for some polynomial p it holds that $\log_2 |S_n^{n-1}| = p(n)$.

Construction 6.4.20 (a $(d, d - 1)$-UOWHF): *Let $f : \{0, 1\}^* \rightarrow \{0, 1\}^*$ be a 1-1 and length-preserving function, and let S_n^{n-1} be a family of hashing functions such that $\log_2 |S_n^{n-1}| = p(n)$, for some polynomial p. (Specifically, suppose that $\log_2 |S_n^{n-1}| \in \{3n - 2, 2n\}$, as in Exercises 22.2 and 23 of Chapter 3.) Then, for every $s \in S_n^{n-1} \equiv \{0, 1\}^{p(n)}$ and every $x \in \{0, 1\}^n$, we define $h'_s(x) \stackrel{\text{def}}{=} h_s(f(x))$.*

Tedious details: *In case $|s| \notin \{p(n) : n \in \mathbb{N}\}$, we define $h'_s \stackrel{\text{def}}{=} h'_{s'}$ where s' is the longest prefix of s satisfying $|s'| \in \{p(n) : n \in \mathbb{N}\}$. We refer to an index selection algorithm that, on input 1^m, uniformly selects $s \in \{0, 1\}^m$.*

That is, $h'_s : \{0, 1\}^{d(|s|)} \to \{0, 1\}^{d(|s|)-1}$, where $d(m)$ is the largest integer n satisfying $p(n) \leq m$. Note that d is monotonically non-decreasing, and that for 1-1 p's, the corresponding d is onto (i.e., $d(p(n)) = n$ for every n).

The following analysis uses, in an essential way, an additional property of the aforementioned families of hashing functions; specifically, we assume that given two pre-image–image pairs, it is easy to uniformly generate a hashing function (in the family) that is consistent with these two mapping conditions. Furthermore, to facilitate the analysis, we use a specific family of hashing functions, presented in Exercise 23 of Chapter 3: Functions in S_n^{n-1} are described by a pair of elements of the finite field $\text{GF}(2^n)$ so that the pair (a, b) describes the function $h_{a,b}$ that maps $x \in \text{GF}(2^n)$ to the $(n - 1)$-bit prefix of the n-bit representation of $ax + b$, where the arithmetic is of the field $\text{GF}(2^n)$. This specific family satisfies all the additional properties required in the next proposition (see Exercise 24).

Proposition 6.4.21: *Suppose that f is a one-way permutation, and that S_n^{n-1} is a family of hashing functions (as defined in Section 3.5.1.1) such that $\log_2 |S_n^{n-1}| = 2n$. Furthermore, suppose that S_n^{n-1} satisfies the following two conditions:*

C1 *All but a negligible fraction of the functions in S_n^{n-1} are 2-to-1.*

C2 *There exists a probabilistic polynomial-time algorithm that, given $y_1, y_2 \in \{0, 1\}^n$ and $z_1, z_2 \in \{0, 1\}^{n-1}$, outputs a uniformly distributed element of $\{s \in S_n^{n-1} : h_s(y_i) = z_i \ \forall i \in \{1, 2\}\}$.*

Then $\{h'_s\}_{s \in \{0,1\}^*}$ as in Construction 6.4.20 is a $(d, d - 1)$-UOWHF for $d(m) = \lfloor m/2 \rfloor$.

Proof Sketch: Intuitively, forming designated collisions under $h'_s \equiv h_s \circ f$ yields the ability to invert f on a random y, because the collisions are due to h_s, which may be selected such that $h_s(y) = h_s(f(x_0))$ *for any given y and x_0.* We stress that typically there are only two pre-images of $h'_s(x_0)$ under h'_s, one being x_0 itself (which is given to the collision-finder) and the other being $f^{-1}(y)$. Thus, the ability to form a designated collision with x_0 yields an ability to invert f on a random y, by selecting a random s such that $h_s(y) = h'_s(x_0)$, and forming a designated collision under h'_s. More precisely, suppose we wish to invert f on a random image y. Then we may invoke a collision-finder, which first outputs some x_0, supply it with a random s satisfying $h_s(y) = h'_s(x_0)$, and hope that it forms a collision (i.e., finds a different pre-image x satisfying $h'_s(x) = h'_s(x_0)$). Indeed, typically, the different pre-image must be $f^{-1}(y)$, which means that whenever the collision-finder succeeds, we also succeed (i.e., invert f on y). Details follow.

Evidently, the proof is by a reducibility argument. Suppose that we are given a probabilistic polynomial-time algorithm A' that forms designated collisions under $\{h'_s\}$, with respect to pre-images produced by a deterministic polynomial-time algorithm A'_0, which maps $p(n)$-bit strings to n-bit strings. Then, we construct an algorithm A that inverts f. On input $y = f(x)$, where $n = |y| = |x|$, algorithm A proceeds as follows:

(1) Select r_0 uniformly in $\{0, 1\}^{p(n)}$, and compute $x_0 = A'_0(r_0)$ and $y_0 = f(x_0)$.

(2) Select s uniformly in $\{s \in S_n^{n-1} : h_s(y_0) = h_s(y)\}$.

(Recall that y is the input to A, and y_0 is generated by A at Step (1).)

(3) Invoke A' on input (s, r_0), and output whatever A' does.

By Condition C2, Step (2) can be implemented in probabilistic polynomial-time.

Turning to the analysis of algorithm A, we consider the behavior of A on input $y = f(x)$ for a uniformly distributed $x \in \{0, 1\}^n$, which implies that y is uniformly distributed over $\{0, 1\}^n$. We first observe that for every fixed r_0 selected in Step (1), if y is uniformly distributed in $\{0, 1\}^n$, then s as determined in Step (2) is almost uniformly distributed in S_n^{n-1}.

> On the distribution of s as selected in Step (2): Fixing $r_0 \in \{0, 1\}^{q(n)}$ means that $y_0 = f(A'_0(r_0)) \in \{0, 1\}^n$ is fixed. Using the pairwise independence property of S_n^{n-1}, it follows that for each $y \in \{0, 1\}^n \setminus \{y_0\}$, the cardinality of $S_y \overset{\text{def}}{=} \{s \in S_n^{n-1} : h_s(y_0) = h_s(y)\}$ equals $|S_n^{n-1}|/2^{n-1}$. Furthermore, in case h_s is 2-to-1, the string s resides in exactly two S_y's (one being S_{y_0}). Recalling that all but a negligible fraction of the h_s's are 2-to-1 (i.e., Condition C1), it follows that each such function is selected with probability $2 \cdot 2^{-n} \cdot (|S_n^{n-1}|/2^{n-1})^{-1} = |S_n^{n-1}|^{-1}$. Other functions (i.e., non-2-to-1 functions) are selected with negligible probability.

By the construction of A (which ignores y in Step (1)), the probability that $f(x_0) = y$ is negligible (but we could have taken advantage of this case, too, by augmenting Step (1) such that if $y_0 = y$, then A halts with output x_0). Note that in case $f(x_0) \neq y$ and h_s is 2-to-1, if A' returns x' such that $x' \neq x_0$ and $h'_s(x') = h'_s(x_0)$, then it holds that $f(x') = y$.

> Justifying the last claim: Let $v \overset{\text{def}}{=} h_s(y)$ and suppose that h_s is 2-to-1. Then, by Step (2) and $f(x_0) \neq y$, it holds that $x = f^{-1}(y)$ and x_0 are *the* two pre-images of $v = h'_s(x) = h'_s(x_0)$ under h'_s, where $h'_s = h_s \circ f$ is 2-to-1 because f is 1-to-1 and h_s is 2-to-1. Since $x' \neq x_0$ is also a pre-image of v under h'_s, it follows that $x' = x$.

We conclude that if A' forms designated collisions with probability $\varepsilon'(n)$, then A inverts f with probability $\varepsilon'(n) - \mu(n)$, where μ is a negligible function (accounting for the negligible probability that h_s is not 2-to-1). (Indeed, we rely on the fact that s as selected in Step (2) is distributed almost uniformly, and furthermore that each 2-to-1 function appears with exectly the right probability.) The proposition follows. ∎

Step II: Constructing $(d', d'/2)$-UOWHFs. We now take the second step on our way, and use any $(d, d - 1)$-UOWHF in order to construct a $(d', d'/2)$-UOWHF. That is, we construct length-restricted UOWHFs that shrink their input by a factor of 2. The construction is obtained by composing a sequence of *different* functions taken from different $(d, d - 1)$-UOWHFs. That is, each function in the sequence shrinks the input by one bit, and the composition of $d'/2$ functions shrinks the initial d'-bit long input by a factor of 2. For simplicity, we assume that the function $d : \mathbb{N} \to \mathbb{N}$ is onto and monotonically non-decreasing. In such a case we denote by $d^{-1}(m)$ the smallest natural number n satisfying $d(n) = m$ (and so $d^{-1}(d(n)) \leq n$).

Construction 6.4.22 (a $(d', d'/2)$-UOWHF): *Let* $\{h_s : \{0, 1\}^{d(|s|)} \to \{0, 1\}^{d(|s|)-1}\}$ $_{s \in \{0,1\}^*}$, *where* $d : \mathbb{N} \to \mathbb{N}$ *is onto and non-decreasing. Then, for every* $\bar{s} = (s_1, ..., s_{\lceil d(n)/2 \rceil})$, *where each* $s_i \in \{0, 1\}^{d^{-1}(d(n)+1-i)}$, *and every* $x \in \{0, 1\}^{d(n)}$, *we define*

$$h'_{s_1,...,s_{\lceil d(n)/2 \rceil}}(x) \stackrel{\text{def}}{=} h_{s_{\lceil d(n)/2 \rceil}}(\cdots h_{s_2}(h_{s_1}(x)) \cdots)$$

That is, letting $x_0 \stackrel{\text{def}}{=} x$, *and* $x_i \leftarrow h_{s_i}(x_{i-1})$ *for* $i = 1, ..., \lceil d(n)/2 \rceil$, *we set* $h'_{\bar{s}}(x_0) = x_{\lceil d(n)/2 \rceil}$. *(Note that* $d(|s_i|) = d(n) + 1 - i$ *and* $|x_i| = d(n) + 1 - i$ *indeed hold.)*

> Tedious details: *We refer to an index selection algorithm that, on input* 1^m, *determines the largest integer* n *such that* $m \geq m' \stackrel{\text{def}}{=} \sum_{i=1}^{\lceil d(n)/2 \rceil} d^{-1}(d(n) + 1 - i)$, *uniformly selects* $s_1, ..., s_{\lceil d(n)/2 \rceil}$ *such that* $s_i \in \{0, 1\}^{d^{-1}(d(n)+1-i)}$, *and* $s_0 \in \{0, 1\}^{m-m'}$, *and lets* $h'_{s_0,s_1,...,s_{\lceil d(n)/2 \rceil}} \stackrel{\text{def}}{=} h'_{s_1,...,s_{\lceil d(n)/2 \rceil}}$.

That is, for $m = |\bar{s}|$, we have $h'_{\bar{s}} : \{0, 1\}^{d(n)} \to \{0, 1\}^{\lfloor d(n)/2 \rfloor}$, where n is the largest integer such that $m \geq \sum_{i=1}^{\lceil d(n)/2 \rceil} d^{-1}(d(n) + 1 - i)$. Thus, $d'(m) = d(n)$, where n is the length of the index in the $(d, d-1)$-UOWHF; that is, we have $h'_{\bar{s}} : \{0, 1\}^{d'(|\bar{s}|)} \to \{0, 1\}^{\lceil d'(|\bar{s}|)/2 \rceil}$, with $d'(|\bar{s}|) = d(n)$. Note that for $d(n) = \Theta(n)$ (as in Construction 6.4.20), it holds that $d'(O(n^2)) \geq d(n)$ and $d'(m) = \Omega(\sqrt{m})$ follows. More generally, if for some polynomial p it holds that $p(d(n)) \geq n \geq d(n)$ (for all n's), then for some polynomial p' it holds that $p'(d'(m)) \geq m \geq d'(m)$ (for all m's), because $d'(d(n) \cdot n) \geq d(n)$. We call such a function sufficiently growing; that is, $d : \mathbb{N} \to \mathbb{N}$ is sufficiently growing if there exists a polynomial p so that for every n it holds that $p(d(n)) \geq n$. (E.g., for every fixed $\varepsilon, \varepsilon' > 0$, the function $d(n) = \varepsilon' n^\varepsilon$ is sufficiently growing.)

Proposition 6.4.23: *Suppose that* $\{h_s\}_{s \in \{0,1\}^*}$ *is a* $(d, d-1)$-UOWHF, *where* $d : \mathbb{N} \to \mathbb{N}$ *is onto, non-decreasing, and sufficiently growing. Then, for some sufficiently growing function* $d' : \mathbb{N} \to \mathbb{N}$, *Construction 6.4.22 is a* $(d', \lceil d'/2 \rceil)$-UOWHF.

Proof Sketch: Intuitively, a designated collision under $h'_{s_1,...,s_{d/2}}$ yields a designated collision under one of the h_{s_i}'s. That is, let $x_0 \stackrel{\text{def}}{=} x$ and $x_i \leftarrow h_{s_i}(x_{i-1})$ for $i = 1, ..., \lceil d(n)/2 \rceil$. Then if given x and $\bar{s} = (s_1, ..., s_{d/2})$, one can find an $x' \neq x$ such that $h'_{\bar{s}}(x) = h'_{\bar{s}}(x')$; then there exists an i so that $x_{i-1} \neq x'_{i-1}$ and $x_i = h_{s_i}(x_{i-1}) = h_{s_i}(x'_{i-1}) = x'_i$, where the x'_j's are defined analogously to the x_j's. Thus, we obtain a designated collision under h_{s_i}. We stress that because $h'_{\bar{s}}$ does not shrink its input too much, the length of s_i is polynomially related to the length of $\bar{s}$ (and thus, forming collisions with respect to h_{s_i} by using the collision-finder for $h'_{\bar{s}}$ yields a contradiction).

The actual proof uses the hypothesis that it is hard to form designated collisions *when one is also given the coins used in the generation of the pre-image* (and not merely the pre-image itself). In particular, we construct an algorithm that forms designated collisions under one of the h_{s_i}'s, when given not only x_{i-1} but also x_0 (which actually yields x_{i-1}). The following details are quite tedious and merely provide an implementation of this idea.

As stated, the proof is by a reducibility argument. We are given a probabilistic polynomial-time algorithm A' that forms designated collisions under $\{h'_{\overline{s}}\}$, with respect to pre-images produced by a deterministic polynomial-time algorithm A'_0 that maps $p'(n)$-bit strings to n-bit strings. We construct algorithms A_0 and A such that A forms designated collisions under $\{h_s\}$ with respect to pre-images produced by algorithm A_0, which maps $p(n)$-bit strings to n-bit strings, for a suitable polynomial p. (Specifically, $p : \mathbb{N} \to \mathbb{N}$ is 1-1 and $p(n) \geq p'(d^{-1}(2d(n))) + n + n \cdot d^{-1}(2d(n))$, where the factor of 2 appearing in the expression is due to the shrinking factor of $h'_{\overline{s}}$.)

We start with the description of A_0, that is, the algorithm that generates pre-images of $\{h_s\}$. Intuitively, A_0 selects a random j, uses A'_0 to obtain a pre-image x_0 of $\{h'_{\overline{s}}\}$, generates random $s_0, \ldots, s_{j-1}$, and outputs a pre-image x_{j-1} of $\{h_{s_j}\}$, computed by $x_i = h_{s_i}(x_{i-1})$ for $i = 1, \ldots, j - 1$. (Algorithm A will be given x_{j-1} (or rather the coins used to generate x_{j-1}) and a random h_{s_j} and will try to form a collision with x_{j-1} under h_{s_j}.)

> Detailed description of A_0: Recall that p' is a polynomial, $d(n) \leq n$ and $d^{-1}(n) = \text{poly}(n)$. Let $p(n) \stackrel{\text{def}}{=} n + n \cdot q(n) + p'(q(n))$, where $q(n) \stackrel{\text{def}}{=} d^{-1}(2d(n))$. On input $r \in \{0, 1\}^{p(n)}$, algorithm A_0 proceeds as follows:
>
> (1) Write $r = r_1 r_2 r_3$ such that $|r_1| = n$, $|r_2| = n \cdot q(n)$, and $|r_3| = p'(q(n))$.
>   Using r_1, determine m in $\{n + 1, \ldots, n \cdot q(n)\}$ and $j \in \{1, \ldots, q(n)\}$ such that both m and j are almost uniformly distributed in the corresponding sets.
> (2) Compute the largest integer n' such that $m \leq \sum_{i=1}^{\lceil d(n')/2 \rceil} d^{-1}(d(n') + 1 - i)$.
> (3) If $d^{-1}(d(n') + 1 - j) \neq n$, then output the $d(n)$-bit long suffix of r_3.
>   (Comment: the output in this case is immaterial to our proof.)
> (4) Otherwise (i.e., $n = d^{-1}(d(n') + 1 - j)$, which is the case we care about), do:
>   (4.1) Let $s_0 s_1 \cdots s_{j-1}$ be a prefix of r_2 such that
> $$|s_0| = m - \sum_{i=1}^{\lceil d(n')/2 \rceil} d^{-1}(d(n') + 1 - i),$$
>   and $|s_i| = d^{-1}(d(n') + 1 - i)$, for $i = 1, \ldots, j - 1$.
>   (4.2) Let $x_0 \leftarrow A'_0(r')$, where r' is the $p'(d^{-1}(d(n')))$-bit long suffix of r_3.
>   (Comment: $x_0 \in \{0, 1\}^{d(n')}$.)
>   (4.3) For $i = 1, \ldots, j - 1$, compute $x_i \leftarrow h_{s_i}(x_{i-1})$.
>   Output $x_{j-1} \in \{0, 1\}^{d(n)}$.
>   (Note that $d(n) = d(n') - (j - 1)$.)

As stated previously, we only care about the case in which Step (4) is applied. This case occurs with noticeable probability, and the description of the following algorithm A refers to it.

Algorithm A will be given x_{j-1} as produced by A_0 (along with, or actually only, the coins used in its generation), as well as a random h_{s_j}, and will try to form a collision with x_{j-1} under h_{s_j}. On input $s \in \{0, 1\}^n$ (viewed as s_j) and the coins given to A_0, algorithm A operates as follows. First, A selects j and $s_0, s_1, \ldots, s_{j-1}$ exactly as A_0 does (which is the reason that A needs the coins used by A_0). Next, A tries to obtain a collision under h_s by invoking $A'(r', s')$, where r' is the sequence of coins that A_0 handed to A'_0 and

$s' = (s_0, s_1, ..., s_{j-1}, s, s_{j+1}, ..., s_{d(n)/2})$, where $s_{j+1}, ..., s_{d(n)/2}$ are uniformly selected by A. Finally, A outputs $h_{s_{j-1}}(\cdots (h_{s_1}(A'(r', s')) \cdots)$.

> **Detailed description of A:** On input $s \in \{0, 1\}^n$ and $r \in \{0, 1\}^{p(n)}$, algorithm A proceeds as follows.

> (1–2) Using r, determine m, j, and n' exactly as done by A_0.
> (3)   If $d^{-1}(d(n') + 1 - j) \neq n$, then abort.
> (4)   Otherwise (i.e., $n = d^{-1}(d(n') + 1 - j)$), do:
>   (4.1) Determine $s_0, s_1, ..., s_{j-1}$ and r' exactly as A_0 does (at its Step (4)).
>   (4.2) Uniformly select $s_{j+1}, ..., s_{\lceil d(n')/2 \rceil}$ such that $s_i \in \{0, 1\}^{d^{-1}(d(n')+1-i)}$,
>   and set $s' = (s_0, s_1, ..., s_{j-1}, s, s_{j+1}, ..., s_{\lceil d(n')/2 \rceil})$.
>   (4.3) Invoke A' on input (s', r'), and obtain $x'_0 \leftarrow A'(s', r')$.
>   (Comment: $x'_0 \in \{0, 1\}^{d(n')}$.)
>   (4.4) For $i = 1, ..., j - 1$, compute $x'_i \leftarrow h_{s_i}(x'_{i-1})$.
>   Output $x'_{j-1} \in \{0, 1\}^{d(n)}$.

Clearly, if algorithms A' and A'_0 run in polynomial-time, then so do A and A_0 (and if p' is a polynomial then so is p). We now lower-bound the probability that A succeeds in forming designated collisions under $\{h_s\}$, with respect to pre-images produced by A_0. We start from the contradiction hypothesis by which the corresponding probability for A' (with respect to A'_0) is non-negligible.

Let use denote by $\varepsilon'(m)$ the success probability of A' on uniformly distributed input $(s', r') \in \{0, 1\}^m \times \{0, 1\}^{p'(m)}$. Let n' be the largest integer so that $m \leq \sum_{i=1}^{\lceil d(n')/2 \rceil} d^{-1}(d(n') + 1 - i)$. Then, there exists a $j \in \{1, ..., d(n')\}$ such that, with probability at least $\varepsilon'(m)/d'(n')$, on input (s', r'), where $s' = s_0, s_1, ..., s_{\lceil d(n')/2 \rceil}$ is as in Construction 6.4.22, A' outputs an $x' \neq x \stackrel{\text{def}}{=} A'_0(r')$ such that $h_{s_{j-1}}(\cdots (h_{s_1}(x')) \cdots) \neq h_{s_{j-1}}(\cdots (h_{s_1}(x)) \cdots)$ and $h_{s_j}(\cdots (h_{s_1}(x')) \cdots) = h_{s_j}(\cdots (h_{s_1}(x)) \cdots)$. Fixing these m, j, and n', let $n = d^{-1}(d(n') + 1 - j)$, and consider what happens when A is invoked on uniformly distributed $(s, r) \in \{0, 1\}^n \times \{0, 1\}^{p(n)}$. With probability at least $\delta(n) \stackrel{\text{def}}{=} 1/(nq(n))^2$ over the possible r's, the values of m and j are determined to equal the aforementioned desired values. Conditioned on this case, A' is invoked on uniformly distributed input $(s', r') \in \{0, 1\}^m \times \{0, 1\}^{p'(m)}$, and so a collision at the j-th hashing function occurs with probability at least $\varepsilon'(m)/d'(n')$. Note that $m = \text{poly}(n)$, $\delta(n) \geq 1/\text{poly}(n)$ and $d'(n') = \text{poly}(n)$. This implies that A succeeds with probability at least $\varepsilon(n) \stackrel{\text{def}}{=} \delta(n) \cdot \frac{\varepsilon'(m)}{d'(n')} = \frac{\varepsilon'(\text{poly}(n))}{\text{poly}(n)}$, with respect to pre-images produced by A_0. Thus, if ε' is non-negligible, then so is ε, and the proposition follows. ∎

Step III: Constructing (Length-Unrestricted) Quasi-UOWHFs That Shrink Their Input by a Factor of Two. The third step on our way consists of using any $(d, d/2)$-UOWHF in order to construct "quasi UOWHFs" that are applicable to any input length but shrink each input to half its length (rather than to a fixed length that only depends on the function description). The resulting construct does not fit Definition 6.4.19, because the function's output length depends on the function's input length, yet the function can be applied to any input length (rather than only to a single length determined by the function's description). Thus, the resulting construct yields a $(d', d'/2)$-UOWHF for *any* polynomially bounded function d' (e.g., $d'(n) = n^2$), whereas in Construction 6.4.22, the function d' is fixed and satisfies $d'(n) \ll n$. The construction itself amounts to parsing the input into blocks and applying the *same* function (taken from a $(d, d/2)$-UOWHF) to each block.

Construction 6.4.24 (a $(d', d'/2)$-UOWHF for any d'): *Let* $\{h_s : \{0, 1\}^{d(|s|)} \to \{0, 1\}^{\lfloor d(|s|)/2 \rfloor}\}_{s \in \{0,1\}^*}$, *where* $d : \mathbb{N} \to \mathbb{N}$ *is onto and non-decreasing. Then, for every* $s \in \{0, 1\}^n$ *and every* $x \in \{0, 1\}^*$, *we define*

$$h'_s(x) \stackrel{\text{def}}{=} h_s(x_1) \cdots h_s(x_t 10^{d(n)-|x_t|-1})$$

where $x = x_1 \cdots x_t$, $0 \le |x_t| < d(n)$ *and* $|x_i| = d(n)$ *for* $i = 1, ..., t - 1$. *The index-selection algorithm of* $\{h'_s\}$ *is identical to the one of* $\{h_s\}$.

Clearly, $|h'_s(x)| = \lceil (|x| + 1)/d(n) \rceil \cdot \lfloor d(n)/2 \rfloor$, which is approximately $|x|/2$ (provided $|x| \ge d(n)$). Furthermore, Construction 6.4.24 satisfies Conditions 1 and 2 of Definition 6.4.18, provided that $\{h_s\}$ satisfies the corresponding conditions of Definition 6.4.19. We thus focus on the hardness to form designated collisions (i.e., Condition 3).

Proposition 6.4.25: *Suppose that* $\{h_s\}_{s \in \{0,1\}^*}$ *is a* $(d, d/2)$-UOWHF, *where* $d : \mathbb{N} \to \mathbb{N}$ *is onto, non-decreasing, and sufficiently growing. Then Construction 6.4.22 satisfies Condition 3 of Definition 6.4.18.*

Proof Sketch: Intuitively, a designated collision under h'_s yields a designated collision under h_s. That is, consider the parsing of each string into blocks of length $d(n)$, as in Construction 6.4.24. Now if, given $x = x_1 \cdots x_t$ and s, one can find an $x' = x'_1 \cdots x'_{t'} \ne x$ such that $h'_s(x) = h'_s(x')$, then $t' = t$ and there exists an i such that $x_i \ne x'_i$ and $h_s(x_i) = h_s(x'_i)$. Details follow.

The actual proof is by a reducibility argument. Given a probabilistic polynomial-time algorithm A' that forms designated collisions under $\{h'_s\}$, with respect to pre-images produced by a polynomial-time algorithm A'_0, we construct algorithms A_0 and A such that A forms designated collisions under $\{h_s\}$ with respect to pre-images produced by algorithm A_0. Specifically, algorithm A_0 invokes A'_0 and uses extra randomness (supplied in its input) to uniformly select one of the $d(n)$-bit long blocks in the standard parsing of the output of A'_0. That is, the random-tape used by algorithm A_0 has the form (r', i), and A_0 outputs the i-th block in the parsing of the string $A'_0(r')$. Algorithm A is derived analogously. That is, given $s \in \{0, 1\}^n$ and the coins $r = (r', i)$ used by A_0, algorithm A invokes A' on input s and r', obtains the output x', and outputs the i-th block in the standard parsing of x'.

Note that whenever we have a collision under h'_s (i.e., a pair $x \ne x'$ such that $h'_s(x) = h'_s(x')$), we obtain at least one collision under the corresponding h_s (i.e., for some i, the i-th blocks of x and x' differ, and yet both blocks are mapped by h_s to the same image). Thus, if algorithm A' succeeds (in forming designated collisions with respect to $\{h'_s\}$)

with probability $\varepsilon'(n)$, then algorithm A succeeds (in forming designated collisions with respect to $\{h_s\}$) with probability at least $\varepsilon'(n)/t(n)$, where $t(n)$ is a bound on the running time of A' (which also upper-bounds the length of the output of A', and so $1/t(n)$ is a lower bound on the probability that the colliding strings differ at a certain uniformly selected block). The proposition follows. ∎

Step IV: Obtaining Full-Fledged UOWHFs. The last step on our way consists of using any quasi-UOWHFs as constructed (in Step III) to obtain full-fledged UOWHFs. That is, we use quasi-UOWHFs that are applicable to any input length but shrink each input to half its length (rather than to a fixed length that only depends on the function description). The resulting construct is a UOWHF (as defined in Definition 6.4.18). The construction is obtained by composing a sequence of *different* functions (each taken from the same quasi-UOWHF); that is, the following construction is analogous to Construction 6.4.22.

Construction 6.4.26 (a UOWHF): *Let* $\{h_s : \{0, 1\}^* \to \{0, 1\}^*\}_{s \in \{0,1\}^*}$, *such that* $|h_s(x)| = |x|/2$, *for every* $x \in \{0, 1\}^{2i \cdot |s|}$ *where* $i \in \mathbb{N}$. *Then, for every* $s_1, \ldots, s_n \in \{0, 1\}^n$ *and every* $t \in \mathbb{N}$ *and* $x \in \{0, 1\}^{2^t \cdot n}$, *we define*

$$h'_{s_1,\ldots,s_n}(x) \stackrel{\text{def}}{=} (t, h_{s_t}(\cdots h_{s_2}(h_{s_1}(x))\cdots))$$

That is, we let $x_0 \stackrel{\text{def}}{=} x$, *and* $x_i \leftarrow h_{s_i}(x_{i-1})$, *for* $i = 1, \ldots, t$.

> Tedious details: *Strings of lengths that are not of the form* $2^t \cdot n$ *are padded into strings of such form in a standard manner. We refer to an index-selection algorithm that, on input* 1^m, *determines* $n = \lfloor \sqrt{m} \rfloor$, *uniformly selects* $s_1, \ldots, s_n \in \{0, 1\}^n$ *and* $s_0 \in \{0, 1\}^{m-n^2}$, *and lets* $h'_{s_0,s_1,\ldots,s_n} \stackrel{\text{def}}{=} h'_{s_1,\ldots,s_n}$.

Observe that $h'_{s_0,s_1,\ldots,s_n}(x) = h'_{s_0,s_1,\ldots,s_n}(x')$ implies that both equal the pair $(t, h_{s_t}(\cdots h_{s_2}(h_{s_1}(x))\cdots))$, where $t = \lceil \log_2(|x|/n) \rceil = \lceil \log_2(|x'|/n) \rceil$. Note that $h'_{s_0,s_1,\ldots,s_n} : \{0, 1\}^* \to \{0, 1\}^{n+\log_2 n}$, and that $m = |s_0, s_1, \ldots, s_n| < (n + 1)^2$.

Proposition 6.4.27: *Suppose that* $\{h_s\}_{s \in \{0,1\}^*}$ *satisfies the conditions of Definition 6.4.18, except that it maps arbitrary input strings to outputs having half the length (rather than a length determined by* $|s|$*). Then Construction 6.4.26 constitutes a collection of UOWHFs.*

The proof of Proposition 6.4.27 is omitted because it is almost identical to the proof of Proposition 6.4.23.

Conclusion. Combining the previous four steps, we obtain a construction of (full-fledged) UOWHFs (based on any one-way permutation). That is, combining Propositions 6.4.21, 6.4.23, 6.4.25, and 6.4.27, we obtain:[35]

---

[35] Actually, there is a minor gap between Constructions 6.4.24 and 6.4.26. In the former we constructed functions that hash every x into a value of length $\lceil (|x| + 1)/d(n) \rceil \cdot \lfloor d(n)/2 \rfloor$, whereas in the latter we used functions that hash every $x \in \{0, 1\}^{2i \cdot n}$ into a value of length $i \cdot n$.

Theorem 6.4.28: *If one-way permutations exist, then universal one-way hash functions exist.*

Note that the *only* barrier toward constructing UOWHFs based on *arbitrary* one-way *functions* is Proposition 6.4.21, which refers to one-way *permutations*. Thus, if we wish to constructs UOWHF based on any one-way function, then we need to present an alternative construction of a $(d, d - 1)$-UOWHF (i.e., an alternative to Construction 6.4.20, which fails in case f is 2-to-1).[36] Such a construction is actually known, and so the following result is known to hold (but its proof it too complex to fit in this work):

Theorem 6.4.29: *Universal one-way hash functions exist if and only if one-way functions exist.*

We stress that the difficult direction is the one referred to earlier (i.e., from one-way functions to UOWHF collections). For the much easier (converse) direction, see Exercise 19.

6.4.3.3. One-Time Signature Schemes Based on UOWHF

Using universal one-way hash functions, we present an alternative construction of one-time signature schemes based on *length-restricted* one-time signature schemes. Specifically, we replace the hash-and-sign paradigm (i.e., Construction 6.2.6) in which collision-free hashing functions were used by the following variant (i.e., Construction 6.4.30) in which universal one-way hash functions are used instead. The difference between the two constructions is that here, the (description of the) hashing function is not a part of the signing and verification keys, but is rather selected on the fly by the signing algorithm (and appears as part of the signature). Furthermore, the description of the hash function is being authenticated (by the signer) together with the hash value. It follows that the forging adversary, which is unable to break the length-restricted one-time signature scheme, must form a designated collision (rather than an arbitrary one). However, the latter is infeasible, too (by virtue of the UOWHF collection in use). We comment that the same (new) construction is applicable to length-restricted signature schemes (rather than to one-time ones): We stress that in the latter case, a new hashing function is selected at random each time the signing algorithm is applied. In fact, we present the more general construction.

Construction 6.4.30 (the Hash-and-Sign Paradigm, Revisited): *Let $\ell, \ell' : \mathbb{N} \to \mathbb{N}$ such that $\ell(n) = \ell'(n) + n$. Let (G, S, V) be an ℓ-restricted signature scheme as in Definition 6.2.1, and $\{h_r : \{0, 1\}^* \to \{0, 1\}^{\ell'(|r|)}\}_{r \in \{0,1\}^*}$ be a collection of functions with an indexing algorithm I (as in Definition 6.4.18). We construct a general signature scheme,*

---

[36] For example, if $f(\sigma, x') = (0, f'(x'))$, for $\sigma \in \{0, 1\}$, then forming designated collisions under Construction 6.4.20 is easy: Given $(0, x')$, one outputs $(1, x')$, and indeed a collision is formed (already under f).

(G', S', V'), with G' identical to G, as follows:

Signing with S': *On input a signing-key s (in the range of $G'_1(1^n)$) and a document $\alpha \in \{0, 1\}^*$, algorithm S' proceeds in two steps:*
1. *Algorithm S' invokes I to obtain $\beta_1 \leftarrow I(1^n)$.*
2. *Algorithm S' invokes S to produce $\beta_2 \leftarrow S_s(\beta_1, h_{\beta_1}(\alpha))$.*
   Algorithm S' outputs the signature (β_1, β_2).

Verification with V': *On input a verifying-key v, a document $\alpha \in \{0, 1\}^*$, and an alleged signature (β_1, β_2), algorithm V' invokes V, and outputs $V_v((\beta_1, h_{\beta_1}(\alpha)), \beta_2)$.*

Recall that secure ℓ-restricted one-time signature schemes exist for any polynomial ℓ, provided that one-way functions exist. Thus, the fact that Construction 6.4.30 requires $\ell(n) > n$ is not a problem. In applying Construction 6.4.30, one should first choose a family of UOWHFs $\{h_r : \{0, 1\}^* \to \{0, 1\}^{\ell'(|r|)}\}_{r \in \{0,1\}^*}$, then determine $\ell(n) = \ell'(n) + n$, and use a corresponding secure ℓ-restricted one-time signature scheme.

Let us pause to compare Construction 6.2.6 with Construction 6.4.30. Recall that in Construction 6.2.6, the function description $\beta_1 \leftarrow I(1^n)$ is produced (and fixed as part of both keys) by the key-generation algorithm. Thus, the function description β_1 is trivially authenticated (i.e., by merely being part of the verification-key). Consequently, in Construction 6.2.6, the S'-signature (of α) equals $S_s(h_{\beta_1}(\alpha))$. In contrast, in Construction 6.4.30 a fresh new (function description) β_1 is selected per each signature, and thus β_1 needs to be authenticated. Hence, the S'-signature equals the pair $(\beta_1, S_s(\beta_1, h_{\beta_1}(\alpha)))$. Since we want to be able to use (length-restricted) *one-time* signatures, we let the signing algorithm authenticate both β_1 and $h_{\beta_1}(\alpha)$ via a single signature. (Alternatively, we could have used two instances of the one-time signature scheme (G, S, V), one for signing the function description β_1 and the other for signing the hash value $h_{\beta_1}(\alpha)$.)

Proposition 6.4.31: *Suppose that (G, S, V) is a secure ℓ-restricted signature scheme and that $\{h_r : \{0, 1\}^* \to \{0, 1\}^{\ell(|r|) - |r|}\}_{r \in \{0,1\}^*}$ is a collection of UOWHFs. Then (G', S', V'), as defined in Construction 6.4.30, is a secure (full-fledged) signature scheme. Furthermore, if (G, S, V) is only a secure ℓ-restricted one-time signature scheme, then (G', S', V') is a secure one-time signature scheme.*

Proof Sketch: The proof follows the underlying principles of the proof of Proposition 6.2.7. That is, forgery with respect to (G', S', V') yields either forgery with respect to (G, S, V) or a collision under the hash function, where in the latter case, a designated collision is formed (in contradiction to the hypothesis regarding the UOWHF). For the furthermore-part, the observation underlying the proof of Proposition 6.4.7 still holds (i.e., the number of queries made by the forger constructed for (G, S, V) equals the number of queries made by the forger assumed (toward the contradiction) for (G', S', V')). Details follow.

Given an adversary A' attacking the complex scheme (G', S', V'), we construct an adversary A that attacks the ℓ-restricted scheme, (G, S, V). The adversary A uses I (the indexing algorithm of the UOWHF collection) and its oracle S_s in order to emulate the oracle S'_s for A'. This is done in a straightforward manner; that is, algorithm A emulates S'_s by using the oracle S_s (exactly as S'_s actually does). Specifically, to answer a query

q, algorithm A generates $a_1 \leftarrow I(1^n)$, forwards $(a_1, h_{a_1}(q))$ to its own oracle (i.e., S_s), and answers with (a_1, a_2), where $a_2 = S_s(a_1, h_{a_1}(q))$. (We stress that A issues a single S_s-query per each S'_s-query made by A'.) When A' outputs a document-signature pair relative to the complex scheme (G', S', V'), algorithm A tries to use this pair in order to form a document-signature pair relative to the ℓ-restricted scheme, (G, S, V). That is, if A' outputs the document-signature pair (α, β), where $\beta = (\beta_1, \beta_2)$, then A will output the document-signature pair (α_2, β_2), where $\alpha_2 \overset{\text{def}}{=} (\beta_1, h_{\beta_1}(\alpha))$.

Assume that with (non-negligible) probability $\varepsilon'(n)$, the (probabilistic polynomial-time) algorithm A' succeeds in existentially forging relative to the complex scheme (G', S', V'). Let $(\alpha^{(i)}, \beta^{(i)})$ denote the i-th query and answer pair made by A', and let (α, β) be the forged document-signature pair that A' outputs (in case of success), where $\beta^{(i)} = (\beta_1^{(i)}, \beta_2^{(i)})$ and $\beta = (\beta_1, \beta_2)$. We consider the following two cases regarding the forging event:

Case 1: $(\beta_1, h_{\beta_1}(\alpha)) \neq (\beta_1^{(i)}, h_{\beta_1^{(i)}}(\alpha^{(i)}))$ for all i's. (That is, the S_s-signed value in the forged signature (i.e., the value $(\beta_1, h_{\beta_1}(\alpha))$) is different from all queries made to S_s.) In this case, the document-signature pair $((\beta_1, h_{\beta_1}(\alpha)), \beta_2)$ constitutes a success in existential forgery relative to the ℓ-restricted scheme (G, S, V).

Case 2: $(\beta_1, h_{\beta_1}(\alpha)) = (\beta_1^{(i)}, h_{\beta_1^{(i)}}(\alpha^{(i)}))$ for some i. (That is, the S_s-signed value used in the forged signature equals the i-th query made to S_s, although $\alpha \neq \alpha^{(i)}$.) Thus, $\beta_1 = \beta_1^{(i)}$ and $h_{\beta_1}(\alpha) = h_{\beta_1^{(i)}}(\alpha^{(i)})$, although $\alpha \neq \alpha^{(i)}$. In this case, the pair $(\alpha, \alpha^{(i)})$ forms a designated collision under $h_{\beta_1^{(i)}}$ (and we do not obtain success in existential forgery relative to the ℓ-restricted scheme). We stress that A' selects $\alpha^{(i)}$ before it is given the description of the function $h_{\beta_1^{(i)}}$, and thus its ability to later produce $\alpha \neq \alpha^{(i)}$ such that $h_{\beta_1}(\alpha) = h_{\beta_1^{(i)}}(\alpha^{(i)})$ yields a violation of the UOWHF property.

Thus, if Case 1 occurs with probability at least $\varepsilon'(n)/2$, then A succeeds in its attack on (G, S, V) with probability at least $\varepsilon'(n)/2$, which contradicts the security of the ℓ-restricted scheme (G, S, V). On the other hand, if Case 2 occurs with probability at least $\varepsilon'(n)/2$, then we derive a contradiction to the difficulty of forming designated collisions with respect to $\{h_r\}$. Details regarding Case 2 follow.

We start with a sketch of the construction of an algorithm that attempts to form designated collisions under a randomly selected hash function. Loosely speaking, we construct an algorithm B' that tries to form designated collisions by emulating the attack of A' on a random instance of (G', S', V') that B' selects by itself. Thus, B' can easily answer any signing-query referred to it by A', but in one of these queries (the index of which is selected at random by B'), algorithm B' will use a hash function given to it from the outside (rather than generating such a function at random by itself). In case A' forges a signature while using this specific function-value pair (as in Case 2), algorithm B' obtains and outputs a designated collision.

We now turn to the actual construction of algorithm B' (which attempts to form designated collisions under a randomly selected hash function). Recall that such an algorithm operates in three stages (see discussion in Section 6.4.3.1): First the algorithm selects a pre-image x_0, next it is given a description of a function h, and finally it is required to output $x \neq x_0$ such that $h(x) = h(x_0)$. We stress that the third stage in the attack is also given the random coins used for producing the pre-image x_0 (at the first stage). Now, on input 1^n, algorithm B' proceeds in three stages:

Stage 1: Algorithm B' selects uniformly $i \in \{1, ..., t(n)\}$, where $t(n)$ bounds the running time of $A'(G_1'(1^n))$ (and thus the number of queries it makes). Next, B' selects $(s, v) \leftarrow G'(1^n)$ and emulates the attack of $A'(v)$ on S_s', while answering the queries of S_s' as follows. All queries except the i-th one are emulated in the straightforward manner (i.e., by executing the program of S_s' as stated). That is, for $j \neq i$, the j-th query, denoted $\alpha^{(j)}$, is answered by producing $\beta_1^{(j)} \leftarrow I(1^n)$, computing $\beta_2^{(j)} \leftarrow S_s(\beta_1^{(j)}, h_{\beta_1^{(j)}}(\alpha^{(j)}))$ (using the knowledge of s), and answering with the pair $(\beta_1^{(j)}, \beta_2^{(j)})$. The i-th query of A', denoted $\alpha^{(i)}$, will be used as the *designated pre-image*. Once $\alpha^{(i)}$ is issued (by A'), algorithm B' completes its first stage (without answering this query), and the rest of the emulation of A' will be conducted by the third stage of B'.

Stage 2: At this point (i.e., after B' has selected the designated pre-image $\alpha^{(i)}$), B' obtains a description of a random hashing function h_r (thus completing its second operation stage). That is, this stage consists of B' being given $r \leftarrow I(1^n)$.

Stage 3: Next, algorithm B' answers the i-th query (i.e., $\alpha^{(i)}$) by applying S_s to the pair $(r, h_r(\alpha^{(i)}))$. Subsequent queries are emulated in the straightforward manner (as in Stage 1). When A' halts, B' checks whether A' has output a valid document-signature pair (α, β) as in Case 2 (i.e., $\beta_1 = \beta_1^{(j)}$ and $h_{\beta_1}(\alpha) = h_{\beta_1^{(j)}}(\alpha^{(j)})$ for some j), and whether the collision formed is indeed on the i-th query (i.e., $j = i$, which means that $h_r(\alpha) = h_r(\alpha^{(i)})$). When this happens, B' outputs α (which is different than $\alpha^{(i)}$), and in doing so it has succeeded in forming a designated collision (with $\alpha^{(i)}$ under h_r).

Now, if Case 2 occurs with probability at least $\frac{\varepsilon'(n)}{2}$ (and A' makes at most $t(n)$ queries), then B' has succeeded in forming a designated collision with probability at least $\frac{1}{t(n)} \cdot \frac{\varepsilon'(n)}{2}$, because the actions of A' are independent of the random value of i. This contradicts the hypothesis that $\{h_r\}$ is UOWHF.

As mentioned earlier, the furthermore-part of the proposition follows by observing that if the forging algorithm A' makes at most one query, then the same holds for the algorithm A constructed in the beginning of the proof. Thus, if (G', S', V') can be broken via a single-message attack, then either (G, S, V) can be broken via a single-message attack or one can form designated collisions (with respect to $\{h_r\}$). In both cases, we reach a contradiction. ∎

Conclusion. Combining the furthermore-part of Proposition 6.4.31, Corollary 6.4.6, and the fact that UOWHF collections imply one-way functions (see Exercise 19), we obtain:

Theorem 6.4.32: *If there exist universal one-way hash functions, then secure one-time signature schemes exist, too.*

6.4.3.4. Conclusions and Comments

Combining Theorems 6.4.28, 6.4.32, and 6.4.9, we obtain:

Corollary 6.4.33: *If one-way permutations exists, then there exist secure signature schemes.*

Like Corollary 6.4.10, Corollary 6.4.33 asserts the existence of secure (public-key) signature schemes, based on an assumption that does *not* mention trapdoors. Furthermore, the assumption made in Corollary 6.4.33 seems weaker than the one made in Corollary 6.4.10. We can further weaken the assumption by using Theorem 6.4.29 (which was stated without a proof), rather than Theorem 6.4.28. Specifically, combining Theorems 6.4.29, 6.4.32, and 6.4.9, we establish Theorem 6.4.1. That is, *secure signature schemes exist if and only if one-way functions exist.* Furthermore, as in the case of MACs (see Theorem 6.3.8), *the resulting signature schemes have signatures of fixed length.*

Comment: The Hash-and-Sign Paradigm, Revisited. We wish to highlight the revised version of the hash-and-sign paradigm that underlies Construction 6.4.30. Similar to the original instantiation of the hash-and-sign paradigm (i.e., Construction 6.2.6), Construction 6.4.30 is useful in practice. We warn that using the latter construction requires verifying that $\{h_r\}$ is a UOWHF (rather than collision-free). The advantage of Construction 6.4.30 over Construction 6.2.6 is that the former relies on a seemingly weaker construct; that is, hardness of forming designated collisions (as in UOWHF) is a seemingly weaker condition than hardness of forming any collision (as in collision-free hashing). On the other hand, Construction 6.2.6 is simpler and more efficient (e.g., one need not generate a new hashing function per each signature).

6.5.* Some Additional Properties

We briefly discuss several properties of interest that some signature schemes enjoy. We first discuss properties that seem unrelated to the original purpose of signature schemes but are useful toward utilizing a signature scheme as a building block toward constructing other primitives (e.g., see Section 5.4.4.4). These (related) properties are having *unique valid signatures* and being *super-secure,* where the latter term indicates the infeasibility of finding a different signature even to a document for which a signature was obtained during the attack. We next turn to properties that offer some advantages in the originally intended applications of signature schemes. Specifically, we consider properties that allow for speeding-up the response-time in some settings (see Sections 6.5.3 and 6.5.4), and a property supporting legitimate revoking of forged signatures (see Section 6.5.5).

6.5.1. Unique Signatures

Loosely speaking, we say that a signature scheme (G, S, V) (either a private-key or a public-key one) has unique signatures if for every possible verification-key v and every document α there is a unique β such that $V_v(\alpha, \beta) = 1$.

Note that this property is related, but not equivalent, to the question of whether or not the signing algorithm is deterministic (which is considered in Exercise 1). Indeed, if the signing algorithm is deterministic, then for every key pair (s, v) and document α, the result of applying S_s to α is unique (and indeed $V_v(\alpha, S_s(\alpha)) = 1$). Still, this does *not* mean that there is no other β (which is never produced by applying S_s to α) such that $V_v(\alpha, \beta) = 1$. On the other hand, the unique signature property may hold even in case the signing algorithm is randomized, but (as mentioned earlier) this randomization can be eliminated anyhow.

Can Secure Signature Schemes Have Unique Signatures? The answer is definitely affirmative, and in fact we have seen several such schemes in the previous sections. Specifically, all private-key signature schemes presented in Section 6.3 have unique signatures. Furthermore, every secure private-key signature scheme can be transformed into one having unique signatures (e.g., by combining deterministic signing as in Exercise 1 with canonical verification as in Exercise 2). Turning to public-key signature schemes, we observe that if the one-way function f used in Construction 6.4.4 is 1-1, then the resulting secure length-restricted one-time (public-key) signature scheme has unique signatures (because each f-image has a unique pre-image). In addition, Construction 6.2.6 (i.e., the basic hash-and-sign paradigm) preserves the unique signature property. Let use summarize all these observations:

Theorem 6.5.1 (Secure Schemes with Unique Signatures):

1. *Assuming the existence of one-way functions, there exist secure message authentication schemes having the unique signature property.*
2. *Assuming the existence of 1-1 one-way functions, there exist secure* length-restricted one-time (*public-key*) *signature schemes having the unique signature property.*
3. *Assuming the existence of 1-1 one-way functions and collision-free hashing collections, there exist secure one-time (*public-key*) signature schemes having the unique signature property.*

In addition, it is known that secure (full-fledged) signature schemes having the unique signature property can be constructed based on a mild variant on the standard RSA assumption (see reference in Section 6.6.5). Still, this leaves open the question of whether or not secure signature schemes having the unique signature property exist if and only if secure signature schemes exist.

6.5.2. Super-Secure Signature Schemes

In case the signature scheme does not possess the unique signature property, it makes sense to ask whether, given a message-signature pair, it is feasible to produce a *different signature to the same message*. More generally, we may ask whether it is feasible for a chosen message attack to produce a different signature to any of the messages to which it has obtained signatures. Such ability may be of concern in some applications (but, indeed, not in the most natural applications). Combining the new concern with the standard notion of security, we derive the following notion, which we call super-security.

A signature scheme is called super-secure if it is infeasible for a chosen message attack to produce a valid message-signature pair that is different from all query-answer pairs obtained during the attack, regardless of whether or not the message used in the new pair equals one of the previous queries. (Recall that ordinary security only requires the infeasibility of producing a valid message-signature pair such that the message part is different from all queries made during the attack.)

Do Super-Secure Signature Schemes Exist? Indeed, every secure signature scheme that has unique signatures is super-secure, but the question is whether super-security may hold for a signature scheme that does not possess the unique signature property. We answer this question affirmatively.

Theorem 6.5.2 (super-secure signature schemes): *Assuming the existence of one-way functions, there exist super-secure (public-key) signature schemes.*

In other words, super-secure signature schemes exist if and only if secure signature schemes exist. We comment that the signature scheme constructed in the following proof does not have the unique signature property.

Proof: Starting from (Part 2 of) Theorem 6.5.1, we can use any 1-1 one-way function to obtain super-secure length-restricted one-time signature schemes. However, wishing to use arbitrary one-way functions, we will first show that universal one-way hashing functions can be used (instead of 1-1 one-way functions) in order to obtain super-secure length-restricted one-time signature schemes. Next, we will show that super-security is preserved by two transformations presented in Section 6.4: specifically, the transformation of *length-restricted* one-time signature schemes into one-time signature schemes (i.e., Construction 6.4.30), and the transformation of the latter to (full-fledged) signature schemes (i.e., Construction 6.4.16). Applying these transformations (to the first scheme), we obtain the desired super-secure signature scheme. Recall that Construction 6.4.30 also uses universal one-way hashing functions, but the latter can be constructed using any one-way function (cf. Theorem 6.4.29).[37]

Claim 6.5.2.1: If there exist universal one-way hashing functions, then for every polynomially-bounded $\ell : \mathbb{N} \to \mathbb{N}$, there exist *super-secure* ℓ-restricted one-time signature schemes.

Proof Sketch: We modify Construction 6.4.4 by using universal one-way hashing functions (UOWHFs) instead of one-way functions. Specifically, for each pre-image placed in the signing-key, we select at random and independently a UOWHF, and place its description both in the signing- and verification-keys. That is, on input 1^n, we uniformly select $s_1^0, s_1^1, ..., s_{\ell(n)}^0, s_{\ell(n)}^1 \in \{0, 1\}^n$ and UOWHFs $h_1^0, h_1^1, ..., h_{\ell(n)}^0, h_{\ell(n)}^1$, and compute $v_i^j = h_i^j(s_i^j)$, for $i = 1, ..., \ell(n)$ and $j = 0, 1$. We let $\bar{s} = ((s_1^0, s_1^1), ..., (s_{\ell(n)}^0, s_{\ell(n)}^1))$,

---

[37] We comment that a simpler proof suffices in case we are willing to use a one-way permutation (rather than an arbitrary one-way function). In this case, we can start from (Part 2 of) Theorem 6.5.1 (rather than prove Claim 6.5.2.1), and use Theorem 6.4.28 (rather than Theorem 6.4.29, which has a more complicated proof).

$\overline{h} = ((h_1^0, h_1^1), ..., (h_{\ell(n)}^0, h_{\ell(n)}^1))$, and $\overline{v} = ((v_1^0, v_1^1), ..., (v_{\ell(n)}^0, v_{\ell(n)}^1))$, and output the key-pair $(s, v) = ((\overline{h}, \overline{s}), (\overline{h}, \overline{v}))$ (or, actually, we may set $(s, v) = (\overline{s}, (\overline{h}, \overline{v}))$). Signing and verification are modified accordingly; that is, the sequence $(\beta_1, ..., \beta_\ell)$ is accepted as a valid signature of the string $\sigma_1 \cdots \sigma_\ell$ (with respect to the verification-key v) if and only if $h_i^{\sigma_i}(\beta_i) = v_i^{\sigma_i}$ for every i. In order to show that the resulting scheme is super-secure under a chosen *one*-message attack, we adapt the proof of Proposition 6.4.5. Specifically, fixing such an attacker A, we consider the event in which A violated the super-security of the scheme. There are two cases to consider:

1. The valid signature formed by A is to the same document for which A has obtained a different signature (via its single query). In this case, for at least one of the UOWHFs contained in the verification-key, we obtain a pre-image (of the image also contained in the verification-key) that is different from the one contained in the signing-key. Adapting the construction presented in the proof of Proposition 6.4.5, we derive (in this case) an ability to form designated collisions (in contradiction to the UOWHF property). We stress that the pre-images contained in the signing-key are selected independently of the description of the UOWHFs (because both are selected independently by the key-generation process). In fact, we obtain a designated collision for a uniformly selected pre-image.

2. The valid signature formed by A is to a document that is different from the one for which A has obtained a signature (via its single query). In this case, the proof of Proposition 6.4.5 yields the ability to invert a randomly selected UOWHF (on a randomly selected image), which contradicts the UOWHF property (as shown in Exercise 19).

Thus, in both cases we derive a contradiction, and the claim follows. $\square$

Claim 6.5.2.2: When applying the revised hash-and-sign construction (i.e., Construction 6.4.30) to a *super-secure* length-restricted signature scheme, the result is a *super-secure* signature scheme. In case the length-restricted scheme is only super-secure under a chosen one-message attack, the same holds for the resulting (length-unrestricted) scheme.

Proof Sketch: We follow the proof of Proposition 6.4.31, and use the same construction of a forger for the length-restricted scheme (based on the forger for the complex scheme). Furthermore, we consider the two forgery cases analyzed in the proof of Proposition 6.4.31:[38]

Case 1: $(\beta_1, h_{\beta_1}(\alpha)) \neq (\beta_1^{(i)}, h_{\beta_1^{(i)}}(\alpha^{(i)}))$ for all i's. In this case, the analysis is exactly as in the original proof. Note that it does not matter whether or not $\alpha \neq \alpha^{(i)}$, since in both subcases we obtain a valid signature for a new string with respect to the

---

[38] Recall that (α, β) denotes the document-signature pair output by the original forger (i.e., for the complex scheme), whereas $(\alpha^{(i)}, \beta^{(i)})$ denotes the i-th query-answer pair (to that scheme). The document-signature pair that we output (as a candidate forgery with respect to a length-restricted scheme) is (α_2, β_2), where $\alpha_2 \stackrel{\text{def}}{=} (\beta_1, h_{\beta_1}(\alpha))$ and $\beta = (\beta_1, \beta_2)$. Recall that a generic valid document-signature for the complex scheme has the form (α', β'), where $\beta' = (\beta_1', \beta_2')$ satisfies $V_v((\beta_1', h_{\beta_1'}(\alpha')), \beta_2') = 1$.

length-restricted signature scheme. Thus, in this case, we derive a violation of the (ordinary) security of the length-restricted scheme.

Case 2: $(\beta_1, h_{\beta_1}(\alpha)) = (\beta_1^{(i)}, h_{\beta_1^{(i)}}(\alpha^{(i)}))$ for some i. The case $\alpha \neq \alpha^{(i)}$ was handled in the original proof (by showing that it yields a designated collision [under $h_{\beta_1^{(i)}}$, which is supposedly a UOWHF]), so here we only handle the case $\alpha = \alpha^{(i)}$. Now, suppose that super-security of the complex scheme was violated; that is, $(\beta_1, \beta_2) \neq (\beta_1^{(i)}, \beta_2^{(i)})$. Then, by the case hypothesis (which implies $\beta_1 = \beta_1^{(i)}$), it must be that $\beta_2 \neq \beta_2^{(i)}$. This means that we derive a violation of the *super*-security of the length-restricted scheme, because β_2 is a different valid S_s-signature of $(\beta_1, h_{\beta_1}(\alpha)) = (\beta_1^{(i)}, h_{\beta_1^{(i)}}(\alpha^{(i)}))$.

> Actually, we have to consider all i's for which $(\beta_1, h_{\beta_1}(\alpha)) = (\beta_1^{(i)}, h_{\beta_1^{(i)}}(\alpha^{(i)}))$ holds, and observe that violation of super-security for the complex scheme means that β_2 must be different from each of the corresponding $\beta_2^{(i)}$'s. Alternatively, we may first prove that with overwhelmingly high probability, all $\beta_1^{(i)}$'s must be distinct.

Thus, in both cases we reach a contradiction to the super-security of the length-restricted signature scheme, which establishes our claim that the resulting (complex) signature scheme must be super-secure. We stress that, as in Proposition 6.4.31, this proof establishes that super-security for one-time attacks is preserved, too (because the constructed forger makes a single query per each query made by the original forger). □

Claim 6.5.2.3: Construction 6.4.16, when applied to super-secure one-time signature schemes, yields super-secure signature schemes.

Proof Sketch: We follow the proof of Proposition 6.4.17, which actually means following the proof of Proposition 6.4.15. Specifically, we use almost the same construction of a forger for the one-time scheme (G, S, V) (based on the forger for the complex scheme (G', S', V')). The only difference is in the last step (i.e., the use of the output), where we consider two forgery cases that are related (but not equal) to the forgery cases analyzed in the proof of Proposition 6.4.15:[39]

1. The *first case* is when the forged signature for the complex scheme (G', S', V') contains an authentication path (for a leaf) that equals some authentication path provided by the signing-oracle (as part of the answer to some oracle-query of the attacker). In this case, the (one-time) verification-key associated with this leaf must be authentic (i.e., equal to the one used by the signing-oracle), and we derive violation of the super-security of the instance of (G, S, V) associated with it. We consider two subcases (regarding the actual document authenticated via this leaf):

   (a) The first subcase is when no oracle-answer has used the instance associated with this leaf for signing an actual document. (This may happen if the instance

---

[39] Recall that forging a signature for the general scheme requires either using an authentication path supplied by the (general) signing-oracle or producing an authentication path different from all paths supplied by the (general) signing-oracle. These are the cases considered here. In contrast, in the proof of Proposition 6.4.15 we considered only the "text part" of these paths, ignoring the question of whether or not the authenticating (one-time) signatures (provided as part of these paths) are equal.

associated with the sibling of this leaf was used for signing an actual document.) In this subcase, as in the proof of Proposition 6.4.15, we obtain (ordinary) forgery with respect to the instance of (G, S, V) associated with the leaf (without making any query to that instance of the one-time scheme).

(b) Otherwise (i.e., the instance associated with this leaf was used for signing an actual document), the forged document-signature pair differs from the query-answer pair that used the same leaf. The difference is either in the actual document or in the part of the complex-signature that corresponds to the one-time signature produced at the leaf (because, by the case hypothesis, the authentication paths are identical). In both subcases this yields violation of the super-security of the instance of (G, S, V) associated with that leaf. Specifically, in the *first sub-subcase,* we obtain a one-time signature to a different document (i.e., violation of ordinary security), whereas in the *second sub-subcase,* we obtain a different one-time signature to the same document (i.e., only a violation of super-security). We stress that in both subcases, the violating signature is obtained after making a single query to the instance of (G, S, V) associated with that leaf.

2. We now turn to the *second case* (i.e., forgery with respect to (G', S', V') is obtained by producing an authentication path different from all paths supplied by the signing-oracle). In this case, we obtain violation of the (one-time) super-security of the scheme (G, S, V) associated with one of the internal nodes (specifically the first node on which the relevant paths differ). The argument is similar (but not identical) to the one given in the proof of Proposition 6.4.15. Specifically, we consider the maximal prefix of the authentication path provided by the forger that equals a corresponding prefix of an authentication path provided by the signing-oracle (as part of its answer). The extension of this path in the complex-signature provided by the forger either uses a different pair of (one-time) verification-keys or uses a different (one-time) signature to the same pair. In the *first subcase,* we obtain a one-time signature to a different document (i.e., violation of ordinary security), whereas in the *second subcase,* we obtain a different one-time signature to the same document (i.e., only a violation of super-security). We stress that in both subcases, the violating signature is obtained after making a single query to the instance of (G, S, V) associated with that internal node.

Thus, in both cases we reach a contradiction to the super-security of the one-time signature scheme, which establishes our claim that the general signature scheme must be super-secure. □

Combining the three claims (and recalling that universal one-way hashing functions can be constructed using any one-way function [cf. Theorem 6.4.29]), the theorem follows. ∎

6.5.3. Off-Line/On-Line Signing

Loosely speaking, we say that a signature scheme (G, S, V) (either a private-key or a public-key one) has an off-line/on-line signing process if signatures are produced in two steps, where the first step is independent of the actual message to be signed. That is, the computation of $S_s(\alpha)$ can be decoupled into two steps, performed by *randomized* algorithms that are denoted S^{off} and S^{on}, respectively, such that $S_s(\alpha) \leftarrow S_s^{\text{on}}(\alpha, S^{\text{off}}(s))$. Thus, one may prepare (or precompute) $S^{\text{off}}(s)$ before the document is known (i.e., "off-line"), and produce the actual signature (on-line) once the document α is presented (by invoking algorithm S^{on} on input $(\alpha, S^{\text{off}}(s))$). This yields improvement in on-line response-time to signing requests, provided that S^{on} is significantly faster than S itself. This improvement is worthwhile in many natural settings in which on-line response-time is more important than off-line processing time.

We stress that S^{off} must be randomized (because, otherwise, $S^{\text{off}}(s)$ can be incorporated in the signing-key). Indeed, one may view algorithm S^{off} as an augmentation of the key-generation algorithm that produces *random* extensions of the signing-key on the fly (i.e., after the verification-key has already been determined). We stress that algorithm S^{off} is invoked once per each document to be signed, but this invocation can take place at any time (and even before the document to be signed is even determined). (In contrast, it may be insecure to reuse the result obtained from S^{off} for two different signatures.)

Can Secure Signature Schemes Employ Meaningful Off-Line/On-Line Signing Algorithms? Of course, any algorithm can be vacuously decoupled into two steps, but we are only interested in meaningful decouplings in which the off-line step takes most of the computational load. It is interesting to note that schemes based on the refreshing paradigm (cf. Section 6.4.2.1) lend themselves to such a decoupling. Specifically, in Construction 6.4.16, only the last step in the signing process depends on the actual document (and needs to be performed on-line). Furthermore, this last step amounts to applying the signing algorithm of a one-time signature scheme, which is typically much faster than all the other steps (which can be performed off-line).[40]

6.5.4. Incremental Signatures

Loosely speaking, we say that a signature scheme (G, S, V) (either a private-key or a public-key one) has an incremental signing process if the signing process can be sped-up when given a valid signature to a (textually) related document. The actual definition refers to a set of text-editing operations such as *delete word* and *insert word* (where more powerful operations like *cutting* a document into two parts and *pasting* two documents may be supported, too). Specifically, we require that given a signing-key, a document-signature pair (α, β), and a sequence of edit operations (i.e., specifying the operation type and its location), one may modify β into a valid signature β' for the

---

[40] For example, when using the one-time signature scheme suggested in Proposition 6.4.7, producing one-time signatures amounts to applying a collision-free hashing function and outputting corresponding parts of the signing-key. This is all that needs to be performed in the on-line step of Construction 6.4.16. In contrast, the off-line step (of Construction 6.4.16) calls for n applications of a pseudorandom function, n applications of the key-generation algorithm of the one-time signature scheme, and n applications of the signing algorithm of the one-time signature scheme.

modified document α' in time proportional to the number of edit operations (rather than proportional to $|\alpha'|$). Indeed, here time is measured in a direct-access model of computation. Of course, the time saved on the "signing side" should not come at the expense of a significant increase in verification time. In particular, verification time should depend only on the length of the final document (and not on the number of edit operations).[41]

An incremental signing process is beneficial in settings where one needs to sign many textually related documents (e.g., in simple contracts, much of the text is almost identical and the few edit changes refer to the party's specific details, as well as to specific clauses that may be modified from their standard form in order to meet the party's specific needs). In some cases, the *privacy of the edit sequence* may be of concern; that is, one may require that the final signature be distributed in a way that only depends on the final document (rather than depending also on documents that "contributed" signatures to the process of generating the final signature).

Can Secure Signature Schemes Employ a Meaningful Incremental Signing Process? Here, meaningful refers to the set of supported text-modification operations. The answer is affirmative, and furthermore, these schemes may even protect the privacy of the edit sequence. In the following, we refer to edit operations that delete/insert fix-length bit-strings called blocks from/to a document (as well as to the cut-and-paste operations mentioned previously).

Theorem 6.5.3 (secure schemes with incremental signing process):

1. *Assuming the existence of one-way functions, there exist secure message-authentication schemes having an incremental signing process that supports block deletion and insertion. Furthermore, the scheme uses a fixed-length authentication tag.*
2. *Assuming the existence of one-way functions, there exist secure* (private-key and public-key) *signature schemes having an incremental signing process that supports block deletion and insertion as well as cut and paste.*

Furthermore, in both parts, the resulting schemes protect the privacy of the edit sequence.

Part 1 is proved by using a variant of an efficient message-authentication scheme that is related to the schemes presented in Section 6.3.1. Part 2 is proved by using an arbitrary secure (private-key or public-key) signature scheme that produces n-bit long signatures to $O(n)$-bit long strings, where n is the security parameter. (Indeed, the scheme need only be secure in the $O(n)$-restricted sense.) The document is stored in the leaves of a 2–3 tree, and the signature essentially consists of the tags of all internal nodes, where each internal node is tagged by applying the basic signature scheme to the tags of its children.

---

[41] This rules out the naive (unsatisfactory) solution of providing a signature of the original document along with a signature of the sequence of edit operations. More sophisticated variants of this naive solution (e.g., refreshing the signature whenever enough edits have occurred) are not ruled out here, but typically they will not satisfy the privacy requirement discussed in the sequel.

One important observation is that a 2–3 tree supports the said operations while incurring only a logarithmic (in its size) cost; that is, by modifying only the links of logarithmically many nodes in the tree. Thus, only the tags of these nodes and their ancestors in the tree need to be modified in order to form the correspondingly modified signature. (Privacy of the edit sequence is obtained by randomizing the standard modification procedure for 2–3 trees.) By analogy to Construction 6.2.13 (and Proposition 6.2.14), the incremental signature scheme is secure.

6.5.5. Fail-Stop Signatures

Loosely speaking, a fail-stop signature scheme is a signature scheme augmented by a (non-interactive) proof system that allows the legitimate signer to prove to anybody that a particular (document,signature)-pair was not generated by him/her. Actually, key-generation involves interaction with an *administrating entity* (which publicizes the resulting verification-keys), rather than just having the user publicize his/her verification-key. In addition, we allow memory-dependent signing procedures (as in Definition 6.4.13).[42] The system guarantees the following four properties, where the first two properties are the standard ones:

1. *Proper operation:* In case the user is honest, the signatures produced by it will pass the verification procedure (with respect to the corresponding verification-key).
2. *Infeasibility of forgery:* In case the user is honest, forgery is infeasible in the standard sense. That is, every feasible chosen message attack may succeed (in generating a valid signature to a new message) only with negligible probability.
3. *Revocation of forged signatures:* In case the user is honest and forgery is committed, the user can prove that indeed forgery has been committed. That is, for every chosen message attack (even a computationally unbounded one)[43] that produces a valid signature to a new message, except for with negligible probability, the user can efficiently convince anyone (which knows the verification-key) that this valid signature was forged (i.e., produced by somebody else).
4. *Infeasibility of revoking unforged signatures:* It is infeasible for a user to create a valid signature and later convince someone that this signature was forged (i.e., produced by somebody else). Indeed, it is possible (but not feasible) for a user to cheat here.

Furthermore, Property 3 (i.e., revocation of forged signatures) holds also in case the administrating entity participates in the forgery and even if it behaves improperly at the key-generation stage. (In contrast, the other items hold *only* if the administrating entity behaves properly during the key-generation stage.)

To summarize, fail-stop signature schemes allow proving that forgery has occurred, and so offer an information-theoretic security guarantee to the potential signers (yet the

---

[42] Allowing memory-dependent signing is essential to the existence of secure fail-stop signature schemes; see Exercise 25.

[43] It seems reasonable to restrict even computationally unbounded adversaries to polynomially many signing requests.

guarantee to potential signature recipients is only a computational one).[44] In contrast, when following the standard semantics of signature schemes, the potential signers have only a computational security guarantee, and the signature recipients have an absolute guarantee: Whenever the verification algorithm accepts a signature, it is by definition an unrevocable one.

Do Secure Fail-Stop Signature Schemes Exist? Assuming the intractability of either the Discrete Logarithm Problem or of integer factorization, the answer is affirmative. Indeed, in fail-stop signature schemes, each document must have super-polynomially many possible valid signatures (with respect to the publicly known verification-key), but only a negligible fraction of these will be (properly) produced by the legitimate signer (who knows a corresponding signing-key, which is not uniquely determined by the verification-key). Furthermore, any strategy (even an infeasible one) is unlikely to generate signatures corresponding to the actual signing-key. On the other hand, it is infeasible given one signing-key to produce valid signatures (i.e., with respect to the verification-key) that do not correspond to the proper signing with this signing-key.

6.6. Miscellaneous

6.6.1. On Using Signature Schemes

Once defined and constructed, signature schemes may be (and are actually) used as building blocks toward various goals that are different from the original motivation. Still, the original motivation (i.e., reliable communication of information) is of great importance, and in this subsection we discuss several issues regarding the use of signature schemes toward achieving it. The discussion is analogous to a similar discussion conducted in Section 5.5.1, but the analogous issues discussed here are even more severe.

Using Private-Key Schemes: The Key-Exchange Problem. As discussed in Section 6.1, using a private-key signature scheme (i.e., a message-authentication scheme) requires the communicating parties to share a secret key. This key can be generated by one party and secretly communicated to the other party by an alternative (expensive) secure and reliable channel. Often, a preferable solution consists of employing a *key-exchange* (or rather *key-generation*) protocol, which is executed over the standard (unreliable) communication channel. We stress that here (unlike in Section 5.5.1) we must consider active adversaries. Consequently, the focus should be on key-exchange protocols that are secure against active adversaries and are called unauthenticated key-exchange protocols (because the messages received over the channel are not necessarily authentic). Such protocols are too complex to be treated in this section, and the interested reader is referred to [29, 30, 15].

---

[44] We refer to the natural convention by which a proof of forgery frees the signer of any obligations implied by the document. In this case, when accepting a valid signature, the recipient is only guaranteed that it is infeasible for the signer to revoke the signature.

Using State-Dependent Message-Authentication Schemes. In many communication settings, it is reasonable to assume that the authentication device may maintain (and modify) a state (e.g., a counter or a clock). Furthermore, in many applications, a changing state (e.g., a clock) must be employed anyhow in order to prevent replay of old messages (i.e., each message is authenticated along with its transmission time). In such cases, state-dependent schemes as discussed in Section 6.3.2 may be preferable. (See further discussion in Section 6.3.2 and analogous discussion in Section 5.5.1.)

Using Signature Schemes: Public-Key Infrastructure. The standard use of (public-key) signature schemes in real-life applications requires a mechanism for providing the verifiers with the signer's authentic verification-key. In small systems, one may assume that each user holds a local record of the verification-keys of all other users. However, this is not realistic in large-scale systems, and so the verifier must obtain the relevant verification-key on the fly in a "reliable" way (i.e., typically, certified by some trusted authority). In most theoretical work, one assumes that the verification-keys are posted and can be retrieved from a public-file that is maintained by a trusted party (which makes sure that each user can post only verification-keys bearing its own identity). Alternatively, such a trusted party may provide each user with a (signed) certificate stating the authenticity of the user's verification-key. In practice, maintaining such a public-file (and/or handling such certificates) is a major problem, and mechanisms that implement these abstractions are typically referred to by the generic term "public-key infrastructure" (PKI). For a discussion of the practical problems regarding PKI deployment, see, e.g., [149, Chap. 13].

6.6.2. On Information-Theoretic Security

In contrast to the bulk of our treatment, which focuses on computationally bounded adversaries, in this section we consider computationally unbounded adversaries. Specifically, we consider computationally unbounded chosen message attacks, but do bound (as usual, by an unknown polynomial) the total number of bits in the signing-queries made by such attackers. We call a (private-key or public-key) signature scheme perfectly secure (or information-theoretically secure) if even such computationally unbounded attackers may succeed (in forgery) only with negligible probability.

It is easy to see that no (public-key) signature scheme may be perfectly secure, *not even in a length-restricted one-time sense.* The reason is that a computationally unbounded adversary that is given a verification-key can find (without making any queries) a corresponding signing-key, which allows it to forge signatures to any message of its choice.

In contrast, *restricted types* of message-authentication schemes (i.e., private-key signature schemes) may be perfectly secure. Specifically, given any polynomial bound on the total number of messages to be authenticated, one may construct a corresponding state-based perfectly secure message-authentication scheme. In fact, a variant of Construction 6.3.11 will do, where a truly random one-time pad is used instead of the pseudorandom sequence generated using the next-step function g. Indeed, this one-time pad will be part of the key, which in turn must be longer than the total number of messages to be authenticated. We comment that the use of a state is essential for allowing several messages to be authenticated (in a perfectly secure manner). (Proofs of both statements can be derived following the ideas underlying Exercise 7.)

6.6.3. On Some Popular Schemes

The reader may note that we have avoided the presentation of several popular signature schemes (i.e., public-key ones). Some of these schemes (e.g., RSA [176] and DSS [160]) seem to satisfy some weak notions of security (i.e., a notion weaker than Definition 6.1.2). Variants of these schemes can be proven to be secure *in the random oracle model*, provided some standard intractability assumptions hold (cf., e.g., [31]). For reasons to be outlined, we choose not to present these results here.

On Using Weaker Definitions. We distinguish between weak definitions that make clear reference to the abilities of the adversary (e.g., one-message attacks, length-restricted message attacks) and weak notions that make hidden and unspecified assumptions regarding what may be beneficial to the adversary (e.g., "forgery of signatures for meaningful documents"). In our opinion, the fact that the hidden assumptions often "feel right" makes them even more dangerous, because it means that they are never seriously considered (and not even formulated). For example, it is often claimed that *existential forgery* (see Section 6.1.4) is "merely of theoretical concern," but these claims are never supported by any evidence or by a specification of the types of forgery that are of "real practical concern." Furthermore, it has been demonstrated that this "merely theoretical" issue yields a real security breach in some important practical applications. Still, weak definitions of security may be useful (i.e., suffice for some applications), provided that they are clearly stated and that one realizes their limitations (and, in particular, their "non-generality"). However, since the current work focuses on generally applicable definitions, we choose not to discuss such weaker notions of security and not to present schemes that can be evaluated only with respect to these weaker notions.[45] The interested reader is referred to [125] for a comprehensive treatment of various (weaker) notions of security (which refer to various types of attacks and success events).

On the Random Oracle Methodology. The *Random Oracle Methodology* [92, 28] consists of two steps: First, one designs an *ideal* system in which all parties (including the adversary) have oracle access to a truly random function, and proves this *ideal* system to be secure (in which case, one says that the system is *secure in the random oracle model*). Next, one replaces the random oracle with a "good cryptographic hashing function," providing all parties (including the adversary) with the succinct description of this function, and hopes that the resulting (actual) scheme is secure.[46] We warn that this hope has no sound justification. Furthermore, there exist encryption and

---

[45] Needless to say, we did not even consider presenting schemes that are not known to satisfy some robust notion of security.

[46] Recall that, in contrast, the methodology of Section 3.6.3 (which is applied often in the current chapter) refers to a situation in which the adversary does not have direct oracle access to the random function, and does not obtain the description of the pseudorandom function used in the latter implementation.

signature schemes that are secure in the Random Oracle Model, but replacing the random function (used in them) by *any* function ensemble yields a totally insecure scheme (cf., [54]).

6.6.4. Historical Notes

As in the case of encryption schemes, the rigorous study of the security of private-key signature schemes (i.e., message-authentication schemes) has lagged behind the corresponding study of public-key signature schemes. The current section is organized accordingly.

6.6.4.1. Signature Schemes

The notion of a (public-key) signature scheme was introduced by Diffie and Hellman [75], who also suggested implementing it using trapdoor permutations. Concrete implementations were suggested by Rivest, Shamir, and Adleman [176] and by Rabin [171]. However, definitions of security for signature schemes were presented only a few years afterward. Still, the abstract notion of a signature scheme as well as the concrete candidate implementations have served as the basis for the development of the theory presented in the current chapter.

A first rigorous treatment of security notions for signature schemes was suggested by Goldwasser, Micali, and Yao [127], but their definition is weaker than the one followed in our text. (Specifically, the adversary's queries in the definition of [127] are determined non-adaptively and obliviously of the public-key.) Assuming the intractability of factoring, they also presented a signature scheme that is secure under their definition. We mention that the security definition of [127] considers existential forgery, and is thus stronger than security notions considered before [127].

A comprehensive treatment of security notions for signature schemes, which culminates in the notion used in our text, was presented by Goldwasser, Micali, and Rivest [125]. Assuming the intractability of factoring, they also presented a signature scheme that is secure (in the sense of Definition 6.1.2). This was the first time that a signature scheme was proven secure under a simple intractability assumption such as the intractability of factoring. Their proof has refuted a folklore (attributed to Ron Rivest) by which no such "constructive proof" may exist (because the mere existence of such a proof was believed to yield a forging procedure).[47] Whereas the (two) schemes

---

[47] The flaw in this folklore is rooted in implicit (unjustified) assumptions regarding the notion of a "constructive proof of security" (based on factoring). In particular, it was implicitly assumed that the signature scheme uses a verification-key that equals a composite number, and that the proof of security reduces the factoring of such a composite N to forging with respect to the verification-key N. In such a case, the folklore suggested that the reduction yields an oracle machine for factoring the verification-key, where the oracle is the corresponding signing-oracle (associated with N), and that the factorization of the verification-key allows for efficiently producing signatures to any message. However, none of these assumptions is justified. In contrast, the verification-key in the scheme of [125] consists of a pair (N, x), and its security is proven by reducing the factoring of N to forging with respect to the verification-key (N, r), where r is randomly selected by the reduction. Furthermore, on input N, the (factoring) reduction produces a verification-key (N, r) that typically does not equal the verification-key (N, x) being attacked, and so being given access to a corresponding signing-oracle does not allow the factoring of N.

of [127] were inherently memory-dependent, the scheme of [125] has a "memoryless" variant (cf. [100] and [125]).

Following Goldwasser, Micali, and Rivest [125], research has focused on constructing secure signature schemes under weaker assumptions. In fact, as noted in [125], their construction of secure signature schemes can be carried out using any collection of *claw-free, trapdoor* permutation pairs. The claw-free requirement was removed in [26], whereas the seemingly more fundamental trapdoor requirement was removed by Naor and Yung [163]. Finally, Rompel showed that one may use arbitrary one-way functions rather than one-way permutations [178], and thus established Theorem 6.4.1. The progress briefly summarized here was enabled by the use of many important ideas and paradigms; some of them were introduced in that body of work and some were "only" revisited and properly formalized. Specifically, we refer to the introduction of the refreshing paradigm in [125], the use of authentication trees (cf., [151, 152], and [125]), the use of the hash-and-sign paradigm (rigorously analyzed in [70]), the introduction of Universal One-Way Hash Functions (and the adaptation of the hash-and-sign paradigm to them) in [163], and the use of one-time signature schemes (cf., [170]).

We comment that our presentation of the construction of signature schemes is different from the one given in any of these cited papers. Specifically, the main part of Section 6.4 (i.e., Sections 6.4.1 and 6.4.2) is based on a variant of the signature scheme of [163], in which collision-free hashing (cf. [70]) is used instead of universal one-way hashing (cf. [163]).

6.6.4.2. Message-Authentication Schemes

Message authentication schemes were first discussed in the information-theoretic setting, where a one-time pad was used. Such schemes were first suggested in [99], and further developed in [188]. The one-time pad can be implemented by a pseudorandom function (or an on-line pseudorandom generator), yielding only computational security, as we have done in Section 6.3.2. Specifically, Construction 6.3.11 is based on [139, 140]. In contrast, in Section 6.3.1 we have followed a different paradigm that amounts to applying a pseudorandom function to the message (or its hashed value), rather than using a pseudorandom function (or an on-line pseudorandom generator) to implement a one-time pad. This alternative paradigm is due to [111], and is followed in works such as [25, 22, 13]. Indeed, following this paradigm, one may focus on constructing generalized pseudorandom function ensembles (as in Definition 3.6.12), based on ordinary pseudorandom functions (as in Definition 3.6.4). See comments on alternative presentations at the end of Sections 6.3.1.2 and 6.3.1.3, as well as in Section C.2 of Appendix C.

6.6.4.3. Additional Topics

Collision-free hashing was first defined in [70]. Construction 6.2.8 is also due to [70], with underlying principles that can be traced to [125]. Construction 6.2.11 is due to [71]. Construction 6.2.13 is due to [153].

Unique signatures and super-security have been used in several works, but they were not treated explicitly before. The notion of off-line/on-line signature schemes was introduced (and first instantiated) in [85]. The notion of incremental crypto-graphic schemes (and, in particular, incremental signature schemes) was introduced and instantiated in [18, 19]. In particular, the incremental MAC of [19] (i.e., Part 1 of Theorem 6.5.3) builds on the message-authentication scheme of [22], and the incremental signature scheme that protects the privacy of the edit sequence is due to [158] (building upon [19]). Fail-stop signatures were defined and constructed in [167].

6.6.5. Suggestions for Further Reading

As mentioned, the work of Goldwasser, Micali, and Rivest contains a comprehensive treatment of security notions for signature schemes [125]. Their treatment refers to two parameters: (1) the type of attack, and (2) the type of forgery that is deemed successful. The most severe type of attack allows the adversary to adaptively select the documents to be signed (as in Definition 6.1.2). The most liberal notion of forgery refers to producing a signature to any document for which a signature was not obtained during the attack (again, as in Definition 6.1.2). Thus, the notion of security presented in Definition 6.1.2 is the strongest among the notions discussed in [125]. Still, in some applications, weaker notions of security may suffice. We stress that one may still benefit from the definitional part of [125], but the constructive part of [125] should be ignored because it is superseded by later work (on which our presentation is based).

Pfitzmann's book [168] contains a comprehensive discussion of many aspects involved in the integration of signature schemes in real-life systems. In addition, her book surveys variants and augmentations of the notion of signature schemes, viewing the one treated in the current book as "ordinary." The focus is on fail-stop signature schemes [168, Chap. 7–11], but much attention is given to the presentation of a general framework [168, Chap. 5] and to a review of other "non-ordinary" schemes [168, Secs. 2.7 and 6.1].

As hinted in Section 6.6.4.2, our treatment of the construction of message-authentication schemes is merely the tip of the iceberg. The interested reader is referred to [186, 139, 140, 35] for details on the "one-time pad" approach, and to [25, 22, 13, 14, 20, 2] for alternative approaches. Constructions and discussion of AXU hashing functions (which are stronger than generalized hashing functions) can be found in [139, 140].

The constructions of universal one-way hash functions presented in Section 6.4.3 use any one-way permutation, and do so in a generic way. The number of applications of the one-way permutation in these constructions is linearly related to the difference between the number of input and output bits in the hash function. In [98], it is shown that as far as generic (black-box) constructions go, this is essentially the best performance that one can hope for.

In continuation of the discussion in Section 6.4.2.4 (regarding the construction of signature schemes based on authentication trees), we refer the reader to [81, 67], in which specific implementations (of a generalization) of Constructions 6.4.14 and 6.4.16 are presented. Specifically, these works utilize an authentication-tree of large degree (rather than binary trees as in Section 6.4.2.2).

In continuation of the discussion in Section 6.5.1, we mention that *signature schemes having unique signatures* are related (but not equivalent) to *verifiable pseudorandom functions* (as defined and constructed in [155]). In particular, the construction in [155] does yield signature schemes having unique signatures, and thus the latter exist under a quite standard assumption (regarding RSA). We comment that signature schemes having unique signatures are stronger than *invariant signature schemes* (as defined in [128] and studied in [21, 128]).

6.6.6. Open Problems

The known construction of signature schemes from *arbitrary* one-way functions [178] is merely a feasibility result. It is indeed an important open problem to provide an alternative construction that may be practical and still utilize an *arbitrary* one-way function. We believe that providing such a construction may require the discovery of important new paradigms.

6.6.7. Exercises

Exercise 1: *Deterministic signing and verification algorithms:*

1. Using a pseudorandom function ensemble, show how to transform any (private-key or public-key) signature scheme into one employing a deterministic signing algorithm.
2. Using a pseudorandom function ensemble, show how to transform any message-authentication scheme into one employing deterministic signing and verification algorithms.
3. Verify that all signature schemes presented in the current chapter employ a deterministic verification algorithm.
4. (By Boaz Barak:) Show that any length-restricted signature scheme can be easily transformed into one employing a deterministic verification algorithm.

   Guideline (for Part 1): Augment the signing-key with a description of a pseudorandom function, and apply this function to the string to be signed in order to extract the randomness used by the original signing algorithm.

   Guideline (for Part 2): Analogous to Part 1. (Highlight your use of the private-key hypothesis.) Alternatively, see Exercise 2.

   Guideline (for Part 4): First transform the signature scheme into one in which all valid signatures are of a length that is bounded by a polynomial in the security parameter (and the length of the messages). Let $\ell(n)$ denote the length of the documents and $m(n)$ denote the length of the corresponding signatures. Next, amplify the verification algorithm such that its error probability is smaller than $2^{-(\ell(n)+m(n)+n)}$. Finally, incorporate the coin tosses of the verification algorithm in the verification-key, making the former deterministic.

Exercise 2: *Canonical verification in the private-key version:* Show that, without loss of generality, the verification algorithm of a private-key signature scheme may consist of comparing the alleged signature to one produced by the verification algorithm itself; that is, the verification algorithm uses a verification-key that equals the signing-key and produces signatures exactly as the signing algorithm.

Why does this claim fail with respect to public-key schemes?

> **Guideline:** Use Part 1 of Exercise 1, and conclude that on a fixed input, the signing algorithm always produces the same output. Use the fact that (by Exercise 7.3) the existence of message-authentication schemes implies the existence of pseudorandom functions, which are used in Part 1 of Exercise 1.

Exercise 3: *Augmented attacks in the private-key case:* In continuation of the discussion in Section 6.1.5.1, consider the definition of an augmented attack (on a private-key signature scheme) in which the adversary is allowed verification-queries.

1. Show that in case the private-key signature scheme has unique valid signatures, it is secure against augmented attacks if and only if it is secure against ordinary attacks (as in Definition 6.1.2).
2. Assuming the existence of secure private-key signature schemes (as in Definition 6.1.2), present such a secure scheme that is insecure under augmented attacks.

> **Guideline (Part 1):** Analyze the emulation outlined in the proof of Proposition 6.1.3. Specifically, ignoring the redundant verification-queries (for which the answer is determined by previous answers), consider the probability that the emulation has gambled correctly on all the verification-queries up to (and including) the *first* such query that should be answered affirmatively.

> **Guideline (Part 2):** Given any secure MAC, (G, S, V), assume without loss of generality that in the key-pairs output by G, the verification-key equals the signing-key. Consider the scheme (G', S', V') (with $G' = G$), where $S'_s(\alpha) = (S_s(\alpha), 0)$, $V'_v(\alpha, (\beta, 0)) = V_v(\alpha, \beta)$, and $V'_v(\alpha, (\beta, i, \sigma)) = 1$ if both $V_v(\alpha, \beta) = 1$ and the i-th bit of v is σ. Prove that (G', S', V) is secure under ordinary attacks, and present an augmented attack that totally breaks it (i.e., obtains the signing-key $s = v$).

Exercise 4: *The signature may reveal the document:* Both for private-key and public-key signature schemes, show that if such secure schemes exist, then there exist secure signature schemes in which any valid signature to a message allows for efficient recovery of the entire message.

Exercise 5: *On the triviality of some length-restricted signature schemes:*

1. Show that for logarithmically bounded ℓ, secure ℓ-restricted private-key signature schemes (i.e., message-authentication schemes) can be trivially constructed (without relying on any assumption).
2. In contrast, show that the existence of a secure ℓ-restricted public-key signature scheme, even for $\ell \equiv 1$, implies the existence of one-way functions.

Guideline (Part 1): On input 1^n, the key-generator uniformly selects $s \in \{0, 1\}^{2^{\ell(n)} \cdot n}$, and outputs the key pair (s, s). View $s = s_1 \cdots s_{2^{\ell(n)}}$, where each s_i is an n-bit long string, and consider any fixed ordering of the $2^{\ell(n)}$ strings of length $\ell(n)$. The signature to $\alpha \in \{0, 1\}^{\ell(n)}$ is defined as s_i, where i is the index of α in the latter ordering.

Guideline (Part 2): Let (G, S, V) be a 1-restricted public-key signature scheme. Define $f(1^n, r) = v$ if, on input 1^n and coins r, algorithm G generates a key-pair of the form $(\cdot, v)$. Assuming that algorithm A inverts f with probability $\varepsilon(n)$, we construct a forger that attacks (G, S, V) as follows. On input a verification key v, the forger invokes A on input v. With probability $\varepsilon(n)$, the forger obtains r such that $f(1^n, r) = v$. In such a case, the forger obtains a matching signing-key s (i.e., (s, v) is output by $G(1^n)$ on coins r), and so can produce valid signatures to any string of its choice.

Exercise 6: *Failure of Construction 6.2.3 in case $\ell(n) = O(\log n)$:* Show that if Construction 6.2.3 is used with a logarithmically bounded ℓ, then the resulting scheme is insecure.

Guideline: Note that by asking for polynomially many signatures, the adversary may obtain two S'_s-signatures that use the same (random) identifier. Specifically, consider making the queries $\alpha\alpha$, for all possible $\alpha \in \{0, 1\}^{\ell(n)}$, and note that if $\alpha\alpha$ and $\alpha'\alpha'$ are S'_s-signed using the same identifier, then we can derive a valid S'_s-signature to $\alpha\alpha'$.

Exercise 7: *Secure MACs imply one-way functions:* Prove that the existence of secure message-authentication schemes implies the existence of one-way functions. Specifically, let (G, S, V) be as in the hypothesis.

1. To simplify the following two items, show that, without loss of generality, $G(1^n)$ uses n coins and outputs a signing-key of length n.
2. Assume first that S is a *deterministic* signing algorithm. Prove that $f(r, \alpha_1, ..., \alpha_m) \stackrel{\text{def}}{=} (S_s(\alpha_1), ..., S_s(\alpha_m), \alpha_1, ..., \alpha_m)$ is a one-way function, where $s = G_1(r)$ is the signing-key generated with coins r, all α_i's are of length $n = |r|$, and $m = \Theta(n)$.
3. Extend the proof to handle *randomized* signing algorithms, thus establishing the main result.

Guideline (Parts 2 and 3): Note that with high probability (over the choice of the α_i's), the m signatures (i.e., $S_s(\alpha_i)$'s) determine a set R such that for every $r' \in R$, it holds that $S_{G_1(r')}(\alpha) = S_s(\alpha)$ for most $\alpha \in \{0, 1\}^n$. (Note that $G_1(r')$ does not necessarily equal s.) Show that this implies that the ability to invert f yields the ability to forge (under a chosen message attack). (Hint: Use m random signing-queries to produce a random image of f, and use the obtained pre-image under f, which contains an adequate signing-key, to forge a signature to a new random message.) The extension to randomized signing is obtained by augmenting the pre-image of the one-way function with the coins used by the m invocations of the signing algorithm.

Exercise 8: *General pseudorandom functions yield general secure MACs:* Using a pseudorandom function ensemble of the form $\{f_s : \{0, 1\}^* \to \{0, 1\}^{|s|}\}_{s \in \{0,1\}^*}$, construct a general secure message-authentication scheme (rather than a length-restricted one).

> **Guideline:** The construction is identical to Construction 6.3.1, except that here we use a general pseudorandom function ensemble rather than the one used there. The proof of security is analogous to the proof of Proposition 6.3.2.

Exercise 9: Consider a generalization of Construction 6.3.5 in which the pseudorandom function is replaced by an arbitrary secure MAC such that on input a signing-key (r, s), a document $\alpha \in \{0, 1\}^{\ell(n)}$ is signed by applying the MAC (with signing-key s) to $h_r(\alpha)$. Show that, for some secure MAC and some collections of hash functions with negligible collision probability, the suggested scheme is insecure.

> **Guideline:** Use the fact that the MAC may reveal the first part of its argument, whereas the hashing function may yield an output value in which the second part is fixed. Furthermore, it may be easy to infer the hashing function from sufficiently many input–output pairs, and it may be easy to find a random pre-image of a given hash function on a given image. Present constructions that satisfy all these conditions, and show how combining them yields the desired result.

Exercise 10: *Easily obtaining pseudorandom functions from certain MACs* (advanced exercise, based on [162]): Let (G, S, V) be a secure message-authentication scheme, and suppose that S is *deterministic*. Furthermore, suppose that $|G_1(1^n)| = n$ and that for every $s, x \in \{0, 1\}^n$ it holds that $|S_s(x)| = \ell(n) \overset{\text{def}}{=} |S_s(1^n)|$. Consider the Boolean function ensemble $\{f_{s_1,s_2} : \{0, 1\}^{|s_1|} \to \{0, 1\}\}_{s_1,s_2}$, where s_1 is selected according to $G_1(1^n)$ and $s_2 \in \{0, 1\}^{\ell(n)}$ is uniformly distributed, such that $f_{s_1,s_2}(\alpha)$ is defined to equal the inner product mod 2 of $S_{s_1}(\alpha)$ and s_2. Prove that this function ensemble is pseudorandom (as defined in Definition 3.6.9 for the case $d(n + \ell(n)) = n$ and $r(n) = 1$).

> **Guideline:** Consider hybrid experiments such that in the i-th hybrid the first i queries are answered by a truly random Boolean function and the rest of the queries are answered by a uniformly distributed f_{s_1,s_2}. (Note that it seems important to use this non-standard order of random versus pseudorandom answers.) Show that distinguishability of the i-th and $i + 1$st hybrids implies that a probabilistic polynomial-time oracle machine can have a non-negligible advantage in the following game. In the game, the machine is first asked to select α; next f_{s_1,s_2} is uniformly selected, and the machine is given s_2 as well as oracle access to S_{s_1} (but is not allowed the query α) and is asked to guess $f_{s_1,s_2}(\alpha)$ (or, equivalently, to distinguish $f_{s_1,s_2}(\alpha)$ from a truly random bit).[48] At this point, one may apply the proof of Theorem 2.5.2,

---

[48] Note that the particular order (of random versus pseudorandom answers in the hybrids) allows this oracle machine to generate the (corresponding) hybrid while playing this game properly. That is, the player answers

and deduce that the said oracle machine can be modified to construct $S_{s_1}(\alpha)$ with non-negligible probability (when given oracle access to S_{s_1} but not being allowed the query α), in contradiction to the security of the MAC.

Exercise 11: Prove that without loss of generality, one can always assume that a chosen message attack makes at least one query. (This holds for general signature schemes as well as for length-restricted and/or one-time ones.)

> **Guideline:** Given an adversary A' that outputs a message-signature pair (α', β') without making any query, modify it such that it makes an arbitrary query $\alpha \in \{0, 1\}^{|\alpha'|} \setminus \{\alpha'\}$ just before producing that output.

Exercise 12: *On perfectly secure one-time message-authentication (MAC) schemes:* By perfect (or information-theoretic) security we mean that even computationally unbounded chosen message attacks may succeed (in forgery) only with negligible probability.

Define perfect (or information-theoretic) security for one-time MACs and length-restricted one-time MACs. (Be sure to bound the length of documents (e.g., by some super-polynomial function) also in the unrestricted case; see Part 3 of the current exercise, as well as Exercise 21.)

Prove the following, without relying on any (intractability) assumptions (which are useless anyhow in the information-theoretic context):

1. For any polynomially bounded and polynomial-time computable function ℓ : $\mathbb{N} \to \mathbb{N}$, perfectly secure ℓ-restricted one-time MACs can be trivially constructed.
2. Using a suitable AXU family of hashing functions, present a construction of a perfectly secure one-time MAC. Furthermore, present such a MAC in which the authentication-tags have fixed length (i.e., depending on the length of the key but not on the length of the message being authenticated).
3. Show that any perfectly secure one-time MAC that utilizes fixed-length authentication-tags and a deterministic signing algorithm yields a generalized hashing ensemble with negligible collision probability. Specifically, for any polynomial p, this ensemble has a $(p, 1/p)$-collision property.

> **Guideline:** For Part 1, combine the ideas underlying Exercise 5.1 and Construction 6.4.4. For Part 2, use the ideas underlying Construction 6.3.11 and the proof of Proposition 6.3.12. For Part 3, given a MAC as in the claim, consider the functions $h_s(x) \stackrel{\text{def}}{=} S_s(x)$, where s is selected as in the key-generation algorithm.

Exercise 13: *Secure one-time* (public-key) *signatures imply one-way functions:* In contrast to Exercise 12, prove that the existence of secure *one-time signature schemes* implies the existence of one-way functions. Furthermore, prove that this holds even

---

the first i queries at random, sets α to equal the $i + 1$st query, uses the tested bit value as the corresponding answer, and uses s_2 and the oracle S_{s_1} to answer the subsequent queries. It is also important that the game be defined such that s_2 is given only after the machine has selected α; see [162].

for 1-restricted signature schemes that are secure (only) under attacks that make no signing-queries.

Guideline: See guideline for Item 2 in Exercise 5.

Exercise 14: Prove that *the existence of collision-free hashing collections implies the existence of one-way functions.*

> **Guideline:** Given a collision-free hashing collection, $\{h_r : \{0, 1\}^* \to \{0, 1\}^{\ell(|r|)}\}_{r \in \{0,1\}^*}$, consider the function $f(r, x) = (r, h_r(x))$, where (say) $|x| = \ell(|r|) + |r|$. Prove that f is a one-way function, by assuming toward the contradiction that f can be efficiently inverted with non-negligible probability, and deriving an efficient algorithm that forms collisions on random h_r's. Given r, form a collision under the function h_r, by uniformly selecting $x \in \{0, 1\}^{\ell(|r|)+|r|}$, and feeding the inverting algorithm with input $(r, h_r(x))$. Observe that with non-negligible probability, a pre-image is obtained, and that only with exponentially vanishing probability this pre-image is (r, x) itself. Thus, with non-negligible probability, we obtain a pre-image $(r, x') \neq (r, x)$ such that $h_r(x') = h_r(x)$.

Exercise 15: Modify Construction 6.2.8 so as to allow the computation of the hash-value of an input string while *processing the input in an on-line fashion*; that is, the implementation of the hashing process should process the input x in a bit-by-bit manner, while storing only the current bit and a small amount of state information (i.e., the number of bits encountered so far and an element of D_s).

> **Guideline:** All that is needed is to redefine $h_{(s,r)}(x) \overset{\text{def}}{=} f_s^{y_t} f_s^{y_{t-1}} \cdots f_s^{y_1}(r)$, where $y_1 \cdots y_t$ is a *suffix*-free encoding of x; that is, for any $x \neq x'$, the coding of x is not a suffix of the coding of x'.

Exercise 16: *Secure MACs that hide the message:* In contrast to Exercise 4, show that if secure message-authentication schemes exist, then there exist such schemes in which it is infeasible (for a party not knowing the key) to extract from the signature any partial information about the message (except for the message length). (Indeed, privacy of the message is formulated as the definition of semantic security of encryption schemes; see Chapter 5.)

> **Guideline:** Combine a message-authentication scheme with an adequate private-key encryption scheme. Refer to such issues as the type of security required of the encryption scheme and why the hypothesis yields the existence of the ingredients used in the construction.

Exercise 17: In continuation of Exercise 16, show that if there exist collision-free hashing functions, then there exist message-authentication schemes in which it is infeasible (for a party not knowing the key) to extract from the signature any partial information about the message *including the message length.* How come we can hide the message length in this context, whereas we cannot do this in the context of encryption schemes?

> **Guideline:** Combine a message-authentication scheme having fixed-length signatures with an adequate private-key encryption scheme. Again, refer to issues as in Exercise 16.

Exercise 18: *Alterntaive formulation of state-based MACs* (by Boaz Barak): For $S = (S', S'')$ and $V = (V', V'')$, consider the following reformulation of Item 2 of Definition 6.3.9: For every pair $(s^{(0)}, v^{(0)})$ in the range of $G(1^n)$, every sequence of messages $\alpha^{(i)}$'s, and every i, it holds that $V'(v^{(i-1)}, \alpha^{(i)}, S'(s^{(i-1)}, \alpha^{(i)})) = 1$, where $s^{(j)} = S''(s^{(j-1)}, 1^{|\alpha^{(j)}|})$ and $v^{(j)} = V''(v^{(j-1)}, 1^{|\alpha^{(j)}|}, 1^{|S'(e^{(j-1)}, 1^{|\alpha^{(j)}|})|})$ for $j = 1, ..., i - 1$. Prove the equivalence of the two formulations.

Exercise 19: Prove that *the existence of collections of UOWHF implies the existence of one-way functions*. Furthermore, show that uniformly chosen functions in any collection of UOWHFs are hard to invert (in the sense of Definition 2.4.3).

> **Guideline:** Note that the guidelines provided in Exercise 14 can be modified to fit the current context. Specifically, the suggested collision-forming algorithm is given uniformly distributed r and x, and invokes the inverter on input $(r, h_r(x))$, hoping to obtain a designated collision with x under h_r. Note that the furthermore-clause is implicit in the proof.

Exercise 20: Assuming the existence of one-way functions, show that there exists a collection of universal one-way hashing functions that is not collision-free.

> **Guideline:** Given a collection of universal one-way hashing functions, $\{f_s : \{0, 1\}^* \to \{0, 1\}^{|s|}\}$, consider the collection $F' = \{f'_s : \{0, 1\}^* \to \{0, 1\}^{|s|}\}$ defined so that $f'_s(x) = (0, f_s(x))$ if the $|s|$-bit long prefix of x is different from s, and $f'_s(sx') = (1, s)$ otherwise. Clearly, F' is not collision-free. Show that F' is a collection of universal one-way hashing functions.

Exercise 21: Show that for every finite family of functions H, there exists $x \neq y$ such that $h(x) = h(y)$ for every $h \in H$. Furthermore, show that for $H = \{h : \{0, 1\}^* \to \{0, 1\}^m\}$, this holds even for $|x|, |y| \leq m \cdot |H|$.

> **Guideline:** Consider the mapping $x \mapsto (h_1(x), ..., h_t(x))$, where $H = \{h_i\}_{i=1}^t$. Since the number of possible images is at most $(2^m)^t$, we get a collision as soon as we consider more than 2^{mt} pre-images.

Exercise 22: *Constructions of Hashing Families with Bounded Collision Probability:* In continuation of Exercise 22.2 in Chapter 3, consider the set of functions S_ℓ^m associated with ℓ-by-m Toeplitz matrix; that is, $h_T(x) = Tx$, where $T = (T_{i,j})$ is a Toeplitz matrix (i.e., $T_{i,j} = T_{i+1,j+1}$ for all i, j). Show that this family has collision probability 2^{-m}. (Note that each ℓ-by-m Toeplitz matrix is specified using $\ell + m - 1$ bits.)

Guideline: Note that we have eliminated the shifting vector b used in Exercise 22.2 of Chapter 3, but this does not affect the relevant analysis.

Exercise 23: *Constructions of Generalized Hashing Families with Bounded Collision Property:* (See definition in Section 6.3.1.3.)

1. Using a variant of the tree-hashing scheme of Construction 6.2.13, construct a generalized hashing ensemble with a $(f, 1/f)$-collision property, where $f(n) = 2^{\sqrt{n}/2}$. (Hint: Use a different hashing function at each level of the tree.)

2. (By Hugo Krawczyk): Show that the tree-hashing scheme of Construction 6.2.13, *where the same hashing function is used in all levels of the tree,* fails in the current context. That is, there exists a hashing ensemble $\{h_r : \{0, 1\}^{2m(|r|)} \to \{0, 1\}^{m(|r|)}\}_r$ with negligible collision probability, such that applying Construction 6.2.13 to it (even with depth two) yields an ensemble with high collision probability.

3. As in Part 2, show that the block-chaining method of Construction 6.2.11 fails in the current context (even for three blocks).

Guideline (Part 1): Let $\{h_r : \{0, 1\}^{2m(|r|)} \to \{0, 1\}^{m(|r|)}\}_r$ be a hashing ensemble with collision probability **cp**. Recall that such ensembles with $m(n) = n/3$ and $cp(n) = 2^{-m(n)}$ can be constructed (see Exercise 22). Then, consider the function ensemble $\{h_{r_1,...,r_{m(n)}} : \{0, 1\}^* \to \{0, 1\}^{2m(n)}\}_{n \in \mathbb{N}}$, where all r_i's are of length n, such that $h_{r_1,...,r_{m(n)}}(x)$ is defined as follows:

1. As in Construction 6.2.13, break x into $t \overset{\text{def}}{=} 2^{\lceil \log_2(|x|/m(n)) \rceil}$ consecutive blocks, denoted $x_1, ..., x_t$, and let $d = \log_2 t$.

2. Let $i = 1, ..., t$, and let $y_{d,i} \overset{\text{def}}{=} x_i$. For $j = d - 1, ..., 1, 0$ and $i = 1, ..., 2^j$, let $y_{j,i} = h_{r_j}(y_{j+1,2i-1}y_{j+1,2i})$. The hash value equals $(y_{0,1}, |x|)$.

The above functions have description length $N \overset{\text{def}}{=} m(n) \cdot n$ and map strings of length at most $2^{m(n)}$ to strings of length $2m(n)$. It is easy to bound the collision probability (for strings of equal length) by the probability of collision occuring in each of the levels of the tree. In fact, for $x_1 \cdots x_t \neq x'_1 \cdots x'_t$ such that $x_i \neq x'_i$, it suffices to bound the sum of the probabilities that $y_{j,\lceil i/2^{d-j} \rceil} = y'_{j,\lceil i/2^{d-j} \rceil}$ holds (given that $y_{j+1,\lceil i/2^{d-(j+1)} \rceil} \neq y'_{j+1,\lceil i/2^{d-(j+1)} \rceil}$) for $j = d - 1, ..., 1, 0$. Thus, this generalized hashing ensemble has a (ℓ, ϵ)-collision property, where $\ell(N) = 2^{m(n)}$ and $\epsilon(N) = m(n) \cdot cp(n)$. We stress that the collision probability of the tree-hashing scheme grows linearly with the depth of the tree (rather than linearly with its size). Recalling that we may use $m(n) = n/3$ and $cp(n) = 2^{-m(n)}$, we obtain (using $N = n^2/3 = 3m(n)^2$) $\ell(N) = 2^{(N/3)^{1/2}} > 2^{(N/4)^{1/2}}$ and $\epsilon(N) < (N/\ell(N)) < 2^{-(N/4)^{1/2}}$ (as desired).

Guideline (Part 2): Given a hashing family as in the hypothesis, modify it into $\{h'_{r,s} : \{0, 1\}^{2m} \to \{0, 1\}^m\}_{r,s}$, where $s \in \{0, 1\}^m$, such that $h'_{r,s}(0^{2m}) = s$, $h'_{r,s}(sv) = 0^m$ for all $v \in \{0, 1\}^m$, and $h'_{r,s}(w) = h_r(w)$ for each other $w \in \{0, 1\}^{2m}$. Note that the new family maintains the collision probability of the original one up to an additive term of $O(2^{-m})$. On the other hand, for every $w \in \{0, 1\}^{2m}$, it holds that $\text{TreeHash}_{r,s}(0^{2m} w) = h'_{r,s}(h'_{r,s}(0^{2m}) h'_{r,s}(w)) = h'_{r,s}(s \, v) = 0^m$, where $v = h'_{r,s}(w)$.

Guideline (Part 3): For $h'_{r,s}$ as in Part 2 and every $v \in \{0, 1\}^m$, it holds that $\text{ChainHash}_{r,s}(0^{2m} v) = h'_{r,s}(h'_{r,s}(0^{2m}) v) = h'_{r,s}(sv) = 0^m$.

Exercise 24: *On the additional properties required in Proposition 6.4.21:* In continuation of Exercise 23 of Chapter 3, show that the function family S_n^{n-1} presented there satisfies the following two properties:

1. All but a negligible fraction of the functions in S_n^{n-1} are 2-to-1.
2. There exists a probabilistic polynomial-time algorithm that, given $y_1, y_2 \in \{0, 1\}^n$ and $z_1, z_2 \in \{0, 1\}^{n-1}$, outputs a uniformly distributed element of $\{s \in S_n^{n-1} : h_s(y_i) = z_i \; \forall i \in \{1, 2\}\}$.

Guideline: Recall that each function in S_n^{n-1} is described by a pair of elements of the finite field $\text{GF}(2^n)$, where the pair (a, b) describes the function $h_{a,b}$ that maps $x \in \text{GF}(2^n)$ to the $(n-1)$-bit prefix of the n-bit representation of $ax + b$, where the arithmetic is of the field $\text{GF}(2^n)$. The first condition follows by observing that the function $h_{a,b}$ is 2-to-1 if and only if $a \neq 0$. The second condition follows by observing that $h_{a,b}(y_i) = z_i$ if and only if $ay_i + b = v_i$ for some v_i that is a single-bit extension of z_i. Thus, generating a pair (a, b), such that $h_{a,b}(y_i) = z_i$ for both i's, amounts to selecting random single-bit extensions v_i's, and (assuming $y_1 \neq y_2$) solving the system $\{ay_i + b = v_i\}_{i=1,2}$ (for the variables a and b).

Exercise 25: *Fail-stop signatures require a memory-dependent signing process:* In continuation of Section 6.5.5, prove that a secure fail-stop signature scheme must employ a memory-dependent signing process (as in Definition 6.4.13).

Guideline: Suppose toward the contradiction that there exists a secure memoryless fail-stop signature scheme. For every signing-key $s \in \{0, 1\}^n$, consider the randomized process P_s in which one first selects uniformly $x \in \{0, 1\}^n$, produces a (random) signature $y \leftarrow S_s(x)$, and outputs the pair (x, y). Show that, given polynomially many samples of P_s, one can find (in exponential time) a string $s' \in \{0, 1\}^n$ such that with probability at least 0.99, the statistical distance between P_s and $P_{s'}$ is at most 0.01. Thus, a computationally unbounded adversary making polynomially many signing queries can find a signing-key that typically produces the same signatures as the true signer. It follows that either these signatures cannot be revoked or that the user may also revoke its own signatures.

CHAPTER SEVEN

General Cryptographic Protocols

The design of secure protocols that implement arbitrarily desired functionalities is a major part of modern cryptography. Taking the opposite perspective, the design of any cryptographic scheme may be viewed as the design of a secure protocol for implementing a suitable functionality. Still, we believe that it makes sense to differentiate between basic cryptographic primitives (which involve little interaction) like encryption and signature schemes, on the one hand, and general cryptographic protocols, on the other hand.

In this chapter we consider *general* results concerning secure *multi*-party computations, where the *two*-party case is an important special case. In a nutshell, these results assert that one can construct protocols for securely computing *any* desirable multi-party functionality (see the following terminology). Indeed, what is striking about these results is their generality, and we believe that the wonder is not diminished by the (various alternative) conditions under which these results hold.

Our focus on the *general* study of secure multi-party computation (rather than on protocols for solving specific problems) is natural in the context of the theoretical treatment of the subject matter. We wish to highlight the importance of this *general* study to practice. Firstly, this study clarifies fundamental issues regarding security in a multi-party environment. Secondly, it draws the lines between what is possible in principle and what is not. Thirdly, it develops general techniques for designing secure protocols. And last, sometimes it may even yield schemes (or modules) that may be incorporated in practical systems. Thus, we believe that the current chapter is both of theoretical and practical importance.

Terminology. The notion of a (multi-party) functionality is central to the current chapter. By an m-ary functionality we mean a random process that maps m inputs to m outputs, where functions mapping m inputs to m outputs are a special case (also referred to as deterministic functionalities). Thus, functionalities are randomized extensions of ordinary functions. One may think of a functionality F as being a probability distribution over (corresponding) functions (i.e., F equals the function $f^{(i)}$ with probability p_i). Alternatively, we think of $F(x_1, ..., x_m)$ as selecting at random a string r, and outputting $F'(r, x_1, ..., x_m)$, where F' is a function mapping $m + 1$ inputs to m outputs.

Teaching Tip. The contents of the current chapter are quite complex. We suggest covering in class only the overview section (i.e., Section 7.1), and consider the rest of this chapter to be advanced material. Furthermore, we assume that the reader is familiar with the material in all the previous chapters. This familiarity is important, not only because we use some of the notions and results presented in these chapters but also because we use similar proof techniques (and do so while assuming that this is *not* the reader's first encounter with these techniques).

Organization. In addition to the overview section (i.e., Section 7.1), the current chapter consists of two main parts:

The first part (i.e., Sections 7.2–7.4) consists of a detailed treatment of general secure *two*-party protocols. Our ultimate goal in this part is to design two-party protocols that withstand any feasible adversarial behavior. We proceed in two steps. First, we consider a benign type of adversary, called *semi-honest*, and construct protocols that are secure with respect to such an adversary (cf. Section 7.3). Next, we show how to force parties to behave in a semi-honest manner (cf. Section 7.4). That is, we show how to transform any protocol, secure in the semi-honest model, into a protocol that is secure against any feasible adversarial behavior. But before presenting these constructions, we present the relevant definitions (cf. Section 7.2).

The second part (i.e., Sections 7.5 and 7.6) deals with general secure *multi*-party protocols. Specifically, in Section 7.5 we extend the treatment presented in the first part to *multi*-party protocols, whereas in Section 7.6 we consider the "private channel model" and present alternative constructions for it.

Although it is possible to skip some of the earlier sections of this chapter before reading a later section, we recommend not doing so. In particular, we recommend reading the overview section (i.e., Section 7.1) before reading any later section.

7.1. Overview

A general framework for casting (m-party) cryptographic (protocol) problems consists of specifying a random process that maps m inputs to m outputs. The inputs to the process are to be thought of as local inputs of m parties, and the m outputs are their corresponding (desired) local outputs. The random process describes the desired functionality. That is, if the m parties were to trust each other (or trust some external party), then they could each send their local input to the trusted party, who would compute the outcome of the process and send to each party the corresponding output. A pivotal question in the area of cryptographic protocols is the extent to which this (imaginary) trusted party can be "emulated" by the mutually distrustful parties themselves. (See illustration in Figure 7.1.)

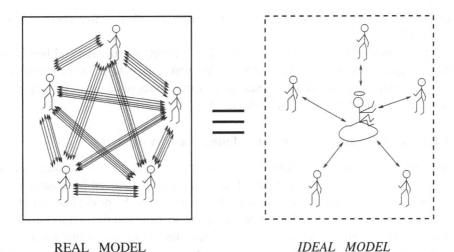

REAL MODEL   *IDEAL MODEL*

Figure 7.1: Secure protocols emulate a trusted party: an illustration.

The results mentioned previously and surveyed later describe a variety of models in which such an "emulation" is possible. The models vary by the underlying assumptions regarding the communication channels, the numerous parameters relating to the extent of adversarial behavior, and the desired level of emulation of the trusted party (i.e., level of "security"). We stress that unless stated differently, the *two*-party case is an important special case of the treatment of the *multi*-party setting (i.e., we consider any $m \geq 2$).

7.1.1. The Definitional Approach and Some Models

Before describing the abovementioned results, we further discuss the notion of "emulating a trusted party," which underlies the definitional approach to secure multi-party computation. The approach can be traced back to the definition of zero-knowledge (see Section 4.3 of Volume 1), and even to the definition of semantic security (see Section 5.2.1). The underlying paradigm (called the simulation paradigm) is that a scheme is secure if whatever a feasible adversary can obtain after attacking it is also feasibly attainable in an "ideal setting." In the case of zero-knowledge, this amounts to saying that whatever a (feasible) verifier can obtain after interacting with the prover on a prescribed valid assertion can be (feasibly) computed from the assertion itself. In the case of multi-party computation, we compare the effect of adversaries that participate in the *execution of the actual protocol* to the effect of adversaries that participate in an *imaginary execution* of a trivial (ideal) protocol for computing the desired functionality *with the help of a trusted party*. If whatever adversaries can feasibly obtain in the former real setting can also be feasibly obtained in the latter ideal setting, then the protocol "emulates the ideal setting" (i.e., "emulates a trusted party"), and so is deemed secure. This means that properties that are satisfied in the ideal setting are also satisfied by a secure protocol that is executed in the real setting. For example, security typically implies the preservation of the *privacy* of the parties' local inputs (beyond whatever is revealed by the local outputs provided to the adversary), and the *correctness* of the honest parties' local outputs (i.e., their consistency with the functionality).

The approach outlined here can be applied in a variety of models, and is used to define the goals of security in these models.[1] We first discuss some of the parameters used in defining various models, and next demonstrate the application of this approach to a couple of important cases (cf. Sections 7.1.1.2 and 7.1.1.3).

7.1.1.1. Some Parameters Used in Defining Security Models

The following parameters are described in terms of the actual (or real) computation. In some cases, the corresponding definition of security is obtained by some restrictions or provisions applied to the ideal model. In all cases, the desired notion of security is defined by requiring that for any adequate adversary in the real model, there exists a corresponding adversary in the corresponding ideal model that obtains essentially the same impact on the computation of the functionality (as the real-model adversary).

- *Set-up assumptions:* Unless differently stated, we make no set-up assumptions (except for the obvious assumption that all parties have copies of the protocol's program). However, in some cases it is assumed that each party knows some information (e.g., a verification-key) corresponding to each of the other parties (or, one may assume the existence of a public-key infrastructure). Another assumption, made more rarely, is that all parties have access to some common (trusted) random string.
- *The communication channels:* Here we refer to issues like the *privacy* and *reliablity* of data sent over the channels, as well as to the availability and the communication features of the channels.

  The standard assumption in the area is that the adversary can tap all communication channels (between honest parties); that is, the channels per se do not provide privacy (i.e., privacy of the data sent over them). In contrast, one may *postulate* that the adversary cannot obtain messages sent between honest parties, yielding the so-called private-channel model. This postulate may be justified in some settings. Furthermore, it may be viewed as a useful abstraction that provides a clean model for study and development of secure protocols. In this respect, it is important to mention that in a variety of settings of the other parameters, the private-channel model can be emulated by ordinary (i.e., "tapped" point-to-point) channels.

  The standard assumption in the area is that the adversary cannot omit, modify, duplicate, or generate messages sent over the communication channels (between honest

---

[1] A few technical comments are in place. Firstly, we assume that the inputs of all parties are of the same length. We comment that as long as the lengths of the inputs are polynomially related, this convention can be enforced by padding. On the other hand, some length restriction is essential for the security results, because (in general) it is impossible to hide all information regarding the length of the inputs to a protocol. Secondly, we assume that the desired functionality is computable in probabilistic polynomial-time, because we wish the secure protocol to run in probabilistic polynomial-time (and a protocol cannot be more efficient than the corresponding centralized algorithm). Clearly, the results can be extended to functionalities that are computable within any given (time-constructible) time bound, using adequate padding.

parties); that is, the channels are postulated to be reliable (in the sense that they guarantee the authenticity of the data sent over them). Furthermore, one may postulate the existence of a broadcast channel. Again, these assumptions can be justified in some settings and emulated in others.

Most work in the area assumes that communication is synchronous and that point-to-point channels exist between every pair of processors. However, one may also consider asynchronous communication and arbitrary networks of point-to-point channels.

- *Computational limitations:* Typically, we consider computationally bounded adversaries (e.g., probabilistic polynomial-time adversaries). However, the private-channel model also allows for (meaningful) consideration of computationally unbounded adversaries.

  We stress that, also in the latter case, security should be defined by requiring that for every real adversary, whatever the adversary can compute after participating in the execution of the actual protocol be computable *within comparable time* (e.g., in polynomially related time) by an imaginary adversary participating in an imaginary execution of the trivial ideal protocol (for computing the desired functionality with the help of a trusted party). Thus, results in the computationally unbounded–adversary model trivially imply results for computationally bounded adversaries.

- *Restricted adversarial behavior:* The most general type of an adversary considered in the literature is one that may corrupt parties to the protocol while the execution goes on, and decide which parties to corrupt based on partial information it has gathered so far. A somewhat more restricted model, which seems adequate in many settings, postulates that the set of dishonest parties is fixed (arbitrarily) before the execution starts (but this set is, of course, not known to the honest parties). The latter model is called non-adaptive as opposed to the adaptive adversary mentioned first.

  An orthogonal parameter of restriction refers to whether a dishonest party takes active steps to disrupt the execution of the protocol (i.e., sends messages that differ from those specified by the protocol), or merely gathers information (which it may later share with the other dishonest parties). The latter adversary has been given a variety of names, such as semi-honest, passive, and honest-but-curious. This restricted model may be justified in certain settings, and certainly provides a useful methodological locus (cf. Section 7.1.3). In the following, we refer to the adversary of the unrestricted model as active; another commonly used name is malicious.

- *Restricted notions of security:* One example is the willingness to tolerate "unfair" protocols in which the execution can be suspended (at any time) by a dishonest party, provided that it is detected doing so. We stress that in case the execution is suspended, the dishonest party does not obtain more information than it could have obtained if the execution were not suspended. What may happen is that some honest parties will not obtain their desired outputs (although other parties did obtain their corresponding outputs), but will rather detect that the execution was suspended. We will say that this restricted notion of security allows abort (or allows premature suspension of the execution).

- *Upper bounds on the number of dishonest parties:* In some models, secure multi-party computation is possible only if a strict majority of the parties are honest.[2] Sometimes even a special majority (e.g., 2/3) is required. General "resilient adversary-structures" have been considered, too (i.e., security is guaranteed in the case that the set of dishonest parties equals one of the sets specified in a predetermined family of sets).

- *Mobile adversary:* In most works, once a party is said to be dishonest it remains so throughout the execution. More generally, one may consider transient adversarial behavior (e.g., an adversary seizes control of some site and later withdraws from it). This model, which will not be further discussed in this work, allows for the construction of protocols that remain secure, even in case the adversary may seize control of all sites during the execution (but never control concurrently, say, more than 10 percent of the sites). We comment that schemes secure in this model were later termed "proactive."

In the rest of this chapter we will consider a few specific settings of these parameters. Specifically, we will focus on non-adaptive, active, and computationally bounded adversaries, and will not assume the existence of private channels. In Section 7.1.1.2 we consider this setting while restricting the dishonest parties to a strict minority, whereas in Section 7.1.1.3 we consider a restricted notion of security for two-party protocols that allows "unfair suspension" of execution (or "allows abort").

7.1.1.2. Example: Multi-Party Protocols with Honest Majority

We consider a non-adaptive, active, computationally bounded adversary, and do not assume the existence of private channels. Our aim is to define multi-party protocols that remain secure provided that the honest parties are in the majority. (The reason for requiring an honest majority will be discussed at the end of this subsection.) For more details about this model, see Section 7.5.1.

Consider any multi-party protocol. We first observe that each party may change its local input before even entering the execution of the protocol. Furthermore, this is also unavoidable when the parties utilize a trusted party Consequently, such an effect of the adversary on the real execution (i.e., modification of its own input prior to entering the actual execution) is not considered a breach of security. In general, whatever cannot be avoided (even) when the parties utilize a trusted party is not considered a breach of security. We wish secure protocols (in the real model) to suffer only from whatever is also unavoidable when the parties utilize a trusted party. Thus, the basic paradigm underlying the definitions of *secure multi-party computations* amounts to saying that the only situations that may occur in the real execution of a secure protocol are those that can also occur in a corresponding ideal model (where the parties may employ a trusted

---

[2] Indeed, requiring an honest majority in the two-party case yields a meaningless model.

party). In other words, the "effective malfunctioning" of parties in secure protocols is restricted to what is postulated in the corresponding ideal model.

When defining secure multi-party protocols (with honest majority), we need to pin-point what cannot be avoided in the ideal model (i.e., when the parties utilize a trusted party). This is easy, because the ideal model is very simple. Since we are interested in executions in which the majority of parties are honest, we consider an ideal model in which any minority group (of the parties) may collude as follows:

1. Firstly, the dishonest minority parties share their original inputs and decide together on replaced inputs to be sent to the trusted party. (The other parties send their respective original inputs to the trusted party. We stress that the communication between the honest parties and the trusted party is not seen by the dishonest colluding minority parties.)
2. Upon receiving inputs from all parties, the trusted party determines the corresponding outputs and sends them to the corresponding parties.
3. Upon receiving the "output message" from the trusted party, each honest party outputs it locally, whereas the dishonest colluding minority parties may determine their outputs based on all they know (i.e., their initial inputs and their received outputs).

Note that such behavior of the minority group is unavoidable in any execution of any protocol (even in the presence of trusted parties). This is the reason that the ideal model was so defined. Now, a *secure multi-party computation with honest majority* is required to emulate this ideal model. That is, the effect of any feasible adversary that controls a minority of the parties in a real execution of the actual protocol can be essentially simulated by a (different) feasible adversary that controls the same parties in the ideal model.

Definition 7.1.1 (secure protocols – a sketch): *Let f be an m-ary functionality and Π be an m-party protocol operating in the real model.*

- *For a real-model adversary A, controlling some minority of the parties* (and tapping all communication channels), *and an m-sequence $\overline{x}$, we denote by* REAL$_{\Pi,A}(\overline{x})$ *the sequence of m outputs resulting from the execution of Π on input $\overline{x}$ under attack of the adversary A.*
- *For an ideal-model adversary A', controlling some minority of the parties, and an m-sequence $\overline{x}$, we denote by* IDEAL$_{f,A'}(\overline{x})$ *the sequence of m outputs resulting from the ideal process described previously, on input $\overline{x}$ under attack of the adversary A'.*

We say that Π securely implements f with honest majority if for every feasible real-model adversary A, controlling some minority of the parties, there exists a feasible ideal-model adversary A', controlling the same parties, so that the probability ensembles $\{$REAL$_{\Pi,A}(\overline{x})\}_{\overline{x}}$ *and* $\{$IDEAL$_{f,A'}(\overline{x})\}_{\overline{x}}$ *are computationally indistinguishable (as in Part 2 of Definition 3.2.7 in Volume 1).*

Thus, security means that the effect of each minority group in a real execution of a secure protocol is "essentially restricted" to replacing its own local inputs (independently of the local inputs of the majority parties) before the protocol starts, and replacing its own local outputs (depending only on its local inputs and outputs) after the protocol terminates. (We stress that in the real execution, the minority parties do obtain additional pieces of information; yet in a secure protocol they gain nothing from these additional pieces of information.)

The fact that Definition 7.1.1 refers to a model without private channels is reflected in the set of possible ensembles $\{\text{REAL}_{\Pi,A}(\overline{x})\}_{\overline{x}}$ that is determined by the (sketchy) definition of the real-model adversary (which is allowed to tap all the communication channels). When defining security in the private-channel model, the real-model adversary is not allowed to tap channels between honest parties, which in turn restricts the set of possible ensembles $\{\text{REAL}_{\Pi,A}(\overline{x})\}_{\overline{x}}$. Thus, the difference between the two models is only reflected in the definition of the real-model adversary. On the other hand, when we wish to define security with respect to passive adversaries, both the scope of the real-model adversaries and the scope of the ideal-model adversaries change. In the real-model execution, all parties follow the protocol, but the adversary may alter the output of the dishonest parties arbitrarily, depending on all their intermediate internal states (during the execution). In the corresponding ideal-model, the adversary is not allowed to modify the *inputs* of dishonest parties (in Step 1), but is allowed to modify their outputs (in Step 3).

We comment that a definition analogous to Definition 7.1.1 can also be presented in case the dishonest parties are not in the minority. In fact, such a definition seems more natural, but the problem is that such a definition cannot be satisfied. That is, most natural functionalities do not have a protocol for computing them securely in case at least half of the parties are dishonest and employ an adequate (active) adversarial strategy. This follows from an impossibility result regarding two-party computation, which essentially asserts that there is no way to prevent a party from prematurely suspending the execution. On the other hand, secure multi-party computation with dishonest majority is possible if (and only if) premature suspension of the execution is not considered a breach of security.

7.1.1.3. Another Example: Two-Party Protocols Allowing Abort

In light of the last paragraph, we now consider multi-party computations in which premature suspension of the execution is not considered a breach of security. For concreteness, we focus here on the special case of two-party computations.[3] For more details about this model, see Section 7.2.3.

Intuitively, in any two-party protocol, each party may suspend the execution at any point in time, and furthermore, it may do so as soon as it learns the desired output. Thus, in case the output of each parties depends on both inputs, it is always possible for one of the parties to obtain the desired output while preventing the other party from fully determining its own output. The same phenomenon occurs even in case the two parties just wish to generate a common random value. Thus, when considering active adversaries in the two-party setting, we do not consider such premature suspension of the execution a breach of security. Consequently, we consider an ideal model where

---

[3] As in Section 7.1.1.2, we consider a non-adaptive, active, computationally bounded adversary.

each of the two parties may "shut down" the trusted (third) party at any point in time. In particular, this may happen after the trusted party has supplied the outcome of the computation to one party but before it has supplied it to the second. That is, an execution in the ideal model proceeds as follows:

1. Each party sends its input to the trusted party, where the dishonest party may replace its input or send no input at all (which may be viewed as aborting).
2. Upon receiving inputs from both parties, the trusted party determines the corresponding outputs and sends the first output to the first party.
3. In case the first party is dishonest, it may instruct the trusted party to halt; otherwise it always instructs the trusted party to proceed. If instructed to proceed, the trusted party sends the second output to the second party.
4. Upon receiving the output message from the trusted party, the honest party outputs it locally, whereas the dishonest party may determine its output based on all it knows (i.e., its initial input and its received output).

A secure two-party computation allowing abort is required to emulate this ideal model. That is, as in Definition 7.1.1, security is defined by requiring that for every feasible real-model adversary A, there exists a feasible ideal-model adversary A', controlling the same party, so that the probability ensembles representing the corresponding (real and ideal) executions are computationally indistinguishable. This means that each party's "effective malfunctioning" in a secure protocol is restricted to supplying an initial input of its choice and aborting the computation at any point in time. (Needless to say, the choice of the initial input of each party may *not* depend on the input of the other party.)

We mention that an alternative way of dealing with the problem of premature suspension of execution (i.e., abort) is to restrict attention to single-output functionalities, that is, functionalities in which only one party is supposed to obtain an output. The definition of secure computation of such functionalities can be identical to Definition 7.1.1, with the exception that no restriction is made on the set of dishonest parties (and, in particular, one may consider a single dishonest party in the case of two-party protocols). For further details, see Section 7.2.3.2.

7.1.2. Some Known Results

We briefly mention some of the models for which *general* secure multi-party computation is known to be attainable; that is, models in which one can construct secure multi-party protocols for computing *any* desired functionality.

7.1.2.1. The Main Results Presented in This Chapter

We start with results that refer to secure two-party protocols, as well as to secure multi-party protocols in the standard model (where the adversary may tap the communication lines).

Theorem 7.1.2 (the main feasibility results – a sketch): *Assuming the existence of enhanced trapdoor permutations* (as in Definition C.1.1 in Appendix C), *general secure multi-party computation is possible in the following three models:*

1. *Passive adversary, for any number of dishonest parties.*
2. *Active adversary that may control only a strict minority of the parties.*
3. *Active adversary, controlling any number of bad parties, provided that suspension of execution is not considered a violation of security.*

In all these cases, the adversary is computationally bounded and non-adaptive. On the other hand, the adversary may tap the communication lines between honest parties (i.e., we do not assume the existence of private channels). The results for active adversaries assume a broadcast channel.

Recall that a broadcast channel can be implemented (while tolerating any number of bad parties) using a signature scheme and assuming a public-key infrastructure (i.e., each party knows the verification-key corresponding to each of the other parties).[4]

Most of the current chapter will be devoted to proving Theorem 7.1.2. In Sections 7.3 and 7.4 we prove Theorem 7.1.2 for the special case of *two parties:* In that case, Part 2 is not relevant, Part 1 is proved in Section 7.3, and Part 3 is proved in Section 7.4. The general case (i.e., of *multi*-party computation) is treated in Section 7.5.

7.1.2.2. Other Results

We next list some other models in which general secure multi-party computation is attainable:

- Making no computational assumptions and allowing computationally unbounded adversaries, but *assuming the existence of private channels,* general secure multi-party computation is possible in the following models:

  1. *Passive adversary that may control only a (strict) minority of the parties.*
  2. *Active adversary that may control only less than one third of the parties.* (Fault-tolerance can be increased to a regular minority if a broadcast channel exists.)

  In both cases the adversary may be adaptive. For details, see Sections 7.6 and 7.7.1.2.
- General secure multi-party computation is possible against an active adaptive, and *mobile* adversary that may control a small constant fraction of the parties at any point in time. This result makes no computational assumptions, allows computationally unbounded adversaries, but *assumes the existence of private channels.*

---

[4] Note that the implementation of a broadcast channel can be cast as a cryptographic protocol problem (i.e., for the functionality $(v, \lambda, ..., \lambda) \mapsto (v, v, ..., v)$, where $v \in \{0, 1\}^*$ and λ denotes the empty string). Thus, it is not surprising that the results regarding active adversaries assume the existence of either such a channel or a setting in which such a channel can be implemented (e.g., either that less than a third of the parties are faulty or that a public-key infrastructure exists). (This reasoning fails if the definition of secure protocols is relaxed such that it does not imply agreement; see [122].)

- *Assuming the intractability of inverting RSA* (or of the DLP), general secure multi-party computation is possible in a model allowing an *adaptive* and active computationally bounded adversary that may control only less than one third of the parties. We stress that this result does not assume the existence of private channels.

Results for asynchronous communication and arbitrary networks of point-to-point channels are also known. For further details, see Section 7.7.5.

7.1.2.3. An Extension and Efficiency Considerations

Secure Reactive Computation. All the aforementioned results extend (easily) to a reactive model of computation in which each party interacts with a high-level process (or application). The high-level process adaptively supplies each party with a sequence of inputs, one at a time, and expects to receive corresponding outputs from the parties. That is, a reactive system goes through (a possibly unbounded number of) iterations of the following type:

- Parties are given inputs for the current iteration.
- Depending on the current inputs, the parties are supposed to compute outputs for the current iteration. That is, the outputs in iteration j are determined by the inputs of the j-th iteration.

A more general formulation allows the outputs of each iteration to depend also on a global state, which is possibly updated at each iteration. The global state may include all inputs and outputs of previous iterations, and may only be partially known to individual parties. (In a secure reactive computation, such a global state may be maintained by all parties in a "secret sharing" manner.) For further discussion, see Section 7.7.1.3.

Efficiency considerations. One important efficiency measure regarding protocols is the number of communication rounds in their execution. The results mentioned earlier were originally obtained using protocols that use an unbounded number of rounds. In some cases, subsequent works obtained secure *constant*-round protocols. Other important efficiency considerations include the total number of bits sent in the execution of a protocol and the local computation time. The communication and computation complexities of the aforementioned protocols are related to the *computational* complexity of the desired functionalities, but alternative relations (e.g., referring to the *communication* complexity of the latter) may be possible.

7.1.3. Construction Paradigms

We briefly sketch three paradigms used in the construction of secure multi-party protocols. We focus on the construction of secure protocols for the model of computationally bounded and non-adaptive adversaries. These constructions proceed in two steps: First, a secure protocol is presented for the model of *passive* adversaries (for any number of dishonest parties), and next, such a protocol is "compiled" into a protocol that is secure in one of the two models of *active* adversaries (i.e., either in a model allowing the adversary to control only a minority of the parties or in a model in which premature suspension of the execution is not considered a violation of security).

Recall that in the model of passive adversaries, all parties follow the prescribed protocol, but at termination, the adversary may alter the output of the dishonest parties depending on all their intermediate internal states (during the execution). In the following, we refer to protocols that are secure in the model of passive (resp., general or active) adversaries by the term passively secure (resp., actively secure).

7.1.3.1. From Passively Secure Protocols to Actively Secure Ones

We show how to transform any passively secure protocol into a corresponding actively secure protocol. The communication model in both protocols consists of a single broadcast channel. Note that the messages of the original (passively secure) protocol may be assumed to be sent over a broadcast channel, because the adversary may see them anyhow (by tapping the point-to-point channels). As for the resulting actively secure protocol, the broadcast channel it uses can be implemented via an (authenticated) Byzantine Agreement protocol (cf. Section 7.5.3.2), thus providing an emulation of this model on the standard point-to-point model (in which a broadcast channel does not exist). We mention that authenticated Byzantine Agreement is typically implemented using a signature scheme (and assuming that each party knows the verification-key corresponding to each of the other parties).

Turning to the transformation itself, the main idea is to use zero-knowledge proofs in order to force parties to behave in a way that is consistent with the (passively secure) protocol. Actually, we need to confine each party to a unique consistent behavior (i.e., according to some fixed local input and a sequence of coin tosses), and to guarantee that a party cannot fix its input (and/or its coins) in a way that depends on the inputs of honest parties. Thus, some preliminary steps have to be taken before the step-by-step emulation of the original protocol can take place. Specifically, the compiled protocol (which, like the original protocol, is executed over a broadcast channel) proceeds as follows:

1. Prior to the emulation of the original protocol, each party commits to its input (using a commitment scheme). In addition, using a zero-knowledge proof-of-knowledge (cf. Section 4.7 of Volume 1), each party also proves that it knows its own input, that is, that it can properly decommit to the commitment it sent. (These zero-knowledge proofs-of-knowledge are conducted sequentially to prevent dishonest parties from setting their inputs in a way that depends on inputs of honest parties.)

2. Next, all parties jointly generate a sequence of random bits for each party such that only this party knows the outcome of the random sequence generated for it, but everybody gets a commitment to this outcome. These sequences will be used as the random-inputs (i.e., sequence of coin tosses) for the original protocol. Each bit in the random-sequence generated for Party X is determined as the exclusive-or of the

outcomes of instances of an (augmented) coin-tossing protocol that Party X plays with each of the other parties.

3. In addition, when compiling (the passively secure protocol to an actively secure protocol) for the model that allows the adversary to control only a minority of the parties, each party shares its input and random-input with all other parties using a Verifiable Secret Sharing protocol (cf. Section 7.5.5). This will guarantee that if some party prematurely suspends the execution, then all the parties can together reconstruct all its secrets and carry on the execution while playing its role.

4. After all these steps have been completed, we turn to the main step in which the new protocol emulates the original one. In each step, each party augments the message determined by the original protocol with a zero-knowledge that asserts that the message was indeed computed correctly. Recall that the next message (as determined by the original protocol) is a function of the sender's own input, its random-input, and the messages it has received so far (where the latter are known to everybody because they were sent over a broadcast channel). Furthermore, the sender's input is determined by its commitment (as sent in Step 1), and its random-input is similarly determined (in Step 2). Thus, the next message (as determined by the original protocol) is a function of publicly known strings (i.e., the said commitments as well as the other messages sent over the broadcast channel). Moreover, the assertion that the next message was indeed computed correctly is an NP-assertion, and the sender knows a corresponding NP-witness (i.e., its own input and random-input, as well as the corresponding decommitment information). Thus, the sender can prove (to each of the other parties) in zero-knowledge that the message it is sending was indeed computed according to the original protocol.

A detailed description is provided in Section 7.4 (see also Section 7.5.4).

7.1.3.2. Passively Secure Computation with "Scrambled Circuits"

The following technique refers mainly to two-party computation. Suppose that two parties, each having a private input, wish to obtain the value of a predetermined two-argument function evaluated at their corresponding inputs, that is, we consider only functionalities of the form $(x, y) \mapsto (f(x, y), f(x, y))$. Further suppose that the two parties hold a circuit that computes the value of the function on inputs of the adequate length. The idea is to have one party construct a "scrambled" form of the circuit so that the other party can propagate encrypted values through the "scrambled gates" and obtain the output in the clear (while all intermediate values remain secret). Note that the roles of the two parties are not symmetric, and recall that we are describing a protocol that is secure (only) with respect to passive adversaries. An implementation of this idea proceeds as follows:

- *Constructing a "scrambled" circuit:* The first party constructs a scrambled form of the original circuit. The scrambled circuit consists of *pairs of encrypted secrets* that correspond to the wires of the original circuit and *gadgets* that correspond to the gates of the original circuit. The secrets associated with the wires entering a gate are used (in the gadget that corresponds to this gate) as keys in the encryption of the secrets associated with the wire exiting this gate. Furthermore, there is a *random correspondence* between each pair of secrets and the Boolean values (of the corresponding wire). That is, wire w is assigned a pair of secrets, denoted (s'_w, s''_w), and there is a random 1-1 mapping, denoted v_w, between this pair and the pair of Boolean values (i.e., $\{v_w(s'_w), v_w(s''_w)\} = \{0, 1\}$).

Each gadget is constructed such that knowledge of a secret that corresponds to each wire entering the corresponding gate (in the circuit) yields a secret corresponding to the wire that exits this gate. Furthermore, the reconstruction of secrets using each gadget respects the functionality of the corresponding gate. For example, if one knows the secret that corresponds to the 1-value of one entry-wire and the secret that corresponds to the 0-value of the other entry-wire, and the gate is an OR-gate, then one obtains the secret that corresponds to the 1-value of the exit-wire.

Specifically, each gadget consists of four templates that are presented in a random order, where each template corresponds to one of the four possible values of the two entry-wires. A template may be merely a double encryption of the secret that corresponds to the appropriate output value, where the double encryption uses as keys the two secrets that correspond to the input values. That is, suppose a gate computing $f : \{0, 1\}^2 \to \{0, 1\}$ has input wires w_1 and w_2, and output wire w_3. Then, each of the four templates of this gate has the form $E_{s_{w_1}}(E_{s_{w_2}}(s_{w_3}))$, where $f(v_{w_1}(s_{w_1}), v_{w_2}(s_{w_2})) = v_{w_3}(s_{w_3})$.

- *Sending the "scrambled" circuit:* The first party sends the scrambled circuit to the second party. In addition, the first party sends to the second party the secrets that correspond to its own (i.e., the first party's) input bits (but not the values of these bits). The first party also reveals the correspondence between the pair of secrets associated with each output (i.e., circuit-output wire) and the Boolean values.[5] We stress that the random correspondence between the pair of secrets associated with each other wire and the Boolean values is kept secret (by the first party).

- *Oblivious Transfer of adequate secrets:* Next, the first party uses a (1-out-of-2) Oblivious Transfer protocol in order to hand the second party the secrets corresponding to the second party's input bits (without the first party learning anything about these bits).

  Loosely speaking, a 1-out-of-k Oblivious Transfer is a protocol enabling one party to obtain one of k secrets held by another party, without the second party learning which secret was obtained by the first party. That is, we refer to the two-party functionality

$$(i, (s_1, ..., s_k)) \mapsto (s_i, \lambda) \tag{7.1}$$

  where λ denotes the empty string.

- *Locally evaluating the "scrambled" circuit:* Finally, the second party "evaluates" the scrambled circuit gate-by-gate, starting from the top (circuit-input) gates (for which it knows one secret per each wire) and ending at the bottom (circuit-output) gates

---

[5] This can be done by providing, for each output wire, a succinct 2-partition (of all strings) that separates the two secrets associated with this wire.

(for which, by construction, the correspondence of secrets to values is known). Thus, the second party obtains the output value of the circuit (but nothing else), and sends it to the first party.

For further details, see Section 7.7.5.

7.1.3.3. Passively Secure Computation with Shares

For any $m \geq 2$, suppose that m parties, each having a private input, wish to obtain the value of a predetermined m-argument function evaluated at their sequence of inputs. Further suppose that the parties hold a circuit that computes the value of the function on inputs of the adequate length, and that the circuit contains only AND- and NOT-gates. Again, the idea is to propagate information from the top (circuit-input) gates to the bottom (circuit-output) gates, but this time the information is different, and the propagation is done jointly by all parties. The idea is to share the value of each wire in the circuit such that all shares yield the value, whereas lacking even one of the shares keeps the value totally undetermined. That is, we use a simple secret-sharing scheme such that a bit b is shared by a random sequence of m bits that sum up to b mod 2. First, each party shares each of its input bits with all parties (by sending each party a random value and setting its own share accordingly).[6] Next, all parties jointly scan the circuit from its input wires to the output wires, processing each gate as follows:

- When encountering a gate, the parties already hold shares of the values of the wires entering the gate, and their aim is to obtain shares of the value of the wire exiting the gate.
- For a NOT-gate, propagating shares through the gate is easy: The first party just flips the value of its share, and all other parties maintain their shares.
- For an AND-gate, propagating shares through the gate requires a secure (i.e., passively secure) multi-party protocol. Since an AND-gate corresponds to multiplication modulo 2, the parties need to securely compute the following randomized functionality (in which the x_i's denote shares of one entry-wire, the y_i's denote shares of the second entry-wire, the z_i's denote shares of the exit-wire, and the shares indexed by i belong to Party i):

$$((x_1, y_1), ..., (x_m, y_m)) \mapsto (z_1, ..., z_2) \tag{7.2}$$

where

$$\sum_{i=1}^{m} z_i = \sum_{i=1}^{m} x_i \cdot \sum_{i=1}^{m} y_i \tag{7.3}$$

That is, the z_i's are random subject to Eq. (7.3).

At the end, each party holds a share of each output wire. The desired output is obtained by letting each party send its share of each output wire to all parties. Thus,

---

[6] For simplicity, we may assume the private-channel model, in which case a value sent to an honest party cannot be read by the adversary.

securely evaluating the entire (arbitrary) circuit "reduces" to securely conducting a specific (very simple) multi-party computation. But things get even simpler: the key observation is that

$$\left(\sum_{i=1}^{m} x_i\right) \cdot \left(\sum_{i=1}^{m} y_i\right) = \sum_{i=1}^{m} x_i y_i + \sum_{1 \le i < j \le m} (x_i y_j + x_j y_i) \qquad (7.4)$$

Thus, the m-ary functionality of Eq. (7.2) and Eq. (7.3) can be computed as follows (where all arithmetic operations are mod 2):

1. Each Party i locally computes $z_{i,i} \overset{\text{def}}{=} x_i y_i$.
2. Next, each pair of parties (i.e., Parties i and j) securely compute random shares of $x_i y_j + x_j y_i$. That is, Parties i and j (holding (x_i, y_i) and (x_j, y_j), respectively), need to securely compute the randomized two-party functionality $((x_i, y_i), (x_j, y_j)) \mapsto (z_{i,j}, z_{j,i})$, where the z's are random subject to $z_{i,j} + z_{j,i} = x_i y_j + y_i x_j$. The latter (simple) two-party computation can be securely implemented using (a 1-out-of-4) Oblivious Transfer. Specifically, Party i uniformly selects $z_{i,j} \in \{0, 1\}$, and defines its four secrets as follows:

Index of the secret	Corresponding value of (x_j, y_j)	Value of the secret (output of Party j)
1	$(0, 0)$	$z_{i,j}$
2	$(0, 1)$	$z_{i,j} + x_i$
3	$(1, 0)$	$z_{i,j} + y_i$
4	$(1, 1)$	$z_{i,j} + x_i + y_i$

Party j sets its input to $2x_j + y_j + 1$, and obtains the secret $z_{i,j} + x_i y_j + y_i x_j$.

(Indeed, for "small" B, any two-party functionality $f : A \times B \to \{\lambda\} \times \{0, 1\}$ can be securely implemented by a single invocation of a 1-out-of-$|B|$ Oblivious Transfer, where the first party defines its $|B|$ secrets in correspondence to the $|B|$ possible values of the input to the second party.)

3. Finally, for every $i = 1, ..., m$, the sum $\sum_{j=1}^{m} z_{i,j}$ yields the desired share of Party i.

A detailed description is provided in Section 7.3 (see also Section 7.5.2).

A related construction. We mention that an analogous construction has been subsequently used in the private-channel model and withstands computationally unbounded active (resp., passive) adversaries that control less than one third (resp., a minority) of the parties. The basic idea is to use a more sophisticated secret-sharing scheme, specifically, via low-degree polynomials. That is, the Boolean circuit is viewed as an arithmetic circuit over a finite field having more than m elements, and a secret element s in the field is shared by selecting uniformly a polynomial of degree $d = \lfloor (m - 1)/3 \rfloor$ (resp., degree $d = \lfloor (m - 1)/2 \rfloor$) having a free-term equal to s, and handing each party the value of this polynomial evaluated at a different (fixed) point (e.g., party i is given the value at point i). Addition is emulated by (local) pointwise addition of the (secret-sharing) polynomials representing the two inputs (using the fact that for polynomials p and q, and any field element e [and in particular $e = 0, 1, ..., m$], it holds that $p(e) + q(e) = (p + q)(e)$). The emulation of multiplication is more involved and requires interaction (because the product of polynomials yields a polynomial of higher degree, and thus the polynomial representing the output cannot be the product of the polynomials representing the two inputs). Indeed, the aim of the interaction is to turn the shares of the product polynomial into shares of a degree d polynomial that has the same free-term as the product polynomial (which is of degree $2d$). This can be done using the fact that the coefficients of a polynomial are a linear combination of its values at sufficiently many arguments (and the other way around), and the fact that one can privately compute any linear combination (of secret values). For further details, see Section 7.6.

7.2.* The Two-Party Case: Definitions

In this section we define security for two models of adversaries for two-party protocols. In both models, the adversary is non-adaptive and computationally bounded (i.e., restricted to probabilistic polynomial-time with [non-uniform] auxiliary inputs). In the first model, presented in Section 7.2.2, we consider a restricted adversary called semi-honest, whereas the general case of malicious adversary is considered in Section 7.2.3. In addition to being of independent interest, the semi-honest model will play a major role in the constructions of protocols for the malicious model (see Sections 7.3 and 7.4).

7.2.1. The Syntactic Framework

A two-party protocol problem is cast by specifying a random process that maps pairs of inputs (one input per each party) to pairs of outputs (one per each party). We refer to such a process as the desired functionality, denoted $f : \{0, 1\}^* \times \{0, 1\}^* \to \{0, 1\}^* \times \{0, 1\}^*$. That is, for every pair of inputs (x, y), the desired output pair is a random variable, $f(x, y)$, ranging over pairs of strings. The first party, holding input x, wishes to obtain the first element in $f(x, y)$; whereas the second party, holding input y, wishes to obtain the second element in $f(x, y)$. A few interesting special cases are highlighted next:

- *Symmetric deterministic functionalities:* This is the simplest general case often considered in the literature. In this case, for some predetermined function, g, both parties wish to obtain the value of g evaluated at the input pair. That is, the functionality they wish to (securely) compute is $f(x, y) \stackrel{\text{def}}{=} (g(x, y), g(x, y))$. For example, they may be interested in determining whether their local inputs are equal (i.e., $g(x, y) = 1$ iff $x = y$) or whether their local inputs viewed as sets are disjoint (i.e., $g(x, y) = 1$ iff for every i either $x_i = 0$ or $y_i = 0$).
- *Input-oblivious randomized functionalities:* Whereas input-oblivious deterministic functionalities are trivial, some input-oblivious randomized functionalities are very interesting. Suppose, for example, that the two parties wish to toss a *fair* coin (i.e.,

such that no party can "influence the outcome" by itself). This task can be cast by requiring that for every input pair (x, y), the output pair $f(x, y)$ is uniformly distributed over $\{(0, 0), (1, 1)\}$.

- *Asymmetric functionalities:* The general case of asymmetric functionalities is captured by functionalities of the form $f(x, y) \stackrel{\text{def}}{=} (f'(x, y), \lambda)$, where $f' : \{0, 1\}^* \times \{0, 1\}^* \to \{0, 1\}^*$ is a randomized process and λ denotes the empty string. A special case of interest is when one party wishes to obtain some predetermined partial information regarding the secret input of the other party, where the latter secret is verifiable with respect to the input of the first party. This task is captured by a functionality f such that $f(x, y) \stackrel{\text{def}}{=} (R(y), \lambda)$ if $V(x, y) = 1$ and $f(x, y) \stackrel{\text{def}}{=} (\bot, \lambda)$ otherwise, where R represents the partial information to be revealed and V represents the verification procedure.[7]

We stress that whenever we consider a protocol for securely computing f, it is implicitly assumed that the protocol correctly computes f when both parties follow the prescribed program. That is, the *joint* output distribution of the protocol, played by honest parties, on input pair (x, y), equals the distribution of $f(x, y)$.

Notation. We let λ denote the empty string and $\bot$ denote a special *error symbol*. That is, whereas $\lambda \in \{0, 1\}^*$ (and $|\lambda| = 0$), we postulate that $\bot \notin \{0, 1\}^*$ (and is thus distinguishable from any string in $\{0, 1\}^*$).

7.2.1.1. Simplifying Conventions

To simplify the exposition, we make the following three assumptions:

1. *The protocol problem has to be solved only for inputs of the same length* (i.e., $|x| = |y|$).
2. *The functionality is computable in time polynomial in the length of the inputs.*
3. *Security is measured in terms of the length of the inputs.*

As discussed next, these conventions (or assumptions) can be greatly relaxed, yet each represents an essential issue that must be addressed.

We start with the first convention (or assumption). Observe that making no restriction on the relationship among the lengths of the two inputs disallows the existence of secure protocols for computing any "non-degenerate" functionality. The reason is that the program of each party (in a protocol for computing the desired functionality) must *either* depend only on the length of the party's input *or* obtain information on the counterpart's input length. In case information of the latter type is not implied by the output value, a secure protocol "cannot afford" to give it away.[8] By using adequate

---

[7] One may also consider the "non-verifiable" case (i.e., $V \equiv 1$), but in this case, nothing can prevent the second party from acting as if its input is different from its "actual" secret input.

[8] The situation is analogous to the definition of secure encryption, where it is required that the message length be polynomially related to the key length. Actually, things become even worse in the current setting because of the possible malicious behavior of parties.

padding, any "natural" functionality can be cast as one satisfying the equal-length convention.[9]

We now turn to the second convention. Certainly, the total running time of a secure two-party protocol for computing the functionality cannot be smaller than the time required to compute the functionality (in the ordinary sense). Arguing as in the case of input lengths, one can see that we need an a priori bound on the complexity of the functionality. A more general approach would be to let such a bound be given explicitly to both parties as an auxiliary input. In such a case, the protocol can be required to run for a time that is bounded by a fixed polynomial in this auxiliary parameter (i.e., the time-complexity bound of f). Assuming that a good upper bound of the complexity of f is time-constructible, and using standard padding techniques, we can reduce this general case to the special case discussed previously: That is, given a general functionality, g, and a time-bound $t : \mathbb{N} \to \mathbb{N}$, we introduce the functionality

$$f((x, 1^i), (y, 1^j)) \stackrel{\text{def}}{=} \begin{cases} g(x, y) \text{ if } i = j = t(|x|) = t(|y|) \\ (\bot, \bot) \text{ otherwise} \end{cases}$$

where $\bot$ is a special error symbol. Now, the problem of securely computing g reduces to the problem of securely computing f, which in turn is polynomial-time computable.

Finally, we turn to the third convention. Indeed, a more general convention would be to have an explicit security parameter that determines the security of the protocol. This general alternative is essential for allowing "secure" computation of finite functionalities (i.e., functionalities defined on finite input domains). We may accommodate the general convention using the special case, postulated previously, as follows. Suppose that we want to compute the functionality f, on input pair (x, y) with security (polynomial in) the parameter s. Then we introduce the functionality

$$f'((x, 1^s), (y, 1^s)) \stackrel{\text{def}}{=} f(x, y),$$

and consider secure protocols for computing f'. Indeed, this reduction corresponds to the realistic setting where the parties first agree on the desired level of security, and only then proceed to compute the function (using this level of security).

Partial functionalities. The first convention postulates that we are actually not considering mapping from the set of all pairs of bit strings, but rather mappings from a certain (general) set of pairs of strings (i.e., $\cup_{n \in \mathbb{N}} \{0, 1\}^n \times \{0, 1\}^n$). Taking this convention one step further, one may consider functionalities that are defined only over a set $R \subseteq \cup_{n \in \mathbb{N}} \{0, 1\}^n \times \{0, 1\}^n$. Clearly, securely computing such a functionality f' can be reduced to computing any of its extensions to $\cup_{n \in \mathbb{N}} \{0, 1\}^n \times \{0, 1\}^n$ (e.g., computing f such that $f(x, y) \stackrel{\text{def}}{=} f'(x, y)$ for $(x, y) \in R$ and $f(x, y) \stackrel{\text{def}}{=} (\bot, \bot)$ otherwise). With one exception (to be discussed explicitly), our exposition only refers to functionalities that are defined over the set of all pairs of strings of equal length.

---

[9] In the sequel, we sometimes take the liberty of presenting functionalities in a form that violates the equal-length convention (e.g., in the case of Oblivious Transfer). Indeed, these formulations can be easily modified to fit the equal-length convention.

An alternative set of conventions. An alternative way of addressing all three concerns discussed previously is to introduce an explicit security parameter, denoted n, and consider the following sequence of functionalities $\langle f^n \rangle_{n \in \mathbb{N}}$. Each f^n is defined over the set of all pairs of bit strings, but typically one considers only the value of f^n on strings of poly(n) length. In particular, for a functionality f as in our main conventions, one may consider $f^n(x, y) \stackrel{\text{def}}{=} f(x, y)$ if $|x| = |y| = n$ and $f^n(x, y) \stackrel{\text{def}}{=} (\bot, \bot)$ otherwise. When following the alternative convention, one typically postulates that there exists a poly(n)-time algorithm for computing f^n (for a generic n), and security is also evaluated with respect to the parameter n. We stress that in this case, the protocol's running time and its security guarantee are only related to the parameter n, and are independent of the length of the input.[10]

7.2.1.2. Computational Indistinguishability: Conventions and Notation

As in Definition 7.1.1, we will often talk of the computational indistinguishability of probability ensembles indexed by strings (as in Part 2 of Definition 3.2.7). Whenever we do so, we refer to computational indistinguishability by (non-uniform) families of polynomial-size circuits. That is, we say that the ensembles, $X \stackrel{\text{def}}{=} \{X_w\}_{w \in S}$ and $Y \stackrel{\text{def}}{=} \{Y_w\}_{w \in S}$, are computationally indistinguishable, denoted $X \stackrel{c}{\equiv} Y$, if the following holds:

For every polynomial-size circuit family, $\{C_n\}_{n \in \mathbb{N}}$, every positive polynomial $p(\cdot)$, every sufficiently large n, and every $w \in S \cap \{0, 1\}^n$,

$$|\Pr[C_n(X_w) = 1] - \Pr[C_n(Y_w) = 1]| < \frac{1}{p(n)} \qquad (7.5)$$

Note that an infinite sequence of w's may be incorporated in the family; hence, the definition is not strengthened by providing the circuit C_n with w as an additional input.[11]

Recall that computational indistinguishability is a relaxation of statistical indistinguishability, where here, the ensembles $X \stackrel{\text{def}}{=} \{X_w\}_{w \in S}$ and $Y \stackrel{\text{def}}{=} \{Y_w\}_{w \in S}$ are statistically indistinguishable, denoted $X \stackrel{s}{\equiv} Y$, if for every positive polynomial $p(\cdot)$, every sufficiently large n and every $w \in S \cap \{0, 1\}^n$,

$$\sum_{\alpha \in \{0,1\}^*} |\Pr[X_w = \alpha] - \Pr[Y_w = \alpha]| < \frac{1}{p(n)} \qquad (7.6)$$

In case the differences are all equal to zero, we say that the ensembles are identically distributed (and denote this by $X \equiv Y$).

---

[10] Consequently, the value of $f^n(x, y)$ may depend only on poly(n)-long prefixes of x and y.

[11] Indeed, here we capitalize on the non-uniformity of the class of potential distinguishers. In case one considers the class of uniform (probabilistic polynomial-time) distinguishers, it is necessary to provide these distinguishers with the distribution's index (i.e., w); see (Part 2 of) Definition 3.2.2.

7.2.1.3. Representation of Parties' Strategies

In Chapter 4, the parties' strategies for executing a given protocol (e.g., a proof system) were represented by interactive Turing machines. In this chapter, we prefer an equivalent formulation, which is less formal and less cumbersome. Specifically, the parties' strategies are presented as functions mapping the party's current view of the interactive execution to the next message to be sent. Recall that the party's view consists of its initial input, an auxiliary initial input (which is relevant only for modeling adversarial strategies), its random-tape, and the sequence of messages it has received so far. A strategy will be called feasible if it is implementable in probabilistic polynomial-time (i.e., the function associated with it is computable in polynomial-time).

As in Chapter 4, it is typically important to allow the adversaries to obtain (non-uniformly generated) auxiliary inputs (cf. Section 4.3.3). Recall that auxiliary inputs play a key role in guaranteeing that zero-knowledge is closed under sequential composition (see Section 4.3.4). Similarly, auxiliary inputs to the adversaries will play a key role in composition theorems for secure protocols, which are pivotal to our exposition and very important in general. Nevertheless, for the sake of simplicity, we often omit the auxiliary inputs from our notations and discussions (especially in places where they do not play an "active" role).

Recall that considering auxiliary inputs (as well as ordinary inputs) without introducing any restrictions (other than on their length) means that we are actually presenting a treatment in terms of non-uniform complexity. Thus, all our assumptions will refer to non-uniform complexity.

7.2.2. The Semi-Honest Model

Loosely speaking, a semi-honest party is one who follows the protocol properly with the exception that it keeps a record of all its intermediate computations. Actually, it suffices to keep the internal coin tosses and all messages received from the other party. In particular, a semi-honest party tosses fair coins (as instructed by its program) and sends messages according to its specified program (i.e., as a function of its input, outcome of coin tosses, and incoming messages). Note that a semi-honest party corresponds to the "honest verifier" in the definitions of zero-knowledge (cf. Section 4.3.1.7).

In addition to the methodological role of semi-honest parties in our exposition, they do constitute a model of independent interest. In particular, deviation from the specified program, which may be invoked inside a complex software application, is more difficult than merely recording the contents of some communication registers. Furthermore, records of these registers may be available through some standard activities of the operating system. Thus, whereas general malicious behavior may be infeasible for many users, semi-honest behavior may be feasible for them (and one cannot assume that they just behave in a totally honest way). Consequently, in many settings, one may assume that although the users may wish to cheat, they actually behave in a semi-honest way. (We mention that the "augmented semi-honest" model, introduced in Section 7.4.4.1, may be more appealing and adequate for more settings.)

In the following, we present two equivalent formulations of security in the semi-honest model. The first formulation capitalizes on the simplicity of the current model and defines security in it by a straightforward extension of the definition of zero-knowledge. The second formulation applies the general methodology outlined in Section 7.1.1. Indeed, both formulations follow the simulation paradigm, but the first does so by extending the definition of zero-knowledge, whereas the second does so by degenerating the general "real-vs.-ideal" methodology.

7.2.2.1. The Simple Formulation of Privacy

Loosely speaking, a protocol *privately computes* f if whatever can be obtained from a party's view of a (semi-honest) execution could be essentially obtained from the input and output available to that party. This extends the formulation of (honest-verifier) zero-knowledge by providing the simulator also with the (proper) output. The essence of the definition is captured by the simpler special case of deterministic functionalities, highlighted in the first item.

Definition 7.2.1 (privacy with respect to semi-honest behavior): *Let* $f : \{0, 1\}^* \times \{0, 1\}^* \to \{0, 1\}^* \times \{0, 1\}^*$ *be a functionality, and* $f_1(x, y)$ *(resp.,* $f_2(x, y)$*) denote the first (resp., second) element of* $f(x, y)$*. Let* Π *be a two-party protocol for computing* f.[12] *The* view *of the first (resp., second) party during an execution of* Π *on* (x, y)*, denoted* $\text{VIEW}_1^\Pi(x, y)$ *(resp.,* $\text{VIEW}_2^\Pi(x, y)$*), is* $(x, r, m_1, ..., m_t)$ *(resp.,* $(y, r, m_1, ..., m_t)$*), where* r *represents the outcome of the first (resp., second) party's internal coin tosses, and* m_i *represents the* i*-th message it has received. The* output *of the first (resp., second) party after an execution of* Π *on* (x, y)*, denoted* $\text{OUTPUT}_1^\Pi(x, y)$ *(resp.,* $\text{OUTPUT}_2^\Pi(x, y)$*), is implicit in the party's own view of the execution, and* $\text{OUTPUT}^\Pi(x, y) = (\text{OUTPUT}_1^\Pi(x, y), \text{OUTPUT}_2^\Pi(x, y))$.

- (deterministic case) *For a deterministic functionality* f*, we say that* Π privately computes f *if there exist probabilistic polynomial-time algorithms, denoted* S_1 *and* S_2*, such that*

$$\{S_1(x, f_1(x, y))\}_{x,y \in \{0,1\}^*} \stackrel{c}{\equiv} \{\text{VIEW}_1^\Pi(x, y)\}_{x,y \in \{0,1\}^*} \tag{7.7}$$

$$\{S_2(y, f_2(x, y))\}_{x,y \in \{0,1\}^*} \stackrel{c}{\equiv} \{\text{VIEW}_2^\Pi(x, y)\}_{x,y \in \{0,1\}^*} \tag{7.8}$$

where $|x| = |y|$*. (Recall that* $\stackrel{c}{\equiv}$ *denotes computational indistinguishability by (non-uniform) families of polynomial-size circuits.)*

- (general case) *We say that* Π privately computes f *if there exist probabilistic polynomial-time algorithms, denoted* S_1 *and* S_2*, such that*

$$\{(S_1(x, f_1(x, y)), f(x, y))\}_{x,y} \stackrel{c}{\equiv} \{(\text{VIEW}_1^\Pi(x, y), \text{OUTPUT}^\Pi(x, y))\}_{x,y} \tag{7.9}$$

$$\{(S_2(y, f_2(x, y)), f(x, y))\}_{x,y} \stackrel{c}{\equiv} \{(\text{VIEW}_2^\Pi(x, y), \text{OUTPUT}^\Pi(x, y))\}_{x,y} \tag{7.10}$$

---

[12] By saying that Π computes (rather than privately computes) f, we mean that the output distribution of the protocol (when played by honest or semi-honest parties) on input pair (x, y) is distributed identically to $f(x, y)$.

We stress that $\text{VIEW}_1^{\Pi}(x, y)$, $\text{VIEW}_2^{\Pi}(x, y)$, $\text{OUTPUT}_1^{\Pi}(x, y)$, and $\text{OUTPUT}_2^{\Pi}(x, y)$ are related random variables, defined as a function of the same random execution. In particular, $\text{OUTPUT}_i^{\Pi}(x, y)$ is fully determined by $\text{VIEW}_i^{\Pi}(x, y)$.

Consider first the deterministic case: Eq. (7.7) (resp., Eq. (7.8)) asserts that the view of the first (resp., second) party, on each possible pair of inputs, can be efficiently simulated based solely on its own input and output. Thus, all that this party learns from the full transcript of the proper execution is effectively implied by its own output from this execution (and its own input to it). In other words, all that the party learns from the (semi-honest) execution is essentially implied by the output itself. Next, note that the formulation for the deterministic case coincides with the general formulation as applied to deterministic functionalities (because, in any protocol Π that computes a deterministic functionality f, it must hold that $\text{OUTPUT}^{\Pi}(x, y) = f(x, y)$, for each pair of inputs (x, y)).[13]

In contrast to the deterministic case, augmenting the view of the semi-honest party by the output of the other party is essential when *randomized* functionalities are concerned. Note that in this case, for any protocol Π that computes a randomized functionality f, it does not necessarily hold that $\text{OUTPUT}^{\Pi}(x, y) = f(x, y)$, because each of the two objects is a random variable. Indeed, these two random variables must be identically (or similarly) distributed, but this does not suffice for asserting, for example, that Eq. (7.7) implies Eq. (7.9). Two disturbing counterexamples follow:

1. Consider the functionality $(1^n, 1^n) \mapsto (r, \lambda)$, where r is uniformly distributed in $\{0, 1\}^n$, and a protocol in which Party 1 uniformly selects $r \in \{0, 1\}^n$, sends it to Party 2, and outputs r. Clearly, this protocol computes the said functionality; alas, intuitively we should not consider this computation private (because Party 2 learns the output of Party 1 although Party 2 is not supposed to learn anything about that output). However, a simulator $S_2(1^n)$ that outputs a uniformly chosen $r \in \{0, 1\}^n$ satisfies Eq. (7.8) (but does not satisfy Eq. (7.10)).

   The point is that Eq. (7.9) and Eq. (7.10) refer to the relation between a party's output and the other party's view in the same execution of the protocol, and require that this relation be maintained in the simulation. As is vividly demonstrated in the aforementioned example, this relation is at the heart of the notion of security: We should simulate a view (of the semi-honest party) that fits the *actual* output of the honest party, and not merely simulate a view that fits the *distribution of the possible* output of the honest party.

2. Furthermore, Eq. (7.9) and Eq. (7.10) require that the party's simulated view fit its actual output (which is given to the simulator). To demonstrate the issue at hand, consider the foregoing functionality, and a protocol in which Party 1 uniformly selects $s \in \{0, 1\}^n$, and outputs $r \leftarrow F(s)$, where F is a one-way permutation. Again, this protocol computes the previous functionality, but it is not clear whether or not we may consider this computation private (because Party 1 learns the pre-image of its own output under F, something it could not have obtained if a trusted party were to

---

[13] Recall that the input pairs (x, y) serve as indices to the distributions in the two ensembles under consideration, and as such they are always given (or incorporated) in the potential distinguisher; see Section 7.2.1.2.

give it the output). Note that a simulator $S_1(1^n, r)$ that uniformly selects $s \in \{0, 1\}^n$ and outputs $(s, F(s))$ satisfies Eq. (7.7) (but does not satisfy Eq. (7.9)).

We comment that the current issue is less acute than the first one (i.e., the one raised in Item 1). Indeed, consider the following alternative to both Eq. (7.7) and Eq. (7.9):

$$\{(S_1(x, f_1(x, y)), f_2(x, y))\}_{x,y} \stackrel{c}{\equiv} \{(\text{VIEW}_1^\Pi(x, y), \text{OUTPUT}_2^\Pi(x, y))\}_{x,y} \quad (7.11)$$

Note that Eq. (7.11) addresses the problem raised in Item 1, but not the problem raised in the current item. *But is the current problem a real one?* Note that the only difference between Eq. (7.9) and Eq. (7.11) is that the former forces the simulated view to fit the output given to the simulator, whereas this is not guaranteed in Eq. (7.11). Indeed, in Eq. (7.11) the view simulated for Party 1 may not fit the output given to the simulator, but the simulated view does fit the output given to the honest Party 2. *Is the former fact of real importance or is it the case that all that matters is the relation of the simulated view to the honest party's view?* We are not sure, but (following a general principle) when in doubt, we prefer to be more careful and adopt the more stringent definition. Furthermore, the stronger definition simplifies the proof of the Composition Theorem for the semi-honest model (i.e., Theorem 7.3.3).

What about Auxiliary Inputs? Auxiliary inputs are implicit in Definition 7.2.1. They are represented by the fact that the definition asks for computational indistinguishability by non-uniform families of polynomial-size circuits (rather than computational indistinguishability by probabilistic polynomial-time algorithms). In other words, indistinguishability also holds with respect to probabilistic polynomial-time machines that obtain (non-uniform) auxiliary inputs.

Private Computation of Partial Functionalities. For functionalities that are defined only for inputs pairs in some set $R \subset \{0, 1\}^* \times \{0, 1\}^*$ (see Section 7.2.1.1), private computation is defined as in Definition 7.2.1, except that the ensembles are indexed by pairs in R.

7.2.2.2. The Alternative Formulation

It is instructive to recast the previous definition in terms of the general ("real-vs.-ideal") framework discussed in Section 7.1.1 (and used extensively in the case of arbitrary malicious behavior). In this framework, one first considers an ideal model in which the (two) parties are joined by a (third) trusted party, and the computation is performed via this trusted party. Next, one considers the real model in which a real (two-party) protocol is executed (and there exist no trusted third parties). A protocol in the real model is said to be *secure with respect to certain adversarial behavior* if the possible real executions with such an adversary can be "simulated" in the corresponding ideal model. The notion of simulation used here is different from the one used in Section 7.2.2.1: The simulation is *not of the view of one party via a traditional algorithm*, but rather *a simulation of the joint view of both parties by the execution of an ideal-model protocol*.

According to the general methodology (framework), we should first specify the ideal-model protocol. In the case of semi-honest adversaries, the ideal model consists of each party sending its input to the trusted party (via a secure private channel), and the third party computing the corresponding output pair and sending each output to the corresponding party. The only adversarial behavior allowed here is for one of the parties to determine its own output based on its input and the output it has received (from the trusted party).[14] This adversarial behavior represents the attempt to learn something from the party's view of a proper execution (which, in the ideal model, consists only of its local input and output). The other (i.e., honest) party merely outputs the output that it has received (from the trusted party).

Next, we turn to the real model. Here, there is a real two-party protocol and the adversarial behavior is restricted to be semi-honest. That is, the protocol is executed properly, but one party may produce its output based on (an arbitrary polynomial-time computation applied to) its view of the execution (as defined earlier). We stress that the only adversarial behavior allowed here is for one of the parties to determine its own output based on its entire view of the proper execution of the protocol.

Finally, we define security in the semi-honest model. A secure protocol for the real (semi-honest) model is such that for every feasible semi-honest behavior of one of the parties, we can simulate the joint outcome (of their real computation) by an execution in the ideal model (where also one party is semi-honest and the other is honest). Actually, we need to augment the definition to account for a priori information available to semi-honest parties before the protocol starts. This is done by supplying these parties with auxiliary inputs.

Note that in both (ideal and real) models, the (semi-honest) adversarial behavior takes place only after the proper execution of the corresponding protocol. Thus, in the ideal model, this behavior is captured by a computation applied to the local input–output pair, whereas in the real model, this behavior is captured by a computation applied to the party's local view (of the execution).

Definition 7.2.2 (security in the semi-honest model): *Let $f : \{0, 1\}^* \times \{0, 1\}^* \to \{0, 1\}^* \times \{0, 1\}^*$ be a functionality, where $f_1(x, y)$ (resp., $f_2(x, y)$) denotes the first (resp., second) element of $f(x, y)$, and let Π be a two-party protocol for computing f.*

- *Let $\overline{B} = (B_1, B_2)$ be a pair of probabilistic polynomial-time algorithms representing parties' strategies for the* ideal model. *Such a pair is* admissible *(in the ideal model) if for at least one B_i we have $B_i(u, v, z) = v$, where u denotes the party's local input, v its local output, and z its auxiliary input. The* joint execution of f under $\overline{B}$ in the ideal model *on input pair (x, y) and auxiliary input z, denoted* $\mathrm{IDEAL}_{f,\overline{B}(z)}(x, y)$, *is defined as $(f(x, y), B_1(x, f_1(x, y), z), B_2(y, f_2(x, y), z))$.*

(That is, if B_i is honest, then it just outputs the value $f_i(x, y)$ obtained from the trusted party, which is implicit in this definition. Thus, our peculiar choice to feed both parties with the same auxiliary input is immaterial, because the honest party ignores its auxiliary input.)

---

[14] We stress that unlike in the malicious model, discussed in Section 7.2.3, here the dishonest (or rather semi-honest) party is not allowed to modify its input (but must hand its actual input to the trusted party).

- Let $\overline{A} = (A_1, A_2)$ *be a pair of probabilistic polynomial-time algorithms representing parties' strategies for the* real model. *Such a pair is* admissible (*in the real model*) *if for at least one* $i \in \{1, 2\}$ *we have* $A_i(\text{view}, \text{aux}) = \text{out}$ *for every* view *and* aux, *where* out *is the output implicit in* view. *The* joint execution of Π under $\overline{A}$ in the real model *on input pair* (x, y) *and auxiliary input* z, *denoted* $\text{REAL}_{\Pi, \overline{A}(z)}(x, y)$, *is defined as* $(\text{OUTPUT}^{\Pi}(x, y), A_1(\text{VIEW}_1^{\Pi}(x, y), z), A_2(\text{VIEW}_2^{\Pi}(x, y), z))$, *where* $\text{OUTPUT}^{\Pi}(x, y)$ *and the* $\text{VIEW}_i^{\Pi}(x, y)$'s *refer to the same execution and are defined as in Definition 7.2.1.*

(Again, if A_i is honest, then it just outputs the value $f_i(x, y)$ obtained from the execution of Π, and we may feed both parties with the same auxiliary input.)

Protocol Π *is said to* securely compute f in the semi-honest model (secure with respect to f and semi-honest behavior) *if for every probabilistic polynomial-time pair of algorithms* $\overline{A} = (A_1, A_2)$ *that is admissible for the real model, there exists a probabilistic polynomial-time pair of algorithms* $\overline{B} = (B_1, B_2)$ *that is admissible for the ideal model such that*

$$\{\text{IDEAL}_{f, \overline{B}(z)}(x, y)\}_{x,y,z} \stackrel{c}{\equiv} \{\text{REAL}_{\Pi, \overline{A}(z)}(x, y)\}_{x,y,z} \tag{7.12}$$

where $x, y, z \in \{0, 1\}^*$ *such that* $|x| = |y|$ *and* $|z| = \text{poly}(|x|)$.

Observe that the definition of the joint execution in the real model prohibits both parties (honest and semi-honest) from deviating from the strategies specified by Π. The difference between honest and semi-honest parties is merely in their actions on the corresponding local views of the execution: An honest party outputs only the output part of the view (as specified by Π), whereas a semi-honest party may output an arbitrary (feasibly computable) function of the view. Note that including the output $f(x, y)$ (resp., $\text{OUTPUT}^{\Pi}(x, y)$) in $\text{IDEAL}_{f, \overline{B}(z)}(x, y)$ (resp., in $\text{REAL}_{\Pi, \overline{A}(z)}(x, y)$) is meaningful only in the case of a randomized functionality f, and is done in order to match the formulation in Definition 7.2.1. We stress that the issue is the inclusion of the output of the dishonest party (see Item 2 in the discussion that follows Definition 7.2.1).

We comment that, as will become clear in the proof of Proposition 7.2.3, omitting the auxiliary input does not weaken Definition 7.2.2. Intuitively, since the adversary is passive, the only affect of the auxiliary input is that it appears as part of the adversary's view. However, since Eq. (7.12) refers to the non-uniform formulation of computational indistinguishability, augmenting the ensembles by auxiliary inputs has no affect.

7.2.2.3. Equivalence of the Two Formulations

It is not hard to see that Definitions 7.2.1 and 7.2.2 are equivalent. That is,

Proposition 7.2.3: *Let* Π *be a protocol for computing* f. *Then,* Π *privately computes* f *if and only if* Π *securely computes* f *in the semi-honest model.*

Proof Sketch: We first show that Definition 7.2.2 implies Definition 7.2.1. Suppose that Π securely computes f in the semi-honest model (i.e., satisfies Definition 7.2.2).

Without loss of generality, we show how to simulate the first party's view. Toward this end, we define the following admissible pair $\overline{A} = (A_1, A_2)$ for the real model: A_1 is merely the identity transformation (i.e., it outputs the view given to it), whereas A_2 (which represents an honest strategy for Party 2) produces an output as determined by the view given to it. We stress that we consider an adversary A_1 that does not get an auxiliary input (or alternatively ignores it). Furthermore, the adversary merely outputs the view given to it (and leaves the possible processing of this view to the potential distinguisher). Let $\overline{B} = (B_1, B_2)$ be the ideal-model adversary guaranteed by Definition 7.2.2. We claim that (using) B_1 (in the role of S_1) satisfies Eq. (7.9), rather than only Eq. (7.7). Loosely speaking, the claim holds because Definition 7.2.2 guarantees that the relation between the view of Party 1 and the outputs of both parties in a real execution is preserved in the ideal model. Specifically, since A_1 is a passive adversary (and Π computes f), the output of Party 1 in a real execution equals the value that is determined in the view (of Party 1), which in turn fits the functionality. Now, Definition 7.2.2 implies that the same relation between the (simulated) view of Party 1 and the outputs must hold in the ideal model. It follows that using B_1 in role of S_1 guarantees that the simulated view fits the output given to the simulator (as well as the output not given to it).

We now show that Definition 7.2.1 implies Definition 7.2.2. Suppose that Π privately computes f, and let S_1 and S_2 be as guaranteed in Definition 7.2.1. Let $\overline{A} = (A_1, A_2)$ be an admissible pair for the real-model adversaries. Without loss of generality, we assume that A_2 merely maps the view (of the second party) to the corresponding output (i.e., $f_2(x, y)$); that is, Party 2 is honest (and Party 1 is semi-honest). Then, we define an ideal-model pair $\overline{B} = (B_1, B_2)$ such that $B_1(x, v, z) \stackrel{\text{def}}{=} A_1(S_1(x, v), z)$ and $B_2(y, v, z) \stackrel{\text{def}}{=} v$. (Note that $\overline{B}$ is indeed admissible with respect to the ideal model.) The following holds (for any infinite sequence of (x, y, z)'s):

$$
\begin{aligned}
\text{REAL}_{\Pi, \overline{A}(z)}(x, y) &= (\text{OUTPUT}^\Pi(x, y), A_1(\text{VIEW}_1^\Pi(x, y), z), A_2(\text{VIEW}_2^\Pi(x, y), z)) \\
&= (\text{OUTPUT}^\Pi(x, y), A_1(\text{VIEW}_1^\Pi(x, y), z), \text{OUTPUT}_2^\Pi(x, y)) \\
&\stackrel{\text{c}}{\equiv} (f(x, y), A_1(S_1(x, f_1(x, y)), z), f_2(x, y)) \\
&= (f(x, y), B_1(x, f_1(x, y), z), B_2(y, f_2(x, y), z)) \\
&= \text{IDEAL}_{f, \overline{B}(z)}(x, y)
\end{aligned}
$$

where the computational indistinguishability (i.e., $\stackrel{\text{c}}{\equiv}$) is due to the guarantee regarding S_1 (in its general form); that is, Eq. (7.9). Indeed, the latter only guarantees $(\text{VIEW}_1^\Pi(x, y), \text{OUTPUT}^\Pi(x, y)) \stackrel{\text{c}}{\equiv} (S_1(x, f_1(x, y)), f(x, y))$, but by incorporating A_1 and z in the potential distinguisher, the soft-equality follows. ∎

Conclusion. This proof demonstrates that the alternative formulation of Definition 7.2.2 is merely a cumbersome form of the simpler Definition 7.2.1. We stress that the reason we have presented the cumbersome form is the fact that it follows the general framework of definitions of security that is used for the malicious adversarial behavior. In the rest of this chapter, whenever we deal with the semi-honest model (for two-party computation), we will use Definition 7.2.1. Furthermore, since much of the text focuses on deterministic functionalities, we will be able to use the simpler case of Definition 7.2.1.

7.2.3. The Malicious Model

We now turn to consider arbitrary feasible deviation from the specified program of a two-party protocol. A few preliminary comments are in place. Firstly, there is no way to force parties to participate in the protocol. That is, a possible malicious behavior may consist of not starting the execution at all, or, more generally, suspending (or aborting) the execution at any desired point in time. In particular, a party can abort at the first moment when it obtains the desired result of the computed functionality. We stress that our model of communication does not allow conditioning of the receipt of a message by one party on the *concurrent* sending of a *proper* message by this party. Thus, no two-party protocol can prevent one of the parties from *aborting when obtaining the desired result* and before its counterpart also obtains the desired result. In other words, it can be shown that perfect fairness – in the sense of both parties obtaining the outcome of the computation concurrently – is not achievable in a two-party computation. We thus give up on such fairness altogether. (We comment that partial fairness is achievable; see Section 7.7.1.1).

Secondly, observe that when considering malicious adversaries, it is not clear what their *input to the protocol* is. That is, a malicious party can enter the protocol with arbitrary input, which may not equal its "true" local input. There is no way for a protocol to tell the "true" local input from the one claimed by a party (or, in other words, to prevent a malicious party from modifying its input). (We stress that these phenomena did not occur in the semi-honest model, for the obvious reason that parties were postulated not to deviate from the protocol.)

In view of this discussion, there are three things we cannot hope to avoid (no matter what protocol we use):

1. Parties refusing to participate in the protocol (when the protocol is first invoked).
2. Parties substituting their local input (and entering the protocol with an input other than the one provided to them).
3. Parties aborting the protocol prematurely (e.g., before sending their last message).

Thus, we shall consider a two-party protocol to be secure if the adversary's behavior in it is essentially restricted to these three actions. Following the real-vs.-ideal methodology (of Section 7.1.1), this means that we should define an ideal model that corresponds to these possible actions, and define security such that the execution of a secure protocol in the real model can be simulated by the ideal model.

7.2.3.1. The Actual Definition

We start with a straightforward implementation of the previous discussion. An alternative approach, which is simpler but partial, is presented in Section 7.2.3.2. (Specifically, the alternative approach is directly applicable only to single-output functionalities, in which case the complications introduced by aborting do not arise. The interested reader may proceed directly to Section 7.2.3.2, which is mostly self-contained.)

The Ideal Model. We first translate the previous discussion into a definition of an ideal model. That is, we will allow in the ideal model whatever cannot possibly be prevented in any real execution. An alternative way of looking at things is that we assume that the the two parties have at their disposal a trusted third party, but even such a party cannot prevent certain malicious behavior. Specifically, we allow a malicious party in the ideal model to refuse to participate in the protocol or to substitute its local input. (Clearly, neither can be prevented by a trusted third party.) In addition, we postulate that the *first* party has the option of "stopping" the trusted party just after obtaining its part of the output, and before the trusted party sends the other output part to the second party. Such an option is not given to the second party.[15] Thus, an execution in the ideal model proceeds as follows (where all actions of both the honest and the malicious parties must be feasible to implement):

Inputs: Each party obtains an input, denoted u.

Sending inputs to the trusted party: An honest party always sends u to the trusted party. A malicious party may, depending on u (as well as on an auxiliary input and its coin tosses), either abort or send some $u' \in \{0, 1\}^{|u|}$ to the trusted party.[16]

The trusted party answers the first party: In case it has obtained an input pair, (x, y), the trusted party (for computing f) first replies to the first party with $f_1(x, y)$. Otherwise (i.e., in case it receives only one input), the trusted party replies to both parties with a special symbol, denoted $\perp$.

The trusted party answers the second party: In case the first party is malicious, it may, depending on its input *and the trusted party's answer,* decide to stop the trusted party. In this case, the trusted party sends $\perp$ to the second party. Otherwise (i.e., if not stopped), the trusted party sends $f_2(x, y)$ to the second party.

Outputs: An honest party always outputs the message it has obtained from the trusted party. A malicious party may output an arbitrary (polynomial-time computable) function of its initial input (auxiliary input and random-tape) and the message it has obtained from the trusted party.

In fact, without loss of generality, we may assume that both parties send inputs to the trusted party (rather than allowing the malicious party not to enter the protocol). This assumption can be justified by letting the trusted party use some default value (or a

---

[15] This asymmetry is due to the non-concurrent nature of communication in the model. Since we postulate that the trusted party sends the answer first to the first party, the first party (but not the second) has the option of stopping the trust party *after* obtaining its part of the output. The second party can only stop the trust party before obtaining its output, but this is the same as refusing to participate. See further discussion at the end of the current subsection.

[16] We comment that restricting the ideal-model adversary (to replacing u by u' of the same length) only strengthens the definition of security. This restriction is essential to our formulation, because (by our convention) the functionality f is defined only for pairs of strings of equal length.

special abort symbol) in case it does not get an input from one of the parties.[17] Thus, the ideal model (computation) is captured by the following definition, where the algorithms B_1 and B_2 represent all possible actions in the model.[18] In particular, $B_1(x, z, r)$ (resp., $B_2(y, z, r)$) represents the input handed to the trusted party by Party 1 (resp., Party 2) having local input x (resp., y) and auxiliary input z and using random-tape r. Indeed, if Party 1 (resp., Party 2) is honest, then $B_1(x, z, r) = x$ (resp., $B_2(y, z, r) = y$). Likewise, $B_1(x, z, r, v) = \bot$ represents a decision of Party 1 to stop the trusted party, on input x (auxiliary input z and random-tape r), after receiving the (output) value v from the trusted party. In this case, $B_1(x, z, r, v, \bot)$ represents the party's local output. Otherwise (i.e., $B_1(x, z, r, v) \neq \bot$), we let $B_1(x, z, r, v)$ itself represent the party's local output. The local output of Party 2 is always represented by $B_2(y, z, r, v)$, where y is the party's local input (z is the auxiliary input, r is the random-tape) and v is the value received from the trusted party. Indeed, if Party 1 (resp., Party 2) is honest, then $B_1(x, z, r, v) = v$ (resp., $B_2(y, z, r, v) = v$).

Definition 7.2.4 (malicious adversaries, the ideal model): *Let $f : \{0, 1\}^* \times \{0, 1\}^* \to \{0, 1\}^* \times \{0, 1\}^*$ be a functionality, where $f_1(x, y)$ (resp., $f_2(x, y)$) denotes the first (resp., second) element of $f(x, y)$. Let $\overline{B} = (B_1, B_2)$ be a pair of probabilistic polynomial-time algorithms representing strategies in the ideal model. Such a pair is* admissible *(in the ideal malicious model) if for at least one $i \in \{1, 2\}$, called* honest, *we have $B_i(u, z, r) = u$ and $B_i(u, z, r, v) = v$, for every possible value of u, z, r, and v. Furthermore, $|B_i(u, z, r)| = |u|$ must hold for both i's. The* joint execution of *f under $\overline{B}$ in the ideal model (on input pair (x, y) and auxiliary input z), denoted* IDEAL$_{f, \overline{B}(z)}(x, y)$, *is defined by uniformly selecting a random-tape r for the adversary, and letting* IDEAL$_{f, \overline{B}(z)}(x, y) \stackrel{\text{def}}{=} \Upsilon(x, y, z, r)$, *where $\Upsilon(x, y, z, r)$ is defined as follows:*

- *In case Party 1 is honest, $\Upsilon(x, y, z, r)$ equals*

$$(f_1(x, y'),\ B_2(y, z, r, f_2(x, y'))),\ \text{where } y' \stackrel{\text{def}}{=} B_2(y, z, r). \tag{7.13}$$

- *In case Party 2 is honest, $\Upsilon(x, y, z, r)$ equals*

$$(B_1(x, z, r, f_1(x', y), \bot),\ \bot)\quad \text{if } B_1(x, z, r, f_1(x', y)) = \bot \tag{7.14}$$

$$(B_1(x, z, r, f_1(x', y)),\ f_2(x', y))\quad \text{otherwise} \tag{7.15}$$

where, in both cases, $x' \stackrel{\text{def}}{=} B_1(x, z, r)$.

---

[17] Both options (i.e., default value or a special abort symbol) are useful, and the choice depends on the protocol designer. In case a special abort symbol is used, the functionality should be modified accordingly, such that if one of the inputs equals the special abort symbol, then the output is a special abort symbol.

[18] As in Definition 7.2.2, we make the peculiar choice of feeding both B_i's with the same auxiliary input z (and the same random-tape r). However, again, the honest strategy ignores this auxiliary input, which is only used by the malicious strategy. Note that unlike in previous definitions, we make the random-tape (of the adversary) explicit in the notation, the reason being that the same strategy is used to describe two different actions of the adversary (rather than a single action, as in Definition 7.2.2). Since these actions may be probabilistically related, it is important that they be determined based on the same random-tape.

Eq. (7.14) and Eq. (7.15) refer to the case in which Party 2 is honest (and Party 1 may be malicious). Specifically, Eq. (7.14) represents the sub-case where Party 1 invokes the trusted party with a possibly substituted input, denoted $B_1(x, z, r)$, and aborts while stopping the trusted party right after obtaining the output, $f_1(B_1(x, z, r), y)$. In this sub-case, Party 2 obtains no output (from the trusted party). Eq. (7.15) represents the sub-case where Party 1 invokes the trusted party with a possibly substituted input, and allows the trusted party to answer Party 2. In this sub-case, Party 2 obtains and outputs $f_2(B_1(x, z, r), y)$. In both sub-cases, the trusted party computes $f(B_1(x, z, r), y)$, and Party 1 outputs a string that depends on both x, z, r and $f_1(B_1(x, z, r), y)$. Likewise, Eq. (7.13) represents possible malicious behavior of Party 2; however, in accordance with the previous discussion, the trusted party first supplies output to Party 1, and so Party 2 does not have a "real" aborting option (analogous to Eq. (7.14)).

Execution in the Real Model. We next consider the real model in which a real (two-party) protocol is executed (and there exist no trusted third parties). In this case, a malicious party may follow an arbitrary feasible strategy, that is, any strategy implementable by a probabilistic polynomial-time algorithm (which gets an auxiliary input). In particular, the malicious party may abort the execution at any point in time, and when this happens prematurely, the other party is left with no output. In analogy to the ideal case, we use algorithms to define strategies in a protocol, where these strategies (or algorithms implementing them) *map partial execution histories to the next message.*

Definition 7.2.5 (malicious adversaries, the real model): *Let f be as in Definition 7.2.4, and Π be a two-party protocol for computing f. Let $\overline{A} = (A_1, A_2)$ be a pair of probabilistic polynomial-time algorithms representing strategies in the real model. Such a pair is* admissible *(with respect to Π) (for the real malicious model) if at least one A_i coincides with the strategy specified by Π. (In particular, this A_i ignores the auxiliary input.) The* joint execution of Π under $\overline{A}$ in the real model *(on input pair (x, y) and auxiliary input z), denoted $\text{REAL}_{\Pi, \overline{A}(z)}(x, y)$, is defined as the output pair resulting from the interaction between $A_1(x, z)$ and $A_2(y, z)$. (Recall that the honest A_i ignores the auxiliary input z, and so our peculiar choice of providing both A_i's with the same z is immaterial.)*

In some places (in Section 7.4), we will assume that the algorithms representing the real-model adversaries (i.e., the algorithm A_i that does not follow Π) are deterministic. This is justified by observing that one may just (consider and) fix the "best" possible choice of coins for a randomized adversary and incorporate this choice in the auxiliary input of a deterministic adversary (cf. Section 1.3.3 of Volume 1).

Security as Emulation of Real Execution in the Ideal Model. Having defined the ideal and real models, we obtain the corresponding definition of security. Loosely speaking, the definition asserts that a secure two-party protocol (in the real model) emulates the ideal model (in which a trusted party exists). This is formulated by saying that admissible adversaries in the ideal model are able to simulate (in the ideal model) the execution of a secure real-model protocol under any admissible adversaries.

Definition 7.2.6 (security in the malicious model): *Let f and Π be as in Definition 7.2.5. Protocol Π is said to* securely compute f *(in the malicious model) if for every probabilistic polynomial-time pair of algorithms $\overline{A} = (A_1, A_2)$ that is admissible for the* real *model (of Definition 7.2.5), there exists a probabilistic polynomial-time pair of algorithms $\overline{B} = (B_1, B_2)$ that is admissible for the* ideal *model (of Definition 7.2.4) such that*

$$\{\mathrm{IDEAL}_{f,\overline{B}(z)}(x, y)\}_{x,y,z} \stackrel{\mathrm{c}}{\equiv} \{\mathrm{REAL}_{\Pi,\overline{A}(z)}(x, y)\}_{x,y,z}$$

where $x, y, z \in \{0, 1\}^*$ such that $|x| = |y|$ and $|z| = \mathrm{poly}(|x|)$. (Recall that $\stackrel{\mathrm{c}}{\equiv}$ denotes computational indistinguishability by (non-uniform) families of polynomial-size circuits.) When the context is clear, we sometimes refer to Π as a secure implementation *of f.*

One important property that Definition 7.2.6 implies is privacy *with respect to malicious adversaries.* That is, all that an adversary can learn by participating in the protocol, while using an arbitrary (feasible) strategy, can be essentially inferred from the corresponding output alone. Another property that is implied by Definition 7.2.6 is correctness, which means that the output of the honest party must be consistent with an input pair in which the element corresponding to the honest party equals the party's actual input. Furthermore, the element corresponding to the adversary must be chosen obliviously of the honest party's input. We stress that both properties are easily implied by Definition 7.2.6, but the latter is not implied by combining the two properties. For further discussion, see Exercise 3.

We wish to highlight another property that is implied by Definition 7.2.6: Loosely speaking, this definition implies that at the end of the (real) execution of a secure protocol, each party "knows" the value of the corresponding input for which the output is obtained.[19] That is, when a malicious Party 1 obtains the output v, it knows an x' (which does not necessarily equal to its initial local input x) such that $v = f_1(x', y)$ for some y (i.e., the local input of the honest Party 2). This "knowledge" is implied by the equivalence to the ideal model, in which the party explicitly hands the (possibly modified) input to the trusted party. For example, say Party 1 uses the malicious strategy A_1. Then the output values (in $\mathrm{REAL}_{\Pi,\overline{A}}(x, y)$) correspond to the input pair $(B_1(x), y)$, where B_1 is the ideal-model adversary derived from the real-model adversarial strategy A_1.

We comment that although Definition 7.2.6 does not talk about transforming admissible $\overline{A}$'s to admissible $\overline{B}$'s, we will often use such phrases. Furthermore, although the definition does not even guarantee that such a transformation is effective (i.e., computable), the transformations used in this work are all polynomial-time computable. Moreover, these transformations consist of generic programs for B_i that use

---

[19] One concrete case where this property plays a central role is in the input-commitment functionality (of Section 7.4.3.6). Specifically, if a secure implementation of this functionality is first used in order to let Party 1 commit to its input, and next, Party 2 uses it in order to commit to its own input, then this property implies that Party 2 cannot just copy the "commitment" made by Party 1 (unless Party 2 knows the input of Party 1).

subroutine (or oracle) calls to the corresponding A_i. Consequently, we sometimes describe these transformations without referring to the auxiliary input, and the description can be completed by having B_i pass its auxiliary input to A_i (in each of its invocations).

Further Discussion. As explained earlier, it is unavoidable that one party can abort the real execution after it (fully) learns its output but before the other party (fully) learns its own output. However, the convention by which this ability is designated to Party 1 (rather than to Party 2) is quite arbitrary. More general conventions (and corresponding definitions of security) may be more appealing, but the current one seems simplest and suffices for the rest of our exposition.[20] An unrelated is issue is that unlike in the treatment of the semi-honest model (cf. Definitions 7.2.1 and 7.2.2), we did not explicitly include the output $f(x, y)$ (resp., OUTPUT$^\Pi(x, y)$) in IDEAL$_{f, \overline{B}(z)}(x, y)$ (resp., in REAL$_{\Pi, \overline{A}(z)}(x, y)$). Note that such an augmentation would not make much sense in the current (malicious) context. Furthermore, recall that this issue is meaningful only in the case of a randomized functionality f, and that its concrete motivation was to simplify the proof of the composition theorem for the semi-honest model (which is irrelevant here). Finally, referring to a third unrelated issue, we comment that the definitional treatment can be extended to partial functionalities.

Remark 7.2.7 (security for partial functionalities): For functionalities that are defined only for input pairs in some set $R \subset \{0, 1\}^* \times \{0, 1\}^*$ (see Section 7.2.1.1), security is defined as in Definition 7.2.6 with the following two exceptions:

1. *When defining the ideal model, the adversary is allowed to modify its input arbitrarily as long as the modified input pair is in R.*
2. *The ensembles considered are indexed by triplets (x, y, z) that satisfy $(x, y) \in R$ as well as $|x| = |y|$ and $|z| = \mathrm{poly}(|x|)$.*

7.2.3.2. An Alternative Approach

A simpler definition of security may be used in the special case of single-output functionalities (i.e., functionalities in which only one party obtains an output). Assume, without loss of generality, that only the first party obtains an output (from the functionality f); that is, $f(x, y) = (f_1(x, y), \lambda)$.[21] In this case, we need not be concerned

---

[20] One alternative convention is to associate with each protocol a binary value indicating which of the two parties is allowed to meaningfully abort. This convention yields a more general (or less restrictive) definition of security, where Definition 7.2.6 is obtained as a special case (in which this value is always required to equal 1). Yet the protocols presented in this work are shown to be secure under the more restrictive definition.

[21] Actually, the treatment of the case in which only the second party obtains an output (i.e., $f(x, y) = (\lambda, f_2(x, y))$) is slightly different. However, also in this case, the event in which the first party aborts after obtaining its (empty) output can be discarded. In this case, this event (of obtaining an a priori fixed output) is essentially equivalent to the party aborting before obtaining output, which in turn can be viewed as replacing its input by a special symbol.

with what happens after the first party obtains its output (because the second party has no output), and thus the complications arising from the issue of aborting the execution can be eliminated. Consequently, computation in the ideal model takes the following form:

Inputs: Each party obtains an input, denoted u.

Sending inputs to the trusted party: An honest party always sends u to the trusted party. A malicious party may, depending on u (as well as on an auxiliary input and its coin tosses), either abort or send some $u' \in \{0, 1\}^{|u|}$ to the trusted party. However, without loss of generality, aborting at this stage may be treated as supplying the trusted party with a special symbol.

The answer of the trusted party: Upon obtaining an input pair, (x, y), the trusted party (for computing f) replies to the first party with $f_1(x, y)$. Without loss of generality, the trusted party only answers the first party, because the second party has no output (or, alternatively, should always output λ).

Outputs: An honest party always outputs the message it has obtained from the trusted party. A malicious party may output an arbitrary (polynomial-time computable) function of its initial input (auxiliary input and its coin tosses) and the message it has obtained from the trusted party.

Thus, the ideal model (computation) is captured by the following definition, where the algorithms B_1 and B_2 represent all possible actions in the model. In particular, $B_1(x, z, r)$ (resp., $B_2(y, z, r)$) represents the input handed to the trusted party by Party 1 (resp., Party 2) having local input x (resp., y), auxiliary input z, and random-tape r. Indeed, if Party 1 (resp., Party 2) is honest, then $B_1(x, z, r) = x$ (resp., $B_2(y, z, r) = y$). Likewise, $B_1(x, z, r, v)$ represents the output of Party 1, when having local input x (auxiliary input z and random-tape r) and receiving the value v from the trusted party, whereas the output of Party 2 is represented by $B_2(y, z, r, \lambda)$. Indeed, if Party 1 (resp., Party 2) is honest, then $B_1(x, z, r, v) = v$ (resp., $B_2(y, z, r, \lambda) = \lambda$).

Definition 7.2.8 (the ideal model): *Let $f : \{0, 1\}^* \times \{0, 1\}^* \to \{0, 1\}^* \times \{\lambda\}$ be a single-output functionality such that $f(x, y) = (f_1(x, y), \lambda)$. Let $\overline{B} = (B_1, B_2)$ be a pair of probabilistic polynomial-time algorithms representing strategies in the ideal model.* Such a pair is admissible *(in the ideal malicious model)* if for at least one $i \in \{1, 2\}$, called honest, we have $B_i(u, z, r) = u$ and $B_i(u, z, r, v) = v$ for all possible u, z, r, and v. Furthermore, $|B_i(u, z, r)| = |u|$ must hold for both i's. The joint execution of f under $\overline{B}$ in the ideal model *(on input pair (x, y) and auxiliary input z), denoted* $\text{IDEAL}_{f, \overline{B}(z)}(x, y)$, *is defined by uniformly selecting a random-tape r for the adversary, and letting* $\text{IDEAL}_{f, \overline{B}(z)}(x, y) \stackrel{\text{def}}{=} \Upsilon(x, y, z, r)$, *where*

$$\Upsilon(x, y, z, r) \stackrel{\text{def}}{=} (B_1(x, z, r, f_1(B_1(x, z, r), B_2(y, z, r))), B_2(y, z, r, \lambda)) \quad (7.16)$$

That is, $\text{IDEAL}_{f,\overline{B}(z)}(x, y) \overset{\text{def}}{=} (B_1(x, z, r, v), B_2(y, z, r, \lambda))$, *where* $v \leftarrow f_1(B_1(x, z, r),$ $B_2(y, z, r))$ *and* r *is uniformly distributed among the set of strings of adequate length.*[22]

We next consider the real model in which a real (two-party) protocol is executed (and there exist no trusted third parties). In this case, a malicious party may follow an arbitrary feasible strategy, that is, any strategy implementable by a probabilistic polynomial-time algorithm. The definition is identical to Definition 7.2.5, and is reproduced here (for the reader's convenience).

Definition 7.2.9 (the real model): *Let* f *be as in Definition 7.2.8, and* Π *be a two-party protocol for computing* f. *Let* $\overline{A} = (A_1, A_2)$ *be a pair of probabilistic polynomial-time algorithms representing strategies in the real model. Such a pair is* admissible (with respect to Π) *(for the real malicious model) if at least one* A_i *coincides with the strategy specified by* Π. *The* joint execution of Π under $\overline{A}$ in the real model *(on input pair* (x, y) *and auxiliary input* z*), denoted* $\text{REAL}_{\Pi,\overline{A}(z)}(x, y)$, *is defined as the output pair resulting from the interaction between* $A_1(x, z)$ *and* $A_2(y, z)$. *(Note that the honest* A_i *ignores the auxiliary input* z.*)*

Having defined the ideal and real models, we obtain the corresponding definition of security. Loosely speaking, the definition asserts that a secure two-party protocol (in the real model) emulates the ideal model (in which a trusted party exists). This is formulated by saying that admissible adversaries in the ideal model are able to simulate (in the ideal model) the execution of a secure real-model protocol under any admissible adversaries. The definition is analogous to Definition 7.2.6.

Definition 7.2.10 (security): *Let* f *and* Π *be as in Definition 7.2.9. Protocol* Π *is said to* securely compute f *(in the malicious model) if for every probabilistic polynomial-time pair of algorithms* $\overline{A} = (A_1, A_2)$ *that is admissible for the* real *model (of Definition 7.2.9), there exists a probabilistic polynomial-time pair of algorithms* $\overline{B} = (B_1, B_2)$ *that is admissible for the* ideal *model (of Definition 7.2.8) such that*

$$\{\text{IDEAL}_{f,\overline{B}(z)}(x, y)\}_{x,y,z} \overset{\text{c}}{\equiv} \{\text{REAL}_{\Pi,\overline{A}(z)}(x, y)\}_{x,y,z}$$

where $x, y, z \in \{0, 1\}^*$ *such that* $|x| = |y|$ *and* $|z| = \text{poly}(|x|)$.

Clearly, as far as single-output functionalities are concerned, Definitions 7.2.6 and 7.2.10 are equivalent (because in this case, the ideal-model definitions coincide). It is also clear from the previous discussions that the two definitions are not equivalent in general (i.e., with respect to two-output functionalities). Still, it is possible to securely implement any (two-output) functionality by using a protocol for securely computing a (related) single-output functionality. That is, the ability to construct secure protocols under Definition 7.2.10 yields the ability to construct secure protocols under Definition 7.2.6.

---

[22] Recall that if B_i is honest, then it passes its input to the trusted party and outputs its response. Thus, our peculiar choice to feed both parties with the same auxiliary input and same random-tape is immaterial, because the honest party ignores both.

Proposition 7.2.11: *Suppose that there exist one-way functions and that any single-output functionality can be securely computed as per Definition 7.2.10. Then any functionality can be securely computed as per Definition 7.2.6.*

Proof Sketch: Suppose that the parties wish to securely compute the (two-output) functionality $(x, y) \mapsto (f_1(x, y), f_2(x, y))$. The first idea that comes to mind is to first let the parties (securely) compute the first output (i.e., by securely computing $(x, y) \mapsto (f_1(x, y), \lambda)$) and next let them (securely) compute the second output (i.e., by securely computing $(x, y) \mapsto (\lambda, f_2(x, y)))$. This solution is insecure, because a malicious party may enter different inputs in the two invocations (not to mention that the approach will fail for randomized functionalities even if both parties are honest). Instead, we are going to let the first party obtain its output as well as an (authenticated and) encrypted version of the second party's output, which it will send to the second party (which will be able to decrypt and verify the value). That is, we will use private-key encryption and authentication schemes, which exist under the first hypothesis, as follows. First, the second party generates an encryption/decryption-key, denoted e, and a signing/verification-key, denoted s. Next, the two parties securely compute the randomized functionality $((x, (y, e, s)) \mapsto ((f_1(x, y), c, t), \lambda)$, where c is the ciphertext obtained by encrypting the plaintext $v = f_2(x, y)$ under the encryption-key e, and t is an authentication-tag of c under the signing-key s. Finally, the first party sends (c, t) to the second party, which verifies that c is properly signed and (if so) recovers $f_2(x, y)$ from it. ∎

7.3.* Privately Computing (Two-Party) Functionalities

Recall that our ultimate goal is to design (two-party) protocols that withstand any feasible adversarial behavior. We proceed in two steps. In this section, we show how to construct protocols for privately computing any functionality, that is, protocols that are secure with respect to the semi-honest model. In Section 7.4, we will show how to compile these protocols into ones that are secure also in the malicious model.

Throughout the current section, we assume that the desired (two-party) functionality (along with the desired input length) is represented by a Boolean circuit. We show how to transform this circuit into a two-party protocol for evaluating the circuit on a given pair of local inputs. The transformation follows the outline provided in in Section 7.1.3.3.[23]

The circuit-evaluation protocol, to be presented in Section 7.3.4, scans the circuit from the input wires to the output wires, processing a single gate in each *basic step*. When entering each basic step, the parties hold *shares* of the values of the input wires of the gate, and when the step is completed, they hold shares of the output wire of the gate. The shares held by each party yield no information about the corresponding values, but combining the two shares of any value allows for reconstructing the value. Each basic step is performed without yielding any additional information; that is, the generation of shares for all wires (and in particular for the circuit's output wires) is performed in

---

[23] Indeed, the current section is essentially a detailed version of Section 7.1.3.3.

a private manner. Put in other words, we will show that privately evaluating the circuit "reduces" to privately evaluating single gates on values shared by both parties.

Our presentation is modular, where the modularity is supported by an appropriate notion of a *reduction*. Thus, we first define such notion, and show that indeed it is suitable to our goals; that is, combining a reduction of (the private computation of) g to (the private computation of) f and a protocol for privately computing f yields a protocol for privately computing g. Applying this notion of a reduction, we reduce the private computation of general functionalities to the private computation of deterministic functionalities, and thus focus on the latter.

We next consider, without loss of generality, the evaluation of Boolean circuits with AND and XOR gates of fan-in 2.[24] Actually, we find it more convenient to consider the corresponding arithmetic circuits over GF(2), where multiplication corresponds to AND and addition to XOR. A value v is shared by the two parties in the natural manner (i.e., the sum of the shares equals v mod 2). We show how to propagate shares of values through any given gate (operation). Propagation through an addition gate is trivial, and we concentrate on propagation through a multiplication gate. The generic case is that the first party holds (a_1, b_1) and the second party holds (a_2, b_2), where $a_1 + a_2$ is the value of one input wire and $b_1 + b_2$ is the value of the other input wire. What we want is to provide each party with a random share of the value of the output wire, that is, a share of the value $(a_1 + a_2) \cdot (b_1 + b_2)$. In other words, we are interested in privately computing the following randomized functionality

$$((a_1, b_1), (a_2, b_2)) \mapsto (c_1, c_2) \tag{7.17}$$

$$\text{where } c_1 + c_2 = (a_1 + a_2) \cdot (b_1 + b_2). \tag{7.18}$$

That is, (c_1, c_2) ought to be uniformly distributed among the pairs satisfying $c_1 + c_2 = (a_1 + a_2) \cdot (b_1 + b_2)$. As shown in Section 7.3.3, this functionality can be privately computed by reduction to a variant of Oblivious Transfer (OT). This variant is defined in Section 7.3.2, where it is shown that this variant can be privately implemented assuming the existence of (enhanced) trapdoor one-way permutations. We stress that the specific functionalities mentioned here are relatively simple (e.g., they have a finite domain). Thus, Section 7.3.4 reduces the private computation of arbitrary (complex) functionalities to the construction of protocols for privately computing a specific simple functionality (e.g., the one of Eq. (7.17) and Eq. (7.18)).

The actual presentation proceeds bottom-up. We first define reductions between (two-party) protocol problems (in the semi-honest model). Next, we define and implement OT, and show how to use OT for privately computing a single multiplication gate. Finally, we show how to use the latter protocol to derive a protocol for privately evaluating the entire circuit.

Teaching Tip. Some readers may prefer to see a concrete protocol (and its privacy analysis) before coping with the abstract notion of a privacy reduction (and a corresponding composition theorem). We advise such readers to read Section 7.3.2 before reading Section 7.3.1.

---

[24] Indeed, negation can be emulated by XORing the given bit with the constant true.

7.3.1. Privacy Reductions and a Composition Theorem

It is time to define what we mean by saying that the private computation of one functionality *reduces* to the private computation of another functionality. Our definition is a natural extension of the standard notion of a reduction as used in the context of ordinary (i.e., one-party) computation. Recall that standard reductions are defined in terms of oracle machines. Thus, we need to consider two-party protocols with oracle access. Here, the oracle is invoked by both parties, each supplying it with one input (or query), and it responds with a pair of answers, one per each party. We stress that the answer-pair depends on the (entire) query-pair.

Definition 7.3.1 (protocols with oracle access): *An* oracle-aided protocol *is an ordinary protocol augmented by pairs of oracle-tapes, one pair per each party, and oracle-call steps defined as follows. Each of the parties may send a special* oracle request *message, to the other party. Such a message is typically sent after this party writes a string, called its* query, *on its own write-only oracle-tape. In response, the other party also writes a string, called its query, on its own oracle-tape and responds to the requesting party with an* oracle call *message. At this point, the oracle is invoked and the result is that a string, not necessarily the same, is written by the oracle on the read-only oracle-tape of each party. This pair of strings is called the* oracle answer.

We stress that the syntax of Definition 7.3.1 allows (only) sequential oracle calls (but not parallel ones). We call the reader's attention to the second item in Definition 7.3.2 that requires that the oracle-aided protocol *privately compute* the functionality, rather than merely computes it.

Definition 7.3.2 (privacy reductions):

- *An oracle-aided protocol is said to be* using the oracle-functionality f *if the oracle answers are according to* f. *That is, when the oracle is invoked, such that the requesting party writes the query* q_1 *and responding party writes the query* q_2, *the answer-pair is distributed as* $f(q_1, q_2)$, *where the requesting party gets the first part* (i.e., $f_1(q_1, q_2)$).[25]

  We require that the length of each query be polynomially related to the length of the initial input.[26]
- *An oracle-aided protocol using the oracle-functionality* f *is said to* privately compute g *if there exist polynomial-time algorithms, denoted* S_1 *and* S_2, *satisfying Eq. (7.9) and Eq. (7.10), respectively, where the corresponding views of the execution of the oracle-aided protocol are defined in the natural manner.*

---

[25] The identity of the requesting party may be determined by the two parties (according to interaction prior to the request). In particular, as in all protocols used in this work, the identity of the requesting party may be fixed a priori.

[26] This requirement guarantees that the security of the oracle calls be related to the security of the high-level protocol.

- *An oracle-aided protocol is said to* privately reduce g to f *if it privately computes g when using the oracle-functionality f. In such a case, we say that g is* privately reducible to f,

We are now ready to state a composition theorem for the semi-honest model.

Theorem 7.3.3 (Composition Theorem for the semi-honest model): *Suppose that g is privately reducible to f and that there exists a protocol for privately computing f. Then there exists a protocol for privately computing g.*

Theorem 7.3.3 can be generalized to assert that if g is privately reducible to f, and f is privately reducible to e, then g is privately reducible to e. See Exercise 5.

Proof Sketch: Let $\Pi^{g|f}$ be a oracle-aided protocol that privately reduces g to f, and let Π^f be a protocol that privately computes f. We construct a protocol Π for computing g in the natural manner; that is, starting with $\Pi^{g|f}$, we replace each invocation of the oracle (i.e., of f) by an execution of the protocol Π^f. Clearly, Π computes g. We need to show that Π privately computes g.

For each $i = 1, 2$, let $S_i^{g|f}$ and S_i^f be the corresponding simulators for the view of Party i (i.e., in $\Pi^{g|f}$ and Π^f, respectively). We construct a simulator S_i, for the view of Party i in Π, in the natural manner. That is, we first run $S_i^{g|f}$ and obtain the (simulated) view of Party i in $\Pi^{g|f}$. This (simulated) view includes queries made by Party i and corresponding answers. (Recall, we have only the part of Party i in the query-answer pair.) Invoking S_i^f on each such "partial query-answer," we fill in the view of Party i for each of these invocations of Π^f. (Note that we rely on the fact that the simulator S_i^f outputs a view that fits the output given to it; see Item 2 in the discussion that follows Definition 7.2.1.)

> A minor technicality: There is a minor inaccuracy in this description, which presupposes that Party i is the party that plays the i-th party in Π^f (i.e., Party 1 is the party in $\Pi^{g|f}$ that requests all oracle calls to f). But, in general, it may be that, in some invocations of Π^f, Party 2 plays the first party in Π^f (i.e., Party 1 is the party in $\Pi^{g|f}$ that requests this particular oracle call). In this case, we should simulate the execution of Π^f by using the simulator that simulates the view of the corresponding party in Π^f (rather than the corresponding party in Π).
>
> Advanced comment: Note that we capitalize on the fact that in the semi-honest model, the execution of the steps of $\Pi^{g|f}$ (inside Π) is independent of the actual executions of Π^f (and depends only on the outcomes of Π^f). This fact allows us to first simulate a transcript of $\Pi^{g|f}$, and next generate simulated transcripts of Π^f. In contrast, in the malicious model, the adversary's actions in $\Pi^{g|f}$ may depend on the transcript of previous executions of Π^f, and thus this simulation strategy will not work in the malicious model (and a more complex simulation strategy will be used).

It is left to show that S_i indeed generates a distribution that (augmented by the value of g) is indistinguishable from the view of Party i (augmented by the output of both parties) in actual executions of Π. Toward this end, we introduce a *hybrid distribution*, denoted H_i. This hybrid distribution represents the view of Party i (and the output of both parties) in an execution of $\Pi^{g|f}$ that is augmented by corresponding invocations of S_i^f. That is, for each query-answer pair, (q, a), viewed by Party i, we augment its view with $S_i^f(q, a)$. In other words, H_i represents the execution of Π, with the exception that the invocations of Π^f are replaced by simulated transcripts.

> Comment: We stress that since g may be a randomized functionality, we should establish that the protocol satisfies the general form of Definition 7.2.1, rather than its simplified form. That is, we consider the joint distribution consisting of the view of Party i and the output of both parties (rather than merely the former). This fact merely makes the phrases more cumbersome, and the essence of the argument may be better captured by assuming that g is deterministic and using the special (simpler) form of Definition 7.2.1. Likewise, in case f is randomized, we have to rely on the general form of Definition 7.2.1 in order to show that the distributions represented by H_i and Π are computationally indistinguishable.

Using the guarantees regarding S_i^f (resp., $S_i^{g|f}$), we show that the distributions corresponding to H_i and Π (resp., H_i and S_i) are computationally indistinguishable. Specifically:

1. *The distributions represented by H_i and Π are computationally indistinguishable*: The reason is that these distributions differ only in that the invocations of Π^f in Π are replaced in H_i by S_i^f-simulated transcripts. Thus, the hypothesis regarding S_i^f implies that the two distributions are computationally indistinguishable (where indistinguishability is measured with respect to the length of the queries, and holds also when measured with respect to the length of the initial inputs).[27] Specifically, one may consider hybrids of Π and H_i such that in the j-th hybrid, the first j invocations of Π^f are real and the rest are simulated. Then distinguishability of neighboring hybrids contradicts the hypothesis regarding S_i^f (by incorporating a possible transcript of the rest of the execution into the distinguisher).

2. *The distributions represented by H_i and S_i are computationally indistinguishable*: The reason is that these distributions are obtained, respectively, from $\Pi^{g|f}$ and $S_i^{g|f}$, by augmenting the latter with invocations of S_i^f. Thus, indistinguishability follows by the hypothesis regarding $S_i^{g|f}$. Specifically, distinguishing H_i and S_i implies distinguishing $\Pi^{g|f}$ and $S_i^{g|f}$ (by incorporating the program S_i^f into the distinguisher).

The theorem follows. ∎

Application: Reducing Private Computation of General Functionalities to Deterministic Ones. Given a general functionality g, we first write it in a way that makes the randomization explicit. That is, we let $g(r, (x, y))$ denote the value of $g(x, y)$ when using coin tosses $r \in \{0, 1\}^{\text{poly}(|x|)}$; that is, $g(x, y)$ is the randomized process consisting of uniformly selecting $r \in \{0, 1\}^{\text{poly}(|x|)}$, and deterministically computing $g(r, (x, y))$. Next, we privately reduce g to a deterministic f, where f is defined as follows:

$$f((x_1, r_1), (x_2, r_2)) \overset{\text{def}}{=} g(r_1 \oplus r_2, (x_1, x_2)) \tag{7.19}$$

---

[27] Here we use the hypothesis (made in the first item of Definition 7.3.2) that the length of each query is polynomially related to the length of the initial input.

Applying Theorem 7.3.3 (while using a straightforward privacy reduction of g to f), we conclude that the existence of a protocol for privately computing the deterministic functionality f implies the existence of a protocol for privately computing the randomized functionality g. For sake of future reference, we explicitly state the privacy reduction of g to f (i.e, the oracle-aided protocol for g given f).

Proposition 7.3.4 (privately reducing a randomized functionality to a deterministic one): *Let g be a randomized functionality, and f be as defined in Eq. (7.19). Then the following oracle-aided protocol privately reduces g to f.*

Inputs: *Party i gets input $x_i \in \{0, 1\}^n$.*

Step 1: *Party i uniformly selects $r_i \in \{0, 1\}^{\text{poly}(|x_i|)}$.*

Step 2 – Reduction: *Party i invokes the oracle with query (x_i, r_i), and records the oracle response.*

Outputs: *Each party outputs the oracle's response.*

We comment that this construction is also applicable in the case of malicious adversaries; see Section 7.4.2.

Proof: Clearly, this protocol, denoted Π, computes g. To show that Π privately computes g, we need to present a simulator for each party view. The simulator for Party i, denoted S_i, is the obvious one. On input (x_i, v_i), where x_i is the local input to Party i and v_i is its local output, the simulator uniformly selects $r_i \in \{0, 1\}^m$, and outputs (x_i, r_i, v_i), where $m = \text{poly}(|x_i|)$. The main observation underlying the analysis of this simulator is that for every fixed x_1, x_2 and $r \in \{0, 1\}^m$, we have $\bar{v} = g(r, (x_1, x_2))$ if and only if $\bar{v} = f((x_1, r_1), (x_2, r_2))$, for every pair (r_1, r_2) satisfying $r_1 \oplus r_2 = r$. Now, let ζ_i be a random variable representing the random choice of Party i in Step 1, and ζ_i' denote the corresponding choice made by the simulator S_i. Then, referring to the general form of Definition 7.2.1 (as we should, since g is a randomized functionality), we show that for every fixed x_1, x_2, r_i and $\bar{v} = (v_1, v_2)$, it holds that

$$\Pr\left[\begin{array}{c} \text{VIEW}_i^\Pi(x_1, x_2) = (x_i, r_i, v_i) \\ \wedge\ \text{OUTPUT}^\Pi(x_1, x_2) = (v_1, v_2) \end{array}\right] = \Pr[(\zeta_i = r_i) \wedge (f((x_1, \zeta_1), (x_2, \zeta_2)) = \bar{v})]$$

$$= \Pr[\zeta_i = r_i] \cdot \frac{|\{r_{3-i} : f((x_1, r_1), (x_2, r_2)) = \bar{v}\}|}{2^m}$$

$$= 2^{-m} \cdot \frac{|\{r : g(r, (x_1, x_2)) = \bar{v}\}|}{2^m}$$

$$= \Pr[\zeta_i' = r_i] \cdot \Pr[g(x_1, x_2) = \bar{v}]$$

$$= \Pr[(\zeta_i' = r_i) \wedge (g(x_1, x_2) = \bar{v})]$$

$$= \Pr\left[\begin{array}{c} S_i(x_i, g_i(x_1, x_2)) = (x_i, r_i, v_i) \\ \wedge\ g(x_1, x_2) = (v_1, v_2) \end{array}\right]$$

where the equalities are justified as follows: the 1st by definition of Π, the 2nd by independence of the ζ_i's, the 3rd by definition of ζ_i and f, the 4th by definition of ζ_i' and g, the 5th by independence of ζ_i' and g, and the 6th by definition of S_i. Thus, the simulated view (and output) is distributed identically to the view (and output) in a real execution. The claim (which only requires these ensembles to be computationally indistinguishable) follows. ∎

7.3.2. The OT_1^k Protocol: Definition and Construction

The (following version of the) *Oblivious Transfer* functionality is a main ingredient of our construction. Let k be a fixed integer ($k = 4$ will do for our purpose), and let $\sigma_1, \sigma_2, ..., \sigma_k \in \{0, 1\}$ and $i \in \{1, ..., k\}$. Then, the (single-output) functionality **1-out-of-k Oblivious Transfer**, denoted OT_1^k, is defined as

$$OT_1^k((\sigma_1, \sigma_2, ..., \sigma_k), i) \;=\; (\lambda, \sigma_i) \tag{7.20}$$

Indeed, 1-out-of-k Oblivious Transfer, is asymmetric. Traditionally, the first player, holding input $(\sigma_1, \sigma_2, ..., \sigma_k)$ is called the *sender*, whereas the second player, holding the input $i \in \{1, ..., k\}$ is called the *receiver*. Intuitively, the goal is to transfer the i-th bit to the receiver, without letting the receiver obtain knowledge of any other bit and without letting the sender obtain knowledge of the identity of the bit required by the receiver.

Using any enhanced trapdoor permutation, $\{f_\alpha : D_\alpha \to D_\alpha\}_{\alpha \in I}$, we present a protocol for privately computing OT_1^k. The following description refers to the algorithms guaranteed by such a collection (see Definition 2.4.5 in Volume 1 and Definition C.1.1 in Appendix C) and to a hard-core predicate b for such a collection (see Section 2.5 of Volume 1). We denote the sender (i.e., the first party) by S and the receiver (i.e., the second party) by R. As discussed in Section 7.2.1, since we are dealing with a finite functionality, we want the security to be stated in terms of an auxiliary security parameter, n, presented to both parties in unary.

Construction 7.3.5 (Oblivious Transfer protocol for semi-honest model):

Inputs: *The sender has input* $(\sigma_1, \sigma_2, ..., \sigma_k) \in \{0, 1\}^k$, *the receiver has input* $i \in \{1, 2, ..., k\}$, *and both parties have the auxiliary security parameter* 1^n.

Step S1: *The sender uniformly selects an index-trapdoor pair, (α, t), by running the generation algorithm, G, on input 1^n. That is, it uniformly selects a random-tape, r, for G and sets $(\alpha, t) = G(1^n, r)$. It sends the index α to the receiver.*

Step R1: *The receiver uniformly and independently selects $x_1, ..., x_k \in D_\alpha$, sets $y_i = f_\alpha(x_i)$ and $y_j = x_j$ for every $j \ne i$, and sends $(y_1, y_2, ..., y_k)$ to the sender. That is:*

1. *It uniformly and independently selects $x_1, ..., x_k \in D_\alpha$, by invoking the domain-sampling algorithm k times, on input α. Specifically, it selects random-tapes, r_j's, for D and sets $x_j = D(\alpha, r_j)$, for $j = 1, ..., k$.*
2. *Using the evaluation algorithm, the receiver sets $y_i = f_\alpha(x_i)$.*
3. *For each $j \ne i$, the receiver sets $y_j = x_j$.*

4. *The receiver sends* $(y_1, y_2, ..., y_k)$ *to the sender.*

(Thus, the receiver knows $f_\alpha^{-1}(y_i) = x_i$, but cannot predict $b(f_\alpha^{-1}(y_j))$ for any $j \neq i$.)

Step S2: *Upon receiving* $(y_1, y_2, ..., y_k)$, *using the inverting-with-trapdoor algorithm and the trapdoor t, the sender computes* $z_j = f_\alpha^{-1}(y_j)$, *for every* $j \in \{1, ..., k\}$. *It sends* $(\sigma_1 \oplus b(z_1), \sigma_2 \oplus b(z_2), ..., \sigma_k \oplus b(z_k))$ *to the receiver.*

Step R2: *Upon receiving* $(c_1, c_2, ..., c_k)$, *the receiver locally outputs* $c_i \oplus b(x_i)$.

We first observe that this protocol correctly computes OT_1^k: This is the case since the receiver's local output (i.e., $c_i \oplus b(x_i)$) satisfies

$$
\begin{aligned}
c_i \oplus b(x_i) &= (\sigma_i \oplus b(z_i)) \oplus b(x_i) \\
&= \sigma_i \oplus b(f_\alpha^{-1}(y_i)) \oplus b(x_i) \\
&= \sigma_i \oplus b(f_\alpha^{-1}(f_\alpha(x_i))) \oplus b(x_i) \\
&= \sigma_i
\end{aligned}
$$

We show next that the protocol indeed privately computes OT_1^k. Intuitively, the sender gets no information from the execution because, for any possible value of i, the senders sees the same distribution; specifically, a sequence of k uniformly and independently distributed elements of D_α. (Indeed, the key observation is that applying f_α to a uniformly distributed element of D_α yields a uniformly distributed element of D_α.) Intuitively, the receiver gains no computational knowledge from the execution since, for $j \neq i$, the only data it has regarding σ_j is the triplet $(\alpha, r_j, \sigma_j \oplus b(f_\alpha^{-1}(x_j)))$, where $x_j = D(\alpha, r_j)$, from which it is infeasible to predict σ_j better than by a random guess. Specifically, we rely on the "enhanced one-way" hypothesis by which, given α and r_j, it is infeasible to find $f_\alpha^{-1}(x_j)$ (or guess $b(f_\alpha^{-1}(x_j))$ better than at random). A formal argument is indeed due and given next.

Proposition 7.3.6: *Suppose that* $\{f_i : D_i \to D_i\}_{i \in I}$ *constitutes a collection of enhanced trapdoor permutations* (as in Definition C.1.1) *and that b constitutes a hard-core predicate for it. Then, Construction 7.3.5 constitutes a protocol for privately computing* OT_1^k (in the semi-honest model).

We comment that the intractability assumption used in Proposition 7.3.6 will propagate to all subsequent results in the current and next section (i.e., Sections 7.3 and 7.4). In fact, the implementation of OT_1^k seems to be the bottleneck of the intractability assumptions used in these sections.

Proof Sketch: Note that since we are dealing with a deterministic functionality, we may use the special (simpler) form of Definition 7.2.1 (which only refers to each party's view). Thus, we will present a simulator for the view of each party. Recall that these simulators are given the local input (which also includes the security parameter) and the local output of the corresponding party. The following schematic depiction of the information flow in Construction 7.3.5 may be useful toward the constructions of these simulators:

	Sender (S)	Receiver (R)
input	$(\sigma_1, ..., \sigma_k)$	i
Step S1	$(\alpha, t) \leftarrow G(1^n)$	
	$\longrightarrow \quad \alpha \quad \longrightarrow$	
Step R1		generates y_j's
	$\longleftarrow (y_1, ..., y_k) \longleftarrow$	(knows $x_i = f_\alpha^{-1}(y_i)$)
Step S2	$c_j = \sigma_j \oplus b(f_\alpha^{-1}(y_j))$	
	$\longrightarrow (c_1, ..., c_k) \longrightarrow$	
R2 (output)	λ	$c_i \oplus b(x_i)$

We start by presenting a simulator for the sender's view. On input $(((\sigma_1, ..., \sigma_k), 1^n), \lambda)$, this simulator randomly selects α (as in Step S1) and generates uniformly and independently $y_1, ..., y_k \in D_\alpha$. That is, let r denote the sequence of coins used to generate α, and assume without loss of generality that the inverting-with-trapdoor algorithm is deterministic (which is typically the case anyhow). Then the simulator outputs $(((\sigma_1, ..., \sigma_k), 1^n), r, (y_1, ..., y_k))$, where the first element represents the party's input, the second its random choices, and the third the (single) message that the party has received. Clearly, this output distribution is *identical* to the view of the sender in the real execution. (This holds because f_α is a permutation, and thus applying it to a uniformly distributed element of D_α yields a uniformly distributed element of D_α.)

We now turn to the receiver. On input $((i, 1^n), \sigma_i)$, the simulator (of the receiver's view) proceeds as follows:

1. Emulating Step S1, the simulator uniformly selects an index-trapdoor pair, (α, t), by running the generation algorithm on input 1^n.
2. As in Step R1, it uniformly and independently selects $r_1, ..., r_k$ for the domain sampler D, and sets $x_j = D(\alpha, r_j)$ for $j = 1, ..., k$. Next, it sets $y_i = f_\alpha(x_i)$ and $y_j = x_j$, for each $j \neq i$.
3. It sets $c_i = \sigma_i \oplus b(x_i)$, and uniformly selects $c_j \in \{0, 1\}$, for each $j \neq i$.
4. Finally, it outputs $((i, 1^n), (r_1, ..., r_k), (\alpha, (c_1, ..., c_k)))$, where the first element represents the party's input, the second its random choices, and the third element represents the two messages that the party has received.

Note that, except for the sequence of c_j's, this output is distributed identically to the corresponding prefix of the receiver's view in the real execution. Furthermore, the said equality holds even if we include the bit c_i (which equals $\sigma_i \oplus b(f_\alpha^{-1}(y_i)) = \sigma_i \oplus b(x_i)$ in the real execution as well as in the simulation). Thus, the two distributions differ only in the values of the other c_j's: For $j \neq i$, in the simulation c_j is uniform and independent of anything else, whereas in the real execution c_j equals

$b(f_\alpha^{-1}(y_j)) = b(f_\alpha^{-1}(x_j))$ (and hence depends on r_j, which determines x_j). However, it is impossible to distinguish the two cases, because x_j is uniformly distributed and the distinguisher is only given α and r_j (but not the trapdoor to f_α). Here is where we use the hypothesis that b is a hard-core of an enhanced collection of trapdoor permutations (as in Definition C.1.1), rather than merely a standard collection of trapdoor permutations. ∎

Other Variants of Oblivious Transfer. A variety of different variants of the Oblivious Transfer functionality were considered in the literature, but most treatments refer to the (more challenging) problem of implementing these variants securely in the malicious model (rather than in the semi-honest model). We briefly mention two of these other variants:

1. Extensions of 1-out-of-k Oblivious Transfer to k secrets that are bit strings rather than single bits.
2. Oblivious Transfer of a single secret (denoted σ) that is to be delivered with probability $1/2$. That is, the randomized functionality that maps (σ, λ) to (λ, σ) with probability $1/2$ and to (λ, λ) otherwise.

Privacy reductions among these variants can be easily constructed (see Exercise 6).

7.3.3. Privately Computing $c_1 + c_2 = (a_1 + a_2) \cdot (b_1 + b_2)$

We now turn to the functionality defined in Eq. (7.17)–(7.18). Recall that this functionality is a randomized mapping $((a_1, b_1), (a_2, b_2)) \mapsto (c_1, c_2)$ satisfying $c_1 + c_2 = (a_1 + a_2) \cdot (b_1 + b_2)$, where the arithmetic is in GF(2). We reduce the private computation of this (finite) functionality to (the private computation of) OT_1^4.

Construction 7.3.7 (privately reducing the functionality of Eq. (7.17)–(7.18) to OT_1^4):

Inputs: *Party i holds $(a_i, b_i) \in \{0, 1\} \times \{0, 1\}$, for $i = 1, 2$.*

Step 1: *The first party uniformly selects $c_1 \in \{0, 1\}$.*

Step 2 – Reduction: *The aim of this step is to privately compute the (residual) deterministic functionality $((a_1, b_1, c_1), (a_2, b_2)) \mapsto (\lambda, f_{a_2,b_2}(a_1, b_1, c_1))$, where $f_{a,b}(x, y, z) \overset{\text{def}}{=} z + (x + a) \cdot (y + b)$. The parties privately reduce the computation of this functionality to OT_1^4. Specifically, Party 1 plays the sender and Party 2 plays the receiver. Using its input (a_1, b_1) and coin c_1, Party 1 sets the sender's input (in the OT_1^4) to equal the 4-tuple*

$$(f_{0,0}(a_1, b_1, c_1), \ f_{0,1}(a_1, b_1, c_1), \ f_{1,0}(a_1, b_1, c_1), \ f_{1,1}(a_1, b_1, c_1)). \quad (7.21)$$

Using its input (a_2, b_2), Party 2 sets the receiver's input (in the OT_1^4) to equal $1 + 2a_2 + b_2 \in \{1, 2, 3, 4\}$.

Thus, the receiver's output will be the $(1 + 2a_2 + b_2)^{\text{th}}$ *element in Eq. (7.21), which in turn equals* $f_{a_2,b_2}(a_1, b_1, c_1)$. *That is:*

Input of Party 2 (i.e., (a_2, b_2))	Receiver's input in OT_1^4 (i.e., $1 + 2a_2 + b_2$)	Receiver's output in OT_1^4 (i.e., $f_{a_2,b_2}(a_1, b_1, c_1)$)
(0, 0)	1	$c_1 + a_1 b_1$
(0, 1)	2	$c_1 + a_1 \cdot (b_1 + 1)$
(1, 0)	3	$c_1 + (a_1 + 1) \cdot b_1$
(1, 1)	4	$c_1 + (a_1 + 1) \cdot (b_1 + 1)$

Recall that $f_{a_2,b_2}(a_1, b_1, c_1) = c_1 + (a_1 + a_2) \cdot (b_1 + b_2)$.

Outputs: *Party 1 outputs* c_1, *whereas Party 2 outputs the result obtained from the* OT_1^4 *invocation.*

We first observe that the reduction is valid; that is, when Party i enters with input (a_i, b_i), the output of Party 2 equals $f_{a_2,b_2}(a_1, b_1, c_1) = c_1 + (a_1 + a_2) \cdot (b_1 + b_2)$, where c_1 is the output of Party 1. That is, the output pair is uniformly distributed among the pairs (c_1, c_2) for which $c_1 + c_2 = (a_1 + a_2) \cdot (b_1 + b_2)$ holds. Thus, each of the local outputs (i.e, of either Party 1 or Party 2) is uniformly distributed, although the two local outputs are dependent of one another (as in Eq. (7.18)). It is also easy to see that the reduction is private. That is,

Proposition 7.3.8: *Construction 7.3.7 privately reduces the computation of Eq. (7.17)–(7.18) to* OT_1^4.

Proof Sketch: Simulators for the oracle-aided protocol of Construction 7.3.7 are easily constructed. Specifically, the simulator of the view of Party 1 has input $((a_1, b_1), c_1)$ (i.e., the input and output of Party 1), which is identical to the view of Party 1 in the corresponding execution (where here c_1 serves as coins to Party 1). Thus, the simulation is trivial (i.e., by the identity transformation). The same also holds for the simulator of the view of Party 2: It gets input $((a_2, b_2), c_1 + (a_1 + a_2) \cdot (b_1 + b_2))$ (i.e., the input and output of Party 2), which is identical to the view of Party 2 in the corresponding execution (where here $c_1 + (a_1 + a_2) \cdot (b_1 + b_2)$ serves as the oracle response to Party 2). Thus, again, the simulation is trivial. We conclude that the view of each party can be perfectly simulated (rather than just be simulated in a computationally indistinguishable manner). The same holds when we also account for the parties' outputs (as required in the general form of Definition 7.2.1), and the proposition follows.[28] ∎

On the Generic Nature of Construction 7.3.7. The idea underlying Step 2 of Construction 7.3.7 can be applied in order to reduce the computation of any deterministic functionality of the form $(x, y) \mapsto (\lambda, f_y(x))$ to 1-out-of-$2^{|y|}$ Oblivious Transfer. Indeed, this reduction is applicable only when y is short (i.e., the number of possible y's is at most polynomial in the security parameter). Specifically, consider the

---

[28] An alternative proof is presented in Exercise 9.

functions $f_y : \{0, 1\}^k \to \{0, 1\}$, for $y \in \{0, 1\}^\ell$ (when in Construction 7.3.7 $\ell = 2$ (and $k = 3$)). Then, privately computing $(x, y) \mapsto (\lambda, f_y(x))$ is reduced to 1-out-of-2^ℓ Oblivious Transfer by letting the first party play the sender with input set to the 2^ℓ-tuple $(f_{0^\ell}(x), ..., f_{1^\ell}(x))$ and the second party play the receiver with input set to the index of y among the ℓ-bit long strings.

7.3.4. The Circuit Evaluation Protocol

We now show that the computation of any deterministic functionality, which is represented by an arithmetic circuit over GF(2), is privately reducible to the functionality of Eq. (7.17)–(7.18). Recall that the latter functionality corresponds to a private computation of multiplication of inputs that are shared by the two parties. We thus refer to this functionality as the multiplication-gate emulation.

Our reduction follows the overview presented in the beginning of this section (i.e., Section 7.3). In particular, the sharing of a bit-value v between the two parties means a uniformly distributed pair of bits (v_1, v_2) such that $v = v_1 + v_2$, where the first party holds v_1 and the second holds v_2. Our aim is to propagate, via private computation, shares of the input-wires of the circuit to shares of all wires of the circuit, so that finally we obtain shares of the output-wires of the circuit.

> Arithmetic circuits – the basics: Recall that an arithmetic circuit over GF(2) is a directed acyclic graph with internal vertices corresponding to gates, where internal vertices are vertices having both incoming and outgoing edges. Without loss of generality, we will consider two types of gates, called addition and multiplication. We will assume that each internal vertex has two incoming edges, called its input-wires, and several outgoing edges called its output-wires. Boolean values are propagated through such gates in the natural manner (i.e., each outgoing wire holds the sum or multiple of the values of the incoming wires of the gate). Vertices with no incoming edges are called sources, and vertices with no outgoing edges are called sinks. Without loss of generality, each source has a single outgoing edge, which is called an input-wire of the circuit, and each sink has a single incoming edge, which is called an output-wire of the circuit. When placing Boolean values on the input-wires of the circuit, the propagation of values through the gates determines values to all output-wires. The function from input values to output values defined this way is called the function computed by the circuit.

> A tedious comment: For the sake of simplicity, we do not provide the circuit with constant values (i.e., 0 and 1). The constant 0 can be easily produced by adding any GF(2) value to itself, but omitting the constant 1 weakens the power of such circuits (because this constant is essential to the computation of non-monotone functions). However, the evaluation of any circuit that uses the constant 1 can be privately reduced to the evaluation of a corresponding circuit that does not use the constant 1.[29]

---

[29] Given a circuit C that uses the constant 1, we derive a circuit C' that lacks constant inputs by introducing an auxiliary variable that is to be set to 1 (and replacing any occurrence of the constant 1 by an occurrence of the new auxiliary variable). Thus, $C(x) = C'(x, 1)$ (or rather $C(x_1, x_2) = C'(1x_1, \sigma x_2)$, for any $\sigma \in \{0, 1\}$). Clearly, the private evaluation of C (on the input pair (x_1, x_2)) is reducible to the private evaluation of C' (e.g., by a single oracle call that asks for the evaluation of C', say, on the input $(1x_1, 0x_2)$).

We will consider an enumeration of all wires in the circuit. The input-wires of the circuit, n per each party, will be numbered 1, 2...., $2n$ so that, for $j = 1, ..., n$, the j-th input of party i corresponds to the $(i - 1) \cdot n + j$-th wire. The wires will be numbered so that the output-wires of each gate have a larger numbering than its input wires. The output-wires of the circuit are clearly the last ones. For the sake of simplicity we assume that each party obtains n output bits, and that the output bits of the second party correspond to the last n wires of the circuit.

Construction 7.3.9 (reducing the evaluation of any circuit to the emulation of a multiplication gate): *For simplicity, we assume that the circuit is either fixed or can be determined in* poly(n)*-time as a function of n, which denotes the length of the input to each party.*[30]

Inputs: *Party i holds the bit string $x_i^1 \cdots x_i^n \in \{0, 1\}^n$, for $i = 1, 2$.*

Step 1 – Sharing the Inputs: Each party (splits and) shares each of its input bits with the other party. *That is, for every $i = 1, 2$ and $j = 1, ..., n$, Party i uniformly selects a bit r_i^j and sends it to the other party as the other party's share of the input wire $(i - 1) \cdot n + j$. Party i sets its own share of the $(i - 1) \cdot n + j^{\text{th}}$ input wire to $x_i^j + r_i^j$.*

Step 2 – Circuit Emulation: Proceeding by the order of wires, the parties use their shares of the two input-wires to a gate in order to privately compute shares for the output-wire(s) of the gate. *Suppose that the parties hold shares to the two input-wires of a gate; that is, Party 1 holds the shares a_1, b_1 and Party 2 holds the shares a_2, b_2, where a_1, a_2 are the shares of the first wire and b_1, b_2 are the shares of the second wire. We consider two cases.*[31]

Emulation of an addition gate: *Party 1 just sets its share of the output-wire of the gate to be $a_1 + b_1$, and Party 2 sets its share of the output-wire to be $a_2 + b_2$.*

Emulation of a multiplication gate: *Shares of the output-wire of the gate are obtained by invoking the oracle for the functionality of Eq. (7.17)–(7.18), where Party 1 supplies the input (query part) (a_1, b_1), and Party 2 supplies (a_2, b_2). When the oracle responds, each party sets its share of the output-wire of the gate to equal its part of the oracle answer. Recall that, by Eq. (7.18), the two parts of the oracle answer sum up to $(a_1 + b_1) \cdot (a_2 + b_2)$.*

Step 3 – Recovering the Output Bits: Once the shares of the circuit-output wires are computed, each party sends its share of each such wire to the party with which the wire is associated. *That is, the shares of the last n wires are sent by Party 1 to Party 2,*

---

[30] Alternatively, we may let the circuit be part of the input to both parties, which essentially means that the protocol is computing the "universal circuit-evaluation" function.

[31] In the text, we implicitly assume that each gate has a single output wire, but this assumption is immaterial and the treatment extends easily to the case that the gates have several output wires. In the case of a multiplication gate, both the natural possibilities (which follow) are fine. The first (more natural) possibility is to invoke the oracle once per each multiplication gate and have each party use the same share for all output wires. The second possibility is to invoke the oracle once per each output-wire (of a multiplication gate).

whereas the shares of the preceding n wires are sent by Party 2 to Party 1. Each party recovers the corresponding output bits by adding up the two shares, that is, the share it had obtained in Step 2 and the share it has obtained in the current step.

Outputs: *Each party locally outputs the bits recovered in Step 3.*

For starters, let us verify that the output is indeed correct. This can be shown by induction on the wires of the circuits. The induction claim is that the shares of each wire sum up to the correct value of the wire. The base case of the induction are the input-wires of the circuits. Specifically, the $(i-1) \cdot n + j$-th wire has value x_i^j, and its shares are r_i^j and $r_i^j + x_i^j$ (indeed, summing up to x_i^j). For the induction step we consider the emulation of a gate. Suppose that the values of the input-wires (to the gate) are a and b, and that their shares a_1, a_2 and b_1, b_2 indeed satisfy $a_1 + a_2 = a$ and $b_1 + b_2 = b$. In the case of an addition gate, the shares of the output-wire were set to be $a_1 + b_1$ and $a_2 + b_2$, indeed satisfying

$$(a_1 + b_1) + (a_2 + b_2) \;=\; (a_1 + a_2) + (b_1 + b_2) \;=\; a + b$$

In the case of a multiplication gate, the shares of the output-wire were set to be c_1 and c_2 such that $c_1 + c_2 = (a_1 + a_2) \cdot (b_1 + b_2)$. Thus, $c_1 + c_2 = a \cdot b$ as required.

Privacy of the Reduction. We now turn to show that Construction 7.3.9 indeed privately reduces the computation of a circuit to the multiplication-gate emulation. That is,

Proposition 7.3.10 (privately reducing circuit evaluation to multiplication-gate emulation): *Construction 7.3.9 privately reduces the evaluation of arithmetic circuits over GF(2) to the functionality of Eq. (7.17)–(7.18).*

Proof Sketch: Note that since we are dealing with a deterministic functionality, we may use the special (simpler) form of Definition 7.2.1 and only refer to simulating the view of each party. Recall that these simulators should produce the view of the party in an oracle-aided execution (i.e., an execution of Construction 7.3.9, which is an oracle-aided protocol). Without loss of generality, we present a simulator for the view of Party 1. This simulator gets the party's input $x_1^1, ..., x_1^n$, as well as its output, denoted $y^1, ..., y^n$. It operates as follows:

1. The simulator uniformly selects $r_1^1, ..., r_1^n$ and $r_2^1, ..., r_2^n$, as in Step 1. (The r_1^j's will be used as the coins of Party 1, which are part of the view of the execution, whereas the r_2^j's will be used as the message Party 1 receives at Step 1.) For each $j \le n$, the simulator sets $x_1^j + r_1^j$ as the party's share of the value of the j-th wire. Similarly, for $j \le n$, the party's share of the $n + j$-th wire is set to r_2^j.
   This completes the computation of the party's shares of all the $2n$ circuit-input wires.
2. The party's shares for all other wires are computed, iteratively gate by gate, as follows:

   - The party's share of the output-wire of an addition gate is set to be the sum of the party's shares of the input-wires of the gate.

- The party's share of the output-wire of a multiplication gate is selected uniformly in $\{0, 1\}$.

(The shares computed for output-wires of multiplication gates will be used as the answers obtained, by Party 1, from the oracle.)

3. For each wire corresponding to an output, denoted y^j, that is available to Party 1, the simulator sets the value z^j to equal the sum of y^j and the party's share of that wire.

4. The simulator outputs

$$((x_1^1, ..., x_1^n), (y^1, ..., y^n), (r_1^1, ..., r_1^n), V^1, V^2, V^3)$$

where $V^1 = (r_2^1, ..., r_2^n)$ corresponds to the view of Party 1 in Step 1 of the protocol, the string V^2 equals the concatenation of the bits selected for the output-wires of multiplication gates (corresponding to the party's view of the oracle answers in Step 2 of a real execution), and $V^3 = (z^1, ..., z^n)$ corresponds to the party's view in Step 3 (i.e., the messages it would have obtained from Party 2 in Step 3 of the execution).

We claim that the output of the simulation is distributed identically to the view of Party 1 in the execution of the oracle-aided protocol. The claim clearly holds with respect to the first four parts of the view; that is, the claim holds with respect to the party's input (i.e., $x_1^1, ..., x_1^n$), its output (i.e., $y^1, ..., y^n$), its internal coin-tosses (i.e., $r_1^1, ..., r_1^n$), and the message obtained from Party 2 in Step 1 (i.e., $(r_2^1, ..., r_2^n) = V^1$). Also, by definition of the functionality of Eq. $(7.17)-(7.18)$, the oracle answers to each party are uniformly distributed independently of (the parts of) the party's queries. Thus, this part of the view of Party 1 is uniformly distributed, identically to V^2. It follows that all *shares held by Party 1* are set by the simulator to have exactly the same distribution as they have in a real execution. This holds, in particular, for the shares of the output wires held by Party 1. Finally, we observe that both in the real execution and in the simulation, adding the latter shares (i.e., the shares of the output wires held by Party 1) to the messages sent by Party 2 in Step 3 (resp., to V^3) yields the corresponding bits of the local output of Party 1. Thus, conditioned on the view so far, V^3 is distributed identically to the messages sent by Party 2 in Step 3. We conclude that the simulation is perfect (not only computationally indistinguishable), and so the proposition follows. ∎

Conclusion. Combining Propositions 7.3.4, 7.3.10, and 7.3.8 with the transitivity of privacy reductions (see Exercise 5), we obtain:

Theorem 7.3.11: *Any functionality is privately reducible to* OT_1^4.

Combining Theorem 7.3.11 and Proposition 7.3.6 with the Composition Theorem (Theorem 7.3.3), we obtain:[32]

---

[32] Alternatively, one may avoid relying on the transitivity of privacy reductions by successively applying the Composition Theorem to derive private protocols first for the multiplication functionality, then for any deterministic functionality, and finally for any functionality. That is, in the first application we use Propositions 7.3.8 and 7.3.6,

Theorem 7.3.12: *Suppose that there exist collections of enhanced trapdoor permutations. Then any functionality can be privately computable* (in the semi-honest model).

For the sake of future usage (in Section 7.4), we point out a property of the protocols underlying the proof of Theorem 7.3.12.

Definition 7.3.13 (canonical semi-honest protocols): *A protocol Π for privately computing the functionality f is called* canonical *if it proceeds by executing the following two stages:*

Stage 1: *The parties privately compute the functionality $(x, y) \mapsto ((r_1, r_2), (s_1, s_2))$, where the r_i's and s_i's are uniformly distributed among all possibilities that satisfy $(r_1 \oplus s_1, r_2 \oplus s_2) = f(x, y)$.*

Stage 2: *Party 2 sends s_1 to Party 1, which responds with r_2. Each party computes its own output; that is, Party i outputs $r_i \oplus s_i$.*

Indeed, the protocols underlying the proof of Theorem 7.3.12 are canonical. Hence,

Theorem 7.3.14: *Suppose that there exist collections of enhanced trapdoor permutations. Then any functionality can be privately computable by a canonical protocol.*

We present two alternative proofs of Theorem 7.3.14: The first proof depends on the structure of the protocols used in establishing Theorem 7.3.11, whereas the second proof is generic and uses an additional reduction.

First Proof of Theorem 7.3.14: Recall that the oracle-aided protocol claimed in Theorem 7.3.11 is obtained by composing the reduction in Proposition 7.3.4 with Constructions 7.3.9 and 7.3.7. The high-level structure of the resulting protocol is induced by the circuit-evaluation protocol (of Construction 7.3.9), which is clearly canonical (with Step 3 fitting Stage 2 in Definition 7.3.13). Indeed, it is important that in Step 3 exactly two messages are sent and that Party 1 sends the last message. The fact that the said oracle-aided protocol is canonical is also preserved when replacing the OT_1^4 oracle by an adequate sub-protocol. ∎

Second Proof of Theorem 7.3.14: Using Theorem 7.3.12, we can first derive a protocol for privately computing the functionality of Stage 1 (in Definition 7.3.13). Augmenting this protocol by the trivial Stage 2, we derive a canonical protocol for privately computing the original functionality (i.e., f itself). ∎

in the second we use Proposition 7.3.10 and the protocol resulting from the first application, and in the last application we use Proposition 7.3.4 and the protocol resulting from the second application.

7.4.* Forcing (Two-Party) Semi-Honest Behavior

Our aim is to use Theorem 7.3.12 (or rather Theorem 7.3.14) in order to establish the main result of this chapter; that is,

Theorem 7.4.1 (main result for the two-party case): *Suppose that there exist collections of enhanced trapdoor permutations. Then any two-party functionality can be securely computable* (in the malicious model).

Theorem 7.4.1 will be established by compiling any protocol for the semi-honest model into an "equivalent" protocol for the malicious model. The current section is devoted to the construction of the said compiler, which was already outlined in Section 7.1.3.1. Loosely speaking, the compiler works by replacing the original instructions by macros that force each party to either effectively behave in a semi-honest manner (hence, the title of the current section) or be detected as cheating (in which case, the protocol aborts).

Teaching Tip. Some readers may prefer to see a concrete protocol (and its security analysis) before getting to the general protocol compiler (and coping with the abstractions used in its exposition). We advise such readers to read Section 7.4.3.1 before reading Sections 7.4.1 and 7.4.2.

7.4.1. The Protocol Compiler: Motivation and Overview

We are given a protocol for the semi-honest model. In this protocol, each party has a local input and uses a uniformly distributed local random-tape. Such a protocol may be used to privately compute some functionality (either a deterministic or a probabilistic one), but the compiler does not refer to this functionality. The compiler is supposed to produce an "equivalent protocol" for the malicious model. That is, any input–output behavior that a malicious adversary can induce by attacking the resulting protocol can also be induced by a semi-honest adversary that attacks the original protocol. To motivate the protocol compiler, let us start by considering what a malicious party may do (beyond whatever a semi-honest party can do).

1. A malicious party may enter the actual execution of the protocol with an input different from the one it is given (i.e., "substitute its input"). As discussed in Section 7.2.3, this is unavoidable. What we need to guarantee is that this substitution is done obliviously of the input of the other party, that is, that the substitution only depends on the original input.
   Jumping ahead, we mention that the *input-commitment* phase of the compiled protocol is aimed at achieving this goal. The tools used here are *commitment schemes* (see Section 4.4.1) and *strong zero-knowledge proofs-of-knowledge* (see Section 4.7.6). Sequential executions of these proofs-of-knowledge guarantee the effective independence of the committed values.
2. A malicious party may enter the actual execution of the protocol with a random-tape that is not uniformly distributed. What we need to do is force the party

to use a random-tape (for the emulated semi-honest protocol) that is uniformly distributed.

The *coin-generation* phase of the compiled protocol is aimed at achieving this goal. The tool used here is an augmented *coin-tossing into the well* protocol, which in turn uses tools as in Item 1.

3. A malicious party may try to send messages different from the ones specified by the original (semi-honest model) protocol. So we need to force the party to send messages as specified by its (already committed) local input and random-tape.

The *protocol-emulation* phase of the compiled protocol is aimed at achieving this goal. The tool used here is *zero-knowledge proof systems* (for NP-statements). In fact, forcing parties to act consistently with some known information is the archetypical application of zero-knowledge proofs.

In accordance with this discussion, the protocols produced by the compiler consist of three phases.

Input-Commitment Phase: Each of the parties commits to its input by using a secure implementation of the input-commitment functionality (to be defined in Section 7.4.3.6). The latter functionality guarantees that the committing party actually knows the value to which it has committed, and that the secrecy of the committed value is preserved. It follows that each party commits to a value that is essentially independent of the value committed to by the other party. Furthermore, the input-commitment functionality provides the committer with the corresponding decommitment information (to be used in the protocol-emulation phase).

Coin-Generation Phase: The parties generate random-tapes for the emulation of the original protocol. Each party obtains the value of the random-tape to be held by it, whereas the other party obtains a commitment to this value. The party holding the value also obtains the corresponding decommitment information. All this is obtained by using a secure implementation of the (augmented) coin-tossing functionality (to be defined in Section 7.4.3.5). It follows that each party obtains a random-tape that is essentially random and independent of anything else.

Protocol Emulation Phase: The parties use a secure implementation of the authenticated-computation functionality (to be defined in Section 7.4.3.4) in order to emulate each step of the original protocol. Specifically, each message transmission in the original protocol is replaced by an invocation of the said sub-protocol (implementing this functionality), where the roles played by the parties and the inputs fed to the sub-protocol are as follows. The party that is supposed to send the message in the original protocol invokes the sub-protocol with an input that consists of its initial input (as committed in the first stage), its random-tape (as generated in the second stage), the decommitment information provided to it in the two corresponding stages, and the sequence of all incoming messages (of the original protocol as emulated so far). The input provided by the other party (i.e., the designated receiver) consists of the commitments it holds for the sender's input and random-tape (received in the first and second stage), as well as the sequence of all messages that it has previously sent to the sender. The functionality guarantees that either the corresponding (next-step) message is delivered or the designated receiver detects cheating.

In order to allow a modular presentation of the compiled protocols, we start by defining an adequate notion of reducibility (where here the oracle-aided protocol needs to be secure in the malicious model rather than in the semi-honest one). We next turn to constructing secure protocols for several basic functionalities, and use the latter to construct secure protocols for the three main functionalities mentioned here. Finally, we present and analyze the actual compiler.

7.4.2. Security Reductions and a Composition Theorem

Analogously to Section 7.3.1, we now define what we mean by saying that one functionality *securely reduces* to another functionality. We use the same definition of an oracle-aided protocol (i.e., Definition 7.3.1), but require such a protocol to be secure in the malicious model (rather than secure in the semi-honest model, as required in Definition 7.3.2). Recall that the basic syntax of an oracle-aided protocol allows sequential (but not parallel) oracle calls. For simplicity of our exposition, we require that the length of each oracle-query can be determined from the length of the initial input to the oracle-aided protocol.

Definition 7.4.2 (security reductions):

- *As in Definition 7.3.2, an oracle-aided protocol is said to be* using the oracle-functionality f *if the oracle answers are according to* f. *However, in accordance with the definition of the ideal model* (for the invoked functionality), *the oracle does not answer both parties concurrently, but rather answers first the real-model party that requested this specific oracle call* (in the oracle-aided protocol). *When receiving its part of the oracle answer, this party* (i.e., the real-model party that requested the oracle call) *instructs the oracle whether or not to respond to the other party.*

  We consider only protocols in which the length of each oracle-query is a polynomial-time computable function of the length of the initial input to the protocol. Furthermore, as in Definition 7.3.2, the length of each query must be polynomially related to the length of the initial input.

  We consider executions of such a protocol by a pair of parties, with strategies represented by probabilistic polynomial-time algorithms A_1 and A_2, such that one of the parties follows the oracle-aided protocol. Such a pair is called admissible. *Analogously to Definition 7.2.5, the* joint execution of an oracle-aided protocol Π with oracle f under $\overline{A} = (A_1, A_2)$ in the real model (on input pair (x, y) and auxiliary input z), *denoted* $\text{REAL}^{f}_{\Pi, \overline{A}(z)}(x, y)$, *is defined as the output pair resulting from the interaction between $A_1(x, z)$ and $A_2(y, z)$, where oracle calls are answered using f. We stress that here the real model corresponds to an execution of an oracle-aided protocol.*

- *An oracle-aided protocol Π using the oracle-functionality f is said to* securely compute g *if a condition analogous to the one in Definition 7.2.6 holds. That is, the* *effect of any admissible real-model strategies as in the previous item can be simulated by admissible strategies for the ideal model, where the ideal model for computing g is exactly as in Definition 7.2.4.*

> More specifically, the oracle-aided protocol Π (using oracle f) is said to **securely compute** g (in the malicious model) if for every probabilistic polynomial-time pair $\overline{A} = (A_1, A_2)$ that is admissible for the *real model of the oracle-aided computation,* there exists a probabilistic polynomial-time pair $\overline{B} = (B_1, B_2)$ that is admissible for the *ideal model* (of Definition 7.2.4) such that
>
> $$\{\text{IDEAL}_{g,\overline{B}(z)}(x, y)\}_{x,y,z} \stackrel{\text{c}}{\equiv} \{\text{REAL}^{f}_{\Pi,\overline{A}(z)}(x, y)\}_{x,y,z}$$
>
> where $x, y, z \in \{0, 1\}^*$ such that $|x| = |y|$ and $|z| = \text{poly}(|x|)$.

- *An oracle-aided protocol is said to* **securely reduce** *g to f if it securely computes g when using the oracle-functionality f. In such a case, we say that g* **is securely reducible to** *f,*

We are now ready to state a composition theorem for the malicious model.

Theorem 7.4.3 (Composition Theorem for the malicious model): *Suppose that g is securely reducible to f and that there exists a protocol for securely computing f. Then there exists a protocol for securely computing g.*

Recall that the syntax of oracle-aided protocols disallows concurrent oracle calls, and thus Theorem 7.4.3 is actually a *sequential composition theorem*. As in the semi-honest case, the Composition Theorem can be generalized to yield transitivity of secure reductions; that is, if g is securely reducible to f and f is securely reducible to e, then g is securely reducible to e (see Exercise 13).

As hinted in Section 7.3.1, the proof of Theorem 7.4.3 is significantly more complex than the proof of Theorem 7.3.3. This does not refer to the construction of the resulting protocol, but rather to establishing its security.

Proof Sketch: Analogously to the proof of Theorem 7.3.3, we are given an oracle-aided protocol, denoted $\Pi^{g|f}$, that securely reduces g to f, and an ordinary protocol Π^f that securely computes f. Again, we construct a protocol Π for computing g in the natural manner; that is, starting with $\Pi^{g|f}$, we replace each invocation of the oracle (i.e., of f) by an execution of the protocol Π^f.

Clearly, Π computes g, and we need to show that Π securely computes g. Specifically, we should present a transformation of real-model adversaries for Π into ideal-model adversaries for g. We have at our disposal two transformations of real-model adversaries (for $\Pi^{g|f}$ and for Π^f) into corresponding ideal-model adversaries (for g and f, respectively). So the first thing we should do is derive, from the real-model adversaries of Π, real-model adversaries for $\Pi^{g|f}$ and for Π^f.

We assume, without loss of generality, that all real-model adversaries output their view of the execution. (Recall that any other output can be efficiently computed from the view, and that any adversary can be easily modified to output its view.)

Let $\overline{A} = (A_1, A_2)$ be an admissible pair of real-model strategies of Π. We first derive from it a pair of strategies $\overline{A}' = (A_1', A_2')$ that represents the behavior of $\overline{A}$ during (each of) the invocations of Π^f. (We stress that we derive a single pair of real-model strategies that represents the behavior of the adversary during all the invocations of Π^f.)[33] Since the honest A_i just behaves according to Π, it follows that the induced A_i' just behaves according to Π^f, which means that A_i' is honest. Thus, we focus on the other (i.e., dishonest) A_i. In this case, the derived A_i' is a real-model adversary of Π^f that gets as auxiliary input the history of the execution of Π up to the current invocation of Π^f. Formally, A_i' takes two inputs, one representing (as usual) the history of the current execution of Π^f, and the other (i.e., an auxiliary one) being the history of the execution of Π up to the current invocation of Π^f. When A_i' completes (or aborts) the current execution of Π^f, it outputs its view of that execution. Loosely speaking, we derive the corresponding ideal-model adversary for f, denoted $\overline{B}' = (B_1', B_2')$, by employing the guaranteed transformation. A few technical difficulties arise and are resolved as follows:

- Party i (i.e., A_i') is not necessarily the party that plays the i-th party in Π^f (i.e., Party 1 is not necessarily the party in $\Pi^{g|f}$ that requests this particular oracle call to f). Furthermore, the identity of the party (in Π^f) played by A_i' is not fixed, but is rather determined by the history of the execution of Π (which is given to A_i' as auxiliary input). In contrast, our definitions refer to adversaries that play a predetermined party. This technical discrepancy can be overcome by considering two versions of A_i', denoted $A_{i,1}'$ and $A_{i,2}'$, such that $A_{i,j}'$ in used (instead of A_i') in case Party i is the party that plays the j-th party in Π^f. Indeed, $A_{i,j}'$ is always used to plays the j-th party in Π^f.
- A minor problem is that A_i may have its own auxiliary input, in which case the resulting A_i' will have two auxiliary inputs (i.e., the first identical to the one of A_i, and the second representing a partial execution transcript of Π). Clearly, these two auxiliary inputs can be combined into a single auxiliary input. (This fact holds generically, but more so in this specific setting in which it is anyhow natural to incorporate the inputs to an adversary in its view of the execution transcript.)
- The last problem is that it is not clear what "initial input" should be given to the adversary A_i' toward its current execution of Π^f (i.e., the input that is supposed to be used for computing f). However, this problem (which is more confusing than real) has little impact on our argument, because what matters is the actual actions of A_i' during the current execution of Π^f, and these are determined based on its (actual) auxiliary input (which represent the history of the execution of Π). Still, the initial inputs for the executions of Π^f have to be defined so that they can be passed to the ideal-model adversary that we derive from A_i'. We may almost set these initial inputs arbitrarily, except that (by our conventions regarding functionalities) we must

---

[33] The simpler alternative of deriving a different pair of (real-model) strategies for each invocation of Π^f would have sufficed for handling oracle-aided protocols that make a constant number of oracle calls. The point is that the corresponding ideal-model strategies (with respect to f) need to be combined into a single real-model strategy for $\Pi^{g|f}$.

set them to strings of correct length (i.e., equal to the length of the other party's f-input). Here we use the hypothesis that this length can be determined from the length of the input to Π itself.[34]

Thus, we have obtained an (admissible) ideal-adversary pair $\overline{B}' = (B_1', B_2')$ corresponding to f such that

$$\{\text{IDEAL}_{f, \overline{B}'(z')}(x', y')\}_{x', y', z'} \stackrel{c}{\equiv} \{\text{REAL}_{\Pi^f, \overline{A}'(z')}(x', y')\}_{x', y', z'} \tag{7.22}$$

We comment that when applying Eq. (7.22), we set the input of the honest party to equal the value on which the sub-protocol (or functionality) was invoked, and set the auxiliary input to equal the current execution transcript of the high-level protocol (as seen by the adversary). (As explained earlier, the setting of the primary input to the dishonest party is immaterial, because the latter determines its actions according to its auxiliary input.)

Our next step is to derive from $\overline{A} = (A_1, A_2)$ a pair of strategies $\overline{A}'' = (A_1'', A_2'')$ that represents the behavior of $\overline{A}$ during the $\Pi^{g|f}$-part of Π. Again, the honest A_i induces a corresponding A_i'' that just behaves according to $\Pi^{g|f}$. Turning to the dishonest A_i, we derive A_i'' by replacing the (real) actions of A_i' that take place in A_i by simulated actions of the ideal-model B_i'. That is, the adversary A_i'' runs machine A_i locally, while interacting with the actual other party of $\Pi^{g|f}$, obtaining the messages that A_i would have sent in a real execution of Π, and feeding A_i with messages that it expects to receive (i.e., messages that A_i would have received in a real execution of Π). The handling of A_i's messages depends on whether they belong to the $\Pi^{g|f}$-part or to one of the invocations of Π^f. The key point is the handling of the latter messages.

Handling Messages of $\Pi^{g|f}$: These messages are forwarded to/from the other party without change. That is, A_i'' uses A_i in order to determine the next message to be sent, and does so by feeding A_i with the history of the execution so far (which contains $\Pi^{g|f}$-part messages that A_i'' has received before, as well as the Π^f-parts that it has generated so far by itself). In particular, if A_i aborts, then so does A_i''.

Handling Messages of Π^f: Upon entering a new invocation of Π^f, the adversary A_i'' sets h_i to record the history of the execution of Π so far. Now, rather than executing Π^f using $A_i'(h_i)$ (as A_i would have done), the adversary A_i'' invokes $B_i'(h_i)$, where B_i' is the ideal-model adversary for f (derived from A_i', which in turn was derived from A_i). Recall that B_i' sends no messages and makes a single oracle-query (which it views as sending a message to its imaginary trusted party). The real-model adversary A_i'' (for the oracle-aided protocol $\Pi^{g|f}$) forwards this query to its own oracle (i.e.,

---

[34] We comment that when using the alternative conventions discussed at the end of Section 7.2.1.1, we may waive the requirement that the query length be determined by the input length. Instead, we postulate that all oracle calls made by the oracle-aided program use the same security parameter as the one with which the program is invoked. On the other hand, under the current conventions, when trying to extend the composition theorem to partial functionalities (or when removing the "length determination" hypothesis), we run into trouble because we need to determine some f-input that fits the unknown f-input of the other party. (This problem can be resolved by introducing an adequate interface to oracle calls.)

f), and feeds B_i' with the oracle answer. At some point B_i' terminates, and A_i'' uses its output to update the simulated history of the execution of Π. In particular, oracle-stopping events caused by $B_i'(h_i)$ (in case Party i requested this specific oracle call) and $\perp$-answers of the oracle (in the other case) are handled in the straightforward manner.

> **On stopping the oracle and $\perp$-answers:** Suppose first that Party i has re-
> quested this specific oracle call. In this case, after receiving the oracle answer
> (which it views as the answer of its trusted party), the ideal-model adversary B_i'
> may stop its trusted party. If this happens, then machine A_i'' instructs its own
> oracle (i.e., f) not to respond to the other party. Next, suppose that Party i is
> the party responding to this specific oracle call (rather than requesting it). In this
> case, it may happen that the oracle is stopped by the other party (i.e., the oracle
> is not allowed to answer Party i). When notified of this event (i.e., receiving a
> $\perp$-answer from its oracle), machine A_i'' feeds $\perp$ as answer to B_i'.

This completes the handling of the current invocation of Π^f.

When A_i halts with some output, A_i'' halts with the same output. Note that $\overline{A}'' = (A_1'', A_2'')$ is admissible as a real-model adversary for the oracle-aided protocol $\Pi^{g|f}$ (which computes g with oracle to f). Thus, we can derive from $\overline{A}''$ a corresponding ideal-model adversary for g, denoted $\overline{B}'' = (B_1'', B_2'')$, by employing the second guaranteed transformation, such that

$$\{\text{IDEAL}_{g,\overline{B}''(z)}(x, y)\}_{x,y,z} \stackrel{c}{\equiv} \{\text{REAL}^f_{\Pi^{g|f},\overline{A}''(z)}(x, y)\}_{x,y,z} \tag{7.23}$$

Thus, given a real-model adversary $\overline{A}$ for Π, we have derived an ideal-model adversary $\overline{B} \stackrel{\text{def}}{=} \overline{B}''$ for g. It is left to show that indeed the following holds:

$$\{\text{IDEAL}_{g,\overline{B}(z)}(x, y)\}_{x,y,z} \stackrel{c}{\equiv} \{\text{REAL}_{\Pi,\overline{A}(z)}(x, y)\}_{x,y,z} \tag{7.24}$$

Note that the left-hand side of Eq. (7.24) equals the left-hand side of Eq. (7.23), so it suffices to show that their corresponding right-hand sides are computationally indistinguishable. But $\text{REAL}_{\Pi,\overline{A}(z)}(x, y)$ differs from $\text{REAL}^f_{\Pi^{g|f},\overline{A}''(z)}(x, y)$ only in that the Π^f- invocations in the former are replaced in the latter by ideal calls to f. However, by Eq. (7.22), each Π^f invocation is computationally indistinguishable from an ideal call to f, where computational indistinguishability holds also with respect to auxiliary inputs (which are used here to represent the execution transcript upto the point of the current invocation). Using a hybrid argument (corresponding to a gradual substitution of Π^f-invocations by ideal calls to f), one can show that $\{\text{REAL}^f_{\Pi^{g|f},\overline{A}''(z)}(x, y)\}_{x,y,z}$ and $\{\text{REAL}_{\Pi,\overline{A}(z)}(x, y)\}_{x,y,z}$ are computationally indistinguishable.[35] This establishes Eq. (7.24), and the theorem follows. ∎

---

[35] Here we use the hypothesis that the query lengths are polynomially related to the length of the input. The issue is that in Eq. (7.22), computational indistinguishability is with respect to the length of the queries (to f), whereas we need computational indistinguishability with respect to the length of the initial inputs. We also highlight the key role of the auxiliary inputs to $\overline{A}'$ and $\overline{B}'$ in this argument (cf. the analysis of the sequential composition of zero-knowledge [i.e., proof of Lemma 4.3.11]).

Security Reduction of General Functionalities to Deterministic Ones. The following reduction will not be used in our compiler, because the compiler refers to protocols (rather to functionalities), and we have already obtained protocols for privately computing general functionalities (by privately reducing them to deterministic ones). Still, we consider it of interest to state that the reduction presented in Proposition 7.3.4 is, in fact, secure in the malicious model.

Proposition 7.4.4 (securely reducing a randomized Functionality to a Deterministic One): *Let g be a randomized functionality, f be as defined in Eq. (7.19), and* Π *be the oracle-aided protocol for g using the oracle f as presented in Proposition 7.3.4. Then* Π *securely computes g.*

Proof Sketch: Suppose, without loss of generality, that Party 1 is malicious, and denote by (x_1', r_1') the query it makes to f. Denoting by x_i the initial input of Party i (in Π), it follows that the oracle answer is $f((x_1', r_1'), (x_2, r_2))$, where r_2 is uniformly distributed (because Party 2 is honest). Recalling that $f((x_1', r_1'), (x_2, r_2)) = g(r_1' \oplus r_2, (x_1', x_2))$, it follows that the oracle answer is distributed identically to $g(x_1', x_2)$. Furthermore, by the definition of Π, all that Party 1 gets is $f_1((x_1', r_1'), (x_2, U_{|r_1'|})) \equiv g_1(x_1', x_2)$. This is easily simulated by a corresponding ideal-model adversary that sets x_1' according to the real-model adversary, and sends x_1' to the trusted third party (which answers according to g). ∎

Remark 7.4.5 (reductions to a set of functionalities): We extend the notion of security reductions to account for protocols that use several oracles rather than one. Specifically, g is securely reducible to a set of functionalities $F = \{f^1, ..., f^t\}$ if there exists an oracle-aided protocol that securely computes g when given oracles $f^1, ..., f^t$. Theorem 7.4.3 also extends to assert that if g is securely reducible to F, and each functionality in F can be securely computed, then so can g. We comment that the entire remark is a matter of semantics, because one can "pack" the set F in one functionality f (e.g., $f((i, x), (i, y)) \stackrel{\text{def}}{=} f^i(x, y)$).

7.4.3. The Compiler: Functionalities in Use

As stated in Section 7.4.1, the protocols produced by our compiler make extensive use of protocols that securely compute three functionalities that are the core of the three corresponding phases of the compiled protocols. In the current section, we explicitly define these functionalities and present protocols for securely computing them.

We start by considering three natural functionalities that are related to the functionalities used by the compiler. Specifically, we first consider the coin-tossing functionality (see Section 7.4.3.1), a *restricted* notion of the authenticated-computation functionality (Section 7.4.3.2), and an "unauthenticated-computation functionality" (called *image transmission* in Section 7.4.3.3). Next, using these three functionalities, we present secure protocols for a *general* notion of authenticated-computation functionality (see Section 7.4.3.4), for an *augmented* notion of coin-tossing (Section 7.4.3.5), and for the

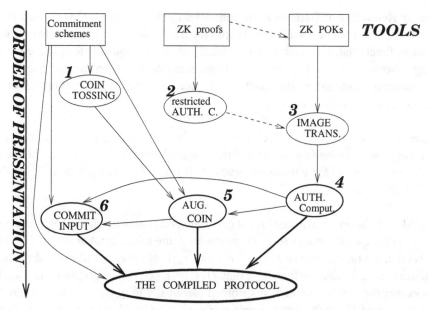

Figure 7.2: The functionalities used in the compiled protocol.

input-commitment functionality (Section 7.4.3.6). The latter three functionalities will be used directly in the compiled protocols (see Figure 7.2, where solid arrows indicate direct and essential use). We comment that although the material in Section 7.4.3.2 is not used directly in the rest of this work, it is instructive to the rest of the current section.

We comment that it is easy to present protocols for *privately* computing all the abovementioned functionalities (in the semi-honest model; see Exercise 11). Our aim, however, is to present (for later use in the compiler) protocols for *securely* computing these functionalities in the malicious model.

Basic Tools and Conventions Regarding Them. Let us recall some facts and notations regarding three tools that we will use:

- *Commitment schemes* (as defined in Definition 4.4.1). For the sake of simplicity, we will use a non-interactive commitment scheme (as in Construction 4.4.2). We assume, for simplicity, that on security parameter n, the commitment scheme utilizes exactly n random bits. We denote by $C_r(b)$ the commitment to the bit b using (security parameter n and) randomness $r \in \{0, 1\}^n$, and by $C(b)$ the value of $C_r(b)$ for a uniformly distributed $r \in \{0, 1\}^n$ (where n is understood from the context).
- *Zero-knowledge proofs of NP-assertions.* We rely on the fact (cf. Theorem 4.4.11) that there exist such proof systems in which the prover strategy can be implemented in probabilistic polynomial-time, when given an NP-witness as auxiliary input. We stress that by this we mean (zero-knowledge) proof systems with negligible soundness error. Furthermore, we rely on the fact that these proof systems have perfect completeness (i.e., the verifier accepts a valid statement with probability 1).

- *Zero-knowledge proofs-of-knowledge of NP-witnesses.* We will use the definition of a *strong* proof of knowledge (see Definition 4.7.13). We again rely on the analogous fact regarding the complexity of adequate prover strategies: That is, strong proofs-of-knowledge that are zero-knowledge exist for any NP-relation, and furthermore, the prover strategy can be implemented in probabilistic polynomial-time, when given an NP-witness as auxiliary input (see Construction 4.7.14).

All these tools are known to exist assuming the existence of one-way 1-1 functions. In fact, the 1-1 requirement can be avoided at the cost of using an interactive commitment scheme.

On the Adversaries Being Considered. For the sake of simplicity, in all the proofs of security presented in this section, we only refer to malicious (real-model) adversaries with no auxiliary input. Furthermore, we will assume that these malicious (real-model) adversaries are deterministic. As discussed in Section 7.2.3.1 (see text following Definition 7.2.5), the treatment of randomized adversaries (with auxiliary inputs) can be reduced to the treatment of deterministic adversaries *with auxiliary inputs,* and so the issue here is actually the fact that we ignore auxiliary inputs. However, in all cases, the extension of our treatment to malicious adversaries with auxiliary input is straight-forward. Specifically, in all cases, we construct ideal-model adversaries by using the real-model adversaries as subroutines. This black-box usage easily supports the extension to adversaries with auxiliary inputs, because all that is needed is to pass the auxiliary-input (given to the ideal-model adversary) to the real-model adversary (which is invoked as a subroutine).

Comments Regarding the Following Exposition. All protocols are presented by specifying the behavior of honest parties, while keeping in mind that dishonest parties may deviate from the specified behavior. Thus, we may instruct one party to send a specific message that satisfies some property and next instruct the other party to check that the message received indeed satisfies this property. When transforming real-model adversaries to ideal-model adversaries, we sometimes allow the latter to halt before invoking the *trusted party.* As discussed in Section 7.2.3.1 (see text preceding Definition 7.2.4), this can be viewed as invoking the trusted party with a special abort symbol, where in this case, the latter responds to all parties with a special abort symbol.

7.4.3.1. Coin-Tossing

We start our assembly of functionalities that are useful for the compiler by presenting and implementing a very natural functionality, which is of independent interest. Specifically, we refer to the coin-tossing functionality $(1^n, 1^n) \mapsto (b, b)$, where b is uniformly distributed in $\{0, 1\}$. This functionality allows a pair of distrustful parties to agree on a common random value.[36]

---

[36] Actually, in order to conform with the convention that the functionality has to be defined for any input pair, we may consider the formulation $(x, y) \mapsto (b, b)$.

Definition 7.4.6 (coin-tossing into the well, basic version): *A* coin-tossing-into-the-well *protocol is a two-party protocol for securely computing* (in the malicious model) *the randomized functionality* $(1^n, 1^n) \mapsto (b, b)$, *where b is uniformly distributed in* $\{0, 1\}$.

That is, in spite of malicious behavior by any one party, a non-aborting execution of a coin-tossing-into-the-well protocol ends with both parties holding the *same uniformly distributed bit, b*. Recall that our definition of security allows $(b, \perp)$ to appear as output in case Party 1 aborts. (It would have been impossible to securely implement the coin-tossing functionality if the definition had not allowed this slackness; see Section 7.7.1.1.) The coin-tossing functionality will not be used directly in the compiled protocols, but it will be used to implement an augmented notion of coin-tossing (see Section 7.4.3.5), which in turn will be used directly in these protocols.

Construction 7.4.7 (a coin-tossing-into-the-well protocol): *For every r, let* $C_r : \{0, 1\} \rightarrow \{0, 1\}^*$.

Inputs: *Both parties get security parameter* 1^n.

Step C1: *Party 1 uniformly selects* $\sigma \in \{0, 1\}$ *and* $s \in \{0, 1\}^n$, *and sends* $c \stackrel{\text{def}}{=} C_s(\sigma)$ *to Party 2.*

To simplify the exposition, we adopt the convention by which failure of Party 1 to send a message (i.e., aborting) is interpreted as an arbitrary bit string, say $C_{0^n}(0)$.

Step C2: *Party 2 uniformly selects* $\sigma' \in \{0, 1\}$, *and sends* σ' *to Party 1.*

Similarly, any possible response of Party 2, including abort, will be interpreted by Party 1 as a bit.[37]

Step C3: *Party 1 outputs the value* $\sigma \oplus \sigma'$, *and sends* (σ, s) *to Party 2.*

Step C4: *Party 2 checks whether or not* $c = C_s(\sigma)$. *It outputs* $\sigma \oplus \sigma'$ *if* $c = C_s(\sigma)$ *and halts with output* $\perp$ *otherwise.*

In contrast to Steps C1–C2, here any illegal answer is interpreted as abort.

Outputs: *Party 1 always outputs* $b \stackrel{\text{def}}{=} \sigma \oplus \sigma'$, *whereas Party 2 either outputs b or* $\perp$.

Intuitively, Steps C1–C2 may be viewed as "tossing a coin into the well." At this point, the value of the coin is determined (essentially as a random value), but only one party knows ("can see") this value. Clearly, if both parties are honest, then they both output the same uniformly chosen bit, recovered in Steps C3 and C4, respectively.

Proposition 7.4.8: *Suppose that C is a bit commitment scheme. Then, Construction 7.4.7 constitutes a coin-tossing-into-the-well protocol.*

Proof Sketch: We need to transform any admissible pair, (A_1, A_2), for the real model into a corresponding pair, (B_1, B_2), for the ideal model. We treat separately each of the

---

[37] These two conventions prevent the parties from aborting the execution before Step C3.

two cases corresponding to the identity of the honest party. Recall that we may assume, for simplicity, that the adversary is deterministic (see discussion toward the end of the preamble of Section 7.4.3). Also, for simplicity, we omit the input 1^n in some places. The following schematic depiction of the information flow in Construction 7.4.7 may be useful toward the following analysis:

	Party 1	Party 2
C1	selects (σ, s)	
	$c \leftarrow C_s(\sigma) \quad \longrightarrow \quad c \quad \longrightarrow$	
C2		selects $\sigma' \in \{0, 1\}$
	$\longleftarrow \quad \sigma' \quad \longleftarrow$	
C3	$b \leftarrow \sigma \oplus \sigma'$	
	$\longrightarrow (\sigma, s) \longrightarrow$	
output	b	b or $\perp$
		(depending on whether $c = C_s(\sigma)$)

We start with the case where *the first party is honest*. In this case, B_1 is determined (by the protocol), and we transform the real-model adversary A_2 into an ideal-model adversary B_2. Machine B_2 will run machine A_2 locally, obtaining the single message that A_2 would have sent in a real execution of the protocol (i.e., $\sigma' \in \{0, 1\}$) and feeding A_2 with the messages that it expects to receive. Recall that A_2 expects to see the messages $C_s(\sigma)$ and (σ, s) (and that B_2 gets input 1^n).

1. B_2 sends 1^n to the *trusted party* and obtains an answer (bit), denoted b, which is uniformly distributed. (Recall that b is also handed to Party 1.)
2. B_2 tries to generate an execution view (of A_2) ending with output b. This is done by repeating the following steps at most n times:

   (a) B_2 uniformly select $\sigma \in \{0, 1\}$ and $s \in \{0, 1\}^n$, and feeds A_2 with $c \stackrel{\text{def}}{=} C_s(\sigma)$. Recall that A_2 always responds with a bit, denoted σ', which may depend on c (i.e., $\sigma' \leftarrow A_2(c)$).

   (b) If $\sigma \oplus \sigma' = b$, then B_2 feeds A_2 with the execution view $(c, (\sigma, s))$, and outputs whatever A_2 does. Otherwise, it continues to the next iteration.

   In case all n iterations were completed unsuccessfully (i.e., without output), B_2 outputs a special failure symbol.

We need to show that for the coin-tossing functionality, denoted f, and for Construction 7.4.7, denoted Π, it holds that

$$\{\text{IDEAL}_{f, \overline{B}}(1^n, 1^n)\}_{n \in \mathbb{N}} \stackrel{c}{\equiv} \{\text{REAL}_{\Pi, \overline{A}}(1^n, 1^n)\}_{n \in \mathbb{N}}$$

In fact, we will show that the two ensembles are *statistically indistinguishable*. We start by showing that the probability that B_2 outputs failure is exponentially small. This is shown by proving that for every $b \in \{0, 1\}$, each iteration of Step 2 succeeds with probability approximately $1/2$. Such an iteration succeeds if and only if $\sigma \oplus \sigma' = b$, that is, if $A_2(C_s(\sigma)) = b \oplus \sigma$, where $(\sigma, s) \in \{0, 1\} \times \{0, 1\}^n$ is uniformly chosen. We have

$$\Pr_{\sigma,s}[A_2(C_s(\sigma)) = b \oplus \sigma]$$

$$= \frac{1}{2} \cdot \Pr[A_2(C(0)) = b] + \frac{1}{2} \cdot \Pr[A_2(C(1)) = b \oplus 1]$$

$$= \frac{1}{2} + \frac{1}{2} \cdot (\Pr[A_2(C(0)) = b] - \Pr[A_2(C(1)) = b])$$

Using the hypothesis that C is a commitment scheme, the second term is a negligible function in n, and so our claim regarding the probability that B_2 outputs failure follows. Letting μ denote an appropriate negligible function, we state the following for future reference:

$$\Pr_{\sigma,s}[A_2(C_s(\sigma)) = b \oplus \sigma] = \frac{1}{2} \pm \mu(n) \qquad (7.25)$$

Next, we show that conditioned on B_2 not outputting failure, the distribution IDEAL$_{f,\overline{B}}(1^n, 1^n)$ is statistically indistinguishable from the distribution REAL$_{\Pi,\overline{A}}(1^n, 1^n)$. Both distributions have the form $(b, A_2(C_s(\sigma), (\sigma, s)))$, with $b = \sigma \oplus A_2(C_s(\sigma))$, and thus both are determined by the (σ, s)-pairs. In REAL$_{\Pi,\overline{A}}(1^n, 1^n)$, all (σ, s)-pairs are equally likely (i.e., each appears with probability $2^{-(n+1)}$); whereas (as proven next) in IDEAL$_{f,\overline{B}}(1^n, 1^n)$, each pair (σ, s) appears with probability

$$\frac{1}{2} \cdot \frac{1}{|S_{\sigma \oplus A_2(C_s(\sigma))}|} \qquad (7.26)$$

where $S_b \overset{\text{def}}{=} \{(x, y) \in \{0, 1\} \times \{0, 1\}^n : x \oplus A_2(C_y(x)) = b\}$ is the set of pairs that pass the condition in Step 2b (with respect to the value b obtained in Step 1). To justify Eq. (7.26), observe that the pair (σ, s) appears as output if and only if it is selected in Step 2a and the trusted party answers with $\sigma \oplus A_2(C_s(\sigma))$, where the latter event occurs with probability $1/2$. Furthermore, the successful pairs, selected in Step 2a and passing the condition in Step 2b, are uniformly distributed in $S_{\sigma \oplus A_2(C_s(\sigma))}$, which justifies Eq. (7.26). We next show that $|S_b| \approx 2^n$, for every $b \in \{0, 1\}$. By Eq. (7.25), for every fixed $b \in \{0, 1\}$ and uniformly distributed $(\sigma, s) \in \{0, 1\} \times \{0, 1\}^n$, the event $(\sigma, s) \in S_b$ (i.e., $\sigma \oplus A_2(C_s(\sigma)) = b$) occurs with probability that is negligibly close to $1/2$, and so $|S_b| = (1 \pm \mu(n)) \cdot \frac{1}{2} \cdot 2^{n+1}$, where μ is a negligible function. Thus, for every pair (σ, s), it holds that $|S_{\sigma \oplus A_2(C_s(\sigma))}| \in \{|S_0|, |S_1|\}$ resides in the interval $(1 \pm \mu(n)) \cdot 2^n$. It follows that the value of Eq. (7.26) is $(1 \pm \mu(n)) \cdot 2^{-(n+1)}$, and so REAL$_{\Pi,\overline{A}}(1^n, 1^n)$ and IDEAL$_{f,\overline{B}}(1^n, 1^n)$ are statistically indistinguishable.

We now turn to the case where *the second party is honest*. In this case, B_2 is determined, and we transform A_1 into B_1 (for the ideal model). On input 1^n, machine B_1 runs machine A_1 locally, obtaining the messages that A_1 would have sent in a real execution of the protocol and feeding A_1 with the single message (i.e., $\sigma' \in \{0, 1\}$) that it expects to receive.

1. B_1 invokes A_1 (on input 1^n). Recall that by our conventions, A_1 always sends a message in Step C1. Let us denote this message (which is supposedly a commitment

using C) by c. Recall that c may be in the range of $C(\sigma)$ for at most one $\sigma \in \{0, 1\}$.

2. Machine B_1 tries to obtain the answers of A_1 (in Step C3) to both possible messages that could be sent in Step C2:

   (a) B_1 feeds A_1 with the (Step C2) message 0 and records the answer, which is either abort or (σ_0, s_0). The case in which $c \neq C_{s_0}(\sigma_0)$ is treated as if A_1 has aborted.

   (b) Rewinding A_1 to the beginning of Step C2, machine B_1 feeds A_1 with the message 1 and records the answer, which is either abort or (σ_1, s_1). (Again, the case in which $c \neq C_{s_1}(\sigma_1)$ is treated as abort.)

   If A_1 aborts in both cases, then machine B_1 aborts with output $A_1(1^n, \sigma')$, for a uniformly chosen $\sigma' \in \{0, 1\}$ (and does so without invoking the *trusted party*, which means that the honest Party 2 receives $\perp$ from the latter).[38] (In the following, we refer to this case as to *Case 0*.) Otherwise, B_1 proceed as follows, distinguishing two cases:

   Case 1: A_1 answers properly (in the previous experiment) for a single 0-1 value, denoted σ'. In this case, we define $\sigma \stackrel{\text{def}}{=} \sigma_{\sigma'}$.

   Case 2: A_1 answers properly for both values. In this case, the values σ_0 and σ_1 (defined in Step 1) must be identical, because $C_{s_0}(\sigma_0) = c = C_{s_1}(\sigma_1)$, whereas the ranges of $C(0)$ and $C(1)$ are disjoint. In this case, we define $\sigma \stackrel{\text{def}}{=} \sigma_0 \, (= \sigma_1)$.

3. Machine B_1 sends 1^n to the *trusted party*, which responds with a uniformly selected value $b \in \{0, 1\}$. Recall that the trusted party has not responded to Party 2 yet, and that B_1 still has the option of stopping the trusted party before it responds to Party 2.

4. In Case 1, machine B_1 *stops the trusted party* if $b \neq \sigma \oplus \sigma'$ (where σ' is as defined in Case 1), and otherwise allows it to send b to Party 2 (in which case $b = \sigma \oplus \sigma'$ holds). In Case 2, machine B_1 sets $\sigma' = b \oplus \sigma$ and allows the *trusted party* to send b to Party 2. Next, in both cases, B_1 feeds σ' to A_1, which responds with the Step C3 message $(\sigma, s_{\sigma'})$. Note that if the trusted party sent b to Party 2, then indeed $\sigma \oplus \sigma' = b$ holds (in both Case 1 and Case 2).

5. Finally, B_1 feeds A_1 with the execution view, $(1^n, \sigma')$, and outputs whatever A_1 does.

We now show that $\text{IDEAL}_{f,\overline{B}}(1^n, 1^n)$ and $\text{REAL}_{\Pi,\overline{A}}(1^n, 1^n)$ are actually *identically distributed*. Consider first the case where A_1 (and so B_1) *never* aborts (i.e., Case 2). In this case, we have

$$\text{IDEAL}_{f,\overline{B}}(1^n, 1^n) = (A_1(1^n, \sigma \oplus b), \, b)$$

$$\text{REAL}_{\Pi,\overline{A}}(1^n, 1^n) = (A_1(1^n, \sigma'), \, \sigma \oplus \sigma')$$

where σ' and b are uniformly distributed in $\{0, 1\}$, and σ is determined by $c = A_1(1^n)$ (i.e., $\sigma = C^{-1}(c)$). Observe that σ' is distributed uniformly independently of σ, and so

---

[38] We comment that whenever B_1 is determined to abort, it need not invoke the trusted party at all, because it (i.e., B_1) can simulate the trusted party's answer by itself. The only reason to invoke the trusted party is to provide Party 2 with an answer that is related to the output of B_1.

$\sigma \oplus \sigma'$ is uniformly distributed over $\{0, 1\}$. We conclude that $(A_1(1^n, \sigma \oplus b), b)$ and $(A_1(1^n, \sigma \oplus (\sigma \oplus \sigma')), \sigma \oplus \sigma')$ are identically distributed.

Next, consider the case that B_1 *always* aborts (due to improper A_1 behavior in Step C3). In this case (i.e., the previous Case 0), B_1 aborts before invoking the trusted party, and so both ensembles are identical (i.e., both equal $(A_1(1^n, \sigma'), \bot)$ for a random σ'). Since A_1 is deterministic (see beginning of the proof), the only case left to consider is where A_1 responds properly (in Step C3) to a single value, denoted σ'. In this case (i.e., Case 1), the *real execution* of Π is completed only if Party 2 sends σ' as its Step C2 message (which happens with probability $1/2$), and is aborted otherwise. Similarly, in the ideal model, the execution is completed (without B_1 aborting) if the trusted party answers with $b = \sigma \oplus \sigma'$ (which happens with probability $1/2$).[39] In both models, the joint non-aborted execution equals $(A_1(1^n, \sigma'), \sigma \oplus \sigma')$, whereas the joint aborted execution equals $(A_1(1^n, \sigma' \oplus 1), \bot)$. ∎

7.4.3.2. Authenticated Computation (Partial Version)

We continue our assembly of functionalities that are useful for the compiler by presenting and implementing another natural functionality, which is of independent interest. Specifically, we refer to the archetypical application of zero-knowledge proofs (cf. Section 4.4.3), which is to solve the following problem. For two predetermined (polynomial-time computable) functions, f and h, a party holding a secret α should send the correct value of $f(\alpha)$ to the other party, which holds $h(\alpha)$, while not revealing anything else to the other party. That is, we are talking about securely computing the functionality $(\alpha, h(\alpha)) \mapsto (\lambda, f(\alpha))$, where typically h is 1-1 (and so the value of its image uniquely determines its preimage).

We stress that the functionality described here has a partial domain; that is, it is not defined over all pairs of inputs (of equal length), but rather only for pairs of the form $(\alpha, h(\alpha))$. This restriction (i.e., definability over a partial domain) coincides with the standard archetypical application of zero-knowledge proofs and is easier to implement. However, this restriction does not suffice for a modular exposition of the compiled protocols (because composition of partial functionalities is more complex than the composition result captured by Theorem 7.4.3). Indeed, in Section 7.4.3.4 we waive the restriction (to the partial domain) and consider an extension of the authenticated computation functionality to arbitrary pairs of (equal-length) strings.

Definition 7.4.9 (authenticated computation, partial version): *Let* $f : \{0, 1\}^* \times \{0, 1\}^* \to \{0, 1\}^*$ *and* $h : \{0, 1\}^* \to \{0, 1\}^*$ *be polynomial-time computable. The h-*authenticated f-computation functionality *is defined by*

$$(\alpha, h(\alpha)) \mapsto (\lambda, f(\alpha)) \tag{7.27}$$

We assume, for simplicity, that h is length preserving. Otherwise, the definition may be modified to consider the functionality $((\alpha, 1^{|h(\alpha)|}), (h(\alpha), 1^{|\alpha|})) \mapsto (\lambda, f(\alpha))$. To

---

[39] Recall that, in this case, σ and σ' are determined by the Step C1 message.

facilitate the implementation, we assume that the function h is one-to-one, as is the case in typical applications. This allows us to use (ordinary) zero-knowledge proofs, rather than strong (zero-knowledge) proofs-of-knowledge. The issue is further discussed in Section 7.4.3.3.

The functionality of Eq. (7.27) is implemented by having Party 1 send $f(\alpha)$ to Party 2, and then prove in zero-knowledge the correctness of the value sent (with respect to the common input $h(\alpha)$). Note that this statement is of the NP type and that Party 1 has the corresponding NP-witness. Actually, the following protocol is *the archetypical* application of zero-knowledge proof systems.

Construction 7.4.10 (authenticated computation protocol, partial version): *Let L be the set of pairs (u, v) satisfying Eq. (7.28) to follow, and (P, V) be an interactive proof for L. Furthermore, suppose that P can be implemented in probabilistic polynomial-time when given an adequate auxiliary-input (i.e., an NP-witness for membership of the common input in L).*

Inputs: *Party 1 gets input $\alpha \in \{0, 1\}^*$, and Party 2 gets input $u = h(\alpha)$.*

Step C1: *Party 1 sends $v \stackrel{\text{def}}{=} f(\alpha)$ to Party 2.*

Step C2: *The parties invoke the proof system (P, V) such that Party 1 plays the prover and Party 2 plays the verifier. The common input to the proof system is (u, v), the prover gets auxiliary input α, and its objective is to prove that*

$$\exists x \quad \text{s.t.} \quad (u = h(x)) \wedge (v = f(x)) \tag{7.28}$$

(Each party locally determines the common input (u, v) according to its own view of the execution so far.)[40] In case the verifier rejects the proof, Party 2 halts with output $\perp$ (otherwise the output will be v).

(Any possible response – including abort – of Party 2 during the execution of this step will be interpreted by Party 1 as a canonical legitimate message.)

Outputs: *In case Party 2 has not halted with output $\perp$ (indicating improper behavior of Party 1), Party 2 sets its local output to v. (Party 1 has no output [or, alternatively, always outputs λ].)*

Observe that the specified strategies are indeed implementable in polynomial-time. In particular, in Step C2, Party 1 supplies the prover subroutine with the NP-witness α such that Eq. (7.28) is satisfied with $x = \alpha$. Also, using the *perfect completeness condition* of the proof system, it follows that if both parties are honest, then neither aborts and the output is as required.

Proposition 7.4.11: *Suppose that the function h is one-to-one and that (P, V) is a zero-knowledge interactive proof (with negligible soundness error) for L. Then, Construction 7.4.10 securely computes* (in the malicious model) *the h-authenticated f-computation functionality of Eq. (7.27).*

---

[40] In particular, Party 1 sets $(u, v) = (h(\alpha), f(\alpha))$, whereas Party 2 sets u according to its own input and v according to the message received in Step C1.

We stress that Proposition 7.4.11 refers to the security of a protocol for computing a partial functionality, as discussed in Remark 7.2.7. In the case of Eq. (7.27), this means that the ideal-model adversary is not allowed to "modify its input" (i.e., it must pass its initial input to the trusted party), because its initial input is the unique value that fits the other party's input.

Proof Sketch: Again, we need to transform any admissible pair, (A_1, A_2), for the real model into a corresponding pair, (B_1, B_2), for the ideal model. We treat separately each of the two cases, corresponding to the identity of the honest party.

We start with the case where *the first party is honest*. In this case, B_1 is determined, and we transform (the real-model adversary) A_2 into (an ideal-model adversary) B_2, which uses A_2 as a subroutine. Recall that B_2 gets input $u = h(\alpha)$, where α is the input of the honest Party 1.

1. B_2 sends u to the *trusted party* and obtains the value v, which equals $f(\alpha)$ for α handed by (the honest) Party 1 to the trusted party. Thus, indeed, B_2 does not modify its input and $(u, v) \in L$. (Recall that Party 1 always obtains λ from the trusted party.)
2. B_2 invokes the simulator guaranteed for the zero-knowledge proof system (P, V), on input (u, v), using (the residual) A_2 as a possible malicious verifier.[41] Note that we are simulating the actions of the prescribed prover P, which in the real protocol is played by the honest Party 1. Denote the obtained simulation transcript by $S = S(u, v)$, where (indeed) A_2 is implicit in the notation.
3. Finally, B_2 feeds A_2 with the alleged execution view (v, S), and outputs whatever A_2 does.

We need to show that for the functionality, denoted F, of Eq. (7.27) and for Construction 7.4.10, denoted Π, it holds that

$$\{\text{IDEAL}_{F,\overline{B}}(\alpha, h(\alpha))\}_{\alpha \in \{0,1\}^*} \stackrel{c}{\equiv} \{\text{REAL}_{\Pi,\overline{A}}(\alpha, h(\alpha))\}_{\alpha \in \{0,1\}^*} \tag{7.29}$$

Let $R(\alpha)$ denote the verifier's view of the real interaction with P on common input $(h(\alpha), f(\alpha))$ and prover's auxiliary input α, where the verifier is played by A_2. Then,

$$\text{REAL}_{\Pi,\overline{A}}(\alpha, h(\alpha)) = (\lambda, \ A_2(h(\alpha), f(\alpha), R(\alpha)))$$

$$\text{IDEAL}_{F,\overline{B}}(\alpha, h(\alpha)) = (\lambda, \ A_2(h(\alpha), f(\alpha), S(h(\alpha), f(\alpha))))$$

However, by the standard formulation of zero-knowledge, it follows that $\{R(\alpha)\}_{\alpha \in \{0,1\}^*}$ and $\{S(h(\alpha), f(\alpha))\}_{\alpha \in \{0,1\}^*}$ are computationally indistinguishable (also when given α as auxiliary input), and so Eq. (7.29) follows.

We now turn to the case where *the second party is honest*. In this case, B_2 is determined, and we transform (real-model) A_1 into (ideal-model) B_1, which uses A_1 as a subroutine. Recall that B_1 gets input $\alpha \in \{0, 1\}^n$.

1. B_1 invokes A_1 on input α. As (implicit) in the protocol, any action of A_1 in Step C1 (including abort) is interpreted as sending a string. Let us denote by v the message sent by A_1 (i.e., $v \leftarrow A_1(\alpha)$).

---

[41] The case in which A_2 executes Step C2 with respect to a different common input is just a special case of a malicious behavior.

2. Intuitively, machine B_1 checks whether or not $v = f(\alpha)$, where α is as in Step 1 (i.e., the input to B_1). Actually, B_1 checks whether or not an honest verifier would have been convinced by (the residual) A_1 that $v = f(\alpha)$ holds, which is equivalent to being convinced that $(h(\alpha), v) \in L$. Specifically, B_1 emulates the execution of Step C2 (i.e., the execution of the proof system (P, V) on common input $(h(\alpha), v)$), while using the strategy A_1 to determine the moves of the (possibly cheating) prover (and playing the honest verifier in a straightforward manner).[42]

Recall that this proof system has negligible soundness error, and so if $(h(\alpha), v)$ does not satisfy Eq. (7.28), this fact is detected with probability $1 - \mu(n)$, where μ is some negligible function. If the verifier (played by B_1 itself) rejects, then machine B_1 aborts (without invoking the *trusted party*).[43] Otherwise, we proceed assuming that $(h(\alpha), v)$ satisfies Eq. (7.28). Note that since h is 1-1 and Eq. (7.28) is satisfied, it must be the case that $v = f(h^{-1}(h(\alpha))) = f(\alpha)$.[44]

3. Assuming that machine B_1 has not aborted, it sends α to the *trusted party* and allows the latter to respond to Party 2. (The trusted party's response will be $f(\alpha) = v$. Again, note that, indeed, B_1 does not modify its input.)

4. Finally, B_1 feeds A_1 with the execution view, which consists of the prover's view of the emulation of Step C2 (produced in Step 2), and outputs whatever A_1 does.

We now show that

$$\{\mathrm{IDEAL}_{F, \overline{B}}(\alpha, h(\alpha))\}_{\alpha \in \{0,1\}^*} \stackrel{c}{\equiv} \{\mathrm{REAL}_{\Pi, \overline{A}}(\alpha, h(\alpha))\}_{\alpha \in \{0,1\}^*} \tag{7.30}$$

Actually, we will show that these two ensembles are statistically indistinguishable, where the statistical difference is due to the case where the real adversary A_1 succeeds in convincing the verifier (played by the honest Party 2) that (u, v) satisfies Eq. (7.28), and yet this claim is false. By the soundness of the proof system, this event happens only with negligible probability. On the other hand, in case (u, v) satisfies Eq. (7.28), we show that $\mathrm{IDEAL}_{F, \overline{B}}(\alpha, h(\alpha))$ and $\mathrm{REAL}_{\Pi, \overline{A}}(\alpha, h(\alpha))$ are identically distributed. Details follow. One key observation is that *the emulation of the proof system* (with prover strategy $A_1(\alpha)$) *performed in Step 2 by B_1 is distributed identically to the real execution of the proof system that takes place in Step C2 of Π.*

Fixing any α, recall that $v \stackrel{\text{def}}{=} A_1(\alpha)$ need not equal $f(\alpha)$, and that $u \stackrel{\text{def}}{=} h(\alpha)$ uniquely determines α (because h is 1-1). We denote by p the probability that $A_1(\alpha)$ (playing a possibly cheating prover) convinces the verifier (played in Step C2 by Party 2) that (u, v) satisfies Eq. (7.28). (Since A_1 is deterministic, $v = A_1(\alpha)$ is fixed and the probability is only taken over the moves of Party 2.) We consider two cases corresponding to the

---

[42] In particular, if A_1 aborts the execution of Step C2, then the honest verifier will not be convinced.

[43] Alternatively, machine B_1 may invoke the trusted party but prevent it from answering Party 2. The difference is immaterial, because Party 1 gets nothing from the trusted party. What matters is that (in either case) Party 2 will get an abort symbol (i.e., $\perp$).

[44] We comment that even if h were not 1-1 but a strong proof-of-knowledge (rather than an ordinary proof system) was used in Step C2, then one could have inferred that Party 1 knows an α' so that $h(\alpha') = u$ and $v = f(\alpha')$, whereas α' does not necessarily equal α. Sending α' to the trusted party in the next (emulation) step, we would have been fine, as it would have (also) meant that the trusted party's response to Party 2 is v.

relation between p and the soundness error-bound function μ associated with the proof system (P, V).[45]

1. Suppose $p > \mu(n)$. In this case, by the soundness condition, it must be the case that $A_1(\alpha) = v = f(\alpha)$, because in this case (u, v) satisfies Eq. (7.28) and so $v = f(h^{-1}(u)) = f(h^{-1}(h(\alpha))) = f(\alpha)$. Thus, in both the real and the ideal model, with probability p, the joint execution view is *non-aborting* and equals $(A_1(\alpha, T), A_1(\alpha)) = (A_1(\alpha, T), f(\alpha))$, where T represents the prover's view of the execution of Step C2 (on common input $(h(\alpha), f(\alpha))$, where the prover is played by $A_1(\alpha)$, and the verifier is honest). On the other hand, in both models, with probability $1 - p$, the joint execution is *aborting* and equals $(A_1(\alpha, T), \perp)$, where T is as before (except that here it is a rejecting execution transcript). Thus, in this case, the distributions in Eq. (7.30) are identical.

    We call the reader's attention to the reliance of our analysis on the fact that the emulation of the proof system (with prover $A_1(\alpha)$) that is performed in Step 2 by B_1 is distributed identically to the real execution of the proof system that takes place in Step C2 of Π.

2. Suppose that $p \leq \mu(n)$. Again, in both models, *aborting* executions are identical and occur with probability $1 - p$. However, in this case, we have no handle on the *non-aborting* executions in the real model (because it is no longer guaranteed that $A_1(\alpha) = f(h^{-1}(u))$ holds in the real non-aborting execution, whereas in the ideal model it still holds that in non-aborting executions, Party 2 outputs $f(\alpha) = f(h^{-1}(u))$). But we do not care, because (in this case) these non-aborting executions occur with negligible probability (i.e., $p \leq \mu(n)$). Thus, in this case, the distribution ensembles in Eq. (7.30) are statistically indistinguishable.

The proposition follows. ∎

We comment that this treatment can be extended to the case that h is a randomized process, rather than a function (as long as the image of h uniquely determines its pre-image). Details are omitted in view of the fact that a much more general treatment will be provided in Section 7.4.3.4.

7.4.3.3. Image Transmission

We now consider the following functionality, called image transmission (or unauthenticated computation):

$$(\alpha, 1^{|\alpha|}) \mapsto (\lambda, f(\alpha)) \tag{7.31}$$

where (as in Section 7.4.3.2) the function f is polynomial-time computable.[46] In contrast to Section 7.4.3.2, the value $f(\alpha)$ is not verifiable (with respect to a value $h(\alpha)$

---

[45] We stress that an explicit error-bound can be associated with all standard zero-knowledge proof systems, and that here we use a system for which μ is negligible. Furthermore, we may use a proof system with error-bound $\mu(n) \stackrel{\text{def}}{=} 2^{-n}$.

[46] Actually, in order to conform with the convention that the functionality has to be defined for any input pair, we may consider the formulation $(\alpha, \beta) \mapsto (\lambda, f(\alpha))$.

that is known to the second party and uniquely determines α). In other words, the value output by Party 2 is only required to be an image of f (corresponding to a pre-image of a given length). Thus, at first glance, one may think that securely computing Eq. (7.31) should be easier than securely computing Eq. (7.27), especially in case f is onto (in which case any string is an f-image). This impression is wrong, because securely computing Eq. (7.31) means emulating an ideal model in which Party 1 knows the string it sends to the trusted party. That is, in a secure protocol for Eq. (7.31), whenever Party 2 outputs some image (of f), Party 1 must know a corresponding pre-image (under f).[47] Still, proving knowledge of a pre-image (and doing so in zero-knowledge) is what a zero-knowledge proof-of-knowledge is all about. Actually, in order to avoid expected probabilistic polynomial-time adversaries, we use zero-knowledge *strong-proof-of-knowledge* (as defined and constructed in Section 4.7.6). We will show that Construction 7.4.10 can be easily adapted in order to yield a secure implementation of Eq. (7.31). Specifically, all that is needed is to use (in Step C2) a zero-knowledge *strong*-proof-of-knowledge (rather than an ordinary zero-knowledge proof), and set h to be a constant function.

Proposition 7.4.12: *Suppose that (P, V) is a zero-knowledge strong-proof-of-knowledge for the relation $R \stackrel{\text{def}}{=} \{(v, w) : v = f(w)\}$, and let h be a constant function. Then, Construction 7.4.10 securely computes* (in the malicious model) *the functionality of Eq. (7.31).*

Proof Sketch: Recall that P is postulated to be implemented in probabilistic polynomial-time when given an adequate auxiliary-input (i.e., a pre-image under f of the common input). For clarity, we reproduce the modified protocol, omitting all mention of the (constant) function h.

Inputs: Party 1 gets input $\alpha \in \{0, 1\}^*$, and Party 2 gets input $1^{|\alpha|}$.

Step C1: Party 1 sends $v \stackrel{\text{def}}{=} f(\alpha)$ to Party 2.

Step C2: Analogously to Construction 7.4.10, the parties invoke the zero-knowledge strong-proof-of-knowledge (for R) such that Party 1 plays the prover and Party 2 plays the verifier. The common input to the proof system is v, the prover gets α as auxiliary input, and its objective is to prove that it knows a w such that $(v, w) \in R$ (i.e., $v = f(w)$). In case the verifier rejects the proof, Party 2 halts with output $\bot$ (otherwise the output will be v).

Outputs: In case Party 2 did not output $\bot$, it halts with output v. (Party 1 has no output.)

The analysis of this protocol, denoted Π, follows the ideas underlying the proof of Proposition 7.4.11. The only significant modification is in the construction of ideal-model adversaries for Party 1.

---

[47] We comment that the same also holds with respect to Eq. (7.27). But there, the knowledge of a pre-image (of the output v under f) is guaranteed by the fact that security implies that the pre-image of v under f must be consistent with $h(\alpha)$, whereas the only such pre-image is α itself, which in turn is the initial input of Party 1 and thus known to it.

Let us first justify why the treatment of the case in which *Party 1 is honest* is exactly as in the proof of Proposition 7.4.11. In this case, we can use exactly the same transformation of the real-model adversary A_2 into an ideal-model adversary B_2, because what this transformation does is essentially invoke the simulator associated with (the residual prover) A_2 on input the string $v = f(\alpha)$ that it obtains from the *trusted party*. Furthermore, the adequateness of this transformation is established by only referring to the adequateness of the (zero-knowledge) simulator, which holds also here.

We now turn to the case where *the second party is honest*. In this case, B_2 is determined, and we transform (real-model) A_1 into (ideal-model) B_1, which uses A_1 as a subroutine. Recall that B_1 gets input $\alpha \in \{0, 1\}^n$:

1. B_1 invokes A_1 on input α. As (implicit) in the protocol, any action of A_1 in Step C1 (including abort) is interpreted as sending a string. Let us denote by v the message sent by A_1 (i.e., $v \leftarrow A_1(\alpha)$).

2. Machine B_1 tries to obtain a pre-image of v under f. Toward this end, B_1 uses the (strong) knowledge-extractor associated with the proof system of Step C2. Specifically, providing the strong knowledge-extractor with oracle access to (the residual prover) $A_1(\alpha)$, machine B_1 tries to extract (from A_1) a string w such that $f(w) = v$. In case the extractor succeeds, B_1 sets $\alpha' \stackrel{\text{def}}{=} w$. Otherwise, B_1 sets $\alpha' \stackrel{\text{def}}{=} \perp$.

3. Machine B_1 now emulates an execution of Step C2. Specifically, it lets $A_1(\alpha)$ play the prover and emulates by itself the (honest) verifier interacting with $A_1(\alpha)$ (i.e., B_1 behaves like A_2).

   - In case the emulated verifier rejects, machine B_1 aborts (without invoking the *trusted party*), and outputs whatever A_1 does (when fed with this emulated proof transcript).
   - Otherwise (i.e., the emulated verifier accepts), if $\alpha' \neq \perp$, then B_1 sends α' to the *trusted party* and allows it to respond to Party 2. (The response will be $f(\alpha')$, which by Step 2 must equal v.) In case $\alpha' = \perp$, this sub-step will fail, and B_1 aborts as in the case that the emulated verifier rejects.

4. Finally, B_1 feeds A_1 with the execution view, which consists of the prover's view of the emulation of Step C2 (produced in Step 3), and outputs whatever A_1 does.

Denoting the functionality of Eq. (7.31) by F, we now show that

$$\{\text{IDEAL}_{F, \overline{B}}(\alpha, 1^{|\alpha|})\}_{\alpha \in \{0,1\}^*} \stackrel{\text{c}}{\equiv} \{\text{REAL}_{\Pi, \overline{A}}(\alpha, 1^{|\alpha|})\}_{\alpha \in \{0,1\}^*} \qquad (7.32)$$

Actually, we will show that these two ensembles are statistically indistinguishable, where the statistical difference is due to the case where the real-model adversary A_1 succeeds in convincing the knowledge-verifier (played by the honest A_2) that it knows a pre-image of v under f, and yet the knowledge-extractor failed to find such a preimage. By definition of strong knowledge-verifiers, such an event may occur only with negligible probability. Loosely speaking, ignoring the rare case in which extraction fails although the knowledge-verifier (played by A_2) is convinced, it can be shown that the distributions $\text{IDEAL}_{f, \overline{B}}((\sigma, r), 1^n)$ and $\text{REAL}_{\Pi, \overline{A}}((\sigma, r), 1^n)$ are identical. Details follow.

Fixing any α, recall that $v \overset{\text{def}}{=} A_1(\alpha)$ need not be an image of f (let alone that it may not equal $f(\alpha)$). We denote by p the probability that $A_1(\alpha)$, playing a possibly cheating prover, convinces the knowledge-verifier (played in Step C2 by Party 2) that it knows a pre-image of v under f. We consider two cases corresponding to the relation between p and the error-bound function μ referred to in Definition 4.7.13:

1. Suppose that $p > \mu(n)$. In this case, by Definition 4.7.13, with probability at least $1 - \mu(n)$, machine B_1 has successfully extracted a pre-image α' (of $v = A_1(\alpha)$ under f). In the real model, with probability p, the joint execution ends up *non-aborting*. By the aforementioned extraction property, in the ideal model, a joint execution is non-aborting with probability $p \pm \mu(n)$ (actually, the probability is at least $p - \mu(n)$ and at most p). Thus, in both models, with probability $p \pm \mu(n)$, a joint execution is non-aborting and equals $(A_1(\alpha, T), A_1(\alpha)) = (A_1(\alpha, T), f(\alpha'))$, where T represents the prover's view of an execution of Step C2 (on common input $f(\alpha') = v = A_1(\alpha)$, where the role of the prover is played by the residual strategy $A_1(\alpha)$ and the verifier is honest). On the other hand, in both models, with probability $1 - p \pm \mu(n)$, the joint execution is *aborting* and equals $(A_1(\alpha, T), \perp)$, where T is as before (except that here it is a rejecting execution transcript). Thus, the statistical difference between the two models is due only to the difference in the probability of producing an aborting execution in the two models, which in turn is negligible.
   We call the reader's attention to the reliance of our analysis on the fact that the emulation of the proof system (with prover $A_1(\alpha)$) performed in Step 2 by B_1 is distributed identically to the real execution of the proof system that takes place in Step C2 of Π.

2. Suppose that $p \leq \mu(n)$. Again, in the real model the non-aborting probability is p, which in this case is negligible. Thus, we ignore these executions and focus on the aborting executions, which occur with probability at least $1 - p \geq 1 - \mu(n)$ in both models. Recalling that aborting executions are identically distributed in both models, we conclude that the statistical difference between the two models is at most $\mu(n)$.

Thus, in both case, the distribution ensembles in Eq. (7.32) are statistically indistinguishable. The proposition follows. ■

7.4.3.4. Authenticated Computation, Revisited

We now generalize the image-transmission functionality to treat the case where Party 2 has some partial information of the input of Party 1. In the extreme case, the information available to Party 2 uniquely determines the input of Party 1 (although obtaining the latter from the former may be infeasible). Thus, in a sense, we revisit the authenticated computation functionality, which was considered in Section 7.4.3.2. The important aspect of the current treatment is that we consider a functionality that is defined on all pairs of (equal-length) strings, rather than a partial functionality (as treated in Section 7.4.3.2).

Definition 7.4.13 (authenticated computation, revisited): *Let* $f : \{0, 1\}^* \times \{0, 1\}^* \rightarrow \{0, 1\}^*$ *and* $h : \{0, 1\}^* \rightarrow \{0, 1\}^*$ *be polynomial-time computable. The h-*authenticated f-computation functionality *is re*defined by

$$
(\alpha, \beta) \mapsto \begin{cases} (\lambda, f(\alpha)) & \text{if } \beta = h(\alpha) \\ (\lambda, (h(\alpha), f(\alpha))) \text{ otherwise} \end{cases} \tag{7.33}
$$

In the intended applications of the h-authenticated f-computation functionality, Party 2 is supposed to input $\beta = h(\alpha)$, and so the first case in Eq. (7.33) holds, provided that both parties are honest. Indeed, if Party 2 is honest, then either it gets the correct value of $f(\alpha)$ (i.e., which fits $h(\alpha)$ known to it) or it gets an indication that Party 1 is cheating. The specific form of the second case was designed to facilitate the implementation, while not causing any harm.[48] What matters is that the outputs in the two cases are different, and so Party 2 can tell whether or not it received the correct value of $f(\alpha)$. We stress that in the intended applications, Party 2 knows $h(\alpha)$ and is supposed to obtain $f(\alpha)$, and so it causes no harm to provide Party 2 with both of them (even in case Party 2 misbehaves and enters an input other than $h(\alpha)$).

We assume again, for simplicity, that h is length preserving, which again can be "enforced" by considering $\alpha' = (\alpha, 1^{|h(\alpha)|})$ and $h'(\alpha') = (h(\alpha), 1^{|\alpha|})$. However, we make no further assumptions concerning the function h, and thus Eq. (7.31) is essentially a special case (obtained by setting $h(\alpha) = 1^{|\alpha|}$).

The functionality of Eq. (7.33) is implemented by having Party 1 use the image-transmission functionality to send the pair $(h(\alpha), f(\alpha))$ to Party 2, which compares the first element to its own input and acts accordingly. That is, we use the following (oracle-aided) protocol:

Construction 7.4.14 (authenticated computation protocol, general version):

Inputs: *Party 1 gets input $\alpha \in \{0, 1\}^*$, and Party 2 gets input $\beta \in \{0, 1\}^{|\alpha|}$.*

Step C1: *Party 1 uses the image-transmission functionality to send the pair $(u, v) \overset{\text{def}}{=} (h(\alpha), f(\alpha))$ to Party 2. That is, the parties invoke the functionality of Eq. (7.31) with respect to the function $g(\alpha) \overset{\text{def}}{=} (h(\alpha), f(\alpha))$, where Party 1 enters the input α and Party 2 is to obtain $g(\alpha)$.*

Step C2: *Assuming that Step C1 was not aborted by Party 1 and that Party 2 receives the pair (u, v) in Step C1, Party 2 outputs v if $u = \beta$ and (u, v) otherwise.*

Outputs: *If not aborted (with output $\perp$), Party 2 sets its local output as directed in Step C2. (Party 1 has no output.)*

We stress that in the oracle invocation (of Step C1), Party i plays the i-th party (with respect to the oracle call). Recall that (unlike Party 2), Party 1 may abort and in particular

---

[48] In contrast, even privately computing the more natural functionality $(\alpha, \beta) \mapsto (\lambda, v)$, where $v = f(\alpha)$ if $\beta = h(\alpha)$ and $v = \lambda$ otherwise, is significantly harder than (securely or privately) implementing Eq. (7.33); see Exercise 12. The difference is that Eq. (7.33) allows for revealing $h(\alpha)$ to Party 2 (specifically in case $h(\alpha) \neq \beta$), whereas the more natural functionality does not allow this.

do so during Step C1. Since Step C1 consists of an oracle invocation, aborting during Step C1 means instructing the oracle not to answer Party 2.

Proposition 7.4.15: *Construction 7.4.14 securely reduces the h-authenticated f-computation functionality of Eq. (7.33) to the image-transmission functionality of Eq. (7.31).*

Proof Sketch: We need to transform any admissible pair, (A_1, A_2), for the real oracle-aided model into a corresponding pair, (B_1, B_2), for the ideal model. We start by assuming that *the first party is honest* and by transforming the real-model adversary A_2 (for the oracle-aided execution) into a corresponding ideal-model adversary B_2. On input β, the latter proceeds as follows:

1. Machine B_2 sends β to the trusted party and obtains the answer, which equals $v \overset{\text{def}}{=} f(\alpha)$ if $\beta = h(\alpha)$ and $(u, v) \overset{\text{def}}{=} (h(\alpha), f(\alpha))$ otherwise, where α is the (unknown to B_2) input of Party 1.[49] In the first case, B_2 sets $u \overset{\text{def}}{=} \beta$, and so in both cases $(u, v) = (h(\alpha), f(\alpha))$.
2. Machine B_2 emulates the protocol, by feeding A_2 with β and the pair (u, v), which A_2 expects to get in Step C1, and outputting whatever the latter outputs (in Step C2).

Note that both the ideal execution under (B_1, B_2) and the real execution (in the oracle-aided model) under (A_1, A_2) yield the output pair $(\lambda, A_2(\beta, (h(\alpha), f(\alpha))))$. Thus, the ideal and real ensembles are identical.

We now turn to the case where *the second party is honest* and transform the real-model adversary A_1 into a corresponding ideal-model adversary B_1. On input α, the latter proceeds as follows:

1. Machine B_1 emulates Step C1 of the protocol, by obtaining from A_1 the input $\alpha' \leftarrow A_1(\alpha)$ (that A_1 wishes to transmit via Eq. (7.31)) and feeding A_1 with the expected answer λ.
2. If A_1 instructs the oracle not to answer Party 2, then B_1 halts without invoking the trusted party. Otherwise, B_1 sends α' to the trusted party and lets it answer Party 2. In both cases, B_1 halts with output equal to the corresponding output of A_1.

Note that if $h(\alpha') = \beta$, where β is the (unknown to B_1) input of Party 2, then the trusted party answers Party 2 with $f(\alpha')$, and otherwise it answers Party 2 with $(h(\alpha'), f(\alpha'))$.

Note that both the ideal execution under (B_1, B_2) and the real execution (in the oracle-aided model) under (A_1, A_2) yield the output pair $(A_1(\alpha, \lambda, \bot), \bot)$ if $A_1(\alpha, \lambda) = \bot$ and $(A_1(\alpha, \lambda), F(A_1(\alpha), \beta))$ otherwise, where $F(\alpha', \beta)$ is as in Eq. (7.33); that is,

---

[49] Recall that, in either case, the trusted party will send Party 1 the answer λ. Also note that the emulation will remain valid regardless of which $|\beta|$-bit long string B_2 sends to the trusted party (because, for any such choice, B_2 will [explicitly] receive $f(\alpha)$, as well as [explicitly or implicitly] receive $h(\alpha)$).

$F(\alpha', \beta) = f(\alpha')$ if $h(\alpha') = \beta$ and $F(\alpha', \beta) = (h(\alpha'), f(\alpha'))$ otherwise. Thus, also here the ideal and real ensembles are identical. ∎

7.4.3.5. Augmented Coin-Tossing

In this section, we generalize the coin-tossing functionality (of Section 7.4.3.1) in two ways. Firstly, we consider the generation of a random $\ell(n)$-bit long string, rather than a single bit. Secondly, we provide the second party with a function of the coin-outcomes obtained by the first party, rather than providing it with the outcomes themselves. That is, for any positive polynomial $\ell : \mathbb{N} \to \mathbb{N}$ and a polynomial-time computable function g, we consider the randomized functionality

$$(1^n, 1^n) \mapsto (r, g(r)), \text{ where } r \text{ is uniformly distributed in } \{0, 1\}^{\ell(n)}. \quad (7.34)$$

Indeed, Definition 7.4.6 is a special case (obtained by setting $\ell(n) \stackrel{\text{def}}{=} 1$ and $g(r) \stackrel{\text{def}}{=} r$). The *augmented coin-tossing functionality* (mentioned in Section 7.4.1) will be derived as a special case (see Proposition 7.4.19). But first we show that Eq. (7.34) can be securely reduced to the set of functionalities presented earlier (see discussion of this notion of a reduction in Remark 7.4.5). That is, we present an oracle-aided protocol that uses two of the latter functionalities (i.e., basic coin-tossing and general authenticated computation), as well as a commitment scheme C. The protocol can be viewed as a "robust" version of Construction 7.4.7 (i.e., simple operations, such as *sending a commitment to a value* and *tossing a coin,* are replaced by corresponding functionalities that prevent various abuses).

Construction 7.4.16 (an oracle-aided protocol for Eq. (7.34)): *For $r_1, ..., r_\ell \in \{0, 1\}^n$ and $\sigma_1, ..., \sigma_\ell \in \{0, 1\}$, we let $\overline{C}_{r_1, ..., r_\ell}(\sigma_1, ..., \sigma_\ell) = (C_{r_1}(\sigma_1), ..., C_{r_\ell}(\sigma_\ell))$.*

Inputs: *Both parties get security parameter 1^n, and set $\ell \stackrel{\text{def}}{=} \ell(n)$.*

Step C1: *Party 1 uniformly selects $\sigma_1, ..., \sigma_\ell \in \{0, 1\}$ and $s_1, ..., s_\ell \in \{0, 1\}^n$, and lets $r' = \sigma_1 \cdots \sigma_\ell$ and $\overline{s} = s_1 \cdots s_\ell$.*

Step C2: *Party 1 uses the image-transmission functionality to send $\overline{c} \stackrel{\text{def}}{=} \overline{C}_{\overline{s}}(r')$ to Party 2. Actually, since image-transmission functionality is a special case of the general authenticated-computation functionality, we use the latter. That is, Party 1 enters Eq. (7.33) with input $(r', \overline{s})$, Party 2 enters with input $1^{\ell + \ell \cdot n}$, and Party 2 is supposed to obtain $f^{(C2)}(r', \overline{s}) \stackrel{\text{def}}{=} \overline{C}_{\overline{s}}(r')$.*

Recall that, by definition, a party cannot abort the execution of an oracle call that was not initiated (requested) by it, and so Party 2 cannot abort Steps C2–C4. For simplicity, we assume that Party 1 does not abort Steps C2 and C3, but it may abort Step C4.

Step C3: *The parties invoke the basic coin-tossing functionality ℓ times to generate a common random string $r'' \in \{0, 1\}^\ell$. That is, in the i-th invocation of the functionality of Definition 7.4.6, the parties obtain the i-th bit of r''.*

Step C4: *Party 1 sets $r \stackrel{\text{def}}{=} r' \oplus r''$, and uses the authenticated-computation functionality to send $g(r)$ to Party 2. Specifically, Party 1 enters Eq. (7.33) with input $(r', \overline{s}, r'')$,*

Party 2 enters with input $(\overline{c}, r'')$, *where* $(\overline{c}, r'')$ *is supposed to equal* $h^{(C4)}(r', \overline{s}, r'') \stackrel{\text{def}}{=}$ $(\overline{C_{\overline{s}}}(r'), r'')$, *and Party 2 is supposed to obtain* $f^{(C4)}(r', \overline{s}, r'') \stackrel{\text{def}}{=} g(r' \oplus r'')$. *In case Party 1 aborts or Party 2 obtains an answer of a different format, which happens if the inputs to the functionality do not match, Party 2 halts with output* $\bot$ *(indicating that Party 1 misbehaved).*

We comment that $r = r' \oplus r''$ *is uniquely determined by* $\overline{c}$ *and* r''.

Outputs: *Party 1 outputs* r, *and Party 2 outputs the value determined in Step C4, which is either* $g(r)$ *or* $\bot$.

We stress that, in all oracle calls, Party 1 is the party initiating (requesting) the call. We comment that more efficient alternatives to Construction 7.4.16 do exist; it is just that we find Construction 7.4.16 easiest to analyze.

Proposition 7.4.17: *Let F be the set of functionalities defined in Definition 7.4.6 and Eq. (7.33), respectively. Then Construction 7.4.16 constitutes a security reduction from the generalized coin-tossing functionality of Eq. (7.34) to F.*

Proof Sketch: We start by assuming that *the first party is honest* and by transforming the real-model adversary A_2 (for the oracle-aided execution) into a corresponding ideal-model adversary B_2. On input 1^n, the latter proceeds as follows:

1. Machine B_2 emulates the local actions of the honest Party 1 in Step C1 of the protocol, by uniformly selecting $r' \in \{0, 1\}^{\ell}$ and $\overline{s} \in \{0, 1\}^{\ell \cdot n}$.
2. Machine B_2 emulates Step C2 of the protocol, by feeding A_2 with $\overline{c} \stackrel{\text{def}}{=} \overline{C_{\overline{s}}}(r')$. (Recall that by our convention, A_2 never aborts.)
3. Machine B_2 emulates Step C3 of the protocol, by uniformly selecting $r'' \in \{0, 1\}^{\ell}$ and feeding A_2 with it.
4. Machine B_2 invokes the trusted party with input 1^n and obtains the answer $g(r)$, for a uniformly distributed $r \in \{0, 1\}^{\ell}$ that is handed to Party 1.[50] Next, machine B_2 obtains the input (or query) of A_2 to the functionality of Step C4. If this input (i.e., $A_2(\lambda, \overline{C_{\overline{s}}}(r'), r'')$, where λ represents the Step 1 emulation of Step C1) does not equal the pair of values $(\overline{C_{\overline{s}}}(r'), r'')$ fed to A_2 in Steps 2–3, then B_2 halts with output $A_2(\lambda, \overline{c}, r'', ((\overline{c}, r''), g(r)))$. Otherwise, B_2 halts with output $A_2(\lambda, \overline{c}, r'', g(r))$.

Note that in both cases, the output of B_2 corresponds to the output of A_2 when fed with the corresponding emulation of Steps C1–C4. In particular, B_2 emulates Step C4 by feeding A_2 either with $g(r)$ or with $(h^{(C4)}(r', \overline{s}, r''), g(r))$, where the decision depends on whether or not $A_2(\lambda, \overline{C_{\overline{s}}}(r'), r'') = (\overline{C_{\overline{s}}}(r'), r'')$. (Recall that $(\overline{C_{\overline{s}}}(r'), r'') = h^{(C4)}(r', \overline{s}, r'')$.) Indeed, B_2 is cheating (in the emulation of Step C4), because A_2 expects to get either $f^{(C4)}(r', \overline{s}, r'') = g(r' \oplus r'')$ or $(h^{(C4)}(r', \overline{s}, r''), g(r' \oplus r''))$, but (as we shall see) this cheating is undetectable.

Let us first assume that the input entered by A_2 to the functionality of Step C4 does fit its view of Steps C2 and C3, an event that occurs with equal probability

---

[50] Indeed, this part of the current step could also take place at an earlier stage.

in both models (because the emulation of Steps C2–C3 is perfect). In this case, the ideal-model execution under (B_1, B_2) yields the pair $(r, A_2(\lambda, \overline{C}(r'), r'', g(r)))$, where r', r'', r are uniformly and independently distributed. On the other hand, the real-model execution (in the oracle-aided model) under (A_1, A_2) yields the pair $(r' \oplus r'', A_2(\lambda, \overline{C}(r'), r'', g(r' \oplus r'')))$, where r' and r'' are as before, which (for $r = r' \oplus r''$) is distributed identically to $(r, A_2(\lambda, \overline{C}(r \oplus r''), r'', g(r)))$. However, due to the hiding property of C, the two ensembles are computationally indistinguishable. In case the input entered by A_2 to the functionality of Step C4 does not fit its view of Steps C2 and C3, the ideal-model execution under (B_1, B_2) yields the pair $(r, A_2(\lambda, \overline{C}(r'), r'', ((\overline{C}(r'), r''), g(r))))$, whereas the real-model execution under (A_1, A_2) yields the pair $(r' \oplus r'', A_2(\lambda, \overline{C}(r'), r'', ((\overline{C}(r'), r''), g(r' \oplus r''))))$, which is distributed identically to $(r, A_2(\lambda, \overline{C}(r \oplus r''), r'', ((\overline{C}(r \oplus r''), r''), g(r))))$. Again, the two ensembles are computationally indistinguishable.

We now turn to the case where *the second party is honest* and transform the real-model adversary A_1 into a corresponding ideal-model adversary B_1. On input 1^n, the latter proceeds as follows:

1. Machine B_1 emulates Step C1 of the protocol, by obtaining $(r', \overline{s}) \leftarrow A_1(1^n)$, which is the query that A_1 will use in Step C2.
2. Machine B_1 emulates Step C2 by doing nothing.
   Note that the real-model adversary A_1 would have made the oracle query $(r', \overline{s})$ and would have obtained λ as an answer.
3. Machine B_1 invokes the *trusted party* (on input 1^n) and obtains a uniformly distributed $r \in \{0, 1\}^\ell$. We stress that at this time, B_1 does not instruct the trusted party whether or not to answer Party 2. Machine B_1 emulates Step C3, by feeding $r'' \stackrel{\text{def}}{=} r \oplus r'$ to A_1.
4. Machine B_1 starts its emulation of Step C4, by checking whether or not the query that A_1 wishes to make (i.e., $A_1(1^n, \lambda, r'')$) fits the tuple $(r', \overline{s}, r'')$ in the sense that it yields the same value $(\overline{C}_{\overline{s}}(r'), r'')$. That is, let $(q', \overline{q}, q'') \stackrel{\text{def}}{=} A_1(1^n, \lambda, r'')$. If $(\overline{C}_{\overline{q}}(q'), q'') = (\overline{C}_{\overline{s}}(r'), r'')$, then B_1 instructs the *trusted party* to answer Party 2, or else B_1 instructs the trusted party to stop (without answering Party 2).[51] Finally, B_1 outputs whatever A_1 does (i.e., $A_1(1^n, \lambda, r'', \lambda)$, where the four inputs of A_1 correspond to its view in each of the four steps).

Note that the output of Party 1 in both the real model (under the A_i's) and the ideal model (under the B_i's) equals $A_1(1^n, \lambda, r'', \lambda)$, where r'' is uniformly distributed (in both models). The issue is the correlation of this output to the output of Party 2, which is relevant only if Party 2 does have an output. Recall that Party 2 obtains an output (in both models) only if the corresponding Party 1 does not abort (or stops the trusted party). Furthermore, in both models, an output is obtained if and only if $(\overline{C}_{\overline{q}}(q'), q'') = (\overline{C}_{\overline{s}}(r'), r'')$ holds, where $(r', \overline{s}) \stackrel{\text{def}}{=} A_1(1^n)$, and $(q', \overline{q}, q'') \stackrel{\text{def}}{=} A_1(1^n, \lambda, r'')$. In particular, $(\overline{C}_{\overline{q}}(q'), q'') =$

---

[51] In particular, if (in contrary to our simplifying assumption) A_1 aborts before Step C4, then the sequence $(q', \overline{q}, q'')$ equals $\perp$ and does not fit $(\overline{C}_{\overline{s}}(r'), r'')$.

$(\overline{C}_{\bar{s}}(r'), r'')$ implies that $(q', q'') = (r', r'')$ and that the inputs entered in Step C4 do match (i.e., $h^{(C4)}(q', \overline{q}, q'') = (\overline{C}_{\bar{s}}(r'), r'')$). This means that in the real model, the output of Party 2 is $f^{(C4)}(q', \overline{q}, q'') = f^{(C4)}(r', \overline{q}, r'') = g(r' \oplus r'')$, whereas in the ideal model, it equals $g(r) = g(r' \oplus r'')$. We conclude that the ideal model perfectly emulates the real model, and the proposition follows. ∎

An Important Special Case. An important special case of Eq. (7.34) is when $g(r, s) = \overline{C}_s(r)$, where $|s| = n \cdot |r|$. This special case will be called the augmented coin-tossing functionality.

Definition 7.4.18 (coin-tossing into the well, augmented): *An* augmented coin-tossing-into-the-well *protocol is a two-party protocol for securely computing the following randomized functionality with respect to some fixed commitment scheme, C, and a positive polynomial* ℓ:

$$(1^n, 1^n) \mapsto ((r, s), \overline{C}_s(r)) \tag{7.35}$$

where (r, s) is uniformly distributed in $\{0, 1\}^{\ell(n)} \times \{0, 1\}^{\ell(n) \cdot n}$.

An augmented coin-tossing protocol is exactly what is needed for the implementation of the coin-generation phase of the compiler. In particular, the string s, included in the output of Party 1, allows it to (later) prove in zero-knowledge statements regarding the actual value, r, committed (to Party 2). This fact will be used in the protocol emulation phase of the compiler.

Proposition 7.4.19: *Let F be as in Proposition 7.4.17, and suppose that C is a commitment scheme. Then Construction 7.4.16, when applied to $g = \overline{C}$, constitutes a secure reduction of the augmented coin-tossing functionality Eq. (7.35) to the set of functionalities F.*

7.4.3.6. Input Commitment

The last component needed for the compiler is a functionality that captures what is required in the input-commitment phase of the compiler. Specifically, we want to force Party 1 to make a random commitment to an input of its choice, while knowing the committed value and the corresponding decommitment. Knowledge of the latter will allow the party to (later) prove in zero-knowledge statements regarding the actual committed value, and this fact will be used in the protocol-emulation phase of the compiler.

Let C be a commitment scheme, and let $\overline{C}$ be defined as in Section 7.4.3.5. We consider the input commitment functionality

$$(x, 1^{|x|}) \mapsto (r, \overline{C}_r(x)), \text{ where } r \text{ is uniformly distributed in } \{0, 1\}^{|x|^2} \tag{7.36}$$

Certainly, the naive protocol of just letting Party 1 send Party 2 a commitment to x does not constitute a secure implementation of Eq. (7.36): This naive suggestion does not guarantee that the output is in the range of the commitment scheme, let alone that it is a random commitment for which Party 1 knows a corresponding decommitment. Thus, the naive protocol must be augmented by mechanisms that address all these concerns. We show that Eq. (7.36) can be securely reduced to the set of functionalities presented in previous subsections.

Construction 7.4.20 (an oracle-aided protocol for Eq. (7.36)):

Inputs: *Party 1 has input $x \in \{0, 1\}^n$, whereas Party 2 gets input 1^n.*

Step C1: *Party 1 selects uniformly $r' \in \{0, 1\}^{n^2}$.*

Step C2: *Party 1 uses the image-transmission functionality to send $c' \overset{\text{def}}{=} \overline{C}_{r'}(x)$ to Party 2. Again, we actually use the authenticated-computation functionality, where Party 1 enters Eq. (7.33) with input (x, r'), Party 2 inputs 1^{n+n^2}, and Party 2 is supposed to obtain $f^{(C2)}(x, r') \overset{\text{def}}{=} \overline{C}_{r'}(x)$. Thus, Steps C1–C2 yield an* initial commitment to the input.

As in Construction 7.4.16, we recall that Party 2 cannot abort Steps C2–C4, and assume that Party 1 does not abort Steps C2 and C3.

Step C3: Generating coins for the final commitment. *The parties use the augmented coin-tossing functionality to obtain the outputs (r, r'') and $c'' \overset{\text{def}}{=} \overline{C}_{r''}(r)$, respectively, where $r \in \{0, 1\}^{n^2}$ and $r'' \in \{0, 1\}^{n^3}$ are uniformly and independently distributed. That is, Party 1 gets (r, r''), while Party 2 gets c''.*

Step C4: Sending the final commitment. *Party 1 uses the authenticated-computation functionality to send $\overline{C}_r(x)$ to Party 2, where (x, r) is uniquely determined by (c', c''). Specifically, Party 1 enters Eq. (7.33) with input (x, r, r', r''), Party 2 enters with input (c', c''), where (c', c'') is supposed to equal $h^{(C4)}(x, r, r', r'') \overset{\text{def}}{=} (\overline{C}_{r'}(x), \overline{C}_{r''}(r))$, and Party 2 is supposed to obtain $f^{(C4)}(x, r, r', r'') \overset{\text{def}}{=} \overline{C}_r(x)$.*

In case Party 1 aborts or Party 2 obtains an answer of a different format, which happens if the inputs to the functionality do not match, Party 2 halts with output $\perp$ (indicating that Party 1 misbehaved).

Outputs: *Party 1 outputs r, and Party 2 outputs the value determined in Step C4, which is either $\overline{C}_r(x)$ or $\perp$.*

Again, more efficient alternatives to Construction 7.4.20 do exist, but we prefer to analyze the one here.

Proposition 7.4.21: *Construction 7.4.20 constitutes a security reduction from Eq. (7.36) to the set of two functionalities defined in Eq. (7.35) and Eq. (7.33), respectively.*

Proof Sketch: We start by assuming that *the first party is honest* and by transforming the real-model adversary A_2 (for the oracle-aided execution) into a corresponding ideal-model adversary B_2. On input 1^n, the latter proceeds as follows:

1. Machine B_2 emulates (the actions of the honest Party 1 in) Step C1 of the protocol, by uniformly selecting $r' \in \{0, 1\}^{n^2}$.

2. Machine B_2 emulates Step C2 of the protocol, by feeding A_2 with $c' \stackrel{\text{def}}{=} \overline{C}_{r'}(0^n)$. (Clearly, B_2 is cheating, because A_2 is supposed to be fed with $\overline{C}(x)$, where x is the (unknown to B_2) input of Party 1. However, A_2 cannot detect this cheating.)

3. Machine B_2 emulates Step C3 of the protocol, by uniformly selecting $s \in \{0, 1\}^{n^2}$ and $r'' \in \{0, 1\}^{n^3}$, and feeding A_2 with $c'' \stackrel{\text{def}}{=} \overline{C}_{r''}(s)$.

4. Machine B_2 invokes the trusted party with input 1^n and obtains the answer $\overline{C}_r(x)$, for a uniformly distributed $r \in \{0, 1\}^{n^2}$ that is handed to Party 1.[52] Next, machine B_2 obtains the input (or query) of A_2 to the functionality of Step C4. If this input (i.e., $A_2(\lambda, c', c'')$) does not equal the pair of values $(c', c'') = (\overline{C}_{r'}(0^n), \overline{C}_{r''}(s))$ fed to A_2 in Steps 2–3, then B_2 halts with output $A_2(\lambda, c', c'', ((c', c''), \overline{C}_r(x)))$. Otherwise, B_2 halts with output $A_2(\lambda, c', c'', \overline{C}_r(x))$.

Note that in both cases, the output of B_2 corresponds to the output of A_2 when fed with the corresponding emulation of Steps C1–C4. In particular, B_2 emulates Step C4 by feeding A_2 with either $\overline{C}_r(x)$ or with $((\overline{C}(0^n), \overline{C}(s)), \overline{C}_r(x))$, where the decision depends on whether or not $A_2(\lambda, \overline{C}_{r'}(0^n), \overline{C}_{r''}(s)) = (\overline{C}_{r'}(0^n), \overline{C}_{r''}(s))$. (Recall that $(\overline{C}_{r'}(0^n), \overline{C}_{r''}(s)) = h^{(C4)}(0^n, s, r', r'')$.) Indeed, on top of cheating in the emulation of Step C2, machine B_2 cheats in the emulation of Step C4, firstly because the decision is supposed to depend on whether or not $A_2(\lambda, \overline{C}_{r'}(x), \overline{C}_{r''}(r)) = (\overline{C}_{r'}(x), \overline{C}_{r''}(r))$, where $(\overline{C}_{r'}(x), \overline{C}_{r''}(r)) = h^{(C4)}(x, r, r', r'')$, and secondly because A_2 expects to get either $\overline{C}_r(x) = f^{(C4)}(x, r, r', r'')$ or $((\overline{C}(x), \overline{C}(r)), \overline{C}_r(x)) \equiv (h^{(C4)}(x, r, r', r''), f^{(C4)}(x, r, r', r''))$. However, as we shall see, this cheating is undetectable.

Let us first assume that the input entered by A_2 to the functionality of Step C4 does fit its view of Steps C2 and C3. In this case, the ideal-model execution under (B_1, B_2) yields the pair $(r, A_2(\lambda, \overline{C}(0^n), \overline{C}(s), \overline{C}_r(x)))$, where r and s are uniformly and independently distributed. On the other hand, the corresponding real-model execution (in the oracle-aided model) under (A_1, A_2) yields the pair $(r, A_2(\lambda, \overline{C}(x), \overline{C}(r), \overline{C}_r(x)))$, where r is as before. However, due to the hiding property of C, the two ensembles are computationally indistinguishable.[53] In case the input entered by A_2 to the functionality of Step C4 does not fit its view of Steps C2 and C3, the ideal-model execution under (B_1, B_2) yields the pair $(r, A_2(\lambda, \overline{C}(0^n), \overline{C}(s), ((\overline{C}(0^n), \overline{C}(s)), \overline{C}_r(x))))$, whereas the corresponding real-model execution under (A_1, A_2) yields the pair $(r, A_2(\lambda, \overline{C}(x), \overline{C}(r), ((\overline{C}(x), \overline{C}(r)), \overline{C}_r(x))))$. Again, the two ensembles are computationally indistinguishable. Since the two cases occur with almost the same probability in both models (because the decision depends on $A_2(\lambda, c', c'')$, where (c', c'') is either $(\overline{C}(0^n), \overline{C}(s))$ or $(\overline{C}(x), \overline{C}(r))$), the outputs in the two models are indistinguishable.

---

[52] Indeed, this part of the current step could also take place at an earlier stage.

[53] In fact, the said ensembles are computationally indistinguishable even when r and s are fixed, rather than being random. That is, the ensembles $\{(\overline{C}(0^{|x|}), \overline{C}(s), \overline{C}_r(x))\}_{x,r,s}$ and $\{(\overline{C}(x), \overline{C}(r), \overline{C}_r(x))\}_{x,r,s}$ are computationally indistinguishable, where (as usual) the distribution's index (x, r, s) is also given to the potential distinguisher. This follows from the computational indistinguishability of $\{(\overline{C}(0^{|x|}), \overline{C}(s))\}_{x,r,s}$ and $\{(\overline{C}(x), \overline{C}(r))\}_{x,r,s}$, which in turn follows from the hiding property of C.

We now turn to the case where *the second party is honest* and transform the real-model adversary A_1 into a corresponding ideal-model adversary B_1. On input x, the latter proceeds as follows:

1. Machine B_1 emulates Step C1 of the protocol, by obtaining r' from $A_1(x)$. Actually, B_1 obtains $(x', r') \leftarrow A_1(x)$, which is the query that A_1 will use in Step C2.
2. Machine B_1 emulates Step C2 by doing nothing.
   Note that the real-model adversary A_1 would have made the oracle query (x', r') and would have obtained λ as an answer.
3. Machine B_1 invokes the *trusted party* on input x', and obtains a uniformly distributed $r \in \{0, 1\}^{n^2}$. We stress that at this time, B_1 does not instruct the trusted party whether or not to answer Party 2. Machine B_1 emulates Step C3, by uniformly selecting $r'' \in \{0, 1\}^{n^3}$ and feeding (r, r'') to A_1.
4. Machine B_1 starts its emulation of Step C4, by checking whether or not the query that A_1 wishes to make (i.e., $A_1(x, \lambda, (r, r''))$) fits the tuple (x', r, r', r'') in the sense that it yields the same value $(\overline{C}_{r'}(x'), \overline{C}_{r''}(r))$. That is, let $(q_1, q_2, s_1, s_2) \overset{\text{def}}{=} A_1(x, \lambda, (r, r''))$. If $(\overline{C}_{s_1}(q_1), \overline{C}_{s_2}(q_2)) = (\overline{C}_{r'}(x'), \overline{C}_{r''}(r))$, then B_1 instructs the *trusted party* to answer Party 2; otherwise B_1 instructs the trusted party to stop (without answering Party 2). Finally, B_1 outputs whatever A_1 does (i.e., $A_1(x, \lambda, (r, r''), \lambda)$, where the four inputs of A_1 correspond to its view in each of the four steps).

Note that the output of Party 1 in both the real model (under the A_i's) and the ideal model (under the B_i's) equals $A_1(x, \lambda, (r, r''), \lambda)$, where $r \in \{0, 1\}^{n^2}$ and $r'' \in \{0, 1\}^{n^3}$ are uniformly and independently distributed (in both models). The issue is the correlation of this output to the output of Party 2, which is relevant only if Party 2 does have an output. Recall that Party 2 obtains an output (in both models) only if the corresponding Party 1 does not abort (or stops the trusted party). Furthermore, in both models, an output is obtained if and only if $(\overline{C}_{s_1}(q_1), \overline{C}_{s_2}(q_2)) = (\overline{C}_{r'}(x'), \overline{C}_{r''}(r))$, where $(x', r') = A_1(x)$ and $(q_1, q_2, s_1, s_2) = A_1(x, \lambda, (r, r''))$. In particular, $(\overline{C}_{s_1}(q_1), \overline{C}_{s_2}(q_2)) = (\overline{C}_{r'}(x'), \overline{C}_{r''}(r))$ implies that $(q_1, q_2) = (x', r)$ and that the inputs entered in Step C4 do match (i.e., $h^{(C4)}(q_1, q_2, s_1, s_2) = (\overline{C}_{r'}(x'), \overline{C}_{r''}(r))$), which means that in the real model, the output of Party 2 is $f^{(C4)}(q_1, q_2, s_1, s_2) = f^{(C4)}(x', r, s_1, s_2) = \overline{C}_r(x')$ (exactly as in the ideal model). We conclude that the ideal model perfectly emulates the real model, and the proposition follows. ∎

7.4.3.7. Summary

Combining Proposition 7.4.8 (resp., Proposition 7.4.12) with suitable results regarding the underlying primitives, we conclude that coin-tossing (resp., image transmission as in Eq. (7.31)) can be securely implemented based on any 1-1 one-way function. Combining Proposition 7.4.15 (resp., Proposition 7.4.19) [resp., Proposition 7.4.21] with the previous results, by using the Composition Theorem (i.e., Theorem 7.4.3 or Remark 7.4.5), we obtain secure implementations of the authenticated-computation functionality (resp., augmented coin-tossing) [resp., input-commitment functionality]. The 1-1 restriction can be waived by using a slightly more cumbersome construction that utilizes the commitment scheme of Construction 4.4.4 (instead of the simple scheme of Construction 4.4.2). We thus state the following for future reference:

Proposition 7.4.22: *Assuming the existence of (non-uniformly strong) one-way functions, the following three functionalities can be securely computed:*

1. *The input-commitment functionality as defined in Eq. (7.36).*
2. *The augmented coin-tossing functionality as defined in Eq. (7.35).*
3. *The authenticated-computation functionality as defined in Eq. (7.33).*

7.4.4. The Compiler Itself

We are now ready to present the compiler. Recall that we are given a protocol, Π, for the semi-honest model, and we want to generate an equivalent protocol Π' for the malicious model. The meaning of the term "equivalent" will be clarified in Section 7.4.4.1. We start by compiling Π into an oracle-aided protocol Π' that uses the three functionalities referred to in Proposition 7.4.22.

We assume, without loss of generality, that on any input of length n, each party to Π tosses $\ell(n) = \text{poly}(n)$ coins. Recall that $\overline{C}$ is a (non-interactive) (string) commitment scheme, derived from the bit commitment scheme C, and that $\overline{C}_r(v)$ denotes the commitment to value v using the random-tape r.

Construction 7.4.23 (the compiled protocol, oracle-aided version): *Given a protocol, Π, for the semi-honest model, we consider the following oracle-aided protocol, Π', for the malicious model:*

Inputs: *Party 1 gets input $x \in \{0, 1\}^n$ and Party 2 gets input $y \in \{0, 1\}^n$.*

Input-Commitment Phase: *Each of the two parties commits to its input by using the input-commitment functionality of Eq. (7.36). Recall that Eq. (7.36) maps the input pair $(u, 1^n)$ to the output pair $(s, \overline{C}_s(u))$, where s is uniformly distributed in $\{0, 1\}^{n^2}$. Thus, each of the parties obtains decommitment information that will allow it to perform its role in the protocol-emulation phase.*

Specifically, we are talking about two invocations of Eq. (7.36). In the first invocation, Party 1 wishing to commit to x, plays the role of the first party in Eq. (7.36), and obtains a uniformly distributed $\rho^1 \in \{0, 1\}^{n^2}$, whereas Party 2 (which plays the role of the second party in Eq. (7.36)) obtains $\gamma^1 \stackrel{\text{def}}{=} \overline{C}_{\rho^1}(x)$. Likewise, in the second invocation, Party 2, wishing to commit to y, plays the role of the first party in Eq. (7.36), and obtains a uniformly distributed $\rho^2 \in \{0, 1\}^{n^2}$, whereas Party 1 (which plays the role of the second party in Eq. (7.36)) obtains $\gamma^2 \stackrel{\text{def}}{=} \overline{C}_{\rho^2}(y)$.

Coin-Generation Phase: *Each of the parties generates a random-tape for the emulation of Π, by invoking the augmented coin-tossing functionality of Eq. (7.35). Recall that this functionality maps the input pair $(1^n, 1^n)$ to the output pair $((r, s), \overline{C}_s(r))$, where (r, s) is uniformly distributed in $\{0, 1\}^{\ell(n)} \times \{0, 1\}^{n \cdot \ell(n)}$. Thus, each party* *obtains the random-tape to be held by it, whereas the other party obtains a commitment to this value. The party holding the random-tape also obtains the randomization used in the corresponding commitment, which it will use in performing its role in the protocol-emulation phase.*

Specifically, we are talking about two invocations of Eq. (7.35). In the first (resp., second) invocation, Party 1 (resp., Party 2) plays the role of the first party in Eq. (7.35), and obtains a uniformly distributed $(r^1, \omega^1) \in \{0, 1\}^{\ell(n)} \times \{0, 1\}^{n \cdot \ell(n)}$ (resp., $(r^2, \omega^2) \in \{0, 1\}^{\ell(n)} \times \{0, 1\}^{n \cdot \ell(n)}$), whereas Party 2 (resp., Party 1) which plays the other role, obtains $\delta^1 \overset{\text{def}}{=} \overline{C}_{\omega^1}(r^1)$ (resp., $\delta^2 \overset{\text{def}}{=} \overline{C}_{\omega^2}(r^2)$).

Protocol-Emulation Phase: *The parties use the authenticated-computation functionality of Eq. (7.33) in order to emulate each step of protocol Π. Recall that, for predetermined functions h and f, this functionality maps the input pair (α, β) to the output pair $(\lambda, f(\alpha))$ if $\beta = h(\alpha)$ and to $(\lambda, (h(\alpha), f(\alpha)))$ otherwise, where the second case is treated as abort.*

The party that is supposed to send a message plays the role of the first (i.e., initiating) party in Eq. (7.33), and the party that is supposed to receive the message plays the role of the second party. Suppose that the current message in Π is to be sent by Party j, and let $u \overset{\text{def}}{=} x$ if $j = 1$ and $u \overset{\text{def}}{=} y$ otherwise. Then the functions h, f and the inputs α, β, for the functionality of Eq. (7.33), are set as follows:

- *The string α is set to equal $(\alpha_1, \alpha_2, \alpha_3)$, where $\alpha_1 = (u, \rho^j)$ is the query and answer of Party j in the oracle call that it initiated in the input-commitment phase, $\alpha_2 = (r^j, \omega^j)$ is the answer that Party j obtained in the oracle call that it initiated in the coin-generation phase, and α_3 is the sequence of messages that Party j obtained so far in the emulation of Π. The string β equals $(\gamma^j, \delta^j, \alpha_3)$, where γ^j and δ^j are the answers that the other party obtained in the same oracle calls in the first two phases (and α_3 is as before).*
  In particular, u is the input to which Party j committed in the input-commitment phase, and r^j is the random-tape generated for it in the coin-generation phase. Together with α_3, they determine the message that is to be sent by Party j in Π. The auxiliary strings ρ^j and ω^j will be used to authenticate u and r^j, as reflected in the following definition of h.
- *The function h is defined such that $h((v_1, s_1), (v_2, s_2), v_3)$ equals $(\overline{C}_{s_1}(v_1), \overline{C}_{s_2}(v_2), v_3)$. Indeed, it holds that $h(\alpha_1, \alpha_2, \alpha_3) = (\overline{C}_{\rho^j}(u), \overline{C}_{\omega^j}(r^j), \alpha_3) = \beta$.*
- *The function f equals the computation that determines the message to be sent in Π. Note that this message is computable in polynomial-time from the party's input (denoted u and being part of α_1), its random-tape (denoted r^j and being part of α_2), and the messages it has received so far (i.e., α_3). Indeed, it holds that $f(\alpha_1, \alpha_2, \alpha_3)$ is the message that Party j should send in Π.*

Recall that the party that plays the receiver in the current oracle call obtains either $f(\alpha)$ or $(h(\alpha), f(\alpha))$. It treats the second case as if the other party has aborted, which is also possible per se.

Aborting: *In case any of the functionalities invoked in any of these phases terminates in an abort state, the party (or parties) obtaining this indication aborts the execution, and sets its output to ⊥. Otherwise, outputs are as follows.*

Outputs: *At the end of the emulation phase, each party holds the corresponding output of the party in protocol Π. The party just locally outputs this value.*

Clearly, in case both parties are honest, the input–output relation of Π′ is identical to that of Π. (We will show that essentially the same also holds in general.) We note that the transformation of Π to Π′ can be implemented in polynomial-time. Finally, replacing the oracle calls by the sub-protocols provided in Proposition 7.4.22 yields a standard protocol for the malicious model.

7.4.4.1. The Effect of the Compiler

As will be shown, given a protocol as constructed in the proof of Theorem 7.3.12, the compiler produces a protocol that securely computes the same functionality. Thus, for any functionality f, the compiler transforms a specific protocol for *privately* computing f (in the semi-honest model) into a protocol for *securely* computing f (in the malicious model). This suffices to establish our main result (i.e., Theorem 7.4.1), yet it does not say what the compiler does when given an arbitrary protocol (i.e., one not constructed as in the proof of Theorem 7.3.12). In order to analyze the action of the compiler, in general, we introduce the following model that is a hybrid of the semi-honest and the malicious models.[54] We call this new model, which is of independent interest, the *augmented semi-honest* model.

Definition 7.4.24 (the augmented semi-honest model): *Let Π be a two-party protocol. An augmented semi-honest behavior (with respect to Π) is a (feasible) strategy that satisfies the following conditions:*

Entering the execution: *Depending on its initial input, denoted u, the party may abort before taking any step in the execution of Π. Otherwise, again depending on u, it enters the execution with any input $u' \in \{0, 1\}^{|u|}$ of its choice. From this point on, u′ is fixed.*

Proper selection of a random-tape: *The party selects the random-tape to be used in Π uniformly among all strings of the length specified by Π. That is, the selection of the random-tape is exactly as specified by Π.*

Proper message transmission or abort: *In each step of Π, depending on its view of the execution so far, the party may either abort or send a message as instructed by Π. We stress that the message is computed as Π instructs based on input u′, the selected random-tape, and all messages received so far.*

---

[54] Indeed, Theorem 7.4.1 will follow as a special case of the general analysis of the compiler (as provided later). See further discussion following the statement of Proposition 7.4.25.

Output: *At the end of the interaction, the party produces an output depending on its entire view of the interaction. We stress that the view consists of the initial input u, the selected random-tape, and all messages received so far.*

A pair of probabilistic polynomial-time strategies, $\overline{C} = (C_1, C_2)$, *is* admissible with respect to Π in the augmented semi-honest model *if one strategy implements* Π *and the other implements an augmented semi-honest behavior with respect to* Π.

The augmented semi-honest model extends the ordinary semi-honest model in allowing adversaries to modify their initial input and to abort the execution at an arbitrary time. The augmented semi-honest model is arguably more appealing than the semi-honest model because in many settings, input modification and aborting can also be performed at a high level, without modifying the prescribed program. In contrast, implementing an effective malicious adversary may require some insight into the original protocol, and it typically requires substitution of the program's code.

Intuitively, the compiler transforms any protocol Π into an (oracle-aided) protocol Π', such that executions of Π' in the malicious model correspond to executions of Π in the augmented semi-honest model. That is:

Proposition 7.4.25 (general analysis of the two-party compiler): *Let* Π' *be the* (oracle-aided) *protocol produced by Construction 7.4.23 when given the protocol* Π, *and let* G *denote the set of the three oracle functionalities that are used by protocol* Π'. *Then, for every pair of probabilistic polynomial-time strategies* $\overline{A} = (A_1, A_2)$ *that are admissible* (with respect to Π') *for the* (real) *malicious model* (of Definition 7.4.2),[55] *there exists a pair of probabilistic polynomial-time strategies* $\overline{B} = (B_1, B_2)$ *that are admissible* with respect to Π *for the augmented semi-honest model* (of Definition 7.4.24), *such that*

$$\{\text{REAL}_{\Pi, \overline{B}(z)}(x, y)\}_{x,y,z} \stackrel{\text{c}}{\equiv} \{\text{REAL}^G_{\Pi', \overline{A}(z)}(x, y)\}_{x,y,z}$$

where $x, y, z \in \{0, 1\}^*$ *such that* $|x| = |y|$ *and* $|z| = \text{poly}(|x|)$.

Proposition 7.4.25 will be applied to protocols as constructed in the proof of Theorem 7.3.12. Actually, we will apply Proposition 7.4.25 to Theorem 7.3.14 (which provides *canonical* protocols for privately computing any functionality). As we shall see (in Section 7.4.4.2), for these *specific* protocols, the augmented semi-honest model (of Definition 7.4.24) can be emulated by the ideal malicious model (of Definition 7.2.4). Thus, we obtain secure (oracle-aided) protocols (with oracle to G) for any functionality, because (schematically speaking) for every functionality f, there exist Π and Π' such that $\text{IDEAL}_{f,\text{malicious}}(x, y)$ equals $\text{REAL}_{\Pi, \text{aug-semi-honest}}(x, y)$, which in turn equals $\text{REAL}^G_{\Pi', \text{malicious}}(x, y)$. (Ordinary secure protocols are obtained by using secure implementations of the oracles in G (which are provided by Proposition 7.4.22).) Thus, Theorem 7.4.1 is proven by combining the properties of the compiler, as stated in

---

[55] Recall the definition of real-model adversaries for an oracle-aided protocol (i.e., Definition 7.4.2) extends the definition of real-model adversaries for ordinary protocols (i.e., Definition 7.2.5).

Proposition 7.4.25, with the properties of specific protocols to be compiled by it. We start by establishing Proposition 7.4.25.

Proof Sketch: Given a pair of strategies, (A_1, A_2), which is admissible with respect to Π' for the real malicious model, we present a corresponding pair, (B_1, B_2), that is admissible with respect to Π for the augmented semi-honest model. In the current proof, the treatment of the two cases for the identity of the honest party is symmetric. Hence, we use a generic symbol for the said identity. (Alternatively, without loss of generality, one may assume that Party 1 is honest.)

We denote by hon the identity of the honest party and by mal the identity of the malicious party (i.e., $\{\mathrm{hon}, \mathrm{mal}\} = \{1, 2\}$). Thus, B_{hon} is determined by Π, and we transform (the malicious adversary) A_{mal} into (an augmented semi-honest adversary) B_{mal}, which uses A_{mal} as a subroutine. In particular, machine B_{mal} will emulate all the oracles that are used in Π' (which is an oracle-aided protocol compiled out of the ordinary protocol Π). On input $u \in \{0, 1\}^n$, machine B_{mal} behaves as follows:

Entering the execution: Machine B_{mal} invokes A_{mal} on input u, and decides whether to enter the protocol, and if so, with what input. Toward this end, machine B_{mal} emulates the input-committing phase of Π', using A_{mal} (as subroutine). Machine B_{mal} obtains from A_{mal} the oracle-query that it makes to the input-committing functionality (initiated by it), and uses this query to determine the replaced input u' (to be used in the rest of the execution). It also provides A_{mal} with the oracle answers that A_{mal} expects to get. Details follow.

Recall that the the input-committing phase consists of two invocations of the input-committing functionality, one by $\mathrm{Party}_{\mathrm{hon}}$ and the other by $\mathrm{Party}_{\mathrm{mal}}$. In each invocation, one party supplies an input and the other party gets a commitment to it (while the first party gets the corresponding commitment coins).

- In the invocation of the input-committing functionality in which $\mathrm{Party}_{\mathrm{hon}}$ commits to its input, machine B_{mal} generates a dummy commitment (supposedly to the input of $\mathrm{Party}_{\mathrm{hon}}$) and feeds it to A_{mal}, which expects to get a commitment (as answer from the oracle). Specifically, B_{mal} uniformly selects $\rho^{\mathrm{hon}} \in \{0, 1\}^{n^2}$, and computes the commitment $\gamma^{\mathrm{hon}} \stackrel{\text{def}}{=} \overline{C}_{\rho^{\mathrm{hon}}}(0^n)$, where 0^n is an arbitrary (dummy) value (which replaces the unknown input of $\mathrm{Party}_{\mathrm{hon}}$). Machine B_{mal} feeds A_{mal} with γ^{hon} (as if γ^{hon} were the oracle answer).
- In the invocation of the input-committing functionality in which $\mathrm{Party}_{\mathrm{mal}}$ commits to its input, machine B_{mal} tries to obtain the committed value (provided by $\mathrm{Party}_{\mathrm{mal}}$) and feeds A_{mal} with decommitment information (which it expects to get). Specifically, B_{mal} obtains the query, denoted u', that A_{mal} makes to the input-committing functionality, and feeds it with a uniformly selected $\rho^{\mathrm{mal}} \in \{0, 1\}^{n^2}$. We stress that B_{mal} will use this u' as its modified input in its (augmented semi-honest) execution of Π.

  In case A_{mal} has aborted this oracle call, machine B_{mal} aborts (i.e., does not enter the execution of Π).

In case B_{mal} did not abort, it enters protocol Π with input u'. Note that this entire step is implemented in polynomial-time, and the resulting u' depends only on u (the initial input of B_{mal}).

Selection of random-tape: B_{mal} selects its random-tape uniformly in $\{0, 1\}^{\ell(n)}$ (as specified by Π), and emulates the execution of the coin-generation phase of Π' ending with this outcome, so as to place A_{mal} in the appropriate state toward the protocol-emulation phase. To achieve the latter goal, machine B_{mal} supplies A_{mal} with the oracle answers that it expects to see. Again, we distinguish between the two oracle calls (to the augmented coin-tossing functionality) made during the coin-generation phase of Π':

- In the invocation of the augmented coin-tossing functionality in which $\text{Party}_{\text{hon}}$ obtains the outcome of the coin-toss, machine B_{mal} generates a dummy commitment (supposedly to the random-tape of $\text{Party}_{\text{hon}}$) and feeds it to A_{mal}, which expects to get a commitment (as answer from the oracle). Specifically, B_{mal} uniformly selects $\omega^{\text{hon}} \in \{0, 1\}^{n \cdot \ell(n)}$, and computes the commitment $\delta^{\text{hon}} \overset{\text{def}}{=} \overline{C}_{\omega^{\text{hon}}}(0^{\ell(n)})$, where $0^{\ell(n)}$ is an arbitrary (dummy) value (which replaces the unknown random-tape of $\text{Party}_{\text{hon}}$). Machine B_{mal} feeds A_{mal} with δ^{hon} (as if δ^{hon} were the oracle answer).
- In the invocation of the augmented coin-tossing functionality in which $\text{Party}_{\text{mal}}$ obtains the outcome of the coin-toss, machine B_{mal} first selects uniformly $r^{\text{mal}} \in \{0, 1\}^{\ell(n)}$ and $\omega^{\text{mal}} \in \{0, 1\}^{n \cdot \ell(n)}$, and feeds A_{mal} with the pair $(r^{\text{mal}}, \omega^{\text{mal}})$. Machine B_{mal} will use r^{mal} as its random-tape in its (augmented semi-honest) execution of Π. If A_{mal} aborts this oracle call, then B_{mal} aborts.

In case B_{mal} did not abort, it will use r^{mal} as its random-tape in the subsequent steps of protocol Π. Note that this entire step is implemented in polynomial-time, and that r^{mal} is selected uniformly in $\{0, 1\}^{\ell(n)}$ independent of anything else.

Subsequent steps – message transmission: Machine B_{mal} now enters the actual execution of Π. It proceeds in this real execution along with emulating the corresponding oracle answers of the authenticated-computation functionality. In a message-transmission step by $\text{Party}_{\text{hon}}$ (in Π), machine B_{mal} obtains from $\text{Party}_{\text{hon}}$ (in the real execution of Π) a message, and emulates the answer given to $\text{Party}_{\text{mal}}$ by the authenticated-computation functionality. In a message-transmission step by $\text{Party}_{\text{mal}}$ in Π, machine B_{mal} computes the message to be sent to $\text{Party}_{\text{hon}}$ (in Π) as instructed by Π, based on the input u' determined earlier, the random-tape r^{mal} selected earlier, and the messages obtained so far from $\text{Party}_{\text{hon}}$ (in Π). It then checks if A_{mal} makes the correct oracle-query, in which case it sends $\text{Party}_{\text{hon}}$ the message just computed, and otherwise it aborts. Details follow:

- In a message-transmission step by $\text{Party}_{\text{hon}}$ (in Π), machine B_{mal} first obtains from $\text{Party}_{\text{hon}}$ (in the real execution of Π) a message, denoted msg. Next, machine B_{mal} obtains from A_{mal} the query that A_{mal} makes to the authenticated-computation functionality. Let us denote this query by $\beta = (q_1, q_2, q_3)$. If $(q_1, q_2) = (\gamma^{\text{hon}}, \delta^{\text{hon}})$ and q_3 equals the sequence of messages sent so far (by B_{mal} to $\text{Party}_{\text{hon}}$), then B_{mal} feeds A_{mal} with the received message msg. Otherwise, B_{mal} feeds A_{mal} with $((\gamma^{\text{hon}}, \delta^{\text{hon}}, \alpha_3), \text{msg})$, where α_3 is the sequence of

---

686

messages sent so far (by B_{mal} to Party$_{\text{hon}}$). (The latter case means that A_{mal} is cheating, but Party$_{\text{hon}}$ does not detect this fact (because it obtains no answer from the authenticated-computation functionality).)

- In a message-transmission step by Party$_{\text{mal}}$ (in Π), machine B_{mal} first computes the message, denoted msg, that it should send (according to Π) on input u' (as determined earlier), random-tape r^{mal} (as recorded earlier), and the messages received so far (from Party$_{\text{hon}}$ in execution of Π). Next, machine B_{mal} obtains from A_{mal} the query that A_{mal} makes to the authenticated-computation functionality. Let us denote this query by $((u'', \rho''), (r'', \omega''), \alpha_3'')$. If $\overline{C}_{\rho''}(u'') = \overline{C}_{\rho^{\text{mal}}}(u')$, $\overline{C}_{\omega''}(r'') = \overline{C}_{\omega^{\text{mal}}}(r^{\text{mal}})$, and α_3'' equals the sequence of messages received so far (from Party$_{\text{hon}}$), then B_{mal} sends the message msg to Party$_{\text{hon}}$. Otherwise, B_{mal} aborts Π. (The latter case means that A_{mal} is cheating in Π', and Party$_{\text{hon}}$ detects this fact and treats it as if Party$_{\text{mal}}$ has aborted in Π'.)

Output: Machine B_{mal} just outputs, whatever machine A_{mal} outputs, given the execution history (in Π') emulated earlier.

Clearly, machine B_{mal} (as described) implements an augmented semi-honest behavior with respect to Π. It is left to show that

$$\{\text{REAL}^{G}_{\Pi', \overline{A}(z)}(x, y)\}_{x,y,z} \stackrel{c}{\equiv} \{\text{REAL}_{\Pi, \overline{B}(z)}(x, y)\}_{x,y,z} \tag{7.37}$$

There is only one difference between the two ensembles referred to in Eq. (7.37): In the first distribution (i.e., $\text{REAL}^{G}_{\Pi', \overline{A}(z)}(x, y)$), the commitments obtained by A_{mal} in the input-commitment and coin-generation phases are to the true input and true random-tape of Party$_{\text{hon}}$. On the other hand, in the second distribution (i.e., $\text{REAL}_{\Pi, \overline{B}(z)}(x, y)$), the emulated machine A_{mal} is given commitments to dummy values (and the actions of B_{mal} are determined accordingly). We stress that, other than this difference, B_{mal} perfectly emulates A_{mal}. However, the difference is "undetectable" (i.e., computationally indistinguishable) due to the hiding property of the commitment scheme. ∎

Composing the oracle-aided protocols produced by the compiler with secure implementations of these oracles (as provided by Proposition 7.4.22), and using the Composition Theorem and Proposition 7.4.25, we obtain:

Corollary 7.4.26 (compilation of two-party protocols): *Assuming the existence of (non-uniformly strong) one-way functions, any two-party protocol Π can be efficiently transformed into a two-party protocol Π' such that the following holds. For every pair of probabilistic polynomial-time strategies $\overline{A} = (A_1, A_2)$ that are admissible (with respect to Π') for the (real) malicious model (of Definition 7.2.5), there exists a pair of probabilistic polynomial-time strategies $\overline{B} = (B_1, B_2)$ that are admissible with respect to Π for the augmented semi-honest model (of Definition 7.4.24), such that*

$$\{\text{REAL}_{\Pi, \overline{B}(z)}(x, y)\}_{x,y,z} \stackrel{c}{\equiv} \{\text{REAL}_{\Pi', \overline{A}(z)}(x, y)\}_{x,y,z}$$

where $x, y, z \in \{0, 1\}^*$ such that $|x| = |y|$ and $|z| = \text{poly}(|x|)$.

7.4.4.2. Canonical Protocols and the Augmented Semi-Honest Model

Recall that a protocol for privately computing some functionality is guaranteed to be *secure with respect to semi-honest behavior*. Thus, a *real semi-honest execution* of this protocol can be emulated by an *ideal semi-honest computation* of the functionality. The question is what happens to such a protocol when it is run under the *augmented* semi-honest model. We now show that for canonical protocols (e.g., the protocols constructed in the proof of Theorem 7.3.12), a *real augmented semi-honest execution of such a protocol can be emulated by an ideal malicious computation of the functionality*. That is, these protocols have the salient property of allowing emulatation of the (wider) class of real augmented semi-honest executions by the (wider) class of ideal malicious computations. Combined with Corollary 7.4.26, this fact means that if one applies the compiler to a canonical protocol Π that privately computes f, then the resulting protocol Π' securely computes f (because malicious executions of Π' can be emulated by augmented semi-honest executions of Π, which in turn can be emulated by the ideal malicious model for f).

Recall that the augmented semi-honest model allows two things that go beyond the semi-honest model: (1) oblivious substitution of inputs, and (2) abort. The first type of behavior has a correspondence in the malicious ideal model, and so poses no problem. To account for the second type of behavior, we need to match an aborting execution in the augmented semi-honest model with an aborting execution in the ideal malicious model. Here is where the extra property of the specific protocols, constructed in the proof of Theorem 7.3.12, comes to help. Specifically, we refer to the fact that these protocols are *canonical*, which means that the output of each party is determined only after it receives the very last message (and no knowledge of the output is obtained before). Thus, aborting before this stage is essentially equivalent to not entering the execution at all, whereas aborting at the last stage is accounted for by the malicious ideal model.

Proposition 7.4.27 (on canonical protocols): *Let Π be a canonical protocol that privately computes the functionality f. Then, for every probabilistic polynomial-time pair $\overline{B} = (B_1, B_2)$ that is admissible for the (real) augmented semi-honest model (of Definition 7.4.24), there exists a probabilistic polynomial-time pair $\overline{C} = (C_1, C_2)$ that is admissible for the ideal malicious model (of Definition 7.2.4) such that*

$$\{\mathrm{REAL}_{\Pi, \overline{B}(z)}(x, y)\}_{x,y,z} \stackrel{c}{\equiv} \{\mathrm{IDEAL}_{f, \overline{C}(z)}(x, y)\}_{x,y,z}$$

where $x, y, z \in \{0, 1\}^*$ such that $|x| = |y|$ and $|z| = \mathrm{poly}(|x|)$.

We comment that the statement of Proposition 7.4.27 implicitly introduces a notion of *security in the augmented semi-honest model*. Indeed, if the real-model adversary is allowed augmented semi-honest behavior, then it is natural to allow a corresponding behavior in the ideal model, which then coincides with the ideal malicious model. Viewed in these terms, Proposition 7.4.27 asserts that *canonical protocols are secure in the augmented semi-honest model*.

Proof Sketch: Recall that canonical protocols (cf. Definition 7.3.13) proceed in two stages, where the first stage yields no information at all (to any semi-honest party) and the second phase consists of the exchange of a single pair of messages (i.e., each party sends a single message). We use the fact that canonical protocols admit a *two-stage* simulation procedure (for the view of a semi-honest party). Such two-stage simulators act as follows:

Input to simulator: A pair (u, v), where u is the initial input of the semi-honest party and v the corresponding local output.

Simulation Stage 1: Based (only) on u, the simulator generates a transcript corresponding to the view of the semi-honest party in the first stage of the canonical protocol Π.

Recall that this is a truncated execution of Π, where the execution is truncated just before the very last message is received by the semi-honest party. We stress that this truncated view, denoted T, is produced without using v.

Simulation Stage 2: Based on T and v, the simulator produces a string corresponding to the last message received by the semi-honest party. The simulator then outputs the concatenation of T and this (last) message.

The reader may easily verify that any canonical protocol has two-stage simulators. Loosely speaking, a simulator as required in Stage 1 is implicit in the definition of a canonical protocol (cf. Definition 7.3.13), and the simulation of Stage 2 is trivial (because Stage 1 in a canonical protocol ends with the parties holding shares of the desired outputs, and Stage 2 consists of each party sending the share required by the other party).

Next, for any protocol having two-stage simulators, given a pair (B_1, B_2) that is admissible with respect to Π for the augmented semi-honest model, we construct a pair, (C_1, C_2) that is admissible for the ideal malicious model. We distinguish two cases, corresponding to the identity of the honest party. The difference between these cases amounts to the possibility of (meaningfully) aborting the execution after receiving the last message (and just before sending the last message). This possibility exists for a dishonest Party 1 but not for a dishonest Party 2 (see Figure 7.3).

We start with the case where Party 1 is honest (and Party 2 is dishonest). In this case, C_1 is determined (by Π), and we need to transform the augmented semi-honest real adversary B_2 into a malicious ideal-model adversary C_2. The latter operates as follows, using the two-stage simulator, denoted S_2, provided for the view of Party 2 in semi-honest executions of Π (which privately computes f). Recall that C_2 gets input $y \in \{0, 1\}^n$.

1. Machine C_2 first determines the input y' to be sent to the trusted party, where y' is determined according to the behavior of B_2 during the entire emulation of the (canonical) protocol Π. In addition, C_2 emulates the messages sent and received by

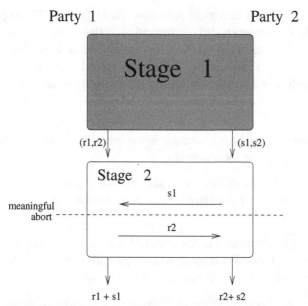

Figure 7.3: Schematic depiction of a canonical protocol.

B_2 during the first phase of Π, and also determines the last message of B_2 (i.e., its single Stage 2-message). This is done as follows:

(a) First, C_2 computes the substituted input with which (the augmented semi-honest adversary) B_2 enters Π. That is, $y' \leftarrow B_2(y)$. In case B_2 aborts, machine C_2 sets $y' = \bot$ (so as to conform with the [simplifying] convention that the ideal-model adversary always sends input to the trusted party).

(b) Next, C_2 invokes the *first stage* of the simulator S_2 in order to obtain the view of the execution of the first stage of Π as seen by a semi-honest party having input y'. Denote this view by T, and note that T includes y'. Machine C_2 extracts from T the random-tape, denoted r, of Party 2. This random-tape will be fixed for the use of B_2.

(c) Using T, machine C_2 emulates the execution of B_2 on input y' and random-tape r, up to the point where Party 2 is to receive the last message (in Π). We stress that this point is just after Party 2 has sent its last message. Thus, the last message of Party 2 (in Π) is determined at this step. To perform the emulation, C_2 feeds B_2 with input y' and random-tape r, and iteratively feeds B_2 with the sequence of (incoming) messages as appearing in the corresponding locations in T. We stress that although T is only the transcript of Stage 1 in Π, it determines all messages of Party 2 in Π (including its single Stage 2 message).

Note that the augmented semi-honest strategy B_2 may abort in such an execution, but in case it does not abort, the messages it sends fit the transcript T. Consequently, the view of (the augmented semi-honest adversary) B_2 in an execution of the first stage of Π is emulated by a prefix of T (which in turn represents the simulated view of a semi-honest party on input y').

690

In case B_2 has aborted the execution (even just before sending the last message, which belongs to Stage 2), machine C_2 *resets* y' to $\perp$.

We stress that y' is determined based only on y, and that C_2 never aborts.

2. Machine C_2 invokes the *trusted party* with input y' and obtains a response, denoted v. (Since the trusted party answers Party 1 first, Party 2 does not have the option of stopping the trusted party before it answers Party 1. But this option is not needed because Party 2 cannot meaningfully abort Π after receiving the last message in it. That is, if B_2 has not aborted so far, then it cannot (meaningfully) abort now, because it has already sent (or rather determined) its last message.)

3. Finally, C_2 determines its output as follows:

   (a) C_2 invokes the *second stage* of the simulator S_2 in order to obtain the last message sent to Party 2. That is, C_2 supplies the simulator with the first-stage transcript T and the output v, and obtains the last message, denoted msg.

   (b) C_2 now emulates the last step of B_2 (i.e., its output computation) by supplying it with the message msg.
   (Note that the last message of B_2 was already determined in Step 1, and so the execution of C_2 ends here.)

The output of C_2 is set to be the output of B_2, regardless if B_2 has aborted or completed the execution.

We need to show that

$$\{\text{REAL}_{\Pi,\overline{B}(z)}(x, y)\}_{x,y,z} \overset{c}{\equiv} \{\text{IDEAL}_{f,\overline{C}(z)}(x, y)\}_{x,y,z} \tag{7.38}$$

Abusing notation, we replace the final value of y' by $B_2(y)$, and get:

$$\{\text{REAL}_{\Pi,\overline{B}}(x, y)\}_{x,y} \equiv \{(\text{OUTPUT}_1^{\Pi}(x, B_2(y)),\ B_2(\text{VIEW}_2^{\Pi}(x, B_2(y))))\}_{x,y}$$

$$\overset{c}{\equiv} \{(f_1(x, B_2(y)),\ B_2(S_2(y, f_2(x, B_2(y)))))\}_{x,y}$$

$$\equiv \{(f_1(x, C_2(y)),\ C_2(y, f_2(x, C_2(y))))\}_{x,y}$$

$$\equiv \{\text{IDEAL}_{f,\overline{C}}(x, y)\}_{x,y}$$

where $S_2(y, v)$ denotes the result of the two-stage simulation. Eq. (7.38) follows. We stress that the first stage of the simulator S_2 is used to determine the value of $y' = B_2(y)$, but unfortunately this fact is not explicit in our notation. An analogous comment holds with respect to the case treated next (where Party 1 is dishonest).

We now turn to the case where Party 2 is totally honest (and Party 1 possibly dishonest). In this case, C_2 is determined, and we need to transform the *augmented semi-honest* real adversary B_1 into a malicious *ideal-model* adversary C_1. The latter operates as follows, using the simulator, denoted S_1, provided for the view of Party 1. Recall that C_1 gets input $x \in \{0, 1\}^n$.

1. Machine C_1 first determines the input x' to be sent to the trusted party, where x' is determined according to the behavior of B_1 during Stage 1 of the (canonical)

protocol Π. In addition, C_1 emulates the messages sent and received by B_1 during the first phase of Π. This is done as in the previous transformation of B_2 to C_2, except that here, the last message of B_1 (i.e., its Stage 2 message) is still undetermined at this step (and can be determined only when given the last message of Party 2, which in turn is obtained only at Step 3).

2. Machine C_1 invokes the *trusted party* with input x' and obtains a response, denoted v.

   We stress that, unlike in the case where Party 2 is dishonest, Party 1 (i.e., C_1) still has the option of stopping the trusted party before it answers Party 2.

3. Next, C_1 invokes the *second stage* of the simulator S_1 in order to obtain the last message sent (by Party 2) to Party 1. It supplies the simulator with the transcript of the first stage and the output v, and obtains the last message, denoted msg.

4. Machine C_1 now emulates the last step of B_1 by supplying it with the message msg. In case B_1 aborts, machine C_1 prevents the *trusted party* from answering Party 2 and aborts. Otherwise, machine C_1 allows the *trusted party* to answer Party 2. We stress that C_1 does not abort in any prior step.

   The output of C_1 is set to be the output of B_1, regardless if B_1 has aborted or completed the execution.

We again need to show that Eq. (7.38) holds. The argument is analogous to the one applied for a dishonest Party 2. Suppose first, for simplicity, that machine B_1 *never aborts*. In such a case, by definition of S_1,

$$\{\text{REAL}_{\Pi,\overline{B}}(x, y)\}_{x,y} \equiv \{(B_1(\text{VIEW}_1^\Pi(B_1(x), y)), \text{OUTPUT}_2^\Pi(B_1(x), y))\}_{x,y}$$

$$\overset{c}{\equiv} \{(B_1(S_1(B_1(x), f_1(B_1(x), y))), f_2(B_1(x), y))\}_{x,y}$$

$$\equiv \{(C_1(x, f_1(C_1(x), y)), f_2(C_1(x), y))\}_{x,y}$$

$$\equiv \{\text{IDEAL}_{f,\overline{C}}(x, y)\}_{x,y}$$

Next, suppose that B_1 always aborts *after receiving the last message,* and before sending its last message to Party 2. In this case, we have

$$\{\text{REAL}_{\Pi,\overline{B}}(x, y)\}_{x,y} \equiv \{(B_1(\text{VIEW}_1^\Pi(B_1(x), y)), \bot)\}_{x,y}$$

$$\overset{c}{\equiv} \{(B_1(S_1(B_1(x), f_1(B_1(x), y))), \bot)\}_{x,y}$$

$$\equiv \{(C_1(x, f_1(C_1(x), y), \bot), \bot)\}_{x,y}$$

$$\equiv \{\text{IDEAL}_{f,\overline{C}}(x, y)\}_{x,y}$$

In the general case, machine B_1 may abort in some executions and not abort in others. Whenever B_1 aborts, it does so before sending its last message (possibly just after receiving the last message). However, both the decision of whether or not to abort and the output at such a case are determined by B_1 based on its view of the execution so far. This view can be simulated by $S_1(B_1(x), f_1(B_1(x), y))$, which in turn is invoked by C_1 in two stages (in Steps 1 and 3, respectively). Thus, Eq. (7.38) holds in this case, too. ∎

7.4.4.3. Conclusion: Proof of Theorem 7.4.1

Essentially, Theorem 7.4.1 follows by combining the following three results: (1) Theorem 7.3.14 providing canonical protocols for privately computing any functionality, (2) the general analysis of the compiler (i.e., Corollary 7.4.26), and (3) the special properties of canonical protocols (i.e., Proposition 7.4.27). Specifically, let f be an arbitrary functionality, Π be a canonical protocol for privately computing f (guaranteed by Theorem 7.3.14), and Π' be the protocol compiled from Π by Construction 7.4.23 (using secure implementations of the functionalities in G). Now, let $\overline{A}$ be admissible for the real *malicious* model (with respect to Π'), let $\overline{B}$ be the real-model adversary (which is admissible with respect to Π in the augmented semi-honest model) derived by Corollary 7.4.26, and $\overline{C}$ be the ideal-model adversary (which is admissible for the malicious model) derived by Proposition 7.4.27. Then

$$\{\text{REAL}_{\Pi',\overline{A}(z)}(x, y)\}_{x,y,z} \stackrel{c}{\equiv} \{\text{REAL}_{\Pi,\overline{B}(z)}(x, y)\}_{x,y,z}$$

$$\stackrel{c}{\equiv} \{\text{IDEAL}_{f,\overline{C}(z)}(x, y)\}_{x,y,z}$$

Theorem 7.4.1 follows. ■

7.5.* Extension to the Multi-Party Case

In this section, we extend the treatment of general secure protocols from the two-party case to the multi-party case. Again, our ultimate goal is to design protocols that withstand any feasible adversarial behavior, and again we proceed in two steps. We first consider a benign type of adversary, called *semi-honest*, and construct protocols that are secure with respect to such an adversary. The definition of this type of adversary is very much the same as in the two-party case. Next, we turn to the case of general adversary behavior, but here (unlike in the two-party case) we consider two different models. The *first model of malicious behavior* mimics the treatment of adversaries in the two-party case; it allows the adversary to control even a majority of the parties, but it does not view the (unavoidable) early abort phenomena as a violation of security. In the *second model of malicious behavior*, we assume that the adversary can control only a strict minority of the parties. In this model, which would have been vacuous in the two-party case, the early abort phenomena can be effectively prevented. We show how to transform protocols secure in the semi-honest model into protocols secure in each of the two malicious-behavior models. As in the two-party case, this is done by forcing parties (in each of the latter models) to behave in an effectively semi-honest manner.

The constructions are obtained by suitable modifications of the constructions used in the two-party case. In fact, the construction of multi-party protocols for the semi-honest model is a minor modification of the construction used in the two-party case. The same holds for the compilation of protocols for the semi-honest model into protocols for the *first* malicious model. When compiling protocols for the semi-honest model into protocols for the *second* malicious model, we will use a new primitive, called

Verifiable Secret Sharing (VSS), in order to "effectively prevent" minority parties from aborting the protocol prematurely. Actually, we shall compile protocols secure in the *first* malicious model into protocols secure in the *second* malicious model.

Our treatment touches upon a variety of issues that were ignored (or are inapplicable) in the two-party case. These issues include the communication model (i.e., the type of communication channels), the consideration of an external adversary, and the way the latter selects dishonest parties (or corrupts parties). In particular, in some models (i.e., postulating private channels and a majority of honest participants), it is possible to obtain secure protocols without relying on any intractability assumptions: See Section 7.6.

Teaching Tip. We strongly recommend reading Sections 7.2–7.4 before reading the current section. In many places in the current section, motivating discussions and technical details are omitted, while relying on the fact that analogue elaboration has appeared in the treatment of the two-party case (i.e., in Sections 7.2–7.4).

7.5.1. Definitions

A multi-party protocol problem is cast by specifying a random process that maps sequences of inputs (one input per each party) to corresponding sequences of outputs. Let m denote the number of parties. It will be convenient to think of m as being fixed, yet one can certainly think of it as an additional parameter. An m-ary functionality, denoted $f : (\{0, 1\}^*)^m \rightarrow (\{0, 1\}^*)^m$, is thus a random process mapping sequences of the form $\overline{x} = (x_1, ..., x_m)$ into sequences of random variables, $f(\overline{x}) = (f_1(\overline{x}), ..., f_m(\overline{x}))$. The semantics is that for every i, the i-th party, initially holds an input x_i, and wishes to obtain the i-th element in $f(x_1, ..., x_m)$, denoted $f_i(x_1, ..., x_m)$. For example, consider deterministic functionalities for computing the maximum, average, or any other statistics of the individual values held by the parties (and see more examples in Exercises 14 and 15). The discussions and simplifying conventions made in Section 7.2.1 apply in the current context, too. Most importantly, we assume throughout this section that all parties hold inputs of equal length; that is, $|x_i| = |x_j|$.

Conventions Regarding the Number of Parties. For simplicity of exposition, we assume throughout our exposition that m is fixed. From time to time, we comment on what is needed in order to derive definitions (and constructions) for the case that m is a parameter. We comment that it is natural to discuss multi-party functionalities that are "uniform," in the sense that there exist (uniform) algorithms for computing them for each value of m (and of course each m-sequence). One such functionality is the "universal functionality" that is given a description of a circuit, as well as a corresponding sequence of inputs. (For example, the circuit may be part of the input of each party, and in case these circuits are not identical, the value of the functionality is defined as a sequence of $\perp$'s.) Indeed, a universal functionality is natural to consider also in the two-party case, but here (in view of the extra parameter m) its appeal is enhanced.

7.5.1.1. The Communication Model and External Adversaries

In the definitional treatment of the two-party case, we viewed one of the communicating parties as an adversary and considered its effect on the protocol's execution. This approach can be extended to the multi-party case, except that here, we may consider coalitions of dishonest parties and their effect on the execution. Alternatively, we may consider an (external) adversary that controls a subset of the parties that participate in the execution. A variety of issues that arise includes the size of this subset, the way it is selected (by the adversary), and the possible effect of the adversary on the communication channels.

The Number of Parties Controlled by the Adversary. In the two-party case, we have focused on the case in which the adversary is identified with one of the participants in the execution. Clearly, the case in which the adversary controls both participants is of no interest, but the case in which the adversary controls none of the participants may be of interest in case the adversary can wire-tap the communication line (as will be discussed). In the multi-party case, we will consider adversaries that control any number of participants.[56] (Of course, when defining security following the "ideal-vs.-real" paradigm, we should insist that the corresponding ideal adversary controls the same set of participants.)

The Selection of Parties Controlled by the Adversary. The notion of an external adversary naturally leads to the issue of how this adversary selects the set of parties that it controls. The basic (and simpler) model postulates that this set is determined before the execution starts (and is, of course, not known to the honest parties). This model is called non-adaptive as opposed to the adaptive model in which the adversary may select the set of parties that it controls *adaptively*, during the execution of the protocol and depending on information it has gathered so far. In this section, we only consider the non-adaptive model, and defer the treatment of the adaptive model to Section 7.7.1.2. We comment that the difference between the non-adaptive model and the adaptive model becomes crucial when the number of parties (i.e., m) is treated as a parameter, rather than being fixed.

The Communication Channels. Throughout this section, we assume a model of synchronous communication. It is natural to assume that the external adversary may tap all communication channels (i.e., specifically, the channels between honest parties). In such a case, even an adversary that controls none of the participants is of interest, because it may potentially gain information about the execution by wire-tapping. However, for the sake of simplicity, we sometimes prefer to present and use definitions that refer to the "private-channel model" (see also Section 7.6); that is, we sometimes presuppose that honest parties may communicate in secrecy (or, put differently, we sometimes assume that adversaries do not tap communication lines between honest parties). We comment that in the non-adaptive model, the issue of implementing the private-channel model

---

[56] Indeed, the case in which the adversary controls all parties is of no interest, and is often ignored.

over the "standard model" (i.e., providing secret communication) is well understood, and can be (easily) decoupled from the main treatment. Specifically, protocols secure in the private-channel model can be compiled to withstand wire-tapping adversaries (by using encryption schemes). Similarly, we assume that messages sent between honest parties arrive intact, whereas one may want to consider adversaries that may inject messages on the communication line between honest parties. Again, this can be counteracted by the use of well-understood paradigms, in this case, the use of signature schemes.

7.5.1.2. The Semi-Honest Model

This model is defined exactly as in the two-party case (see Section 7.2.2.1). Recall that a semi-honest party is one who follows the protocol properly, with the exception that it keeps a record of all its intermediate computations. Loosely speaking, a multi-party protocol privately computes f if whatever a *set* (or a *coalition*) of semi-honest parties can obtain after participating in the protocol could be essentially obtained from the input and output *of these very parties*. Thus, the only difference between the current definition and the one used in the two-party case is that we consider the gain of a coalition (rather than of a single party) from participating in the protocol.

Definition 7.5.1 (privacy with respect to semi-honest behavior, without wire-tapping):
Let $f : (\{0, 1\}^*)^m \to (\{0, 1\}^*)^m$ *be an m-ary functionality, where* $f_i(x_1, ..., x_m)$ *denotes the i-th element of* $f(x_1, .., x_m)$. *For* $I = \{i_1, ..., i_t\} \subseteq [m] \stackrel{\text{def}}{=} \{1, ..., m\}$, *we let* $f_I(x_1, ..., x_m)$ *denote the subsequence* $f_{i_1}(x_1, ..., x_m), ..., f_{i_t}(x_1, ..., x_m)$. *Let* Π *be an m-party protocol for computing* f.[57] *The* view *of the i-th party during an execution of* Π *on* $\overline{x} = (x_1, ..., x_m)$, *denoted* $\text{VIEW}_i^\Pi(\overline{x})$, *is defined as in Definition 7.2.1, and for* $I = \{i_1, ..., i_t\}$, *we let* $\text{VIEW}_I^\Pi(\overline{x}) \stackrel{\text{def}}{=} (I, \text{VIEW}_{i_1}^\Pi(\overline{x}), ..., \text{VIEW}_{i_t}^\Pi(\overline{x}))$.

- (deterministic case) *In case f is a deterministic m-ary functionality, we say that* Π privately computes f *if there exists a probabilistic polynomial-time algorithm, denoted S, such that for every* $I \subseteq [m]$, *it holds that*

$$\{S(I, (x_{i_1}, ..., x_{i_t}), f_I(\overline{x}))\}_{\overline{x} \in (\{0,1\}^*)^m} \stackrel{c}{\equiv} \{\text{VIEW}_I^\Pi(\overline{x})\}_{\overline{x} \in (\{0,1\}^*)^m} \quad (7.39)$$

- (general case) *We say that* Π privately computes f *if there exists a probabilistic polynomial-time algorithm, denoted S, such that for every* $I \subseteq [m]$, *it holds that*

$$\{(S(I, (x_{i_1}, ..., x_{i_t}), f_I(\overline{x})), f(\overline{x}))\}_{\overline{x} \in (\{0,1\}^*)^m} \quad (7.40)$$
$$\stackrel{c}{\equiv} \{(\text{VIEW}_I^\Pi(\overline{x}), \text{OUTPUT}^\Pi(\overline{x}))\}_{\overline{x} \in (\{0,1\}^*)^m}$$

where $\text{OUTPUT}^\Pi(\overline{x})$ *denotes the output sequence of all parties during the execution represented in* $\text{VIEW}_I^\Pi(\overline{x})$.

---

[57] As in Section 7.2, by saying that Π computes (rather than privately computes) f, we mean that the output distribution of the protocol (when played by honest or semi-honest parties) on the input sequence $(x_1, ..., x_m)$ is distributed identically to $f(x_1, ..., x_m)$.

Eq. (7.40) asserts that the view of the parties in I can be efficiently simulated based solely on their inputs and outputs. Note that $\text{VIEW}_I^{\Pi}(\overline{x})$ includes only the *local* views of parties in I, and does not include the messages sent between pairs of honest parties. Thus, Definition 7.5.1 refers to the case in which the semi-honest parties do not (or cannot) wire-tap the channels between honest parties (and, hence, is labeled "without wire-tapping"), which is equivalent to assuming the existence of "private channels." To deal with the case of wire-tapping, one just needs to augment $\text{VIEW}_I^{\Pi}(\overline{x})$ with the transcript of the messages sent between all the pairs of honest parties. In this case, it is more natural to consider an external adversary that obtains the views of all parties in I, as well as all messages sent over all channels.

Definition 7.5.1 can be easily adapted to deal with a varying parameter m, by taking advantage of the current order of quantifiers (i.e., "there exists an algorithm S such that for every I").[58] We also note that the simulator can certainly handle the trivial cases in which either $I = [m]$ or $I = \emptyset$. (The case $I = [m]$ is always trivial, whereas the case $I = \emptyset$ is trivial only because here we consider the case of no wire-tapping.)

As in the two-party case, Definition 7.5.1 is equivalent to a definition that can be derived by following the real-vs.-ideal paradigm (analogously to the treatment in Section 7.2.2.2).

7.5.1.3. The Two Malicious Models

We now turn to consider arbitrary feasible deviation of parties from a specified multi-party protocol. As mentioned earlier, one may consider two alternative models:

1. A model in which the number of parties that deviate from the protocol is arbitrary. The treatment of this case extends the treatment given in the two-party case. In particular, in this model, one cannot prevent malicious parties from aborting the protocol prematurely, and the definition of security has to account for this fact (if it is to have a chance of being met).

2. A model in which the number of parties that deviate from the protocol is strictly less than half the total number of parties. The definitional treatment of this case is simpler than the treatment given in the two-party case. In particular, one may – in some sense – (effectively) prevent malicious parties from aborting the protocol prematurely.[59] Consequently, the definition of security is "freed" from the need to account for early stopping, and thus is simpler.

We further assume (toward achieving a higher level of security) that malicious parties may communicate (without being detected by the honest parties), and may thus coordinate their malicious actions. Actually, it will be instructive to think of all malicious parties as being controlled by one (external) adversary. Our presentation follows the

---

[58] Note that for a fixed m, it may make as much sense to reverse the order of quantifiers (i.e., require that "for every I there exists an algorithm S_I").

[59] As we shall see, the assumption that malicious parties are in a minority opens the door to effectively preventing them from aborting the protocol immaturely. This will be achieved by letting the majority parties have (together!) enough information so as to be able to emulate the minority parties in case the latter abort.

ideal-vs.-real emulation paradigm introduced and used in the previous sections. The difference between the two malicious models is reflected in a difference in the corresponding *ideal models,* which captures the different types of benign behaviors that a secure protocol is aimed at achieving. Another difference is in the number of malicious parties considered in each model.

The first malicious model. Following the discussion in Section 7.2.3, we conclude that three things cannot be avoided in the first malicious model:

1. Malicious parties may refuse to participate in the protocol (when the protocol is first invoked). Actually, as explained in Section 7.2.3, this behavior may be viewed as a special case of input substitution (as discussed in the next item).
2. Malicious parties may substitute their local inputs (and enter the protocol with inputs other than the ones provided to them from the outside).
3. Malicious parties may abort the protocol prematurely (e.g., before sending their last message).

Accordingly, the ideal model is derived by a straightforward generalization of Definition 7.2.4. In light of this similarity, we allow ourselves to be quite terse. To simplify the exposition, we assume that for every I, first the trusted party supplies the adversary with the I-part of the output (i.e., the value of f_I), and only next is it possibly allowed (at the adversary's discretion) to answer the other parties. Actually, as in the two-party case, the adversary has the ability to prevent the trusted party from answering all parties only in the case where it controls Party 1.[60]

Definition 7.5.2 (the ideal model – first malicious model): *Let* $f : (\{0, 1\}^*)^m \to (\{0, 1\}^*)^m$ *be an m-ary functionality. For* $I = \{i_1, ..., i_t\} \subseteq [m] \stackrel{\text{def}}{=} \{1, ..., m\}$, *let* $\overline{I} = [m] \setminus I$ *and* $(x_1, ..., x_m)_I = (x_{i_1}, ..., x_{i_t})$. *A pair* (I, B), *where* $I \subseteq [m]$ *and* B *is a probabilistic polynomial-time algorithm, represents an adversary in the ideal model. The joint execution of* f *under* (I, B) *in the ideal model (on input* $\overline{x} = (x_1, ..., x_m)$ *and auxiliary input* z*), denoted* $\text{IDEAL}^{(1)}_{f, I, B(z)}(\overline{x})$, *is defined by uniformly selecting a random-tape* r *for the adversary, and letting* $\text{IDEAL}^{(1)}_{f, I, B(z)}(\overline{x}) \stackrel{\text{def}}{=} \Upsilon(\overline{x}, I, z, r)$, *where* $\Upsilon(\overline{x}, I, z, r)$ *is defined as follows:*

- *In case Party 1 is honest (i.e., $1 \notin I$),*

$$\Upsilon(\overline{x}, I, z, r) \stackrel{\text{def}}{=} (f_{\overline{I}}(\overline{x}'), \; B(\overline{x}_I, I, z, r, f_I(\overline{x}'))), \tag{7.41}$$

where $\overline{x}' \stackrel{\text{def}}{=} (x_1', ..., x_m')$ *such that* $x_i' = B(\overline{x}_I, I, z, r)_i$ *for* $i \in I$ *and* $x_i' = x_i$ *otherwise.*
- *In case Party 1 is not honest (i.e., $1 \in I$), $\Upsilon(\overline{x}, I, z, r)$ equals*

$$(\perp^{|\overline{I}|}, \; B(\overline{x}_I, I, z, r, f_I(\overline{x}'), \perp)) \quad \text{if } B(\overline{x}_I, I, z, r, f_I(\overline{x}')) = \perp \tag{7.42}$$

$$(f_{\overline{I}}(\overline{x}'), \; B(\overline{x}, I, z, r, f_I(\overline{x}'))) \quad \text{otherwise} \tag{7.43}$$

---

[60] As in the two-party case, this convention is rather arbitrary; see the discussion at the end of Section 7.2.3.1.

where, in both cases, $\overline{x}' \overset{\text{def}}{=} (x_1', ..., x_m')$ *such that* $x_i' = B(\overline{x}_I, I, z, r)_i$ *for* $i \in I$ *and* $x_i' = x_i$ *otherwise.*

In all cases, the trusted party is invoked with possibly substituted inputs, denoted $\overline{x}' = (x_1', ..., x_m')$, where $x_i' \neq x_i$ only if $i \in I$. Eq. (7.42) represents the case where the trusted party is stopped right after supplying the adversary with the I-part of the output (i.e., $f_I(\overline{x}')$). This case is allowed only when $1 \in I$, and so Party 1 can always be "blamed" when this happens.[61] Equations (7.41) and (7.43) represent the cases where the trusted party is invoked with possibly substituted inputs, but is allowed to answer all parties. We stress that either all honest parties get their output or all are notified that the trusted party was stopped by the adversary. As usual, the definition of security is obtained by requiring that for every feasible adversary in the real model, there exists a corresponding adversary in the ideal model that achieves the same effect. Specifically, in the real model, the adversary may tap all communication lines and determine (adaptively) all the outgoing messages of all dishonest parties.

Definition 7.5.3 (Security in the first malicious model): *Let f be as in Definition 7.5.2, and Π be an m-party protocol for computing f.*

- *The* joint execution of Π under (I, A) in the real model *(on input a sequence $\overline{x} = (x_1, ..., x_m)$ and auxiliary input z), denoted* $\text{REAL}_{\Pi, I, A(z)}(\overline{x})$, *is defined as the output sequence resulting from the interaction between the m parties, where the messages of parties in I are computed according to $A(\overline{x}_I, I, z)$ and the messages of parties in $\overline{I} \overset{\text{def}}{=} [m] \setminus I$ are computed according to Π.[62] Specifically, the messages of malicious parties (i.e., parties in I) are determined by the adversary A based on the initial inputs of the parties in I, the auxiliary input z, and all messages sent so far by all parties (including messages received by the honest parties [i.e., parties in $\overline{I}$]).*
- *Protocol Π is said to* securely compute f *(in the first malicious model) if for every probabilistic polynomial-time algorithm A (representing a real-model adversary strategy), there exists a probabilistic polynomial-time algorithm B (representing an ideal-model adversary strategy), such that for every $I \subseteq [m]$*

$$\{\text{IDEAL}^{(1)}_{f, I, B(z)}(\overline{x})\}_{\overline{x}, z} \overset{\text{c}}{\equiv} \{\text{REAL}_{\Pi, I, A(z)}(\overline{x})\}_{\overline{x}, z}$$

When the context is clear, we sometimes refer to Π as an implementation *of f.*

We stress that the ideal-model adversary (i.e., B) controls exactly the same set of parties (i.e., I) as the the real-model adversary (i.e., A). Definition 7.5.3 (as well as the following Definition 7.5.4) refers to an adversary that may wire-tap all communication channels. This is reflected in the definition of $\text{REAL}_{\Pi, I, A(z)}(\overline{x})$, which allows A to determine its actions based on all messages communicated so far. (Thus, for $m = 2$, Definition 7.5.3 is stronger than Definition 7.2.6, because [unlike the latter] the former also refers to the

---

[61] In fact, in the protocols presented in this work, early abort is always due to malicious behavior of Party 1. By Definition 7.5.3, this translates to malicious behavior of Party 1 in the ideal model.

[62] To fit the format used in Definition 7.5.2, the outputs of the parties (in $\text{REAL}_{\Pi, I, A(z)}(\overline{x})$) are arranged such that the outputs of the honest parties appear on the left-hand side.

case $I = \emptyset$, which is non-trivial because it refers to an adversary that may wire-tap the communication channel.) In order to derive a definition for the private-channel model, one should modify the definition of $\text{REAL}_{\Pi, I, A(z)}(\overline{x})$, such that A's actions may depend only on the messages received by parties in I.

The Second Malicious Model. In the second model, where malicious parties are in a strict minority, the early-abort, phenomena can be effectively prevented. Thus, in this case, there is no need to "tolerate" early-abort, and consequently our definition of security requires "proper termination" of executions. This is reflected in the definition of the ideal model, which actually becomes simpler.[63]

Definition 7.5.4 (security in the second malicious model, assuming an honest majority): *Let f and Π be as in Definition 7.5.3:*

- *The ideal-model adversary is defined as in Definition 7.5.2, except that the abort case captured by Eq. (7.42) is not allowed. The corresponding joint computation in the ideal model, under (I, B), is denoted by $\text{IDEAL}^{(2)}_{f, I, B(z)}(\overline{x})$.*
- *The real-model adversary is defined exactly as in Definition 7.5.3. However, we will only consider the case where such adversary controls strictly less than $m/2$ parties.*
- *Protocol Π is said to* **securely compute** *f (in the second malicious model) if for every probabilistic polynomial-time algorithm A* (representing a real-model adversary strategy), *there exists a probabilistic polynomial-time algorithm B* (representing an ideal-model adversary strategy), *such that for every $I \subset [m]$ such that $|I| < m/2$, it holds that*

$$\{\text{IDEAL}^{(2)}_{f, I, B(z)}(\overline{x})\}_{\overline{x}, z} \overset{c}{\equiv} \{\text{REAL}_{\Pi, I, A(z)}(\overline{x})\}_{\overline{x}, z}$$

When the context is clear, we sometimes refer to Π as an **implementation** *of f.*

We stress that in Definition 7.5.4, we consider only adversaries that control a strict minority of the parties.

Discussion. The two alternative malicious models give rise to two appealing and yet fundamentally incomparable notions of security. Put in other words, there is a trade-off between the willingness to put up with early-abort (i.e., not consider it a breach of security) and requiring the protocol to be robust also against malicious coalitions controlling a majority of all parties. The question of which notion of security is preferable depends on the application (or on the setting). In some settings, one may prefer to be protected from malicious majorities, while giving up the guarantee that parties cannot abort the protocol prematurely (while being detected doing so). On the other hand, in settings in which a strict majority of the parties can be trusted to follow the protocol, one may obtain the benefit of effectively preventing parties to abort the protocol prematurely. We stress that all definitions are easily adapted to deal with a varying parameter m.

---

[63] In this case, the definition extends the one presented in Section 7.2.3.2.

7.5.2. Security in the Semi-Honest Model

Our construction of private multi-party protocols (i.e., secure versus semi-honest behavior) for any given multi-argument functionality follows the presentation of the two-party case. For simplicity, we think of the number of parties m as being fixed. The reader may verify that the dependence of our constructions on m is at most polynomial.

Our protocol construction adapts the one used in the two-party case (see Section 7.3). That is, we consider a GF(2) circuit for evaluating the (deterministic) m-ary functionality f, and start by letting each party share its input bits with all other parties, such that the sum of all shares equals the input bit. Next, scanning the circuit from its input wires to its output wires, we propagate shares through the circuit gates, by using a suitable private computation. As in the two-party case, we focus on the propagation of shares through multiplication gates. That is, for Party i holding bits a_i and b_i, we wish to conduct a private computation such that this party ends up with a random bit c_i and $(\sum_{i=1}^{m} a_i) \cdot (\sum_{i=1}^{m} b_i) = \sum_{i=1}^{m} c_i$ holds. More precisely, we are interested in privately computing the following randomized m-ary functionality:

$$((a_1, b_1), ..., (a_m, b_m)) \mapsto (c_1, ..., c_m) \quad \text{uniformly in } \{0, 1\}^m \quad (7.44)$$

$$\text{subject to } \sum_{i=1}^{m} c_i = \sum_{i=1}^{m} a_i \cdot \sum_{i=1}^{m} b_i . \quad (7.45)$$

Thus, all that we need to do on top of Section 7.3 is to provide a private m-party computation of this functionality. This is done by privately reducing, for arbitrary m, the computation of Eq. (7.44)–(7.45) to the computation of the same functionality for the case $m = 2$, which in turn coincides with Eq. (7.17)–(7.18). But first we need to define an appropriate notion of a reduction. Indeed, the new notion of a reduction is merely a generalization of the notion presented in Section 7.3.1.

7.5.2.1. A Composition Theorem

We wish to generalize the notion of privacy reduction presented in Section 7.3.1 (in the context of two-party [semi-honest] computation). Here, the reduction is an m-party protocol that may invoke a k-ary functionality in its oracle calls, where $k \leq m$. In case $k < m$, an oracle call also needs to specify the set of parties who are to provide the corresponding k inputs. Actually, the oracle call needs to specify the order of these parties (i.e., which party should supply which input, etc.). (We note that the ordering of parties also needs to be specified in case $k = 2$, and indeed this was done implicitly in Section 7.3.1, where the convention was that the party who makes the oracle request is the one supplying the first input. In case $k > 2$, such a convention does not determine the correspondence between parties and roles, and thus in the following we use an explicit mechanism for defining the correspondence.)

Definition 7.5.5 (*m-party protocols with k-ary oracle access*): *As in the two-party case, an* oracle-aided protocol *is an ordinary protocol augmented by a pair of oracle-tapes per each party, and oracle-call steps defined as follows. Each of the m parties* *may send a special* oracle-request *message to all other parties. The oracle-request message contains a sequence of k distinct parties, called the* request sequence, *that are to supply queries in the current oracle call. In response, each party specified in the request sequence writes a string, called its* query, *on its own write-only oracle-tape, and responds to the requesting party with an* oracle-call *message. At this point, the oracle is invoked and the result is that a string, not necessarily the same, is written by the oracle on the read-only oracle-tape of each of the k specified parties. This k-sequence of strings is called the* oracle answer.

One may assume, without loss of generality, that the party who invokes the oracle is the one who plays the role of the first party in the reduction (i.e., the first element in the request sequence is always the identity of the party that requests the current oracle call).

Definition 7.5.6 (multi-party privacy reductions):

- *An m-party oracle-aided protocol is said to be* using the k-*ary oracle-functionality f if the oracle answers are according to f. That is, when the oracle is invoked with request sequence $(i_1, ..., i_k)$, and the query sequence $q_1, ..., q_k$ is supplied by parties $i_1, ..., i_k$, the answer sequence is distributed as $f(q_1, ..., q_k)$. Specifically, party i_j in the m-party protocol* (the one which supplied q_j), *is the one which obtains the answer part $f_j(q_1, ..., q_k)$. As in Definition 7.3.2, we require that the length of each query be polynomially related to the length of the initial input.*
- *An m-party oracle-aided protocol using the k-ary oracle-functionality f is said to* privately compute *g if there exists a polynomial-time algorithm, denoted S, satisfying Eq. (7.40), where the corresponding views are defined in the natural manner.*
- *An m-party oracle-aided protocol is said to* privately reduce *the m-ary functionality g to the k-ary functionality f if it privately computes g when using the oracle-functionality f. In such a case, we say that g* is privately reducible *to f,*

We are now ready to generalize Theorem 7.3.3:

Theorem 7.5.7 (Composition Theorem for the multi-party semi-honest model): *Suppose that the m-ary functionality g is privately reducible to the k-ary functionality f, and that there exists a k-party protocol for privately computing f. Then there exists an m-party protocol for privately computing g.*

As in the two-party case, the Composition Theorem can be generalized to yield transitivity of privacy reductions; that is, if g is privately reducible to f and f is privately reducible to e, then g is privately reducible to e.

Proof Sketch: The construction supporting the theorem is identical to the one used in the proof of Theorem 7.3.3: Let $\Pi^{g|f}$ be an oracle-aided protocol that privately reduces g to f, and let Π^f be a protocol that privately computes f. Then, a protocol Π for computing g is derived by starting with $\Pi^{g|f}$, and replacing each invocation of the oracle by an execution of Π^f. Clearly, Π computes g. We need to show that it privately computes g (as per Definition 7.5.1).

We consider an arbitrary (non-trivial) set $I \subseteq [m]$ of semi-honest parties in the execution of Π, where the trivial cases (i.e., $I = \emptyset$ and $I = [m]$) are treated (differently) in a straightforward manner. Note that for $k < m$ (unlike the situation in the two-party case), the set I may induce different sets of semi-honest parties in the different executions of Π^f (replacing different invocations of the oracle). Still, our "uniform" definition of simulation (i.e., uniform over all possible sets of semi-honest parties) keeps us away from trouble. Specifically, let $S^{g|f}$ and S^f be the simulators guaranteed for $\Pi^{g|f}$ and Π^f, respectively. We construct a simulation S, for Π, in the natural manner. On input $(I, \overline{x}_I, f_I(\overline{x}))$, we first run $S^{g|f}(I, \overline{x}_I, f_I(\overline{x}))$, and obtain the view of the semi-honest coalition $I \neq \emptyset$ in $\Pi^{g|f}$. This view includes the sequence of all oracle-call requests made during the execution, which in turn consists of the sequence of parties that supply query-parts in each such call. The view also contains the query-parts supplied by the parties in I, as well as the corresponding answer-parts. For each such oracle call, we denote by J the subset of I that supplied query-parts in this call and invoke S^f, providing it with the subset J, as well as with the corresponding J-parts of the queries and answers. Thus, we fill up the view of I in the current execution of Π^f. (Recall that S^f can also handle the trivial cases in which either $|J| = k$ or $|J| = 0$.)

It is left to show that S indeed generates a distribution indistinguishable from the view of semi-honest parties in actual executions of Π. As in the proof of Theorem 7.3.3, this is done by introducing a *hybrid distribution*, denoted H. This hybrid distribution represents the view of the parties in I (and output of all parties) in an execution of $\Pi^{g|f}$ that is augmented by corresponding invocations of S^f. In other words, H represents the execution of Π, with the exception that the invocations of Π^f are replaced by simulated transcripts. Using the guarantees regarding S^f (resp., $S^{g|f}$), we show that the distributions corresponding to H and Π (resp., H and S) are computationally indistinguishable. The theorem follows. ∎

7.5.2.2. Privately Computing $\sum_i c_i = (\sum_i a_i) \cdot (\sum_i b_i)$

We now turn to the m-ary functionality defined in Eq. $(7.44)-(7.45)$. Recall that the arithmetic is that of GF(2), and so $-1 = +1$, and so forth. The key observation is that

$$\left(\sum_{i=1}^{m} a_i \right) \cdot \left(\sum_{i=1}^{m} b_i \right) = \sum_{i=1}^{m} a_i b_i + \sum_{1 \leq i < j \leq m} \left(a_i b_j + a_j b_i \right) \tag{7.46}$$

$$= (1 - (m-1)) \cdot \sum_{i=1}^{m} a_i b_i + \sum_{1 \leq i < j \leq m} (a_i + a_j) \cdot (b_i + b_j)$$

$$= m \cdot \sum_{i=1}^{m} a_i b_i + \sum_{1 \leq i < j \leq m} (a_i + a_j) \cdot (b_i + b_j) \tag{7.47}$$

where the last equality relies on the specifics of GF(2). Now, looking at Eq. (7.47), we observe that each party, i, can compute (by itself) the term $m \cdot a_i b_i$, whereas each 2-subset, $\{i, j\}$, can privately compute shares to the term $(a_i + a_j) \cdot (b_i + b_j)$ by invoking the two-party functionality of Eq. (7.17)–(7.18). This leads to the following construction:

Construction 7.5.8 (privately reducing the m-party computation of Eq. (7.44)–(7.45) to the two-party computation of Eq. (7.17)–(7.18)):

Inputs: *Party i holds $(a_i, b_i) \in \{0, 1\} \times \{0, 1\}$, for $i = 1, ..., m$.*

Step 1 – Reduction: *Each pair of parties, (i, j), where $i < j$, invokes the 2-ary functionality of Eq. (7.17)–(7.18). Party i provides the input pair, (a_i, b_i), whereas Party j provides (a_j, b_j). Let us denote the oracle response to Party i by $c_i^{\{i,j\}}$, and the response to Party j by $c_j^{\{i,j\}}$.*

Step 2: *Party i sets $c_i = m a_i b_i + \sum_{j \neq i} c_i^{\{i,j\}}$.*
Indeed, $m a_i b_i = 0$ if m is even and $m a_i b_i = a_i b_i$ otherwise.

Outputs: *Party i outputs c_i.*

We first observe that this reduction is valid; that is, the output of all parties indeed sum up to what they should. It is also easy to see that the reduction is private. That is,

Proposition 7.5.9: *Construction 7.5.8 privately reduces the computation of the m-ary functionality given by Eq. (7.44)–(7.45) to the computation of the 2-ary functionality given by Eq. (7.17)–(7.18).*

Proof Sketch: We construct a simulator, denoted S, for the view of the parties in the oracle-aided protocol, denoted Π, of Construction 7.3.7. Given a set of semi-honest parties, $I = \{i_1, ..., i_t\}$ (with $t < m$), and a sequence of inputs $(a_{i_1}, b_{i_1}), ..., (a_{i_t}, b_{i_t})$ and outputs $c_{i_1}, ..., c_{i_t}$, the simulator proceeds as follows:

1. For each pair, $(i, j) \in I \times I$ where $i < j$, the simulator uniformly selects $c_i^{\{i,j\}} \in \{0, 1\}$ and sets $c_j^{\{i,j\}} = c_i^{\{i,j\}} + (a_i + a_j) \cdot (b_i + b_j)$.
2. Let $\bar{I} \stackrel{\text{def}}{=} [m] \setminus I$, and let ℓ be the largest element in $\bar{I}$. (Such an $\ell \in [m]$ exists since $|I| < m$.)

    (a) For each $i \in I$ and each $j \in \bar{I} \setminus \{\ell\}$, the simulator uniformly selects $c_i^{\{i,j\}} \in \{0, 1\}$.
    (b) For each $i \in I$, the simulator sets $c_i^{\{i,\ell\}} = c_i + m a_i b_i + \sum_{j \notin \{i, \ell\}} c_i^{\{i,j\}}$, where the latter $c_i^{\{i,j\}}$'s are as generated in Steps 1 and 2a.

3. The simulator outputs all $c_i^{\{i,j\}}$'s generated here. That is, it outputs the sequence of $c_i^{\{i,j\}}$'s corresponding to all $i \in I$ and $j \in [m] \setminus \{i\}$.

We claim that the output of the simulator is distributed identically to the view of the parties in I during the execution of the oracle-aided protocol. Furthermore, we claim that for every such I, every $\overline{x} = ((a_1, b_1), ..., (a_m, b_m))$, and every possible outcome $(c_1, ..., c_m)$ of the functionality f of Eq. (7.44)–(7.45), it holds that the conditional distribution of $S(I, \overline{x}_I, f_I(\overline{x}))$ is distributed identically to the conditional distribution of $\text{VIEW}_I^{\Pi}(\overline{x})$.

To prove this claim, we first note that $f(\overline{x})$ is uniformly distributed over the m-bit, long sequences that sum up to $c \overset{\text{def}}{=} (\sum_i a_i) \cdot (\sum_i b_i)$. The same holds also for the outputs of the parties in protocol Π, because the sequence of the outputs of Parties $1, ..., m - 1$ is uniformly distributed over $\{0, 1\}^{m-1}$ (due to the contribution of $c_i^{\{i,m\}}$ to the output of Party i), whereas the sum of all m outputs equals c. Turning to the conditional distributions (i.e., conditioning on $f(\overline{x}) = (c_1, ..., c_m) = \text{OUTPUT}^{\Pi}(\overline{x})$), we show that the sequence of $c_i^{\{i,j\}}$'s (for $i \in I$) is distributed identically in both distributions (i.e., in the execution view and in the simulation). Specifically, in both cases, the sequence $(c_i^{\{i,j\}})_{i \in I, j \in [m] \setminus \{i\}}$ is uniformly distributed among the sequences satisfying $c_i^{\{i,j\}} + c_j^{\{i,j\}} = (a_i + a_j) \cdot (b_i + b_j)$ (for each $i \in I$ and $j \neq i$) and $\sum_{j \neq i} c_i^{\{i,j\}} = c_i + m a_i b_i$ (for each $i \in I$).

> Details: Consider the distribution of the sub-sequence $(c_i^{\{i,j\}})_{i \in I, j \in [m] \setminus \{i, \ell\}}$, where $\ell \in \overline{I}$ is as in the preceding. In both cases, the conditioning (on $f(\overline{x}) = (c_1, ..., c_m) = \text{OUTPUT}^{\Pi}(\overline{x})$) does not affect this distribution, because the $c_i^{\{i,\ell\}}$'s are missing. Thus, in both cases, this sub-sequence is uniformly distributed among the sequences satisfying $c_i^{\{i,j\}} + c_j^{\{i,j\}} = (a_i + a_j) \cdot (b_i + b_j)$ (for each $i \neq j \in I$). Furthermore, in both cases, the $c_i^{\{i,\ell\}}$'s are set such that $\sum_{j \neq i} c_i^{\{i,j\}} = c_i + m a_i b_i$ holds.

The proposition follows. ∎

7.5.2.3. The Multi-Party Circuit-Evaluation Protocol

For sake of completeness, we explicitly present the m-party analogue of the protocol of Section 7.3.4. Specifically, we show that the computation of any deterministic functionality, which is expressed by an arithmetic circuit over GF(2), is privately reducible to the functionality of Eq. (7.44)–(7.45).

Our reduction follows the overview presented in the beginning of this section. In particular, the sharing of a bit-value v between m parties means a uniformly selected m-sequence of bits $(v_1, ..., v_m)$ satisfying $v = \sum_{i=1}^{m} v_i$, where the i-th party holds v_i. Our aim is to propagate, via private computation, shares of the input wires of the circuit to shares of all wires of the circuit, so that finally we obtain shares of the output-wires of the circuit.

We will consider an enumeration of all wires in the circuit. The input-wires of the circuit, n per each party, will be numbered $1, 2..., m \cdot n$ such that, for $j = 1, ..., n$, the j-th input of Party i corresponds to the $(i - 1) \cdot n + j^{\text{th}}$ wire. The wires will be numbered so that the output-wires of each gate have a larger numbering than its input wires. The output-wires of the circuit are the last ones. For the sake of simplicity, we assume that each party obtains n output bits, and that the j-th output bit of the i-th party corresponds to wire $N - (m + 1 - i) \cdot n + j$, where N denotes the size of the circuit.

Construction 7.5.10 (privately reducing any deterministic m-ary functionality to the functionality of Eq. (7.44)–(7.45), for any $m \geq 2$): *For simplicity, we assume that the circuit is either fixed or can be determined in* $\text{poly}(n + m)$-*time as a function of n and m, where n denotes the length of the input to each party.*

Inputs: *Party i holds the bit string* $x_i = x_i^1 \cdots x_i^n \in \{0, 1\}^n$, *for* $i = 1, ..., m$.

Step 1 – Sharing the Inputs: Each party splits and shares each of its input bits with all other parties. *That is, for every* $i = 1, ..., m$ *and* $j = 1, ..., n$, *and every* $k \neq i$, *Party i uniformly selects a bit* $r_k^{(i-1)n+j}$ *and sends it to Party k as the party's share of input-wire* $(i - 1) \cdot n + j$. *Party i sets its own share of the* $(i - 1) \cdot n + j^{\text{th}}$ *input wire to* $x_i^j + \sum_{k \neq i} r_k^{(i-1)n+j}$.

Step 2 – Circuit Emulation: Proceeding by the order of wires, the parties use their shares of the two input wires to a gate in order to privately compute shares for the Output-wire of the gate. *Suppose that the parties hold shares to the two input-wires of some gate; that is, for* $i = 1, ..., m$, *Party i holds the shares* a_i, b_i, *where* $a_1, ..., a_m$ *are the shares of the first wire and* $b_1, ..., b_m$ *are the shares of the second wire. We consider two cases:*

Emulation of an addition gate: *Each party, i, just sets its share of the output-wire of the gate to be* $a_i + b_i$.

Emulation of a multiplication gate: *Shares of the output-wire of the gate are obtained by invoking the oracle for the functionality of Eq. (7.44)–(7.45), where Party i supplies the input* (query-part) (a_i, b_i). *When the oracle responds, each party sets its share of the output-wire of the gate to equal its part of the oracle answer.*

Step 3 – Recovering the Output Bits: Once the shares of the circuit-output wires are computed, each party sends its share of each such wire to the party with which the wire is associated. *That is, for* $i = 1, ..., m$ *and* $j = 1, ..., n$, *each party sends its share of wire* $N - (m + 1 - i) \cdot n + j$ *to Party i. Each party recovers the corresponding output bits by adding up the corresponding m shares; that is, it adds the share it had obtained in Step 2 to the* $m - 1$ *shares it has obtained in the current step.*

Outputs: *Each party locally outputs the bits recovered in Step 3.*

As in the two-party case, one can easily verify that the output of the protocol is indeed correct. Specifically, by using induction on the wires of the circuits, one can show that the shares of each wire sum up to the correct value of the wire. Indeed, for $m = 2$, Construction 7.5.10 coincides with Construction 7.3.9. The privacy of Construction 7.5.10 is also shown by extending the analysis of the two-party case; that is, analogously to Proposition 7.3.10, one can show that Construction 7.5.10 privately reduces the computation of a circuit to the multiplication-gate emulation.

Proposition 7.5.11: *Construction 7.5.10 privately reduces the evaluation of arithmetic circuits over* $\text{GF}(2)$, *representing an m-ary deterministic functionality, to the functionality of Eq. (7.44)–(7.45).*

Proof Sketch: Just follow the proof of Proposition 7.3.10, treating the parties in I analogously to the way that Party 1 is treated there. In treating the output wires of parties in I (i.e., Step 3 in the simulation), note that the shares of parties in I and the known output value uniquely determine the shares received in Step 3' of the protocol only if $|I| = m - 1$ (as was the case in the proof of Proposition 7.3.10). Otherwise (i.e., for $|I| < m - 1$), the shares sent (in Step 3 of the protocol) by parties in $\bar{I}$ should be selected uniformly among all sequences that (together with the shares of parties in I) add up to the given output value. ∎

7.5.2.4. Conclusion: Private Computation of Any Functionality

As in Section 7.3, we may privately reduce the computation of a general (randomized) m-ary functionality, g, to the computation of the deterministic m-ary functionality, f, defined by

$$f((x_1, r_1), ..., (x_m, r_m)) \overset{\text{def}}{=} g(\oplus_{i=1}^{m} r_i, (x_1, ..., x_m)) \tag{7.48}$$

where $g(r, \bar{x})$ denotes the value of $g(\bar{x})$ when using coin-tosses $r \in \{0, 1\}^{\text{poly}(|\bar{x}|)}$ (i.e., $g(\bar{x})$ is the randomized process consisting of uniformly selecting $r \in \{0, 1\}^{\text{poly}(|\bar{x}|)}$, and deterministically computing $g(r, \bar{x})$). Combining this fact with Propositions 7.5.11, 7.5.9, and 7.3.8 (and using the transitivity of privacy reductions), we obtain:

Theorem 7.5.12: *Any m-ary functionality is privately reducible to* OT_1^4.

Combining Theorem 7.5.12 and Proposition 7.3.6 with the Composition Theorem (Theorem 7.5.7), we conclude that *if enhanced trapdoor permutations exist, then any m-ary functionality is privately computable*. As in the two-party case, we wish to highlight a useful property of the protocols underlying the latter fact. Indeed, we refer to a notion of canonical m-party computation that extends Definition 7.3.13.

Definition 7.5.13 (canonical semi-honest multi-party protocols): *A protocol Π for privately computing the m-ary functionality f is called* canonical *if it proceeds by executing the following two stages:*

Stage 1: *The parties privately compute the functionality $\bar{x} \mapsto ((r_1^1, ..., r_m^1), ..., (r_1^m, ..., r_m^m))$, where the r_j^i's are uniformly distributed among all possibilities that satisfy $(\oplus_{i=1}^{m} r_1^i, ..., \oplus_{i=1}^{m} r_m^i) = f(\bar{x})$.*

Stage 2: *For $i = 2, ..., m$ and $j \in [m] \setminus \{i\}$, Party i sends r_j^i to Party j. Next, Party 1 sends r_j^1 to Party j, for $j = 2..., m$. Finally, each party computes its own output; that is, for $j = 1..., m$, Party j outputs $\oplus_{i=1}^{m} r_j^i$.*

Indeed, the protocols underlying the proof of Theorem 7.5.12 are essentially canonical.[64] Hence,

Theorem 7.5.14: *Suppose that there exist collections of enhanced trapdoor permutations. Then any functionality can be privately computable by a canonical protocol.*

We comment that the said protocols happen to maintain their security *even if the adversary can wire-tap all communication lines*. This follows from the fact that *privacy with respect to wire-tapping adversaries* happens to hold for all privacy reductions presented in the current section, as well as for the protocols presented in Section 7.3.

7.5.3. The Malicious Models: Overview and Preliminaries

Our aim is to use Theorem 7.5.14 in order to establish the main result of this section; that is,

Theorem 7.5.15 (main result for the multi-party case): *Suppose that there exist collections of enhanced trapdoor permutations. Then any m-ary functionality can be securely computable in each of the two malicious models, provided that a public-key infrastructure exists in the network.*[65]

The theorem will be established in two steps. First, we compile any protocol for the semi-honest model into an "equivalent" protocol for the first malicious model. This compiler is very similar to the one used in the two-party case. Next, we compile any protocol for the first malicious model into an "equivalent" protocol for the second malicious model. The heart of the second compiler is a primitive, which is alien to the two-party case, called Verifiable Secret Sharing (VSS). For simplicity, we again think of the number of parties m as being fixed. The reader may again verify that the dependence of our constructions on m is at most polynomial.

To simplify the exposition of the multi-party compilers, we describe them as producing protocols for a communication model consisting of a single broadcast channel (and no point-to-point links). In this model, in each communication round, only one (predetermined) party may send a message, and this message arrives to all parties. We stress that only this predetermined party may send a message in the said round (i.e., the message is "authenticated" in the sense that each other party can verify that, indeed, the message was sent by the designated sender). Such a broadcast channel can be implemented via an (authenticated) Byzantine Agreement protocol, thus providing an emulation of the broadcast model on the standard point-to-point model (in which a broadcast channel does not exist).

---

[64] This assertion depends on the exact implementation of Step 3 of Construction 7.5.10, and holds provided that Party 1 is the last party to send its shares to all other parties.

[65] That is, we assume that each party has generated a pair of keys for a signature scheme and has publicized its verification-key (so that it is known to all other parties). This set-up assumption can be avoided if the network is augmented with a broadcast channel.

Recall that our goal is to transform protocols that are secure in the semi-honest *point-to-point model* into protocols that are secure in the two malicious *broadcast models*. Starting with (semi-honestly secure) protocols that operate in the point-to-point communication model, we first derive equivalent protocols for the broadcast-channel model, and only next we apply the two compilers, where each compiler takes and produces protocols in the broadcast-channel model (which are secure with respect to a corresponding type of adversaries). Thus, the full sequence of transformations establishing Theorem 7.5.15 (based on Theorem 7.5.14) is as follows:

- We first use the *pre-compiler* (of Section 7.5.3.1) to transform a protocol Π_0 that privately computes a functionality f in the (private-channel) point-to-point model into a protocol Π_0' that privately computes f in the broadcast model (where no private point-to-point channels exist).

  Note that, since we refer to semi-honest behavior, we do not gain by having a broadcast channel, and we may only lose by the elimination of the private point-to-point channels (because this allows the adversary to obtain all messages sent). However, the protocols presented in Section 7.5.2 happen to be secure in the semi-honest broadcast model,[66] and so this pre-compiler is actually not needed (provided we start with these specific protocols, rather than with arbitrary semi-honestly secure protocols).

- Using the *first compiler* (of Section 7.5.4), we transform Π_0' (which is secure in the semi-honest model) into a protocol Π_1' that is secure in the *first malicious model*.

  We stress that both Π_0' and Π_1' operate and are evaluated for security in a communication model consisting of a single broadcast channel. The same holds also for Π_2' mentioned next.

- Using the *second compiler* (of Section 7.5.5), we transform Π_1' (which is secure in the first malicious model) into a protocol Π_2' that is secure in the *second malicious model*.

- Finally, we use the *post-compiler* (of Section 7.5.3.2) to transform each of the protocols Π_1' and Π_2', which are secure in the first and second malicious models when communication is via a broadcast channel, into corresponding protocols, Π_1 and Π_2, for the standard point-to-point model. That is, Π_1 (resp., Π_2) securely computes f in the first (resp., second) malicious model in which communication is via standard point-to-point channels.

  We stress that security holds even if the adversary is allowed to wire-tap the (point-to-point) communication lines between honest parties.

We start by discussing the security definitions for the broadcast communication model and by presenting the aforementioned pre-compiler and the post-compiler. Once this is

---

[66] As noted at the very end of Section 7.5.2, these protocols also happen to be secure against semi-honest adversaries that do wire-tape all communication channels. These protocols can be trivially converted to work in the broadcast model by letting the honest parties ignore broadcast messages that are not intended for them. Indeed, in the resulting protocol, the adversary receives all messages (including those intended for other parties), but it could also obtain these messages in the original protocol by wire-tapping all point-to-point channels.

done, we turn to the real core of this section: the two compilers (which are applied to protocols that operate in the broadcast model).

Definitions. Indeed, security in the broadcast model was not defined so far. However, the three relevant definitions for the broadcast communication model are easily derived from the corresponding definitions given in Section 7.5.1, where a point-to-point communication model was used. Specifically, in defining security in the semi-honest model, one merely includes the entire transcript of the communication over the (single) broadcast channel in each party's view. Similarly, when defining security in the two malicious models, one merely notes that the "real execution model" (i.e., $\text{REAL}_{\Pi, I, A}$) changes (since the protocol is now executed over a different communication media), whereas the "ideal model" (i.e., $\text{IDEAL}_{f, I, B}^{(1)}$ or $\text{IDEAL}_{f, I, B}^{(2)}$) remains intact.

7.5.3.1. Pre-Compiler (Emulating Private Channels)

It is easy to (securely) emulate a set of (private) point-to-point communication channels over a (single) broadcast channel. All that one needs to do is use a secure public-key encryption scheme. Specifically, a protocol Π that operates in the (private) point-to-point communication model is emulated as follows. First, each party randomly generates a pair of encryption/decryption keys, posts the encryption-key on the broadcast channel, and keeps the decryption-key secret. Next, any party instructed (by Π) to send a message, msg, to Party i encrypts msg using the encryption-key posted by Party i, and places the resulting ciphertext on the broadcast channel (indicating that it is intended for Party i). Party i recovers msg by using its decryption-key and proceeds as directed by Π. Denote the resulting protocol by Π'. In the following, we merely consider the effect of this transformation in the semi-honest model.

Proposition 7.5.16 (pre-compiler): *Suppose that there exist collections of enhanced trapdoor permutations. Then any m-ary functionality is privately computable in the broadcast communication model. Furthermore, the protocol is canonical.*

Proof Sketch: Let f be an m-ary functionality, and Π be a protocol (guaranteed by Theorem 7.5.14) for privately computing f in the (private-channel) point-to-point communication model. Given a trapdoor permutation, we construct a secure public-key encryption scheme and use it to transform Π into Π' as described previously.

To simulate the view of parties in an execution of Π' (taking place in the broadcast communication model), we first simulate their view in an execution of Π (taking place in the point-to-point communication model). We then encrypt each message sent by a party that belongs to the semi-honest coalition, as this would be done in an execution of Π'. Note that we know both the message and the corresponding encryption-key. We do the same for messages received by semi-honest parties. All that remains is to deal with messages, which we do not know, sent between two honest parties. Here, we merely place an encryption of an arbitrary message. This concludes the description of the "broadcast-model" simulator.

The analysis of the latter simulator combines the guarantee given for the "point-to-point simulator" and the guarantee that the encryption scheme is secure. That is, the ability to distinguish the output of the broadcast-model simulator from the execution view (in the broadcast model) yields either (1) the ability to distinguish the output of the "point-to-point" simulator from the execution view (in the point-to-point model) or (2) the ability to distinguish encryptions under the public-key encryption scheme being used. In both cases we reach contradiction to our hypothesis. ∎

7.5.3.2. Post-Compiler (Emulating a Broadcast Channel)

Here we go the other way around (i.e., from the broadcast model to the point-to-point model). We are given a protocol that securely computes (in one of the two malicious models) some functionality, where the protocol uses a broadcast channel. We wish to convert this protocol into an equivalent one that works in a point-to-point communication model. (Actually, we do not go all the way back, because we do not assume these point-to-point lines to provide private communication.) Thus, all we need to do is emulate a broadcast channel over a point-to-point network and do so in the presence of malicious parties, which reduces to solving the celebrated Byzantine Agreement problem. However, we have signature schemes at our disposal, and so we merely need to solve the much easier problem known as *authenticated Byzantine Agreement*. For the sake of self-containment, we define the problem and present a solution.

Authenticated Byzantine Agreement. We presuppose a synchronous point-to-point model of communication and a signature scheme infrastructure. That is, each party knows the verification-key of all other parties. Party 1 has an input bit, denoted σ, and its objective is to let all honest parties agree on the value of this bit. In case Party 1 is honest, the other parties must agree on its actual input, but otherwise they may agree on any value (as long as they agree).

Construction 7.5.17 (Authenticated Byzantine Agreement): *Let m denote the number of parties. We assume that the signature scheme in use has signature of length that depends only on the security parameter, and not on the length of the message to be signed.*[67]

Phase 1: *Party 1 signs its input and sends the resulting input-signature pair to all parties. Party 1 may terminate at this point.*

Definition: *A message is called (v, i)-authentic if it has the form $(v, s_{p_1}, ..., s_{p_i})$, where $p_1 = 1$, all p_j's are distinct, and for every $j = 1, ..., i$, the string s_{p_j} is accepted as a signature to $(v, s_{p_1}, ..., s_{p_{j-1}})$ relative to the verification-key of party p_j.*

Observe that when Party 1 follows the protocol with input v, at Phase 1 it sends a $(v, 1)$-authentic message to each party. For every $i \geq 2$, if $(v, s_{p_1}, ..., s_{p_i})$ is (v, i)-authentic, then $(v, s_{p_1}, ..., s_{p_{i-1}})$ is $(v, i - 1)$-authentic.

---

[67] Such a signature scheme can be constructed given any one-way function. In particular, one may use Construction 6.4.30. Maintaining short signatures is important in this application, because we are going to iteratively sign messages consisting of (the concatenation of an original message and) prior signatures.

Phase $i = 2, ..., m$: *Each honest party* (other than Party 1) *inspects the messages it has received at Phase $i - 1$, and forwards signed versions of the $(\cdot, i - 1)$-authentic messages that it has received. Specifically, for every $v \in \{0, 1\}$, if Party j has received a $(v, i - 1)$-authentic message $(v, s_{p_1}, ..., s_{p_{i-1}})$ such that all p_k's are different from j, then it appends its signature to the message and sends the resulting (v, i)-authentic message to all parties.*

We stress that for each value of v, Party j sends at most one (v, i)-authentic message to all parties. Actually, it may refrain from sending (v, i)-authentic messages if it has already sent (v, i')-authentic messages for some $i' < i$.

Termination: *Each honest party* (other than Party 1) *evaluates the situation as follows:*

1. *If, for some $i_0, i_1 \in [m]$ (which are not necessarily different), it has received both a $(0, i_0)$-authentic message and a $(1, i_1)$-authentic message, then it decides that Party 1 is malicious and outputs an error symbol, say $\bot$.*
2. *If, for a single $v \in \{0, 1\}$ and some i, it has received a (v, i)-authentic message, then it outputs the value v.*
3. *If it has never received a (v, i)-authentic message, for any $v \in \{0, 1\}$ and i, then it decides that Party 1 is malicious and outputs an error symbol, say $\bot$.*

We comment that in the Distributed Computing literature, an alternative presentation is preferred in which if a party detects cheating by Party 1 (i.e., in Cases 1 and 3), then the party outputs a default value, say 0, rather than the error symbol $\bot$.

The protocol can be easily adapted to handle non-binary input values. For the sake of efficiency, one may instruct honest parties to forward at most two authentic messages that refer to different values (because this suffices to establish that Party 1 is malicious).

Proposition 7.5.18: *Assuming that the signature scheme in use is unforgeable, Construction 7.5.17 satisfies the following two conditions:*

1. *It is infeasible to make any two honest parties output different values.*
2. *If Party 1 is honest, then it is infeasible to make any honest party output a value different from the input of Party 1.*

The claim holds regardless of the number of dishonest parties and even if dishonest parties abort the execution.

In other words, Proposition 7.5.18 asserts that Construction 7.5.17 is essentially a secure implementation of the ("broadcast") functionality $(v, \lambda, ..., \lambda) \mapsto (v, v, ..., v)$. In particular, the case in which the honest parties output $\bot$ can be accounted for by the abort of an ideal-model adversary playing Party 1. We note that security as used here is incomparable to security in either of the two malicious models. On the one hand, we do not provide security with respect to an external adversary that only taps the communication lines while not controlling any of the parties. That is, we do not provide secrecy with respect to an external adversary, and indeed, this feature is not required by the post-compiler (presented in the proof of Proposition 7.5.19). On the other hand, we do provide security in the (stronger) sense of the second malicious model but do so *without limiting the number of dishonest parties*. That is, for any number of dishonest parties, the protocol effectively prevents dishonest parties from aborting (because abort is treated as sending some illegal message). In particular, the case in which Party 1 does not even enter the execution is treated as the case in which it sent illegal messages.

Proof Sketch: Fixing any j and v, suppose that in Phase $i - 1$, Party j receives a $(v, i - 1)$-authentic message, and assume that i is the smallest integer for which this happens. For this event to happen, it must be that $i \leq m$, because the message must contain $i - 1$ signatures from different parties (other than Party j itself).[68] In such a case, if Party j is honest, then it will send an authentic (v, i)-message in Phase i ($i \leq m$), and so all parties will receive an authentic (v, i)-message in Phase i. Thus, for every v, if an honest party sees a $(v, \cdot)$-authentic message, then so do all other honest parties, and Part 1 follows. Part 2 follows by observing that if Party 1 is honest and has input v, then all honest parties see a $(v, 1)$-authentic message. Furthermore, none can see a (v', i)-authentic message, for $v' \neq v$ and any i. ∎

Proposition 7.5.19 (post-compiler): *Suppose that one-way functions exist. Then any m-ary functionality that is securely computable in the first* (resp., second) *malicious broadcast model is also securely computable in the first* (resp., second) *malicious point-to-point model, provided that a public-key infrastructure exists in the network.*

Proof Sketch: The idea is to replace any broadcast message sent in the original protocol by an execution of the Authenticated Byzantine Agreement (AuthBA) protocol. This idea needs to be carefully implemented because it is not clear that the security of AuthBA is preserved under multiple executions, and thus applying Proposition 7.5.18 per se will not do. The problem is that the adversary may use authenticated messages sent in one execution of the protocol in order to fool some parties in a different execution. This attack can be avoided in the current context by using identifiers (which can be assigned consistently by the higher-level protocol) for each of the executions of the AuthBA protocol. That is, authentic messages will be required to bear the distinct identifier of the corresponding AuthBA execution (and all signatures will be applied to that identifier as well). Thus, authentic messages of one AuthBA execution will not be authentic in any other AuthBA execution. It follows that the proof of Proposition 7.5.18 can be extended to our context, where sequential executions of AuthBA (with externally assigned distinct identifiers) take place.

The proof of security transforms any real-model adversary for the point-to-point protocol to a real-model adversary for the broadcast-channel protocol. In particular, the latter determines the messages posted on the broadcast channel exactly as an honest party determines the values delivered by the various executions of AuthBA. In the transformation, we assume that each instance of the AuthBA sub-protocol satisfies the conditions stated in Proposition 7.5.18 (i.e., it delivers the same value to all

---

[68] Note that the said message cannot contain a signature of Party j due to the minimality of i: If the $(v, i - 1)$-authentic message had contained a signature of Party j, then for some $i' < i$, Party j would have received a $(v, i' - 1)$-authentic message in Phase $i' - 1$.

honest parties, and this value equals the one entered by the honest sender). In case the assumption does not hold, we derive a forger for the underlying signature scheme. ∎

7.5.4. The First Compiler: Forcing Semi-Honest Behavior

We follow the basic structure of the compiler presented in Section 7.4 for the two-party case. Adapting that compiler to the multi-party setting merely requires generalizing the implementation of each of the three phases (of the compiled two-party protocols). Following is a high-level description of the multi-party protocols generated by the corresponding compiler. Recall that all communication, both in the input protocol as well as in the one resulting from the compilation, is conducted merely by posting messages on a single broadcast channel.

Input-commitment phase: Each of the parties commits to its input bits. This will be done using a multi-party version of the input-commitment functionality of Eq. (7.36).

Intuitively, malicious parties may (abort or) substitute their inputs during this phase, but they may do so depending only on the value of the inputs held by malicious parties.

Coin-generation phase: The parties generate random-tapes for each of the parties. These random-tapes are intended to serve as the coins of the corresponding parties in their emulation of the semi-honest protocol. Each party obtains the random-tape to be held by it, whereas the other parties obtain commitments to this value. This will be done using a multi-party version of the augmented coin-tossing functionality of Eq. (7.35).

Intuitively, malicious parties may abort during this phase, but otherwise they end up with a uniformly distributed random-tape.

Protocol emulation phase: The parties emulate the execution of the semi-honest protocol with respect to the inputs committed in the first phase and the random-tapes selected in the second phase. This will be done using a multi-party version of the authenticated-computation functionality of Eq. (7.33). The fact that the original protocol is executed over a broadcast channel is used here.

Intuitively, malicious parties may abort during this phase, but otherwise they end up sending messages as directed by the semi-honest protocol.

In order to implement these phases, we define natural generalizations of the input-commitment, coin-tossing, and authenticated-computation functionalities (of the two-party case), and present secure implementations of them in the current (first malicious) multi-party model. The original definitions and constructions are obtained by setting $m = 2$. We start again by defining an adequate notion of reducibility, which allows a modular presentation of the compiled protocols.

7.5.4.1. Security Reductions and a Composition Theorem

Analogously to Section 7.5.2.1, we now define what we mean by saying that one functionality is *securely reducible* to another functionality. We use the same definition of an oracle-aided protocol (i.e., Definition 7.5.5), but require such a protocol to be secure in the first malicious model (rather than be secure in the semi-honest model). As in the two-party case, we require that the length of each oracle-query can be determined from the length of the initial input to the oracle-aided protocol.

Definition 7.5.20 (Security Reductions in the First Malicious Model):

- *As in Definition 7.5.6, an m-party oracle-aided protocol is said to be* using the k-party oracle-functionality f *if the oracle answers are according to f. However, in accordance with the definition of the* (first) *ideal model* (for the invoked functionality), *the oracle does not answer all parties concurrently, but rather answers first the real-model party that requested this specific oracle call* (in the oracle-aided protocol). *When receiving its part of the oracle answer, the party that requested the oracle call instructs the oracle whether or not to respond to the other parties.*

  We consider only protocols in which the length of each oracle-query is a polynomial-time computable function of the length of the initial input to the protocol. Furthermore, the length of each query must be polynomially related to the length of the initial input.

  Analogously to Definition 7.5.3, the joint execution of an oracle-aided protocol Π with oracle f under (I, A) in the real model (on input sequence $\overline{x} = (x_1, ..., x_m)$ and auxiliary input z), *denoted* $\text{REAL}^f_{\Pi, I, A(z)}(\overline{x})$, *is defined as the output sequence resulting from the interaction between the m parties, where the messages of parties in I are computed according to $A(\overline{x}_I, z)$, the messages of parties not in I are computed according to Π, and the oracle calls are answered according to f.*

- *An oracle-aided protocol Π, using the oracle-functionality f, is said to* securely compute g (in the first malicious model) *if a condition analogous to the one in Definition 7.5.3 holds. That is, the effect of any efficient real-model adversary as in the previous item can be simulated by a corresponding ideal-model adversary, where the ideal model for computing g is exactly as in Definition 7.5.2.*

  > More specifically, the oracle-aided protocol Π (using oracle f) is said to *securely compute* g (in the first malicious model) if for every probabilistic polynomial-time A, there exists a probabilistic polynomial-time B such that for every $I \subseteq [m]$
  >
  > $$\{\text{IDEAL}^{(1)}_{g, I, B(z)}(\overline{x})\}_{\overline{x}, z} \overset{\text{c}}{\equiv} \{\text{REAL}^f_{\Pi, I, A(z)}(\overline{x})\}_{\overline{x}, z}$$

- *An oracle-aided protocol is said to* securely reduce g to f (in the first malicious model) *if it securely computes g (in the first malicious model) when using the oracle-functionality f. In such a case, we say that g is* securely reducible to f,

Indeed, when it is clear from the context, we often omit the qualifier "in the first malicious model."

We are now ready to state a composition theorem for the first multi-party malicious model.

Theorem 7.5.21 (Composition Theorem for the first multi-party malicious model):
Suppose that the m-ary functionality g is securely reducible to the k-ary functionality f and that there exists a k-party protocol for securely computing f. Then there exists an m-party protocol for securely computing g.

Recall that the syntax of oracle-aided protocols disallows concurrent oracle calls, and thus Theorem 7.5.21 is actually a *sequential composition theorem*. As in the two-party case, the Composition Theorem can be generalized to yield transitivity of secure reductions and to account for reductions that use several oracles rather than one.

Proof Sketch: Analogously to the proof of previous composition theorems, we are given an oracle-aided protocol, denoted $\Pi^{g|f}$, that securely reduces g to f, and an ordinary protocol Π^f that securely computes f. Again, we construct a protocol Π for computing g in the natural manner; that is, starting with $\Pi^{g|f}$, we replace each invocation of the oracle (i.e., of f) by an execution of the protocol Π^f. Clearly, Π computes g, and we need to show that Π securely computes g. This is proven by merely generalizing the proof of Theorem 7.4.3 (i.e., the two-party case). The only point that is worthwhile stressing is that the real-model adversary for Π^f, derived from the real-model adversary for Π, is constructed obliviously of the set of parties I that the adversary controls.[69] As in the proof of Theorem 7.5.7, we determine the set of parties for every such invocation of Π^f, and rely on the fact that security holds with respect to adversaries controlling any subset of the k parties participating in an execution of Π^f. In particular, the security of an invocation of Π^f by parties $P = \{p_1, ..., p_k\}$ holds also in case $I \cap P = \emptyset$, where it means that a real-model adversary (which controls no party in P) learns nothing by merely tapping the broadcast channel.[70] ∎

7.5.4.2. Secret Broadcast

In order to facilitate the implementation of some functionalities, we introduce the following secret-broadcast functionality:

$$(\alpha, 1^{|\alpha|}, ..., 1^{|\alpha|}) \mapsto (\alpha, \alpha, ..., \alpha) \tag{7.49}$$

At first glance, it seems that Eq. (7.49) is trivially implementable by Party 1 posting α on the broadcast channel. This solution is "secure" as long as the (real-model) adversary controls a non-empty set of parties, but fails in case the adversary controls none of the parties and yet can tap the broadcast channel. That is, the trivial solution does not provide secrecy with respect to an external adversary (which taps the channel but controls none of the parties and thus is not supposed to learn the value sent by Party 1 to all other parties). Note that secrecy with respect to an external adversary also arises in a subtle way when we do not care about it a priori (e.g., see the proof of Theorem 7.5.21).

Proposition 7.5.22: *Assuming the existence of trapdoor permutations, there exists a secure implementation of Eq. (7.49) in the first malicious model.*

---

[69] Unlike in the two-party case, here we cannot afford to consider a designated adversary for each subset of parties.
[70] Security holds also in the other extreme case, where $I \cap P = P$, but it is not meaningful in that case.

Proof Sketch: The first idea that comes to mind is to let each party generate a pair of keys for a public-key encryption scheme and broadcast the encryption-key, and then let Party 1 broadcast the encryption of its input under each of these encryption-keys. The problem with this protocol is that it is no longer guaranteed that all parties receive the same value. One solution is to let Party 1 provide zero-knowledge proofs (to each of the parties) that the posted ciphertexts are consistent (i.e., encrypt the same value), but the implementation of this solution is not straightforward (cf. Construction 7.5.24). An alternative solution, adopted here, is to use the encryption scheme in order to emulate a set of private (point-to-point) channels, as in Section 7.5.3.1, and run an authenticated Byzantine Agreement on this network. Since we have an ordinary broadcast channel at our disposal, we do not need to assume an initial set-up that corresponds to a public-key infrastructure, but can rather generate it on the fly. The resulting protocol is as follows:

1. Each party generates a pair of keys for a signature scheme and posts the verification-key on the broadcast channel. This establishes the public-key infrastructure as relied upon in Construction 7.5.17.
2. Each party generates a pair of keys for a public-key encryption scheme and posts the encryption-key on the broadcast channel. This effectively establishes a network of private (point-to-point) channels to be used in Step 3.
3. The parties invoke the authenticated Byzantine Agreement protocol of Construction 7.5.17 in order to let Party 1 broadcast its input to all other parties. All messages of this protocol are sent in encrypted form, where each message is encrypted using the encryption-key posted in Step 2 by the designated receiver.

Combining the ideas underlying the proofs of Propositions 7.5.16 and 7.5.18 (and considering two cases corresponding to whether I is empty or not), the current proposition follows. ∎

7.5.4.3. Multi-Party Authenticated Computation

We start our assembly of multi-party functionalities by presenting and implementing a multi-party generalization of the authenticated-computation functionality of Eq. (7.33).

Definition 7.5.23 (authenticated computation, multi-party version): *Let $f : \{0, 1\}^* \times \{0, 1\}^* \to \{0, 1\}^*$ and $h : \{0, 1\}^* \to \{0, 1\}^*$ be polynomial-time computable. The h-authenticated f-computation m-party functionality is defined by*

$$(\alpha, \beta_2, ..., \beta_m) \mapsto (\lambda, v_2, ..., v_m) \tag{7.50}$$

where $v_i \stackrel{\text{def}}{=} f(\alpha)$ if $\beta_i = h(\alpha)$ and $v_i \stackrel{\text{def}}{=} (h(\alpha), f(\alpha))$ otherwise, for each i.[71]

---

[71] Indeed, an alternative multi-party generalization may require that all v_i's equal $f(\alpha)$ if $\beta_2 = \cdots = \beta_m = h(\alpha)$ and equal $(h(\alpha), f(\alpha))$ otherwise. However, this alternative generalization seems harder to implement, whereas Eq. (7.50) suffices for our application.

Note that the obvious reduction of Eq. (7.50) to the two-party case (i.e., to Eq. (7.33)) does not work (see Exercise 16). As in the two-party case, we will securely reduce Eq. (7.50) to an adequate multi-party generalization of the image-transmission functionality and provide a secure implementation of the latter. We start by implementing the adequate multi-party generalization of the image-transmission functionality, defined as follows:

$$(\alpha, 1^{|\alpha|}, ..., 1^{|\alpha|}) \mapsto (\lambda, f(\alpha), ..., f(\alpha)) \tag{7.51}$$

Indeed, Eq. (7.51) is essentially a special case of Eq. (7.50). We stress that in a secure implementation of Eq. (7.51), either all parties obtain the same f-image or they all obtain an indication that Party 1 has misbehaved. Thus, the honest parties must be in agreement regarding whether or not Party 1 has misbehaved, which makes the generalization of the two-party protocol less obvious than it may seem. In particular, the fact that we use a proof system of perfect completeness plays a central role in the analysis of the multi-party protocol. The same holds with respect to the fact that all messages are sent using (secret) broadcast (and so the honest parties agree on their value). Together, these two facts imply that any party can determine whether some other party has "justifiably rejected" some claim, and this ability enables the parties to reach agreement regarding whether or not Party 1 has misbehaved.

Construction 7.5.24 (image-transmission protocol, multi-party version): *Let $R \stackrel{\text{def}}{=} \{(v, w) : v = f(w)\}$. For simplicity, we assume that f is length-regular; that is, $|f(x)| = |f(y)|$ for every $|x| = |y|$.*

Inputs: *Party 1 gets input $\alpha \in \{0, 1\}^*$, and each other party gets input 1^n, where $n = |\alpha|$.*

Step C1: *Party 1 secretly broadcasts $v \stackrel{\text{def}}{=} f(\alpha)$. That is, Party 1 invokes Eq. (7.49) with input v, whereas each other party enters the input $1^{|f(1^n)|}$ and receives the output v.*

Step C2: *For $i = 2, ..., m$, Parties 1 and i invoke a zero-knowledge strong-proof-of-knowledge system for R such that Party 1 plays the prover and Party i plays the verifier. The common input to the proof system is v, the prover gets α as auxiliary input, and its objective is to prove that it knows a w such that $(v, w) \in R$ (i.e., $v = f(w)$). In case the verifier rejects the proof, Party i sends the coins used by the verifier so that all other parties can be convinced of its justifiable rejection, where the latter corresponds to the view of the verifier in a rejecting interaction. All messages of the proof system are sent using the secret broadcast functionality.*

Outputs: *For $i = 2, ..., m$, if Party i sees some justifiable rejection, then it outputs $\bot$; otherwise it outputs v. (Party 1 has no output.)*

Agreement on whether or not Party 1 has misbehaved is reduced to the decision whether or not *some* verifier has justifiably rejected in Step C2, where of the latter decision depends on information available to all parties. A key observation is that if Party 1 is honest, then no party can justifiably reject its proof in Step C2, because the proof system has perfect completeness (which means that there exists no random-tape that makes the verifier reject a claim by an honest prover). Note that Construction 7.5.24 is actually an oracle-aided protocol, using the secret broadcast oracle. Consequently, if the real-model adversary controls none of the parties, then it learns nothing (as opposed to what might have happened if we were to use an ordinary broadcast in Steps C1 or C2).

Proposition 7.5.25: *Suppose that the proof system, (P, V), used in Step C2 is indeed a zero-knowledge strong-proof-of-knowledge for the relation R. Then Construction 7.5.24 securely reduces Eq. (7.51) to Eq. (7.49).*

Proof Sketch: The proof extends the two-party case treated in Proposition 7.4.12. Here, we transform any real-model adversary A into a corresponding ideal-model adversary B, where both get the set I as auxiliary input. The case $I = \emptyset$ is handled by relying on the secret broadcast functionality (which implies that in this case, the real-model adversary, which refers to an oracle-aided protocol in which all messages are sent using Eq. (7.49), gets nothing). Otherwise, the operation of B depends on whether or not $1 \in I$, which corresponds to the cases handled in the two-party case.

As in the two-party case, when transforming real-model adversaries to ideal-model adversaries, we sometimes allow the latter to halt before invoking the *trusted party*. This can be viewed as invoking the trusted party with a special abort symbol, where in this case, the latter responds to all parties with a special abort symbol.

We start with the case where *the first party is honest,* which means here that $1 \notin I$. In this case, the input to B consists essentially of 1^n, where $n = |\alpha|$, and it operates as follows (assuming $I \neq \emptyset$):

1. Acting on behalf of each party in I, the ideal-model adversary B sends $1^{|\alpha|}$ to the *trusted party* and obtains the answer v, which equals $f(\alpha)$ for α handed (to the trusted party) by (the honest) Party 1. Thus, indeed, $(v, \alpha) \in R$. (Recall that Party 1 always obtains λ from the trusted party, but the other parties in $\bar{I} = [m] \setminus I$ obtain v.)

2. For $i = 2, ..., m$, machine B invokes the simulator guaranteed for the zero-knowledge proof system (P, V), on input v, using (the residual) A as a possible malicious verifier. Note that we are simulating the actions of the prescribed prover P, which in the real protocol is played by the honest Party 1. Once one simulation is finished, its transcript becomes part of the history fed to A in subsequent simulations. Denote the obtained sequence of simulation transcripts by $S = S(v)$.

3. Finally, B feeds A with the alleged execution view (v, S) and outputs whatever A does.

The computational indistinguishability of the output of the real-model adversary under (A, I) and the output of the ideal-model adversary under (B, I) follows from the guaranteed quality of the zero-knowledge simulator. In addition, we need to consider the outputs of the honest parties (i.e., the parties in $\bar{I}$), and specifically the outputs of parties in $\bar{I} \setminus \{1\}$ (since Party 1 has no output). (Indeed, this is an issue only if $\bar{I} \setminus \{1\} \neq \emptyset$, which is the reason that this issue did not arise in the two-party case.) In the ideal-model execution, each party in $\bar{I} \setminus \{1\}$ outputs $v = f(\alpha)$, and we have to prove that the same occurs in the real-model execution (when Party 1 is honest). This follows from the perfect completeness of (P, V), as discussed earlier.

We now turn to the case where *the first party is dishonest* (i.e., $1 \in I$). In this case, the input to B includes α, and it operates as follows (ignoring the easy case $I = [m]$):

1. B invokes A on input α, and obtains the Step C1 message, denoted v, that A instructs Party 1 to send (i.e., $v = A(\alpha)$). As (implicit) in the protocol, any action of A in Step C1 (including abort) is interpreted as sending a string.

2. B tries to obtain a pre-image of v under f. Toward this end, B uses the (strong) knowledge-extractor associated with (P, V). Specifically, providing the strong knowledge-extractor with oracle access to (the residual prover) $A(\alpha)$, machine B tries to extract (from A) a string w such that $f(w) = v$. This is done for each of the $|\bar{I}|$ executions of the proof system in which the verifier is played by an honest party, while updating the history of A accordingly.[72] In case the extractor succeeds (in one of these $|\bar{I}|$ attempts), machine B sets $\alpha' \stackrel{\text{def}}{=} w$. Otherwise, B sets $\alpha' \stackrel{\text{def}}{=} \bot$.

3. B now emulates an execution of Step C2. Specifically, for each $i \in \bar{I}$, machine B lets the adequate residual A play the prover, and emulates by itself the (honest) verifier interacting with A (i.e., B behaves as a honest Party i). (The emulation of the proofs given to parties in I is performed in the straightforward manner.) Next, B decides whether or not to invoke the trusted party and let it respond to the honest parties. This decision is based on all the $m - 1$ emulated proofs.

    - In case any of the $m - 1$ emulated verifiers rejects justifiably, machine B aborts (without invoking the *trusted party*), and outputs whatever A does (when fed with these emulated proof transcripts).
    - Otherwise (i.e., no verifier rejects justifiably), we consider two sub-cases:

        (a) If $\alpha' \neq \bot$, then B sends α' (on behalf of Party 1) to the *trusted party* and allows it to respond the honest parties. (The response will be $f(\alpha')$, which by Step 2 must equal v.)
        (b) Otherwise (i.e., $\alpha' = \bot$, indicating that extraction has failed), B fails. (Note that this means that in Step 3 the verifier was convinced, while in Step 2 the extraction attempt has failed.)

4. Finally, B feeds A with the execution view, which contains the prover's view of the emulation of Step C2 (produced in Step 3), and outputs whatever A does.

As in the two-party case (see proof of Proposition 7.4.12), the real-model execution differs from the ideal-model execution only in case the real-model adversary A succeeds in convincing the knowledge-verifier (which is properly emulated for any $i \in \bar{I}$) that it knows a pre-image of v under f, and yet the knowledge-extractor failed to find such a pre-image. By definition of strong knowledge-verifiers, such an event may occur only with negligible probability. ∎

---

[72] If necessary (i.e., $|\bar{I}| \neq \{2, ..., |\bar{I}| + 1\}$), we also emulate the interleaved proofs that are given to parties in I. This is performed in the straightforward manner (i.e., by letting A emulate both parties in the interaction).

Securely Reducing Authenticated Computation to Image Transmission. Analogously to the two-party case, we securely reduce Eq. (7.50) to Eq. (7.51).

Construction 7.5.26 (multi-party authenticated computation, oracle-aided protocol):

Inputs: *Party 1 gets input $\alpha \in \{0, 1\}^*$, and Party $i \neq 1$ gets input $\beta_i \in \{0, 1\}^{|\alpha|}$.*

Step C1: *Party 1 uses the (multi-party) image-transmission functionality to send the pair $(u, v) \stackrel{\text{def}}{=} (h(\alpha), f(\alpha))$ to the other parties. That is, the parties invoke the functionality of Eq. (7.51), where Party 1 enters the input α and Party i is to obtain $g(\alpha) \stackrel{\text{def}}{=} (h(\alpha), f(\alpha))$.*

Step C2: *Assuming that Step C1 was not aborted by Party 1 and that Party i receives the pair (u, v) in Step C2, Party i outputs v if $u = \beta_i$ and (u, v) otherwise.*

Outputs: *If not aborted (with output $\perp$), Party $i \neq 1$ sets its local output as directed in Step C2. (Party 1 has no output.)*

Extending the proof of Proposition 7.4.15 (to apply to Construction 7.5.26), and using Propositions 7.5.25 and 7.5.22, we obtain:

Proposition 7.5.27: *Assuming the existence of trapdoor permutations, the h-authenticated f-computation m-party functionality of Eq. (7.50) can be securely implemented in the first malicious model.*

Proof Sketch: We focus on the analysis of Construction 7.5.26, which extends the proof of Proposition 7.4.15. As in the proof of Proposition 7.5.25, when extending the proof of the two-party setting, the two cases (in the proof) correspond to whether or not Party 1 is honest (resp., $1 \notin I$ or $1 \in I$). Again, we discard the case $I = \emptyset$, where here the justification is that the oracle-aided protocol does not use the broadcast channel at all (and so no information is available to the real-model adversary in this case). The case $1 \notin I \neq \emptyset$ is handled exactly as the case that Party 1 is honest in the proof of Proposition 7.4.15 (i.e., B sends the β_i's it holds to the trusted party, obtains $h(\alpha)$ (either explicitly or implicitly) and $f(\alpha)$, where α is the input of Party 1, and uses $(h(\alpha), f(\alpha))$ to emulate the real execution). In case $1 \in I$, we need to extend the two-party treatment a little, because we also have to emulate the oracle answer given (in Step C1) to dishonest parties (different from Party 1, which gets no answer). However, this answer is determined by the query α' made in Step C1 by Party 1, and indeed, we merely need to feed A with the corresponding oracle answer $(h(\alpha'), f(\alpha'))$. The rest of the treatment is exactly as in the two-party case. The proposition follows. ∎

Comment: Pure Oracle-Aided Protocols. Note that Construction 7.5.26 makes no direct use of its communication channel, but is rather confined to the invocation of oracles and local computations. Such an oracle-aided protocol is called pure. Note that most oracle-aided protocols presented in Section 7.4 are pure. An important property of pure oracle-aided protocols is that an adversary that controls none of the parties and only wire-taps the communication channel gets no information, and so this case can be discarded (as done in the proof of Proposition 7.5.27).[73] In fact, Construction 7.5.24 is also a pure oracle-aided protocol (by virtue of its use of the secret broadcast functionality).

7.5.4.4. Multi-Party Augmented Coin-Tossing

In this section, we generalize the augmented coin-tossing functionality (of Section 7.4.3.5) to the multi-party setting. More generally, for any positive polynomial $\ell : \mathbb{N} \to \mathbb{N}$ and a polynomial-time computable function g, we consider the randomized m-ary functionality

$$(1^n, ..., 1^n) \mapsto (r, g(r), ..., g(r)), \tag{7.52}$$

where r is uniformly distributed in $\{0, 1\}^{\ell(n)}$. We securely reduce Eq. (7.52) to the multi-party authenticated-computation functionality. We note that the following construction is different from the one used in the two-party case:

Construction 7.5.28 (an oracle-aided protocol for Eq. (7.52)): *Let C be a commitment scheme and $\overline{C}_{r_1,...,r_\ell}(\sigma_1, ..., \sigma_\ell) = (C_{r_1}(\sigma_1), ..., C_{r_\ell}(\sigma_\ell))$ be as in Construction 7.4.16.*

Inputs: *Each party gets input 1^n and sets $\ell \stackrel{\text{def}}{=} \ell(n)$.*

Step C1: *For $i = 1, .., m$, Party i uniformly selects $r_i \in \{0, 1\}^\ell$ and $s_i \in \{0, 1\}^{\ell \cdot n}$.*

Step C2: *For $i = 1, .., m$, Party i uses the image-transmission functionality to send $c_i \stackrel{\text{def}}{=} \overline{C}_{s_i}(r_i)$ to all parties. Actually, Party i enters Eq. (7.50) with input (r_i, s_i); each other party enters with input $1^{\ell + \ell \cdot n}$, which is supposed to equal $h^{(C2)}(r_i, s_i) \stackrel{\text{def}}{=} 1^{|r_i| + |s_i|}$, and is supposed to obtain $f^{(C2)}(r_i, s_i) \stackrel{\text{def}}{=} \overline{C}_{s_i}(r_i)$. Abusing notation, let us denote by c_i the answer received by each party, where c_i may equal $\bot$ in case Party i has aborted the i-th oracle call. Thus, in Steps C1–C2, each party commits to a random string. Without loss of generality, we assume that no party aborts these steps (i.e., we treat abort as if it were some legitimate default action).*

Step C3: *For $i = 2, .., m$ (but not for $i = 1$), Party i uses the authenticated-computation functionality to send r_i to all parties. That is, Party i enters Eq. (7.50) with input (r_i, s_i); each other party enters with input c_i, where c_i is supposed to equal $h^{(C3)}(r_i, s_i) \stackrel{\text{def}}{=} \overline{C}_{s_i}(r_i)$, and is supposed to obtain $f^{(C3)}(r_i, s_i) \stackrel{\text{def}}{=} r_i$. If Party i aborts the oracle call (that it has invoked) or some Party j obtains an answer of a different format, which happens in case the inputs of these two parties do not match, then Party j halts with output $\bot$. Otherwise, Party j obtains $f^{(C3)}(r_i, s_i) = r_i$ and sets $r_i^j = r_i$. (For simplicity, let $r_j^j \stackrel{\text{def}}{=} r_j$.)*

Thus, in this step, each party (except Party 1), reveals the ℓ-bit long string to which it has committed in Step C2. The correctness of the revealed value is guaranteed by the definition of the authenticated-computation functionality, which is used here

---

[73] Recall that in Section 7.4 we did not consider such external adversaries, and thus the notion of pure oracle-aided protocols was neither discussed nor used.

instead of the straightforward way of disclosing the decommitment information. It follows that for every $j \in [m]$, if Party j is honest and did not halt, then $r_i^j = r_i$ for every $i \in [m] \setminus \{1\}$, where r_i is the value committed by Party i in Step C3.

Step C4: *In case Party 1 did not halt (and so $r_i^1 = r_i$ for every $i \in [m]$), Party 1 uses the authenticated-computation functionality to send $g(\oplus_{i=1}^m r_i^1)$ to all parties. Details follow:*

For $j = 1, ..., m$, Party j sets $r^j \stackrel{\text{def}}{=} \oplus_{i=2}^m r_i^j$. Note that in case Party j did not halt, it holds that $r_i^j = r_i$ (for every $i \in [m]$), and so $r^j = \oplus_{i=2}^m r_i = r^1$. Thus, $\oplus_{i=1}^m r_i^1 = r_1 \oplus r^1$.

Party 1 sets $r \stackrel{\text{def}}{=} r_1 \oplus r^1$ and uses the authenticated-computation functionality to send $g(r)$ to all parties. Specifically, Party 1 enters Eq. (7.50) with input (r_1, s_1, r^1); each (other) Party j enters with input (c_1, r^j), where (c_1, r^j) is supposed to equal $h^{(C4)}(r_1, s_1, r^1) \stackrel{\text{def}}{=} (\overline{C}_{s_1}(r_1), r^1)$, and is supposed to obtain $f^{(C4)}(r_1, s_1, r^1) \stackrel{\text{def}}{=} g(r_1 \oplus r^1)$, which equals $g(r)$. In case Party 1 aborts or Party j obtains an answer of a different format, which happens if the inputs to the functionality do not match, Party j halts with output $\perp$ (indicating that Party 1 misbehaved).

Outputs: *Unless halted in Step C3 (with output $\perp$), Party 1 outputs r, and Party $j \neq 1$ outputs the value determined in Step C4, which is either $g(r)$ or $\perp$.*

In case $m = 2$, Construction 7.5.28 yields an alternative protocol for Eq. (7.34), that is, a protocol that is fundamentally different from the one in Construction 7.4.16.

Proposition 7.5.29: *Construction 7.5.28 securely reduces Eq. (7.52) to Eq. (7.50).*

Proof Sketch:[74] We transform any real-model adversary A (for the oracle-aided execution) into a corresponding ideal-model adversary B. The operation of B depends on whether or not Party 1 is honest (i.e., $1 \in \bar{I}$), and we ignore the trivial cases of $I = \emptyset$ and $I = [m]$. In case $1 \in \bar{I}$ (i.e., Party 1 is honest), machine B proceeds as follows:

1. Machine B emulates the local actions of the honest parties in Step C1. In particular, it uniformly selects (r_i, s_i) for each $i \in \bar{I}$ (including $i = 1$).
2. For every $i \in \bar{I}$, machine B emulates the i-th sub-step of Step C2 by feeding A with the corresponding $c_i = \overline{C}_{s_i}(r_i)$ (as if it were the answer of the i-th oracle call). For every $i \in I$, machine B obtains the input (r_i, s_i) that A enters (on behalf of Party i) to the i-th oracle call of Step C2, and feeds A with adequate emulations of the oracle answers (to other parties in I).
3. For every $i \in \bar{I} \setminus \{1\}$, machine B emulates the i-th sub-step of Step C3 by feeding A with a sequence in $\{r_i, (c_i, r_i)\}^{|I|}$ that corresponds to whether or not each Party $j \in I$ has entered the input c_i (defined in Step 2). For every $i \in I$, machine B obtains the input (r_i', s_i') that A enters (on behalf of Party i) to the i-th oracle call of Step C3, records whether or not $\overline{C}_{s_i}(r_i) = \overline{C}_{s_i'}(r_i')$, and feeds A with adequate emulations of the oracle answers.

---

[74] As in the proof of Proposition 7.5.25, we sometimes present ideal-model adversaries that halt before invoking the *trusted party*. This can be viewed as invoking the trusted party with a special abort symbol.

For every $i \in \bar{I}$, machine B sets $r_i^1 = r_i$. For every $i \in I$, machine B sets $r_i^1 = r_i$ if $\overline{C}_{s_i}(r_i) = \overline{C}_{s_i'}(r_i')$ and *aborts* otherwise (while outputting whatever A outputs [when Party 1 halts in Step C3]). Note that for every i, this setting of r_i^1 agrees with the setting of r_i^1 in the protocol. In particular, B aborts if and only if (the honest) Party 1 would have halted in the corresponding (emulated) execution of Step C3.[75]

4. In case B did not abort, it invokes the trusted party with input 1^n and obtains the answer $g(r)$, where r is the uniformly distributed ℓ-bit string handed to Party 1. Next, machine B emulates Step C4 by feeding each dishonest party with either $g(r)$ or $((c_1, r^1), g(r))$, where $r^1 \stackrel{\text{def}}{=} \oplus_{i=2}^m r_i^1$. The choice is determined by whether or not (in Step C4) this party has entered the input (c_1, r^1). (Note that we cheat in the emulation of the oracle answer in Step C4; specifically, we use $g(r)$ rather than $g(r_1 \oplus r^1)$.) Finally, machine B outputs whatever A does.

We stress that in this case (i.e., $1 \notin I$), machine B may possibly abort only before invoking the trusted party (which satisfies the security definition). Observe that the only difference between the ideal-model execution, under B and the real-model execution under A is that in the ideal-model execution, an independently and uniformly distributed $r \in \{0, 1\}^\ell$ is used (in the emulation of Step C4), whereas in the real-model execution, r (as used in Step C4) is set to $\oplus_{i=1}^m r_i^1 = r_1 \oplus r^1$. That is, in the ideal-model, r_1 is independent of r and r^1, whereas in the real-model, $r_1 = r \oplus r^1$, where $g(r)$ and $r^1 = r^i$ (for every i) are known to the adversary (and r appears in the joint-view). Thus, in addition to its possible affect on r (in the real model), the only (other) affect that r_1 has on the joint-view is that the latter contains $c_1 = \overline{C}(r_1)$. In other words, (the joint-views in) the real model and the ideal model differ only in whether c_1 is a commitment to $r \oplus r^1$ or to a uniformly and independently distributed string, where r and r^1 are explicit in the joint-view. By the hiding property of C, this difference is undetectable.

We now turn to the case that $1 \in I$ (i.e., Party 1 is dishonest). The treatment of this case differs in two main aspects. First, unlike in the previous case, here the real-model adversary (which controls Party 1) obtains all r_i's, and so we must guarantee that in the ideal-model execution, the trusted party's answer (to Party 1) equals $\oplus_{i=1}^m r_i$. Second, unlike in the previous case, here the real-model adversary may effectively abort Step C4 (i.e., abort after obtaining the outcome), but this is easy to handle using the ideal-model adversary's ability to instruct the trusted party not to respond the honest parties. Returning to the first issue, we present a different way of emulating the real-model execution.[76] Specifically, we will cheat in our emulation of the honest parties and use (in Step 1–2) commitments to the value 0^ℓ, rather than commitments to the corresponding r_i's, which will be determined only at the end of Step 2. Details follow:

1. Machine B starts by invoking the trusted party and obtains a uniformly distributed $r \in \{0, 1\}^\ell$. At this time, B does not decide whether or not to allow the trusted party to answer the honest parties.

---

[75] Indeed, in Step C3, Party 1 halts if and only if for some i, the input that Party 1 enters to the i-th sub-step (which in turn equals the value $c_i = \overline{C}_{s_i}(r_i)$ that Party 1 has obtained in the i-th sub-step of Step C2) does not fit the input (r_i', s_i') that is entered by Party i (i.e., iff $c_i \neq \overline{C}_{s_i'}(r_i')$).

[76] We comment that the alternative emulation strategy can also be used in case Party 1 is honest.

In addition, B emulates the local actions of the honest parties in Step C1 by uniformly selecting only the s_i's, for each $i \in \bar{I}$.

2. For every $i \in \bar{I}$, machine B emulates the i-th sub-step of Step C2 by feeding A with $c_i = \overline{C}_{s_i}(0^\ell)$. For every $i \in I$, machine B obtains the input (r_i, s_i) that A enters (on behalf of Party i) to the i-th oracle call of Step C2. Finally, B uniformly selects all other r_i's (i.e., for i's in $\bar{I}$) such that $\oplus_{i=1}^m r_i = r$ holds; for example, for each $i \in \bar{I} \setminus \{1\}$, select $r_i \in \{0,1\}^\ell$ uniformly, and set $r_1 = r \oplus (\oplus_{i=2}^m r_i)$.

3. For every $i \in \bar{I}$, machine B emulates the i-th sub-step of Step C3 by feeding A with a sequence in $\{r_i, (c_i, r_i)\}^{|I|}$ that corresponds to whether or not each Party $j \in I$ has entered the input c_i. Note that the fact that c_i is unlikely to be a commitment to r_i is irrelevant here. The rest of this step (i.e., the determination of the r_i^1's) is as in the case that Party 1 is honest. In particular, we let B *halt* if some Party $i \in I$ behaves improperly (i.e., invokes the corresponding oracle with input that does not fit c_i as recorded in the emulation of Step C2).

The next step is performed only in case B did not abort. In this case, $r_i^1 = r_i$ holds for every $i = 2, ..., m$, and $r = r_1 \oplus (\oplus_{i=2}^m r_i^1)$ follows.

4. Next, machine B emulates Step C4 and determines whether or not A instructs Party 1 to abort its oracle call (in Step C4). The decision is based on whether or not the oracle query (q_1, q_2, q_3) of Party 1 (in Step C4) matches the oracle query (r_i, s_i) it made in Step C2 and the value of $\oplus_{i=2}^m r_i^1$ as determined in Step 3 (i.e., whether or not $\overline{C}_{q_2}(q_1) = \overline{C}_{s_i}(r_i)$ and $q_3 = \oplus_{i=2}^m r_i^1$). If Party 1 aborts, then B prevents the trusted party from answering the honest parties, and otherwise B allows the trusted party to answer. (Indeed, in case the trusted party answers Party $i \neq 1$, the answer is $g(r)$.) In addition, B emulates the answers of the Step C4 oracle call to the dishonest parties (as in the case that Party 1 is honest). Finally, machine B outputs whatever A does.

Observe that the only difference between of the ideal-model execution under B and the real-model execution under A is that in the former, commitments to 0^ℓ (rather than to the r_i's, for $i \in \bar{I}$) are delivered in Step C2. However, by the hiding property of C, this difference is undetectable. ∎

An Important Special Case. An important special case of Eq. (7.52) is the case that $g(r, s) = \overline{C}_s(r)$, where $|s| = n \cdot |r|$. This special case will be called the augmented (m-party) coin-tossing functionality. That is, for *some fixed* commitment scheme, C, and a positive polynomial ℓ, we consider the m-ary functionality:

$$(1^n, ..., 1^n) \mapsto ((r, s), \overline{C}_s(r), ..., \overline{C}_s(r)) \tag{7.53}$$

where (r, s) is uniformly distributed in $\{0,1\}^{\ell(n)} \times \{0,1\}^{\ell(n) \cdot n}$. Combining Propositions 7.5.27 and 7.5.29, we get:

Proposition 7.5.30: *Assuming the existence of trapdoor permutations, the augmented coin-tossing functionality of Eq. (7.53) can be securely implemented in the first malicious model.*

7.5.4.5. Multi-Party Input Commitment

The last functionality needed for the first multi-party compiler is a multi-party generalization of the input-commitment functionality of Section 7.4.3.6. Specifically, for C and $\overline{C}$ as in Section 7.5.4.4, we consider the m-party input-commitment functionality

$$(x, 1^{|x|}, ..., 1^{|x|}) \mapsto (r, \overline{C}_r(x), ..., \overline{C}_r(x)), \tag{7.54}$$

where r is uniformly distributed in $\{0, 1\}^{|x|^2}$. By combining a straightforward generalization of Construction 7.4.20 with Propositions 7.5.27 and 7.5.30, we get:

Proposition 7.5.31: *Assuming the existence of trapdoor permutations, the input-commitment functionality of Eq. (7.54) can be securely implemented in the first malicious model.*

Proof Sketch: Starting from Construction 7.4.20, we replace each oracle call to a two-party functionality by a call to the corresponding multi-party functionality. That is, in Step C2 Party 1 uses the image-transmission (or rather the authenticated-computation) functionality to send $c' \stackrel{\text{def}}{=} \overline{C}_{r'}(x)$ to all other parties, in Step C3 an augmented coin-tossing is used to provide Party 1 with a random pair (r, r'') whereas each other party gets $c'' \stackrel{\text{def}}{=} \overline{C}_{r''}(r)$, and in Step C4 Party 1 uses the authenticated-computation functionality to send $\overline{C}_r(x)$ to all other parties. Each of the other parties acts exactly as Party 2 acts in Construction 7.4.20.

The security of the resulting multi-party oracle-aided protocol is established as in the two-party case (treated in Proposition 7.4.21). As in the previous analysis of multi-party protocols that generalize two-party ones, the two cases here are according to whether or not Party 1 is honest (resp., $1 \notin I$ or $1 \in I$). Finally, composing the oracle-aided protocol with secure implementations of the adequate multi-party functionalities (as provided by Propositions 7.5.27 and 7.5.30), the proposition follows. ∎

7.5.4.6. The Compiler Itself

We are now ready to present the first multi-party compiler. Given a multi-party protocol, Π, for the semi-honest model, we want to generate an "equivalent" protocol Π' for the first malicious model. Recall that the given protocol operates in a communication model consisting of a single broadcast channel. The compiled protocol will operate in the same communication model. As in the two-party case, we first present an oracle-aided version of the compiled protocol (which will actually be a *pure* oracle-aided protocol, and thus the communication model is actually irrelevant for discussing the oracle-aided version of the compiled protocol). The compiled protocol is a generalization of the one presented in Construction 7.4.23 (for $m = 2$), and the reader is referred there for additional clarifications.

Construction 7.5.32 (The first multi-party compiler, oracle-aided version): *Given an m-party protocol, Π, for the semi-honest model* (using a single broadcast channel), *the* *compiler produces the following oracle-aided m-party protocol, denoted Π', for the first malicious model:*

Inputs: *Party i gets input $x^i \in \{0, 1\}^n$.*

Input-Commitment Phase: *Each of the parties commits to its input by using the input-commitment functionality of Eq. (7.54). That is, for $i = 1, ..., m$, Party i invokes Eq. (7.54), playing the role of the first party with input x^i, and obtains the output ρ^i, whereas each other party obtains $\gamma^i \stackrel{\text{def}}{=} \overline{C}_{\rho^i}(x^i)$.*

Coin-Generation Phase: *The parties generate random-tapes for the emulation of Π. Each party obtains the random-tape to be held by it, whereas each other party obtains a commitment to this value. This is done by invoking the augmented coin-tossing functionality of Eq. (7.53). That is, for $i = 1, ..., m$, Party i invokes Eq. (7.53), playing the role of the first party, and obtains the output (r^i, ω^i), whereas each other party obtains $\delta^i \stackrel{\text{def}}{=} \overline{C}_{\omega^i}(r^i)$.*

Protocol-Emulation Phase: *The parties use the authenticated-computation functionality of Eq. (7.50) in order to emulate each step of protocol Π. The party that is supposed to send (i.e., broadcast) a message plays the role of the first party in Eq. (7.50), and the other parties play the other roles. Suppose that the current message in Π is to be sent by Party j. Then the functions h, f and the inputs $\alpha, \beta_2, ..., \beta_m$, for the functionality of Eq. (7.50), are set as follows (analogously to their setting in Construction 7.4.23):*

- *The string α is set to equal $(\alpha_1, \alpha_2, \alpha_3)$, where $\alpha_1 = (x^j, \rho^j)$ is the query and answer of Party j in the oracle call that it initiated in the input-commitment phase, $\alpha_2 = (r^j, \omega^j)$ is the answer that Party j obtained in the oracle call that it initiated in the coin-generation phase, and α_3 is the sequence of messages that Party j obtained so far in the emulation of Π. Each β_i equals $\beta \stackrel{\text{def}}{=} (\gamma^j, \delta^j, \alpha_3)$, where γ^j and δ^j are the answers that the other parties obtained in the same oracle calls in the first two phases (and α_3 is as previously).*
  Note that since Π operates over a single broadcast channel, all parties receive exactly the same messages.
- *The function h is defined such that $h((v_1, s_1), (v_2, s_2), v_3)$ equals $(\overline{C}_{s_1}(v_1), \overline{C}_{s_2}(v_2), v_3)$. Indeed, it holds that $h(\alpha_1, \alpha_2, \alpha_3) = \beta$.*
- *The function f equals the computation that determines the message to be sent in Π. Note that this message is computable in polynomial-time from the party's input (denoted x^j and being part of α_1), its random-tape (denoted r^j and being part of α_2), and the messages it has received so far (i.e., α_3). Indeed, it holds that $f(\alpha_1, \alpha_2, \alpha_3)$ is the message that Party j should send in Π.*

Recall that each party that plays a receiver in the current oracle call obtains either $f(\alpha)$ or $(h(\alpha), f(\alpha))$. It treats the second case as if the sending party has aborted, which is also possible per se.

Aborting: *In case any of the functionalities invoked in any of the above phases termi-nates in an abort state, the parties obtaining this indication abort the execution and set their output to $\perp$. Otherwise, outputs are as follows.*

Outputs: *At the end of the emulation phase, each party holds the corresponding output of the party in protocol Π. The party just locally outputs this value.*

We note that both the compiler and the protocols produced by it are efficient, and that their dependence on m is polynomially bounded.

7.5.4.7. Analysis of the Compiler

The effect of Construction 7.5.32 is analyzed analogously to the effect of Construction 7.4.23. In view of this similarity, we combine the two main steps (in the analysis) and state only the end result:

Theorem 7.5.33 (Restating half of Theorem 7.5.15): *Suppose that there exist collections of enhanced trapdoor permutations. Then any m-ary functionality can be securely computable in the* first *malicious model* (using only point-to-point communication lines), *provided that a public-key infrastructure exists in the network. Furthermore, security holds even if the adversary can read all communication among honest parties.*

Proof Sketch: We start by noting that the definition of the *augmented semi-honest model* (i.e., Definition 7.4.24) applies without any change to the multi-party context (also in case the communication is via a single broadcast channel). Recall that the *augmented semi-honest model* allows parties to enter the protocol with modified inputs (rather than the original ones) and abort the execution at any point in time. We stress that in the multi-party augmented semi-honest model, an adversary controls all non-honest parties and coordinates their input modifications and abort decisions. As in the two-party case, other than these non-proper actions, the non-honest parties follow the protocol (as in the semi-honest model).

The first significant part of the proof is showing that the compiler of Construction 7.5.32 transforms any protocol Π into a protocol Π' such that executions of Π' in the first malicious real model can be emulated by executions of Π in the augmented semi-honest model (over a single broadcast channel). This part is analogous to Proposition 7.4.25, and its proof is analogous to the proof presented in the two-party case. That is, we transform any real-model adversary (A, I) for Π' into a corresponding augmented semi-honest adversary, (B, I), for Π. The construction of B out of A in analogous to the construction of B_{mal} out of A_{mal} (carried out in the proof of Proposition 7.4.25): Specifically, B modifies inputs according to the queries that A makes in the input-committing phase, uniformly selects random-tapes (in accordance with the coin-generation phase), and aborts in case the emulated machine does so. Thus, B, which is an augmented semi-honest adversary, emulates the malicious adversary A.

The second significant part of the proof is showing that canonical protocols (as provided by Theorem 7.5.14) have the property that their execution in the augmented semi-honest model can be emulated in the (first) malicious ideal model of Definition 7.5.2. This part is analogous to Proposition 7.4.27, and its proof is analogous to the proof presented in the two-party case.

Thus, given any m-ary functionality f, we first (use Theorem 7.5.14 to) obtain a canonical protocol Π that privately computes f. (Actually, we use the version of Π that operates over a single broadcast channel, as provided by the pre-compiler [i.e., Proposition 7.5.16].) Combining the two parts, we conclude that when feeding Π to the compiler of Construction 7.5.32, the result is an oracle-aided protocol Π' such that executions of Π' in the (first) malicious real model can be emulated in the ideal model of Definition 7.5.2. Thus, Π' securely computes f in the first malicious model.

We are almost done, but there are two relatively minor issues to address. First, Π' is an oracle-aided protocol rather than an ordinary one. However, an ordinary protocol that securely computes f can be derived by using secure implementations of the oracles used by Π' (as provided by Propositions 7.5.27, 7.5.30, and 7.5.31). Second, Π' operates in the broadcast-channel communication model, whereas we claimed a protocol in the point-to-point communication model. This gap is bridged by using the post-compiler (i.e., Proposition 7.5.19). ∎

7.5.5. The Second Compiler: Effectively Preventing Abort

We now show how to transform any protocol for securely computing some functionality in the *first* malicious model into a protocol that securely computes the same functionality in the *second* malicious model. We stress that again, all communication, both in the input protocol as well as in the one resulting from the compilation, is conducted by posting messages on a single broadcast channel.

The current compiler has little to do with anything done in the two-party case. The only similarity is at a technical level; that is, in using a secure implementation of the authenticated-computation functionality. The main novelty is in the use of a new ingredient, called *Verifiable Secret Sharing* (VSS).

It is interesting to note that we use implementations of the authenticated-computation functionality (of Eq. (7.50)) and of VSS that are ("only") secure *in the first malicious model*. It is what we add on top of these implementations that makes the resulting protocol secure *in the second malicious model*. Following is a high-level description of the multi-party protocols generated by the current compiler. Recall that the input to the compiler is a protocol secure in the *first* malicious model (and so the random-tape and actions mentioned here refer to this protocol).[77]

The sharing phase: Each party shares its input and random-tape with all the parties such that any strict majority of parties can retrieve their value, whereas no minority group can obtain any knowledge of these values. This is done by using Verifiable Secret Sharing (VSS).

---

[77] In our application, we feed the current compiler with a protocol generated by the first compiler. Still, the random-tape and protocol actions mentioned here refer to the secure protocol compiled by the first compiler, not to the semi-honest protocol from which it was derived.

Intuitively, the malicious parties (which are *in a strict minority*) are effectively pre-vented from aborting the protocol by the following conventions:

- If a party aborts the execution prior to completion of the sharing phase, then the honest parties (which are in the majority) will set its input and random-tape to some default value and will carry out the execution ("on its behalf").
- If a party aborts the execution after the completion of the sharing phase, then the honest (majority) parties will reconstruct its input and random-tape and will carry out the execution ("on its behalf"). The ability of the majority parties to reconstruct the party's input and random-tape relies on the properties of VSS.

The fact that communication is conducted over a broadcast channel, as well as the abovementioned conventions, guarantee that the (honest) majority parties will always be in consensus as to which parties have aborted (and what messages were sent).

Protocol-emulation phase: The parties emulate the execution of the original protocol with respect to the input and random-tapes shared in the first phase. This will be done using a secure (*in the first malicious model*) implementation of the authenticated-computation functionality of Eq. (7.50).

We start by defining and implementing the only new tool needed; that is, Verifiable Secret Sharing.

7.5.5.1. Verifiable Secret Sharing

Loosely speaking, a Verifiable Secret Sharing scheme is (merely) a secure (in the *first* malicious model) implementation of a secret-sharing functionality. Thus, we first define the latter functionality.

Definition 7.5.34 (Secret-Sharing Schemes): *Let $t \leq m$ be positive integers. A t-out-of-m Secret-Sharing Scheme is a pair of algorithms, $G_{m,t}$ and $R_{m,t}$, satisfying the following conditions:*[78]

Syntax: *The* share-generation algorithm, $G_{m,t}$, *is a* probabilistic *mapping of secret bits to m-sequences of* shares; *that is, for every $\sigma \in \{0, 1\}$, the random variable $G_{m,t}(\sigma)$ is distributed over $(\{0, 1\}^*)^m$. The recovering algorithm, $R_{m,t}$, maps t-sequences of pairs in $[m] \times \{0, 1\}^*$ into a single bit, where $[m] \stackrel{\text{def}}{=} \{1, ..., m\}$.*

The recovery condition: *For any $\sigma \in \{0, 1\}$, any sequence $(s_1, ..., s_m)$ in the range of $G_{m,t}(\sigma)$, and any t-subset $\{i_1, ..., i_t\} \subseteq [m]$, it holds that*

$$R_{m,t}((i_1, s_{i_1}), ..., (i_t, s_{i_t})) = \sigma$$

The secrecy condition: *For any $(t-1)$-subset $I \subset [m]$, the distribution of the I-components of $G_{m,t}(\sigma)$ is independent of σ. That is, for any $I = \{i_1, ..., i_{t-1}\} \subset [m]$, let $g_I(\sigma)$ be defined to equal $((i_1, s_{i_1}), ..., (i_{t-1}, s_{i_{t-1}}))$, where $(s_1, ..., s_m) \leftarrow G_{m,t}(\sigma)$.*

---

[78] At this point, we place no computational requirements on $G_{m,t}$ and $R_{m,t}$. Typically, when m is treated as a parameter, these algorithms will operate in time that is polynomial in m.

Then we require that for any such I, the random variables $g_I(0)$ and $g_I(1)$ are identically distributed.

Indeed, an m-out-of-m secret-sharing scheme is implicit in the construction presented in Section 7.5.2: To share a bit σ, one just generates m random bits that sum up to σ (mod 2). Efficient t-out-of-m secret-sharing schemes do exist for any value of $t \leq m$. The most popular one, which uses low-degree polynomials over finite fields, is presented next.

Construction 7.5.35 (Shamir's t-out-of-m secret-sharing scheme): *Find the smallest prime number, denoted p, that is bigger than m, and consider arithmetic over the finite field GF(p).*[79] *The share-generating algorithm consists of uniformly selecting a degree $t - 1$ polynomial over GF(p) with free term equal to σ, and setting the i-th share to be the value of this polynomial at i. The recovering algorithm consists of finding (by interpolation) the unique degree $t - 1$ polynomial that fits the given values and outputting its free term.*

Construction 7.5.35 is analyzed in Exercise 17. Getting back to our subject matter, we derive the basic definition of verifiable secret sharing.

Definition 7.5.36 (Verifiable Secret Sharing, basic version): *A verifiable secret sharing (VSS) scheme* with parameters (m, t) *is an m-party protocol that implements* (i.e., securely computes in the first malicious model) *the share-generation functionality of some t-out-of-m secret-sharing scheme. That is, let $G_{m,t}$ be a share-generation algorithm of some t-out-of-m secret-sharing scheme. Then the corresponding share-generation functionality that the VSS securely computes* (in the first malicious model) *is*

$$((\sigma, 1^n), 1^n, ..., 1^n) \mapsto G_{m,t}(\sigma) \tag{7.55}$$

Actually, it will be more convenient to use an augmented notion of Verifiable Secret Sharing. The augmentation provides each party with an auxiliary input that determines the secret σ (as in a commitment scheme), and allows Party 1 to later conduct *authenticated computations* relative to the auxiliary inputs given to the other parties. Furthermore, each party is provided with a certificate of the validity of its own share (relative to the auxiliary inputs given to the other parties). We seize the opportunity to generalize the definition, such that it refers to the sharing of strings (of a priori known length), rather than to the sharing of single bits. From this point on, when we say Verifiable Secret Sharing (or VSS), we mean the notion defined next (rather the the weaker form in Definition 7.5.36).

Definition 7.5.37 (Verifiable Secret Sharing, revised): *Given a share-generation algorithm $G_{m,t}$ of some t-out-of-m secret-sharing scheme, we extend it to handle*

---

[79] By the Fundamental Theorem of Number Theory, $p \leq 2m$. Thus, p can be found by merely (brute-force) factoring all integers between $m + 1$ and $2m$.

n-bit long strings; that is, $G_{m,t}(\sigma_1, ..., \sigma_n) \stackrel{\text{def}}{=} (s_1, ..., s_m)$, *where* $s_i = s_{i,1} \cdots s_{i,n}$ *and* $(s_{1,j}, ..., s_{m,j}) \leftarrow G_{m,t}(\sigma_j)$ *for every* $i = 1, ..., m$ *and* $j = 1, ..., n$. *Suppose that* $G_{m,t}(\alpha) \in (\{0, 1\}^{\ell(|\alpha|)})^m$, *and let* C *be a commitment scheme and* $\overline{C}$ *be as in Construction 7.5.28. Consider the corresponding* (augmented) *share-generation functionality*

$$(\alpha, 1^{|\alpha|}, ..., 1^{|\alpha|}) \mapsto ((\overline{s}, \overline{\rho}), (s_2, \rho_2, \overline{c}), ..., (s_m, \rho_m, \overline{c})) \tag{7.56}$$

$$\text{where } \overline{s} \stackrel{\text{def}}{=} (s_1, ..., s_m) \leftarrow G_{m,t}(\alpha), \tag{7.57}$$

$$\overline{\rho} \stackrel{\text{def}}{=} (\rho_1, ..., \rho_m) \in \{0, 1\}^{m \cdot \ell(|\alpha|)^2} \tag{7.58}$$

$$\text{is uniformly distributed,}$$

$$\text{and } \overline{c} \stackrel{\text{def}}{=} (\overline{C}_{\rho_1}(s_1), ..., \overline{C}_{\rho_m}(s_m)). \tag{7.59}$$

Then any m-party protocol that securely computes Eq. (7.56)−(7.59) *in the* first *malicious model is called a* verifiable secret sharing (VSS) scheme with parameters (m, t).

Observe that each party may demonstrate (to each other party) the validity of its "primary" share (i.e., the s_i) with respect to the globally held $\overline{c}$, by revealing the corresponding ρ_i. We shall be particularly interested in VSS schemes with parameters $(m, \lceil m/2 \rceil)$; that is, $t = \lceil m/2 \rceil$. The reason for this focus is that we assume throughout this section that the malicious parties are in strict minority. Thus, by the secrecy requirement, setting $t \geq m/2$ guarantees that the (less than $m/2$) dishonest parties are not able to obtain any information about the secret from their shares. On the other hand, by the recovery requirement, setting $t \leq \lceil m/2 \rceil$ guarantees that the (more than $m/2$) honest parties are able to efficiently recover the secret from their shares. Thus, in the sequel, whenever we mention VSS without specifying the parameters, we mean the VSS with parameters $(m, \lceil m/2 \rceil)$, where m is understood from the context.

Clearly, by Theorem 7.5.33, verifiable secret sharing schemes exist, provided that enhanced trapdoor permutations exist. Actually, to establish the existence of VSS, we merely need to apply the first compiler to the straightforward protocol that privately computes Eq. (7.56)−(7.59); see Exercise 10. For the sake of subsequent reference, we state the latter result.

Proposition 7.5.38: *Suppose that trapdoor permutations exist. Then for every* $t \leq m$, *there exists a verifiable secret-sharing scheme with parameters* (m, t).

Note that the assumption used in Proposition 7.5.38 is (merely) the one needed for the operation of the first compiler, which amounts to the assumption needed for implementing the functionalities used in Construction 7.5.32.

7.5.5.2. The Compiler Itself

We are now ready to present the second compiler. Recall that we are given a multi-party protocol, Π, that is secure in the *first* malicious model, and we want to generate an "equivalent" protocol Π' for the *second* malicious model. Also recall that both the given protocol and the one generated by the compiler operate in a communication model consisting of a *single broadcast channel*. Finally, we note that the generated protocol uses sub-protocols that are secure with respect to the first malicious model (and yet the entire protocol will be analyzed with respect to the second malicious model).[80]

Construction 7.5.39 (The second multi-party compiler): *Let $t \stackrel{\text{def}}{=} \lceil m/2 \rceil$. Given an m-party protocol, Π, for the* first *malicious model, the compiler produces the following m-party protocol, denoted Π', for the* second *malicious model.*

Inputs: *Party i gets input $x^i \in \{0, 1\}^n$.*

Random-Tape: *Party i uniformly selects a* random-tape, *denoted $r^i \in \{0, 1\}^{c(n)}$, for the emulation of Π.*

The Sharing Phase: *Each party shares its input and random-tape with all the parties, using a Verifiable Secret Sharing scheme. That is, for $i = 1, ..., m$, Party i invokes the VSS scheme playing the first party with input $x^i r^i$, while the other parties play the roles of the other parties in Eq. $(7.56) - (7.59)$ with input $1^{n+c(n)}$.*

Regarding the i-th VSS invocation,[81] we denote the output that Party i obtains by $(\overline{s}^i, \overline{\rho}^i)$, and the outputs that each other Party j obtains by $(s_j^i, \rho_j^i, \overline{c}^i)$, where $\overline{s}^i = (s_1^i, ..., s_m^i) \leftarrow G_{m,t}(x^i r^i)$, $\overline{\rho}^i = (\rho_1^i, ..., \rho_m^i)$ is uniformly distributed, $\overline{c}^i = (c_1^i, ..., c_m^i)$, and $c_k^i = \overline{C}_{\rho_k^i}(s_k^i)$. Note that either all honest parties get the correct outcome or they all detect that Party i is cheating and set their outcome to $\perp$.

Handling Abort: If Party i aborts the i-th VSS invocation, which means that all honest parties received the outcome $\perp$, then the honest parties set its input and random-tape to some default value; that is, they set their record of the input and random-tape of Party i (which are otherwise unknown to them) to some default value. Note that by definition, the VSS scheme is secure in the first malicious model, and thus all honest parties agree on whether or not the VSS initiator (i.e., Party i) has aborted.[82]

---

[80] For this reason, we cannot utilize a composition theorem for the second malicious model. We comment that such a composition theorem would anyhow be more restricted than Theorem 7.5.21. One issue is that the second malicious model depends on a bound on the fraction of dishonest parties. Thus, if the m-party oracle-aided protocol invokes a k-ary functionality with $k < m$, then the bound (on the fraction of dishonest parties) may be violated in the sub-protocol that replaces the latter. For this reason, when dealing with the second malicious model, one should confine the treatment to m-party oracle-aided protocols that use m-ary (rather than k-ary) functionalities.

[81] Indeed, this notation is slightly inconsistent with the one used in Definition 7.5.37. Here, Party i plays the first party in the VSS, and being consistent with Definition 7.5.37 would required calling its share s_1^i rather than s_i^i. Consequently, the share of Party j in this invocation would have been denoted $s_{\pi_i(j)}^i$, where $\pi_i(j)$ is the role that Party j plays in this invocation. However, such notation would have made our exposition more cumbersome.

[82] This is reflected in the corresponding ideal-model adversary that either makes all honest parties detect abort (i.e., output $\perp$) or allows all of them to obtain (and output) the corresponding entries in a valid m-sequence.

We stress that in case Party i aborts the i-th VSS invocation, its (default) input and random-tape become known to all parties. Since the entire execution takes place over a broadcast channel, each party can determine by itself what messages Party i should send in a corresponding execution of Π. *Thus, there is actually no need to send actual messages on behalf of Party i.*

Protocol-Emulation Phase: *The parties emulate the execution of protocol* Π *with respect to the input and random-tapes shared in the first phase. This will be done by using a secure* (in the first malicious model) *implementation of the authenticated-computation functionality of Eq. (7.50).*

That is, Party i, which is supposed to send a message in Π, *plays the role of the first party in Eq. (7.50), and the other parties play the other roles. The inputs* $\alpha, \beta_2, ..., \beta_m$ *and the functions* h, f, *for the functionality of Eq. (7.50), are set as follows:*

- *The string* $\alpha = (\alpha_1, \alpha_2)$ *is set such that* $\alpha_1 = (x^i r^i, \overline{s}^i, \overline{\rho}^i)$ *and* α_2 *equals the concatenation of all previous messages sent in the emulation of previous steps of* Π. *Recall that* $(x^i r^i, (\overline{s}^i, \overline{\rho}^i))$ *is the input–output pair of Party i in the i-th invocation of the VSS.*
- *The string* β_j *equals* $\beta \stackrel{\text{def}}{=} (\overline{c}^i, \alpha_2)$, *where* α_2 *is as in previous item. Recall that* $\overline{c}^i$ *is part of the output that each other party got in the i-th invocation of the VSS.*
- *The function* h *is defined such that* $h((z, (s_1, ..., s_m), (r_1, ..., r_m)), \gamma) = ((\overline{C}_{r_1}(s_1), ..., \overline{C}_{r_m}(s_m)), \gamma)$. *Indeed,* $h(\alpha_1, \alpha_2) = \beta$.
- *The function* f *is set to be the computation that determines the message to be sent in* Π. *Note that this message is computable in polynomial-time from the party's input* (denoted x^i), *its random-tape* (denoted r^i), *and the previous messages posted so far* (i.e., α_2).

As a result of the execution of the authenticated-computation sub-protocol, each party either gets an indication that Party i aborted or determines the message that Party i should have sent in a corresponding execution of Π. *By the definition of security in the first malicious model, all honest parties agree on whether or not Party i aborted, and in case it did not abort, they also agree on the message it sent.*

Handling Abort: *If a party aborts when playing the role of the first party in an invocation of Eq. (7.50) during the emulation phase, then the majority parties recover its* (actual) *input and random-tape, and carry out the execution on its behalf. Specifically, if Party j detects that Party i has aborted, then it broadcasts the pair* (s^i_j, ρ^i_j) *that it has obtained in the sharing phase, and each party uses the* correctly *decommitted shares* (i.e., the s^i_j's) *to reconstruct* $x^i r^i$.

We note that the completion of the sharing phase (and the definition of VSS) guarantee that the majority parties hold shares that yield the input and random-tape of any party. Furthermore, the correct shares are verifiable by each of the other parties, and so reconstruction of the initial secret is efficiently implementable whenever a majority of parties wishes to do so.

Outputs: *At the end of the emulation phase, each party holds the corresponding output of the party in protocol Π. The party just locally outputs this value.*

Note that the VSS scheme is implicitly used as a commitment scheme for the value of $x^i r^i$; that is, $\bar{c}^i = (c_1^i, ..., c_m^i)$ serves as a commitment to the sequence of shares $(s_1^i, ..., s_m^i)$, which in turn determine $x^i r^i$. Actually, the main steps in the emulation phase only refer to this aspect of the VSS, whereas only the abort-handling procedure refers to the additional aspects (e.g., the fact that Party j holds the value of the share s_j^i that is determined by the commitment c_j^i, as well as the corresponding decommitment information).

Comment. Applying the two (multi-party protocol) compilers one after the other is indeed wasteful. For example, we enforce proper emulation (via the authenticated-computation functionality) twice: first with respect to the semi-honest protocol, and next with respect to the protocol resulting from the first compiler. Indeed, more efficient protocols for the second malicious model could be derived by omitting the authenticated-computation protocols generated by the first compiler (and having the second compiler refer to the actions of the semi-honest protocol). Similarly, one can omit the input-commit phase in the first compiler. In general, feeding the second compiler with protocols that are secure in the first malicious model is an overkill; see further discussion subsequent to Proposition 7.5.42.

7.5.5.3. Analysis of the Compiler

Our aim is to establish the following:

Theorem 7.5.40 (Restating the second half of Theorem 7.5.15): *Suppose that there exist collections of enhanced trapdoor permutations. Then any m-ary functionality can be securely computable in the* second *malicious model* (using only point-to-point communication lines), *provided that a public-key infrastructure exists in the network. Furthermore, security holds even if the adversary can read all communication among honest parties.*

As will be shown here, given a protocol as guaranteed by Theorem 7.5.33, the second compiler produces a protocol that securely computes (in the second malicious model) the same functionality. Thus, for any functionality f, the compiler transforms protocols for securely computing f in the first malicious model into protocols for securely computing f in the second malicious model. This suffices to establish Theorem 7.5.40, yet it does not say what the compiler does when given an arbitrary protocol (i.e., one not provided by Theorem 7.5.33). In order to analyze the action of the second compiler, in general, we introduce the following model that is a hybrid of the semi-honest and the two malicious models. We call this new model the *second-augmented semi-honest* model. Unlike the (first) *augmented semi-honest* model (used in the analysis of the first compiler [see proof of Theorem 7.5.33]), the new model allows a dishonest party to select its random-tape arbitrarily, but does *not* allow it to abort.

Definition 7.5.41 (the second-augmented semi-honest model): *Let* Π *be a multi-party protocol. A coordinated strategy for parties* I *is admissible as a* second-augmented semi-honest behavior (*with respect to* Π) *if the following holds:*

Entering the execution: *Depending on their initial inputs and in coordination with each other, the parties in* I *may enter the execution of* Π *with any input of their choice.*

Selection of random-tape: *Depending on their inputs and in coordination with each other, the parties in* I *may arbitrarily select their random-tapes for the execution of* Π.

Here and in the previous step, the parties in I *may employ randomized procedures, but the randomization in their procedures is not to be confused with the random-tapes for* Π *selected in the current step.*

Proper message transmission: *In each step of* Π, *depending on its view so far, the designated (by* Π) *party sends a message as instructed by* Π. *We stress that the message is computed as* Π *instructs based on the party's (possibly modified) input, its (possibly non-uniformly selected) random-tape, and the messages received so far, where the input and random-tape are as set in the previous two steps.*

Output: *At the end of the interaction, the parties in* I *produce outputs depending on their entire view of the interaction. We stress that the view contains their initial inputs and all messages sent over all channels.*[83]

Intuitively, the compiler transforms any protocol Π into a protocol Π' so that executions of Π' in the second malicious model correspond to executions of Π in the second augmented semi-honest model. That is:

Proposition 7.5.42 (general analysis of the second multi-party compiler): *Let* Π' *be the m-party protocol produced by the compiler of Construction 7.5.39, when given the protocol* Π. *Then for every probabilistic polynomial-time adversary* A *for the second malicious model, there exists a probabilistic polynomial-time strategy* B *that is admissible (with respect to* Π) *in the second-augmented semi-honest model (of Definition 7.5.41), such that for every* $I \subset [m]$ *with* $|I| < m/2$

$$\{\text{REAL}_{\Pi,I,B(z)}(\overline{x})\}_{\overline{x},z} \overset{\text{c}}{\equiv} \{\text{REAL}_{\Pi',I,A(z)}(\overline{x})\}_{\overline{x},z}$$

Proposition 7.5.42 can be viewed as asserting that *if* Π *is secure in the second-augmented semi-honest model, then* Π' *is secure in the second malicious model*, where by the former term we mean that for every real-model adversary B that is admissible (with respect to Π) in the second-augmented semi-honest model, there exists an ideal-model adversary C as per Definition 7.5.4 such that $\{\text{IDEAL}^{(2)}_{f,I,C(z)}(\overline{x})\}_{\overline{x},z} \overset{\text{c}}{\equiv} \{\text{REAL}_{\Pi,I,B(z)}(\overline{x})\}_{\overline{x},z}$ (for every I). Proposition 7.5.42 will be applied to protocols that securely compute a functionality in the first malicious model. As we shall see, for such protocols, the second augmented semi-honest model (of Definition 7.5.41) can be emulated by the second ideal malicious

---

[83] This model is applicable both when the communication is via a single broadcast channel and when the communication is via point-to-point channels that can be wire-tapped by the adversary.

model (of Definition 7.5.4). Thus, Theorem 7.5.40 will follow. We start by establishing Proposition 7.5.42:

Proof Sketch: Given a real-model adversary A (for Π'), we present a corresponding adversary B that is admissible with respect to Π for the second augmented semi-honest model. We stress two points. First, whereas A may abort some parties, the adversary B may not do so (as per Definition 7.5.41). Second, we may assume that the number of parties controlled by A (and thus by B) is less than $m/2$ (because nothing is required otherwise).

Machine B will use A as well as the ideal-model adversaries derived (as per Definition 7.5.3) from the behavior of A in the various sub-protocols invoked by Π'. We stress that these ideal-model adversaries are of the first malicious model. Furthermore, machine B will also emulate the behavior of the trusted party in these ideal-model emulations (without communicating with any trusted party; there is no trusted party in the augmented semi-honest model). Thus, the following description contains an implicit special-purpose composition theorem (in which sub-protocols that are secure in the first malicious model are used to implement the oracles of an oracle-aided protocol that is secure in the second malicious model):

Entering the execution and selecting a random-tape: B invokes A (on the very input supplied to it) and decides with what input and random-tape to enter the execution of Π. Toward this end, machine B emulates the execution of the sharing phase of Π', using A (as subroutine). Machine B supplies A with the messages it expects to see, thus emulating the honest parties in Π', and obtains the messages sent by the parties in I (i.e., those controlled by A). We stress that this activity is internal to B and involves no real interaction (of B in Π).

Specifically, B emulates the executions of the VSS protocol in an attempt to obtain the values that the parties in I share with all parties. The emulation of each such VSS-execution is done by using the ideal-model adversary derived from (the residual real-model malicious adversary) A. We stress that in accordance with the definition of VSS (i.e., security in the first malicious model), the ideal-model adversary derived from (the residual) A is in the first malicious model and may abort some parties. Note that (by Definitions 7.5.3 and 7.5.2) this may happen only if the initiator of the VSS is dishonest. In case the execution initiated by some party aborts, its input and random-tape are set to the default value (as in the corresponding abort-handling procedure of Π'). Details follow:

- In an execution of VSS initiated by an honest party (i.e., in which an honest party plays the role of the first party in VSS), machine B obtains the corresponding augmented shares (available to I).[84] Machine B will use an arbitrary value, say $0^{n+c(n)}$, as the first party's input for the current emulation of the VSS (because the real value is unknown to B). In emulating the VSS, machine B will use the ideal-model adversary, denoted A', that emulates the behavior of A in this VSS (in Π'), when given the history so far. We stress that since the initiating

---

[84] These will be used in the emulation of future message-transmission steps.

party of the VSS is honest, this ideal-model adversary (i.e., A') cannot abort any party.

Invoking the ideal-model adversary A', and emulating both the honest (ideal-model) parties and the trusted party, machine B obtains the outputs of all parties (i.e., and in particular, the output of the initiating party). That is, machine B emulates the sharing of value $0^{n+c(n)}$ by the initiating party and emulates the response of the trusted oracle (i.e., by setting $\bar{s} \leftarrow G_{m,t}(0^{n+c(n)})$, uniformly selecting $\bar{\rho}$ of adequate length, and computing the outputs as in Eq. $(7.56)-(7.59)$).

- In an execution of VSS initiated by a party in I (i.e., a dishonest party plays the role of the first party in VSS), machine B obtains the corresponding input and random-tape of the initiator, as well as the randomization used in the commitment to it. As before, machine B uses the derived ideal-model adversary, denoted A', to emulate the execution of the VSS. Recall that A' emulates the behavior of A in the corresponding execution of the VSS.

Suppose that we are currently emulating the instance of VSS initiated by Party i, where $i \in I$. Then B invokes A' on input $x^i r^i$ (i.e., the initial input and random-tape of Party i), and emulating both the honest (ideal-model) parties and the trusted party, machine B obtains the outputs of all parties (including the "VSS-randomization" (i.e., $(\bar{s}^i, \bar{\rho}^i)$)) handed to Party i which is in I). A key point is that machine B has obtained, while emulating the trusted party, the input handed by A' to the trusted party. This value is recorded as the modified input and random-tape of Party i.

In case the emulated machine did not abort the initiator (i.e., Party i), machine B records the previous value, as well as the randomization used by B (as trusted party) in the execution of VSS. Otherwise (i.e., A aborts Party i in the invocation of VSS initiated by it), the input and random-tape of Party i are set to the default value (as in Π'). In either case, B concatenates the emulation of the VSS to the history of the execution of A.

Thus, inputs and random-tapes are determined for all parties in I, depending only on their initial inputs. (All this is done before entering the actual execution of Π.) Furthermore, the view of machine A in the sharing phase of Π' has been emulated, and the VSS-randomizations (i.e., the pairs $(\bar{s}^i, \bar{\rho}^i)$) used in the sharing of all values have been recorded by B. (Actually, it suffices to record the VSS-randomization handed to dishonest parties and the commitments made on behalf of honest ones; these will be used in the emulation of the message-transmission steps of Π', where the VSS-randomization will be used only in case the corresponding party aborts.)

Subsequent steps – message transmission: Machine B now enters the actual execution of Π (with inputs and random-tapes for I-parties as determined earlier). It proceeds in this real execution of Π, along with emulating the corresponding executions of the authenticated computation of Eq. (7.50) (which are invoked in Π').

In a message-transmission step by an honest party in Π, machine B obtains a message from this honest party (in the real execution of Π) and emulates an execution of the authenticated-computation protocol resulting in this message as output. In a message-transmission step by a dishonest party in Π, machine B computes the message to be sent as instructed by Π, based on the input and random-tape determined in the previous stage and the messages obtained so far (in Π). In addition, B emulates an execution of the authenticated-computation protocol resulting in this message as output. The emulation of each execution of the authenticated-computation protocol, which securely computes (in the first malicious model) the functionality Eq. (7.50), is done by using the malicious ideal-model adversary derived from A. The fact that in these emulations machine B also emulates the trusted party allows it to set the outcome of the authenticated-computation protocol to fit the message being delivered. We stress that the fact that a (dishonest) party may abort some parties in these emulations of Π' does *not* result in aborting the real execution of Π (and is merely reflected in the transcript of these emulations). Details follow:

- In a message-transmission step by an honest party in Π, machine B first obtains from this party (in the real execution of Π) a message, denoted msg. This completes all that is done in this step with respect to communication in Π.

  Next, machine B proceeds in emulating the corresponding message-transmission sub-protocol of Π'. Firstly, machine B derives the ideal-model adversary, denoted A', which corresponds to the behavior of A in the corresponding execution of the authenticated-computation sub-protocol (executed by protocol Π'). Invoking the ideal-model adversary A', and emulating both the honest (ideal-model) parties and the trusted party, machine B sets the trusted party's replies (to parties in I) to equal either msg or (β, msg), where β is as in Construction 7.5.39.[85] The decision concerning which reply to deliver to each party in I depends on the input that this party hands to the trusted party (or rather the input that A' hands on its behalf): If the party hands the correct value β, then it receives msg; otherwise it receives (β, msg).

  Note that the emulation of the authenticated-computation sub-protocol is carried out so as to produce an output in $\{\mathrm{msg}, (\beta, \mathrm{msg})\}^{|I|}$, where msg does not necessarily fit the output of the authenticated-computation functionality of Eq. (7.50) on the corresponding *dummy* inputs. However, the machine A' used in the emulation cannot detect that we are cheating because the inputs that A' gets (i.e., commitments to dummy values) are computationally indistinguishable from the correct inputs (i.e., commitments to values that correspond to the unknown input and random-tape of the corresponding honest party).

  Finally, B concatenates the emulation of the authenticated-computation sub-protocol to the history of the execution of A. (Note that since the initiator of the authenticated-computation sub-protocol is honest, abort is not possible here, by definition of the first ideal model.)

---

[85] Recall that $\beta = (\overline{c}^i, \alpha_2)$, where $\overline{c}^i$ is the commitment produced by the VSS that was invoked by Party i, which is assumed to be the sender in the current message-transmission step, and α_2 equals the sequence of messages sent so far in the emulated execution of Π.

- In a message-transmission step by a dishonest party in Π, machine B first computes the message to be sent according to Π. This message is computed based on the input and random-tape determined (and recorded) in the emulation of the sharing phase of Π' and the messages received so far (in the execution of Π). Denote the resulting message by $\mathtt{msg}$. Machine B completes the execution of this step in Π by posting $\mathtt{msg}$ on the broadcast channel.

  Next, machine B proceeds in emulating the corresponding authenticated-computation sub-protocol of Π'. Firstly, machine B derives the ideal-model adversary, denoted A'. Invoking A' and emulating both the honest (ideal-model) parties and the trusted party, machine B produces an emulation of the corresponding execution of the authenticated-computation protocol. The input (for the transmitting party) used by B in this emulation equals the value recorded in the emulation of (the corresponding VSS in) the sharing phase of Π'.

  Note that this emulation (of the corresponding authenticated-computation sub-protocol of Π') either produces the very same message $\mathtt{msg}$ (or a pair $(\beta, \mathtt{msg})$ as above) or aborts the sender. In the latter case, we emulate the abort-handling procedure of Π', by using the corresponding VSS-randomization (as recorded in the sharing phase of Π'). In both cases, B concatenates the emulation of the authenticated-computation protocol (and possibly also the abort-handling procedure) to the history of the execution of A.

Note that each message-transmission step is implemented in polynomial-time, and each message posted is computed exactly as instructed by Π. (We stress again that the emulation of an aborting event in Π' does not result in aborting the execution of any party in Π.)

Output: Machine B just outputs whatever machine A outputs given the execution history composed (or actually emulated) as in the previous steps.

Clearly, machine B (described here) implements a second-augmented semi-honest behavior with respect to Π. It is left to show that

$$\{\mathrm{REAL}_{\Pi',I,A}(\overline{x})\}_{\overline{x}} \stackrel{c}{\equiv} \{\mathrm{REAL}_{\Pi,I,B}(\overline{x})\}_{\overline{x}} \tag{7.60}$$

There are two differences between the two ensembles referred to in Eq. (7.60):

1. In the first distribution (i.e., $\mathrm{REAL}_{\Pi',(A,I)}(\overline{x})$), secure (in the first malicious model) protocols implementing VSS and authenticated computation (of Eq. $(7.56) - (7.59)$ and Eq. (7.50), respectively) are executed; whereas in the second distribution (i.e., $\mathrm{REAL}_{\Pi,(B,I)}(\overline{x})$), these executions are emulated using the corresponding ideal-model adversaries.
2. The emulation of Eq. (7.50) in $\mathrm{REAL}_{\Pi,(B,I)}(\overline{x})$ is performed with a potentially wrong input, specifically, with commitments to dummy values, rather than to the correct values.

However, these differences are computationally undetectable. ∎

Proof of Theorem 7.5.40: Given an m-ary functionality f, let Π be an m-party proto-col, as guaranteed by Theorem 7.5.33, for securely computing f in the *first* malicious model. (Actually, we merely need a protocol operating in the broadcast channel [rather than point-to-point] communication model.) We now apply the compiler of Construction 7.5.39 to Π and derive a protocol Π'. By Proposition 7.5.42, for any efficient real-model adversary A (for Π'), there exists an efficient admissible behavior (with respect to Π) in the second-augmented semi-honest model, denoted B, such that for every $I \subset [m]$ with $|I| < m/2$

$$\{\text{REAL}_{\Pi',I,A}(\overline{x})\}_{\overline{x}} \stackrel{c}{\equiv} \{\text{REAL}_{\Pi,I,B}(\overline{x})\}_{\overline{x}} \tag{7.61}$$

One key observation is that B constitutes a benign form of a real-model adversarial behavior with respect to Π (which is certainly allowed by the first malicious model). Specifically, the malicious behavior of B amounts to replacing inputs and random-tapes arbitrarily, and executing Π with these replaced values and without aborting any party. Thus, by the security of Π (in the first malicious model), the real-model adversary B can be emulated by an ideal-model adversary C that operates in the first ideal model (and so may potentially abort parties). However, since B does not abort parties, then neither does C (except with negligible probability). It follows that C is essentially an admissible ideal-model adversary for the second malicious party, or, more accurately, C behaves in a way that is statistically close to a second ideal-model adversary C' (which behaves as C except that it never aborts). Combining Eq. (7.61) with the latter observations, we obtain (for every $|I| < m/2$)

$$\{\text{REAL}_{\Pi',I,A}(\overline{x})\}_{\overline{x}} \stackrel{c}{\equiv} \{\text{REAL}_{\Pi,I,B}(\overline{x})\}_{\overline{x}}$$
$$\stackrel{c}{\equiv} \{\text{IDEAL}^{(1)}_{f,I,C}(\overline{x})\}_{\overline{x}}$$
$$\stackrel{s}{\equiv} \{\text{IDEAL}^{(2)}_{f,I,C'}(\overline{x})\}_{\overline{x}}$$

We are almost done. The only problem is that Π' operates in the communication model of a single broadcast channel. As in the proof of Theorem 7.5.33, this problem is resolved by applying the post-compiler (i.e., Proposition 7.5.19). ∎

7.6.* Perfect Security in the Private Channel Model

In this section, we present an alternative treatment of general secure multi-party protocols. Specifically, we assume the existence of private channels between each pair of parties and present protocols that are "perfectly secure" (i.e., perfectly emulate a trusted party), and we do so without relying on any intractability assumptions. However, security holds only in case the honest parties are in a strict majority, and thus the current treatment is not meaningful for the two-party case. Let us summarize the *Pros* and *Cons* of the current treatment in comparison to the treatment offered in Section 7.5:

PROS: Abstracting away computational issues. In particular:

1. Making no intractability assumptions.
2. Emulating a trusted party in a perfect sense (rather than in a computationally indistinguishable sense), even with respect to computationally unbounded adversaries.

CONS: Limited applicability. In particular:

1. A strict majority of honest parties is required (even for withstanding semi-honest adversaries). Thus, the current treatment is inapplicable to the two-party case.
2. Perfectly private channels are postulated to exist.

Again, our ultimate goal is to design protocols that withstand any feasible adversarial behavior, and again we proceed in two steps: first dealing with the semi-honest model and next with the malicious model. However, here, protocols for the malicious model are derived by extending the ideas that underlie the semi-honest protocols, rather than by compiling the latter.

7.6.1. Definitions

We consider both the semi-honest and the malicious models, where in both cases we refer to explicit bounds on the number of dishonest parties. Furthermore, in both cases, we consider a communication network consisting of point-to-point channels that cannot be wire-taped by the adversary. Finally, in both models, we require the relevant probability ensembles to be statistically indistinguishable, rather than (only) computationally indistinguishable.

Security in the Semi-Honest Model. The following definition is derived from Definition 7.5.1 by restricting the number of dishonest parties and strengthening the indistinguishability requirement.

Definition 7.6.1 (t-privacy of m-party protocols): *Let f be an m-ary functionality, and Π be an m-party protocol for computing f. As in Definition 7.5.1, we denote the joint-view of the parties in $I \subseteq [m]$ by* $\text{VIEW}_I^\Pi(\overline{x})$, *and the corresponding output sequence of all parties by* $\text{OUTPUT}^\Pi(\overline{x})$. *We say that Π t-privately computes f if there exists a probabilistic polynomial-time algorithm, denoted S, such that for every $I \subset [m]$ of cardinality at most t, it holds that*

$$\{(S(I, \overline{x}_I, f_I(\overline{x})), f(\overline{x}))\}_{\overline{x} \in (\{0,1\}^*)^m}$$
$$\stackrel{\text{s}}{\equiv} \{(\text{VIEW}_I^\Pi(\overline{x}), \text{OUTPUT}^\Pi(\overline{x}))\}_{\overline{x} \in (\{0,1\}^*)^m} \tag{7.62}$$

where $\overline{x}_I$ and f_I denote projections of the corresponding m-ary sequence on the coordinates in I. In case the ensembles in Eq. (7.62) are identically distributed, we say that the emulation is perfect.

We stress that Eq. (7.62) requires statistical indistinguishability, whereas the analogue requirement in Definition 7.5.1 is of computational indistinguishability. As in

Definition 7.5.1, the view of parties in I does *not* include messages sent among parties in $\bar{I} \stackrel{\text{def}}{=} [m] \setminus I$.

Security in the Malicious Model. Analogously, the following definition is derived from Definition 7.5.4 by restricting the number of dishonest parties, disallowing wire-tapping, and strengthening the indistinguishability requirement. Recall that Definition 7.5.4 refers to security in the *second* malicious model, which is reflected in the choice of the ideal model. We further strengthen the definition by allowing computationally unbounded real-model adversaries, and by requiring the corresponding ideal-model adversaries to be of "comparable complexity" (i.e., have polynomially related running time). Specifically, we say that algorithm B has comparable complexity to algorithm A if there exists a polynomial p such that for every y, it holds that $\text{time}_B(y) \leq p(\text{time}_A(y))$, where $\text{time}_A(y)$ (resp., $\text{time}_B(y)$) denotes the number of steps taken by A (resp., B) on input y.

Definition 7.6.2 (*t-security of m-party protocols*): *Let f, Π, and $\text{IDEAL}^{(2)}_{f,I,B(z)}(\bar{x})$ be exactly as in Definition 7.5.4. The real-model adversary is defined as in Definitions 7.5.3 and 7.5.4, except that here, the real-model adversary A does not see messages sent among honest parties (i.e., parties in $\bar{I}$). We say that Π* t-securely computes f *if for every probabilistic algorithm A* (representing a real-model adversary strategy), *there exists a probabilistic algorithm of comparable complexity B* (representing an ideal-model adversary strategy), *such that for every $I \subset [m]$ of cardinality at most t, it holds that*

$$\{\text{IDEAL}^{(2)}_{f,I,B(z)}(\bar{x})\}_{\bar{x},z} \stackrel{\text{s}}{\equiv} \{\text{REAL}_{\Pi,I,A(z)}(\bar{x})\}_{\bar{x},z} \tag{7.63}$$

In case the ensembles in Eq. (7.63) are identically distributed, we say that the emulation is perfect.

We stress that Eq. (7.63) requires statistical indistinguishability, whereas the analogue requirement in Definition 7.5.4 is of computational indistinguishability. More importantly, we make no computational restrictions regarding the real-model adversary, and require the corresponding ideal-model adversary to be of comparable complexity. The latter requirement is very important: It prevents obviously bad protocols (see Exercise 18), and it guarantees that Definition 7.6.2 is actually a strengthening of Definition 7.5.4 (see Exercise 19).

7.6.2. Security in the Semi-Honest Model

The following construction of t-private m-party protocols, for $t < m/2$, is a modification of the construction presented in Section 7.5.2 (which in turn generalized the construction presented in the two-party case [i.e., Section 7.3]). Recall that the core of these constructions is the privately computed *propagation of shares* of bits through a circuit that represents the desired computation. In the previous cases (see Sections 7.3 and 7.5.2), we used a very simple m-out-of-m secret-sharing scheme (i.e., a bit was shared by m random bits that sum up to the value of the secret bit). Here, we use the more sophisticated $(t + 1)$-out-of-m secret-sharing scheme of Construction 7.5.35 (i.e., a bit is shared by the values of a random degree t polynomial with free term that equals the value of the secret bit). Thus, our focus is on propagating these types of shares through the circuit, and on doing so via a t-private computation. Again, the heart of the construction is performing the propagation through a single multiplication gate.

Let us clarify this discussion by being more specific about the details. We fix some prime $p > m$ and consider polynomials of degree t over $GF(p)$.[86] Recall that the value of such a polynomial at $t + 1$ arbitrary (known) points allows for recovery of the polynomial and specifically its free term. On the other hand, the value of a random (degree t) polynomial at t arbitrary (known) points does not reveal information about the value of the free term of the polynomial. Thus, each party will share each of its input bits with all other parties, by uniformly selecting a random (degree t) polynomial with free term equal to the value of this bit, and hand to Party i the value of this polynomial at point i.

Suppose that the parties hold the shares of two $GF(p)$ values and wish to derive shares of the sum of these values, where all arithmetic operations refer to $GF(p)$. Then letting each party add the two shares it holds yields the desired shares. That is, suppose that the values u and v are shared using the (degree t) polynomials $a(\cdot)$ and $b(\cdot)$, such that $u = a(0)$ and $v = b(0)$, and Party i holds the shares $a_i = a(i)$ and $b_i = b(i)$. Then the $a_i + b_i$'s are shares of a polynomial $c(\cdot)$ that has free term $u + v$ (i.e., letting $c(z) = a(z) + b(z)$, it holds that $c(i) = a_i + b_i$ and $c(0) = u + v$). Furthermore, the degree of $c(\cdot)$ is at most t. Thus, we are able to propagate shares through an addition gate, and we do so in a totally private manner (because only local computations are used).

It is appealing to try to do the same in case of multiplication (rather than addition). Indeed, the entire argument goes through, except that the corresponding polynomial c may have a degree greater than t (but not more than $2t$). Thus, we need a more sophisticated way of propagating shares through multiplication gates. Using the same notations (as previously), we consider the following (randomized) process:

Construction 7.6.3 (t-private m-party protocol for propagating shares through a multiplication gate): *Recall that $t < m/2$, and so $2t \leq m - 1$.*

Input: *Party i enters with input (a_i, b_i), where $a_i = a(i)$ and $b_i = b(i)$ for degree t polynomials $a(\cdot)$ and $b(\cdot)$.*

The protocol itself proceeds as follows:

1. *For every i, Party i (locally) computes $c_i \leftarrow a_i \cdot b_i$.*

   Indeed, these c_i's are the values of the polynomial $c(z) \overset{\text{def}}{=} a(z) \cdot b(z)$ at the corresponding i's, and $c(0) = u \cdot v$. However, c may have degree $2t$ (rather than at most t).

2. *For every i, Party i shares c_i with all other parties. That is, Party i selects uniformly a polynomial q_i of degree t such that $q_i(0) = c_i$, and sends $q_i(j)$ to Party j, for every j.*

---

[86] Here and in the following, when we say a degree d polynomial, we actually mean a polynomial of degree at most d.

Motivation: *Extrapolation of the c_i's yields the value of $c(0) = u \cdot v$. In the following we will let each party perform the corresponding operation on the shares it obtained. We will show that this will yield shares with the desired properties.*

Recall that by the Extrapolation Theorem, *there exist constants $\gamma_1, ..., \gamma_m$ such that for every polynomial q of degree $m - 1$ it holds that*

$$q(0) = \sum_{i=1}^{m} \gamma_i q(i) \tag{7.64}$$

(Specifically, $\gamma_i = -(1)^{i+1} \cdot \binom{m}{i}$.)

3. *For every j, Party j (locally) computes $d_j \leftarrow \sum_{i=1}^{m} \gamma_i q_i(j)$, where $\gamma_1, ..., \gamma_m$ are the extrapolation constants satisfying Eq. (7.64), and $q_i(j)$ is the share that Party j received from Party i in Step 2.*

Output: *Party i exits with output d_i.*

It is quite clear that Construction 7.6.3 yields no information about u and v to any coalition of t (or fewer) parties. The reason is that the only new information obtained by t parties (i.e., t shares of each of the other c_i's) yields no information about the polynomials a and b (because it yields no information about these c_i's). It is also clear that every sequence of t of the d_i's is uniformly distributed (because the values of the q_i's at any t points are uniformly distributed). What is less clear is that the d_i's are indeed admissible shares of the desired value (i.e., $d_i = d(i)$ for some degree t polynomial d having free term $u \cdot v$). This fact will be established next.

Fact 7.6.4: *Let the d_i's be defined as in Construction 7.6.3, and $t < m/2$. Then there exists a degree t polynomial, d, such that $d(0) = a(0) \cdot b(0)$ and $d(i) = d_i$ for $i = 1, ..., m$.*

Proof: Consider the formal polynomial $q(z) \stackrel{\text{def}}{=} \sum_{i=1}^{m} \gamma_i q_i(z)$, where the q_i's are the polynomials selected at Step 2. Since each q_i has degree t, this holds also for q. For every $j = 1, ..., m$, by Step 3, we have $d_j = \sum_{i=1}^{m} \gamma_i q_i(j) = q(j)$, where the second equality is due to the definition of q. Finally, note that

$$q(0) = \sum_{i=1}^{m} \gamma_i q_i(0)$$

$$= \sum_{i=1}^{m} \gamma_i c_i$$

$$= \sum_{i=1}^{m} \gamma_i \cdot a(i) \cdot b(i)$$

$$= a(0) \cdot b(0)$$

where the second equality is by Step 2, the third equality is by Step 1, and the last equality is by the Extrapolation Theorem (applied to the $2t \leq m - 1$ degree polynomial $a(z) \cdot b(z)$). ∎

Conclusion. Using Fact 7.6.4, for $t < m/2$, one can show (see Exercise 23) that Construction 7.6.3 constitutes a t-private computation of the (partial) m-ary functionality

$$((a(1), b(1)), ..., (a(m), b(m))) \mapsto (r(1), ..., r(m)) \qquad (7.65)$$

where a and b are degree t polynomials and r is a uniformly distributed degree t polynomial with free term equal to $a(0) \cdot b(0)$. By a straightforward adaptation of Construction 7.5.10 and its analysis, it follows that any m-ary functionality can be t-privately reduced to Eq. (7.65). Finally, by using a suitable Composition Theorem, we obtain:

Theorem 7.6.5: *For $t < m/2$, any m-ary functionality is t-privately computable. Furthermore, the emulation is perfect.*

In contrast, very few m-ary functionalities are t-privately computable for $t \geq m/2$. In particular, the only m-ary Boolean-valued functions that are $m/2$-privately computable are linear combinations of Boolean-valued functions of the individual inputs (i.e., $f(x_1, ..., x_m) = \sum_{i=1}^{m} c_i f^{(i)}(x_i) \bmod 2$).

7.6.3. Security in the Malicious Model

In order to deal with the malicious model, we replace Construction 7.6.3 with a more robust protocol that t-securely computes Eq. (7.65). In particular, the protocol should withstand a possible modification of t of the inputs (which, in particular, may not fit the domain of the functionality as partially defined earlier). This turns out to be possible, provided $t < m/3$, and so we get:

Theorem 7.6.6: *For $t < m/3$, any m-ary functionality is t-securely computable. Furthermore, the emulation is perfect.*

We briefly sketch the ideas that underlie the proof of Theorem 7.6.6. Let us first assume that $t < m/4$, and note that Steps 2–3 of Construction 7.6.3 constitute a t-private computation of the (partial) m-ary functionality

$$(c(1), ..., c(m)) \mapsto (r(1), ..., r(m)) \qquad (7.66)$$

where c is a degree $2t$ polynomial and r is a uniformly distributed degree t polynomial with free term equal to $c(0)$. We wish to t-securely compute Eq. (7.66). Let us first consider the related task of t-securely computing $c(0)$. Construction 7.5.10 suggests that $c(0)$ can be computed by extrapolation of the $c(i)$'s, and that extrapolation is a linear function, which (as such) can be t-privately computed (see Exercise 20). However, when some parties are malicious, simple extrapolation will fail. What we need is a "robust extrapolation" procedure, which corresponds to error correction of Reed-Solomon codes, which in turn is a linear function of the given sequence.

Specifically, this task is to find the free term of the unique degree $2t$ polynomial (i.e., c) that fits at least $m - t$ of the inputs (i.e., the correct $c(i)$'s), and we can perform this task in a t-secure manner. (The desired polynomial is indeed unique, because otherwise we get two different degree $2t$ polynomials that agree on $m - 2t \geq 2t + 1$ of the inputs.) Finally, observe that the parties can t-securely generate shares of a random degree t polynomial with free term equal to zero. Combining the two linear computations, one obtains the desired t-secure implementation of Eq. (7.66), provided that $t < m/4$.

In order to handle the case $m/4 \leq t < m/3$, we have to work directly with Eq. (7.65), rather than with Eq. (7.66); that is, we use the fact that the parties actually hold the shares of two degree t polynomials, rather than only the product of these shares (which corresponds to shares of a degree $2t$ polynomial).

7.7. Miscellaneous

7.7.1.* Three Deferred Issues

In this section, we briefly discuss three important issues that were avoided (for the sake of simplicity) in previous sections.

7.7.1.1. Partial Fairness, or On Exchanging Secrets

As commented upon in Section 7.2.3, in general, no two-party protocol can guarantee *perfect fairness;* that is, it cannot be guaranteed that one party obtains its desired output if and only if the other party obtains its own desired output. Intuitively, an adversary may always abort at the first possible time at which it obtains its output, and this means that one of the parties may obtain the desired output while the other party does not quite get its own output. In fact, in the specific (two-party and multi-party) protocols that we have presented, this phenomenon occurs in an extreme sense; that is, Party 1 gets the output before any other party gains any knowledge regarding its own output. As we will show, the severity of this phenomenon can be reduced (but, as shown in [65], cannot be totally eliminated). That is, "partial fairness" (alas, not "perfect fairness") may be achieved in some sense. In the rest of this section, we focus on two-party protocols, but similar treatment can be applied to multi-party protocols (lacking an honest majority).

A general framework for obtaining partial fairness consists of first computing shares of both desired outputs, and next gradually revealing pieces of these shares, such that a party reveals the next piece only if its counterpart has revealed the previous piece. The parties should be able to verify the correctness of the revealed pieces, which can be achieved by generating also commitments to these pieces (and asking the revealing party to also provide the corresponding decommitment information). Thus, for a functionality f, which without loss of generality satisfies $|f_1(x, y)| = |f_2(x, y)|$, we may proceed in two stages:

1. *The parties securely compute shares of the desired outputs of f.* Specifically, the parties securely compute the functionality

$$(x, y) \mapsto ((v_1 \oplus s_1, s_2, r_1, c), (s_1, v_2 \oplus s_2, r_2, c))$$

where $(v_1, v_2) \leftarrow f(x, y)$, the s_i's are uniformly distributed in $\{0, 1\}^{|v_i|}$, and $c \leftarrow \overline{C}_{r_1 \oplus r_2}(v_1, v_2)$, for uniformly distributed $r_1, r_2 \in \{0, 1\}^{|v_1, v_2|^2}$. Note that at this stage, each individual party obtains no knowledge of the desired outputs, but together they hold (verifiable) secrets (i.e., the $v_i \oplus s_i$'s and s_i's) that yield both outputs.

2. *The parties gradually exchange the secrets that they hold.* That is, Party 1 reveals pieces of s_2 in exchange for pieces of s_1 (revealed by Party 2), where one piece of s_2 is revealed per one piece of s_1. The pieces are revealed by using a secure computation of an adequate functionality. Suppose that Party i is supposed to obtain the piece $\pi_i(s_i)$, where π_i may be a (predetermined) Boolean function or a randomized process. Then the parties securely compute the functionality that maps $((a_1, a_2, \rho_1, \gamma_1), (b_1, b_2, \rho_2, \gamma_2))$ to $(\pi_1(b_1), \pi_2(a_2))$ if $\gamma_1 = \gamma_2 = \overline{C}_{\rho_1 \oplus \rho_2}(a_1 \oplus b_1, a_2 \oplus b_2)$ and to (λ, λ) otherwise. Indeed, each party enters this secure computation with the input it has received in the first stage; that is, Party 1 (resp., Party 2) enters with input $(v_1 \oplus s_1, s_2, r_1, c)$ (resp., $(s_1, v_2 \oplus s_2, r_2, c)$).

The entire approach (and, in particular, the gradual exchange of secrets) depends on a satisfactory definition of a *piece of a secret*. Such a definition should satisfy two properties: (1) Given sufficiently many pieces of a secret, one should be able to recover the secret, whereas (2) getting yet another piece of the secret contributes little to the knowledge of the secret. We admit that we do not know of a definition (of a piece of a secret) that is "uncontroversially satisfactory"; still, some suggestions (for what these pieces of information may be) seem quite appealing. For example, consider the randomized process π that maps the n-bit long secret $\sigma_1 \cdots \sigma_n$ to the n-bit long string $\tau_1 \cdots \tau_n$, such that $\tau_i = \sigma_i$ with probability $\frac{1}{2} + \varepsilon$ and $\tau_i = 1 - \sigma_i$ otherwise, for every i, independently.[87] Then each piece carries $O(n\varepsilon^2)$ bits of information, whereas after seeing t such pieces of the secret, one can guess it with success probability at least $1 - n \cdot \exp(-t\varepsilon^2)$, which for $t = O(n/\varepsilon^2)$ means practically obtaining the secret. However, if Party 1 knows that $s_1 \in \{0^n, 1^n\}$, whereas Party 2 only knows that $s_2 \in \{0, 1\}^n$, then $\pi(s_1)$ seems more meaningful to Party 1 than $\pi(s_2)$ is to Party 2. *Is it really so* or *is the proposed exchange actually fair?* Note that things are even more complex (than they seem), because the uncertainty of the parties is actually not information-theoretic but rather computational.

---

[87] An alternative randomized process π maps the n-bit string s to the random pair (r, b), such that r is uniformly distributed in $\{0, 1\}^n$ and $b \in \{0, 1\}$ equals the inner product (mod 2) of s and r with probability $\frac{1}{2} + \varepsilon$ (and the complementary value otherwise). In this case, each piece carries $O(\varepsilon^2)$ bits of information about s, whereas after seeing $O(n/\varepsilon^2)$ such pieces, one practically obtains s.

7.7.1.2. The Adaptive Model

The definitions presented in Section 7.5.1 referred to adversaries, called *non-adaptive*, that control a predetermined set of parties (which, of course, is not known to the honest parties).[88] In this section, we consider a stronger type of adversaries, called *adaptive,* that can select the parties that they control as the execution proceeds. To demonstrate the power of adaptive adversaries, consider an m-party protocol in which Party 1 uniformly selects an $m/3$-subset J of the parties, publicizes J, and shares its own input with the parties in J as a whole (i.e., it hands each Party j in J a random r_j such that $\sum_{j \in J} r_j$ equals its own input). Treating m as a parameter, this protocol (for computing nothing) is secure with respect to Definition 7.5.4, essentially because for every set I of fewer than $m/2$ parties, it holds that the probability that a random $m/3$-subset J is contained in I is exponentially vanishing in m. However, an adaptive adversary that selects the set of parties that it controls to equal the publicized set J obtains the input of Party 1 without controlling it (and, hence, demonstrates that the protocol is insecure with respect to adaptive adversaries).

In general, an adaptive adversary is one that can decide which parties to *corrupt* (i.e., seize control of) during the course of the execution of the protocol. Potentially, such an adaptive decision may be more beneficial to the adversary than an oblivious decision. Security in the adaptive model means that even an adaptive adversary cannot gain from the execution more than what is unavoidable (even in the presence of a trusted party).

To actually define security with respect to adaptive adversaries, we should first define an adequate ideal model, which corresponds to what is unavoidable when considering adaptive adversaries. The crucial point is that even in an ideal-model execution, the adversary may select the parties that it controls adaptively and based on the information it has gathered so far (i.e., the inputs of the parties controlled so far).[89] We stress that once the adversary seizes control of a party, it learns the party's initial input (and in the real model, it also learns its random-tape and the messages that this party has received so far).

When defining the result of such an ideal-model execution, we also include in it the set of parties that the adversary controls. The same is done when defining the result of the real-model execution. Consequently, when we require that the ideal-model execution can emulate the real-model execution, the executions must refer to the same (or computationally indistinguishable) sets of controlled parties. Actually, one should also consider the order in which the controlled parties are selected. To clarify this discussion, let use consider an extension of Definition 7.5.4 (i.e., the second malicious model) to the adaptive model.

Definition 7.7.1 (security in the malicious adaptive model, a sketch): *Let f and Π be as in Section 7.5.1, and t be a bound on the number of parties that the adversary is allowed to control* (e.g., $t < m/2$).

---

[88] The issue of adaptivity also arises, but in a more subtle way, in the case of two-party protocols.

[89] The non-adaptive model can be viewed as a special case in which the adversary selects the parties that it controls up-front, before learning any information regarding the current execution. But in general (in the adaptive model), only the choice of the first controlled party is oblivious of the execution.

- *A t-adaptive ideal-model adversary is a randomized process that operates in up-to $t + 1$ steps, which are partitioned into two main* phases. *In each step of the* first phase, *based on the information available to it, the adversary decides whether to seize control of another party or to move to the second phase. In the first case, the adversary also determines the identity of the new party to be controlled and obtains its local input. In the second case, the adversary invokes the trusted party and supplies the trusted party with inputs of its choice corresponding to the parties that it currently controls. At this point, the other parties supply the trusted party with their original inputs, and the trusted party determines the corresponding outputs and provides each party with its corresponding output, where the adversary receives all the outputs of parties that it controls.*[90]

  In each step of the second phase, *based on the information available to it, the adversary decides whether or not to seize control of another party and if so also determines its identity. Consequently, the adversary receives the local input and output of this party. The* joint computation in the ideal model, *under an adaptive adversary, is defined as the concatenation of the outputs of the uncontrolled parties, the adversary's output, and the sequence of the parties on which the adversary gained control.*

- *A t-adaptive real-model adversary is a randomized strategy that corresponds to an attack on the actual execution of the protocol. Such an adversary may adaptively select up to t parties it wishes to control, obtain their current view of the execution (as per Definition 7.2.1), and determine their actions. The adversary may select some parties before the actual execution starts, some parties during the actual execution, and some after it has terminated, as long as the total number of selected parties is at most t. The* joint computation in the real model, *under an adaptive adversary, is defined as the concatenation of the outputs of the uncontrolled parties, the adversary's output, and the sequence of the parties on which the adversary gained control.*

- *Protocol Π for computing f is called t-adaptively* secure *if for every feasible t-adaptive real-model adversary A, there exists a feasible t-adaptive ideal-model adversary B, such that the joint computation in the real model under A is computationally indistinguishable from the joint computation in the ideal model under B.*

We stress that in the real model, when the adversary seizes control of a party, it gets the party's view of the execution so far (where the party's view is as defined in Definition 7.2.1). In particular, the protocol's possible instructions to erase certain data does not affect the party's view, which always contains its input, its random-tape, and all messages it has received so far. A weaker notion of security postulates that when the adversary seizes control of a party, it only gets the current values of the party's local variables as determined by the protocol (in which case, the adversary does not obtain

---

[90] As in Definition 7.5.4 (and unlike in Definition 7.5.2), the trusted party always answers all parties; that is, the adversary has no option of preventing the trusted party from answering the honest parties. Recall that here the trusted party is invoked (by the adversary) at the time the adversary decides that it controls enough parties.

data that was explicitly erased by an instruction of the protocol). Our definitional choice is motivated by the fear that the past values of the party's local variables (i.e., the party's view as per Definition 7.2.1) may be available somewhere on its computing system; see analogous discussion in Section 7.2.2 (regarding the semi-honest model).

Theorem 7.7.2 (main results regarding adaptively secure protocols):

1. In the private channel model, *any m-ary functionality can be computed in a $\lfloor (m-1)/3 \rfloor$-adaptively secure manner. Furthermore, as in Theorem 7.6.6, the emulation is perfect.*
2. *Assuming the intractability of inverting RSA (or of the DLP), any m-ary functionality can be computed in a $\lfloor (m-1)/3 \rfloor$-adaptively secure manner,* even when the adversary can tap all communication lines.

Part 1 follows by extending the proof of Theorem 7.6.6, that is, by observing that the protocols used toward proving the latter result are in fact adaptively secure. Proving Part 2 is more problematic. In particular, a straightforward application of the pre-compiler described in Section 7.5.3.1 seems to fail. The source of trouble is that standard encryption schemes, which may be used to emulate *private* (point-to-point) channels over *ordinary* (point-to-point) channels, effectively "commit" to the single value that was sent (which is a problem because of messages sent between honest parties that are later corrupted by the adversary). Intuitively, the solution is to use non-standard encryption schemes (i.e., "non-committing" ones). The latter can be constructed using trapdoor permutations with certain additional properties.

7.7.1.3. Reactive Systems

Our treatment so far has focused on functionalities that represent standard (multi-party) computations, mapping (sequences of) inputs to (sequences of) outputs. A more general treatment may refer to (multi-party) reactive systems that iteratively respond to inputs presented from the outside. Furthermore, the functionalities of these reactive systems may depend on a (global) state that they maintain and update. This global state may not be known to any individual party (but is rather the concatenation of the local states that the individual parties maintain and update). Thus, we view (multi-party) reactive systems as iterating the following steps (for an a priori unbounded number of times):[91]

- Parties are given inputs for the current iteration; that is, in the j-th iteration Party i is given input $x_i^{(j)}$. In addition, there is a global state: The global state at the beginning of the j-th iteration is denoted $s^{(j)}$, where the initial global state is empty (i.e., $s^{(1)} = \lambda$).
- Depending on the current inputs and the global state, the parties are supposed to compute outputs for the current iteration, as well as update the global state. That is,

---

[91] As usual, the number of iterations (and the length of the inputs) must be polynomial in the security parameter. Furthermore, the length of the global state (at any time) must also be polynomial in the security parameter.

the outputs in iteration j are determined by the $x_i^{(j)}$'s, for all i's, and $s^{(j)}$. The new global state, $s^{(j+1)}$, is determined similarly (i.e., also based on $x_i^{(j)}$'s and $s^{(j)}$).

As it is an abstraction, one may think of the global state as being held by a trusted party. In other words, reactive systems are captured by reactive functionalities in which the trusted party maintains a state and interacts with the actual parties in iterations. Indeed, in each iteration, the trusted party obtains an input from each party, responds (as directed by the reactive functionality) with corresponding outputs, depending also on its state, and updates its state. Note that the latter formulation fits a definition of an ideal model (for computing the reactive functionality), whereas a (real-model) reactive protocol must emulate this augmented notion of a trusted party. Thus, the reactive protocol should emulate the iterative computation of outputs *while maintaining the state of the imaginary trusted party*. Indeed, it is natural to have the real-model parties use a secret-sharing scheme in order to maintain the latter state (such that the state remains unknown to individual parties and even to a bounded number of dishonest parties). In fact, we need to use a verifiable secret-sharing scheme (see Section 7.5.5.1), because dishonest parties should be prevented from (illegally) modifying the (system's) state (except from the predetermined effect of the choice of their own inputs).

This discussion suggests that the secure implementation of reactive functionalities can be reduced to the secure implementation of ordinary (i.e., non-reactive) functionalities. For example, we refer to security in the second malicious model, as defined in Definition 7.5.4 (for ordinary functionalities). That is, we postulate that a majority of the parties are honest and require that the dishonest parties cannot (effectively) abort the execution. In such a case, we use a verifiable secret-sharing scheme in which only a majority of the pieces yield the secret. Once a verifiable secret-sharing scheme is fixed and the (system's) state is shared using it, the computation of each iteration of the reactive system can be cast as an ordinary functionality. The latter maps sequences of the form $((x_1, s_1), ..., (x_m, s_m))$, where x_i denotes the current input of Party i and s_i denotes its share of the current state, to the sequence $((y_1, r_1), ..., (y_m, r_m))$, where y_i denotes the next output of Party i and r_i denotes its share of the updated state.

We conclude that the results regarding secure computation of ordinary (i.e., non-reactive) computations can be extended to reactive systems (thus obtaining secure implementations of the latter).

7.7.2.* Concurrent Executions

A natural problem regarding cryptographic protocol is whether (or to what extent) they preserve their security when executed concurrently. The problems that arise with respect to the preservation of zero-knowledge (see Section C.5.1) are merely an indication to the type of problems that we may encounter. The lesson to be learned (even from that brief discussion) is that *an adversary attacking several concurrent executions of the same protocol may be able to cause more harm than by attacking a single execution* (or several sequential executions) of the same protocol.

7.7.2.1. Definitions

One may say that a protocol is concurrently secure if whatever the adversary may obtain by invoking and controlling parties in real *concurrent executions of the protocol* is also obtainable by a corresponding adversary that controls corresponding parties making *concurrent functionality calls* to a trusted party (in a corresponding ideal model). More generally, one may consider concurrent executions of many sessions of *several* protocols, and say that a *set of protocols* is concurrently secure if whatever the adversary may obtain by invoking and controlling such real concurrent executions is also obtainable by a corresponding adversary that invokes and controls concurrent calls to a trusted party (in a corresponding ideal model). Consequently, a protocol is said to be secure with respect to concurrent compositions if adding this protocol to *any set* of concurrently secure protocols yields a set of concurrently secure protocols.

A much more appealing approach has been recently suggested by Canetti [51]. Loosely speaking, he suggests considering a protocol to be secure (hereafter referred to as *environmentally secure*)[92] only if it remains secure when executed within any (feasible) environment. The notion of an environment is a generalization of the notion of an auxiliary-input; in a sense, the environment is an auxiliary oracle (or rather a state-dependent oracle) that the adversary may access. In particular, the environment may represent other executions of various protocols that are taking place concurrently (to the execution that we consider). We stress that the environment is not supposed to assist the proper execution of the protocol (and, in fact, honest parties merely obtain their inputs from it and return their outputs to it). In contrast, potentially, the environment may assist the adversary in attacking the execution. Following the simulation paradigm, we say that a protocol is environmentally secure if any feasible *real-model adversary attacking the protocol, with the assistance of any feasible environment,* can be emulated by a corresponding *ideal-model adversary that uses the same environment,* while making similar queries to the environment. In the following formulation, the environment is implemented by a (non-uniform) family of polynomial-size circuits, and is also responsible for providing the parties with inputs and for trying to distinguish the real-model execution from the ideal-model execution.

Definition 7.7.3 (Environmentally Secure Protocols, a rough sketch): *Let f be an m-ary functionality and Π be an m-party protocol, and consider the following real and ideal models:*

- *As usual, a* real-model *adversary controls some of the parties in an execution of the protocol Π. In addition to executing Π, all parties can communicate with an arbitrary interactive process, which is called an* environment. *Honest parties only communicate with the environment before the execution starts and when it ends; they merely obtain their inputs from the environment and pass their outputs to it. In contrast, dishonest parties* (controlled by the adversary) *may communicate freely with the environment and do so concurrently with the entire execution of Π.*

---

[92] The term used in [51] is *Universally Composable*, but we believe that a reasonable sense of "universal composability" is only a corollary of the suggested definition.

- *An* ideal-model *adversary controls some of the parties in an ideal computation assisted by a trusted party that behaves according to the functionality f. In addition, all parties can communicate with an environment* (as in the real model). *Indeed, the dishonest parties may communicate extensively with the environment before and after their single communication with the trusted party, whereas the honest parties merely obtain their inputs from the environment and pass their outputs to it.*

We say that Π *is an environmentally secure protocol for computing f if for every probabilistic polynomial-time real-model adversary A there exists a probabilistic polynomial-time ideal-model adversary B, such that for any subset $I \subset [m]$ of adequate cardinality,[93] no family of polynomial-size circuits $E = \{E_n\}_{n \in \mathbb{N}}$ can distinguish the case in which it interacts with parties in the real-model execution of Π under adversary (I, A) from the case in which it interacts with parties in the ideal-model computation of f under adversary (I, B). Schematically,*

$$\{\text{IDEAL}_{f,I,B(1^n),E_n}\}_{n \in \mathbb{N}} \stackrel{\text{c}}{\equiv} \{\text{REAL}_{\Pi,I,A(1^n),E_n}\}_{n \in \mathbb{N}}$$

where $\text{IDEAL}_{f,I,B(1^n),E_n}$ (resp., $\text{REAL}_{\Pi,I,A(1^n),E_n}$) *denotes the output of E_n after interacting with the ideal-model* (resp., real-model) *execution under* (I, B) (resp., (I, A)).

As hinted earlier, the environment may account for other executions of various protocols that are taking place concurrently with the main execution being considered. Definition 7.7.3 implies that such environments cannot distinguish the real execution from an ideal one. This means that anything that the real-model adversary gains from the execution of the protocol and any environment (representing other concurrent executions) can also be obtained by an adversary operating in the ideal model and having access to the same environment. Thus, each *single* execution of an environmentally secure protocol can be replaced by an ideal oracle call to the corresponding functionality, without affecting the other concurrent executions. Furthermore, one can *simultaneously* replace all these concurrent executions by ideal oracle calls and use a hybrid argument to show that the behavior is maintained. (One needs to use the fact that a single replacement does not affect the other concurrent executions, even in case some of the other executions are in the real model and the rest are in the ideal model.) It follows that *environmentally secure protocols are secure with respect to concurrent compositions* [51]. We wonder whether the reverse direction holds.

7.7.2.2. Constructions

The main positive result currently known is that environmentally secure protocols for any functionality can be constructed for settings in which more than two-thirds of the active parties are honest (cf. [51]). This holds unconditionally for the private-channel model and under standard assumptions (e.g., allowing the construction of public-key encryption schemes) for the standard model (i.e., without private channel).

---

[93] Thus, the definition should actually specify an additional parameter bounding the number of parties that may be controlled by the adversary.

The immediate consequence of this result is that general environmentally secure multi-party computation is possible, provided that more than two-thirds of the parties are honest.

In contrast, general environmentally secure *two-party* computation is not possible (in the standard sense).[94] Still, one can salvage general environmentally secure two-party computation in the following reasonable model: Consider a network that contains servers that are willing to participate (as "helpers," possibly for a payment) in computations initiated by a set of (two or more) users. Now, suppose that two users wishing to conduct a secure computation can agree on a set of servers such that each user believes that more than two-thirds of the servers (in this set) are honest. Then, with the active participation of this set of servers, the two users can compute any functionality in an environmentally secure manner.

Another reasonable model where general environmentally secure *two-party* computation is possible is the shared random-string model [59]. In this model, all parties have access to a universal random string (of length related to the security parameter). We stress that the entity trusted to post this universal random string is not required to take part in any execution of any protocol, and that all executions of all protocols may use the same universal random string.

7.7.3. Concluding Remarks

In this chapter, we have presented a host of definitions of security for multi-party protocols (especially for the case of more than two parties). Furthermore, some of these definitions are incomparable to others (i.e., they neither imply the others nor are implied by them), and there seems to be no single definition that may be crowned as the central one.

For example, as stated in Section 7.5.1.3, the security definitions for the two malicious (multi-party) models (i.e., Definitions 7.5.3 and 7.5.4) are incomparable and there is no generic reason to prefer one over the other. Actually, one could formulate a natural definition that implies both Definitions 7.5.3 and 7.5.4. We refer to waiving the bound on the number of dishonest parties in Definition 7.5.4 (or, equivalently, eliminating the abort as an admissible option in the ideal model underlying Definition 7.5.3). That is, the resulting definition is free of the annoying restrictions (or provisions) that were introduced in each of the previous definitions. The "only" problem with the resulting definition is that it cannot be satisfied (in general), whereas each of the previous definitions could be satisfied. Thus, for the first time in this work, we have reached a situation in which a natural (and general) definition cannot be satisfied, and we are forced to choose between two weaker alternatives, where each of these alternatives carries fundamental disadvantages (beyond the fact that security holds only with respect to probabilistic polynomial-time adversaries).

In general, the current chapter carries a stronger flavor of compromise (i.e., recognizing inherent limitations and settling for a restricted meaningful goal) than previous

---

[94] Of course, some specific two-party computations do have environmentally secure protocols. See [51] for several important examples (e.g., key exchange).

chapters. In contrast to the impression given in other parts of this work, it is now obvious that we cannot get all that we may want. Instead, we should study the alternatives and go for the one that best suits our real needs.

Indeed, as stated in the preface, the fact that we can define a cryptographic goal does not mean that we can satisfy it as defined. In case we cannot satisfy the initial definition, we should search for acceptable relaxations that can be satisfied. These relaxations should be defined in a clear manner so that it would be obvious what they achieve and what they fail to achieve. Doing so will allow a sound choice of the relaxation to be used in a specific application. That is, the choice will have to be a circumstantial rather than a generic one. This seems to be a good point at which to end the current work.

A good compromise is one in which
the most important interests of all parties are satisfied.
Adv. Klara Goldreich-Ingwer (1912–2004)

7.7.4. Historical Notes

The main results presented in this chapter (i.e., Theorems 7.4.1 and 7.5.15) are due to Yao [191] and to Goldreich, Micali, and Wigderson [117, 118], treating the two-party and multi-party cases, respectively. Unfortunately, the original papers do not provide a satisfactory presentation of these results. In particular, these papers lack adequate definitions of security (which were developed only later) and provide only rough sketches of the constructions and no proofs of their security. Still, the conference version of [117] provides a rough sketch of the compilation of protocols for the semi-honest model into protocols for the malicious model, by using zero-knowledge proofs (which are the main focus of [117]) to "force" malicious parties to behave in a semi-honest manner. Yao's work [191] presents a construction that can be used to derive two-party protocols for privately computing any desirable functionality, whereas the second paper of Goldreich et. al. [118] presents a different construction for the multi-party case.

Our presentation reverses the chronological order (in which these results were discovered). Firstly, our treatment of the two-party case is derived, via some degeneration, from the treatment of the multi-party case (in [117, 118]). Secondly, we start by treating the semi-honest models and only later compile protocols for this model into protocols for the malicious models. We note that (following [118]) our presentation of the main protocols is essentially symmetric, whereas Yao's original protocol for the two-party case [191] is asymmetric (with respect to the two parties). The latter asymmetry has its own merits as demonstrated in [27, 165, 143].

In treating the semi-honest model, we follow the framework of Goldreich, Micali, and Wigderson [118], while adapting important simplifications due to [129] and [120]. In presenting the "semi-honest to malicious" compilers (or the paradigm of "forcing" semi-honest behavior), we follow the outline provided in [117, FOCS Version, Sec. 4] and [118, Sec. 5]. We comment that the original sources (i.e., [117, 118]) are very terse, and that full details were only provided in [107]. Our treatment differs from [107] in using a higher level of modularity, which is supported by composition theorems for the malicious models.

As stated earlier, a satisfactory definitional treatment of secure multi-party computation was provided after the presentation of the constructions of [117, 118, 191]. The basic approach was developed by Micali and Rogaway [157] and Beaver [10, 11],[95] and reached maturity in Canetti's work [50], which provides a relatively simple, flexible, and comprehensive treatment of the (basic) definitions of secure multi-party computation. In particular, the composition theorems that we use are essentially taken from [50].

A variety of cryptographic tools is used in establishing the main results of this chapter. Firstly, we mention the prominent role of Oblivious Transfer in the protocols developed for the semi-honest model.[96] An Oblivious Transfer protocol was first suggested by Rabin [172], but our actual definition and implementation follow the ideas of Even, Goldreich, and Lempel [84] (as further developed in the proceedings version of [117]). Several ingredients play a major role in the compilation of protocols secure in the semi-honest model into generally secure protocols (for the malicious models). These include *commitment schemes, zero-knowledge proofs-of-knowledge, verifiable secret sharing* (introduced by Chor, Goldwasser, Micali, and Awerbuch [63]), and *secure coin-flipping* (introduced by Blum [37]).

The Private Channel Model. In contrast to the bulk of this chapter (as well as the bulk of the entire work), the private channel model (treated in Section 7.6) allows the presentation of results that do not rely on intractability assumptions. These results (e.g., Theorem 7.6.6) were obtained by Ben-Or, Goldwasser, and Wigderson [34] and Chaum, Crépeau, and Damgård [62]. These works were done after the results of Yao [191] and Goldreich, Micali, and Wigderson [117, 118] were known, with the explicit motivation of obtaining results that do not rely on intractability assumptions. Our presentation is based on [34] (cf. [97]). The essential role of the bound on the number of dishonest parties (even in the semi-honest model) was studied in [64] and subsequent works.

7.7.5. Suggestions for Further Reading

As hinted, Yao's alternative treatment of the two-party case offers some advantages over the treatment presented in Section 7.3. A sketch of Yao's construction is provided in Section 7.1.3.2. For more details, see [177].

---

[95] The approach of Goldwasser and Levin [121] is more general: It avoids the definition of security (with respect to a given functionality) and defines instead a notion of *protocol robustness*. Loosely speaking, a protocol is robust if whatever an arbitrary malicious adversary can obtain by attacking it can also be obtained by a very benign adversarial behavior.

[96] Subsequent results by Kilian [137] further demonstrate the importance of Oblivious Transfer in this context.

The aforementioned results were originally obtained using protocols that use a polynomial number of rounds. In some cases, subsequent works obtained secure *constant*-round protocols (e.g., in the case of multi-party computations with honest majority [27], and in the case of two-party computations allowing abort [143]).

We have mentioned (e.g., in Section 7.7.1.1) the impossibility of obtaining fairness in secure computations without an honest majority. These statements are backed by the impossibility of implementing a fair two-party coin-toss, as proven in [65].

We have briefly discussed the notion of adaptive adversaries. A more detailed discussion of the definitions is provided in [50], which builds on [49]. For a proof of Theorem 7.7.2, the reader is referred to [49, 53]. For a study of adaptive versus non-adaptive security, the reader is referred to [52].

Our treatment of multi-party protocols assumes a synchronous network with point-to-point channels between every pair of parties. Results for asynchronous communication and arbitrary networks of point-to-point channels were presented in [33, 49] and [78], respectively.

General secure multi-party computation in a model of transient adversarial behavior was considered in [166]. In this model, the adversary may seize control of each party during the protocol's execution, but can never control more than (say) 10 percent of the parties at any point in time. We comment that schemes secure in this model were later termed "proactive" (cf., [57]).

Whenever we have restricted the adversary's control of parties, we have done so by bounding the cardinality of the set of controlled parties. It is quite natural to consider arbitrary restrictions on the set of controlled parties (i.e., that this set belongs to a family of sets against which security is guaranteed). The interested reader is referred to [131].

For further discussion of Byzantine Agreement, see any standard textbook on Distributed Computing (e.g., [3, 147]). We mention that whereas plain m-party Byzantine Agreement can tolerate at most $\lfloor (m - 1)/3 \rfloor$ malicious parties, Authenticated Byzantine Agreement can tolerate any number of malicious parties (see Construction 7.5.17, which follows [80]). The problems arising when composing Authenticated Byzantine Agreement are investigated in [144].

7.7.6. Open Problems

Recall that by Theorem 7.5.12, one can privately reduce any functionality to Oblivious Transfer. Furthermore, the compilation of protocols that are secure in the semi-honest model into protocols that are secure in the malicious models only requires one-way functions and private channels, whereas the latter can be emulated using secure communication protocols (e.g., secure public-key encryption schemes). Since Oblivious Transfer implies the existence of the latter (see Exercise 7), general secure computation is reducible to Oblivious Transfer. Thus, determining the complexity assumptions required for the implementation of Oblivious Transfer seems to be of key importance. In particular, we have shown that Oblivious Transfer can be implemented using enhanced trapdoor permutations (see Proposition 7.3.6). We wonder whether the enhanced requirement can be omitted (i.e., whether ordinary trapdoor permutations may suffice).[97] For further discussion of enhanced trapdoor permutations, see Section C.1 in Appendix C.

7.7.7. Exercises

Exercise 1: *Oblivious sampling:* Suppose that both parties hold a function (or circuit) that defines a distribution in the natural way and wish to obtain a sample from this distribution without letting any party learn the corresponding pre-image. Cast this problem as one of securely computing a corresponding functionality, treating differently the case in which the function (or circuit) is fixed and the case in which it is given as input to both parties. Consider also the case in which only the first party is to obtain the output.

Exercise 2: *Oblivious signing:* In continuation of Exercise 1, consider the case in which the distribution to be sampled is determined by the inputs of both parties. For example, consider the task of *oblivious signing* in which one party wishes to obtain the signature of the second party to some document without revealing the document to the signer (i.e., the document is the input of the first party, whereas the signing-key is the input of the second party).

Exercise 3: *Privacy and Correctness:* Referring to the discussion that follows Definition 7.2.6, consider the following definitions of (partial) privacy and correctness (with respect to malicious adversaries). Partial privacy is defined as a restriction of Definition 7.2.6 to the adversary's component of the random variables $\text{REAL}_{\Pi,\overline{A}(z)}(x, y)$ and $\text{IDEAL}_{f,\overline{B}(z)}(x, y)$, whereas partial correctness coincides with a restriction of Definition 7.2.6 to the honest party's component of these random variables.

1. Show that both properties are implied by Definition 7.2.6, but that even their combination does not imply Definition 7.2.6.
2. Why were both properties qualified by the term "partial"?

> **Guideline (Item 1):** Note that computational indistinguishability of ensembles of pairs implies computational indistinguishability of the ensembles resulting by projection to each coordinate, but the converse does not necessarily hold.

> **Guideline (Item 2):** This is related to the need to use the general formulation of Definition 7.2.1 for randomized functionalities; see the discussion that follows Definition 7.2.1.

Exercise 4: *On the importance of the length convention:* Show that if the equal-length convention is omitted from definitions like Definition 7.2.1 and 7.2.6, then they cannot be satisfied for many natural functionalities. That is, consider these definitions when the ensembles are indexed by the set of all pairs of strings, rather than by the set of pairs of equal-length strings.

---

[97] Partial progress toward this goal is reported in Haitner's work "Implementing Oblivious Transfer using collection of dense trapdoor permutations" (proceedings of the first *Theory of Cryptography Conference*, 2004).

Guideline: (Here, privacy and security refer to the notions obtained when omitting the equal-length convention.) Show that the functionality $(x, y) \mapsto (f(x, y), f(x, y))$, where $f(x, y) \overset{\text{def}}{=} 1$ if $|x| = |y|$ and $f(x, y) \overset{\text{def}}{=} 0$ otherwise, cannot be *privately computed*. Show that $(x, y) \mapsto (|y|, |x|)$ can be *privately computed* but tthat he simple protocol in which Party 1 sends $|x|$ to Party 2 (and Party 2 sends $|y|$ to Party 1) fails to *securely compute* it. Challenge: Try to show that the latter functionality cannot be securely computed.

Exercise 5: *Transitivity of privacy reductions:* Show that if f is privately reducible to f', and f' is privately reducible to f'', then f is privately reducible to f''. Note that Theorem 7.3.3 is obtained as a special case (e.g., by setting f'' to be the identity mapping).

Guideline: Generalize the proof of Theorem 7.3.3. Specifically, let $\Pi^{f|f'}$ (resp., $\Pi^{f'|f''}$) be an oracle-aided protocol for f (resp., f') using oracle f' (resp., f''). Composing these two protocols, obtain and analyze the oracle-aided protocol $\Pi = \Pi^{f|f''}$.

Exercise 6: *Variants of Oblivious Transfer:* In continuation of Section 7.3.2, consider the following two variants of Oblivious Transfer.

1. For functions $k, \ell : \mathbb{N} \to \mathbb{N}$, consider the extension of 1-out-of-k Oblivious Transfer to $k(n)$ secrets each of length $\ell(n)$, where n is the security parameter.
2. For a function $\ell : \mathbb{N} \to \mathbb{N}$, consider the Oblivious Transfer of a single $\ell(n)$-bit long secret (denoted σ) that is to be delivered with probability $1/2$; that is, the randomized functionality that maps (σ, λ) to (λ, σ) with probability $1/2$ and to (λ, λ) otherwise.

Assuming that k and ℓ are polynomially bounded and efficiently computable, present privacy reductions between all these variants. Specifically, show a privacy reduction of the extended 1-out-of-k Oblivious Transfer to the original 1-out-of-2 Oblivious Transfer of bits, and between 1-out-of-2 Oblivious Transfer of ℓ-bit long secrets and Oblivious Transfer of a single $\ell(n)$-bit long secret.

Guideline: Note that you are asked only to present oracle-aided protocols that are secure in the semi-honest model. The only non-obvious reduction is from 1-out-of-2 Oblivious Transfer to single-secret Oblivious Transfer (OT), presented next. The first party randomly selects $r_1, r_2 \in \{0, 1\}^{\ell(n)}$, and the parties invoke OT twice where the first party inputs r_1 in the first time and r_2 in the second time. If the second party wishes to obtain the i-th secret, for $i \in \{1, 2\}$, then it says OK if and only if it has obtained r_i but not r_{3-i}. Otherwise, the parties repeat the experiment. Once the second party says OK, the first party sends it the pair $(\sigma_1 \oplus r_1, \sigma_2 \oplus r_2)$, where the σ_j's are the actual secrets.

Exercise 7: *Oblivious Transfer implies secure communication protocols:* A secure communication protocol is a two-party protocol that allows the parties to communicate in secrecy even when the communication line is tapped by an adversary (see Exercise 1 of Chapter 5). Show that any 1-out-of-2 Oblivious Transfer (with security with respect to the semi-honest model) implies the existence of a secure communication protocol. Recall that the latter implies the existence of one-way functions.

> **Guideline:** To transmit a bit σ, the sender invokes the 1-out-of-2 Oblivious Transfer with input $(\sigma, 0)$, while the receiver sets its input to 1 and gets σ (i.e., the sender's first bit in the OT). Observe that "privacy with respect to the sender" implies that (the sender and thus also) the adversary cannot distinguish the case where the receiver enters 1 from the case where it enters 2. Likewise, "privacy with respect to the receiver" implies that, in the (fictitious) case where the receiver enters 2, the adversary (like the receiver) cannot tell whether the sender enters $(0, 0)$ or $(1, 0)$. Thus, also in the (real) case where the receiver enters 1, the adversary cannot tell whether the sender enters $(0, 0)$ or $(1, 0)$.

Exercise 8: *Privately reducing OT to the functionality of Eq.* $(7.17) - (7.18)$: Show that 1-out-of-2 Oblivious Transfer can be privately reduced to the functionality of Eq. $(7.17) - (7.18)$.

> **Guideline:** Reduce 1-out-of-2 OT to $((s_1, s_2), (r_1, r_2)) \mapsto (\lambda, s_1 r_1 + s_2 r_2)$, and reduce the latter to Eq. $(7.17) - (7.18)$.

Exercise 9: *Alternative analysis of Construction 7.3.7:* The said construction can be decoupled into two reductions. First, the functionality of Eq. $(7.17) - (7.18)$ is reduced to the deterministic functionality $((a_1, b_1, c_1), (a_2, b_2)) \mapsto (\lambda, f_{a_2, b_2}(a_1, b_1, c_1))$, where $f_{a,b}(x, y, z) \stackrel{\text{def}}{=} z + (x + a) \cdot (y + b)$, and next the latter is reduced to OT_1^4. Present each of these reductions and prove that each is a privacy reduction.

> **Guideline:** When analyzing the second reduction, use the fact that it is used to compute a deterministic functionality and that thus, the simpler form of Definition 7.2.1 can be used.

Exercise 10: *Some functionalities that are trivial to privately compute:* Show that each of the following types of functionalities has a trivial protocol for privately computing it (i.e., using a single message):

1. Each deterministic functionality that only depends on the input of one party (i.e., $(x, 1^{|x|}) \mapsto (f_1(x), f_2(x))$ for arbitrary functions f_1 and f_2).
2. Each randomized functionality of the form $(x, 1^{|x|}) \mapsto (g(x), f(x, g(x)))$, where g is any randomized process and f is a function.

Generalize these functionality types and their treatment to the multi-party case.

Exercise 11: In continuation of Exercise 10, show that all six functionalities introduced in Section 7.4.3 are trivial to compute in a private manner.

> **Guideline:** Note that the restricted authenticated-computation functionality of Eq. (7.27) and the image-transmission functionality of Eq. (7.31) fit Item 1, whereas the basic and augmented coin-tossing functionalities, as well as the input-commitment functionality, fit Item 2. What about Eq. (7.33)?

Exercise 12: *On the difficulty of implementing more natural versions of authenticated computation:* Consider the functionality $(\alpha, \beta) \mapsto (\lambda, v)$, where $v = f(\alpha)$ if $\beta = h(\alpha)$ and $v = \lambda$ otherwise. We call this functionality the natural auth-comp.

1. Show that the equality functionality (i.e., $(\alpha, \beta) \mapsto (\chi, \chi)$, where $\chi = 1$ if $\beta = \alpha$ and $\chi = 0$ otherwise) is privately reducible to a special case of natural auth-comp.
2. Show that Oblivious Transfer is privately reducible to a special case of natural auth-comp. Conclude that there can be no trivial protocol for privately computing the latter (e.g., a protocol that privately computes natural auth-comp implies the existence of one-way functions).

    Guideline (Part 2): Privately reduce the single-secret (bit) version of Oblivious Transfer to the special case of natural auth-comp in which $h(\alpha)$ (resp., $f(\alpha)$) equals the first (resp., second) bit of α. On input a secret bit σ, Party 1 sets its oracle-query to 1σ and Party 2 sets its query to a uniformly selected bit (and so if the latter equals $h(1\sigma) = 1$, then Party 2 gets $f(1\sigma) = \sigma$, and otherwise it gets λ).

Exercise 13: *Transitivity of security reductions:* Show that if f is securely reducible to f', and f' is securely reducible to f'', then f is securely reducible to f''. Note that Theorem 7.4.3 is obtained as a special case (e.g., by setting f'' to be the identity mapping).

    Guideline: See Exercise 5.

Exercise 14: *Voting, Elections, and Lottery:* Write a specification for some social procedure (e.g., voting, elections, or lottery), and cast it as a multi-party functionality. Note that allowing appeals and various forms of interaction requires a reactive functionality (see Section 7.7.1.3), which in turn can be reduced to a standard (non-reactive) functionality.

Exercise 15: *Threshold Cryptography:* Loosely speaking, Threshold Cryptography is concerned with allowing a set of parties to share the ability to perform certain (cryptographic) operations (cf. [74, 96]). For example, suppose that we wish m parties to hold shares of a signing-key (with respect to some signature scheme), such that every t of these parties (but not fewer) can generate signatures to documents of their choice. Cast this example as a multi-party functionality. (The same holds for other versions of Threshold Cryptography.)

Exercise 16: *Failure of a simple protocol for multi-party authenticated computation:* Consider the m-party oracle-aided protocol for computing Eq. (7.50) in which, for $i = 2, ..., m$, Parties 1 and i invoke Eq. (7.33), with Party 1 entering the input α and Party i entering the input β_i. Show that this oracle-aided protocol does not constitute a secure implementation of Eq. (7.50).

Exercise 17: *Analysis of Shamir's Secret-Sharing Scheme:* Prove that Construction 7.5.35 satisfies the conditions of Definition 7.5.34.

    Guideline: For every sequence $(u_1, v_1), ..., (u_\ell, v_\ell)$, where the u_i's are distinct, consider the set of degree $d \geq \ell - 1$ polynomials q that satisfy $q(u_i) = v_i$ for

$i = 1, ..., \ell$. Denoting the unknown coefficients of q by q_j's, observe that each equality $q(u_i) = v_i$ yields a linear equation for the q_j's (i.e., $\sum_{j=0}^{d} u_i^j \cdot q_j = v_i$). Furthermore, the equations are linearly independent, and so the solution space has cardinality $p^{d+1-\ell}$. Indeed, it is important to consider these equations as referring to the variables q_j's and the constants u_i's, rather than the other way around.

Exercise 18: *On the importance of comparable complexity in the definition of perfect security:* Consider a modification of Definition 7.6.2 such that the ideal-model adversary is not required to be of comparable complexity to the real-model adversary. Present protocols that are deemed "secure" under the modified definition although they are insecure under the original definition (as well as under Definition 7.5.4).

Guideline: Consider any protocol for computing the functionality $(x, 1^{|x|}, ..., 1^{|x|}) \mapsto (f(x), f(x), ..., f(x))$, where f is a one-way permutation. Show that such a protocol, even the trivial (and *bad*) one in which Party 1 sends its input (in the clear) to everybody, is deemed "secure" under the modified definition. In particular, an ideal-model adversary that does not control (resp., controls) Party 1 can recover the input of Party 1 (resp., the substituted input of Party 1) in exponential time by inverting f on any party's output.

Exercise 19: *Perfect security implies ordinary security:* Show that Definition 7.6.2 implies Definition 7.5.4.

Guideline: Observe that if A is polynomial-time and B has complexity comparable to A, then B is polynomial-time.

Exercise 20: *Private computation of linear functions:* For any fixed m-by-m matrix M, over a finite field, show that the m-ary functionality $\bar{x} \mapsto \bar{x}M$ can be m-privately computed (as per Definition 7.6.1).

Guideline: For starters, consider first the functionality $(x_1, ..., x_m) \mapsto (\sum_{i=1}^{m} c_i x_i, 0, ..., 0)$, where the c_i's are fixed constants. Show that the following protocol is m-private: First, each party shares its input with all other parties (by uniformly selecting shares that sum up to its input and sending a share to each party). Next, each party computes the linear combination of the shares it has received. Finally, each party sends the result to Party 1. Note that this computation would be t-private if we were to use sharing via a degree t polynomial.

Exercise 21: *Private generation of vectors in a linear subspace:* For M as in Exercise 20, show that the m-ary functionality $(\lambda, ..., \lambda) \mapsto \bar{r}$, such that $\bar{r}$ is a random m-ary vector satisfying $\bar{r}M = 0^m$ can be m-privately computed (as per Definition 7.6.1).

Guideline: Consider the generating matrix, denoted G, of the subspace defined by (the parity-check) matrix M. Suppose that G has rank k (i.e., G is a full-rank k-by-m matrix). Show that, without loss of generality, the k-by-k left submatrix of G equals the identity matrix. Privately reduce the generation task to the functionality of Exercise 20.

Exercise 22: *Alternative presentation of t-private computation of Eq. (7.66):*

1. In continuation of Exercises 20 and 21, given M_1 and M_2, consider the m-ary functionality $\bar{x} \mapsto \bar{x} M_1 + \bar{r}$, such that $\bar{r}$ is a random m-ary vector satisfying $\bar{r} M_2 = 0^m$. Show that this functionality can be m-privately computed.
2. Show that the functionality of Eq. (7.66) is a special case of the class of functionalities considered in Item 1.

Guideline (Item 1): Note that privately computing each of the two terms of $\bar{x} M_1 + \bar{r}$, separately, will not do. Instead, one has to combine the ideas underlying these constructions. Defining G as in Exercise 21, our aim is to privately compute $\bar{x} \mapsto \bar{x} M_1 + \bar{s} G$, where $\bar{s}$ is a uniformly distributed k-element long sequence. Assuming, without loss of generality, that the k-by-k left submatrix of G is of full rank, we can rewrite the functionality as $\bar{x} \mapsto \bar{x} M' + \bar{s} G'$, where the k-by-k left submatrix of G' is the identity matrix and the m-by-k left submatrix of M' is the all-zero matrix. Recall that we know how to privately compute each of the two terms of $\bar{x} M' + \bar{s} G'$, separately; but again this will not do. Instead, we combine these two computations so as not to yield information about the value of the individual terms. As a warm-up, consider privately computing the functionality $((x_1, y_1), ..., (x_m, y_m)) \mapsto (x_1, y_1, ..., x_m, y_m) M$, where M is a fixed $2m$-by-m matrix.

Guideline (Item 2): Show that the computation of the free term of the polynomial c can be captured by an adequate M_1, whereas the generation of the values of a random degree t polynomial with free-term equal to zero can be captured by an adequate M_2.

Exercise 23: *Analysis of Construction 7.6.3:* For $t < m/2$, show that Construction 7.6.3 constitutes a protocol that t-privately computes Eq. (7.65).

Guideline: Consider, without loss of generality, $I = \{1, ..., t\}$. The simulator is given an input sequence $((a_1, b_1), ..., (a_t, b_t))$ and an output sequence $(r_1, ..., r_t)$, and needs to emulate the messages that the parties in I obtain at Step 2. This can be done by randomly selecting degree t polynomials q_j''s that are consistent with these sequences and letting the messages that Party i obtains equal $q_1'(i), ..., q_m'(i)$. Specifically, for $i = 1, .., t$, the polynomial q_i' is selected like q_i (i.e., uniformly among the t polynomials having free-term $a_i b_i$); for $i = t + 1, .., m - 1$, the polynomial q_i' is selected uniformly among all t polynomials, and q_m' is selected such that $\sum_{j=1}^{m} \gamma_j q_j'(i) = r_i$ holds for all $i \in [t]$.

Corrections and Additions
to Volume 1

There is no 100% guarantee in the world;
whoever wants 100% guarantee should not build anything.
Eng. Isidor Goldreich (1906–1995)

In this appendix, we list a few corrections and additions to the previous chapters of this work (which appeared in [108]).

C.1. Enhanced Trapdoor Permutations

Recall that a collection of trapdoor permutations, as defined in Definition 2.4.5, is a collection of permutations, $\{f_\alpha\}_\alpha$, accompanied by four probabilistic polynomial-time algorithms, denoted I, S, F, and B (for *index, sample, forward,* and *backward*), such that the following (syntactic) conditions hold:

1. On input 1^n, algorithm I selects a random n-bit long index α of a permutation f_α, along with a corresponding trapdoor τ;
2. On input α, algorithm S *samples* the domain of f_α, returning an almost uniformly distributed element in it;
3. For x in the domain of f_α, given α and x, algorithm F returns $f_\alpha(x)$ (i.e., $F(\alpha, x) = f_\alpha(x)$);
4. For y in the range of f_α if (α, τ) is a possible output of $I(1^n)$, then, given τ and y, algorithm B returns $f_\alpha^{-1}(y)$ (i.e., $B(\tau, y) = f_\alpha^{-1}(y)$).

The hardness condition in Definition 2.4.5 refers to the difficulty of inverting f_α on a uniformly distributed element of its range, when given only the range element and α. That is, let $I_1(1^n)$ denote the first element in the output of $I(1^n)$ (i.e., the index); then for every probabilistic polynomial-time algorithm A (resp., every non-uniform family of polynomial-size circuit $A = \{A_n\}_n$), every positive polynomial p, and all sufficiently large n's,

$$\Pr[A(I_1(1^n), f_{I_1(1^n)}(S(I_1(1^n)))) = S(I_1(1^n))] < \frac{1}{p(n)} \qquad \text{(C.1)}$$

Namely, A (resp., A_n) fails to invert f_α on $f_\alpha(x)$, where α and x are selected by I and S as here. An equivalent way of writing Eq. (C.1) is

$$\Pr[A(I_1(1^n), S'(I_1(1^n), R_n)) = f_{I_1(1^n)}^{-1}(S'(I_1(1^n), R_n))] < \frac{1}{p(n)} \qquad \text{(C.2)}$$

where S' is the residual two-input (deterministic) algorithm obtained from S when treating the coins of the latter as an auxiliary input, and R_n denotes the distribution of the coins of S on n-bit long inputs. That is, A fails to invert f_α on x, where α and x are selected as earlier.

Although this definition suffices for many applications, in some cases we will need an enhanced hardness condition. Specifically, we will require it to be hard to invert f_α on a random input x (in the domain of f_α), *even when given the coins used by S in the generation of x*. (Note that given these coins (and the index α), the resulting domain element x is easily determined.)

Definition C.1.1 (enhanced trapdoor permutations): *Let* $\{f_\alpha : D_\alpha \to D_\alpha\}$ *be a collection of trapdoor permutations as in Definition 2.4.5. We say that this collection is* enhanced (*and call it an* enhanced collection of trapdoor permutations) *if for every probabilistic polynomial-time algorithm A, every positive polynomial p, and all sufficiently large n's,*

$$\Pr[A(I_1(1^n), R_n) = f_{I_1(1^n)}^{-1}(S'(I_1(1^n), R_n))] < \frac{1}{p(n)} \qquad \text{(C.3)}$$

where S' is as in the foregoing discussion. The non-uniform version is defined analogously.

We comment that the RSA collection (presented in Section 2.4.3.1 and further discussed in Section 2.4.4.2) is, in fact, an *enhanced* collection of trapdoor permutations,[1] provided that RSA is hard to invert in the same sense as assumed in Section 2.4.3.1. In contrast, the Rabin Collection (as defined in Section 2.4.3) does not satisfy Definition C.1.1 (because the coins of the sampling algorithm give away a modular square root of the domain element). Still, the Rabin Collection can be easily modify to yield an *enhanced* collection of trapdoor permutations, provided that factoring is hard (in the same sense as assumed in Section 2.4.3). Actually, we present

---

[1] Here and in the following, we assume that sampling Z_N^*, for a composite N, is trivial. However, sampling Z_N^* (or even Z_N) by using a sequence of unbiased coins is not that trivial. The straightforward sampler may take $\ell \stackrel{\text{def}}{=} 2\lfloor \log_2 N \rfloor$ random bits, view them as an integer in $i \in \{0, 1, ..., 2^\ell - 1\}$, and output $i \bmod N$. This yields an almost uniform sample in Z_N. Also note that given an element $e \in Z_N$, one can uniformly sample an $i \in \{0, 1, ..., 2^\ell - 1\}$ such that $i \equiv e \pmod{N}$. Thus, the actual sampler does not cause trouble with respect to the enhanced hardness requirement.

two such possible modifications:

1. *Modifying the functions.* Rather than squaring modulo the composite N, we consider the function of raising to the power of 4 modulo N. It can be shown that the resulting permutations over the quadratic residues modulo N satisfy Definition C.1.1, provided that factoring is hard. Specifically, given N and a random $r \in Z_N$, the ability to extract the 4th root of $r^2 \bmod N$ (modulo N) yields the ability to factor N, where the algorithm is similar to the one used in order to establish the intractability of extracting square roots.

2. *Changing the domains.* Rather than considering the permutation induced (by the modular squaring function) on the set Q_N of the quadratic residues modulo N, we consider the permutations induced on the set M_N, where M_N contains all integers in $\{1, ..., N/2\}$ that have Jacobi symbol modulo N that equals 1. Note that as in the case of Q_N, each quadratic residue has a unique square root in M_N (because exactly two square roots have a Jacobi symbol that equals 1 and their sum equals N).[2] However, unlike Q_N, membership in M_N can be determined in polynomial-time (when given N without its factorization). Thus, sampling M_N can be done in a straightforward way, which satisfies Definition C.1.1.

   Actually, squaring modulo N is a 1-1 mapping of M_N to Q_N. In order to obtain a permutation over M_N, we modify the function a little, such that if the result of modular squaring is bigger than $N/2$, then we use its additive inverse (i.e., rather than outputting $y > N/2$, we output $N - y$).

We comment that the special case of Definition 2.4.5 in which the domain of f_α equals $\{0, 1\}^{|\alpha|}$ is a special case of Definition C.1.1 (because, without loss of generality, the sampling algorithm may satisfy $S'(\alpha, r) = r$). Clearly, the RSA and the Rabin collections can be slightly modified to fit the former special case.

Correction to Volume 1. Theorems 4.10.10, 4.10.14, and 4.10.16 (which in turn are based on Remark 4.10.6) refer to the existence of certain non-interactive zero-knowledge proofs. The claimed non-interactive zero-knowledge proof systems can be constructed by assuming the existence of an *enhanced* collection of trapdoor permutations. However, in contrast to the original text, it is not known how to derive these proof systems based on the existence of a (regular) collection of trapdoor permutations. See further discussion in Section C.4.1.

Open Problem. *Is it possible to convert any collection of trapdoor permutations into an enhanced one?* An affirmative answer will resolve open problems stated in Sections 7.7.6 and C.4.1, which refer to the assumptions required for General Secure Multi-Party Computation and various types of Non-Interactive Zero-Knowledge proofs, respectively.

---

[2] As in the case of Q_N, we use the fact that -1 has Jacobi symbol 1.

C.2. On Variants of Pseudorandom Functions

The focus of Section 3.6 was on a special case of pseudorandom functions, hereafter referred to as the fixed-length variant. For some function $\ell : \mathbb{N} \to \mathbb{N}$ (e.g., $\ell(n) = n$), these functions map $\ell(n)$-bit long strings to $\ell(n)$-bit long strings, where n denotes the lengths of the function's seed. More general definitions were presented in Section 3.6.4. In particular, functions mapping strings of *arbitrary length* to $\ell(n)$-bit long strings were considered. Here, we refer to the latter as the variable-length variant.

A natural question regarding these variants is how to *directly* (or efficiently) transform functions of the fixed-length variant into functions of the variable-length variant.[3] Exercises 30 and 31 in Chapter 3 *implicitly suggest such a transformation,* and so does Proposition 6.3.7. Because of the interest in this natural question, we next state the actual result explicitly.

Proposition C.2.1: *Let $\{f_s : \{0, 1\}^{\ell(|s|)} \to \{0, 1\}^{\ell(|s|)}\}_s$ be a (fixed-length) pseudorandom function ensemble, and $\{h_r : \{0, 1\}^* \to \{0, 1\}^{\ell(|r|)}\}_r$ be a generalized hashing ensemble with a $(t, 1/t)$-collision property,[4] for some super-polynomial function $t : \mathbb{N} \to \mathbb{N}$. Then $\{g_{s,r} = f_s \circ h_r\}_{s,r:|s|=|r|}$ is a (variable-length) pseudorandom function ensemble.*

Proof Idea: The proofs of Propositions 6.3.6 and 6.3.7 actually establish Proposition C.2.1. ∎

Comment. Alternative constructions of variable-length pseudorandom functions based on fixed-length pseudorandom functions are presented in [25, 22, 13]. In these works, the fixed-length pseudorandom functions are applied to each block of the input, and so the number of applications is linearly related to the input length (rather than being a single one). On the other hand, these works do not use variable-length hashing. Indeed, these works presuppose that a fixed-length pseudorandom function (rather than a variable-length one) is non-expensive (and, in practice, is available as an off-the-shelf product).

C.3. On Strong Witness Indistinguishability

Unfortunately, we have to withdraw two claims regarding *strong* witness indistinguishable proofs as defined in Definition 4.6.2.[5] Specifically, in general, *strong* witness

---

[3] An indirect construction may use the fixed-length variant in order to obtain a one-way function, and then construct the variable-length variant using this one-way function. Needless to say, this indirect construction is very wasteful.

[4] Recall that the $(t, 1/t)$-collision property means that for every $n \in \mathbb{N}$ and every $x \neq y$ such that $|x|, |y| \leq t(n)$, the probability that $h_r(x) = h_r(y)$ is at most $1/t(n)$, where the probability is taken over all possible choices of $r \in \{0, 1\}^n$ with uniform probability distribution.

[5] We comment that the notion of *strong* witness indistinguishability was introduced by the author at a late stage of writing [108].

indistinguishability is not closed under parallel composition (and so Lemma 4.6.7 is wrong). Consequently, contrary to what is stated in Theorem 4.6.8, we do not know whether there exist constant-round public-coin proofs with negligible error that are *strong* witness indistinguishable for languages out of $\mathcal{BPP}$.[6] Before discussing the reasons for withdrawing these claims and the consequences of doing so, we stress that the flaws pointed out here only refer to *strong* witness indistinguishability and not to (regular) witness indistinguishability. That is, as stated in Lemma 4.6.6, (regular) witness indistinguishability is closed under parallel composition, and thus the part of Theorem 4.6.8 that refers to regular witness indistinguishability is valid (i.e., providing constant-round public-coin proofs with negligible error that are witness indistinguishable for $\mathcal{NP}$).

Notation. To facilitate the rest of the discussion, we let WI stand for "(regular) witness indistinguishability" and strong-WI stand for "strong witness indistinguishability."

C.3.1. On Parallel Composition

A counter-example to Lemma 4.6.7 can be derived by using the protocol presented at the end of Section 4.5.4.1 (and assuming the existence of one-way functions); that is, this protocol is (zero-knowledge and hence) strong-WI, but executing it twice in parallel (on the same common input) is not strong-WI. Tracing the error in the reasoning outlined in Section 4.6.2, we stress a fundamental difference between WI and strong-WI. Under the former (i.e., under the definition of WI), the indistinguishability of executions, in which the prover uses one out of two possible NP-witnesses (for the same common input), holds even when the (adversary) verifier is given these two NP-witnesses. The analogous claim does not necessarily hold for strong-WI, because these two NP-witnesses (even presented in random order) may allow for distinguishing one possible common input from the other (provided that these two possibilities are *not* identical, unlike in the case of WI). Now, observe that the single-session adversary constructed in the proof of Lemma 4.6.6 needs to get the NP-witnesses that correspond to the other sessions in order to emulate these sessions. However, these other NP-witnesses may determine the two possible NP-witnesses for the current session, and so the indistinguishability of the executions of the current session is no longer guaranteed. Furthermore, the other NP-witnesses may even uniquely determine the NP-witness (or the input triple) used in the current session. Indeed, the source of trouble is in the possible dependence among the NP-witnesses used in the various sessions. Consequently, we can resurrect parallel compositions (of strong-WI) for the special case in which the NP-witnesses used in the various sessions are independently distributed. Actually, we need statistical independence among the (entire) input triples used in the various sessions.

Lemma C.3.1 (Parallel Composition for Strong Witness Indistinguishability, Revisited): *Let $L \in \mathcal{NP}$, R_L, (P, V), Q, R_L^Q, and P_Q be as in Lemma 4.6.6, and suppose*

---

[6] Theorem 4.6.8 does not mention the public-coin condition, but the construction that is supposed to support it is of the public-coin type. Note that constant-round zero-knowledge protocols are presented in Section 4.9, but these are in relaxed models and are not of the public-coin type.

that (P, V) is strong witness indistinguishable. Then for every two probability en-
sembles $\{(\overline{X}_n^1, \overline{Y}_n^1, \overline{Z}_n^1)\}_{n \in \mathbb{N}}$ and $\{(\overline{X}_n^2, \overline{Y}_n^2, \overline{Z}_n^2)\}_{n \in \mathbb{N}}$ such that $\overline{X}_n^j = (X_{n,1}^j, ..., X_{n,Q(n)}^j)$,
$\overline{Y}_n^j = (Y_{n,1}^j, ..., Y_{n,Q(n)}^j)$, and $\overline{Z}_n^j = (Z_{n,1}^j, ..., Z_{n,Q(n)}^j)$, where $(X_{n,i}^j, Y_{n,i}^j, Z_{n,i}^j)$ is inde-
pendent of $(X_{n,k}^\ell, Y_{n,k}^\ell, Z_{n,k}^\ell)_{k \neq i, \ell \in \{1,2\}}$, the following holds:

> *If $\{(\overline{X}_n^1, \overline{Z}_n^1)\}_{n \in \mathbb{N}}$ and $\{(\overline{X}_n^2, \overline{Z}_n^2)\}_{n \in \mathbb{N}}$ are computationally indistinguishable,*
> *then so are $\{\langle P_Q(\overline{Y}_n^1), V_Q^*(\overline{Z}_n^1)\rangle(\overline{X}_n^1)\}_{n \in \mathbb{N}}$ and $\{\langle P_Q(\overline{Y}_n^2), V_Q^*(\overline{Z}_n^2)\rangle(\overline{X}_n^2)\}_{n \in \mathbb{N}}$,*
> *for every probabilistic polynomial-time machine V_Q^*.*

We stress that the components of $\overline{Y}_n^j$ (resp., $\overline{Z}_n^j$) may depend on the corresponding components of $\overline{X}_n^j$, but they are independent of the other components of $\overline{Y}_n^j$ (resp., $\overline{Z}_n^j$), as well as of the other components of $\overline{X}_n^j$. Note that statistical independence of this form holds vacuously in Lemma 4.6.6, which refers to fixed sequences of strings. Lemma C.3.1 is proved by extending the proof of Lemma 4.6.6. Specifically, we consider hybrids as in the original proof, and construct a verifier V^* that interacts with P on the i-th session (or copy), while emulating all the other sessions (resp., copies). Toward this emulation, we provide V^* with the corresponding $Q(n) - 1$ components of both $\overline{Y}_n^j$'s (as well as of both $\overline{X}_n^j$'s and $\overline{Z}_n^j$'s). Fixing the best possible choice for these $Q(n) - 1$ components, we derive a verifier that interacts with P and contradicts the hypothesis that (P, V) is strong witness indistinguishable. The key point is that revealing (or fixing) the other $Q(n) - 1$ components of both $\overline{Y}_n^j$'s does not allow for distinguishing the i-th component of $\overline{X}_n^1$ and $\overline{Z}_n^1$ from the i-th component of $\overline{X}_n^2$ and $\overline{Z}_n^2$.

C.3.2. On Theorem 4.6.8 and an Afterthought

Unfortunately, Theorem 4.6.8 is proved by a parallel composition that refers to the same common input (and the same NP-witness). Thus, Lemma C.3.1 is not applicable, and consequently we do not know whether the part of Theorem 4.6.8 that refers to *strong* witness indistinguishable proofs is valid (when referring to public-coin proofs). This is indeed an interesting open problem.

We comment that one can reduce the construction of constant-round (public-coin) *strong* witness indistinguishable proofs with negligible error for $\mathcal{NP}$ to the construction of such proofs for the special case in which the two X_n^j's (and Y_n^j's) are identically distributed (and the Z_n^j's are only computationally indistinguishable). Consider, for example, the following protocol:

1. The prover sends a commitment to the value 0.

2. Using a (regular) witness indistinguishable proof (as provided by Theorem 4.6.8), the prover proves that either the common input is in the language or the string sent at Step 1 is a commitment to 1.
   Let us denote by T_n^j the transcript of the execution of this step, when the common input is X_n^j (and the parties use auxiliary inputs Y_n^j and Z_n^j, respectively). It can

be proven that the T_n^j's are computationally indistinguishable (by considering what happens if at Step 1 the prover sends a commitment to 1).

3. Using a *strong* witness indistinguishable proof (which is indeed the missing component or the sub-protocol to which the current protocol is reduced), the prover proves that the string sent at Step 1 is a commitment to 0.

   Note that it suffices to show that the verifier cannot distinguish the two possible transcript distributions of the current step, where both possible distributions refer to executions with the same common input (i.e., the commitment) and the same prover's auxiliary input (i.e., the decommitment information). In contrast, these two distributions (of executions) refer to two different distributions of the verifier's auxiliary input (i.e., either T_n^1 or T_n^2), which are indistinguishable.

The foregoing reduction demonstrates that the notion of strong witness indistinguishability actually refers to issues that are fundamentally different from witness indistinguishability. Specifically, the issue is whether or not the interaction with the prover helps to distinguish between two possible distributions of some auxiliary information (which are indistinguishable without such an interaction). Furthermore, this issue arises also in case the prover's auxiliary inputs (i.e., the "witnesses") are identically distributed.

C.3.3. Consequences

In view of the fact that we do not have constant-round public-coin strong witness indistinguishable proofs with negligible error for $\mathcal{NP}$, we suggest replacing the use of such proofs with some cumbersome patches. A typical example is the construction of non-oblivious commitment schemes (i.e., Theorem 4.9.4).

Non-Oblivious Commitment Schemes. We begin the discussion by noting that the specific formulation appearing in Definition 4.9.3 is wrong. One should partition the commit phase into two sub-phases, such that the second sub-phase is a proof-of-knowledge of the input and coins used by the sender at the first sub-phase, which in turn should constitute (by itself) a commitment scheme. That is, the view in the relation displayed in Definition 4.9.3 should be the view of the first sub-phase (rather than the view of the entire commit phase). In fact, for the *current implementation,* we need a relaxed definition in which one only proves knowledge of the input (but not of the coins) used by the sender at the first sub-phase. We stress that the input value proved to be known must be such that it is impossible for the sender to later decommit to a different value. Indeed, in the relaxed form, we do not require a later decommitment to be at all possible; we only require that if decommitment takes place, then the outcome should match the said input value. Note that this relaxed form suffices for the proof presented in Section 4.9.2.2.

Next, we modify the construction used in the proof of Theorem 4.9.4 as follows. First, rather than sending one ordinary commitment to the input, we send many such (independent) commitments. Secondly, rather than using a (constant-round) proof-of-knowledge with negligible error, we use one that has constant error. The point is that such a (constant-round) proof-of-knowledge that is zero-knowledge (and, hence, strong witness indistinguishable) is known. We invoke this proof system many times, in parallel, where each invocation is applied to a different commitment. Thus, we can apply Lemma C.3.1 and conclude that these executions are strong witness indistinguishable (where the witnesses are the coins used in the ordinary commitments), and therefore, the entire protocol constitutes a (complicated) commitment scheme. Finally, one can establish the non-oblivious property by using the knowledge-extractor associated with the proof system. Note that we can only extract the committed input and part of the coins used at the first stage (i.e., the coins used in some of the ordinary commitments but not necessarily the coins used in all of them). Furthermore, it may be that we also accept in case the sequence of strings sent at the first stage does not correspond to any legitimate sequence (i.e., of commitments to the same value). However, if we extract one value, then it is impossible for the sender to later decommit to a different value, because the extracted value always fits at least one of the individual commitments.

Other Applications. Fortunately, Theorem 4.9.4 is the only place where *strong* witness indistinguishable proofs are used in this work. We believe that in many other applications of *strong* witness indistinguishable proofs, an analogous modification can be carried out (in order to salvage the application). A typical example appears in [7]. Indeed, the current situation is very unfortunate, and we hope that it will be redeemed in the future. Specifically, we propose the following open problem:

Open Problem. *Construct constant-round* public-coin *strong witness indistinguishable proofs* (and proofs-of-knowledge) *with negligible error for* $\mathcal{NP}$, or prove that this cannot be done. Recall that zero-knowledge *arguments* of this nature are known [5]. The challenge is in providing such *proofs*.

C.4. On Non-Interactive Zero-Knowledge

In retrospect, it appears that Section 4.10 is too laconic. As is usually the case, laconic style gives rise to inaccuracies and gaps, which we wish to address here. (See also Section C.6.)

C.4.1. On NIZKs with Efficient Prover Strategies

In continuation of Remark 4.10.6 and following [32], we briefly discuss the issues that arise when we wish to implement Construction 4.10.4 by an efficient prover. Recall that Remark 4.10.6 outlines such an implementation, while using a family of trapdoor permutations of the form $\{f_\alpha : \{0, 1\}^{|\alpha|} \to \{0, 1\}^{|\alpha|}\}_{\alpha \in \overline{I}}$, where the index-set $\overline{I}$ is efficiently recognizable. Unfortunately, no family of trapdoor permutations of this particular form (and, in particular, with an efficiently recognizable $\overline{I}$) is known. Thus, we first extend the treatment to the case in which $\overline{I}$ is not necessarily efficiently recognizable. The problem we encounter is that the prover may select (and send) a function that is not in the family (i.e., an α not in $\overline{I}$). In such a case, the function is not necessarily 1-1, and, consequently, the soundness property may be violated. This concern can be addressed by using a (simple) non-interactive (zero-knowledge) proof for establishing that the function is "typically 1-1" (or, equivalently, is "almost onto the designated range"). The proof proceeds by presenting pre-images (under the function) of random elements specified in the reference string. Note that for any fixed polynomial p, we can only prove that the function is 1-1 on at least a $1 - (1/p(n))$ fraction of the designated range (i.e., $\{0, 1\}^n$), yet this suffices for moderate soundness of the entire proof system (which in turn can be amplified by repetitions). For further details, consult [32].

Although the known candidate trapdoor permutations can be modified to fit this form, we wish to further generalize the result such that any *enhanced* trapdoor permutation (as in Definition C.1.1) can be used. This can be done by letting the reference string consist of the coin sequences used by the domain-sampling algorithm (rather than of elements of the function's domain). By virtue of the enhanced hardness condition (i.e., Eq. (C.3)), the security of the hard-core is preserved, and so is the zero-knowledge property.

As stated at the end of Section C.1, in contrast to what was claimed in Remark 4.10.6, we do not known how to extend the construction to arbitrary (rather than enhanced) trapdoor permutations. This leads to the following open problem.

Open Problem. *Under what intractability assumptions is it possible to construct non-interactive zero-knowledge proofs with efficient prover strategies for any set in $\mathcal{NP}$? In particular, does the existence of arbitrary collections of trapdoor permutations suffice?* We comment that the assumption used here affects the assumption used in (general) constructions of public-key encryption schemes that are secure under chosen ciphertext attacks (see, e.g., Theorem 5.4.31).

C.4.2. On Unbounded NIZKs

The preliminary discussion is Section 4.10.3.1 reduces the general treatment to a treatment of assertions of a priori bounded length, but the former is not defined formally. To close this gap, we note that a definition that covers assertions of a priori unbounded length can be derived from Definition 4.10.11 by considering inputs in $\cup_{i=1}^{\text{poly}(n)} L_i$, rather than in L_{n^ε}. In view of the key role of efficient provers in this setting, it is also adequate to present a definition that covers this aspect. This can be done analogously to the formulations used in the following Proposition C.4.1.

The proof of Proposition 4.10.13 relies on the fact that witness indistinguishability of non-interactive protocols is preserved under parallel composition *even if the same reference string is used in all copies*. That is, we claim and use the following result (where R is typically an NP-relation):

Proposition C.4.1: *Let P be a probabilistic polynomial-time algorithm such that for every infinite sequence of triples of the form $\overline{t} \stackrel{\text{def}}{=} (x, u, v)$, where $(x, u), (x, v) \in R$, it holds that $\{(U_{\text{poly}(|x|)}, P(x, u, U_{\text{poly}(|x|)}))\}_{\overline{t}}$ and $\{(U_{\text{poly}(|x|)}, P(x, v, U_{\text{poly}(|x|)}))\}_{\overline{t}}$*

are computationally indistinguishable.[7] *Then for every polynomial p and every infinite sequence of sequences of the form $\bar{s} \stackrel{\text{def}}{=} (x_1, ..., x_t, u_1, ..., u_t, v_1, ..., v_t)$, where $n \stackrel{\text{def}}{=} |x_1| = \cdots = |x_t|$, $t \stackrel{\text{def}}{=} p(n)$ and $(x_j, u_j), (x_j, v_j) \in R$ for $j = 1, .., t$, it holds that the ensembles $\{(U_{\text{poly}(n)}, P(x_1, u_1, U_{\text{poly}(n)}), ..., P(x_t, u_t, U_{\text{poly}(n)}))\}_{\bar{s}}$ and $\{(U_{\text{poly}(n)}, P(x_1, v_1, U_{\text{poly}(n)}), ..., P(x_t, v_t, U_{\text{poly}(n)}))\}_{\bar{s}}$ are computationally indistinguishable.*

We stress that the same reference string (i.e., $U_{\text{poly}(n)}$) is used in all invocations of the prover P. Thus, Proposition C.4.1 does not refer to multiple samples of computationally indistinguishable ensembles (nor even to independent samples from a sequence of computationally indistinguishable pairs of ensembles, as would have been the case if the various invocations were to use independently distributed reference strings). Still, Proposition C.4.1 can be established by using the hybrid technique. The key observation is that, given a single proof with respect to some reference string along with the reference string (as well as the relevant sequence $\bar{s}$), one can efficiently generate all the other proofs (with respect to the same reference string). Indeed, the *internal coins* used by P in each of these proofs are independent.

C.4.3. On Adaptive NIZKs

In Definition 4.10.15, the *adaptive zero-knowledge* condition should be quantified only over efficiently computable input-selection strategies. Furthermore, it seems that also the witness-selection strategies should be restricted to ones implemented by polynomial-size circuits. The revised form is presented in Definition 5.4.22.

A few words regarding the proof of Theorem 4.10.16 seem appropriate. The (two-stage) simulation procedure itself is sketched in footnote 29 (of Chapter 4). Recall that at the first stage, we generate matrices at random, and replace the useful matrices with all-zero matrices (i.e., matrices of f-images that have pre-images with hard-core value equal to zero). In the second stage, when given an adaptively chosen graph, we reveal all elements of all non-useful matrices and the required elements of the useful matrices (i.e., the non-edges), where revealing an element means revealing the corresponding f-pre-image. In establishing the quality of this simulation procedure, we rely on the hypothesis that the input graph, as well as a Hamiltonian cycle in it, are determined by a polynomial-size circuit.[8] Loosely speaking, assuming toward the contradiction that the simulation can be distinguished from the real proof, we construct a circuit that distinguishes a sequence of random $f(x)$'s with $b(x) = 0$ from a sequence of random $f(x)$'s with $b(x) = 1$. This "b-value distinguisher" places the tested f-images in the suitable entries (i.e., those corresponding to the predetermined Hamiltonian cycles) of useful matrices, fills up the rest of the entries of the useful matrices with elements it generates in $\{f(x) : b(x) = 0\}$, and fills the entries of non-useful matrices with random f-images that it generates (conditioned on their yielding non-useful matrices). We stress

---

[7] Recall that the distinguisher is also given the index of the distribution, which in this case is the triple $\bar{s}$.

[8] Indeed, here is where we use the fact that the corrected definition (see Definition 5.4.22) refers only to input-selection and witness-selection strategies that can be implemented by polynomial-size circuits.

that the simulator generates f-images by selecting random pre-images and applying f to each of them, and so it knows the pre-images and can reveal them later. Next, the simulator determines the input graph and the corresponding Hamiltonian cycle (by using the abovementioned polynomial-size circuit) and acts as the real prover. Finally, it feeds the original distinguisher with the corresponding output. Observe that in case the given sequence of $f(x)$'s satisfies $b(x) = 0$ (resp., $b(x) = 1$) for each $f(x)$, the "b-value distinguisher" produces outputs distributed exactly as in the simulation (resp., the real proof).

C.5. Some Developments Regarding Zero-Knowledge

A recent result by Barak [5] calls for reevaluation of the significance of all negative results regarding black-box zero-knowledge[9] (as defined in Definition 4.5.10). In particular, relying on standard intractability assumptions, Barak presents round-efficient public-coin zero-knowledge arguments for $\mathcal{NP}$ (using non-black-box simulators), whereas only $\mathcal{BPP}$ can have such *black-box* zero-knowledge arguments (see comment following Theorem 4.5.11). It is interesting to note that Barak's simulator works in strict (rather than expected) probabilistic polynomial-time, addressing an open problem mentioned in Section 4.12.3. Barak's result is further described in Section C.5.2

In Section C.5.1, we review some recent progress in the study of the preservation of zero-knowledge under concurrent composition. We seize the opportunity to provide a wider perspective on the question of the preservation of zero-knowledge under various forms of protocol composition operations.

We mention that the two problems discussed in this section (i.e., the "preservation of security under various forms of protocol composition" and the "use of the adversary's program within the proof of security") arise also with respect to the security of other cryptographic primitives. Thus, the study of zero-knowledge protocols serves as a good benchmark for the study of various problems regarding cryptographic protocols.

C.5.1. Composing Zero-Knowledge Protocols

A natural question regarding zero-knowledge proofs (and arguments) is whether or not the zero-knowledge condition is preserved under a variety of composition operations. Three types of composition operation were considered in the literature: *sequential composition, parallel composition,* and *concurrent composition.* We note that the preservation of zero-knowledge under these forms of composition not only is interesting for its own sake but also sheds light on the preservation of the security of general protocols under these forms of composition.

We stress that when we talk of the composition of protocols (or proof systems), we mean that the honest users are supposed to follow the prescribed program (specified in the protocol description) that refers to a single execution. That is, the actions of

---

[9] Specifically, one should reject the interpretation, offered in Section 4.5 (see Sections 4.5.0, 4.5.4.0, and 4.5.4.2), by which negative results regarding black-box zero-knowledge indicate the inherent limitations of zero-knowledge.

honest parties in each execution are independent of the messages they received in other executions. The adversary, however, may coordinate the actions it takes in the various executions, and in particular, its actions in one execution may also depend on messages it received in other executions.

Let us motivate the asymmetry between the postulate that honest parties act independently in different executions and the absence of such an assumption with respect to the adversary's actions. Typically, coordinating actions in different executions is difficult but not impossible. Thus, it is desirable to use stand-alone protocols that preserve security under "composition" (as defined earlier), rather than to use protocols that include inter-execution coordination actions. Note that at the very least, inter-execution coordination requires users to keep track of all executions that they perform. Actually, trying to coordinate honest executions is even more problematic than it seems, because one may need to coordinate executions of *different* honest parties (e.g., all employees of a big corporation or an agency under attack), which in many cases is highly unrealistic. On the other hand, the adversary attacking the system may be willing to go to the extra trouble of coordinating its attack in the various executions of the protocol.

For $T \in \{\texttt{sequential}, \texttt{parallel}, \texttt{concurrent}\}$, we say that a protocol is T-zero-knowledge if it is zero-knowledge under a composition of type T. The definitions of T-zero-knowledge are derived from the standard definition by considering appropriate adversaries (i.e., adversarial verifiers), that is, adversaries that can initiate a polynomial number of interactions with the prover, where these interactions are scheduled according to the type T.[10] The corresponding simulator (which, as usual, interacts with nobody) is required to produce an output that is computationally indistinguishable from the output of such a type T adversary.

C.5.1.1. Sequential Composition

Sequential composition refers to a situation in which the protocol is invoked (polynomially) many times, where each invocation follows the termination of the previous one. At the very least, security (e.g., zero-knowledge) should be preserved under sequential composition, or else the applicability of the protocol is highly limited (because one cannot safely use it more than once).

We mention that whereas the "simplified" version of zero-knowledge (i.e., without auxiliary inputs, as in Definition 4.3.2) is not closed under sequential composition (see [113]), the actual version (i.e., with auxiliary inputs, as in Definition 4.3.10) is closed under sequential composition (see Section 4.3.4). We comment that the same phenomenon arises when trying to use a zero-knowledge proof as a sub-protocol inside larger protocols. Indeed, it is for these reasons that the augmentation of the "basic" definition by auxiliary inputs was adopted in all subsequent works.[11]

---

[10] Without loss of generality, we may assume that the adversary never violates the scheduling condition; it may instead send an illegal message at the latest possible adequate time. Furthermore, without loss of generality, we may assume that all the adversary's messages are delivered at the latest possible adequate time.

[11] The preliminary version of Goldwasser, Micali, and Rackoff's work [124] uses the "basic" definition (i.e., Definition 4.3.2), whereas the final version of that work as well as most subsequent works use the augmented

C.5.1.2. Parallel Composition

Parallel composition refers to a situation in which (polynomially) many instances of the protocol are invoked at the same time and proceed at the same pace. That is, we assume a synchronous model of communication, and consider (polynomially) many executions that are totally synchronized, such that the i-th message in all instances is sent exactly (or approximately) at the same time. (Natural extensions of this model are discussed here as well as at the end of Section C.5.1.3.)

It turns out that, in general, zero-knowledge is not closed under parallel composition. A simple counter-example (to the "parallel composition conjecture") is outlined in Section 4.5.4.1 (following [113]). This counter-example consists of a simple protocol that is zero-knowledge (in a strong sense) but is not closed under parallel composition (not even in a very weak sense).[12]

We comment that in the 1980s, parallel composition was studied mainly in the context of *round-efficient error reduction* (cf. [91, 113]); that is, the aim was to construct full-fledged zero-knowledge proofs (with negligible soundness error) by composing (in parallel) a basic zero-knowledge protocol of high (but bounded away from 1) soundness error. Since alternative ways of constructing constant-round zero-knowledge proofs (and arguments) were found (cf. [112, 90, 47]), interest in parallel composition (of zero-knowledge protocols) has died. In retrospect, this was a conceptual mistake, because parallel composition (and mild extensions of this notion) capture the preservation of security in a fully synchronous (or almost fully synchronous) communication network. We note that the almost fully synchronous communication model is quite realistic in many settings, although it is certainly preferable not to assume even weak synchronism.

Although, in general, zero-knowledge is not closed under parallel composition, under standard intractability assumptions (e.g., the intractability of factoring), there exist zero-knowledge protocols for $\mathcal{NP}$ that are closed under parallel composition. Furthermore, these protocols have a constant number of rounds (cf. [109] for proofs and [82] for arguments).[13] Both results also extend to concurrent composition in a synchronous communication model, where the extension is in allowing protocol invocations to start at different times (and, in particular, executions may overlap but not run simultaneously).

We comment that parallel composition is also problematic in the context of reducing the soundness error of arguments (cf. [24]), but our focus here is on the zero-knowledge aspect of protocols, regardless of whether they are proofs, arguments, or neither.

C.5.1.3. Concurrent Composition (with and without Timing)

Concurrent composition generalizes both sequential and parallel composition. Here (polynomially) many instances of the protocol are invoked at arbitrary times and proceed

---

definition (i.e., Definition 4.3.10). In some works, the "basic" definition is used for simplicity, but typically one actually needs and means the augmented definition.

[12] The presentation in Section 4.5.4.1 is in terms of two protocols, each being zero-knowledge, such that executing them in parallel is not zero-knowledge. These two protocols can be easily combined into one protocol (e.g., by letting the second party determine, in its first message, which of the two protocols to execute).

[13] In the case of parallel zero-knowledge *proofs*, there is no need to specify the soundness error because it can always be reduced via parallel composition. As mentioned later, this is not the case with respect to arguments.

at an arbitrary pace. That is, we assume an asynchronous (rather than synchronous) model of communication.

In the 1990s, when extensive two-party (and multi-party) computations became a reality (rather than a vision), it became clear that it is (at least) desirable that cryptographic protocols maintain their security under concurrent composition (cf. [77]). In the context of zero-knowledge, concurrent composition was first considered by Dwork, Naor, and Sahai [82]. Actually, two models of concurrent composition were considered in the literature, depending on the underlying model of communication (i.e., a *purely asynchronous model* and an *asynchronous model with timing*).

Concurrent Composition in the Pure Asynchronous Model. Here we refer to the standard model of asynchronous communication. In comparison to the timing model, the pure asynchronous model is a simpler model, and using it requires no assumptions about the underlying communication channels. However, it seems harder to construct concurrent zero-knowledge protocols for this model. In particular, for a while it was not known whether concurrent zero-knowledge proofs for $\mathcal{NP}$ exist at all (in this model). Under standard intractability assumptions (e.g., the intractability of factoring), this question was affirmatively resolved by Richardson and Kilian [175]. Following their work, research has focused on determining the round-complexity of concurrent zero-knowledge proofs for $\mathcal{NP}$. Currently, this question is still open, and the state of the art regarding it is as follows:

- Under standard intractability assumptions, every language in $\mathcal{NP}$ has a concurrent zero-knowledge proof with *almost logarithmically* many rounds (cf. [169], building upon [138], which in turn builds over [175]). Furthermore, the zero-knowledge property can be demonstrated by using a black-box simulator (see the definition in Section 4.5.4.2 and the discussion in Section C.5.2).
- Black-box simulators cannot demonstrate the concurrent zero-knowledge property of non-trivial proofs (or arguments) having significantly less than logarithmically many rounds (cf. Canetti et al. [58]).[14]
- Recently, Barak [5] demonstrated that the "black-box simulation barrier" can be bypassed. With respect to concurrent zero-knowledge, he obtained only the following partial result: Under standard intractability assumptions, every language in $\mathcal{NP}$ has a constant-round zero-knowledge argument (rather than proof) that maintains security as long as an a priori bounded (polynomial) number of executions take place concurrently. (The length of the messages in his protocol grows linearly with this a priori bound.)

Thus, it is currently unknown whether or not *constant-round* arguments for $\mathcal{NP}$ may be concurrent zero-knowledge (in the pure asynchronous model).

---

[14] By *non-trivial* proof systems we mean ones for languages outside $\mathcal{BPP}$, whereas by *significantly less than logarithmic* we mean any function $f : \mathbb{N} \to \mathbb{N}$ satisfying $f(n) = o(\log n / \log \log n)$. In contrast, by *almost logarithmic* we mean any function f satisfying $f(n) = \omega(\log n)$.

Concurrent Composition under the Timing Model. A model of naturally limited asynchronousness (which certainly covers the case of parallel composition) was introduced by Dwork, Naor, and Sahai [82]. Essentially, they assume that each party holds a local clock such that the relative clock rates are bounded by an a priori known constant, and they consider protocols that employ time-driven operations (i.e., time-out incoming messages and delay outgoing messages). The benefit of the timing model is that it seems easier to construct concurrent zero-knowledge protocols for it. Specifically, using standard intractability assumptions, *constant-round* arguments and proofs that are concurrent zero-knowledge under the timing model do exist (cf. [82] and [109], respectively). The disadvantages of the timing model are discussed next.

The timing model consists of the *assumption* that talking about the actual timing of events is meaningful (at least in a weak sense) and of the *introduction of time-driven operations*. The timing assumption amounts to postulating that each party holds a local clock and knows a global bound, denoted $\rho \geq 1$, on the relative rates of the local clocks.[15] Furthermore, it is postulated that the parties know a (pessimistic) bound, denoted Δ, on the message-delivery time (which also includes the local computation and handling times). In our opinion, these timing assumptions are most reasonable, and are unlikely to restrict the scope of applications for which concurrent zero-knowledge is relevant. We are more concerned about the effect of the time-driven operations introduced in the timing model. Recall that these operations are the time-out of incoming messages and the delay of outgoing messages. Furthermore, *typically* the delay period is at least as long as the time-out period, which in turn is at least Δ (i.e., the time-out period must be at least as long as the pessimistic bound on message-delivery time so as not to disrupt the proper operation of the protocol). This means that the use of these time-driven operations yields a slowing down of the execution of the protocol (i.e., running it at the rate of the pessimistic message-delivery time, rather than at the rate of the actual message-delivery time, which is typically much faster). Still, in the absence of more appealing alternatives (i.e., a constant-round concurrent zero-knowledge protocol for the pure asynchronous model), the use of the timing model may be considered reasonable. (We comment than other alternatives to the timing model include various set-up assumptions; cf. [55, 72].)

Back to Parallel Composition. Given our opinion about the timing model, it is not surprising that we consider the problem of parallel composition almost as important as the problem of concurrent composition in the timing model. Firstly, it is quite reasonable to assume that the parties' local clocks have approximately the same rate, and that drifting is corrected by occasional clock synchronization. Thus, it is reasonable to assume that the parties have an approximately good estimate of some global time. Furthermore, the global time may be partitioned into phases, each consisting of a constant number of rounds, so that each party wishing to execute the protocol just delays its invocation to the beginning of the next phase. Thus, concurrent execution

---

[15] The rate should be computed with respect to reasonable intervals of time; for example, for Δ as defined next, one may assume that a time period of Δ units is measured as Δ' units of time on the local clock, where $\Delta/\rho \leq \Delta' \leq \rho\Delta$.

of (constant-round) protocols in this setting amounts to a sequence of (time-disjoint) almost parallel executions of the protocol. Consequently, proving that the protocol is parallel zero-knowledge suffices for concurrent composition in this setting.

Relation to Resettable Zero-Knowledge. Going to the other extreme, we mention that there exists a natural model of zero-knowledge that is even stronger than concurrent zero-knowledge (even in the pure asynchronous model). Specifically, "resettable zero-knowledge" as defined in [55] implies concurrent zero-knowledge.

C.5.2. Using the Adversary's Program in the Proof of Security

Recall that the definition of zero-knowledge proofs states that whatever an efficient adversary can compute after interacting with the prover can be efficiently computed from scratch by a so-called *simulator* (which works without interacting with the prover). Although the simulator may depend arbitrarily on the adversary, the need to present a simulator for each feasible adversary seems to require the presentation of a universal simulator that is given the adversary's strategy (or program) as another auxiliary input. The question addressed in this section is how the universal simulator can use the adversary's program.

The adversary's program (or strategy) is actually a function that determines for each possible view of the adversary (i.e., its input, random choices, and the message it has received so far) which message will be sent next. Thus, we identify the adversary's program with this next-message function. As stated previously, until very recently, all universal simulators (constructed toward demonstrating zero-knowledge properties) have used the adversary's program (or rather its next-message function) as a black-box (i.e., the simulator invoked the next-message function on a sequence of arguments of its choice). Furthermore, in view of the presumed difficulty of "reverse-engineering" programs, it was commonly believed that nothing is lost by restricting attention to simulators, called black-box simulators, that only make black-box usage of the adversary's program. Consequently, Goldreich and Krawczyk conjectured that impossibility results regarding black-box simulation represent inherent limitations of zero-knowledge itself, and studied the limitations of the former [113].

> In particular, they showed that parallel composition of the protocol of Construction 4.4.7 (as well as of any constant-round public-coin protocol) *cannot be proven to be zero-knowledge using a black-box simulator,* unless the language (i.e., 3-Colorability) is in $\mathcal{BPP}$. In fact, their result refers to any constant-round public-coin protocol with negligible soundness error, regardless of how such a protocol is obtained. This result was taken as strong evidence toward the conjecture that a constant-round public-coin protocol with negligible soundness error *cannot be zero-knowledge* (unless the language is in $\mathcal{BPP}$).

> Similarly, as mentioned in Section C.5.1.3, it was shown that protocols of a sublogarithmic number of rounds *cannot be proven to be concurrent zero-knowledge via a black-box simulator* [58]. Again, this was taken as evidence toward the conjecture that such protocols cannot be *concurrent zero-knowledge.*

In contrast to these conjectures (and to the reasoning underlying them), Barak showed how to construct non-black-box simulators and obtained several results that were known to be unachievable via black-box simulators [5]. In particular, under standard intractability assumptions (see also [7]), he presented constant-round public-coin zero-knowledge arguments with negligible soundness error for any language in $\mathcal{NP}$. (Moreover, the simulator runs in strict polynomial-time, which is impossible for black-box simulators of non-trivial constant-round protocols [9].) Furthermore, these protocols preserve zero-knowledge under a fixed[16] polynomial number of concurrent executions, in contrast to the result of [58] (regarding black-box simulators) that also holds in that restricted case. Thus, Barak's result calls for the reevaluation of many common beliefs. Most concretely, it says that results regarding black-box simulators do not reflect inherent limitations of zero-knowledge (but rather an inherent limitation of a natural way of demonstrating the zero-knowledge property). Most abstractly, it says that there are meaningful ways of using a program other than merely invoking it as a black-box.

Does this means that a method was found to "reverse-engineer" programs or to "understand" them? We believe that the answer is negative. Barak [5] is using the adversary's program in a significant way (i.e., more significant than just invoking it), without "understanding" it. *So, how does he use the program?*

The key idea underlying Barak's protocol [5] is to have the prover prove that either the original NP-assertion is valid or that he (i.e., the prover) "knows the verifier's residual strategy" (in the sense that it can predict the next verifier message). Indeed, in a real interaction (with the honest verifier), it is infeasible for the prover to predict the next verifier message, and so computational soundness of the protocol follows. However, a simulator that is given the code of the verifier's strategy (and not merely oracle access to that code) can produce a valid proof of the disjunction by properly executing the sub-protocol using its knowledge of an NP-witness for the second disjunctive. The simulation is computational indistinguishable from the real execution, provided that one cannot distinguish an execution of the sub-protocol in which one NP-witness (i.e., an NP-witness for the original assertion) is used from an execution in which the second NP-witness (i.e., an NP-witness for the auxiliary assertion) is used. That is, the sub-protocol should be a *witness indistinguishable* argument system (see Sections 4.6 and 4.8). We warn the reader that the actual implementation of this idea requires overcoming several technical difficulties (cf. [5, 7]).

Perspective. In retrospect, taking a wide perspective, it should not come as a surprise that the program's code yields extra power beyond black-box access to it. Feeding a program with its own code (or part of it) is the essence of the diagonalization technique, and this, too, is done without reverse engineering. Furthermore, various non-black-box techniques have appeared before in the cryptographic setting, but they were used in the more natural context of *devising an attack* on an (artificial) insecure scheme (e.g., toward

---

[16] The protocol depends on the polynomial that bounds the number of executions, and thus is not known to be concurrent zero-knowledge (because the latter requires fixing the protocol and then considering any polynomial number of concurrent executions).

proving the failure of the "Random Oracle Methodology" [54] and the impossibility of software obfuscation [8]). In contrast, in [5] (and [6]), the code of the adversary is being used within a sophisticated proof of security. What we wish to highlight here is that *non-black-box usage of programs is also relevant to proving* (rather than to disproving) *the security of systems.*

Digest: Witness Indistinguishability and the FLS-Technique

The foregoing description (of [5]), as well as several other sophisticated constructions of zero-knowledge protocols (e.g., [89, 175]), make crucial use of a technique introduced by Feige, Lapidot, and Shamir [89], which in turn is based on the notion of witness indistinguishability (introduced by Feige and Shamir [91]). This technique, hereafter referred to as the FLS-technique, was used in Construction 4.10.12, but we wish to further discuss it next.

Following is a sketchy description of a special case of the FLS-technique, whereas the abovementioned application uses a more general version (which refers to proofs-of-knowledge, as defined in Section 4.7).[17] In this special case, the technique consists of the following construction schema, which uses witness indistinguishable protocols for $\mathcal{NP}$ in order to obtain zero-knowledge protocols for $\mathcal{NP}$. On common input $x \in L$, where L is the NP-set defined by the witness relation R, the following two steps are performed:

1. The parties generate an instance x' for an auxiliary NP-set L', where L' is defined by a witness relation R'. The generation protocol in use must satisfy the following two conditions:

   (a) If the verifier follows its prescribed strategy, then no matter which feasible strategy is used by the prover, with high probability, the protocol's outcome is a NO-instance of L'.

   (b) There exists an efficient (non-interactive) procedure for producing a (random) transcript of the generation protocol *along with an NP-witness for the corresponding outcome* (which is a YES-instance of L'), such that the produced transcript is computationally indistinguishable from the transcript of a real execution of the protocol.

2. The parties execute a *witness indistinguishable* protocol for the set L'' defined by the witness relation $R'' = \{((u, u'), (v, v')) : (u, v) \in R \lor (u', v') \in R'\}$. The sub-protocol is such that the corresponding prover can be implemented in probabilistic polynomial-time, given an NP-witness for $(u, u') \in L''$. The sub-protocol is invoked on common input (x, x'), where x' is the outcome of Step 1, and the sub-prover

---

[17] In the general case, the generation protocol may generate an instance x' in L', but it is infeasible for the prover to obtain a corresponding witness (i.e., a w' such that $(x', w') \in R'$). In the second step, the sub-protocol in use ought to be a proof-of-knowledge, and computational soundness of the main protocol will follow (because otherwise, the prover, using a knowledge-extractor, can obtain a witness for $x' \in L'$).

is invoked with the corresponding NP-witness as auxiliary input (i.e., with (w, λ), where w is the NP-witness for x given to the main prover).

The computational soundness of this protocol follows by Property (a) of the generation protocol (i.e., with high probability $x' \notin L'$, and so $x \in L$ follows by the soundness of the protocol used in Step 2). To demonstrate the zero-knowledge property, we first generate a simulated transcript of Step 1 (with outcome $x' \in L'$), along with an adequate NP-witness (i.e., w' such that $(x', w') \in R'$), and then emulate Step 2 by feeding the sub-prover strategy with the NP-witness (λ, w'). Combining Property (b) of the generation protocol and the witness indistinguishability property of the protocol used in Step 2, the simulation is indistinguishable from the real execution.

C.6. Additional Corrections and Comments

Regarding Constriction 4.10.7 and the Proof of Proposition 4.10.9. The current description of the setting of the mapping of the input graph G to the Hamiltonian matrix H (via the two mappings π_1 and π_2) is confusing and even inaccurate. Instead, one may identify the rows (resp., columns) of H with $[n]$ and use a single permutation π over $[n]$ (which supposedly maps the vertices of G to those of H).[18] Alternatively, one may compose this permutation π with the two (1-1) mappings ϕ_i's (where $\phi_i : [n] \to [n^3]$ is as in the original text), and obtain related π_i's (i.e., $\pi_i(v) = \phi_i(\pi(v))$), which should be used as in the original text. We stress that the real prover determines π to be an isomorphism between the Hamiltonian cycle of G and the Hamiltonian cycle of H, whereas the simulator selects π at random.

Arguments-of-Knowledge. In continuation of Sections 4.7 and 4.9.2, we mention that the round-efficient argument system of [90] is actually an "argument-of-knowledge" (with negligible error). The interested reader is referred to [9] for further improvements regarding such proof systems. Essentially, using a relaxed (yet satisfactory) definition of an argument-of-knowledge, the latter work presents a constant-round zero-knowledge argument-of-knowledge with *strict* (rather than expected) probabilistic polynomial-time simulator and knowledge-extractor.

Some Missing Credits. The sequential composition lemma for zero-knowledge protocols (i.e., Lemma 4.3.11) is due to [119]. The notions of *strong* witness indistinguishability (Definition 4.6.2) and *strong* proofs-of-knowledge (Section 4.7.6), and the Hidden Bit Model (Section 4.10.2) have first appeared in early versions of this work.

---

[18] The identification is via the two mappings ϕ_1 and ϕ_2 mentioned in the original text. We stress that these mappings only depend on the matrix M that contains H.

C.7. Additional Mottoes

Motto for Section 3.2

> *Indistinguishable things are identical*
> *(or should be considered as identical).*

The Principle of Identity of Indiscernibles
G. W. Leibniz (1646–1714)

(Leibniz admits that counter-examples to this principle are conceivable but will not occur in real life because God is much too benevolent.)

Motto for Chapter 4

> *A: Please.*
> *B: Please.*
> *A: I insist.*
> *B: So do I.*
> *A: OK then, thank you.*
> *B: You are most welcome.*

A protocol for two Italians to pass through a door.
Source: Silvio Micali, 1985.

(The protocol is zero-knowledge because it can be simulated without knowing any of the secrets of these Italians; in fact, the execution is independent of their secrets as well as of anything else.)

Bibliography

[1] W. Alexi, B. Chor, O. Goldreich, and C. P. Schnorr. RSA/Rabin Functions: Certain Parts Are as Hard as the Whole. *SIAM Journal on Computing*, Vol. 17, April 1988, pages 194–209.

[2] J. H. An and M. Bellare. Constructing VIL-MACs from FIL-MACs: Message Authentication under Weakened Assumptions. In *Crypto99*, Springer Lecture Notes in Computer Science (Vol. 1666), 1999, pages 252–269.

[3] H. Attiya and J. Welch. *Distributed Computing: Fundamentals, Simulations and Advanced Topics*. London: McGraw-Hill, 1998.

[4] E. Bach and J. Shallit. *Algorithmic Number Theory* (Volume I: Efficient Algorithms). Cambridge, MA: MIT Press, 1996.

[5] B. Barak. How to Go Beyond the Black-Box Simulation Barrier. In *42nd IEEE Symposium on Foundations of Computer Science*, 2001, pages 106–115.

[6] B. Barak. Constant-Round Coin-Tossing with a Man in the Middle or Realizing the Shared Random-String Model. In *43th IEEE Symposium on Foundations of Computer Science*, 2002, pages 345–355.

[7] B. Barak and O. Goldreich. Universal Arguments and Their Applications. In the *17th IEEE Conference on Computational Complexity*, 2002, pages 194–203.

[8] B. Barak, O. Goldreich, R. Impagliazzo, S. Rudich, A. Sahai, S. Vadhan, and K. Yang. On the (Im)possibility of Software Obfuscation. In *Crypto01*, Springer-Verlag Lecture Notes in Computer Science (Vol. 2139), 2001, pages 1–18.

[9] B. Barak and Y. Lindell. Strict Polynomial-Time in Simulation and Extraction. In *34th ACM Symposium on the Theory of Computing*, 2002, pages 484–493.

[10] D. Beaver. Foundations of Secure Interactive Computing. In *Crypto91*, Springer-Verlag Lecture Notes in Computer Science (Vol. 576), 1992, pages 377–391.

[11] D. Beaver. Secure Multi-Party Protocols and Zero-Knowledge Proof Systems Tolerating a Faulty Minority. *Journal of Cryptology*, Vol. 4, 1991, pages 75–122.

[12] M. Bellare. A Note on Negligible Functions. *Journal of Cryptology*, Vol. 15, 2002, pages 271–284.

[13] M. Bellare, R. Canetti, and H. Krawczyk. Pseudorandom Functions Revisited: The Cascade Construction and Its Concrete Security. In *37th IEEE Symposium on Foundations of Computer Science*, 1996, pages 514–523.

[14] M. Bellare, R. Canetti, and H. Krawczyk. Keying Hash Functions for Message Authentication. In *Crypto96,* Springer Lecture Notes in Computer Science (Vol. 1109), 1996, pages 1–15.

[15] M. Bellare, R. Canetti, and H. Krawczyk. Modular Approach to the Design and Analysis of Authentication and Key Exchange Protocols. In *30th ACM Symposium on the Theory of Computing,* 1998, pages 419–428.

[16] M. Bellare, A. Desai, D. Pointcheval, and P. Rogaway. Relations among Notions of Security for Public-Key Encryption Schemes. In *Crypto98,* Springer Lecture Notes in Computer Science (Vol. 1462), 1998, pages 26–45.

[17] M. Bellare and O. Goldreich. On Defining Proofs of Knowledge. In *Crypto92,* Springer-Verlag Lecture Notes in Computer Science (Vol. 740), 1992, pages 390–420.

[18] M. Bellare, O. Goldreich, and S. Goldwasser. Incremental Cryptography: The Case of Hashing and Signing. In *Crypto94,* Springer-Verlag Lecture Notes in Computer Science (Vol. 839), 1994, pages 216–233.

[19] M. Bellare, O. Goldreich, and S. Goldwasser. Incremental Cryptography and Application to Virus Protection. In *27th ACM Symposium on the Theory of Computing,* 1995, pages 45–56.

[20] M. Bellare, O. Goldreich, and H. Krawczyk. Stateless Evaluation of Pseudorandom Functions: Security Beyond the Birthday Barrier. In *Crypto99,* Springer Lecture Notes in Computer Science (Vol. 1666), 1999, pages 270–287.

[21] M. Bellare and S. Goldwasser. New Paradigms for Digital Signatures and Message Authentication Based on Non-Interative Zero-Knowledge Proofs. In *Crypto89,* Springer-Verlag Lecture Notes in Computer Science (Vol. 435), 1990, pages 194–211.

[22] M. Bellare, R. Guerin, and P. Rogaway. XOR MACs: New Methods for Message Authentication Using Finite Pseudorandom Functions. In *Crypto95,* Springer-Verlag Lecture Notes in Computer Science (Vol. 963), 1995, pages 15–28.

[23] M. Bellare, S. Halevi, A. Sahai, and S. Vadhan. Trapdoor Functions and Public-Key Cryptosystems. In *Crypto98,* Springer Lecture Notes in Computer Science (Vol. 1462), 1998, pages 283–298.

[24] M. Bellare, R. Impagliazzo, and M. Naor. Does Parallel Repetition Lower the Error in Computationally Sound Protocols? In *38th IEEE Symposium on Foundations of Computer Science,* 1997, pages 374–383.

[25] M. Bellare, J. Kilian, and P. Rogaway. The Security of Cipher Block Chaining. In *Crypto94,* Springer-Verlag Lecture Notes in Computer Science (Vol. 839), 1994, pages 341–358.

[26] M. Bellare and S. Micali. How to Sign Given Any Trapdoor Function. *Journal of the ACM,* Vol. 39, 1992, pages 214–233.

[27] D. Beaver, S. Micali, and P. Rogaway. The Round Complexity of Secure Protocols. In *22nd ACM Symposium on the Theory of Computing,* 1990, pages 503–513.

[28] M. Bellare and P. Rogaway. Random Oracles Are Practical: A Paradigm for Designing Efficient Protocols. In *1st Conf. on Computer and Communications Security,* ACM, 1993, pages 62–73.

[29] M. Bellare and P. Rogaway. Entity Authentication and Key Distribution. In *Crypto93,* Springer-Verlag Lecture Notes in Computer Science (Vol. 773), 1994, pages 232–249.

[30] M. Bellare and P. Rogaway. Provably Secure Session Key Distribution: The Three Party Case. In *27th ACM Symposium on the Theory of Computing,* 1995, pages 57–66.

[31] M. Bellare and P. Rogaway. The Exact Security of Digital Signatures: How to Sign with RSA and Rabin. In *EuroCrypt96,* Springer Lecture Notes in Computer Science (Vol. 1070), 1996, pages 399–416.

[32] M. Bellare and M. Yung. Certifying Permutations: Noninteractive Zero-Knowledge Based on Any Trapdoor Permutation. *Journal of Cryptology,* Vol. 9, 1996, pages 149–166.

[33] M. Ben-Or, R. Canetti, and O. Goldreich. Asynchronous Secure Computation. In *25th ACM Symposium on the Theory of Computing,* 1993, pages 52–61. See details in [49].

[34] M. Ben-Or, S. Goldwasser, and A. Wigderson. Completeness Theorems for Non-Cryptographic Fault-Tolerant Distributed Computation. In *20th ACM Symposium on the Theory of Computing,* 1988, pages 1–10.

[35] J. Black, S. Halevi, H. Krawczyk, T. Krovetz, and P. Rogaway. UMAC: Fast and Secure Message Authentication. In *Crypto99,* Springer Lecture Notes in Computer Science (Vol. 1666), 1999, pages 216–233.

[36] M. Blum. How to Exchange Secret Keys. *ACM Trans. Comput. Sys.,* Vol. 1, 1983, pages 175–193.

[37] M. Blum. Coin Flipping by Phone. In *the 24th IEEE Computer Conference (CompCon),* February 1982, pages 133–137. See also *SIGACT News,* Vol. 15, No. 1, 1983.

[38] L. Blum, M. Blum, and M. Shub. A Simple Secure Unpredictable Pseudo-Random Number Generator. *SIAM Journal on Computing,* Vol. 15, 1986, pages 364–383.

[39] M. Blum, A. De Santis, S. Micali, and G. Persiano. Non-Interactive Zero-Knowledge Proof Systems. *SIAM Journal on Computing,* Vol. 20, No. 6, 1991, pages 1084–1118. (Considered the journal version of [40].)

[40] M. Blum, P. Feldman, and S. Micali. Non-Interactive Zero-Knowledge and Its Applications. In *20th ACM Symposium on the Theory of Computing,* 1988, pages 103–112. See [39].

[41] M. Blum and S. Goldwasser. An Efficient Probabilistic Public-Key Encryption Scheme Which Hides All Partial Information. In *Crypto84,* Springer-Verlag Lecture Notes in Computer Science (Vol. 196), 1985, pages 289–302.

[42] M. Blum and S. Micali. How to Generate Cryptographically Strong Sequences of Pseudo-Random Bits. *SIAM Journal on Computing,* Vol. 13, 1984, pages 850–864. Preliminary version in *23rd IEEE Symposium on Foundations of Computer Science,* 1982.

[43] J. B. Boyar. Inferring Sequences Produced by Pseudo-Random Number Generators. *Journal of the ACM,* Vol. 36, 1989, pages 129–141.

[44] G. Brassard. A Note on the Complexity of Cryptography. *IEEE Trans. on Inform. Th.,* Vol. 25, 1979, pages 232–233.

[45] G. Brassard. Quantum Information Processing: The Good, the Bad and the Ugly. In *Crypto97,* Springer Lecture Notes in Computer Science (Vol. 1294), 1997 pages 337–341.

[46] G. Brassard, D. Chaum, and C. Crépeau. Minimum Disclosure Proofs of Knowledge. *Journal of Computer and System Science,* Vol. 37, No. 2, 1988, pages 156–189. Preliminary version by Brassard and Crépeau in *27th IEEE Symposium on Foundations of Computer Science,* 1986.

[47] G. Brassard, C. Crépeau, and M. Yung. Constant-Round Perfect Zero-Knowledge Computationally Convincing Protocols. *Theoretical Computer Science,* Vol. 84, 1991, pages 23–52.

[48] C. Cachin and U. Maurer. Unconditional Security Against Memory-Bounded Adversaries. In *Crypto97,* Springer Lecture Notes in Computer Science (Vol. 1294), 1997, pages 292–306.

[49] R. Canetti. *Studies in Secure Multi-Party Computation and Applications.* Ph.D. thesis, Department of Computer Science and Applied Mathematics, Weizmann Institute of Science, Rehovot, Israel, June 1995. Available from http://theory.lcs.mit.edu/~tcryptol/BOOKS/ran-phd.html.

[50] R. Canetti. Security and Composition of Multi-party Cryptographic Protocols. *Journal of Cryptology,* Vol. 13, No. 1, 2000, pages 143–202.

[51] R. Canetti. Universally Composable Security: A New Paradigm for Cryptographic Protocols. In *42nd IEEE Symposium on Foundations of Computer Science,* 2001, pages 136–145. Full version (with different title) is available from *Cryptology ePrint Archive,* Report 2000/067.

[52] R. Canetti, I. Damgard, S. Dziembowski, Y. Ishai, and T. Malkin. On Adaptive Versus Non-Adaptive Security of Multiparty Protocols. *Journal of Cryptology,* forthcoming.

[53] R. Canetti, U. Feige, O. Goldreich, and M. Naor. Adaptively Secure Multiparty Computation. In *28th ACM Symposium on the Theory of Computing,* 1996, pages 639–648.

[54] R. Canetti, O. Goldreich, and S. Halevi. The Random Oracle Methodology, Revisited. In *30th ACM Symposium on the Theory of Computing,* 1998, pages 209–218.

[55] R. Canetti, O. Goldreich, S. Goldwasser, and S. Micali. Resettable Zero-Knowledge. In *32nd ACM Symposium on the Theory of Computing,* 2000, pages 235–244.

[56] R. Canetti, S. Halevi, and A. Herzberg. How to Maintain Authenticated Communication in the Presence of Break-Ins. *Journal of Cryptology,* Vol. 13, No. 1, 2000, pages 61–106.

[57] R. Canetti and A. Herzberg. Maintaining Security in the Presence of Transient Faults. In *Crypto94,* Springer-Verlag Lecture Notes in Computer Science (Vol. 839), 1994, pages 425–439.

[58] R. Canetti, J. Kilian, E. Petrank, and A. Rosen. Black-Box Concurrent Zero-Knowledge Requires $\tilde{\Omega}(\log n)$ Rounds. In *33rd ACM Symposium on the Theory of Computing,* 2001, pages 570–579.

[59] R. Canetti, Y. Lindell, R. Ostrovsky, and A. Sahai. Universally Composable Two-Party and Multi-Party Secure Computation. In *34th ACM Symposium on the Theory of Computing,* 2002, pages 494–503.

[60] L. Carter and M. Wegman. Universal Hash Functions. *Journal of Computer and System Science,* Vol. 18, 1979, pages 143–154.

[61] D. Chaum. Blind Signatures for Untraceable Payments. In *Crypto82.* New York: Plenum Press, 1983, pages 199–203.

[62] D. Chaum, C. Crépeau, and I. Damgård. Multi-party Unconditionally Secure Protocols. In *20th ACM Symposium on the Theory of Computing,* 1988, pages 11–19.

[63] B. Chor, S. Goldwasser, S. Micali, and B. Awerbuch. Verifiable Secret Sharing and Achieving Simultaneity in the Presence of Faults. In *26th IEEE Symposium on Foundations of Computer Science,* 1985, pages 383–395.

[64] B. Chor and E. Kushilevitz. A Zero-One Law for Boolean Privacy. *SIAM J. on Disc. Math.,* Vol. 4, 1991, pages 36–47.

[65] R. Cleve. Limits on the Security of Coin Flips When Half the Processors Are Faulty. In *18th ACM Symposium on the Theory of Computing,* 1986, pages 364–369.

[66] J. D. Cohen and M. J. Fischer. A Robust and Verifiable Cryptographically Secure Election Scheme. In *26th IEEE Symposium on Foundations of Computer Science,* 1985, pages 372–382.

[67] R. Cramer and I. Damgård. New Generation of Secure and Practical RSA-Based Signatures. In *Crypto96,* Springer Lecture Notes in Computer Science (Vol. 1109), 1996, pages 173–185.

[68] R. Cramer and V. Shoup. A Practical Public-Key Cryptosystem Provably Secure Against Adaptive Chosen Ciphertext Attacks. In *Crypto98,* Springer-Verlag Lecture Notes in Computer Science (Vol. 1462), 1998, pages 13–25.

[69] C. Crépeau. Efficient Cryptographic Protocols Based on Noisy Channels. In *EuroCrypt97,* Springer, Lecture Notes in Computer Science (Vol. 1233), 1997, pages 306–317.

[70] I. Damgård. Collision Free Hash Functions and Public Key Signature Schemes. In *EuroCrypt87,* Springer-Verlag Lecture Notes in Computer Science (Vol. 304), 1988, pages 203–216.

[71] I. Damgård. A Design Principle for Hash Functions. In *Crypto89*, Springer-Verlag Lecture Notes in Computer Science (Vol. 435), 1990, pages 416–427.

[72] I. Damgård. Concurrent Zero-Knowledge in Easy in Practice: Theory of Cryptography Library, 99-14, June 1999. http://philby.ucsd.edu/cryptolib. See also "Efficient Concurrent Zero-Knowledge in the Auxiliary String Model" (in *Eurocrypt'00*, 2000).

[73] A. De Santis, G. Di Crescenzo, R. Ostrovsky, G. Persiano, and A. Sahai. Robust Non-interactive Zero-Knowledge. In *Crypto01*, Springer Lecture Notes in Computer Science (Vol. 2139), 2001, pages 566–598.

[74] Y. Desmedt and Y. Frankel. Threshold Cryptosystems. In *Crypto89*, Springer-Verlag Lecture Notes in Computer Science (Vol. 435), 1990, pages 307–315.

[75] W. Diffie and M. E. Hellman. New Directions in Cryptography. *IEEE Trans. on Info. Theory*, IT-22, Nov. 1976, pages 644–654.

[76] H. Dobbertin. The Status of MD5 after a Recent Attack. In *CryptoBytes*, RSA Lab., Vol. 2, No. 2, 1996, pages 1–6.

[77] D. Dolev, C. Dwork, and M. Naor. Non-Malleable Cryptography. In *23rd ACM Symposium on the Theory of Computing*, 1991, pages 542–552. Full version available from authors.

[78] D. Dolev, C. Dwork, O. Waarts, and M. Yung. Perfectly Secure Message Transmission. *Journal of the ACM*, Vol. 40 (1), 1993, pages 17–47.

[79] D. Dolev and A. C. Yao. On the Security of Public-Key Protocols. *IEEE Trans. on Inform. Theory*, Vol. 30, No. 2, 1983, pages 198–208.

[80] D. Dolev and H. R. Strong. Authenticated Algorithms for Byzantine Agreement. *SIAM Journal on Computing*, Vol. 12, 1983, pages 656–666.

[81] C. Dwork and M. Naor. An Efficient Existentially Unforgeable Signature Scheme and Its Application. *Journal of Cryptology*, Vol. 11 (3), 1998, pages 187–208

[82] C. Dwork, M. Naor, and A. Sahai. Concurrent Zero-Knowledge. In *30th ACM Symposium on the Theory of Computing*, 1998, pages 409–418.

[83] S. Even and O. Goldreich. On the Security of Multi-party Ping-Pong Protocols. In *24th IEEE Symposium on Foundations of Computer Science*, 1983, pages 34–39.

[84] S. Even, O. Goldreich, and A. Lempel. A Randomized Protocol for Signing Contracts. *CACM*, Vol. 28, No. 6, 1985, pages 637–647.

[85] S. Even, O. Goldreich, and S. Micali. On-line/Off-line Digital Signatures. *Journal of Cryptology*, Vol. 9, 1996, pages 35–67.

[86] S. Even, A.L. Selman, and Y. Yacobi. The Complexity of Promise Problems with Applications to Public-Key Cryptography. *Information and Control*, Vol. 61, 1984, pages 159–173.

[87] S. Even and Y. Yacobi. Cryptography and NP-Completeness. *In Proceedings of 7th ICALP*, Springer-Verlag Lecture Notes in Computer Science (Vol. 85), 1980, pages 195–207. See [86].

[88] U. Feige, A. Fiat, and A. Shamir. Zero-Knowledge Proofs of Identity. *Journal of Cryptology*, Vol. 1, 1988, pages 77–94.

[89] U. Feige, D. Lapidot, and A. Shamir. Multiple Non-Interactive Zero-Knowledge Proofs under General Assumptions. *SIAM Journal on Computing*, Vol. 29 (1), 1999, pages 1–28.

[90] U. Feige and A. Shamir. Zero-Knowledge Proofs of Knowledge in Two Rounds. In *Crypto89*, Springer-Verlag Lecture Notes in Computer Science (Vol. 435), 1990, pages 526–544.

[91] U. Feige and A. Shamir. Witness Indistinguishability and Witness Hiding Protocols. In *22nd ACM Symposium on the Theory of Computing*, 1990, pages 416–426.

[92] A. Fiat and A. Shamir. How to Prove Yourself: Practical Solution to Identification and Signature Problems. In *Crypto86*, Springer-Verlag Lecture Notes in Computer Science (Vol. 263), 1987, pages 186–189.

[93] M. Fischer, S. Micali, C. Rackoff, and D. K. Wittenberg. An Oblivious Transfer Protocol Equivalent to Factoring. Unpublished manuscript, 1986. Preliminary versions were presented in *EuroCrypt84* and in the *NSF Workshop on Mathematical Theory of Security,* Endicott House, 1985.

[94] A. M. Frieze, J. Håstad, R. Kannan, J. C. Lagarias, and A. Shamir. Reconstructing Truncated Integer Variables Satisfying Linear Congruences. *SIAM Journal on Computing,* Vol. 17, 1988, pages 262–280.

[95] M. R. Garey and D. S. Johnson. *Computers and Intractability: A Guide to the Theory of NP-Completeness.* New York: W. H. Freeman and Company, 1979.

[96] P. S. Gemmell. An Introduction to Threshold Cryptography. In *CryptoBytes,* RSA Lab., Vol. 2, No. 3, 1997, pages 7–12.

[97] R. Gennaro, M. Rabin, and T. Rabin. Simplified VSS and Fast-Track Multiparty Computations with Applications to Threshold Cryptography. In *17th ACM Symposium on Principles of Distributed Computing,* 1998, pages 101–112.

[98] R. Gennaro and L. Trevisan. Lower Bounds on the Efficiency of Generic Cryptographic Constructions. In *41st Symposium on Foundations of Computer Science,* 2000, pages 305–313.

[99] E. N. Gilbert, F. J. MacWilliams, and N. J. A. Sloane. Codes Which Detect Deception. *Bell Syst. Tech. J.,* Vol. 53, 1974, pages 405–424.

[100] O. Goldreich. Two Remarks Concerning the GMR Signature Scheme. In *Crypto86,* Springer-Verlag Lecture Notes in Computer Science (Vol. 263), 1987, pages 104–110.

[101] O. Goldreich. *Foundation of Cryptography – Class Notes.* Preprint, Spring 1989. See [102]. Superseded by the current work.

[102] O. Goldreich. *Lecture Notes on Encryption, Signatures and Cryptographic Protocol.* Extracts from [101]. Available from http://www.wisdom.weizmann.ac.il/~oded /foc.html. Superseded by the current work.

[103] O. Goldreich. A Note on Computational Indistinguishability. *Information Processing Letters,* Vol. 34, May 1990, pages 277–281.

[104] O. Goldreich. A Uniform Complexity Treatment of Encryption and Zero-Knowledge. *Journal of Cryptology,* Vol. 6, No. 1, 1993, pages 21–53.

[105] O. Goldreich. *Foundation of Cryptography – Fragments of a Book.* February 1995. Available from http://www.wisdom.weizmann.ac.il/~oded/foc.html. Superseded by the current work.

[106] O. Goldreich. *Modern Cryptography, Probabilistic Proofs and Pseudorandomness.* Algorithms and Combinatorics series, Vol. 17. Heidelberg: Springer, 1999.

[107] O. Goldreich. *Secure Multi-Party Computation.* Unpublished manuscript, 1998. Available from http://www.wisdom.weizmann.ac.il/~oded/foc.html. Superseded by the current work.

[108] O. Goldreich. *Foundation of Cryptography – Basic Tools.* New York: Cambridge University Press, 2001.

[109] O. Goldreich. Concurrent Zero-Knowledge With Timing, Revisited. In *34th ACM Symposium on the Theory of Computing,* 2002, pages 332–340.

[110] O. Goldreich, S. Goldwasser, and S. Micali. How to Construct Random Functions. *Journal of the ACM,* Vol. 33, No. 4, 1986, pages 792–807.

[111] O. Goldreich, S. Goldwasser, and S. Micali. On the Cryptographic Applications of Random Functions. In *Crypto84,* Springer-Verlag Lecture Notes in Computer Science (Vol. 263), 1985, pages 276–288.

[112] O. Goldreich and A. Kahan. How to Construct Constant-Round Zero-Knowledge Proof Systems for NP. *Journal of Cryptology,* Vol. 9, No. 2, 1996, pages 167–189. Preliminary versions date to 1988.

[113] O. Goldreich and H. Krawczyk. On the Composition of Zero-Knowledge Proof Systems. *SIAM Journal on Computing,* Vol. 25, No. 1, February 1996, pages 169–192.

[114] O. Goldreich and L. A. Levin. Hard-Core Predicates for Any One-Way Function. In *21st ACM Symposium on the Theory of Computing,* 1989, pages 25–32.

[115] O. Goldreich and Y. Lindell. Session-Key Generation Using Human Passwords. In *Crypto01,* Springer-Verlag Lecture Notes in Computer Science (Vol. 2139), 2001, pages 408–432.

[116] O. Goldreich, Y. Lustig, and M. Naor. On Chosen Ciphertext Security of Multiple Encryptions. *Cryptology ePrint Archive,* Report 2002/089, 2002.

[117] O. Goldreich, S. Micali, and A. Wigderson. Proofs That Yield Nothing but Their Validity or All Languages in NP Have Zero-Knowledge Proof Systems. *Journal of the ACM,* Vol. 38, No. 1, 1991, pages 691–729. Preliminary version in *27th IEEE Symposium on Foundations of Computer Science,* 1986.

[118] O. Goldreich, S. Micali, and A. Wigderson. How to Play Any Mental Game – A Completeness Theorem for Protocols with Honest Majority. In *19th ACM Symposium on the Theory of Computing,* 1987, pages 218–229.

[119] O. Goldreich and Y. Oren. Definitions and Properties of Zero-Knowledge Proof Systems. *Journal of Cryptology,* Vol. 7, No. 1, 1994, pages 1–32.

[120] O. Goldreich and R. Vainish. How to Solve Any Protocol Problem – An Efficiency Improvement. In *Crypto87,* Springer Verlag Lecture Notes in Computer Science (Vol. 293), 1988, pages 73–86.

[121] S. Goldwasser and L. A. Levin. Fair Computation of General Functions in Presence of Immoral Majority. In *Crypto90,* Springer-Verlag Lecture Notes in Computer Science (Vol. 537), 1991, pages 77–93.

[122] S. Goldwasser and Y. Lindell. Secure Computation Without Agreement. In *16th International Symposium on Distributed Computing* (DISC), Springer-Verlag Lecture Notes in Computer Science (Vol. 2508), 2002, pages 17–32.

[123] S. Goldwasser and S. Micali. Probabilistic Encryption. *Journal of Computer and System Science,* Vol. 28, No. 2, 1984, pages 270–299. Preliminary version in *14th ACM Symposium on the Theory of Computing,* 1982.

[124] S. Goldwasser, S. Micali, and C. Rackoff. The Knowledge Complexity of Interactive Proof Systems. *SIAM Journal on Computing,* Vol. 18, 1989, pages 186–208. Preliminary version in *17th ACM Symposium on the Theory of Computing,* 1985.

[125] S. Goldwasser, S. Micali, and R. L. Rivest. A Digital Signature Scheme Secure Against Adaptive Chosen-Message Attacks. *SIAM Journal on Computing,* Vol. 17, No. 2, April 1988, pages 281–308.

[126] S. Goldwasser, S. Micali, and P. Tong. Why and How to Establish a Private Code in a Public Network. In *23rd IEEE Symposium on Foundations of Computer Science,* 1982, pages 134–144.

[127] S. Goldwasser, S. Micali, and A. C. Yao. Strong Signature Schemes. In *15th ACM Symposium on the Theory of Computing,* 1983, pages 431–439.

[128] S. Goldwasser and R. Ostrovsky. Invariant Signatures and Non-Interactive Zero-Knowledge Proofs Are Equivalent. In *Crypto92,* Springer-Verlag Lecture Notes in Computer Science (Vol. 740), 1992, pages 228–245.

[129] S. Haber and S. Micali. Private communication, 1986.

[130] J. Håstad, R. Impagliazzo, L. A. Levin, and M. Luby. A Pseudorandom Generator from Any One-way Function. *SIAM Journal on Computing,* Vol. 28, No. 4, 1999, pages 1364–1396. Preliminary versions by Impagliazzo et al. in *21st ACM Symposium on the Theory of Computing* (1989) and Håstad in *22nd ACM Symposium on the Theory of Computing* (1990).

[131] M. Hirt and U. Maurer. Complete Characterization of Adversaries Tolerable in Secure Multi-party Computation. *Journal of Cryptology,* Vol. 13, No. 1, 2000, pages 31–60.

[132] R. Impagliazzo and M. Luby. One-Way Functions Are Essential for Complexity Based Cryptography. In *30th IEEE Symposium on Foundations of Computer Science,* 1989, pages 230–235.

[133] R. Impagliazzo and S. Rudich. Limits on the Provable Consequences of One-Way Permutations. In *21st ACM Symposium on the Theory of Computing,* 1989, pages 44–61.

[134] A. Juels, M. Luby, and R. Ostrovsky. Security of Blind Digital Signatures. In *Crypto97,* Springer-Verlag Lecture Notes in Computer Science (Vol. 1294), 1997, pages 150–164.

[135] J. Kahn, M. Saks, and C. Smyth. A Dual Version of Reimer's Inequality and a Proof of Rudich's Conjecture. In *15th IEEE Conference on Computational Complexity,* 2000, pages 98–103.

[136] J. Katz and M. Yung. Complete Characterization of Security Notions for Probabilistic Private-Key Encryption. In *32nd ACM Symposium on the Theory of Computing,* 2000, pages 245–254.

[137] J. Kilian. Basing Cryptography on Oblivious Transfer. In *20th ACM Symposium on the Theory of Computing,* 1988, pages 20–31.

[138] J. Kilian and E. Petrank. Concurrent and Resettable Zero-Knowledge in Poly-logarithmic Rounds. In *33rd ACM Symposium on the Theory of Computing,* 2001, pages 560–569.

[139] H. Krawczyk. LFSR-Based Hashing and Authentication. In *Crypto94,* Springer-Verlag Lecture Notes in Computer Science (Vol. 839), 1994, pages 129–139.

[140] H. Krawczyk. New Hash Functions For Message Authentication. In *EuroCrypt95,* Springer-Verlag Lecture Notes in Computer Science (Vol. 921), 1995, pages 301–310.

[141] A. Lempel. Cryptography in Transition. *Computing Surveys,* Vol. 11, No. 4, Dec. 1979, pages 285–303.

[142] Y. Lindell. A Simpler Construction of CCA2-Secure Public-Key Encryption under General Assumptions. In *EuroCrypt03,* Springer Lecture Notes in Computer Science (Vol. 2656), 2003, pages 241–254.

[143] Y. Lindell. Parallel Coin-Tossing and Constant-Round Secure Two-Party Computation. In *Crypto01,* Springer Lecture Notes in Computer Science (Vol. 2139), 2001, pages 171–189.

[144] Y. Lindell, A. Lysyanskaya, and T. Rabin. On the Composition of Authenticated Byzantine Agreement. In *34th ACM Symposium on the Theory of Computing,* 2002, pages 514–523.

[145] M. Luby. *Pseudorandomness and Cryptographic Applications.* Princeton, NJ: Princeton University Press, 1996.

[146] M. Luby and C. Rackoff. How to Construct Pseudorandom Permutations from Pseudorandom Functions. *SIAM Journal on Computing,* Vol. 17, 1988, pages 373–386.

[147] N. Lynch. *Distributed Algorithms.* San Mateo, CA: Morgan Kaufmann Publishers, 1996.

[148] U. Maurer. Secret Key Agreement by Public Discussion from Common Information. *IEEE Trans. on Inform. Th.,* Vol. 39, No. 3, May 1993, pages 733–742.

[149] A. J. Menezes, P. C. van Oorschot, and S. A. Vanstone. *Handbook of Applied Cryptography.* Boca Raton, FL: CRC Press, 1996.

[150] R. C. Merkle. Secure Communication over Insecure Channels. *CACM,* Vol. 21, No. 4, 1978, pages 294–299.

[151] R. C. Merkle. Protocols for Public Key Cryptosystems. In *Proceedings of the 1980 Symposium on Security and Privacy,* 1980, pages 122–134.

[152] R. C. Merkle. A Digital Signature Based on a Conventional Encryption Function. In *Crypto87,* Springer-Verlag Lecture Notes in Computer Science (Vol. 293), 1987, pages 369–378.

[153] R. C. Merkle. A Certified Digital Signature Scheme. In *Crypto89,* Springer-Verlag Lecture Notes in Computer Science (Vol. 435), 1990, pages 218–238.

[154] R. C. Merkle and M. E. Hellman. Hiding Information and Signatures in Trapdoor Knapsacks. *IEEE Trans. Inform. Theory,* Vol. 24, 1978, pages 525–530.

[155] S. Micali, M. O. Rabin, and S. Vadhan. Verifiable Random Functions. In *40th IEEE Symposium on Foundations of Computer Science,* 1999, pages 120–130.

[156] S. Micali, C. Rackoff, and B. Sloan. The Notion of Security for Probabilistic Cryptosystems. *SIAM Journal on Computing,* Vol. 17, 1988, pages 412–426.

[157] S. Micali and P. Rogaway. Secure Computation. In *Crypto91,* Springer-Verlag Lecture Notes in Computer Science (Vol. 576), 1992, pages 392–404.

[158] D. Micciancio. Oblivious Data Structures: Applications to Cryptography. In *29th ACM Symposium on the Theory of Computing,* 1997, pages 456–464.

[159] National Bureau of Standards. Data Encryption Standard (DES). *Federal Information Processing Standards,* Publ. 46, 1977.

[160] National Institute for Standards and Technology. Digital Signature Standard (DSS). *Federal Register,* Vol. 56, No. 169, Aug. 1991.

[161] M. Naor. Bit Commitment Using Pseudorandom Generators. *Journal of Cryptology,* Vol. 4, 1991, pages 151–158.

[162] M. Naor and O. Reingold. From Unpredictability to Indistinguishability: A Simple Construction of Pseudorandom Functions from MACs. In *Crypto98,* Springer-Verlag Lecture Notes in Computer Science (Vol. 1464), 1998, pages 267–282.

[163] M. Naor and M. Yung. Universal One-Way Hash Functions and their Cryptographic Application. *21st ACM Symposium on the Theory of Computing,* 1989, pages 33–43.

[164] M. Naor and M. Yung. Public-Key Cryptosystems Provably Secure Against Chosen Ciphertext Attacks. In *22nd ACM Symposium on the Theory of Computing,* 1990, pages 427–437.

[165] R. Ostrovsky, R. Venkatesan, and M. Yung. Secure Commitment Against Powerful Adversary: A Security Primitive Based on Average Intractability. In *Proceedings of the 9th Symposium on Theoretical Aspects of Computer Science (STACS92),* 1992, pages 439–448.

[166] R. Ostrovsky and M. Yung. How to Withstand Mobile Virus Attacks. In *10th ACM Symposium on Principles of Distributed Computing,* 1991, pages 51–59.

[167] T. P. Pedersen and B. Pfitzmann. Fail-Stop Signatures. *SIAM Journal on Computing,* Vol. 26, No. 2, 1997, pages 291–330. Based on several earlier works (see first footnote in the paper).

[168] B. Pfitzmann. *Digital Signature Schemes (General Framework and Fail-Stop Signatures).* Springer-Verlag Lecture Notes in Computer Science (Vol. 1100), 1996.

[169] M. Prabhakaran, A. Rosen, and A. Sahai. Concurrent Zero-Knowledge Proofs in Logarithmic Number of Rounds. In *43rd IEEE Symposium on Foundations of Computer Science,* 2002, pages 366–375.

[170] M. O. Rabin. Digitalized Signatures. In *Foundations of Secure Computation,* R. A. DeMillo et al., eds. New York: Academic Press, 1977, pages 155–168.

[171] M. O. Rabin. Digitalized Signatures and Public Key Functions as Intractable as Factoring. TR-212, LCS, MIT, 1979.

[172] M. O. Rabin. How to Exchange Secrets by Oblivious Transfer. Tech. Memo TR-81, Aiken Computation Laboratory, Harvard University, 1981.

[173] T. Rabin and M. Ben-Or. Verifiable Secret Sharing and Multi-party Protocols with Honest Majority. In *21st ACM Symposium on the Theory of Computing,* 1989, pages 73–85.

[174] C. Rackoff and D. R. Simon. Non-Interactive Zero-Knowledge Proof of Knowledge and Chosen Ciphertext Attack. In *Crypto91,* Springer Verlag Lecture Notes in Computer Science (Vol. 576), 1991, pages 433–444.

[175] R. Richardson and J. Kilian. On the Concurrent Composition of Zero-Knowledge Proofs. In *EuroCrypt99,* Springer-Verlag Lecture Notes in Computer Science (Vol. 1592), 1999, pages 415–413.

[176] R. Rivest, A. Shamir, and L. Adleman. A Method for Obtaining Digital Signatures and Public Key Cryptosystems. *CACM,* Vol. 21, Feb. 1978, pages 120–126.

[177] P. Rogaway. The Round Complexity of Secure Protocols. Ph.D. thesis, MIT June 1991. Available from http://www.cs.ucdavis.edu/~rogaway/papers.

[178] J. Rompel. One-Way Functions Are Necessary and Sufficient for Secure Signatures. In *22nd ACM Symposium on the Theory of Computing,* 1990, pages 387–394.

[179] A. Sahai. Non-Malleable Non-Interactive Zero Knowledge and Achieving Chosen-Ciphertext Security. In *40th IEEE Symposium on Foundations of Computer Science,* 1999, pages 543–553.

[180] A. Sahai. Improved Constructions Achieving Chosen-Ciphertext Security. Unpublished manuscript, 2001. See [73].

[181] A. Shamir. On the Cryptocomplexity of Knapsack systems. In *11th ACM Symposium on the Theory of Computing,* 1979, pages 118–129.

[182] A. Shamir. How to Share a Secret. *CACM,* Vol. 22, Nov. 1979, pages 612–613.

[183] A. Shamir. A Polynomial-Time Algorithm for Breaking the Merkle-Hellman Cryptosystem. In *23rd IEEE Symposium on Foundations of Computer Science,* 1982, pages 145–152.

[184] A. Shamir, R. L. Rivest, and L. Adleman. Mental Poker. TM-125, LCS, MIT, 1979.

[185] C. E. Shannon. Communication Theory of Secrecy Systems. *Bell System Technical Journal,* Vol. 28, 1949, pages 656–715.

[186] D. Stinson. Universal Hashing and Authentication Codes. *Designs, Codes and Cryptography,* Vol. 4, 1994, pages 369–380.

[187] S. Vadhan. Constructing Locally Computable Extractors and Cryptosystems in the Bounded Storage Model. *Journal of Cryptology,* Vol. 17, No. 1, 2004, pages 43–77.

[188] M. Wegman and L. Carter. New Hash Functions and Their Use in Authentication and Set Equality. *Journal of Computer and System Science,* Vol. 22, 1981, pages 265–279.

[189] A. D. Wyner. The Wire-Tap Channel. *Bell System Technical Journal,* Vol. 54, No. 8, Oct. 1975, pages 1355–1387.

[190] A. C. Yao. Theory and Application of Trapdoor Functions. In *23rd IEEE Symposium on Foundations of Computer Science,* 1982, pages 80–91.

[191] A. C. Yao. How to Generate and Exchange Secrets. In *27th IEEE Symposium on Foundations of Computer Science,* 1986, pages 162–167.

Index